Legal Borderlands

Legal borderlands

Legal Borderlands

Law and the Construction of American Borders

Edited by

Mary L. Dudziak

& Leti Volpp

The Johns Hopkins University Press
Baltimore

 Published 2006
Printed in the United States of America on acid-free paper
9 8 7 6 5 4 3 2

The Johns Hopkins University Press
2715 North Charles Street
Baltimore, Maryland 21218-4363
www.press.jhu.edu

ISBN 0-8018-8414-4 (pbk. : alk. paper)

Library of Congress Control Number: 2006920142

A catalog record for this book is available from the British Library.

For more information about *American Quarterly*, please see:
www.press.jhu.edu/journals/american_quarterly/

Cover Design: William Longhauser
Front cover: "El Bordo," photograph by Julián Varela Gassol, www.intertlan.com. Photograph of the metal wall built in 1994 by the United States Immigration and Naturalization Service (INS), separating Tijuana, Mexico, and San Diego, California, and extending inland for sixty-six miles. "*Alto a Guardian*" (Stop Operation Gatekeeper) refers to the INS program Operation Gatekeeper, which is blamed for increasing deaths among migrants crossing the border. The letters are composed of images of skulls, each representing a person who died trying to cross the border.
Back cover: "Illegal Immigrant with an Anklecuff," photograph by David Turnley, © 2005 Corbis.

Contents

Preface *vii*
Marita Sturken

Introduction / 1
Mary L. Dudziak and Leti Volpp

Law's Borders

At the Boundaries of Law: Executive Clemency, Sovereign Prerogative, and the Dilemma of American Legality / 19
Austin Sarat

Borders of Identity

Racial Naturalization / 41
Devon W. Carbado

Notes toward a Queer History of Naturalization / 67
Siobhan B. Somerville

Outlawing "Coolies": Race, Nation, and Empire in the Age of Emancipation / 85
Moon-Ho Jung

Between "Oriental Depravity" and "Natural Degenerates": Spatial Borderlands and the Making of Ordinary Americans / 111
Nayan Shah

Toward a History of Statelessness in America / 135
Linda K. Kerber

In the Shadow of NAFTA: *Y tu mamá también* Revisits the National Allegory of Mexican Sovereignty / 159
María Josefina Saldaña-Portillo

Borders of Territory

The Edges of Empire and the Limits of Sovereignty: American Guano Islands / 187
Christina Duffy Burnett

Romantic Sovereignty: Popular Romances and the American Imperial State in the Philippines / 213
Andrew Hebard

Where Is Guantánamo? / 239
Amy Kaplan

Borders of Power

Canton Is Not Boston: The Invention of American Imperial Sovereignty / 267
Teemu Ruskola

Liberation under Siege: U.S. Military Occupation and Japanese Women's Enfranchisement / 293
Lisa Yoneyama

Between Camps: Eastern Bloc "Escapees" and Cold War Borderlands / 319
Susan L. Carruthers

The Biopolitics of Security: Oil, Empire, and the Sports Utility Vehicle / 351
David Campbell

"Setting the Conditions" for Abu Ghraib: The Prison Nation Abroad / 381
Michelle Brown

Contributors 407
Index 413

Preface

This special issue of *American Quarterly, Legal Borderlands: Law and the Construction of American Borders*, marks an unprecedented collaboration of scholars in the interdisciplinary fields of legal studies and American studies. As investigations into the way that law has shaped and policed the borders of the United States, these essays examine the historical significance of law in the border-making of the nation. The essays of *Legal Borderlands* demonstrate how the borders that define the reach of power of the United States are often murky and complex; they are not simply physical boundaries, but borders of and within identities, borders of power relations, and borders within and outside the nation-state. They show us that in the context of colonial ventures, immigration, military occupation, and empire, the law is more than a means of regulation; it is a key factor in the construction of national identity.

The breadth and interdisciplinary reach of this issue is testimony to the immense ambition and intellectual acumen of guest editors Mary L. Dudziak and Leti Volpp, who have brought together an extraordinary group of scholars and shaped their work into a deep and rewarding conversation, one that points to the emergence of a field of legal American studies in itself. This issue is the result of a worthy and deeply gratifying collaboration between *American Quarterly* and the Hart Institute for American History at Pomona College. The Hart Institute sponsored the Legal Borderlands symposium at Pomona College in September 2004, which set this issue into motion, and has helped to sponsor the special issue. We are very grateful to Helena M. Wall, director of the Hart Institute and an *American Quarterly* managing board member, for her crucial guidance on this project and her invaluable support for it.

This special issue has benefited immensely from the wise counsel and steady input of a broad range of *American Quarterly* editors, board members, and staff members, including associate editors Katherine Kinney, Barry Shank, and Raúl Villa, and managing board members Fred Moten and Helena Wall, who read all the submissions and offered incisive and helpful feedback on the essays. The editors have also benefited from valuable editorial input generously provided by Muneer Ahmad, David Eng, Rip Smith, and Chris Stone. We are grateful to American Studies Association President Shelley Fisher

Fishkin, Elazar Barkan, Katherine Franke, Neil Gotanda, Inderpal Grewal, Cheryl Harris, George Sánchez, Miguel Tinker Salas, and Robert Williams, who made important contributions as participants in the symposium. The *American Quarterly* managing board has helped to shepherd this process, including additional board members Eric Avila, Judith Jackson Fossett, Carla Kaplan, Bruce Robertson, John Carlos Rowe, Shelly Streeby, and Henry Yu.

This issue would never have come to fruition without the reliable and skilled labor of the graduate students who run the *American Quarterly* office. *American Quarterly* managing editor Hillary Jenks has been amazingly talented in coordinating this complex editing process, and *AQ* staff members Michelle Commander, Kristiane Joy, Orlando Serrano, Sean Slusser, Matt Storing, Wendy Cheng for her work on the index, Hong Vu, and Cynthia Willis provided invaluable support labor. We thank Stacey Lynn, our skilled and patient copyeditor, William Longhauser, who produced the exquisite cover design, and Hart Institute staff members Michele Palstring and Evelyn Khalili, who ran the Legal Borderlands symposium with exceptional efficiency.

Finally, we are grateful for the funding support that we have received from the James Irvine Foundation through the Program in American Studies and Ethnicity, and from the Provost's Office; Dean Joseph Aoun and the College of Letters, Arts, and Sciences; Dean Matthew Spitzer and the Law School; the Center on Law, History, and Culture; and Dean Geoffrey Cowan and the Annenberg School for Communication at the University of Southern California.

—Marita Sturken, Editor, *American Quarterly*

Legal Borderlands

Introduction

Mary L. Dudziak and Leti Volpp

On the coast, at the California-Mexico border, a rusted sheath of metal extends from the beach into the ocean, dividing the waves. There, grains of sand become attributes of different sovereignties. Two nations are brought together at this edge; at the same time, their inhabitants are marked with national identities; they come together wearing the marks of sovereignty inscribed by the border. Yet while it classifies and codifies subjects, the border cannot contain sovereignty itself. The border marks a space that American power proceeds from.

The metal edge on the beach descends into the ocean. From the beach it looks as if it might extend to the horizon, dividing the ocean floor. There are borders, not marked by metal, throughout the ocean. They mark a nation's territorial waters, a sovereignty of currents and of sea life. The boundaries around U.S. territorial waters are not outlined by physical structures; they exist on the shelves of law libraries, their dimensions defined in treaties. Instead of a metal edge, there are words on a page.

The words that place seashells into the category of American sovereignty are the technology of law. Such words are attached not only to unseeable ocean borders. They are embedded in the metal edge on the beach; they are inscribed on bodies on either side. Law defines national borders; it delineates the consequence of borders for the peoples within them. It does not contain sovereign power, but law has an imprint on national power wherever it is exercised.

This volume interrogates law's role in constituting American borders. One project of American studies scholarship has been to explore American culture and history in relation to the rest of the world.[1] But the global turn in American studies raises new questions about the boundaries of the field and of the reach of "America" itself. Once we view the United States in a global context, once territory—formerly the implicit boundary around American studies—is decentered, it becomes important to ask what the frame is around "American" studies, and to ask how, in a global context, U.S. borders and identities are constructed. Law is one window through which to look at the construction of American borders. Law is an important technology in the drawing of dividing lines between American identities and the boundaries (or lack of boundaries) around American global power. Borders are constructed in law, not only through formal legal controls on entry and exit but also through the construction of rights of citizenship and noncitizenship, and the regulation or legitimation of American power in other parts of the world.

The essays in this volume highlight the multiple ways law figures in American borders. Law has always been there in borderlands writing, although law and American studies scholars have often operated in separate intellectual spaces.[2] It was not at the surf, but in the desert spaces of what we call the Southwest, that Gloria Anzaldúa powerfully rendered the force of law in the role of *la migra*, the border patrol. "In the fields, *la migra*," she writes.

> My aunt saying, "*No corran*, don't run. They'll think you're *del otro lao*." In the confusion, Pedro ran, terrified of being caught. He couldn't speak English, couldn't tell them he was fifth generation American. *Sin papeles*—he did not carry his birth certificate to work in the fields. *La migra* took him away while we watched. *Se lo llevaron.* He tried to smile when he looked back at us, to raise his fist. But I saw the shame pushing his head down, I saw the terrible weight of shame hunch his shoulders. They deported him to Guadalajara by plane. The furthest he'd ever been to Mexico was Reynosa, a small border town opposite Hidalgo, Texas, not far from McAllen. Pedro walked all the way to the Valley. *Se lo llevaron sin un centavo al pobre. Se vino andando desde Guadalajara.*[3]

The U.S. border with Mexico is the most iconic American border, a space that has been the subject of much powerful scholarship.[4] As Sonia Saldívar-Hull has written, Anzaldúa's *Borderlands* "focuses on a specific geographic locale—the U.S.–Mexico border, and presents a specific history—that of Mexican origin U.S. Chicanas." Yet Anzaldúa's analysis goes beyond this, and "opens up a radical way of restructuring the way we study history."[5] Through the work of Anzaldúa and others, this geographic space opens up a way of thinking that writers in this volume take to other locales—spaces on the edge of American sovereignty and internal places at the heart of American identity.

What is "law" on these borders? It is *la migra*, the border patrol. It is the Department of Homeland Security, embodied in the firm hands of the airport security worker across your chest. It is there in the police lights that pull over an African American driver who has crossed an unmarked border into a neighborhood where he seems not to belong, marking internal American spaces. Law can be a force that maintains borders, encountered with varying degrees of pain.

Law also creates spaces within which border meetings come about. Law creates opportunities, new identities that we might seek. It gives us a way to announce to the state that we are joined together, as a family, or in a community that shares particular ideals. We pass laws both to manage the terrain within the state and as an expression of who we are as a people, within our borders. Law can also be a tool drawn upon to challenge state power. We might see in law not an inescapable hegemony, but a role in an ascribed identity. Law does mark bodies (as citizen, as alien), but it can also be drawn upon in constructions of self.

In a world where state power seems borderless, law follows the state in its transnational sojourns. It cannot hold back state power; instead law provides the state with a language for its global actions.

In borderland spaces, we can see what law *does* in American history and American culture. In some legal scholarship, law plays the role of tagalong, following changes in society that are seen as more fundamental.[6] Law's role in border regions makes apparent that the relationship between law and society is more dynamic. Mae Ngai demonstrates this in her book *Impossible Subjects*, showing the ways law produces categories that then are seen as social problems in need of legal regulation.[7] The transnational labor market at the U.S.–Mexico border appears, not as a natural phenomenon, but fueled by labor needs of large-scale agriculture in the west, and by legal restrictions on Asian immigration to the United States. Once immigration was funneled into the *bracero* temporary worker program or through restrictive immigration quotas, preexisting migration outside these bounds became "illegal." At the same time, the border itself, a fluid, transnational space, was militarized and patrolled. Through legal and policy developments, the problem of "illegal" immigration is structured and produced. In this example, law does not respond to natural forces outside the law; instead it responds to a social context constructed, in part, through law.

Legal Borderlands

What, then, is a *legal* borderland? We might start with the role of law in borderlands that are geographic places. Borderlands can be contact zones between distinct physical spaces; they can be interstitial zones of hybridization. They can constitute spaces that challenge paradigms and that therefore reveal the criteria that determine what fits in those paradigms. Borderlands can also function not as literal physical spaces but as contact zones between ideas, as spaces of ideological ambiguity that can open up new possibilities of both repression and liberation.[8]

Legal borderlands can be physical territories with an ambiguous legal identity, such as U.S. territories where the Constitution does not follow the flag, or

Guantánamo. Their ambiguity seems to render them sites of abnormal legal regulation, placing them on the edge of the law. But we can also draw upon the idea of legal borderlands to demarcate ideological spaces or gaps, holes in the imagining of America, where America is felt to be "out of place," contexts in which, in spite of American ideals of democracy and rights, violations of the law are routinized, such as in the space of the prison. The supposition that these spaces are exceptional, rather than the norm, enables the continued belief that "the story of America is the story of the rule of law," for stories of the violation of the rule of law are explained through their location in those physical spaces or their placement in those ideological gaps.[9]

Law also helps define the boundaries of American national identity. That American identity and law are conflated is indisputable. But American ideology incorporates a particular vision of law, which is law as the rule of law, and law as the guarantor of democracy, equality, and freedom. Americans believe that their law *is* the rule of law. U.S. history most often renders America as the guarantor of freedoms and rights. Thus, Americanization projects are understood as projects of democratization. And yet sovereign power includes the power to suspend the rule of law. To harmonize suspension with the idea of law, suspension is characterized as a state of exception, and is rationalized in the name of national security.[10] This volume develops the concept of legal borderlands in part to consider spaces of exception that illustrate disjunctures between American identity and the rule of law.

The essays in this volume demonstrate that there is a necessary outside to this notion of the United States as the embodiment of the rule of law. American history is marked by episodes that can be simultaneously conceptualized as violations of the law and as actions sanctioned by law; violations of law are as fully a part of America as what we consider to be its democratic inside. Ruptures in the guarantees of rights have been as central to actual practice as the guarantees have been to American ideology. American national mythology has continued through safeguarding borders of American identity; maintaining the center as mainstream, acceptable, and normal; and differentiating the edge, through marking out the wild and uncultivated.[11] But, as these essays illustrate, we also must acknowledge that slavery, the living dead in prison camps, and a nation in a multiracial hierarchy are a product of America's relationship to the law.

The essays in this volume are organized thematically to illustrate different forms of legal borders. They begin by considering the borders of law itself, where law begins and ends; move to consider borders of identity created by the legal regulation of bodies; turn to examine law's defining of territory and sovereignty; and conclude with essays on law's role in constituting the borders, or lack of borders, of American global power.

Law's Borders

An exploration of law and borders must begin with a discussion of the borders of law itself. Law plays a key role in American borders, but as it does so, law is not a stable technology, a tool easily seen, whose capacities and limits are apparent.[12] Austin Sarat examines law's borders in his essay "At the Boundaries of Law: Executive Clemency, Sovereign Prerogative, and the Dilemma of American Legality." It is the very idea that the rule of law is central to American identity that requires us to interrogate law's limits, he argues. Sarat's focus is on the tension between law and sovereignty. "Sovereignty troubles the rule of law by being at once prior to and yet a product of it," he suggests. He examines sovereignty in the context of executive clemency, where "law authorizes a kind of lawlessness." Acts of clemency, he argues, "are quintessentially sovereign acts in that they are authorized by law as moments when officials can 'decide who shall be removed from the purview of the law.'"[13] Because clemency removes things from the domain of law, clemency reveals law's boundaries.

To examine clemency, Sarat turns to Alexander Hamilton's defense of the practice, against Blackstone's critique of clemency as a power of monarchy, in debates over the U.S. Constitution. Hamilton's embrace of clemency turned in part on his image of America, a nation faced with difficulties, but one that might "welcome its enemies back into the fold." Sarat then examines court rulings on clemency. Here he finds instability and arbitrariness amid the attempts of judges to tame clemency through law. This very potential for arbitrariness and abuse marks the status of clemency in law's borderland.

Clemency, as a legal borderland, helps to illuminate what might be at the center of law, or a "rule of law," itself. As Sarat puts it, "the rule of law is replete with gaps, fissures, and failures, places where law runs up against national interest or sovereign prerogative. Its boundaries are unclear, uncertain, unchartable. And, in many places, law runs out, law gives way." The places where law runs out are not places where we lose our way, but instead where we might find it, for "it is in its bleeding borders that law itself, and with it American identity, is constructed, contested, and made meaningful."

Borders of Identity

The shackled foot on the back cover of this volume, belonging to a woman in immigration detention, reminds us how bodies are policed in the service of maintaining national borders. Which bodies can enter and which bodies are expelled, and the attempted enforcement of those decisions, bounds American identity through the incorporation of some and the exclusion of others.

The typical narrative of America as a nation of immigrants foregrounds a liberal story of social contract and choice, whereby immigrants are welcomed and then easily assimilate as citizens. Race sharply disrupts this narrative, given the facts of slavery, territorial dispossession, forced removals, and racial bars to immigration and naturalization. But this disruption is conventionally presumed not to threaten national myths of freedom and democracy, and to be rectified through the passage of time and progress.[14] The essays in this section challenge both presumptions, in excavating and interpreting foundational but little-known dimensions of the restrictions of movement and membership of bodies, and in asserting that the inclusion of citizens is in fact predicated upon exclusion.

One way to consider citizenship is to note the hydraulic relationship between the inclusion of some persons as citizens and the exclusion of other persons as the citizens' opposite—as aliens or, post 9/11, as terrorists. But another important and understudied dynamic is the manner in which inclusion and exclusion can be experienced by the same bodies. Devon Carbado, in his essay, "Racial Naturalization," addresses the paradox of black American identity, whereby the black American is included as a citizen, and is presumed to belong to America, but also experiences exclusion as racially subordinate. He labels this phenomenon an "inclusionary form of exclusion."

Carbado seeks to reconceptualize the relationship between black Americans and naturalization. To this purpose, he reformulates the concept of naturalization, from its formal and doctrinal understandings as the process through which one becomes an American citizen, to a social process producing American racial identity, fueled by racism. Tracing the inclusive exclusion of blacks in America to the Supreme Court decision in *Dred Scott*, he notes how enslaved blacks were excluded from citizenship but included as property, which he analogizes to unincorporated territories in the Insular Cases, described as "foreign in a domestic sense," not incorporated but "appurtenant thereto as a possession." The granting of formal citizenship through the Fourteenth Amendment naturalized blacks as citizens, and included them into an American identity, but an explicitly racially subordinate American identity, visible today in the delimiting of black social movement through the police practice of stop-

and-frisk. Carbado's essay helps us understand why racism not only "divides us as Americans" but consolidates American national identity, as it "binds us as a nation in a multiracial hierarchy."

If Carbado's essay fills one important gap in studies of naturalization, Siobhan Somerville's "Notes toward a Queer History of Naturalization" addresses another. Somerville usefully divides the concept of citizenship in the nation from citizenship in the state; the former could be considered citizenship as a matter of identity—the kinship, belonging, or bond that joins a people and differentiates them from others. Citizenship in the state is also called formal citizenship, namely the processes that determine legal membership in a territorial community. As she indicates, work on citizenship and sexuality has attended much more closely to citizenship in the nation than to citizenship in the state. But rules of formal citizenship must be understood also as sexualized.

National borders are not only material and territorial; they are also rhetorical. Conventional renderings of our national narrative cast the immigrant as the desiring subject, longing to come to and belong to America. Somerville examines how the state also functions as a site of affective power, whereby it selects objects of desire and produces them as citizens. Naturalization is presumed to function as a salutary corrective to birthright citizenship, as modeled along the lines of contract and choice rather than ascriptive, accidental characteristics based upon blood. This essay casts a powerful challenge to that presumption, in discerning how, at the inception of the American nation, naturalization did not escape a sexualized logic of belonging. Rather, in the early national period, naturalization depended upon the transmission of citizenship through biological reproduction and presumed only certain subjects as "naturalizable," as capable of "surviving or reproducing as if native." Thus, sexuality has stood at the core of determining which bodies can be incorporated into belonging.

In his essay "Outlawing 'Coolies': Race, Nation, and Empire in the Age of Emancipation," Moon-Ho Jung similarly demonstrates the insights produced by examining together what are considered disparate sites of inquiry. Slavery and immigration are typically studied as separate phenomena and historical processes (unless slavery is studied as a form of forced migration). Jung analyzes legislative attempts to outlaw "coolies" in the nineteenth century to show that the complex origins of U.S. immigration restrictions in fact lay in struggles to demarcate the legal boundary between slavery and freedom. Thus, he questions conventional readings of anti-"coolie" agitation as stemming from anti-Chinese rancor in California, and instead defines it as the culmination of debates over the slave trade and slavery.

"Coolies," Jung argues, were not "a people but a conglomeration of racial imaginings" that emerged in the era of emancipation. Linked with slavery, the banning of the importation of "coolies" allowed immigration restriction to proceed in the name of freedom. The power of this association of immigration and freedom helps explain the perennial contradiction of how U.S. immigration law is imagined to have been historically unfettered, but with certain exceptions. Jung's focus on "coolies" also provides an important piece of the story of American exceptionalism: the moral imperative to prohibit slavery and coolieism around the world rationalized U.S. expansionism abroad, from China and Cuba in the 1850s to the Philippines in the 1890s. Thus, as Jung asserts, the locating, defining, and outlawing of "coolies" helped produce the historical transition of America from a slaveholding nation to a nation of immigrants, and from an empire of manifest destiny to a liberating empire. We can see the legacy of this transition today in the form of a preemptive war in the name of freedom.

Nayan Shah, in "Between 'Oriental Depravity' and 'Natural Degenerates': Spatial Borderlands and the Making of Ordinary Americans," focuses upon the lived experiences and regulation of the bodies of migrants once within the terrain of the United States. He newly examines little-known sodomy, statutory rape, and vagrancy cases in California in the early twentieth century wherein Asian men, perceived as the importers of unnatural sexual practices, were prosecuted for intergenerational, working class, and same-sex relations with adolescent boys. While the "foreigner" and the "degenerate" were not doctrinal categories, they functioned discursively to identify and explain moral peril. American identity consolidated around the normal masculine through the casting out of perverse behavior, ascribed to Asian men. The cases show an intense desire to contain and fix social boundaries and status, which, Shah argues, was both impossible and the product of an irremediable insecurity.

This site of legal regulation—the streets, alleys, boardinghouses, labor camps, and ranches where migrant workers congregated—functioned as what Shah calls a borderland space, a location characterized by police surveillance and anxiety about unruly, uncontained behavior that troubled categories and boundaries. In this sense, the space of the borderland functions as the shadow side, the other, to what is presumed to be the space of the normal. The borderland is the opposite of what we believe to be American normality.

If the borderland and American normality function as spatial opposites, what then is the opposite of the citizen? The citizen is considered the paradigmatic member, one who possesses full rights in the nation state. Linda Kerber, in "Toward a History of Statelessness in America," suggests that we understand the citizen's other not to be the citizen of another country, but to be the stateless person, the "man without a country." The relationship between the citizen and the stateless person, she asserts, may be in some sense necessary: the state "needs its negation in order to know itself." As she documents, when Americans invented a political structure in which to practice the fundamental rights of mankind, they were simultaneously devising structures that fundamentally deprived a large segment of the population of their human rights. Thus, her essay troubles the assumption of "we the people": at its founding core, some Americans could be considered stateless. Kerber also contradicts the assumption of America as an ever expanding circle of citizenship that can embrace all members over time; today, she writes, increasing numbers of people lack secure citizenship.

Hannah Arendt famously wrote that citizenship is nothing less than "the right to have rights."[15] This formulation would suggest that if one possesses formal citizenship, one's state will enforce one's rights, and that it is the lack of formal citizenship that has produced the nightmare of statelessness. But Kerber productively argues that it is not enough to possess formal citizenship if citizenship does not ensure the civil rights of a citizen. In a system of inequality among nation states, citizenship in a state cannot ensure that a prisoner receives the right to counsel at Guantánamo. Economic vulnerability, especially along the lines of gender, also creates what Kerber would consider de facto statelessness, a precarious existence characterized by the failure of one's state to protect. Statelessness, she writes, is most usefully understood not only as a status but as a practice, made and remade through daily vulnerabilities that render one not a citizen.

María Josefina Saldaña-Portillo, in her essay "In the Shadow of NAFTA: *Y tu mamá también* Revisits the National Allegory of Mexican Sovereignty," importantly asks us to consider the relationship between nation states in her examination of the vulnerabilities created by a treaty, the North American Free Trade Agreement (NAFTA). NAFTA involved what she labels a "fiction of development"—that territorial borders could be porous to goods and capital, but closed to those laborers whose impoverishment is often the result of NAFTA-style development. For the nearly three million new immigrants from Mexico who have traveled to the United States post-NAFTA, the treaty is not a story of the success of development, but a story of displacement and diaspora and, for those who are undocumented in the United States, a life on the borders of legality.

Saldaña-Portillo also analyzes what NAFTA has meant for Mexicans, especially the rural subaltern experiencing structural adjustment. For Mexicans, the eroding of sovereignty over territory created through NAFTA and the structural adjustments that have ensued have created cultural and political transformations that she argues cannot be captured through economic indicators and statistics. Here she turns to an incisive reading of scenes in the film *Y tu mamá también* (2001), which chronicle the subaltern's movement from periphery to center: from fishing village to tourist resort, from Michoacán to Mexico City, from Mexico City to the United States. The film registers the effects of NAFTA in everyday life and death, in brutal migration, and in the erosion of Mexican sovereignty, in the form of the loss of the dream of a nationalist state that will provide work and protect workers. Saldaña-Portillo reminds us that legal changes wrought by NAFTA have radically altered the social geography of the borderland of Mexico and the United States.

Borders of Territory

Legal borderlands can be understood as physical zones where, as Andrew Hebard writes, the "territorial and legal limits of the United States are being negotiated." These physical zones can exist within the fifty states and Washington, D.C.—for example within the space of U.S. prisons—or outside, in the form of an unincorporated territory such as the Commonwealth of the Northern Mariana Islands. In either case they inevitably implicate the relationship between American identity and democracy and the rule of law. Because American identity and democracy are fused, sites where the rule of law is suspended, revoked, or never implemented constitute what we could consider spaces of exception. These spaces of exception, so long as they carry the appellation "American," require some kind of legitimation for the suspension of normal democratic processes, either through the dehumanization of those who do not receive those rights or through the obliteration from the imagination of those spaces, disappeared in a Bermuda Triangle of collective memory.

All three essays in this section raise the question of empire and challenge the idea of American exceptionalism, particularly the presumption that America stands as an exception to the history of imperialism. The idea of American exceptionalism has permitted the notion that the United States is limited to the territorial boundaries of the nation-state; what happens "outside" those boundaries does not implicate the same level of concern for the rule of law, democracy, and full rights. Thus, if Guantánamo is a prison camp, or if the United States fails to guarantee equal citizenship to residents of U.S. territories, the narrative of exceptionalism holds that this does not implicate America itself and its commitment to the rule of law and individual rights.

The belief in American exceptionalism has been fueled by the failure of the United States to claim sovereignty over other nations to the extent that Western European powers did. But imperial powers have also disclaimed sovereignty in the service of imperialism, as contradictory as this might seem. Christina Duffy Burnett, in her essay "The Edges of Empire and the Limits of Sovereignty: American Guano Islands," persuasively shows how American imperialism has, in part, consisted of efforts to impose limits upon expansion. While, as she writes, we tend to associate imperialism with "the expansion of territory, the projection of power, and the imposition of sovereignty," American imperialism has also involved the circumscribing of power to reduce the responsibilities that come with sovereignty.

Burnett mines the history of the American Guano Islands, as "seemingly insignificant" places in the history of American expansion, to show the wide range of formal, legal practices of boundary management that attended territorial expansion. The Guano Islands—uninhabited but rich with fertilizer that led to a nineteenth-century craze for guano—were legally categorized as appertaining to the United States, belonging to yet not a part of the United States. The uncertainty of the status of appurtenance created a flexibility to implement control without responsibility. As with Guantánamo, the limiting of federal power, by reducing the responsibility of the federal government to protect those on annexed territory, is no less an imperialist move than the extension of sovereignty to that territory.

If Burnett shows us that imperialism can be not just about expansion but about limits, Andrew Hebard, in his essay "Romantic Sovereignty: Popular Romances and the American Imperial State in the Philippines," reminds us that imperialism was also about mundane legal and bureaucratic work. As he notes, other scholars have linked imperialism to the literary aesthetic of the romance, aligning the imaginary of an imperial nation to the imaginary of the romance. But Hebard argues that conventions of both romance and realism were reflected in the work of imperialism, which involved both extraordinary and undemocratic acts of violence as well as seemingly ordinary norms of colonial administration.

Imperial administration involved a necessary contradiction, an ambivalence between bureaucratic governance and violence. Violence, says Hebard, was seen paradoxically as both incongruous to civil governance and necessary for its instantiation in the U.S. colony of the Philippines, apparent through the simultaneous existence of both military and civil rule. The Philippines could be independent only when there was no longer a need for tutelage and intervention; the narrative of U.S. imperialism in the Philippines explained violence through a story of progress and benevolence. Thus, the violence necessary to maintaining colonial rule became a convention within a romantic narrative of progress. This was the common sense of U.S. imperialism.

The contemporary common sense of American empire appears in the United States' relationship to Guantánamo. Amy Kaplan, in her essay "Where Is Guantánamo?," writes against the notion of Guantánamo as a strange aberration, as a legal black hole, or a prison beyond the law. Instead, she argues, Guantánamo lies at the heart of American empire; Guantánamo is America. Kaplan traces the history of Guantánamo as a strategic colonial site to which the United States gained an indefinite lease with jurisdiction and control, but purportedly without sovereignty. The disclaiming of this sovereignty permits the United States government to argue that neither the Constitution nor international human rights treaties apply to U.S. treatment of the prisoners on Guantánamo.

Burnett and Kaplan together show that the ambiguity of the relationship of Guantánamo to the United States is the legacy of the Insular Cases, wherein the Supreme Court ruled in several cases beginning in 1901 that the Constitution only sometimes follows the flag: the United States could rule over distant territories and peoples with impunity and without constitutional restraint.[16] Thus, while Guantánamo is considered today to be a disturbing aberration, Guantánamo is in fact the norm in how the United States has practiced empire throughout history, through choosing to define certain spaces as beyond legal protection, spaces where the United States could govern without normal legal constraints. Kaplan argues that Guantánamo is not extraordinary; rather it appears ordinary when we examine the historical relationship of the United States to territory it seeks to control without constitutional responsibility.

Borders of Power

If state power proceeds from, but is not limited by, the geographic space mapped as "America," how are boundaries of American power drawn? Are there boundaries, or has the globe itself become an American space? Does law play a role in negotiating the terms of American power in the world? Long before the idea of "preemptive war" entered American political discourse and before the Abu Ghraib prison in Iraq came to define a new level of depravity in global perceptions of Americans, there was little faith in the idea that law and legal institutions served as an enforceable brake in the arena of global politics. Law does not provide a boundary around the powers of sovereignty, but instead provides a language within which state power is invoked. The essays in this section engage the question of where in the world American legal ideas and institutions operate, and examine how legal categories play a role in constructing an American sphere in the world and in defining the terms of entry to that sphere.

Empire is usually thought of as the ultimate expression of a nation's power in other regions of the world. The essence of empire is the conquest of foreign territory, and imperial power is exercised through control of that territory. The essays on borders of territory show that American exercise of imperial power has also involved a disclaiming of sovereign power over territory that it in fact controls. In this section, Teemu Ruskola, in "Canton Is Not Boston: The Invention of American Imperial Sovereignty," introduces a third way of conceptualizing empire, and along the way reframes the way we might think of nations themselves.

The role of American law outside of U.S. territory depends on how other regions of the world are imagined and understood. In the nineteenth century, suggests Ruskola, the world was not divided only into the categories of sovereign and "savage." Although this binary categorization constituted the primary justification for Western colonialism—the physical occupation and control of "savage" territories—there was a third category of "semicivilized" peoples. Such peoples might possess a degree of sovereignty, yet they could not impose their laws on the "civilized," even when the "civilized" came within the borders of their territory. This practice of Western extraterritorial jurisdiction constituted a form of borderless, nonterritorial imperialism.

Ruskola traces the history of the United States' first trade treaty with China, negotiated at gunpoint in 1844, to show how the United States became the leading practitioner of extraterritorial imperialism throughout the Asia-Pacific region. The imperial character of the American exercise of law was illustrated by its unilateral character. While Americans relied upon international law to force China to enter into "free" trade relations, they simultaneously used international law to justify the prohibition on Chinese immigration. The law of nations, Ruskola writes, was "thus seen to give Americans *both* the right to exclude Chinese from the United States *and* the right to 'open' China for the entry of Americans." Ultimately, he argues, the American power exercised through extraterritoriality was attached "to the *bodies* of American citizens—each one of them representing a floating island of American sovereignty."

In contrast, post–World War II Japan was, for the United States, a more traditional site of empire, a nation occupied by a victorious military power. As Lisa Yoneyama describes it, Japan became a site not only for the exercise of American military power, but also for the construction of American norms of equality and liberation. In "Liberation under Siege: U.S. Military Occupation and Japanese Women's Enfranchisement," Yoneyama takes on the provocative question of the use of American power in post–World War II Japan to achieve the enfranchisement and liberation of women. Her focus is not on the occupation itself, but on how the memory of the occupation has come to be constructed, and the way the liberation of women came to be central to that historical memory.

During the war, the U.S. press represented Japanese women as the "modern girl," the woman warrior. The stereotype of the submissive and obedient Japanese woman appeared near the end of the war, and was central to occupation-era constructions of Japanese culture in the American press. The occupation was celebrated as having brought American-style rights and liberation to oppressed women. Later, postwar women in Japan and the United States were thought to be ensconced in domesticity. The press portrayed American women as motivated by choice, while Japanese women were depicted as bound by a culture that frustrated the realization of Western ideas of equality. The enduring story Yoneyama draws from this narrative is the way the occupation, viewed as the source of emancipation for Japanese women, serves to justify contemporary warfare as a means of bringing rights to oppressed women in Afghanistan and Iraq. Preemptive war creates a state of unfreedom, paradoxically in the name of liberation.

Freedom and its opposite were central categories in the construction of the cold war world. During the early years of the cold war, the world was thought to be divided into two categories, two camps: the "free world," and the Soviet bloc, which was thought to embody enslavement, godlessness, and a rejection of other "Western" values. As Europe turned to postwar rebuilding, the United States emerged as the "leader of the free world." The barrier between East and West was imagined as an "iron curtain," and nations militarized physical borders. Borders became iconic spaces, places of dramatic encounters between cold war adversaries. Across these spaces passed the subjects of Susan Carruthers's essay, the escapees.

In "Between Camps: Eastern Bloc 'Escapees' and Cold War Borderlands," Carruthers argues that the U.S. government essentially created the category of cold war escapees by encouraging flight from the Soviet bloc. The fact that escapees would risk their lives in crossing militarized cold war borders helped to dramatically underscore the difference between the free world and its adversary. Yet these refugees, invited across the wall, were not fully welcome in the United States itself. U.S. immigration law required refugees to have documentation that escapees rarely possessed, and the number of refugee visas was decreased. While they sought entry to the United States, many escapees found themselves instead in refugee camps, where they were imagined as temporary sojourners awaiting a Soviet collapse so that they could return home. The escapee, for Carruthers, was an "impossible subject," "assigned the task of advertising the desirability of U.S. citizenship while being largely excluded from its entitlements."[17]

In Carruthers's essay, American power is shown to be exercised at a border—between East and West, between worlds—that was physically manifest in Europe. The legal subject, the escapee, is configured both in international law and in U.S. domestic politics. As an idea, the escapee thus crossed political categories. David Campbell's legal subject, the sports utility vehicle (SUV), traverses American freeways, its movement enabled by law, global politics, and a culture of desire for mobility and security.

The war in Iraq has sometimes been loosely linked with American oil consumption, particularly the preference of American drivers for large, gas-guzzling vehicles epitomized by the sports utility vehicle. Beneath the loose political rhetoric, how has oil, a strategic resource, figured in American national security policy? And why is it that high-consumption vehicles are associated with a security-oriented consumer culture? Campbell views oil not in the economistic terms common in American political discourse, which focus principally on the supply of oil. Instead, he argues that analyses of supply are insufficient because they ignore the question of the cultural production of a desire for oil. American desire for oil, Campbell argues, is tied to the centrality of mobility to American culture. This leads passenger vehicles to be the greatest consumers of oil in the United States.

While other essays in this volume address sovereign power, Campbell focuses on biopolitical power, which is distinguished from sovereign power by its focus on preserving the life of the population rather than the safety of the sovereign or the security of territory. In response to Hardt and Negri's argument that distinct national identities are fading, Campbell argues that "the sense of fading national colors is being resisted by the reassertion of national identity boundaries through foreign policy's writing of danger in a range of cultural sites."[18] The cultural site in this essay is the American freeway, occupied by the SUV. As Campbell illustrates, the SUV is a phenomenon enabled by law, defined as a "light truck" in U.S. environmental law and therefore exempt from the emissions standards applicable to cars. The SUV provides American consumers with a capacity for vehicular freedom that they desire but seldom actually use. Consumers defend their choice of fuel inefficient vehicles by invoking the idea that freedom from government regulation of consumer choices is central to American identity. This shows us, according to

Campbell, "the way that individual choices are part of a biopolitical whole with geopolitical consequences."

The legal narrative in Campbell's story is a tragic one, for the regulatory regime designed to decrease energy consumption created a category (light trucks/SUVs) that undermines the law's purpose. The consequences go beyond U.S. borders. The SUV, Campbell argues, "is the vehicle of empire"; it is "a materialization of American's global security attitude, functioning as a gargantuan capsule of excess consumption in an uncertain world."

Campbell's SUV-driving Americans, riding roughshod over international environmental treaties, would seem to portray the United States at the apex of its global power. Michelle Brown's essay brings us to a contemporary paradox. It was American global power that enabled the United States to take power in Iraq and to control the Abu Ghraib prison there. And it was the actions of Americans torturing and humiliating Iraqi prisoners at Abu Ghraib that now threaten American legitimacy. Abu Ghraib raises the question of whether this exercise of power leads to the conditions for its own limitation.

The idea of a rule of law, the idea that law can contain power, has perhaps been most threatened within the walls of Abu Ghraib. Here, the power of one nation is exercised in another through the control of prisoners by their captors. The story that emerges from Abu Ghraib would seem the opposite of the story of liberation Yoneyama finds in constructions of postwar Japan, as the prison is exposed as a site of torture. Yet in "'Setting the Conditions' for Abu Ghraib: The Prison Nation Abroad," Brown argues that conflicting understandings of the prison torture photos were constructed through law. Two legal frames dominated the understanding of the scandal. One focused on individual culpability, the idea that the soldiers who abused Iraqi prisoners were rogue elements in an otherwise lawful regime. The second frame focused instead on the dispersal of authority across a network of government and private actors, under pressure in a post-9/11 context.

While Abu Ghraib is often cast as an exceptional site, Brown sets it in the broader context of American prison policy, and sees the "war on terror" in the context of other "wars without end," against drugs and crime. Abu Ghraib, she argues, renders "the fundamental contradictions of imprisonment in a democratic context acutely visible." Ultimately Abu Ghraib falls into a contradictory space, "a legal borderland filled with spectral violence, a space packed with people and yet profoundly empty of its humanity."

* * *

As these essays go to press, new tensions have arisen over the border fence on the beach at San Diego and Mexico. In the name of homeland security, construction of a stronger fence has been ordered, despite objections about its impact on the environment. There, the metal edge, which had seemed as a scar upon the beach, is now recast as a nostalgic image. The divider is now reconfigured as an agent protecting the coastline, the sea life, and nesting birds.[19] Legal borders can be like this fence upon the beach. We might slip through their passageways, or burrow underneath; we might travel around them; we might fortify them or tear them down; we might simply reimagine them. Whatever their weight upon our imaginations, these borders, these tracings of law, are indelible on the American horizon.

Notes

1. For works that examine American studies in a global or "postnational" context, see Shelley Fisher Fishkin, "Crossroads of Cultures: The Transnational Turn in American Studies—Presidential Address to the American Studies Association, November 12, 2004," *American Quarterly* 57.1 (March 2005):17–58; Amy Kaplan, "Violent Belongings and the Question of Empire Today—Presidential Address to the American Studies Association, October 17, 2003," *American Quarterly* 56.1 (March 2004): 1–18; John Carlos Rowe, ed., *Post-Nationalist American Studies* (Berkeley: University of California Press, 2000); Donald E. Pease and Robyn Wiegman, eds., *The Futures of American Studies* (Durham, N.C.: Duke University Press, 2002).
2. One example of work that brings legal studies and cultural borderland analysis together is Carl Gutierrez-Jones, *Rethinking the Borderlands: Between Chicano Culture and Legal Discourse* (Berkeley: University of California Press, 1995).
3. Gloria Anzaldúa, *Borderlands/La Frontera: The New Mestiza*, 2nd ed. (San Francisco: Aunt Lute Books, 1999), 26. Special thanks to Shelley Fisher Fishkin for highlighting Anzaldúa's work, and this passage in particular, at the Legal Borderlands symposium.
4. For other works engaging the U.S.-Mexico border and the border region, see José David Saldívar, *Border Matters: Remapping American Cultural Studies* (Berkeley: University of California Press, 1997); David G. Gutiérrez, *Walls and Mirrors: Mexican Americans, Mexican Immigrants, and the Politics of Ethnicity* (Berkeley: University of California Press, 1995); Neil Foley, *The White Scourge: Mexicans, Blacks, and Poor Whites in Texas Cotton Culture* (Berkeley: University of California Press, 1998).
5. Sonia Saldívar-Hull, "Introduction to the Second Edition," Anzaldúa, *Borderlands/La Frontera*, 2.
6. See Michael J. Klarman, *From Jim Crow to Civil Rights: The Supreme Court and the Struggle for Racial Equality* (New York: Oxford University Press, 2004); William E. Nelson, *The Legalist Reformation: Law, Politics, and Ideology in New York, 1920–1980* (Chapel Hill: University of North Carolina Press, 2001).
7. Mae Ngai, *Impossible Subjects: Illegal Aliens and the Making of Modern America* (Princeton, N.J.: Princeton University Press, 2004).
8. Akhil Gupta and James Ferguson, "Beyond 'Culture': Space, Identity, and the Politics of Difference," in *Culture, Power, Place: Explorations in Critical Anthropology*, ed. Akhil Gupta and James Ferguson (Durham, N.C.: Duke University Press, 1997), 33–51; Susan Bibler Coutin, "Illegality, Borderlands, and the Space of Nonexistence," in *Globalization Under Construction: Governmentality, Law and Identity*, ed. Richard Warren Perry and Bill Maurer (Minneapolis: University of Minnesota Press, 2003), 171–202; and Mehnaaz Momen, "Are You a *Citizen*? Insights from Borderlands," *Citizenship Studies* 9 (2005): 323–34.

9. Sarat, "At the Boundaries of Law," this issue. See also Austin Sarat, Lawrence Douglas, and Martha Merrill Umphrey, eds., *The Limits of Law* (Stanford, Calif.: Stanford University Press, 2005).
10. See Giorgio Agamben, *Homo Sacer: Sovereign Power and Bare Life*, trans. Daniel Heller-Roazen (Stanford, Calif.: Stanford University Press, 1998); Carl Schmitt, *Political Theology: Four Chapters on the Concept of Sovereignty*, trans. George Schwab (1922; Cambridge, Mass.: MIT Press, 1985). On the relationship between the use of exceptional measures and the rule of law, see Nasser Hussain, *The Jurisprudence of Emergency: Colonialism and the Rule of Law* (Ann Arbor: University of Michigan Press, 2003). On the American national security justification for the state of exception, see Kim Lane Scheppele, "Law in a Time of Emergency: States of Exception and the Temptations of 9/11," *University of Pennsylvania Journal of Constitutional Law* 6 (2004): 1001–83. On the suppression of civil liberties, see Ellen Schrecker, *Many Are the Crimes: McCarthyism in America* (Boston: Little, Brown, 1998); Peter Irons, *Justice at War* (New York: Oxford University Press, 1983).
11. Mehnaaz Momen, "Are You a *Citizen*?"
12. Stuart A. Scheingold, *The Politics of Rights : Lawyers, Public Policy, and Political Change*, 2nd ed. (Ann Arbor: University of Michigan Press, 2004).
13. Sarat quotes Andrew Norris, "Introduction: Giorgio Agamben and the Politics of the Living Dead," in *Politics, Metaphysics, and Death: Essays on Giorgio Agamben's Homo Sacer*, unpublished ms., 2003, 15.
14. There is, of course, much scholarship critically examining the tension between American ideology and practices. See Rogers Smith, *Civic Ideals: Conflicting Visions of Citizenship in U.S. History* (New Haven, Conn.: Yale University Press, 1999); Desmond King, *The Liberty of Strangers: Making the American Nation* (New York: Oxford University Press, 2004).
15. Hannah Arendt, *The Origins of Totalitarianism* (London: Andre Deutsch, 1986), 295–296.
16. For a discussion of the Insular Cases, see Christina Duffy Burnett, "Appendix: A Note on the Insular Cases," in *Foreign in a Domestic Sense: Puerto Rico, American Expansion, and the Constitution*, ed. Christina Duffy Burnett and Burke Marshall (Durham, N.C.: Duke University Press, 2001).
17. Carruthers's "impossible subjects" is a reference to Ngai, *Impossible Subjects*.
18. See Michael Hardt and Antonio Negri, *Empire* (Cambridge, Mass.: Harvard University Press, 2000).
19. John M. Broder, "With Congress's Blessing, a Border Fence May Finally Push Through to the Sea," *New York Times*, July 4, 2005, A8.

At the Boundaries of Law: Executive Clemency, Sovereign Prerogative, and the Dilemma of American Legality

Austin Sarat

As territorial boundaries erode or become more permeable under the pressure of globalization, the temptation to seek other kinds of demarcations, what might be called "conceptual borders," intensifies.[1] These conceptual borders sometimes help to maintain an old cultural and political geography and to separate "self" from "other," "our nation" from "theirs."[2] Such borders, as Margaret Montoya argues, are particularly important today as "an epistemic space for the exploration of cultural production."[3] More than ever they require critical examination.

For the United States, no set of conceptual boundaries is more important, or in need of critical examination, than those associated with the idea of the rule of law. Today, as in the past, Americans pride themselves on their commitment to the rule of law.[4] This commitment is deeply rooted, or so the story goes, in America's history, and it has been renewed from one generation to the next. From Tocqueville's observation that "the spirit of the laws which is produced in the schools and courts of justice, gradually permeates . . . into the bosom of society"[5] to the present, numerous commentators have said that America has the "principled character . . . of a Nation of people who aspire to live according to the rule of law."[6]

Invocations of the rule of law as a constitutive boundary separating this country from the rest of the world are pervasive.[7] Thus Ronald Cass, former dean of the Boston University Law School, observes that the commitment to the rule of law is "central to our national self-definition . . . For most of the world . . . the nation most immediately associated with the rule of law—is the United States of America. The story of America . . . is *uniquely* the story of law" (emphasis added).[8] The philosopher Michael Oakeshott suggests that "The rule of law is the single greatest condition of our freedom, removing from us that great fear which has overshadowed so many communities, the fear of the power of our own government."[9] Similarly, Henry Cisneros argues that "the fundamental identity of the U.S. is not an identity based on how people look, what language they learnt first or over how many generations they absorbed Anglo-Protestant values. Rather it is based upon acceptance of the rule of law."[10]

Current controversies surrounding the war on terror and American intervention in Iraq have brought rule of law rhetoric to a fevered pitch, with public officials and commentators uncritically linking it to America's boundary-marking values and arguments about America's distinctiveness. Typical was the recent statement of Jonathan Lippman, Chief Administrative Judge of the State of New York, who said, "The rule of law is what separates us from those who seek to defeat our democratic institutions and way of life through violence and terror."[11] Commenting on the scandal at Abu Ghraib, former defense secretary William Cohen argued, "The strength of this country is its insistence that we adhere to the rule of law."[12] A particularly bellicose version of such arguments took the following form: "The rule of law separates civilized societies from despotic societies. Unlike Iraq, the United States is a nation of laws, not men . . . Yet if we blatantly violate the Constitution by pursuing an undeclared war, we violate the rule of law."[13]

References to the rule of law point toward a set of related concepts summarized in the idea that, as Cass puts it, "something other than the mere will of the individual deputized to exercise government powers must have primacy."[14] Cass identifies several core ideas that compose the rule of law. The first, "fidelity to rules," is that "rules tell officials how, to what ends, and within what limits they may exercise power,"[15] or that "government in all its actions is bound by rules fixed and announced beforehand," such that the rule of law makes possible a "principled predictability" in the actions of government.[16] Where rules govern, they must emanate from "valid authority"[17] and impose meaningful constraints on officials.[18]

In this essay I examine the issue of borders and borderlands in regard to the rule of law itself. I look at the way courts and judges chart the boundaries of legality as they wrestle with sovereignty and sovereign prerogative. Sovereignty troubles the rule of law by being at once prior to and yet a product of it. Sovereignty in a constitutional democracy exists in a legal borderland, where ideas of principled predictability and meaningful constraints on officials meet their limits.

I take up one example of sovereignty prerogative, namely executive clemency, and examine its treatment in and by law. Executive clemency provides an arena in which to examine how law explains and justifies gaps in its facade of principled predictability and constraint. As we will see, in its dealings with executive clemency, law authorizes a kind of lawlessness, or acknowledges the limited ability of rules to tell officials how, when, and why they may exercise the power accorded to them. Here we see law constructing and policing its own boundaries, boundaries within which, on its own account, prerogative power cannot be contained. In the jurisprudence of clemency we find law's borderland and, as in all borderlands, uncertainty and anxiety as well as possibility and opportunity.[19]

Sovereign Prerogative in Constitutional Democracy

Giorgio Agamben suggests that the essence of sovereign prerogative, like executive clemency, is its embodiment of the power to decide on an exception and remove a subject from the purview of "regular" law.[20] In the use of such a terminology, of course, Agamben draws on Carl Schmitt's famous definition, "the sovereign is he who decides on the state of exception."[21] This definition contains Schmitt's interest in the personal element of political decisions and in the agonistic and borderline relation of exception and norm. Schmitt's understanding of the exception is related to a state of emergency, a situation of economic and political crisis that imperils the state and requires the suspension of regular law and rules to resolve.

Executive clemency, of course, does not generally deal in terms of imminent peril or collapse; its usual idiom is one of mercy and not danger. And yet the two situations are not entirely dissimilar, as they both cannot be fully subsumed by the rule of law and thus require broad discretionary power.[22] As Schmitt repeatedly emphasizes, *this situation of danger can never be exhaustively anticipated or codified in advance*, and thus the suspension of law that it requires has to be the result of a conscious decision. Here, Schmitt says, "resides the essence of the state's sovereignty, which must be juridically defined correctly, not as the monopoly to coerce or to rule, but as the monopoly to decide."[23] Sovereignty cannot, of course, live without the concept of norm that it subtends and is parasitical upon, but that only highlights its agonistic relation to the rule of law.

The exception is, as Agamben puts it, "a kind of exclusion," and he says that "what is excluded from the general rule is an individual case. . . . [W]hat is excluded . . . is not, on account of being excluded, absolutely without relation to the rule. On the contrary, what is excluded in the exception maintains itself in relation to the rule in the form of the rule's suspension. *The rule applies to the exception in no longer applying, in withdrawing from it.*"[24] Acts of sovereignty such as executive clemency create exceptions, exclusions, but as Agamben notes, the exception does not "subtract itself from the rule; rather the rule, suspending itself, gives rise to the exception and, maintaining itself in relation to the exception, first constitutes itself as a rule."[25] Acts of clemency are quintessentially sovereign acts in that they are authorized by law as moments when officials can "decide who shall be removed from the purview of the law."[26] They mark the boundaries of the rule of law even as they do work that law requires.

Recently, Jacques Derrida has taken up this same theme in exploring clemency, pardon, and forgiveness. Derrida too recognizes that all of them are caught in a tension that he describes in several ways, starting with the addressees to whom clemency, pardon, and forgiveness might be offered. "It is important," he says, "to analyze at base the tension . . . between on the one hand the idea . . . of the unconditional, gracious, infinite . . . pardon, accorded to the guilty precisely as guilty, without compensation, even to one who does not repent or ask for pardon, and on the other hand . . . a conditional pardon, proportionate to the recognition of fault, to remorse and the transformation of the sinner who asks, then, explicitly, for pardon."[27] In Derrida's view, all such acts carry with them the specter of the impossible, the infinite, the unearned act of grace. Thus the tension between the unconditional and the conditional is "irreconcilable and indissociable."[28]

Derrida describes the borderland life of clemency in various other ways as well. Clemency exists in tension between acts and persons, in the ways acts become an irreducible sign of the persons who perform them and of persons who refuse to be reduced to the aggregate of their deeds. When we pardon, this dual reference—act or person—is always in place. "Does one pardon something," he asks, "a crime, a fault, a wrong, meaning an act or a moment which does not exhaust the incriminated person and at the limit is not confounded with the guilty who remains irreducible to it. Or rather does one pardon someone, absolutely, no longer marking then the limit between the wrong, the moment of the fault, and on the other hand, the person one holds responsible or guilty?"[29] This is a question that Derrida insists must be left "open."[30]

He turns to law to name in yet another way clemency's liminal status. Like Agamben, he is fascinated by the relationship between sovereignty and law and sees in the pardon what he calls "the right of grace."[31] To speak in the language of rights is to locate clemency on the terrain of law, yet *this* right works precisely by inscribing in law "a power above the law." Clemency, Derrida says, is "Law above the law."[32] Like Agamben, Derrida thinks of the exception as an inscription in the field of law itself, as marking the boundary where lawlessness becomes lawful.[33] "The right of grace is . . . the exception of the right, the exception of the right is situated at the summit or the foundation of the juridicio-political. In the body of the sovereign, it incarnates that which founds, sustains or raises, more highly, with the unity of the nation, the guaranty of the constitution, the conditions and the exercise of the law."[34]

In these arguments, Derrida considers the compatibility of clemency with democracy and calls attention to the reappropriation of the "right of grace" and the idea of sovereignty in "the republican heritage."[35] Democracies, he argues, claim to "secularize" clemency.[36] Yet the relation between democracy and clemency has long been recognized to be a troubled one. Thus the great English legal commentator William Blackstone wrote that "in democracies . . . this power of pardon can never subsist; for there nothing higher is acknowledged than the magistrate who administers the laws."[37] Like Blackstone, others worry that such a power, which allows executives "to insult the laws, to protect crimes, to indemnify, and by indemnifying, to encourage criminals," is indeed "extraordinary" in a democratic political system.[38]

Defending Lawful Lawlessness in the American Constitution

Writing in 1788, Alexander Hamilton sought to respond to concerns of the kind raised by Blackstone and others, explaining and defending the power to grant "reprieves and pardons for offenses against the United States" solely in the president of the United States.[39] Although the original versions of the New York and Virginia plans that provided the frameworks for debate at the Constitutional Convention included no provisions for pardon, revisions to both plans eventually did.[40] Yet unlike the president's power as commander-in-chief of the army and navy, a constitutional provision the propriety of which, in Hamilton's view, was "so evident in itself . . . that little need be said to explain or enforce it,"[41] the president's power to pardon was not self-evident.

The need for explanation and defense arose because granting such a power to the chief executive meant breaching the boundary between the rule of law and monarchical privilege. It meant importing traditional ideas of sovereignty into a document dedicated to constructing a government of limited powers.[42] As Blackstone noted, the power to grant reprieves and pardons was "one of the great advantages of monarchy in general; that there is a magistrate, who has it in his power to extend mercy, whenever he thinks it is deserved: holding a court of equity in his own breast, to soften the rigour of the general law, in such criminal cases as merit an exception from punishment."[43]

Saying that clemency issues from a "court of equity," Blackstone highlights its complex and unstable relationship to constitutionalism and the rule of law.[44] Like all sovereign prerogative, its essence is discretionary. Its efficacy is bound up to its very disregard of declared law.[45] Thus more than half a century before Blackstone, Locke famously defined prerogative as the "power to act according to discretion, for the public good, without the prescription of the Law, and sometimes even against it. . . . [T]here is a latitude left to the Executive power, to do many things of choice, which the Laws do not prescribe."[46] More recently, following Locke, John Harrison described clemency as "the power of doing good without a rule." In his view, "[pardons] should be like lightening bolts . . . because their incidence . . . cannot be accounted for in advance by the imperfect approximations on which legal rules are based."[47] Here we see yet again tensions between sovereign power and America's rule of law ideals, tensions that arise in part from sovereignty's ambiguous relation to legality.

Like the king acting "in a superior sphere," lodging the power to pardon exclusively in the president meant that even in a constitutional democracy the fate of persons convicted of crimes would be dependent ultimately on the "*sole fiat*" of a single person;[48] this was hardly the image of a government of laws and not of persons that Hamilton sought to defend. Yet defend it he did, claiming that what he called "the benign prerogative of pardoning . . . (unlike almost every other government power in the new constitution) should be as little as possible fettered."[49]

Hamilton constructed his defense of the pardon power around several propositions. First, he noted that without such a power "justice would wear a countenance too sanguinary and cruel."[50] To the framers, the power to pardon was necessary because of the way the law was applied. In England, it was common for minor offenses to carry a sentence of death, with pardon by the king being the only way to avoid the punishment. Judges often applied a death sentence, having no choice, but applied for a Royal Pardon in the same breadth. This is what Hamilton was referring to when, in Federalist 74, he mentioned "necessary severity" and "unfortunate guilt."[51]

Second, he argued that having such awesome responsibility concentrated in one person would inspire in the chief executive "scrupulousness and caution."[52] Yet such faith in the ennobling power of responsibility does not fit easily with a constitution designed to insure that "ambition . . . (would) counteract ambition" or the recognition that "if men were angels, no government would be necessary. If angels were to govern men, neither external nor internal controls on government would be necessary."[53]

Third, Hamilton focuses particularly, and revealingly, on the need for executives to have the power to pardon in cases of treason, which he rightly describes as "a crime leveled at the immediate being of the society."[54] As if to underline the connection between clemency and national emergency, Hamilton reminds his readers that "treason will often be connected with seditions which embrace a large proportion of the community."[55] And it is a "well-timed" offer of clemency, Hamilton contended, deriving neither from the "dilatory process of convening the legislature" nor its fractious deliberations, which in the "critical moments" of "seasons of insurrection or rebellion . . . may restore the tranquility of the commonwealth; and which, if suffered to pass unimproved, it may never be possible afterwards to recall."[56]

Hamilton connects the power to pardon to the construction of a boundary between the rebel and the loyalist. But the boundary he constructs is permeable, not fixed, and acts of mercy and gestures of compassion provide the occasion for its crossing.[57] He imagines an America beset with threats and turmoil, yet the America he imagines need not make rebels into permanent enemies or exiles. Hamilton's America would welcome its enemies back into the fold through devices constructed in order that boundaries might be breached and divisions overcome.

Hamilton's writings, and his imaginings of America, point to the richness and promise of executive clemency as a site to explore law's borderlands and its role in the construction of national boundaries. In its basic operations, of course, law attempts to create, police, and occasionally to transgress social, spatial, and temporal boundaries.[58] The preeminent declaration of a legal system—its announcement of its own existence—is a proclamation of jurisdictional boundaries within which its authority prevails.[59] This definition of a geographical space is matched by the declaration of temporal boundaries (statutes of limitation, ages of minority and majority, retroactive or prospective application of statutes or case law) within which legal authority is exercised.[60] Within law's spatial-temporal grid, complex systems of classification are established, creating additional boundaries that define individuals, communities, acts, and norms: Who is a criminal? A citizen? A victim of negligence? An individual or group entitled to legal protection or remedy?

Precisely because it is a power established and sanctioned by law that cannot be subject to legal rules, clemency marks a boundary of law itself. Examining the jurisprudence of clemency allows us to see the way law constructs its own boundaries and the boundaries of the commitment to rule by law that has been so central to the articulation of America's national myths and identities. As we will see, the equity of which Blackstone speaks springs from the body of sovereignty, as if originating well beyond any place the law could know or inhabit, yet it "depends on the law getting a chance to get the right result; (these) actions are . . . derivative of the law, secondary, complementary, and equitable."[61] "Derivative," "secondary," "complementary"—this language situates clemency in the borderland of law or at a fault line in the fabric of legality, waiting to do work that law requires. It is, in this sense, law's necessary other.

This other helps constitute the boundaries of law even as it reminds us of their uncertain, porous quality. It also generates anxieties as we confront that uncertainty and porousness. Its specter haunts a society whose self-conception is so closely tied to its alleged commitment to rule by law.

Clemency in the Courts: Charting Law's Borderland

American history has been marked by judges' repeated attempts to come to terms with sovereign prerogative and clemency, to name their relationship to democratic legality.[62] Some believe that history to be marked by change from a less legalized to a more legalized conception, seeing an emergent, if not fully realized, triumph of law over clemency,[63] of clemency's incorporation within the boundaries of legality. Yet the prerogative has, in fact, hardly been displaced. For every judge who finds resources to contain clemency's alegality in our legal tradition, others continue to acknowledge and defer to that alegality.[64]

This fact highlights the place of pardon, commutation, and amnesty in law's barely chartable borderland. Law cannot quite contain the exception, nor can it renounce the effort to do so. The judicial corpus gives clemency its due as an opening/a fissure in legal life and seems to take some comfort that in granting clemency this status, it is asserting the continuing supremacy of law. What is most apparent in the judiciary's efforts is its inability to find a stable register in which either to tame or fully liberate clemency, to incorporate it into, or exile it from, the province of law. Thus clemency marks a limit of law, one that law itself acknowledges. Yet in this acknowledgment law seeks to incorporate its limit, police its boundary, and define the terms on which its boundary can be crossed.

Instability has been present from the start. It is found in Chief Justice John Marshall's typically magisterial pronouncements in the first clemency case to reach the United States Supreme Court.[65] *United States v. Wilson* brought to the Court President Andrew Jackson's pardon of a robber for "the crime for which he has been sentenced to death" and the question of what would happen when Wilson, for breathtakingly inexplicable reasons, "did not wish in any manner to avail himself, in order to avoid the sentence in this particular case, of the pardon referred to."[66] Wilson's refusal put the courts in a bind of almost novelistic proportions, requiring them to determine whether a pardon could unseal the fate of a criminal against his wish to see it sealed.

Adopting the "principles" and "rules" of English law, Marshall described a pardon of the kind rendered by President Jackson as "an act of grace, proceeding from the power entrusted with the execution of the laws."[67] This grace is seemingly beyond the reach of legal compulsion or regulation; it is a grace freely given or withheld, finding its only home, as Blackstone might put it, in "a court of equity in . . . [the president's] own breast."[68]

Yet in the next moment of Marshall's opinion he tries to bring pardons back onto the terrain of law, describing them using legal language—promises, contracts, property. A pardon, he says, "is the private, though official act of the executive magistrate, delivered to the individual for whose benefit it is intended."[69] Blurring the lines of public duty and private act, Marshall says that a pardon is "a constituent part of the judicial system" but that it is a "private deed."[70] Sounding the idiom of modern contract law, if a pardon is rejected by the person to whom it is "tendered" it cannot be valid; "we have discovered no power in a court to force it on him."[71] The force of law suddenly lacks force. The force from which the pardon is exempted and from which it seeks to exempt Wilson cannot save Wilson's life should he not wish it saved.[72] The sovereign's godlike prerogative to spare life is rendered impotent by his subject's humble refusal.

For Marshall the "public" interest in the pardon that President Jackson granted was insufficient to override a private, contractual transaction between the one who offers grace and the one who decides whether to accept it. Marshall says that a pardon not pleaded by its intended recipient in a court of competent authority "cannot be noticed by the judges."[73]

But judges "notice" pardons all the time, regularly repeating a ritual in which they ceremoniously accept jurisdiction, thereby asserting clemency's place within law's boundaries. Sometimes they confidently pronounce the law's ability to control clemency. More often they avoid, defer, or refuse to use the "force" of the law to discipline, regulate, or regularize it.

A little more than twenty years after *Wilson*, the Supreme Court dealt with the question of whether the president could impose conditions on pardons. In *Ex parte Wells*, a murderer under a death sentence received and accepted from President Fillmore "a pardon of the offence of which he was convicted, upon condition that he be imprisoned during his natural life, that is, the sentence of death is hereby commuted to imprisonment for life in the penitentiary at

Washington."[74] The murderer subsequently sought review of his prison sentence. Taking up Justice Marshall's contractual imagery, Wells contended that his acceptance of the condition was invalid because it was undertaken while under the "duress" of imprisonment.[75]

The Court began its decision by acknowledging that, while the power to pardon was expressly provided for in the Constitution, "No statute has ever been passed regulating it in cases of conviction by the civil authorities. In such cases, the President has acted exclusively under the power as it is expressed in the constitution."[76] And, in an interesting assertion of law's dominion over pardon, Justice Wayne turned to language and usage, differentiating the way the term *pardon* is understood in "common parlance" from its legal meaning. In the former, pardon is forgiveness, release, remission; forgiveness for an offence, whether it be one for which the person committing it is liable in law or otherwise; release from pecuniary obligation, as where it is said, I pardon you your debt; or it is the remission of a penalty, to which one may have subjected himself by the nonperformance of an undertaking or contract, or when a statutory penalty in money has been incurred, and it is remitted by a public functionary having power to remit it.[77]

Yet "in the law," Wayne continued, "it has different meanings, which were as well understood when the constitution was made as any other legal word in the constitution now is."[78] Such a thing as a pardon "without a designation of its kind is not known in the law. Time out of mind, in the earliest books of the English law, every pardon has its particular denomination. They are general, special, or particular, conditional or absolute, statutory, not necessary in some cases, and in some grantable of course."[79] Wayne continued, as if uncertain that enough had been or could be said to show the subservience of clemency to law,

> It meant that the power was to be used according to law; that is, as it had been used in England, and these States when they were colonies; not because it was a prerogative power, but as incidents of the power to pardon particularly when the circumstances of any case disclosed such uncertainties as made it doubtful if there should have been a conviction of the criminal, or when they are such as to show that there might be a mitigation of the punishment without lessening the obligation of vindicatory justice. Without such a power of clemency, to be exercised by some department or functionary of a government, it would be most imperfect and deficient in its political morality, and in that attribute of Deity whose judgments are always tempered with mercy.[80]

Wayne's equation of clemency with mercy provides a touchstone for understanding its place in law's borderland. Rules can, of course, authorize officials to grant mercy and/or assign that power to one institution or another, but mercy itself cannot be completely rule governed.[81] It is precisely its status outside of rule that makes it an "attribute of Deity" and that means that it will always be accompanied by the anxiety that, in any constitutional democracy, accompanies the recognition of lawless power.

The anxiety-generating language of mercy reappeared when, in 1866, the Supreme Court again took up the president's power to pardon, this time upholding clemency for a confederate legislator who had been a pardoned "for all offences by him committed, arising from participation, direct or implied, in the said Rebellion."[82] The issue before the Court was whether that pardon exempted him from being subject to an act of Congress requiring persons wanting to practice law to swear that they had "not yielded a voluntary support to any pretended government, authority, power, or constitution, within the United States, hostile or inimical thereto."[83]

Speaking of the president's pardon power, Justice Field gave legal sanction to its lawlessness. "The power thus conferred," Field said,

> is unlimited, with the exception [in cases of impeachment]. It extends to every offence known to the law, and may be exercised at any time after its commission, either before legal proceedings are taken, or during their pendency, or after conviction and judgment. This power of the President is not subject to legislative control. Congress can neither limit the effect of his pardon, nor exclude from its exercise any class of offenders. The benign prerogative of mercy reposed in him cannot be fettered by any legislative restrictions.[84]

While pardon cannot, as Field conceives of it, be subject to rule in the normal sense of that word, he leaves unstated the scope of judicial review. His silence about the power of courts in relation to pardons is most telling. In silence he registers law's profound uncertainty and ambivalence about even the diminished form of sovereign prerogative left to executives in constitutional democracy, reserving for the courts an unstated, perhaps unstateable, role.

In the early twentieth century the Supreme Court returned to clemency, again registering its borderland legal status. In *Ex parte Grossman* Chief Justice Taft conjured once more the merciful sovereign authorized by law to exercise an unfettered discretion.[85] Our Constitution, he said, "confers this discretion on the highest officer in the nation in confidence that he will not abuse it."[86] Two years later, in a case some commentators see as a turning point from Marshall's ambivalent conception of clemency as at once an act of grace and a kind of private contract, a unanimous Supreme Court joined Justice Holmes in denying the claim that commutation of a death sentence to one of life imprisonment "cannot be done without the convict's consent."[87] The Court rejected the idea that informed Marshall's view, namely, that in order to be valid, a pardon had to be presented to a court.

Holmes spoke in distinctly un-Marshallian terms, finally asserting, or so it seemed, law's control over clemency by characterizing clemency as a matter of constitutional moment. "A pardon in our days," Holmes asserted, "is not a private act of grace from an individual happening to possess power. It is a part of the Constitutional scheme. When granted it is the determination of the ultimate authority that the public welfare will be better served by inflicting less than what the judgment fixed."[88] Here the juxtaposition of the phrases "an individual happening to possess power" and "the ultimate authority" is particularly striking, seeming to place clemency fully within a legal order whose constant presence authorizes it. Clemency, as Holmes understood it, springs not from a court of equity in the sovereign's breast, but rather from a set of considerations by one expressly charged to act for the "public."[89]

"Just as the original punishment," Holmes writes,

> would be imposed without regard to the prisoner's consent and in the teeth of his will, whether he liked it or not, the public welfare, not his consent, determines what shall be done. So far as a pardon legitimately cuts down a penalty, it affects the judgment imposing it. No one doubts that a reduction of the term of an imprisonment or the amount of a fine would limit the sentence effectively on the one side and on the other would leave the reduced term or fine valid and to be enforced, and that the convict's consent is not required. When we come to the commutation of death to imprisonment for life it is hard to see how consent has any more to do with it than it has in the cases first put. Supposing that Perovich did not accept the change, he could not have got himself hanged against the Executive order. Supposing that he did accept, he could not affect the judgment to be carried out. The considerations that led to the modification had nothing to do with his will.[90]

Holmes's reliance on a complete parallel between punishment and commutation misses the full impact of constitutional democracy on sovereignty, which splits sovereign prerogative, reserving clemency for executive action, while removing punishment from its purview. Yet Holmes rightly reminds us that the power over death is not left with the individual whose life the government wishes to dispose or to preserve. The sovereign right to spare life is recognized even as sovereignty is domesticated, and thus rendered less fearsome, by the requirements of due process.

Other courts have come close to Holmes in asserting law's dominion over sovereign prerogative, asserting for example, that pardon or commutation must be "exercised in a lawful and proper manner"[91] or that the clemency power is not "limitless" and that it must be exercised "in the public interest" and in a way that does not violate "the Bill of Rights which expressly reserved to the 'individual' certain fundamental rights."[92] Yet most courts continue to hold that the law imposes no substantive limitations on the grounds on which chief executives can grant clemency. Thus in an 1872 Virginia case, that state's supreme court likened clemency to "the authority to suspend the operation of laws,"[93] and, fifty years later, the Kansas Supreme Court said that "when the court's attention is called to pardon it will not inquire into the motives which prompted the pardoning official to issue the pardon, for to do so would be to usurp the pardoning power." It portrayed clemency as an act of mercy properly used to repair injustices that occasionally arise in "a just government,"[94] yet concluded that clemency always "is in derogation of the law."[95] In a 1977 decision, the Supreme Court of Florida endorsed "the following excerpt from *American Jurisprudence*: 'An executive may grant a pardon for good reasons or bad, or for any reason at all, and his act is final and irrevocable.'"[96] Or, as the United States Court of Appeals for the Sixth Circuit explained in a 1997 decision, "the very nature of clemency is that it is grounded solely in the will of the dispenser. He need give no reasons for granting it, or for denying it. . . . The governor may agonize over every petition; he may glance at one or all such petitions and toss them away."[97] Saying that clemency is rooted solely in "the will" of the dispenser seems to be about as straightforward an acknowledgment as one can imagine of the tension between clemency and the rule of law.

But the uncertain history of law and clemency did not end in these apparent judicial repudiations of Holmes. One of the most revealing statements of the continuing trouble that clemency poses for the rule of law and for constitutional democracy, of the spectral presence of both Marshall and Holmes in law's attitude toward it, is found in an Oklahoma case that arose in the early twentieth century. In that case, *Ex parte Crump*,[98] the Court of Criminal Appeals of Oklahoma explored the relationship of sovereignty and death, only here the death imagined is the death of law at the hands of a sovereign's uncheckable prerogative power.

"A pardon," the court said, echoing Marshall as well as Holmes "is an act of grace and mercy bestowed by the state, through its chief executive, upon offenders against its laws. Yet a pardon properly granted is also an act of justice, supported by a wise public policy. While the power to pardon, parole, reprieve, or commute after conviction for offenses against the state is a matter of executive discretion, this discretion should be exercised on public considerations alone."[99] This lawless discretion can and should be guided by conventions dictated by the design of government and prudence. "An executive officer . . . does not sit as a court of appeal from the Legislature. If he believes the law under which a prisoner is suffering to be unwise or unjust, still this opinion cannot incline him to grant a pardon, because the power which makes and unmakes laws is not in him, and officially he is required to look upon the law as just and wise, however his private opinion may revolt."[100]

Failure to abide by those conventions, the court suggests, could be deadly for the very law that authorizes executive clemency. "The granting of pardons is discretionary in its nature. . . . If it comes to be understood that a single man, entrusted with the high function of pardon, can open all the prisons of the country and let every guilty person go free, thus at a blow striking down the law itself . . ., the most disastrous consequences to liberty and law will sooner or later follow. Such a conclusion is itself the annihilation of law and only upon law can liberty repose."[101] Yet, as if conceding law's powerlessness to prevent its own annihilation, the court says that "this sort of executive abuse will not authorize the courts to decline giving effect to the executive pardon. . . . No court has the power to review the action of the executive in granting a pardon, for that would be the exercise of the pardoning power in part, and . . . would be a manifest usurpation of authority."[102]

A recent Supreme Court decision reiterated *Crump's* acknowledgment of clemency's existence at the boundaries of legality. In *Ohio Adult Parole Authority v. Woodard*, the Court heard a challenge to the long-held view that clemency could not be subject to due process standards applicable to other executive and administrative acts.[103] Ohio is one of a number of states that have endeavored to alleviate some of the anxiety about the executive's clemency power by elaborating an administrative framework that diffuses responsibility for all clemency decisions.[104] It requires that in death cases, the Ohio Adult Parole Authority hold hearings on any requests for clemency and make a recommendation to the governor prior to his decision. An inmate denied clemency sued, claiming that the parole authority's procedures violated, among other things, the due process clause of the Fourteenth Amendment.

Justice Rehnquist responded by reaffirming a posture of judicial deference in respect to clemency.[105] He rejected the respondent's contention that the statutory establishment of the parole authority's clemency procedures created a "life" interest any different from the interest "adjudicated at trial and sentencing."[106] But the core of his argument was his recognition that to subject clemency to due process would be to effectively extinguish it. In explaining the threat that Woodard's claim posed, Rehnquist endorsed Marshall's clemency as "grace" conception. "The process respondent seeks would be inconsistent with the heart of executive clemency, which is a grant of clemency as a matter of grace, thus allowing the executive to consider a wide range of factors not comprehensible by earlier judicial proceedings and sentencing determinations."[107] Rehnquist asserted that clemency is not part of the "adjudicatory process," while anxiously reiterating his view of the danger that legalization posed to executive prerogative. "Here the executive's authority would cease to be a matter of grace committed to the executive authority if it were constrained by the sort of procedural requirements that respondent urges."[108]

That Rehnquist's opinion garnered no majority gives further evidence of clemency's borderland status.[109] Concurring with the holding that the respondent had no cognizable due process claim, Justice O'Connor nonetheless insisted that "some *minimal* procedural safeguards apply to clemency proceedings."[110] Yet she was not able to name what those procedures might be and could imagine judicial intervention only in cases of the most transparent and unreasoning arbitrariness, for example, "a scheme where a state official flipped a coin to determine whether to grant clemency, or in a case where the State arbitrarily denied a prisoner any access to its clemency process."[111] Justice Stevens added to this list of barely imaginable horrors when he stated that "no one would contend that a governor could ignore the commands of the Equal Protection Clause and use race, religion, or political affiliation as a standard for granting or denying clemency."[112]

O'Connor and Stevens looked executive prerogative in the eye and blinked, insisting that, at least in some minimal but barely speakable way, clemency be rescued from its liminal status in a society dedicated to the rule of law. Yet it is precisely a legally uncontrollable arbitrariness that the clemency power requires us to imagine. Such arbitrariness and potential abuse of power generates doubt about, and criticism of, clemency and marks its status in law's borderland.

Conclusion

In June 2003, Mexico sued the United States in the International Court of Justice, alleging that some of this country's death penalty practices and procedures violated international law.[113] In the arguments before the court, the status of clemency in marking law's border and its status in the netherworld of the rule of law were again on display. Thus, the Mexican government alleged that the clemency process in the United States was inadequate in insuring opportunities for review and reconsideration of criminal convictions required by international law. Describing American practices, Mexico adopted Chief Justice Marshall's view, alleging that "clemency . . . is standardless, secretive, and immune from judicial oversight." It is "an executive act of grace and not a matter of right . . . (in which) Governors and parole boards across the United States have virtually unfettered discretion."[114] Not surprisingly, the American response echoed Holmes, confidently asserting law's ability to govern clemency. "Mexico is wrong" the United States claimed. "While the clemency procedures of the fifty states of the United States are not uniform . . ., these procedures are an integral part of the existing 'laws and regulations' of the United States." "Clemency in the modern era," it continued, "has been viewed less as a means of grace and more as a part of the constitutional scheme for ensuring justice and fairness in the legal process."[115]

This argument revisits and reiterates sovereign prerogative's uncertain legal status and highlights the equally uncertain boundaries of the rule of law itself. Indeed, if clemency has any resonance at all with the remainder of our constitutional scheme, that resonance is to be found in "the jurisprudence of emergency," which authorizes responses to grave threats to the nation.[116] There can be no doubt that the clemency power itself springs from the same source that has recently seen the president of the United States try to install military tribunals and remove altogether subjects from the purview of the civil courts by declaring them "enemy combatants."[117]

Both clemency and the emergency power remind us that the boundaries of legality are less stable and secure than those who enlist the rule of law to name what it means to be an American, or to justify America's overseas adventures, are willing to admit. Today additional reminders seem to be everywhere. Thus, even as some praise America for being uniquely dedicated to the rule of law, the United States refuses to submit to the jurisdiction of the International Criminal Court.[118] Americans hold themselves out as uniquely situated to defend the values and virtues of legality in a lawless world, yet we transfer detainees to other nations to allow them to be interrogated using techniques that would be unlawful under domestic law.[119] We assert the importance of our commitment to law in defining our national identity, yet until recently we defied international legal norms governing, for example, the execution of juvenile offenders.[120]

As these examples show, the rule of law is replete with gaps, fissures, and failures, places where law runs up against national interest or sovereign prerogative. Its boundaries are unclear, uncertain, unchartable. And, in many places, law runs out, law gives way. Indeed as Abraham Lincoln argued more than a century ago, the survival of constitutional democracy may at times require a form, if you will, of "constitutional dictatorship."[121] Like Lincoln's "constitutional dictatorship," the jurisprudence of clemency in a nation committed to the rule of law illustrates, in Dwight Conquergood's phrase, that "borders bleed, as much as they contain,"[122] and that it is in its bleeding borders that law itself, and with it American identity, is constructed, contested, and made meaningful.

Notes

I am grateful to participants in the conference on Legal Borderlands, Hart Institute, Pomona College, September 10–11, 2004; to Mary Dudziak; to Leti Volpp; and to two anonymous reviewers for helpful comments on an earlier draft of this essay.

1. See Patricia Goff, "Invisible Borders: Economic Liberalization and National Identity," *International Studies Quarterly* 44 (December 2000): 533. As Jacobsen notes, "Particularly striking is the fading role of a territory in defining a people (as in the nation-state), at least in the West, and the subsequent 'deterritorialization of identity.'" David Jacobson, "New Frontiers: Territory, Social Spaces, and the State," *Sociological Forum* 12 (1997): 121, 124.
2. "The borders of a settled nation-state substantially define our sense of political identity and justify a marked ethical partiality towards our fellow nationals." Michael Kenny, "Global Civil Society: A Liberal-Republican Argument," *Review of International Studies* 29 (2003): 119.
3. Margaret Montoya, "Border/ed Identities: Narrative and the Social Construction of Legal and Personal Identities," in *Crossing Boundaries: Traditions and Transformations in Law and Society Research*, ed. Austin Sarat, Marianne Constable, David Engel, Valerie Hans, and Susan Lawrence (Evanston, Ill.: Northwestern University Press, 1998), 131.
4. William F. Buckley Jr., "Strange Uses of Tolerance," *San Diego Union-Tribune*, January 27, 1985, C2.
5. Alexis de Tocqueville, *Democracy in America*, vol. 1 (New York: Knopf, 1945), 278.
6. See *Planned Parenthood v. Casey*, 505 U.S. 833, 868 (1992).
7. Samuel Huntington, *The Clash of Civilizations and the Remaking of World Order* (New York: Simon & Schuster, 1996), 311.
8. Ronald Cass, *The Rule of Law in America* (Baltimore: Johns Hopkins University Press, 2001), xii.
9. Michael Oakeshott, *Rationalism in Politics and Other Essays* (Indianapolis: Liberty Press, 1991), 389.
10. Henry Cisneros, "Extra Spice for American Culture," *Financial Times of London*, May 24, 2004, 17. See also Marci Hamilton, "The Rule of Law: Even As We Try to Export the Ideal of Justice by Law, Not Whim, Some in America Resist That Very Ideal" at writ.news.findlaw.com/hamilton/20031023.html (accessed May 27, 2005).
11. See Jonathan Lippman, "Preserving Safety and Access to the Courts," *New York Law Journal* 83 (April 30, 2004): 9.
12. Ann Parks, "Former Secretary of Defense Shares Views on War, Business, and the Rule of Law," *The Daily Record*, May 17, 2004. See also Law Tribune Advisory Board, "Are We Still the Land of the Free," *Connecticut Law Tribune*, April 12, 2004, 19.
13. Ron Paul, "War in Iraq, War on the Rule of Law?" *Texas Straight Talk* at www.house.gov/paul/tst/tst2002/tst082602.htm, (accessed May 27, 2005). See also "Our Opinions: Ignoring Detainees Rights Weakens U.S. Principles," *The Atlanta Journal Constitution*, May 18, 2004, 10A; and John Hutson, "Rule of Law: Guantanamo Offers U.S. A Chance to Showcase Ideal of Due Process," *The Recorder*, January 16, 2004, 4.
14. Cass, *The Rule of Law in America*, 3. See also Richard Fallon, "'The Rule of Law' as a Concept in Constitutional Discourse," *Columbia Law Review* 97 (1997): 1.
15. Cass, *The Rule of Law in America*, 4.
16. Ibid., 7.
17. Ibid., 12.
18. Ibid., 17.
19. For a discussion of the uncertainty and anxiety as well as possibility and opportunity found in borderlands, see Thomas W. Wilson, ed. *Border Identities: Nation and State at International Borders* (Cambridge: Cambridge University Press, 1998).
20. Giorgio Agamben, *Homo Sacer: Sovereign Power and Bare Life*, trans. Daniel Heller-Roazen (Stanford: Stanford University Press, 1998).
21. Carl Schmitt, *Political Theology: Four Chapters on the Concept of Sovereignty*, 2nd ed., trans. George Schwab (1932; reprint, Cambridge, Mass.: M.I.T Press, 1985), 5.
22. For a different view, see Bruce Ackerman, "The Emergency Constitution," *Yale Law Journal* 113 (2004): 1029.
23. Schmitt, *Political Theology*, 13.
24. Agamben, *Homo Sacer*, 17–18.
25. Agamben, *Homo Sacer*, 18. Agamben's *Homo Sacer* points to the formative and continuing influence of a vision of sovereignty that is by no means completely extinguished either by new forms of autho-

rization (electoral democracy) or new forms of adjudication (the rule of law). Agamben is distinctly less useful, however, in understanding the historical mutations and contemporary arrangements that reshape and replace such a sovereign power. One of the main transformations that Agamben neglects is that ideas of constitutionalism and the rule of law develop by essentially splitting *vitae et necis potestatem.* The power to punish (to authorize and to impose) is stripped away from the executive and vested in the legislature and courts. This is, of course, the well-known notion of a "separation of powers," which is constitutive of the very idea of limited government in the West. Indeed, for Montesquieu, the limitation that "the king cannot judge" saved even an absolutist monarch in the West from becoming "oriental despotism." Charles de Secondat Baron de Montesquieu, *The Spirit of the Laws* [1748], ed. and trans. Anne M. Cohler et al. (Cambridge: Cambridge University Press, 1989), bk. 11, 147. This splitting makes executive clemency today part of a received constitutional schema and not just some archaic residual of a once absolute power.

26. Andrew Norris, "Introduction: Giorgio Agamben and the Politics of the Living Dead," in *Politics, Metaphysics, and Death: Essays on Giorgio Agamben's Homo Sacer*, unpublished ms., 2003, 15.
27. See Jacques Derrida, "The Century and the Pardon," *Le Mondes des Debats*, no. 9 (December 1999), 5. Found at www.excitingland.com/fixion/pardonEng.htm (accessed June 28, 2005).
28. Ibid., 9.
29. Ibid., 6. William Blackstone, writing about the effect of pardon on the legal and political status of its recipients, said that "the effect of such pardon by the king is to make the offender a new man . . . as to give him a new credit and capacity." *Commentaries on the Laws of England: A Facsimile of the First Edition of 1765–1769* (Chicago: University of Chicago Press, 1979), vol. 4, 397–402.
30. Derrida, "The Century and the Pardon," 6.
31. Ibid, 9.
32. Ibid.
33. "The non-juridical dimension of forgiveness, and of the unforgivable—there where it suspends and interrupts the usual order of law—has not in fact come to inscribe itself, inscribe its interruption in law itself." See Jacques Derrida, "To Forgive: The Unforgivable and the Imprescriptable," in *Questioning God*, ed. John Caputo, Mark Dooley, and Michael Scanlon (Bloomington: Indiana University Press, 2001), 25–26.
34. Ibid., 10.
35. Ibid., 9.
36. Ibid. "The only inscription of forgiveness in law," Derrida says, ". . . is no doubt the right to grant clemency, the kingly right of theological-political origin that survives in modern democracies." See "To Forgive," 32.
37. Blackstone, *Commentaries*, vol. 4, 397–402.
38. See James Wilson, "Executive Department, Lectures in Law," in *2 The Works of James Wilson*, ed. Robert McCloskey (Cambridge: Harvard University Press, 1967), 442–44.
39. Alexander Hamilton, "Federalist 74," *The Federalist: A Commentary on the Constitution of the United States* (New York: The Modern Library, 1956), 482.
40. "Presidential Pardons," *Jurist* at jurist.law.pitt.edu/pardonslist.htm (accessed May 27, 2005).
41. Hamilton, "Federalist 74," 482.
42. The original definition of sovereignty in the West comes from the Roman law maxim *vitae et necis potestatem*, the power over life and death. Thus the opening sentence of Foucault's final section of the *History of Sexuality*, vol. 1, says that "for a long time, one of the characteristic privileges of sovereign power was the right to decide life and death." Michel Foucault, *The History of Sexuality: An Introduction*, trans. Robert Hurley (New York: Viking, 1990), 135.
43. Blackstone, *Commentaries on the Laws of England*, vol. 4, 397–402. Executive mercy was introduced into English jurisprudence in the seventh century on the grounds that all offenses are committed against the king's peace, and since it is he who is injured by fighting in his house, he alone should possess the power of forgiveness. See Stuart Gorin, "Presidential Pardons and Constitutional Authority," http://www.scoop.co.nz/stories/WO0103/S00027.htm (accessed June 28, 2005).
44. When Blackstone mentioned a court of equity, he was undoubtedly thinking of the actual courts of equity in his time. They developed in distinction to the common law courts with their elaborate, even byzantine, system of rules, pleadings, and writs, of the court of Chancery. See J. H. Baker, *An Introduction to English Legal History* (London: Butterworths, 1990), 122–28. And although by the time Blackstone wrote the *Commentaries* equity had hardened into law, he knew well the common under-

standing that "Chancery was not a court of law but a court of conscience . . . [and] the essence of equity as a corrective to the rigour of laws was that is should not be tied to rules." Ibid.

45. Austin Sarat and Nasser Hussain, "On Lawful Lawlessness: George Ryan, Executive Clemency, and the Rhetoric of Sparing Life," *Stanford Law Review* 56 (2004): 1307.
46. John Locke, *Second Treatise on Civil Government*, ed. and with an introduction by C. B. Macpherson (Indianapolis: Hackett,1980), sec. 159–60. "The Rulers," John Locke observed, "should have a Power . . . to mitigate the severity of the Law, and Pardon some Offenders: For the end of Government being the preservation of all, as much as may be, even the guilty are to be spared, where it can prove no prejudice to the innocent."
47. See John Harrison, "Pardon as Prerogative," *Federal Sentencing Reporter* 13 (2000–2001): 147, 148.
48. Hamilton, "Federalist 74," 482.
49. Ibid.
50. Ibid.
51. Ibid.
52. Ibid.
53. Ibid., 337.
54. Ibid., 483.
55. Ibid.
56. Ibid.
57. "Frontiers and boundaries, in addition to separating territories, have social functions, too, such as differentiation, connection, and regulation. . . . In the same vein, one can see frontiers as barriers, passages, filters, or gateways between different human—cultural and political—worlds." See Victor Segesvary, *World State, Nation States, or Non-Centralized Institutions? A Vision of Politics in the Future* (Latham, Md. : University Press of America, 2003), 22. As Frank Munger observes, "Boundaries may mark sites of many kinds of activities, for example, merger or elimination of differences . . . or renewal of, or contestation between, differences." See Frank Munger, "Mapping Law and Society," in *Crossing Boundaries: Traditions and Transformations in Law and Society Research*, ed. Austin Sarat, Marianne Constable, David Engel, Valerie Hans, and Susan Lawrence (Evanston: Northwestern University Press, 1998), 22.
58. See Richard Ford, "Law's Territory (A History of Jurisdiction)," in *The Legal Geographies Reader*, ed. Nicholas Blomley, David Delaney, and Richard Ford (Oxford: Blackwell, 2001), 200.
59. Ibid.
60. As Anderson notes, "Perceptions of territorial limits and territorial constraints are part of social and political processes. A sense of territory is an element (although the characteristics of this element have yet to be established) of what it is to be human. Human consciousness and social organization are profoundly conditioned by territory and frontiers. Boundary-making may be seen as part of the natural history of the human species." Malcolm Anderson, *Frontiers: Territory and State Formation in the Modern World* (Cambridge: Polity Press, 1996), 112.
61. William Miller, "Clint Eastwood and Equity: Popular Culture's Theory of Revenge," in *Law in the Domains of Culture*, ed. Austin Sarat and Thomas R. Kearns (Ann Arbor: University of Michigan Press, 1998), 175.
62. For a more complete treatment of this history, see Austin Sarat, *Mercy on Trial: What It Means to Stop an Execution* (Princeton: Princeton University Press, 2005), chap. 3.
63. See, for example, Victoria Palacios, "Faith in Fantasy: The Supreme Court's Reliance on Commutation to Ensure Justice in Death Penalty Cases," *Vanderbilt Law Review* 49 (1996): 311, 335–36.
64. Typical is the remark of Justice Frankfurter, who said, "It is not for this Court even remotely to enter into the domain of clemency reserved by the Constitution exclusively to the President." See *Rosenberg v. United States*, 346 U.S. 322 (1953).
65. See *United States v. Wilson*, 32 U.S. 150, 160 (1833).
66. Ibid., 159.
67. Ibid.
68. Blackstone, *Commentaries on the Laws of England*, vol. 4, 397–402.
69. *Wilson*, 32 U.S. at 160–61.
70. Ibid.
71. Ibid., 161.

72. On the force of law, see Jacques Derrida, "Force of Law: The Mystical Foundation of Authority," *Cardozo Law Review* 11 (1990): 919.
73. *Wilson*, 32 U.S. at 163.
74. *Ex parte Wells*, 59 U.S. 307 (1856).
75. Ibid.
76. Ibid., 309.
77. Ibid., 309–10.
78. Ibid., 310.
79. Ibid.
80. Ibid.
81. Emilios Christodoulidis, "The Irrationality of Merciful Legal Judgment: Exclusionary Reasoning and the Question of the Particular," *Law and Philosophy* 18 (1999), 215, 218. Christodoulidis contends that mercy demonstrates an "irreconcilability with law" in that it is "located in the space between law—law's justice—and particularity." Mercy, he says, "must provide its own criteria for judgment." Mercy, Johnson notes, allows "for the individuation between cases where the universal law cannot." Also see Clara Ann Hage Johnson, "Entitled to Clemency: Mercy in the Criminal Law," *Law and Philosophy* 10 (1991): 109, 115.
82. *Ex parte Garland*, 71 U.S. 333, 336 (1866).
83. Ibid., 376.
84. Ibid., 371. See also *Armstrong v. United States*, 80 U.S. 154, 155–56 (1872), and *United States v. Klein*, 80 U.S. 128, 142 (1872).
85. *Ex parte Grossman*, 267 U.S. 87, 120–21 (1925).
86. Ibid., 121.
87. *Biddle v. Perovich*, 274 U.S. 480, 485 (1927).
88. Ibid., 486.
89. See P. E. Digeser, "Justice, Forgiveness, Mercy, and Forgetting: The Complex Meaning of Executive Pardoning," *Capital University Law Review* 31 (2003): 161, 165. Digeser says pardon is a form of "political forgiveness . . . [which] is wholly public."
90. *Biddle*, 274 U.S., 486–87
91. *Schick v. Reed*, 483 F.2d 1266, 1267 (1973).
92. *Hoffa v. Saxbe*, 378 F. Supp. 1221, 1231 (1974).
93. *Lee v. Murphy*, 63 Va. 789, 798 (1872).
94. *Jamison v. Flanner*, 116 Kan. 624, 632 (1924).
95. Ibid., 630, 632. As the Supreme Court of Tennessee put it, "Executive clemency operates outside the letter of the law." See *Workman v. Tennessee*, 22 S.W.3d 807, 812 (2000). Or, in the words of Judge Arnold of the United States District Court for the Eastern District of Arkansas, grants of clemency "are by definition acts of grace, bestowed on no fixed basis and according to no ascertainable standards. They are manifestations of mercy, not of the operation of law." See *Rogers v. Britton*, 476 F. Supp 1036, 1039 (1979).
96. *Sullivan v. Askew*, 348 So.2d 312, 315.
97. *In re Sapp*, 118 F.3d 460, 465 (6th Cir. 1997). See *Otey v. State*, 485 N.W.2d 153, 166 (Neb. 1992) (the Nebraska Board of Pardons has "unfettered discretion" to grant or deny a commutation "for any reason or no reason at all"). Also *Joubert v. Nebraska Board of Pardons*, 87 F. 3d 966 (8th Cir. 1996).
98. *Ex parte Crump*, 135 P.428 (Okla. Crim. App. 1913).
99. Ibid., 430.
100. Ibid.
101. Ibid.
102. Ibid. See also *Herrera v. Collins*, 506 U.S. 390 (1993). In that case Chief Justice Rehnquist quotes Blackstone approvingly on the sovereign's "power to extend mercy, whenever he thinks it is deserved" and embraces Marshall's "pardon is an act of grace" conception of clemency. See *Herrera*, 412.
103. *Ohio Adult Parole Authority v. Woodard*, 523 U.S. 272 (1998).
104. See Adam Gershowitz, "The Diffusion of Responsibility in Capital Clemency," *Journal of Law and Politics* 17 (2001): 669, 673.
105. "Rarely, if ever (are clemency decisions) appropriate subjects for judicial review." See *Woodard*, 523 U.S., 276.
106. Ibid., 279.

107. *Woodard*, 523 U.S., 280–81.
108. Ibid., 285.
109. Various commentators and courts also disagree on what *Woodard* stands for, some seeing Rehnquist's no due process as the correct reading of the holding, others insisting that O'Connor's minimal due process garnered a majority. See David Olson, "Second-Guessing the Quality of Mercy: Due Process in State Executive Clemency Proceedings," *Harvard Journal of Law and Public Policy* 22 (1999): 1009. Also Kenneth Williams, "The Deregulation of the Death Penalty," *Santa Clara Law Review* 40 (2000): 677, 719; Kobil, "Chance and the Constitution," 573.
110. Ibid., 289. Some courts have also taken notice of the division in *Woodard*. See *Duvall v. Keating*, 162 F.3d 1058, 1060 (10th Cir. 1998), and *Workman v. Bell*, 245 F.3d 849, 852 (6th Cir. 2001). Other courts seem to have embraced O'Connor's minimal due process approach. See, for example, *Sellers v. State*, 973 P.2d 894, 896 (Okla. Crim. App. 1999); *Anderson v. Davis*, 279 F.3d 674, 676 (9th Cir. 2002); *Faulder v. Texas Bd. of Pardons and Paroles*, 178 F.3d 343, 344 (5th Cir. 1999); and *Duvall v. Keating*, 162 F.3d 1058. Nonetheless, in most cases the courts have found that whatever procedure was or was not provided passed constitutional muster. For an important exception, see *McGee v. Arizona State Board of Pardons and Paroles*, 376 P.2d 779, 781 (Ariz. 1962).
111. *Woodard*, 523 U.S., XX.
112. Ibid., 292 (Stevens dissenting). See Mark Strasser, "Some Reflections on the President's Pardon Power," *Capital University Law Review* 31 (2003): 143, 153–59. Strasser argues that Stevens's imagined cases are "not the kinds of cases that might reasonably be expected to occur."
113. Memorial of Mexico (June 20, 2003) submitted in the *Case Concerning Avena and Other Mexican Nationals, Mexico v United States of America*. Found at www.worldii.org/int/cases/ICJ/2003/2.html (accessed May 27, 2005).
114. Ibid., 101, 104.
115. Counter-Memorial of the United States (November 3, 2003) submitted in the *Case Concerning Avena and Other Mexican Nationals, Mexico v United States of America*, 112–13. Found at www.worldii.org/int/cases/ICJ/2003/2.html (accessed June 28, 2005).
116. Nasser Hussain, *The Jurisprudence of Emergency: Colonialism and the Rule of Law* (Ann Arbor: University of Michigan Press, 2003).
117. For a recent repudiation of that effort, see *Hamdi v. Rumsfeld*, 124 S. Ct. 2633 (2004).
118. For one explanation of this refusal, see Senator Jon Kyl, "U.S. Troops Must Not Be at the Mercy of an 'International Criminal Court,'" *RealClearPolitics* (December 14, 2004). Found at www.realclearpolitics.com/Commentary/com_12_14_04_jk.html (accessed June 28 2005).
119. See Dana Priest, "CIA–Drafted Memo Allows Transfer of Detainees from Iraq," *The Washington Post*, October 24, 2004. Found at http://www.boston.com/news/world/articles/2004/10/24/cia_drafted_memo_allows_transfer_of_detainees_from_iraq?mode=PF (accessed May 27, 2005).
120. See "USA: Time to Stop Executing Juvenile Offenders and Join the Modern World," Report of Amnesty International, August 15, 2001. Found at http://web.amnesty.org/library/Index/ENGAMR511212001?open&of=ENG-USA (accessed May 27, 2005).
121. The term is from the title of Clinton Rossiter's book. See Clinton L. Rossiter, *Constitutional Dictatorship: Crisis Government in Modern Democracies* (Princeton, N.J.: Princeton University Press, 1948).
122. Dwight Conquergood, "Rethinking Ethnography: Toward a Critical Cultural Politics," *Communication Monographs* 58 (1991): 94.

Racial Naturalization

Devon W. Carbado

Prologue: Notes of a Naturalized Son

A few years ago, I pledged allegiance to the United States of America—that is to say, I became an American citizen. Before that, I was a permanent resident of America and a citizen of the United Kingdom.

Yet I became a black American long before I acquired American citizenship. Unlike citizenship, black racial naturalization was always available to me, notwithstanding the fact that I tried to make myself unavailable for that particular Americanization process.

But I became a black American anyway. Resistance to this naturalization was futile. It is part of a broader social practice wherein all of us are Americanized and made socially intelligible via racial categorization. My intelligibility was skin deep. Epidermal. Visually inscribed on my body. I could not cross (pass) the phenotypic borders of blackness.

And I could not escape black racial social meaning. That I had a dream did not matter. The politics of distinction, or self-presentation strategies with the intraracial signification "I am the New Negro," did not help.[1] Out of racial necessity, my American black identity developed one interpellation after another.

Nor could I count on color blindness to protect me. That veil of ignorance became racially transparent.[2] Color blindness helps to prevent African Americans from becoming black no more.[3] Its racial ideology casts all of us in an ongoing national drama, an "American Dilemma."[4]

A significant part of this drama is acted out on the streets in the context of police interactions; there is no dearth of black men in leading roles. One of my earliest performances occurred only a few months after I purchased my first car, a yellow, convertible Triumph Spitfire. My brother and I were stopped by the police while driving in Inglewood, a predominantly black neighborhood in Los Angeles.

After we were forced to exit the car and sit on the pavement, I questioned whether we had done anything wrong: "We have a right to know, don't we? We're not criminals after all." Today I might have acted differently, less defiantly, but my strange career with race within the racial borders of America had only just begun. It had not occurred to me that my encounter with these officers was potentially life threatening. This was one of my many racial blind spots. Eventually, I would develop my second sight.

The officer discerned that I was not American. Presumably, my accent provided the clue, but my lack of racial etiquette—mouthing off to white police officers in a "high crime" area in the middle of the night—might also have suggested that I was an outsider with respect to the racial dynamics of police encounters, that I had not internalized the racial survival strategy of performing obedience for the police.[5]

The officer looked at my brother and me, seemingly puzzled. He needed more information to racially process us, to make sense of what he might have experienced as a moment of racial incongruity—that we were not quite not black. While there was no disjuncture between the phenotypic cues for black identity and how we *looked*, our *performance* of blackness could have created a racial indeterminacy problem that had to be fixed. The officer could see—with his inner eyes[6]—that we had the souls of black folk.[7] He simply needed to confirm our racial stock so that he could freely trade on our blackness.

"Where are you guys from?"

"The U.K."

"The what?"

"England."

"You were born in England?"

"Yes."

We were still strange fruit.[8] Our racial identity had to be grounded.

"Where are your parents from?"

"The West Indies."

At last, we were racially intelligible. Our English identity had been dislocated—falsified—or at least buried among our diasporic roots. Black was our country.

"How long has he been in America?" the officer wanted to know, pointing at me.

"About a year," my brother responded.

"Well, tell him that if he doesn't want to find himself in jail, he should shut the fuck up."

The history of racial violence in his words existentially moved us.[9] We were now squarely within a subregion of the borders of American blackness. Unwillingly, we were participating in a naturalization ceremony within which our submission to authority both reflected and reproduced black American racial subjectivity. We were being pushed and pulled through the racial body of America to be born again. A new motherland awaited us. Eventually we would belong to her. Her racial burden was to make us naturalized sons.[10]

And naturalized sons we became. Other police interactions facilitated this Americanization. They, too, helped to integrate us into an American black identity. I recount one more episode here.

My brothers and my brother-in-law had just arrived from England. On our way from the airport, we stopped at my sister's apartment, which was in a predominantly white neighborhood.

After letting us in, my sister left to do some errands. One of my brothers went into the kitchen to make tea. When the kettle continued whistling, and my brother did not respond to our calls to turn it off, my other brother went to see what was going on. Finally the whistling stopped, but neither of my brothers returned. My brother-in-law and I were convinced that my brothers were engaged in some sort of prank. Together, we went into the kitchen. At the door were two police officers. Guns drawn, they instructed us to exit the apartment. With our hands in the air, we did so.

Outside, both of my brothers were pinned against the wall: at gunpoint. There were eight officers. Each was visibly edgy, nervous, and apprehensive. Passersby comfortably engaged in conspicuous racial consumption. The racial product was a familiar public spectacle: white law enforcement officers disciplining black men. The currency of their stares purchased for them precisely what it took away from us: race pleasure and a sense of racial comfort and safety. This racial dialectic is a natural part of, and helps to sustain, America's racial economy, an economy within which racial bodies are differentially valued, made into property, and invested with social meaning. No doubt, our policed presence confirmed what the onlooking racial interpellators already "knew": that we were criminals.

"What's going on?," my brother-in-law inquired. The officer responded that they had received a call from a neighbor that several black men had entered an apartment with guns.

"Do you have any drugs?"

"Of course not. Look, this is a mistake." The officers (white men) did not believe us (would not listen). We were trapped inside their racial imagination. Our only escape was to prove that, in a social meaning sense, we were not what, phenotypically, quite obviously we were: black. Our look—or, in Fanonian terms, *the* look—was unmistakable.[11]

"May we search the apartment?"

"Sure," my brother in-law "consented." "Whatever it takes to get this over."

Two officers entered the apartment. After about two minutes, they came out shaking their heads, presumably signaling that they were not at a crime scene. Based on bad information—information that was *presumed* to be good—they had made an error.

"Sometimes these things happen." Sometimes? The "things" to which the officers referred happen all the time. Indeed, they have a name: the color line. We were its problem. There was no mystique about that.[12]

"Look, we're really sorry about this, but when we get a call that there are [black] men with guns, we take it quite seriously. Again, we really are sorry for the inconvenience." With that racial excuse, they departed. Our privacy had been invaded, we experienced a loss of dignity, and our race had been established—once more—as a crime of identity.

But that was our law enforcement cross to bear. In other words, the police were simply doing their job: acting on racial intelligence. And we were simply shouldering our racial burden: responding to the racial prerequisite that we prove our noncriminality. The borders of the color line had been protected. Entry had been simultaneously denied and granted. We were being included in one American experience (police harassment) and excluded from another (police protection). We had participated in a naturalization ceremony whose purpose was to make us a particular kind of American subject.

We went inside, drank our tea, and didn't talk much about what had transpired. Perhaps we were too shocked. Perhaps we needed time to recover our dignity, to repossess our bodies. Perhaps we knew that the incident was part of a broader social process to welcome us to and include us in America. Perhaps we understood that we were already Americans, that our race had naturalized us.

We relayed the incident to my sister. She was furious. "Bloody bastards!" She lodged a complaint with the Beverly Hills Police Department. She called the local paper. She contacted the NAACP. "No, nobody was shot." "No, they were not physically abused." "Yes, I suppose everyone is alright." Of course, nothing became of her complaints. After all, the police were "protecting and serving." We, like other blacks in America, were necessary casualties of the war against crime. Eventually, we would learn that we were impossible witnesses to police abuse, that within the racial borders of the United States, policed black identity is a national and natural resource—an American reserve that can be mined to fuel our anxieties about race, place, and crime.[13]

Introduction

Much of the literature on race and naturalization laws has as its point of departure Ian Haney López's extremely important book *White by Law*.[14] In it,

López explicates and theorizes the so-called prerequisite cases, cases that reveal the racial terms upon which courts granted American citizenship. What interests López is both the fact that whiteness operated as a prerequisite in naturalization jurisprudence and the shifting ways in which it did so—moving back and forth, according to López, between justifications based on science and justifications based on common sense. In large part, López's project is to answer, among other questions, the following: "How did the courts define who was white? What reasons did they offer, and what do those rationales tell us about the nature of whiteness? What do the cases reveal about the legal construction of race? . . . Do these cases afford insights into white racial identity as it exists today? What, finally, *is* white?"[15]

Yet there is another question one might ask about the prerequisite cases, the answer to which theoretically underwrites this essay: How precisely is naturalization operating within these cases? The dominant answer to this question is that naturalization operates in the prerequisite cases largely to deny American citizenship to people the courts construct as nonwhite.[16] That answer is certainly right, but it is based on a formal and doctrinal understanding of naturalization—namely, that it is a process through which a person becomes an American citizen.

However, more is going on in the prerequisite cases than race-based denials of citizenship. In these cases, courts naturalize (rather than simply construct) whiteness itself. The prerequisite cases are significant not only because they reveal the racial terms upon which people became (and sometimes unbecame) white by law; they are significant as well because they naturalized whiteness as the normative identity for citizenship. In the prerequisite cases, law establishes whiteness as American identity, and racism facilitates this naturalization.

Reading the prerequisite cases in this way broadens our understanding of naturalization. More particularly, this reading helps us to conceive of naturalization not simply as a formal process that produces American citizenship but also as a social process that produces American racial identities. Under this view of naturalization, Americanization and racial formation are not oppositional. They go hand in hand. It is precisely this relationship between Americanization and racial identity formation that is the subject of this essay.[17]

More specifically, I advance three broad claims: first, that racism is a naturalization process through which people become Americans; second, that historically the law has structured (though not exhausted) the racial terms of this naturalization; and third, that racial naturalization is simultaneously a process of exclusion and inclusion. Underwriting these claims is a distinction between American identity, on the one hand, and American citizenship, on the other. American citizenship here means formal citizenship, or citizenship as legal status.[18] American identity means the capacity, as a racial subject, to be a representative body—figuratively and materially—for the nation. Historically, Asian Americans, even those with formal American citizenship, have lacked this representational capacity.[19] By and large, Asian Americans have experienced a kind of national identity displacement or racial extraterritorialization.

Disaggregating American citizenship from American identity reveals that American identity does not require American citizenship, and that American citizenship does not guarantee American identity. Citizenship is neither a necessary nor sufficient condition for American identity, and American identity is neither a necessary nor sufficient condition for citizenship. Thus, one can be included in the category of people with American citizenship and be excluded from the category of people perceived to have an American identity. Racial naturalization produces these inclusions and exclusions. Consider, for example, the internment of people of Japanese ancestry during World War II. While most of the people the government interned were *included* in the category of formal citizenship, they were *excluded* from the category of American identity. Notwithstanding their formal citizenship status, they were perceived to be foreigners. One can think of Japanese Americans in this context as citizen aliens (as distinct from illegal aliens), a status that is forged at the interstices of an inclusive exclusion: inclusion in American citizenship and exclusion from American identity.

In a sense, my aim is to elaborate the foregoing example to demonstrate more generally how racial naturalization produces inclusionary forms of exclusion. This demonstration undermines the dominance of two sets of equivalencies: (1) the inclusion-equality equivalency (or the notion that inclusion and equality go hand in hand) and (2) the exclusion-inequality equivalency (or the notion that exclusion and inequality go hand in hand). One might reasonably read this intervention as broadening and racializing Giorgio Agamben's notion of "bare life." Agamben writes that

> the protagonist . . . is bare life, that is, the life of *homo sacer* (sacred man), who *may be killed and yet not sacrificed*, and whose essential function in modern politics we intend to assert. An obscure figure of archaic Roman law, in which human life is included in the juridical order . . . solely in the form of its exclusion (that is, of its capacity to be killed), has thus offered the key by which not only the sacred texts of sovereignty but also the very codes of political power will unveil their mysteries.[20]

Implicit in Agamben's conception of bare life is the notion that inclusion can be a social vehicle for exclusion and that inclusive exclusions can have constitutive power. This understanding allows us to conceive of blackness itself as a form of bare life. Simply put, the notion is this: blackness has often been included in the juridical order solely in the form of its exclusion (that is, its capacity to be subordinated). This inclusive exclusion historically has positioned black people both inside and outside America's national imagination—as a matter of law, politics, and social life. Blackness, in this sense, might be thought of as an insular identity; like Puerto Rico, blackness is foreign in a domestic sense. This racial liminality—outside and inside the borders of the American body, not quite not American—is precisely what I enlist the term *racial naturalization* to convey. To borrow from Gloria Anzaldúa, racial naturalization produces a borderlands space within which "you are at home, a stranger."[21]

As will become clear, the foregoing claims eschew the rubric of second-class citizenship. By and large, the literature on second-class citizenship understands this status to be constituted by (a) the acquisition of the legal or formal rights of citizenship (such as the right to vote) and (b) economic and social inequality. Thus, in the context of Jim Crow, both black Americans and Japanese Americans were second-class citizens; while both groups had acquired formal citizenship, or citizenship as legal status, neither group had achieved social equality.

This essay avoids the language of second-class citizenship because the process of naturalization it describes does not necessarily culminate in, and is not exhausted by the acquisition of, formal citizenship status.[22] In short, one need not be an American citizen to racially belong to America. To racially belong to America as a nonwhite is to experience racial inequality. To become an American citizen is often to cross the border into, not outside of, this racial inequality.

The above claim is not intended to suggest that people of color experience only racism in America. Nor is the argument that the American national identity is constituted only by racism. Because significant racial progress has been made in the United States, the weight of racism on our national identity, and in the lives of people of color, has significantly diminished. Still, racism persists in the United States—rarely in its Jim Crow iteration, to be sure—but the practice persists nonetheless. Examining the relationship between racism and Americanization helps to explain why—namely, that racism not only divides us as Americans; it also binds us as a nation in a multiracial hierarchy.

Models of Naturalization

Studies of naturalization principally appear in three forms, each of which is situated within an immigration framework that conceives of naturalization as a formal legal process through which a noncitizen acquires American citizenship. This framework conflates American citizenship and American identity, obscuring the role racism plays in producing and sustaining both. Instead, we should understand racism itself as a naturalizing phenomenon.

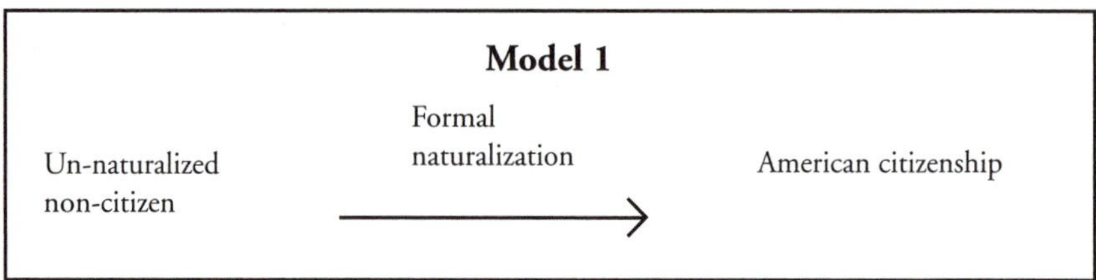

The first model of naturalization is perhaps both the simplest and the one with the most ideological currency. The basic idea is this: the immigrant moves from unnaturalized noncitizen to American citizen by a formal and bureaucratic naturalization process. Significant in this model is the fact that American identity and citizenship are inextricably linked. In other words, under this model, American identity does not exist outside of citizenship, and citizenship necessarily carries within it an American identity. The conflation of citizenship and American identity signifies both social inclusion and legal status. That is, under Model 1, becoming an American citizen effectuates a move not only from noncitizen to citizen, a transition that confers rights, privileges, and responsibilities. Becoming an American citizen also effectuates a move from outsider (or social exclusion) to insider (or social inclusion), a transition that, according to this model, confers the possibility, if not guarantee, of equality in social position and economic status.

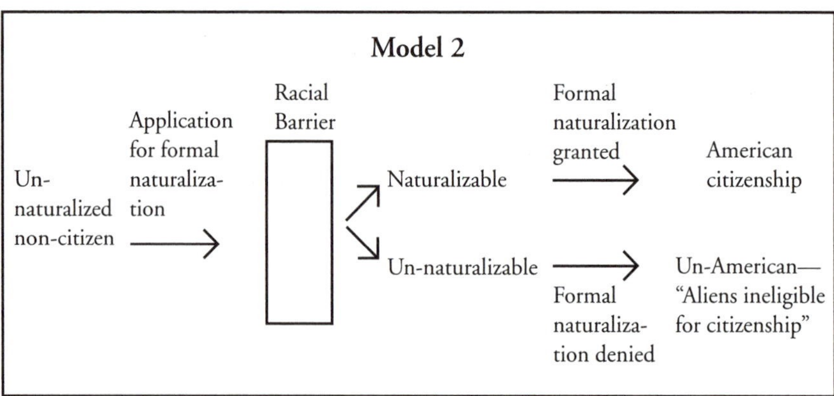

The second model exposes the racial legacy of naturalization. More particularly, it reveals that, historically, the legal borders of naturalization have been racialized. This racialization created two trajectories: the naturalizable trajectory and the unnaturalizable trajectory. The former became American citizens, the latter became un-American—more exactly, "aliens ineligible for citizenship." This is precisely the story of Asian naturalization. Racial naturalization laws moved Asian immigrants from unnaturaliz*ed* noncitizens to unnaturaliz*able* noncitizens. The juridical and ideological effect of this move was the production of all people of Asian ancestry as presumptively foreign and thus un-American.[23] In other words, as a result of racial naturalization laws, people of Asian ancestry became un-American by law. This status helped to create the social and legal conditions of possibility for the internment of Japanese Americans.

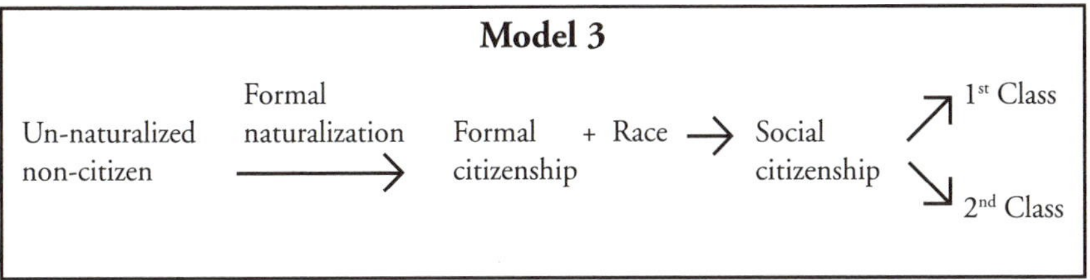

The third model lays naturalization onto broader social processes of race. The basic aim of this model is to demonstrate that race is implicated in naturalization not only as a prerequisite—that is, as a basis for determining who gets to become an American citizen. Race also determines the kind of American citizenship status one occupies. Under this model, everyone who is naturalized acquires formal citizenship, a status that confers a set of rights and privileges—for example, the right to vote. According to this model, formal citizenship interacts with race to produce social citizenship, a status that attempts to track the social conditions—economic, political, educational—of people's lives. The model delineates two categories of social citizenship: first class and second class. The former signifies a privileged social position in society, the latter a marginal position. The fundamental idea this model conveys is that naturalization occurs in a racial context, and this context shapes how citizenship is experienced. To make the point more concretely, while a white Frenchman and a black Ethiopian would, under formal citizenship, have the same formal rights and privileges, they would not necessarily have the same social citizenship.

While each of the foregoing models is useful, none invites us to think about the relationship between race and naturalization *outside of* a formal immigration process. Model 1 ignores race altogether and presents a race-neutral picture of naturalization. Model 2's engagement with race is historical, and the analysis is situated solely within the context of naturalization law. While Model 3 maps naturalization onto broader societal racial dynamics, that mapping does not conceive of naturalization itself as a racialization process. Under Model 3, the unnaturalized person is first naturalized into a formal citizenship status via a legal process, and then, through an entirely separate social process, racialized into a social citizenship status (first- or second-class citizenship). Central to the theory of naturalization I am offering is the notion that racialization is itself a form of naturalization and, further, that this naturalization does not require and is not exhausted by the acquisition of formal citizenship. The following diagram attempts to capture this.

	Formal citizenship	**American identity**	**Equality**
Japanese ancestry/Internment	YES	NO	NO
Black slave identity	NO	YES	NO
Contemporary black identity	YES	YES	NO

The diagram delineates three identity categories: Japanese ancestry identity in the context of internment, black identity in the context of slavery, and contemporary black identity. The diagram then pursues three questions with respect to each: whether holders of the identity (1) acquired formal citizenship status, (2) were intelligible as Americans, that is, had the capacity as a racialized body to represent the nation, and (3) experienced social equality. While many (though not all) people of Japanese ancestry were in fact formal citizens in the context of internment, they were not perceived to be Americans.

A similar point can be made about blacks in the context of slavery. While slaves were not citizens, they were intelligible as Americans—more particularly, as inferior beings that belonged to America. Slavery was a kind of forced naturalization, a process in which blacks were simultaneously denationalized from Africa and domesticated to (but never fully incorporated in) America.[24] *Dred Scott* was the key case in enacting this denationalization and domestication.[25]

Roughly, *Dred Scott* held in 1856 that people of African ancestry—whether free or slave—were not, and could never become, citizens of the United States.[26] This decision, and the language the Court employed to articulate it—that "the civilized and enlightened portions of the world" considered blacks "so far inferior, that they had no rights which the white man was bound to respect"—has earned *Dred Scott* an anticanonical status.[27] Central to the conception of *Dred Scott* as an anticanonical case is the notion that Justice Taney's opinion represents an extreme example of racial exclusion. Indeed, because of the racially subordinating positions the Court stakes out, Christopher Eisgruber suggests that the case is "almost certainly the worst judicial ruling in American constitutional history."[28] Yet precisely why this is so remains to be fully articulated. *Dred Scott* is problematic not only because it excludes people of African ancestry (from citizenship) but also because it includes them (as American [property]).[29] *Dred Scott's* inclusive exclusion establishes legal and normative precedent for the conception of African Americans as foreign in a domestic sense.

The specific phrase "foreign in a domestic sense" comes from Justice White's concurrence in *Downes v. Bidwell*, one of the Insular Cases that characterized Puerto Rico as neither foreign nor a part of the United States.[30] According to Justice White,

> while in an international sense Porto Rico was not a foreign country, since it was subject to the sovereignty of and was owned by the United States, it was foreign to the United States in a domestic sense, because the island had not been incorporated into the United States, but was merely appurtenant thereto as a possession.[31]

In the context of slavery, blacks were similarly positioned vis-à-vis the nation-state. That is, under slavery, blacks were "subject to the sovereignty of and . . . [were] owned by the United States." Moreover, with respect to citizenship, blacks had "not been incorporated into the United States, but . . . [were] merely appurtenant thereto as a possession." This is the manner in which slaves were "foreign in a domestic sense" or American aliens. The following brief discussion of *Dred Scott* makes this liminal status more apparent. Consider the two interrelated claims upon which Justice Taney builds his argument that blacks were not (and could never become) citizens of the United States. Claim 1: People of African ancestry are not, strictly speaking, foreigners. Perhaps the clearest manifestation of this idea is Justice Taney's juxtaposition of slaves with Indians. According to Taney, the situation of this population [African slaves] was altogether unlike that of the Indian race. The latter, it is true, formed no part of the colonial communities, and never amalgamated with them in social connections or in government. But although they were uncivilized, they were yet a free and independent people, associated together in nations or tribes, and governed by their own laws.[32]

In further distinguishing the Indians, the Court explains that the nation treated Indians as foreign governments, "as much so as if an ocean had separated the red man from the white . . . [T]he people who compose these Indian political communities have always been treated as foreigners not living under our government."[33] Taney extraterritorializes Indians (people who were actually here) and intraterritorializes blacks (people who had in fact been separated from white inhabitants by an ocean). Taney invites us to conclude that, unlike Indians, blacks were *not* foreigners; they "were living under our government" as a subordinate class.[34]

And one gets the sense that Taney does indeed conceive of slave identity as a kind of American class status, a status that was defined by complete domination. Implicit in his opinion is the notion that the American identity or class position of blacks was co-extensive with their involuntary servitude. The terms upon which they were included in the United States constituted the very terms of their exclusion. Thus, while people of African ancestry "had no rights which the white man was bound to respect"[35] (signaling their exclusion), "the African race . . . born in the country, did owe allegiance to the government" (signaling a kind of inclusion).[36] Slavery both denationalized blacks from Africa and Americanized them. The notion that blacks might belong to Africa—owe allegiance to one of *its* nations—is completely unintelligible in Justice Taney's opinion. As Neil Gotanda puts it, "The social categorization and hence social identity of the former slaves was not Yoruba, Hausa, or even African, but Negro or black."[37] Anthony Farley makes a similar point, observing that the middle passage was an experience in which "all manner of nations went into the wombs of those terrible ships to be born again 'as blacks' after a transatlantic labor-of-hate."[38] Part of the discursive violence of *Dred Scott* is the ease with which it eliminates the African identity of slaves. "No one of that race had ever migrated to the United States voluntarily; all of them had been brought here as articles of merchandise."[39] Taney's suggestion seems to be that the involuntary nature of slavery and its racial exclusivity is precisely what provided people of African ancestry their American identity—that is to say, naturalized them. Understood in this way, people of African ancestry became American via slavery. Slavery substantially diminished, if not eliminated, the formal status of Africans as foreigners.

Claim 2: While people of African ancestry are not, strictly speaking, foreigners, nor are they citizens—"constituent members of this sovereignty."[40] According to Taney, people of African ancestry "are not included, and were not intended to be included, under the word 'citizens' in the Constitution."[41] Informing Taney's reasoning, once again, are the twin notions of black inferiority and subordination. Taney argues that at the time the Constitution was written, blacks were "considered as a subordinate and inferior class of being . . ., who had been subjugated by the dominant race, and whether emancipated or not, yet remained subject to their authority, and had no rights or privileges but such as those who held the power and the government might choose to grant them."[42] For Taney, black inferiority and subordination precluded blacks from being citizens.

Read together, the foregoing two claims demonstrate that, for Taney, blacks were neither foreigners nor citizens. The Court recognizes that slaves were from somewhere else, but the terms upon which they came to the United States eliminated any prior national belonging and created a new one: slave status within the American nation-state. In this sense, African people's rebirth as slaves did not render them stateless. Slaves existed within, not outside of, the boundaries of America's national identity. Indeed, as Taney makes clear, slaves owed allegiance to and were subjects of the United States. Slaves had a place—a social position—in the political and constitutional order of the nation.[43] They were nonforeign-noncitizen—a status that had at least marginal (re)cognizability as an American identity. Not from "here" (America), not, for purposes of constitutional law, foreign, and with no claim to "there" (Africa), slaves were not quite not American, not quite not foreign; they were foreign in a domestic sense.[44]

If slavery inaugurated the inclusive exclusion that characterizes the Americanization of black people, the legacy of slavery perpetuates it. In fact, neither the granting of formal citizenship to blacks nor the eradication of Jim Crow has eliminated the constitutive role racism plays in naturalizing black people into their subordinate American identities. To put the point more directly, inclusion in the category of formal citizenship has not meant exclusion from racial inequality. Notwithstanding the doctrinal death of *Dred Scott* and the repudiation of *Plessy* (a case I discuss more fully below), the social intelligibility of African Americans as Americans remains directly linked to racial subordination. Indeed, almost 150 years after *Dred Scott*, black people still become Americans through (not in spite of) racism. Because of racism, black people, even today, express some iteration of what Zora Neale Hurston expressed many years ago: "I remember the very day that I became colored."[45] In remembering her social birth as an American Negro, Hurston is remembering her racial naturalization.

Dred Scott usefully demonstrates why we might conceptualize racism as a naturalization process. I want to more fully explain why this conceptualization is productive. To do so, I offer a simple definition of racial naturalization and then broaden it to distinguish between de jure and de facto racial naturalization.

De Jure and De Facto Racial Naturalization

A simple definition of naturalization is that it is the process through which people become American. If it is understood that part of becoming American is being forced into a particular racial identity and developing an epistemology about race, then racial naturalization is a process or experience in which that identity formation and knowledge production occurs. To put the point slightly differently, racial naturalization is what produces and renders intelligible race-based American identities. How the Irish became white is a story about racial naturalization; and the representational moves from African to slave to Negro to colored, and so on, are moves effectuated by racial naturalization. They are moves within the borders of American identity, moves that Americanized black people. This is the sense in which the experience of racism is a naturalizing one. It socializes people to become, and understand themselves as, American via their experiences with race. While there is a vast literature delineating how racism prevents people from becoming American, little attention has been paid to how racism *makes* people American. My hope is that the examples of racial naturalization I offer below will further our understanding of this latter phenomenon.

Broadly speaking, there are two forms of racial naturalization: de jure racial naturalization and de facto racial naturalization. Both forms, operating independently and collaboratively, produce, normalize, and render (re)cognizable race-based American identities. I discuss each form in turn.

De Jure Racial Naturalization

De jure racial naturalization occurs when race is intentionally and explicitly used to establish an American identity. Jim Crow politics and law reflect this. Consider, for example, *Plessy v. Ferguson*, in which, roughly, the Supreme Court declares racial segregation constitutional.[46] This case is most commonly understood as excluding blacks from American identity. My suggestion here, however, is that the case can also be conceptualized as a case about inclusion, and more specifically about inclusion in an American identity. Significantly, there is no dispute in the case about the status of blacks either as Americans or as citizens. The Fourteenth Amendment took care of the latter, overruling *Dred Scott* and declaring that "all persons born or naturalized in the United States . . . are citizens of the United States."[47]

Nowhere in the *Plessy* opinion does its author, Justice Brown, suggest that blacks are un-American. At all times in Justice Brown's opinion, blacks are intelligible as Americans. Indeed, the juridical effect of Justice Brown's analysis is the naturalization of blacks into an American identity—that is, the racial position they will occupy *as Americans.* According to Justice Brown, the Fourteenth Amendment "could not have been intended to abolish distinctions based upon color, or to enforce social . . . equality, or a commingling of the two races upon terms unsatisfactory to either."[48] For Justice Brown, segregation is a constitutive part of the American identity, and black people reside within, not outside of, the boundaries of this racial body.

Even Justice Harlan's *Plessy* dissent, which argues that racial segregation is unconstitutional, reflects formal racial naturalization. Consider the following two passages from this dissent.

Passage 1:

> The white race deems itself to be the dominant race in this country. And so it is, in prestige, in achievements, in education, in wealth, and in power. So, I doubt not that it will continue to be for all time, if it remains true to its great heritage.[49]

When reading this passage, one has to remind oneself that Justice Harlan is arguing against, not for, racial segregation. The significance of the passage for our purpose is that it advances the idea that "for all time" black American identity will be subordinate to white American identity. While in Harlan's view, the law should be employed neither to separate the races nor to create a dominant race, he is comfortable with a society in which there is both racial segregation and racial dominance.

In the above passage and elsewhere, Harlan goes out of his way to make clear that eliminating racial segregation as a matter of law would not lead to substantive equality for blacks as a matter of social fact. "For social equality no more exists between two races when traveling in a passenger coach or a public highway than when members of the same races sit by each other in a street car."[50] Like Justice Brown's majority opinion, Justice Harlan's dissent naturalizes black people into a subordinate but cognizable American identity. For Justice Brown, this naturalization may occur as a matter of formal law; for Justice Harlan, it should occur only as a matter of private social practice. In both opinions, then, blacks are recognized and recognizable as both citizens and Americans, and this racial recognition presupposes black marginalization.

Consider now Passage 2:

> There is a race so different from our own that we do not permit those belonging to it to become citizens of the United States. Persons belonging to it are, with few exceptions, absolutely excluded from our country. I allude to the Chinese race. But by the statute in question a Chinaman can ride in the same passenger coach with white citizens of the United States.[51]

One could read this passage as being concerned only with citizenship. But I want to suggest that it is not only citizenship that is being denied here, but also access to an American identity. People of Chinese ancestry are "so different from our own" that they cannot, even as a subordinate group, comfortably fit within the borders of the American body.

Justice Harlan's representation of the Chinese as unalterably different in his *Plessy* dissent rehearsed a position he would stake out two years later in *United States v. Wong Kim Ark*.[52] The question in that case was whether the Citizenship Clause of the Fourteenth Amendment applied to persons of Chinese ancestry. In a sense, the issue was about naturalization. Prior to the ratification of the Fourteenth Amendment, blacks were not citizens of the United States. The Fourteenth Amendment naturalized them. (The more standard articulation is that the Fourteenth Amendment conferred citizenship.) The question for the Court was whether the amendment similarly naturalized people of Asian ancestry born in the United States. The Court answered the question in the affirmative, and Justice Harlan (joining the opinion of Justice Fuller) dissented.[53] For our purposes, two aspects of this dissent are significant.

First, the dissent clearly understands the Fourteenth Amendment as a naturalization amendment. According to the dissent:

> In providing that persons born or naturalized in the United States, and subject to the jurisdiction thereof, are citizens, the 14th Amendment undoubtedly had particular reference to securing citizenship to the members of the colored race, whose servile status had been obliterated by the 13th Amendment, and who had been born in the United States, but were not and never had been subject to any foreign power. *They were not aliens (and even if they could be so regarded, this* [the Fourteenth Amendment] *operated as a collective naturalization)*, and their political status could not be affected by any change of the laws for the naturalization of individuals.[54]

The passage rehearses a conception of slaves that Justice Taney articulated in *Dred Scott*: in the context of slavery blacks occupied a liminal status, neither citizen nor alien. The Fourteenth Amendment naturalized them.

The second significant aspect of the dissent is its discourse about the Chinese. The dissent reproduces Chinese subalternity as unalterably different, noting what it perceived to be the serious social problems that could arise from "large numbers of Chinese laborers, of a distinct race and religion, remaining strangers in the land, residing apart by themselves, tenaciously adhering to the customs and usages of their own country, unfamiliar with our institutions, and apparently incapable of assimilating with our people."[55] The dissent is not simply denying citizenship here; it is denying any claim people of Chinese ancestry might make to an American identity. Unlike blacks, the Chinese did not have the liminal status of domestic foreigners, a status that can be disaggregated from and has intelligibility outside of formal citizenship. Indeed, in neither the *Plessy* dissent nor the *Wong Kim Ark* dissent are people of Chinese ancestry perceived to be domestic in any sense at all. Both dissents produce the Chinese as utterly and completely foreign and alien—not simply noncitizen, but also non-American. Moreover, in both dissents, the seeds for this racial production are sown in a juridical field that naturalizes blacks as a subordinated group with both American citizenship and American identity.

De Facto Racial Naturalization

De facto racial naturalization occurs when race is implicitly being used to establish, solidify, or sediment race-based American identities. Police interactions often perform this function. Consider, for example, the so-called stop-and-frisk practice. Consistent with Fourth Amendment law, police officers may stop and subject to questioning any person about whom they have "reasonable suspicion" to believe to be engaged in criminality.[56] Further, officers may frisk any person about whom they have reasonable suspicion to believe is armed and dangerous. Lower than probable cause, reasonable suspicion is a relatively easy evidentiary burden for police officers to meet.[57] In other words, an officer will have little difficulty justifying his stop-and-frisk decisions.

Because of racial stereotypes, every time a police officer stops a black person, blackness is reestablished and consumed as a crime of identity. This is so whether or not the officer's decision to stop is informed by race. For quite apart from the officer's intentionality, people could believe that stopping African Americans makes sense given the common notion that blacks are more criminally inclined than other groups.

A similar racial logic—that black people are more dangerous than people from other racial backgrounds—sanctions the frisking of African Americans. Simultaneously, the practice of frisking entrenches this racial logic and reifies black dangerousness: black people must be dangerous given the extent to which the police frisk them.

Significantly, the stop-and-frisk representation of black people as criminal and dangerous is not just an external phenomenon in the sense that it confirms people's suspicions about, and in effect re-creates, black criminality and dangerousness. There is an internal phenomenon as well. Because of the pervasive nature of stop-and-frisk, black people often experience these moments as a natural and constitutive part of their American identity. Discourses on what it means to be both black and American almost always reference some aspect of stop-and-frisk. Rather than undermine black American identity or citizenship, then, the stop-and-frisk practice actually facilitates both. Indeed, to the extent that the deployment of stop-and-frisk against blacks is based on stereotypes, the practice renders blacks more, not less, intelligible as Americans. This is at least one sense in which stop-and-frisk is a naturalization ritual. More broadly, the practice establishes the terms and conditions upon which black people will experience their American identities and be understood as Americans.

I should be clear to point out that the naturalizing effects of police interactions are manifested not only in what police officers do but in how suspects respond. These, too, are moments in Americanization. Part of becoming a black American is being socialized into performing obedience for the police. In their book *The Race Trap: Smart Strategies for Effective Racial Communication in Business and in Life*, Robert L. Johnson and Steven Simring offer the following obedience strategies for black people who are stopped by the police:

> * Don't argue the Fourth Amendment . . . [A]t the point you are stopped it is important to maintain control of your emotions and your behavior.
> * Don't be sarcastic or condescending to the officer. Always be cooperative and polite.
> * Don't display anger—even if it's justified.[58]

Presumably, everyone feels some pressure to be polite and courteous in the context of police encounters. Presumably, everyone employs technologies of the self. Each of us negotiates the pressures of governmentality. But for blacks, the pressure to be polite, and the self-discipline and self-regulation it engenders, is often experienced as a survival strategy. The reason relates to stereotypes. To the extent that blacks are perceived to be criminal and dangerous and that both of these perceptions invite police surveillance and control, there is an incentive for blacks to direct their performance of obedience toward disconfirming or negating stereotypes.

One way blacks may attempt to negate or disconfirm stereotypes is to consent to more police searches than they otherwise would. If, for example, Toney, a black man, consents to the search of his person and the search yields nothing, Toney may believe that he has demonstrated that he is not criminal, disconfirming or negating the stereotype that he is. Another strategy Toney might employ is to respond to questions such as "Where are you going?" "Where are you coming from?" and "What are you doing in this part of town?" under circumstances in which, as a matter of formal law, he is not required to do so.

Toney may believe that answering questions of the foregoing sort sends a clear signal that he has nothing to hide, that he is not in fact "up to no good."[59]

One can think of stereotype-negation strategies in the Marxian sense as a kind of surplus compliance. Surplus compliance is productive ("surplus") not only in the social sense of helping to make the stop play out smoothly; it is productive in an affective sense as well, creating a sense of comfort, ease, and naturalness to the stop. More generally, surplus compliance is naturalizing in that it reflects and reproduces a "normal" way of being American and a "normal" understanding of a particular American identity. From the perspective of the police, black people are supposed to perform surplus compliance; it is "natural" (sometimes articulated as "rational") to expect them to do so. From the perspective of black people, surplus compliance is a constitutive part of their American lives—an existential "what is." The Americanizing economy of police interactions not only creates the racial demand for and supply of surplus compliance, but it profits from the production of this racial obedience.

Conclusion

My argument has been that American identity and American citizenship do not necessarily go hand in hand, that racial naturalization constitutes both, and that racial naturalization ought to be understood as a process or experience through which people enter the imagined American community as cognizable racial subjects. Explicit in this claim is a conception of racism itself as a technology of naturalization. Indeed, it is precisely through racism that our American racial identities come into being. Put differently, racism plays a significant role in socially situating and defining us *as Americans*. Our sense of ourselves as Americans, of others as Americans, and of the nation itself, is inextricably linked to racism.

I do not mean to suggest that we are overdetermined by racism—that, as a result of racism, we have no agency. My point is simply that racism helps to determine who we are as Americans and how we fit into the social fabric of American life. Racism, in other words, is always already a part of America's social script, a script within which there are specific racial roles or identities for all of us. None of us exists outside of or is unshaped by the American culture racism helps to create and sustain.

To some extent, my conception of racial naturalization is linked to a claim Toni Morrison advances in "On the Backs of Blacks." Morrison's point of departure is a critique of Elia Kazan's critically acclaimed *America, America*. She writes:

> Fresh from Ellis Island, Stavros gets a job shining shoes at Grand Central Terminal. It is the last scene of Elia Kazan's film *America, America,* the story of a young Greek's fierce determination to immigrate to America. Quickly, but as casually as an afterthought, a young black man, also a shoe shiner, enters and tries to solicit a customer. He is run off the screen—"Get out of here! We're doing business here!"–and silently disappears.
> This interloper into Stavros's workplace is crucial in the mix of signs that make up the movie's happy-ending immigrant story: a job, a straw hat, an infectious smile—and a scorned black. It is the act of racial contempt that transforms this charming Greek into an entitled white. Without it, Stavros's future as an American is not at all assured.[60]

Morrison powerfully reveals the nature of Stavros's racialized journey into American identity. Indeed, the scene depicts Stavros's social rebirthing as an American—which is to say, his racial naturalization. Through the deployment of a recognizable American social practice—antiblack racism—Stavros is born again. He becomes a (white) American out of the racial body of northern racism.

Significantly, this transition in Stavros's identity does not require the acquisition of formal citizenship status. Stavros becomes a white American by social practice, not by law.[61] While formal naturalization and citizenship might never be available to Stavros, he can (and does) become racially naturalized by simply shoring up his whiteness, and positioning himself against black subalternity.

Morrison's analysis might lead one to conclude that the episode she describes figures Stavros's, but not the shoe shiner's, Americanization. My own view, however, is that the encounter naturalizes the shoe shiner as well. More than merely reflect the shoe shiner's black American identity, the encounter actually produces it. When it is kept in mind that Kazan's *America, America* takes place in the early 1900s, a period during which African American racial subordination was utterly and completely normative, it becomes clear that Stavros's displacement of the shoe shiner rehearses an American script that is both inclusive and familiar. The shoe shiner's part in this script is to experience racial subordination. Stavros's is to practice it. Both are included in the drama, and both are Americanized by it.

In this sense, Kazan's representation of the black shoe shiner reflects more than a problem of racial exclusion. It reveals what I have been calling an inclusive exclusion. Stavros's "Get out of here" includes the black shoe shiner into a recognizable American social position—that of the American Negro. This social position is in turn subordinated to Stavros's newly acquired status as a white American. In other words, Stavros's attainment of white American identity depends upon an exclusion of the black shoe shiner ("Get out of here"), and that exclusion is precisely what renders the shoe shiner intelligible as an

American. Indeed, it is through Stavros's exclusion that the shoe shiner reexperiences his American belonging.

What I am suggesting, in short, is that the scene around which Morrison frames her argument naturalizes Stavros *and* the black shoe shiner. The event assimilates both, drawing them into an American reality that both precedes and is enacted by the racial roles they perform. Morrison is only half right, then, when she asserts that "becoming [white] American is based on . . . an exclusion of me." The concept of racial naturalization disarticulates racism from exclusion. It conceives of racism as a social process that *includes* everyone, naturalizing us into different but recognizable American racial positions, both as citizens and noncitizens. None of us is excluded from this process. None of us is outside of it. None of us is left behind.

Conceiving of racial naturalization in this way has at least two benefits. First, it provides another theoretical vehicle to make the point that racism is endemic to American society, that, historically, racism has been formative of, and not simply oppositional to, American democracy.[62] Second, the concept helps to disrupt our tendency to engage in racial compartmentalism. By racial compartmentalism I mean the application of particular racial paradigms (such as immigration) to understand the racial experiences of particular racial groups (such as Latinas/os). As a result of racial compartmentalism, blacks disappear in the context of discussions about immigration law and policy, and Asian Americans disappear in the context of discussions about racial profiling.[63] Racial compartmentalism makes it possible to study *Korematsu v. United States* and never engage, or even reference, the fact that the constitutionality of Japanese American internment was litigated in the context of Jim Crow.[64] And because of racial compartmentalism, it is acceptable to study the racial failures of Reconstruction and never engage, or even acknowledge, the fact that these failures occur in the context of Chinese exclusion.[65] If, like Nikhil Pal Singh, we understand the color line as "an internal border"[66]—or, to pluralize his conception, a series of borders—it becomes more difficult for us to ignore or elide the multiracial social dynamics of inclusion and exclusion.[67]

Conceptualizing the color line as an internal border (or a series of borders) provides a way of highlighting the fact that racial identification *is* a form of documentation. How we cross the borders of the color line and where socially we end up are functions of the racial identification we carry. Perhaps not surprisingly, then, historically, racial identification (like other forms of identification) has raised evidentiary questions about falsification, standards of proof, and methods of authentication—in short, questions about the "real" and the "copy."

To the extent that we understand race as a form of identification, it becomes apparent that problems of migration (social movement across marked boundaries), documentation ("papers"/identifications), and national membership (noncitizen, citizen, American identity) do not end at the physical borders of America. These problems are a part of the broader social landscape of America. Consider this point with respect to Latinas/os. The racial identification of this group as both "illegal" and "alien" is a problem within, and not simply a problem at the physical borders of, the nation-state.[68] Thus we have the phenomenon of factory surveys, or raids of workplaces with significant representation of Latina/o employees by U.S. immigration officials. These raids, within the nation's interior, suggest that the color line operates both as a fixed checkpoint (at the physical borders of the United States) and as a roving patrol (within the interior).[69]

Problematizing the color line in terms of documentation has implications for black experiences as well. Specifically, this framing brings into sharp relief the ways in which documentation has served as an important technology for policing physical and social boundary-crossings by blacks. *Dred Scott* is a useful starting place for elaborating this point.

A little-discussed aspect of *Dred Scott* is Justice Taney's concern about the relationship between citizenship and black freedom of movement. Specifically, Taney worried that if blacks were granted citizenship,

> it would exempt them from the operation of the special laws and from the police regulations which they considered to be necessary for their own safety. It would give to persons of the negro race, who were recognized as citizens in any one State of the Union, the right to enter every other State whenever they pleased, singly or in companies, without pass or passport, and without obstruction, to sojourn there as long as they pleased, to go where they pleased at every hour of the day or night without molestation, unless they committed some violation of the law for which a white man would be punished.[70]

Justice Taney need not have worried. The conferral of citizenship to blacks did not enable black freedom of movement "without pass or passport, and without obstruction." Indeed, just last year, the Supreme Court ruled that, with no more than "reasonable suspicion" (which again is a lower evidentiary showing than probable cause) police officers may require a suspect to identify himself, and states may criminalize a suspect's failure to do so.[71] While everyone is affected by this law, African Americans are particularly vulnerable given racial assumptions about crime and criminality. Against a backdrop of racial stereotypes, the Supreme Court's pronouncement creates an incentive for police officers to both stop black people and request that they produce identification. The cumulative effect of such requests is a reduction in black peoples' freedom to "go where they please . . . at every hour of the day or night without molestation."

There is another more general way in which documents are implicated in black people's vulnerability to police encounters. The absence of documents—a driver's license or an identification card—undermines the perceived truthfulness of a black person's claim of noncriminality or innocence. As John Torpey observes, "Identity documents reveal a massive illiberality, a presumption of their bearers' guilt when called upon to identify themselves. The use of such documents by states indicates their fundamental suspicion that people will lie when asked who or what they are."[72] Because in the context of policing this suspicion is racialized, undocumented black people have a kind of illegal identity, that of a presumptive criminal. Without papers and the background check it enables, this presumption of criminality is difficult to rebut.

None of this is to say that physical documents alone will *necessarily* be enough to prove innocence. No amount of documentation (papers) can overcome strong racial investments or the perceived authenticity of racial identity. Put another way, if we think of race as a type of "paper" worn, inscribed, or lacerated onto the body, the presumptive authenticity of *this* form of documentation, and what it reads, in terms of social meaning, will not always be undermined by more traditional forms of identification.

***

Racial naturalization is a provisional concept. It is not intended to exhaust our understanding of racial formation. Its aim is more limited: to link, rather than disaggregate, racism and Americanization, and to employ that nexus to complicate how we think about inclusion, exclusion, and American belonging.

Notes

For comments on and conversations about this essay, I thank Saloni Mathur, Cheryl Harris, Nancy Postero, Gowri Ramachandran, David Goldberg, Gillian Lester, Michael Salman, Gabriele Schwab, Mitu Gulati, Kimberlé Crenshaw, Philomena Essed, Sora Han, Luke Harris, and Carol Anne Tyler. I am particularly grateful to Mary Dudziak and Leti Volpp for encouraging me to pursue this project and for providing feedback along the way, and to Marita Sturken for reading several drafts. Finally, I thank Nicholas Espíritu, Kevin Green, and Charles D'Itri for providing invaluable research assistance. Funding for this project was provided by the University of California, Los Angeles School of Law, the University of California Humanities Institute (Cloning Cultures Work Group), and the Alphonso Fletcher Sr. Fellowship Program.

1. See *The New Negro: An Interpretation*, ed. Alain Locke (New York: A. and C. Boni, 1925).
2. See John Rawls, *A Theory of Justice* (Cambridge, Mass.: Harvard University Press, 1971).
3. See George Schuyler, *Black No More: Being an Account of the Strange and Wonderful Workings of Science in the Land of the Free, A.D. 1933–1940* (Boston: Northeastern University Press, 1989).
4. See Gunnar Myrdal, *An American Dilemma: The Negro Problem and Modern Democracy* (New York: Harper & Brothers, 1944).
5. Jim Crow required blacks to perform a kind of racial etiquette for whites. A classic example is the domestic worker who implicitly understands that a racial condition of her employment is that she signal happiness (by, for example, singing or smiling) while performing her work.
6. See Ralph Waldo Ellison, *Invisible Man* (New York: Random House, 1952), 1 (referring to the "inner eye" as the "eye . . . with which they look through their physical eyes upon reality").
7. See W. E. B. DuBois, *The Souls of Black Folk: Authoritative Text, Contexts, Criticism*, ed. Henry Louis Gates and Terri Hume Oliver (1903; New York: W. W. Norton, 1999), 10.
8. Billie Holiday, *Strange Fruit* (Commodore, 1939).
9. See J. L. Austin, *How to Do Things with Words* (Oxford: Clarendon Press, 1975).
10. See Richard Wright, *Native Son* (New York: Harper & Brothers, 1940).
11. See Frantz Fanon, *Black Skin, White Masks*, trans. Charles Lam Markmann (New York: Grove Press, 1967), 113.
12. See Betty Friedan, *The Feminine Mystique* (New York: Norton, 1963).
13. This narrative, as well as the narrative articulated in the conclusion, draws heavily from and builds on an earlier work. See Devon W. Carbado, "(E)racing the Fourth Amendment" *Michigan Law Review* 100 (2002): 946.
14. Ian F. Haney López, *White by Law: The Legal Construction of Race* (New York: New York University Press, 1996).
15. López, *White by Law*, 3 (emphasis in original).
16. See John Tehranian, "Performing Whiteness: Naturalization Litigation and the Construction of Racial Identity in America," *Yale Law Journal* 109 (January 2000): 817–848.
17. See Paul Gilroy, *"There Ain't No Black in the Union Jack": The Cultural Politics of Race and Nation* (London: Hutchinson, 1987).
18. See also Linda Bosniak, "Citizenship Denationalized," *Indiana Journal of Global Legal Studies* 7 (2000): 447, 452.
19. See Leti Volpp, "The Citizen and the Terrorist," *UCLA Law Review* 49 (June 2002): 1597–98.
20. Giorgio Agamben, *Homo Sacer: Sovereign Power and Bare Life*, ed. Daniel Heller-Roazen (Stanford, Calif.: Stanford University Press, 1998), 8.
21. Gloria Anzaldúa, "To Live in the Borderlands," in *Borderlands/La Frontera: The New Mestiza* (San Francisco: Aunt Lute, 1987), 194.
22. Note that there are other reasons one might eschew the concept of second-class citizenship, including, but not limited to, the notion that the concept assumes that one can move from first- to second-class citizenship, an understanding that obscures the fact that first- and second-class citizenship are co-constitutive. The point is that one need not be an American citizen of any sort to be subject to racial naturalization; noncitizens are subject to this process as well. Nor does being a citizen necessarily bar one from the experience.
23. See Robert S. Chang, "Dreaming in Black and White: Racial-Sexual Policing in *The Birth of a Nation, The Cheat*, and *Who Killed Vincent Chin*?" *Asian Law Journal* 5 (May 1998): 41–61.
24. See Neil Gotanda, "Towards Repeal of Asian Exclusion: *The Magnuson Act of 1943, The Act of July 2, 1946, The Presidential Proclamation of July 4, 1946, The Act of August 9, 1946*, and *The Act of August 1, 1950*," in *Asian Americans and Congress: A Documentary History*, ed. Hyung-Chan Kim (Westport, Conn.: Greenwood Press, 1996), 309, 320.
25. *Dred Scott v. Sandford*, 60 U.S. 393 (1856).
26. The court also held that the federal government lacked constitutional authority to prohibit slavery in its territories. *Dred Scott*, 395–96.
27. Ibid., 407.
28. Christopher L. Eisgruber, "The Dred Scott Story: Originalism's Forgotten Past," in *Constitutional Law Stories*, ed. Michael C. Dorf (New York: Foundation Press, 2004), 151.
29. See Michael Hardt and Antonio Negri, *Empire* (Cambridge, Mass.: Harvard University Press, 2000), 171. Hardt and Negri write that "African American slaves could be neither completely included nor

entirely excluded. Black slavery was paradoxically both an exception to and a foundation of the Constitution."

30. 182 U.S. 244 (1901).
31. Ibid., 341–42 (Justice White concurring).
32. *Dred Scott v. Sanford*, 403, n. 25.
33. Ibid., 404.
34. To substantiate this point, elsewhere in the opinion the Court draws on state law to explicitly distinguish people of African ancestry from aliens. "The alien is excluded, because, being born in a foreign country, he cannot be a member of the community until he is naturalized. But why are the African race, born in the State, not permitted to share in one of the highest duties of the citizen?" Taney's answer: black people "form . . . no part of the sovereignty of the State." Ibid., 415.
35. Ibid., 407.
36. Ibid., 420.
37. Gotanda, "Towards Repeal of Asian Exclusion," 320, n. 24.
38. Anthony Paul Farley, "All Flesh Shall See It Together," *Chicano-Latino Law Review* 19 (spring 1998): 163, 167.
39. *Dred Scott v. Sanford*, 411, n. 25.
40. Ibid., 404.
41. Ibid.
42. Ibid., 404–5.
43. Several provisions of the Constitution implicate slavery.
44. For an interesting discussion of how black experiences immediately following slavery can broaden how we think about immigration and foreignness, see Kunal M. Parker, "Making Blacks Foreigners: The Legal Construction of Former Slaves in Post-Revolutionary Massachusetts," *Utah Law Review* 2001.1 (2001): 75–124.
45. Zora Neale Hurston, "How It Feels to Be Colored Me," in *"I Love Myself When I Am Laughing and Then Again When I Am Looking Mean and Impressive": A Zora Neale Hurston Reader*, ed. Alice Walker (Old Westbury, N.Y.: Feminist Press, 1979).
46. 163 U.S. 537 (1896).
47. Fourteenth Amendment, U.S. Constitution.
48. *Plessy v. Ferguson*, 544, n. 43.
49. Ibid., 559.
50. Ibid., 561.
51. Ibid. I have problematized these passages elsewhere. See Devon W. Carbado, "Race to the Bottom," *UCLA Law Review* 49 (June 2002): 1283–1312. Others have as well. See Ronald S. Sullivan Jr., "Multiple Ironies: Brown at 50," *Howard Law Journal* 47 (fall 2003): 23–57; Gabriel J. Chin, "The *Plessy* Myth: Justice Harlan and the Chinese Cases," *Iowa Law Review* 82 (October 1996): 151, 171–82; Cheryl I. Harris, "The Story of *Plessy v. Ferguson*: The Death and Resurrection of Racial Formalism," in *Constitutional Law Stories*, 181, n. 28. Each of these investigations, including my own, discusses *Plessy* along the lines of the racial exclusion thesis.
52. 169 U.S. 649 (1898).
53. Ibid., 705–32.
54. Ibid., 727 (my emphasis).
55. Ibid., 731 (citing *Fong Yue Ting v. United States*, 149 U. S. 698, 717 (1893).
56. *Terry v. Ohio*, 392 U.S. 1 (1968).
57. See Carbado, "(E)Racing the Fourth Amendment," 13.
58. Robert L. Johnson and Steven Simring, *The Race Trap: Smart Strategies for Effective Racial Communication in Business and in Life* (New York: Harper Business, 2002): 121.
59. For a complete articulation of this argument, see Carbado, "(E)racing the Fourth Amendment," 13.
60. Toni Morrison, "On the Backs of Blacks," in *Arguing Immigration: The Debate Over the Changing Face of America*, ed. Nicolaus Mills (New York: Touchstone, 1994), 97.
61. Of course, law is playing a role here. My point is that it is not a formal immigration-naturalization regime that is effectuating the shift in Stavros's identity.
62. See, generally, Derrick Bell, *And We Are Not Saved: The Elusive Quest for Racial Justice* (New York: Basic Books, 1989).

63. But see Lolita K. Buckner, "Tricky Magic: Blacks as Immigrants and the Paradox of Foreignness," *DePaul Law Review* 49 (1999): 85–137 (discussing the black experience as an immigrant experience).
64. 323 U.S. 214 (1944).
65. Erika Lee, *At America's Gates: Chinese Immigration During the Exclusion Era, 1882–1943* (Chapel Hill: University of North Carolina Press, 2003).
66. Nikhil Pal Singh, *Black Is a Country: Race and the Unfinished Struggle for Democracy* (Cambridge, Mass.: Harvard University Press, 2004).
67. See Carbado, "Race to the Bottom," n. 51.
68. I purposefully separate "illegal" and "alien" from the expression "illegal alien" to make clear that the terms have stand-alone racial signification.
69. In *United States v. Martinez-Fuerte*, 428 U.S. 543 (1976), the Supreme Court ruled that "apparent Mexican ancestry" alone, with no other indicia of suspicion, was sufficient grounds to detain individuals at fixed checkpoints near the border. The Court distinguished this holding from its ruling the year before, in *United States v. Brignoni-Ponce*, 422 U.S. 873 (1975), that apparent Mexican ancestry alone was not sufficient justification for a "seizure" in which the officers were on a "roving patrol" for suspected violations of immigration law.
70. *Dred Scott v. Sanford*, 416–17, n. 25.
71. *Hiibel v. Sixth Judicial Dist. Court of Nevada*, Humboldt County 124 S. Ct. 2451, 2458 (2004).
72. John Torpey, *The Invention of the Passport: Surveillance, Citizenship, and the State* (Cambridge: Cambridge University Press, 2000), 166.

Notes toward a Queer History of Naturalization

Siobhan B. Somerville

Questions of citizenship and national belonging have long been understood to be embedded within structures of desire and affect. For better or worse, in the words of Benedict Anderson, "nations inspire love, and often profoundly self-sacrificing love."[1] Lauren Berlant has usefully connected this discourse of national love to the context of immigration in the United States. As she writes, "Immigration discourse is a central technology for the reproduction of patriotic nationalism: not just because the immigrant is seen as without a nation or resources and thus as deserving of pity or contempt, but because the immigrant is defined as *someone who desires America*."[2] It is important to note that Berlant is discussing dominant views of the immigrant, which have been complicated, of course, by our knowledge that immigrants do not necessarily or even typically migrate voluntarily, but are often compelled to relocate because of violence or coercion, whether physical, psychic, economic, or political. Yet, for all of its inaccuracy, the myth of America as the immigrant's beloved is a powerful one, shaping not only popular cultural representations (as Berlant demonstrates), but also, as I discuss here, legislation and policymaking in the United States.

Although studies of nationalism and sexuality have had a central place within queer studies for more than a decade, the field has only recently begun to focus specifically on the role of immigration and naturalization in setting the terms for discourses of sexual citizenship and national belonging in the United States.[3] These studies not only extend the possibilities of queer scholarship by placing race, migration, and nation at the center of analysis, but also offer a bracing corrective to the fields of migration studies and citizenship studies, which have tended to assume that immigrants are heterosexual or/and that queer subjects are already legal citizens.[4] Challenging this tendency, much of the new scholarship employs ethnographic and sociological methods to chart the impact of queer migrants on U.S. culture and politics. Alternatively, others focus on the histories and practices of heteronormative institutions and discourses that have shaped constructions of citizens and noncitizens. In other words, while some work focuses on queers crossing borders, other studies have analyzed how ideologies of the nation have actively queered particular migrants, regardless of their sexual orientation.

For the most part, this work on citizenship, immigration, and naturalization has attended more closely to the nation than the state. This emphasis may result, in part, from the influence of Foucault, whose formulation of power directs attention away from the state.[5] It may also stem from the traditional ways that the distinctions between the state and nation have been theorized.[6] The state, for instance, is usually understood to be a juridical formation with some territorial component. In contrast, "nation," derived from the Latin root *nasci* (to be born), has traditionally been associated with a sense of kinship, a primordial belonging, or, in the words of one theorist, "a psychological bond that joins a people and differentiates it, in the subconscious conviction of its members, from all other people in a most vital way."[7] The emphasis on affective, "primordial," and familial bonds in models of the nation has made it a visible site of queer critique, which has demonstrated that the familial, heteronormative model of the nation is an ideological effect, rather than a prepolitical truth.[8]

But queer studies has focused less frequently and consistently on the ways that the state itself (rather than the nation) might be understood as sexualized and sexualizing.[9] As Davina Cooper notes, few scholars have explored "the ways in which sexuality as a disciplinary structure, identity and culture shapes state form and practice."[10] Cooper argues that "although dominant discourses identify the state as asexual, and the state works to maintain this ideological image, from the perspective of oppositional discourse, the sexual surplus possessed by the state pervades state practices."[11] Likewise, Jacqueline Stevens points out the stakes of understanding the state as an institution embedded in, not separate from, the sexual: "Once it is understood that the most fundamental structures of the modern state—the rules regulating marriage and immigration—are what enable the state to reproduce itself and what make possible the power relations associated with nationality, ethnicity, race, and family roles, then it is clear that piecemeal approaches to eradicating certain inequalities will not work."[12] Furthermore, scholars have recently begun to consider the myriad ways in which particular state practices promote and produce various forms of sexuality. Eithne Luibhéid, for instance, has identified the immigration control apparatus itself as "a key site for the production and reproduction of sexual categories, identities, and norms within relations of inequality."[13]

I want to return to the construction of the immigrant "as someone who desires America" and linger on it in light of these provocative insights about the mutually constitutive relationship between sexuality and state form and practice. To what extent, for instance, does the construction of a desiring immigrant obscure the ways that the state itself, through immigration and naturalization policy, sets the terms of this imagined love, actively distinguishing between which immigrants' desire will be returned and which will be left unrequited? To what extent does the presumed lovability of the United States distract us from, among other things, the state's own construction of certain immigrants and citizens as "lovable," and others as inappropriate objects for the nation's love? And what would it mean to understand the historical production of "undesirables" as a process of "queering" certain immigrants' imagined desire?

To approach these questions, I look at one of the "fundamental structures of the modern state"—the legal production of the naturalized citizen—at a specific moment in U.S. history, the early national period. Because of a tendency to focus on territorial borders as the site of national exclusion or inclusion, immigration has been a privileged site for scholarship on citizenship in American studies. However, as this special issue emphasizes, "borders are constructed in law not only through formal legal controls on entry and exit but also through the construction of rights of citizenship and noncitizenship."[14] If we consider the question of borders to be discursive as well as material or territorial, it is possible to see that the process of naturalization raises questions about the juridical production of American borders in ways that are distinct from those surrounding questions of immigration. Although in popular U.S. parlance naturalization tends to be linked implicitly to immigration, it is crucial to keep distinct the histories and processes of naturalization and immigration.[15] We might then recast Berlant's questions about the immigrant to consider the specific figure of the alien who seeks naturalization. To what extent has the naturalization process been understood within economies of desire? And to what extent have narratives about naturalization obscured or exposed the state's attachment to particular embodiments of desirable citizens? How have these narratives been entangled with or detached from questions about sexuality and reproduction?

My aim is to begin to trace a queer history of naturalization as a particular (and often contradictory) state practice through which citizens have been produced in the United States. My primary sources include early national juridical texts concerning naturalization, such as the Naturalization Act of 1790, as well as contemporary commentaries on these laws. It is important to note, however, that I do not regard laws themselves as transparent statements of state power; rather, as I will demonstrate, if we attend to the specific textual aspects of these laws, including metaphorical language and narrative logic, we may see the ways that the state itself functions as a site of affective power. In other words, we might shift our focus from whether or not the alien is "someone who desires America," and instead pay attention to the ways in which the state selects its own objects of desire and produces them as citizens.

It is generally understood that, historically, the United States has reproduced its citizenry in two ways: first, through "birthright citizenship"; and, second, through naturalization. In existing scholarship, the distinction drawn between these two models of producing citizens has centered on the question of consent. Birthright citizenship is a nonconsensual means of granting citizenship, linked to feudal, hierarchical models of allegiance. In contrast, naturalization is understood as a consensual process of conferring citizenship, associated with Lockean and later Enlightenment models of a contractual relationship between citizen and state, principles that have been seen as fundamental to liberal democracies.[16] Peter Schuck and Rogers Smith refer to this tension as "one between the rival principles of ascription and consent."[17] Thus, birthright citizenship as an ascriptive model confers status upon a child based on factors that are not under her/his control, such as place of birth or biological parentage. Naturalization, on the other hand, enacts a contractual relationship, a voluntary allegiance based on mutual consent between the immigrant and the state. In the United States, the individual establishes that contract with the state by taking a public oath, the full text of which currently reads:

> I hereby declare, on oath, that I absolutely and entirely renounce and abjure all allegiance and fidelity to any foreign prince, potentate, state or sovereignty, of whom or which I have heretofore been a subject or citizen; that I will support and defend the Constitution and laws of the United States of America against all enemies, foreign and domestic; that I will bear true faith and allegiance to the same; that I will bear arms on behalf of the United States when required by the law; that I will perform noncombatant service in the armed forces of the United States when required by the law; that I will perform work of national importance under civilian direction when required by the law; and that I take this obligation freely without any mental reservation or purpose of evasion; so help me God.[18]

Unlike birthright citizenship, then, naturalized citizenship is produced through this self-conscious, presumably voluntary declaration of the citizen's agreement to the terms of this contract with the state. Perhaps not coincidentally, in form, language, and effect, the oath of allegiance has similarities to traditional vows of marriage: both are speech acts that transform the speaker's legal status; both use the language of "fidelity" and "obligation"; and both establish an exclusive—one might even say "monogamous"—relationship to the other party.

In fact, the echoes of monogamous marriage vows in the oath of allegiance suggest another way that we might contrast birthright citizenship and naturalization, by focusing on how the sexual is situated in each. As the term suggests, birthright citizenship entails the literal production of citizens through sexual reproduction. In the United States, citizenship is granted at birth to anyone born within the nation's territory (regardless of the citizenship status of the child's parents) or to any child of a U.S. citizen (regardless of the place of birth).[19] Notably, the United States is somewhat anomalous in granting the first kind of birthright citizenship (*jus soli*, being born within the nation's territory); most nations, especially in Europe, assign citizenship at birth according to the citizenship status of at least one parent (*jus sanguinis*).[20] Nevertheless, both forms of birthright citizenship are seemingly "natural" or organic forms of the production of citizens through sexual reproduction. In contrast, naturalization presumably entails the nonsexual production of national subjects, so that citizenship is acquired rather than ascribed. In a self-consciously performative process, naturalization takes place through speech acts (oaths and pledges of allegiance) adjudicated by the state.[21] In this way, there appears to be something very queer at the heart of the naturalization process, a performance whose very theatricality exposes the constructed nature of citizenship itself. At least, that is one way to describe the radical potential of naturalization: to enact a purely consensual form of citizenship, without any necessary relationship to sexual reproduction or ancestry.

Yet, even though naturalization is theoretically a performative, nonreproductive model of producing citizens, the very term *naturalization* demonstrates the difficulties that modern states have had in imagining the full potential of that process.[22] Instead of breaking with a model of citizenship based on bloodline, the very language of naturalization has historically been encumbered with assumptions about a heterosexual, reproductive subject, and so tends to reinforce the model of an organic, sexually reproduced citizenry. As I argue, we should be more skeptical of the distinction typically drawn between birthright citizenship and naturalization—ascriptive versus consensual—and attend to the ways that the opposition between the two models actually serves to mask how both have historically been embedded within (hetero)sexualized understandings of production. Despite its potential to make good on the liberal promise of consent, even naturalization cannot escape a logic of belonging that depends on the transmission of citizenship through biological reproduction. This is not simply because legislation has tended to instantiate exclusionary ideologies of identity (race, gender, class, sexual orientation) that have "spoiled" the liberal promise of citizenship in the United States, but also, and perhaps more stubbornly, because this blood logic is embedded within the very metaphors through which such a form of producing citizenship is imagined.

There is no question that historically naturalization has been central to the ways in which models of consensual citizenship have been imagined, codified, and popularized in the United States. In fact, some historians have argued that the principles inherent in the naturalization process—that the relationship between an individual and government was contractual and voluntary, rather than natural and perpetual—provided a model for the founders' creation of a liberal democracy in the United States.[23] The Declaration of Independence, for instance, self-consciously insists upon the principles of citizenship by contract rather than ascribed subjecthood: "Governments are instituted among men, deriving their just powers from the consent of the governed." In fact, we might read the Declaration of Independence itself as performing a kind of collective naturalization for the inhabitants of the new nation. The founders declare that they intend "to dissolve the political bands" that tie them to England, finally pledging that

> [we . . .] do, in the name and by the authority of the good people of these colonies solemnly publish and declare, That these United Colonies are, and of right ought to be, FREE AND INDEPENDENT STATES; that they are absolved from all allegiance to the British crown and that all political connection between them and the state of Great Britain is, and ought to be, totally dissolved.[24]

By renouncing "allegiance" to the king and "political connection" to the state of Great Britain, the Declaration functions as an oath of renunciation, the formal legal means by which, to this day, a citizen may expatriate him/herself from his existing loyalty.[25] Simultaneously, in form and language, the Declaration also functions as an oath of allegiance, which is the final step in the process of naturalization. When the signers "mutually pledge to each other our lives, our fortunes, and our sacred honor," they perform their exclusive loyalty to the new United States and no other sovereignty.

While a model of naturalized citizenship implicitly shaped the theory and form of the Declaration of Independence, it also occupied an explicit place in the founders' justification for establishing a new nation. In the catalog of grievances against George III, the Declaration complains "that he has endeavoured to prevent the population of these States; for that purpose obstructing the Laws for Naturalization of Foreigners; refusing to pass others to encourage their migrations hither, and raising the conditions of new Appropriations of Lands."[26] This line reminds us that very different material conditions attended immigration in the eighteenth century, something we tend to forget within the current politics of migration and globalization. As James H. Kettner notes in his classic study of the history of naturalization in the United States, "The desire for military security, the persistent need for labor, and the generally acknowledged benefits of population growth led the colonists to grant extensive inducements to foreign immigrants by way of naturalization."[27] Although occasional restrictive measures were passed in the colonial period, they tended to be short-lived; in general, voluntary immigration seemed to be encouraged rather than policed by American authorities in the seventeenth and eighteenth centuries.[28]

In its first century of existence, then, the U.S. federal government imagined itself as a state that desired immigrants and new citizens. Before the exclusionary legislation of the late nineteenth century, immigration and naturalization do not appear to have been very active issues on federal lawmakers' agendas (though, of course, nativist movements held significant sway in other arenas beyond the federal sphere during the same period, particularly in local political, economic, and cultural struggles).[29] Although it is hard for us to imagine, there did not exist any federal apparatus in the United States for administering immigration until 1891, when Congress assigned responsibility for implementing national immigration policy to an office housed within the Treasury Department. Federal procedures for naturalization were not standardized until 1906, when Congress combined the immigration and naturalization functions of the federal government into the Bureau of Immigration and Naturalization, housed within the Department of Commerce and Labor.[30] The 1906 law also specified that federal courts, rather than state and local courts, should have jurisdiction over naturalization. Before 1906, however, individual states administered naturalization procedures and set the specific provisions of laws concerning citizenship, particularly whether and under what circumstances aliens could buy property. These provisions and procedures could vary widely from state to state and region to region, so that certain aliens might be able to become citizens in, say, Connecticut but not Virginia. These inconsistencies appeared not to trouble federal lawmakers, as long as individual state laws did not come into conflict with the relatively loose federal policy.

In the first century of the United States, then, federal immigration and naturalization policy was relatively decentralized and unregulated. Historians have tended to locate the origins of more repressive (and now more familiar) federal policy on immigration and naturalization in the late nineteenth century, with explicitly exclusionary laws that defined immigration in negative terms. In 1875, with the Page Act, Congress passed the first federal legislation that enumerated specific types of people who were excluded from entry into the United States. Illicit sexuality was at the center of the legislators' attention: the Page Act prohibited women "imported for the purposes of prostitution."[31] Although the legislation was aimed at the traffic in *all* "immoral women," the figure of the prostitute in this law was, in fact, inherently racialized, because the Page Act required U.S. consuls to ensure that any immigrant from China, Japan, or other Asian countries was not under contract for "lewd and immoral purposes."[32] Seven years later, in 1882, Congress passed the first legislation that used race as an explicit criterion for exclusion, the Chinese Exclusion Act, which barred all Chinese immigrants from entry into the United States and thus from citizenship.[33]

When compared with these restrictions of the late nineteenth century, earlier U.S. policy may seem to have encouraged immigration and naturalization, but in fact the first federal law on naturalization was implicitly exclusionary. In 1790, Congress set down "An Act to establish an uniform Rule of Naturalization," which stated:

> *Be it enacted by the Senate and House of Representatives of the United States of America in Congress assembled,* That any alien, being a free white person, who shall have resided within the limits and under the jurisdiction of the United States for the term of two years, may be admitted to become a citizen thereof, on application to any common law court of record, in any one of the states wherein he shall have resided for the term of one year at least, and making proof to the satisfaction of such court, that he is a person of good character, and taking the oath or affirmation prescribed by law, to support the constitution of the United States, which oath or affirmation such court shall administer; and the clerk of such court shall record such application, and the proceedings thereon; and thereupon such person shall be considered as a citizen of the United States. And the children of such persons so naturalized, dwelling within the United States, being under the age of twenty-one years at the time of such naturalization, shall also be considered as citizens of the United States. And the children of citizens of the United States, that may be born beyond sea, or out of the limits of the United States, shall be considered as natural born citizens; *Provided,* That the right of citizenship shall not descend to persons whose fathers have never been resident in the United States: *Provided* also, That no person heretofore proscribed by any state, shall be admitted a citizen as aforesaid, except by an act of the legislature of the state in which such person was proscribed.[34]

This law clearly and quite self-consciously restricted naturalization to "free white persons," thus racializing naturalized American citizenship at the very moment in which it was codified as a legal status. In fact, the 1790 act was the first federally enacted law that referred to race explicitly.[35] While the precise meaning of "white" has never been stable in the enforcement of this law, historically, the naturalization process has been embedded in an explicit policy of racial exclusion and the logic of white supremacy.[36] (After the Civil War, the "white person" restriction of naturalization came under attack, and, although there were efforts to do away with it completely, Congress simply modified it in 1870, when it extended the right to naturalize to "persons of African nativity or African descent," a law that recognized freed African American slaves, but that maintained discriminatory policies against other racial groups.[37]) The reference to "free" also indicates how the 1790 naturalization law anticipated questions about the status of two groups who might potentially claim citizenship status: indentured servants and slaves. Indentured servitude was a form of contract (usually) in which servants voluntarily surrendered their freedom for a set number of years.[38] Paradoxically, they exercised the right of contract—understood as a constitutive exercise of the liberal subject's freedom—in order to become temporarily "unfree." Slavery, on the other hand, is a relationship established by force rather than consent and, of course, was inconsistent with classical liberal theory. The Naturalization Act of 1790 reinforced the assumption that slaves were not potential citizens—whether by birthright or naturalization: slave status removed an individual from being recognized as a potential participant in a contractual or consensual relationship with the state (except as property). Slaves, along with the larger category of people not considered "white," were thus constructed as "unnaturalizable."

The glaring racialization of naturalized citizenship in the 1790 act and its indirect reference to slavery may blind us temporarily to the other ways that this legislation implicitly constructs prospective citizens. Notice, for instance, that, following its delineation of the court procedures for naturalization, the act turns to the citizenship status of children: "And the children of such persons so naturalized, dwelling within the United States, being under the age of twenty-one years at the time of such naturalization, shall also be considered as citizens of the United States. And the children of citizens of the United States, that may be born beyond sea, or out of the limits of the United States, shall be considered as natural born citizens." What these passages make clear is that this earliest juridical statement on naturalization presumed that the prospective citizen would be not only white and free but also a (potential) parent. That may not seem remarkable, but when put in the context of the stated purpose of the law—to establish a uniform rule of naturalization—the second statement about children seems oddly misplaced, since it outlines a rule not of naturalization but of birthright citizenship (the principle of *jus sanguinis*, granting citizenship through blood relation). By identifying *jus sanguinis* as the exception that needs to be spelled out in the law, the act also establishes that the default mode of becoming a "natural born citizen" is to be born within the territorial limits of the United States (*jus soli*, granting citizenship through place of birth).

What I want to call attention to in this passage is the way that ("natural born") citizens and "naturalized persons" are imagined to *have* children. That is, the seemingly abstract citizen invoked here is actually one who is also delineated through his/her (sexually) reproductive capacity, a capacity that, like the racial prerequisite, curiously re-embodies this seemingly abstract national subject. As the first law outlining naturalization as an ostensibly consensual and contractual relationship between the citizen and the state, the 1790 act contains within it assumptions about biological kinship that seem to revert, contradictorily, to an ascriptive process of conferring citizenship through the accident of birth.

The 1790 act thus seems to confuse two different logics of national belonging—blood and contract. This confusion, I want to suggest, indicates an ambivalence about the model of naturalized citizenship articulated in the first part of the law, one that represents, on its own, a more performative model of citizenship. The act's shift in attention toward children suggests that lawmakers were unable to imagine a truly nonascriptive model of citizenship. The reference to *jus sanguinis* seems to derail the act's attempt to narrate a model of contractual citizenship, but this derailment serves an important function, allowing an older model of allegiance based on biological kinship to prevail in the face of the law's earlier narrative of a citizen bound to the state by nothing more than contract. The reference to (white) (sexual) reproduction reanimates a more (literally) familiar model—and perhaps a more familiar affect—of national belonging produced through bloodlines.

Here it is helpful to look at the full range of meanings of the word "naturalization" and to consider why and how this particular term came to be associated with this presumably contractual/consensual form of conferring citizenship. According to the *Oxford English Dictionary*, to "naturalize" means generally "to make native." The object of the verb, it suggests, can be a foreigner or immigrant, a word or phrase, a plant or animal. In definitions regarding the term's usage with plants or animals, the meaning becomes more subtle: to naturalize is "to introduce (a plant or animal) to a place where it is not indigenous, but in which it may survive and reproduce as if it were native; to plant (a bulb, etc.) so that it requires no cultivation and becomes self-propagating, giving the effect of wild growth."[39] The process of naturalization, then, is one in which the difference between the indigenous and the imported becomes effaced. And, crucially, the key means by which this effacement is achieved is reproduction: to become "native" is to "require . . . no cultivation" and to become "self-propagating." In other words, biological reproduction becomes a key sign by which the naturalized organism passes as indigenous. Note that the important outcome of the process is to achieve the "effect of wild growth." This part of the definition suggests that there is nothing inherently indigenous or natural about "wild growth" itself: we can not know whether any particular "wild growth" is an "effect" produced and performed through artificial means or whether it was there all along. And sexual reproduction is the mechanism by which this effect is achieved: we know that an organism has been fully naturalized—and might as well be indigenous—by its successful self-propagation, presumably through sexual reproduction.[40]

This is another way of saying that "naturalization" is a metaphor, one that imagines the political and natural worlds as analogous and inextricably linked.[41] This metaphor circulated widely in discourses of citizenship in the early republic. It was deployed, for instance, by J. Hector St. John de Crèvecoeur in *Letters from an American Farmer* (1782), a series of semiautobiographical, semifictional reflections on American life directed "to the people of England."[42] At one point in the well-known chapter titled "What is an American?" Crèvecoeur, who himself had emigrated from France to New York (via Quèbec) in 1759, describes the process by which a European becomes American: "Every industrious European who transports himself here may be compared to a sprout growing at the foot of a great tree; it enjoys and draws but a little portion of sap; wrench it from the parent roots, transplant it, and it will become a tree bearing fruit also."[43] Here, the language of reproduction suffuses Crèvecoeur's organic image: the immigrant's European origins are its "parent roots" and his fulfillment of the naturalization process is evidenced in his ability to thrive not simply as a full-grown tree, but a reproductive one that "bear[s] fruit." Like the plant whose ability to be "self-propagating" demonstrates its success at naturalization within a new climate, the immigrant is imagined by Crèvecoeur as achieving full status as an American citizen through his ability to thrive and bear evidence of his reproductive capacity.

Crèvecoeur, of course, did not have a monopoly on the analogy between political and natural worlds, which was a common trope in eighteenth-century political thought more broadly. While Crèvecoeur uses the metaphor to present a romanticized view of immigration and naturalization (at least in the early part of his *Letters*), his contemporary Thomas Jefferson approaches the same issue in a more scientific fashion in *Notes on the State of Virginia* (1787), his wide-ranging compendium of statistical information, natural history, and philosophical thought. The most extended discussion of immigration appears in Query VIII, on "Population," in which Jefferson offers numerical data on the historical and existing populations of Virginia and compares different models for increasing its citizenry. In the process, he boldly articulates the assumed desire of the new nation toward immigration, but then takes a skeptical stance toward it: "The present desire of America is to produce rapid population by as great importation of foreigners as possible. But is this founded in good policy?"[44] Jefferson clearly recognizes the state as an affective realm: America "desires" an increase in population (and therefore desires immigrants). Jefferson then ponders the relative costs and benefits of, on the one hand, the "importation of foreigners" and, on the other, "natural propagation." To determine which makes better policy, he presents, in true Enlightenment fashion, a statistical comparison of the two methods, calculating that it would take twenty-seven and a quarter years to double the existing "stock" of Virginia but noting that the population could be doubled in a single year through immigration. If it is true that "the present desire of America is to produce rapid population," then it seems obvious that the best and most efficient option is to encourage immigration. Questioning his own mathematical logic, however, Jefferson argues that there are hidden costs in relying on immigration to increase the population:

> [Immigrants] will bring with them the principles of the [monarchical] governments they leave, imbibed in their early youth; or, if able to throw them off, it will be in exchange for an unbounded licentiousness, passing, as is usual, from one extreme to another. It would be a miracle were they to stop precisely at the point of temperate liberty. These principles, with their language, they will transmit to their children. In proportion to their numbers, they will share with us the legislation. They will infuse into it their spirit, warp and bias its direction, and render it a heterogeneous, incoherent, distracted mass. (84–85)

Jefferson denies any existing heterogeneity by projecting the blame for the "warp[ed]" and "bias[ed]" deformation of politics onto immigrants. Echoing the 1790 act, Jefferson takes for granted that these immigrant citizens are reproductive, destined to transmit to their children both the "principles" and "language" of monarchical governments, which they have "imbibed" (like mother's milk) "in their early youth." In this scenario, political ideologies are inevitably transmitted through biological reproduction.

As Jefferson's alarmist language about a "heterogeneous, incoherent, distracted mass" signals, he rejects immigration and recommends "natural propagation" as a way to secure a "more homogeneous, more peaceable, more durable" government (85). Despite the numerical data that seem to favor immigration and despite Jefferson's own espoused commitment to the prin-

	Proceeding on our present stock.	Proceeding on a double stock.
1781	567,614	1,135,228
1808¼	1,135,228	2,270,456
1835½	2,270,456	4,540,912
1862¾	4,540,912	

Figure 1.
Jefferson's comparison of "natural propagation" and "importation of foreigners" as methods for population growth. Thomas Jefferson, *Notes on the State of Virginia*, ed. and with intro. by William Peden (Chapel Hill: University of North Carolina Press, 1982), 155.

ciples of liberal democracy, he ultimately seems persuaded not by scientific or political argumentation, but rather by emotion, a fear that compels him toward a "safer" (but hardly rational) conclusion.[45] Thus, Jefferson appears to frame his discussion as a choice between two methods of increasing population—"natural [biological] propagation" versus immigration—but that distinction masks the ways that the production of citizenship in either instance remains unimaginable outside of biological models, even in the mind of a thinker as committed as Jefferson is to shaking off the residue of feudal models of belonging.

My goals in this essay have been to begin to construct a history of the state's production of citizens through naturalization in the United States and to explore the ways in which this practice has been fundamentally sexualized. In doing so, I am aware that citizenship, as a relation of belonging, is not reducible to the state; there are differences between citizenship as a formal status in the law and as a substantive category of belonging. Yet it is important to consider how the state functions as a site of affective power that has shaped the conditions of possibility for the production of U.S. citizens. By focusing on these codifications of and commentaries on immigration and naturalization in the early national period, I have highlighted a moment during which legal mechanisms for producing citizens were being formulated, often through the use of metaphors, such as naturalization, that shaped those laws in contradictory ways. Naturalization, of course, was certainly not the only state practice of the early national period that contradicted the Revolution's goals of establishing a contractual, rather than familial, model of allegiance and belonging. The continued legitimation of slavery through law was one of the most visible contradictions of the tenets of liberal theory that guided the formation of the early United States. Linda Kerber has demonstrated that these liberal ideals of consent and contract also foundered in the juridical construction of women's rights, particularly the system of coverture, which transferred a woman's civic identity and the use of her property to her husband at marriage. As Kerber notes, "The generation of men who radically transgressed inherited understandings of the relationship between kings and men, fathers and sons, and who radically reconstructed many basic elements of law, nevertheless refused to destabilize the law governing relations between husbands and wives, mothers and children."[46] To recognize those lawmakers' actions as a series of refusals serves as a useful reminder that these policies and procedures were not inevitable and that they might have been (and still may be) imagined in different ways.

Given the founders' emphasis on a model of citizenship based on active consent, rather than passive inheritance, it would have been consistent with that principle for acquired citizenship (i.e., naturalization) to have become the default model, rupturing inherited logics of kinship and blood as the primary basis for political belonging. Yet even the most contract-based articulations of citizenship in the early national period—from the Naturalization Act of 1790 to Jefferson's *Notes*—repeatedly revert to the logic of sexual reproduction, perhaps as a way to contain social panic about the potential political disintegration associated with the contractual production of citizens. In a recent commentary, Stevens has identified queer theory and activism as a site for the critique of "intergenerational structures of identities" and has envisioned its potential to effect "a revolution against all forms of state boundaries . . . the unhindered movement and full-fledged development of capacities regardless of one's birthplace or parentage."[47] Although I'm not sure that Stevens would necessarily make this connection, the revolutionary tone and vision of her description of queer theoretical and political projects uncannily echoes the professed goals of classical liberal theory at its most radical potential. In the texts that I have analyzed here, we see the limits of social contract ideology as it has actually been enacted and embodied: the liberal project of putting into practice a model of consensual citizenship stumbles when it confronts its own queer potential (and perhaps inherent demand) to detach political belonging from (hetero)sexual reproduction.

Notes

I thank Lisa Cohen, Lauren Goodlad, Regina Kunzel, Trish Loughran, Leslie Reagan, Joe Valente, and Leti Volpp for their generous comments on earlier drafts of this essay. Marita Sturken and the two anonymous readers for *American Quarterly* also made helpful suggestions that strengthened the final version. I have benefited greatly from discussions with participants in the September 2003 conference on "Sexual Worlds, Political Cultures," sponsored by the Social Science Research Council, as well as audiences at the University of Illinois, Urbana-Champaign, Purdue University, Concordia University in Montreal, the University of Alabama, the DeBartolo Conference on Eighteenth-Century Studies, and the annual conference of the Law and Society Association.

1. Benedict Anderson, *Imagined Communities: Reflections on the Origin and Spread of Nationalism*, rev. ed. (1983; London: Verso, 1991), 141.
2. Lauren Berlant, *The Queen of America Goes to Washington City: Essays on Sex and Citizenship* (Durham, N.C.: Duke University Press, 1997), 195.
3. For an excellent example of scholarship on the surveillance and production of sexual identities via immigration, see Eithne Luibhéid, *Entry Denied: Controlling Sexuality at the Border* (Minneapolis: University of Minnesota Press, 2002). Legal studies scholars have also produced a number of important studies in this area. See, for instance, Robert J. Foss, "The Demise of the Homosexual Exclusion: New Possibilities for Gay and Lesbian Immigration," *Harvard Civil Rights–Civil Liberties Law Review* 29 (1994): 439–75; and Shannon Minter, "Sodomy and the Public Morality Offenses Under U.S. Immigration Law: Penalizing Lesbian and Gay Identity," *Cornell International Law Journal* 26 (1993): 771–818.
4. See Eithne Luibhéid, "Introduction: Queering Migration and Citizenship," *Queer Moves: Sexuality, International Migration, and the Contested Boundaries of U.S. Citizenship*, ed. Eithne Luibhéid and Lionel Cantú (Minneapolis: University of Minnesota Press, 2005), ix–xlvi.
5. See Michel Foucault, *The History of Sexuality*, vol. 1 (New York: Vintage, 1978), trans. Robert Hurley.
6. Jacqueline Stevens argues that the distinction between the nation and the state may be misleading: "Despite the apparent tension between the experience of law (artifice) versus nature as the underlying bond of the political community, the state (or political society) are [*sic*] not concepts at odds with the logic of the nation." She argues instead that "the 'state' and 'nation' are two sides of the same familial coin . . . The family rhetoric of the state-nation is not obscure, metaphysical, or difficult to locate. The familial nation exists through practices and often legal documents that set out the kinship rules for particular political societies." Jacqueline Stevens, *Reproducing the State* (Princeton, N.J.: Princeton University Press, 1999), 108.
7. Walker Connor, "A Nation Is a Nation, Is a State, Is an Ethnic Group, Is a . . .," in *Nationalism*, ed. John Hutchinson and Anthony D. Smith (New York: Oxford University Press, 1994), 36. See also Clifford Geertz, *The Interpretation of Cultures* (New York: Basic Books, 1973).
8. See, for instance, Berlant, *The Queen of America*; Philip Brian Harper, Anne McClintock, José Esteban Muñoz, and Trish Rosen, eds., "Queer Transexions of Race, Nation, and Gender," *Social Text* 52–53 (1997); Andrew Parker, Mary Russo, Doris Sommer, and Patricia Yaeger, eds., *Nationalisms and Sexualities* (New York: Routledge, 1992); Elizabeth A. Povinelli and George Chauncey, eds., "Thinking Sexuality Transnationally," *GLQ* 5.4 (1999); Eve Kosofsky Sedgwick, "Nationalisms and Sexualities: As Opposed to What?" in *Tendencies* (Durham, N.C.: Duke University Press, 1993), 143–53; George Mosse, *Nationalism and Sexuality: Respectability and Abnormal Sexuality in Modern Europe* (New York: Fertig, 1985); Lauren Berlant, "National Brands/National Body: Imitation of Life," in *Comparative American Identities: Race, Sex, and Nationality in the Modern Text*, ed. Hortense J. Spillers (New York: Routledge, 1991), 110–40; and Cindy Patton and Benigno Sánchez-Eppler, eds., *Queer Diasporas* (Durham, N.C.: Duke University Press, 2000).
9. Michael Warner has noted that "queer politics has developed little in the way of an agenda for the state." Michael Warner, "Something Queer about the Nation-State," *Publics and Counterpublics* (New York: Zone Books, 2002), 221. Warner contrasts queer activism with a kind of activism that involves "routine interaction with the state," which he associates with lesbian and gay approaches. "Negotiation with state agencies, as a normal kind of activism, is typically organized by ideas of minority politics, community representation, and state coordination of special interests" (212).
10. Davina Cooper, *Power in Struggle: Feminism, Sexuality and the State* (Buckingham: Open University Press, 1995), 1. In her essay "Queering the State," Lisa Duggan has also stressed the urgency of such a project: "Tracing out in a concrete way the extent of the state's involvement in promoting heterosexuality would be a useful, though enormous, project." See Lisa Duggan and Nan D. Hunter, *Sex Wars: Sexual Dissent and Political Culture* (New York: Routledge, 1995), 189. For an especially well-crafted example of such a project, see Margot Canady, "Building a Straight State: Sexuality and Social Citizenship under the 1944 G.I. Bill," *Journal of American History* 90.3 (2003): 935–957.
11. Cooper, *Power in Struggle*, 78 n. 21.
12. Stevens, *Reproducing the State*, xv.
13. Luibhéid, *Entry Denied*, x.

14. Call for Papers, "Legal Borderlands: Law and the Construction of American Borders," *American Quarterly* 56.1 (March 2001).
15. Margot Canaday helpfully reminded me about this point when I first began research in this area. Delinking naturalization from immigration helps make visible the other forms of naturalization that do not necessarily take place through immigration, such as collective naturalization through territorial annexation.
16. For a helpful discussion of four different perspectives on models of U.S. citizenship—"rights, consent, contract, and community"—see T. Alexander Aleinikoff, "Theories of Loss of Citizenship," *Michigan Law Review* 84 (1985–1986): 1471–503.
17. Peter H. Schuck and Rogers M. Smith, *Citizenship without Consent: Illegal Aliens in the American Polity* (New Haven, Conn.: Yale University Press, 1985), 9.
18. "Naturalization Oath of Allegiance to the United States of America," http://www.uscis.gov/graphics/aboutus/history/teacher/oath.htm (accessed July 6, 2005). A uniform oath of allegiance was not standardized in the United States until 1929, at which time a signed oath also became a standard part of naturalization procedures. See "Standardization of the Language of the Oath of Allegiance," http://www.uscis.gov/graphics/aboutus/history/articles/OATH.htm (accessed July 6, 2005).
19. It is important to note, however, that rules of birthright citizenship continue to be contested in ways that demonstrate the ongoing centrality of marriage and gender difference to U.S. laws on nationality. In the case of children born abroad and "out of wedlock" when only one biological parent is a U.S. citizen, birthright citizenship is transmitted automatically to the child only if the citizen parent is the mother, not the father. This rule was recently upheld by the Supreme Court in the case of *Tuan Anh Nguyen v. Immigration and Naturalization Service* (2001). As Linda Kerber points out in her essay in this volume, the ruling confirms that, in essence, "men representing the U.S. abroad have the Court's permission to father children out of wedlock and abandon them," 741.
20. According to Polly J. Price, "the United States, Great Britain, and many Latin American countries have historically favored *jus soli* over *jus sanguinis* as a rule for acquisition of citizenship by birth." However, Great Britain repealed *jus soli* in 1981 with the *British Nationality Act.* Price also notes that "no nation relies exclusively on one of these principles to determine who is a natural-born subject or citizen." See Polly J. Price, "Natural Law and Birthright Citizenship in Calvin's Case (1608)," *Yale Journal of Law and the Humanities* 9.1 (1997): 77 n. 15.
21. As Judith Butler explains: "Within speech act theory, a performative is that discursive practice that enacts or produces that which it names." Although it may appear that the subject speaking holds the power to enact what it wills, Butler insists that instead this power is actually derived from the conventions of authority that the speaker cites. See Judith Butler, *Bodies That Matter: On the Discursive Limits of "Sex"* (New York: Routledge, 1993), 12–16.
22. My thinking about these questions has benefited enormously from Stevens's persuasive arguments in *Reproducing the State.* In a chapter on "The Nation and the Tragedy of Birth," Stevens focuses her attention primarily on birthright citizenship, except for a paragraph in which she briefly discusses naturalized citizenship: "non-kinship membership practices are parasitic on the family model . . . Birth is experienced as the real way of becoming a citizen. No one says of citizenship by birthright in the United States: 'It's as good as a green card,' but the opposite is true" (147). Stevens's brief mention of naturalization helpfully points the way to the questions that I am placing at the center of my work here.
23. See, for example, James H. Kettner, *The Development of American Citizenship, 1608–1870* (Chapel Hill: University of North Carolina Press, 1978), 10.
24. Merrill Jensen, ed., *The Documentary History of the Ratification of the Constitution,* vol. 1, *Constitutional Documents and Records, 1776–1787* (Madison: State Historical Society of Wisconsin, 1976), 73–74.
25. The current oath of renunciation states: "I desire to make a formal renunciation of my American nationality, as provided by section 349(a)(5) of the *Immigration and Nationality Act,* and pursuant thereto I hereby absolutely and entirely renounce my United States nationality together with all the rights and privileges and all duties of allegiance and fidelity thereunto pertaining." "Oath of Renunciation of the Nationality of the United States," http://usembassy-australia.state.gov/consular/oathrenunciation.pdf (accessed July 6, 2005). See Section 349(a)(5) of the Immigration and Nationality Act, 66 Stat. 268, as amended by P.L. 95–432, of October 10, 1978, 92 Stat. 1046.
26. Jensen, *The Documentary History,* vol. 1, 73–74.
27. Kettner, *The Development of American Citizenship,* 106.
28. Ibid., 110.

29. On particular nativist movements in the early nineteenth century, see, for example, Sean Wilentz, *Chants Democratic: New York City and the Rise of the American Working Class, 1788–1850* (New York: Oxford University Press, 1984), 266–71, 315–25.
30. Marian L. Smith, "Overview of INS History," http://uscis.gov/graphics/aboutus/history/articles/oview.htm (accessed July 6, 2005), originally published in *A Historical Guide to the U.S. Government*, ed. George T. Kurian (New York: Oxford University Press, 1998).
31. "An Act Supplementary to the Acts in Relation to Immigration," 43rd Cong., 2nd sess., (March 3, 1875), 141.
32. Nancy F. Cott, *Public Vows: A History of Marriage and the Nation* (Cambridge, Mass.: Harvard University Press, 2000), 136; and Sucheng Chan, "The Exclusion of Chinese Women, 1870–1943," in *Entry Denied: Exclusion and the Chinese Community in America, 1882–1943*, ed. Sucheng Chan (Philadelphia: University of Pennsylvania Press, 1991), esp. 105–9.
33. This was also one of the first instances when Congress legislated immigration and naturalization together. Prior to this act, Congress had legislated separately regarding the two processes, with one congressional committee drafting nationality law and, beginning in the late nineteenth century, another committee addressing immigration law.
34. 1st Cong., 2nd sess. (March 26, 1790), *Cong. Rec.*, 103–4.
35. The other was the first federal Militia Act, passed in 1792, which required states to limit enrollment in their militias to "every free able-bodied white male citizen"; 1 Stat. 271 (1792). See Stephen A. Siegel, "The Federal Government's Power to Enact Color-Conscious Laws: An Originalist Inquiry," *Northwestern University Law Review* 92 (1998): 522–23.
36. Ian F. Haney López, *White by Law: The Legal Construction of Race* (New York: New York University Press, 1996), 1.
37. Quoted in Haney López, *White by Law*, 43–44.
38. Indentured servants typically signed a contract (or "indenture") before departure from their home country. Other kinds of voluntary servitude involving immigrants ("customary servants" and "German redemptioners") involved contracts negotiated not prior to immigration, but upon landing. See Russell R. Menard, "Transitions to African Slavery in British America, 1630–1730: Barbados, Virginia and South Carolina," in *Migrants, Servants and Slaves: Unfree Labor in Colonial British America* (Burlington, Vt.: Ashgate, 2001), 37.
39. See the entry for "naturalize" in the *Oxford English Dictionary*, http://dictionary.oed.com (accessed July 6, 2005).
40. From 1737 until the early nineteenth century, the most widely used method of plant classification was that developed by Carl Linnaeus, who centered his system on the perceived sexual difference in plants (which he understood to be either male or female). However, as Londa Schiebinger points out, "though eighteenth-century botanists were correct to recognize that many plants do reproduce sexually, they gave undue primacy to sexual reproduction and heterosexuality," because most plants are "hermaphroditic," with both male and female parts in the same organism. See Londa Schiebinger, *Nature's Body: Gender in the Making of Modern Science* (Boston: Beacon Press, 1993), 21–22.
41. The term *naturalizing* apparently was first used in an act of 23 Eliz. I (1581), according to Kettner, *The Development of American Citizenship*, 30 n. 2.
42. J. Hector St. John de Crèvecoeur, *Letters from an American Farmer* (London, 1782), n.p. Based on information from English Short Title Catalogue. "Eighteenth Century Collections Online" at http://galenet.galegroup.com/servlet/ECCO (accessed August 19, 2005).
43. Crèvecoeur, *Letters*, 69.
44. Thomas Jefferson, *Notes on the State of Virginia*, ed. and with introduction by William Peden (Chapel Hill: University of North Carolina Press, 1982), 83.
45. It is interesting that Jefferson had a keen interest in natural history, particularly botany. He introduced and naturalized a number of foreign crops to the United States, including upland rice, olives, the cork oak, plus more than a hundred different kinds of garden plants, including trees, shrubs, roses, and perennials. Powell Glass, "Jefferson and Plant Introduction," *The National Horticultural Magazine* 23.3, July 1944, 127–31. I intend to explore the connection between Jefferson's views on political and botanical naturalization in future research.
46. Linda K. Kerber, "The Paradox of Women's Citizenship in the Early Republic: The Case of *Martin v. Massachusetts*, 1805," *American Historical Review* 97.2 (1992): 351.
47. Jacqueline Stevens, "The Politics of LGBTQ Scholarship," *GLQ* 10.2 (2004): 225.

Outlawing "Coolies": Race, Nation, and Empire in the Age of Emancipation

Moon-Ho Jung

A vote for Chinese exclusion would mean a vote against slavery, against "cooly importation," a U.S. senator from California warned in 1882. "An adverse vote now is to commission under the broad seal of the United States, all the speculators in human labor, all the importers of human muscle, all the traffickers in human flesh, to ply their infamous trade without impediment under the protection of the American flag, and empty the teeming, seething slave pens of China upon the soil of California!" The other senator from California added that those who had been "so clamorous against what was known as African slavery" had a moral obligation to vote for Chinese exclusion, "when we all know that they are used as slaves by those who bring them to this country, that their labor is for the benefit of those who practically own them." A "coolie," or "cooly," it seemed, was a slave, pure and simple. Representative Horace F. Page (California) elaborated on the same point in the other chamber, branding the "Chinese cooly contract system" and polygamy the "twin relic[s] of the barbarism of slavery." The United States was "the home of the down-trodden and the oppressed," he declared, but "not the home for millions of cooly slaves and serfs who come here under a contract for a term of years to labor, and who neither enjoy nor practice any of our religious characteristics."[1]

Some of their colleagues demanded clarification. If the bill aimed to exclude "coolies," why did it target Chinese laborers wholesale? New England Republicans, in particular, challenged the conflation of "coolies" and "laborers." "All coolies are laborers," inquired a Massachusetts representative, "but are all Chinese laborers coolies?" Somewhat flustered, Page claimed that they were synonymous in China and California, where Chinatowns overflowed with "coolies and women of a class that I would not care to mention in this presence." His reply failed to sway the bill's detractors, who assailed its indiscriminate prohibition of Chinese immigration. With the Civil War and Reconstruction fresh in everyone's memory, Senator George F. Hoar of Massachusetts vowed never to "consent to a denial by the United States of the right of every man who desires to improve his condition by honest labor—his labor being no man's property but his own—to go anywhere on the face of the earth that he pleases." There were limits to "honest labor" though. Echoing a sentiment common among the dissenting minority, Hoar called for more exacting words that would strike only at "the evil" associated with "the coming of these people from China, especially the importation of coolies." "It is not importation, but immigration; it is not importation, but the free coming; it is not the slave, or the apprentice, or the prostitute, or the leper, or the thief," he argued, "but the laborer at whom this legislation strikes its blow."[2]

These congressional debates remind us of the extent to which slavery continued to define American culture and politics after emancipation. The language of abolition infused the proceedings on Chinese exclusion, with no legislator challenging the federal government's legal or moral authority to forbid "coolies" from entering the reunited, free nation. Indeed, by the 1880s, alongside the prostitute, there was no more potent symbol of chattel slavery's enduring legacy than the "coolie," a racialized and racializing figure that anti-Chinese (and putatively pro-Chinese) lawmakers condemned.[3] A stand against "coolies" was a stand for America, for freedom. There was no disagreement on that point. The legal exclusion of Chinese laborers in 1882 and the subsequent barrage of anti-Asian laws reflected and exploited this consensus in American culture and politics: "coolies" fell outside the legitimate borders of the United States.

This consensus took root in the decades before the Civil War and the abolition of slavery, a result not so much of anti-Chinese rancor in California but of U.S. imperial ambitions in Asia and the Caribbean and broader struggles to demarcate the legal boundary between slavery and freedom. A year before Abraham Lincoln delivered the Emancipation Proclamation on January 1, 1863, he emblematized this consensus by signing into law a bill designed to divorce "coolies" from America, a little known legislation that reveals the complex origins of U.S. immigration restrictions. While marking the origination of the modern immigration system, Chinese exclusion also signified the culmination of preceding debates over the slave trade and slavery, debates that had turned the attention of proslavery and antislavery Americans not only to Africa and the U.S. South but also to Asia and the Caribbean. There, conspicuously and tenuously at the border between slavery and freedom, they discovered "coolies," upon whom they projected their manifold desires. "Coolies," however, were not a people but a conglomeration of racial imaginings that emerged worldwide in the era of slave emancipation.[4] Ambiguously and then unfailingly linked with slavery and the Caribbean in American culture, "coolies" would eventually make possible the passage of the nation's first restrictions on immigration under the banner of "freedom" and "immigration." The legal and cultural impulse to prohibit "coolies," at home and abroad, also enabled the U.S. nation-state to proclaim itself as "free" and to deepen and defend its imperial presence in Asia and the Americas. Outlawing "coolies," in short, proved pivotal in the reproduction of race, nation, and empire in the age of emancipation.

"Coolies" and Freedom

The word *coolie* was a product of European expansion into Asia and the Americas, embodying the contradictory imperial imperatives of enslavement and emancipation. Of Tamil, Chinese, or other origin, the term was initially popularized in the sixteenth century by Portuguese sailors and merchants across Asia and later was adopted by fellow European traders on the high seas and in port cities. By the eighteenth century, *coolie* had assumed a transcontinental definition of an Indian or Chinese laborer, hired locally or shipped abroad. The word took on a new significance in the nineteenth century, as the beginnings of abolition remade "coolies" into indentured laborers in high demand across the world, particularly in the tropical colonies of the Caribbean. Emerging out of struggles over British emancipation and Cuban slavery in particular, *coolies* and *coolieism*—defined as "the importation of coolies as labourers into foreign countries" by the late nineteenth century—came to denote the systematic shipment and employment of Asian laborers on sugar plantations formerly worked by enslaved Africans.[5] It was during this era of emancipation and Asian migration that the term *cooly* entered the mainstream of American culture, symbolized literally by its relocation from the appendix to the main body of Noah Webster's American dictionary in 1848.[6]

By then, like the word, the idea of importing "coolies" as indentured laborers to combat the uncertainties of emancipation circulated widely around the world. Even before the permanent end to slavery in the British Empire in 1838, sugar planters from the French colony of Bourbon and the British colony of Mauritius, both islands in the Indian Ocean, had begun transporting South Asian workers to their plantations. These initiatives inspired John Gladstone to inquire into the feasibility of procuring a hundred "coolies" for at least five years of labor on his sugar estates in British Guiana. Doubting that black "apprentices"—the status forced upon former slaves for six years in 1834—would work much longer, Gladstone contended that planters had "to endeavor to provide a portion of other labourers whom we might use as a set-off, and when the time for it comes, make us, as far as possible, independent of our negro population." "Coolies" were his solution. A British firm foresaw no difficulty in extending its business from Mauritius to the West Indies, "the natives being perfectly ignorant of the place they go to or the length of voyage they are undertaking." In May 1838, five months before "apprenticeship" came to a premature end, 396 South Asian "coolies" arrived in British Guiana, launching a stream of migrant labor that flowed until World War I.[7]

What happened to the "Gladstone coolies," as they came to be known, exposed a contradiction inherent in coolieism that would bedevil and befuddle planters and government officials in the Americas for decades. Did the recruitment and employment of "coolies" represent a relic of slavery or a harbinger of freedom? Early reports decidedly indicated the former. Upon the complaints registered by the British Anti-Slavery Society, British Guiana authorities established a commission to investigate conditions on the six plantations to which the "Gladstone coolies" had been allotted. Witnesses testified that overseers brutally flogged and extorted money from laborers under their supervision. By the end of their contracts in 1843, a quarter of the migrants had died and the vast majority of the survivors elected to return to India. Only sixty remained in British Guiana. Undaunted, the colony's sugar planters proceeded with plans to expand the experiment, but met resistance in India and London. The Indian governor-general prohibited further emigration at the end of 1838, a policy that the secretary for the colonies refused to amend in 1840. "I am not prepared to encounter the responsibility of a measure which may lead to a dreadful loss of life on the one hand," the secretary explained, "or, on the other, to a new system of slavery."[8]

Figure 1.
Woodcut of a plantation manager's house in British Guiana by "a clever Chinese immigrant" that conveys "the grievances likely to arise under the Coolie system." Groups of South Asian and Chinese migrant workers sit bound, supplying their blood to the manager and his family up above and the plantation owners in Britain. From Edward Jenkins, *The Coolie: His Rights and Wrongs* (New York: George Routledge and Sons, 1871), 8.

Such inauspicious beginnings failed to derail the mission that Gladstone had inaugurated; West Indian planters soon found a sympathetic hearing in London. They could have their migrant laborers, as long as the state regulated all phases of recruitment, transportation, and employment. Applied to African "immigrants"—those "liberated" from slave smugglers and pressured into indentureship—and then to Asian "coolies" in the 1840s, state intervention was championed in British political circles as the guarantor of freedom. For a time, despite persistent protests and investigations, the employment of "coolies" appeared to signal a departure from the evils of the slave trade, from

coercion and servitude, sanctified by voluntary contracts, legal rights, and public subsidies and enforced by the imperial and colonial state apparatus. In practice, however, the system placed a preponderance of power in the hands of planters and their allies, to the detriment of indentured workers who faced criminal prosecution for violating civil contracts. State enforcement on behalf of employers—along with rampant extralegal practices like kidnapping, deception, and corporal punishment—more often than not eclipsed state protection of workers. These contradictions notwithstanding, London and the colonial regimes in India and the West Indies worked together, albeit contentiously at times, to institute the mass migration of laborers bound to five-year indentures as a mainstay of postemancipation life by the 1860s. Coolieism thus became associated with emancipation, but not even the highest aspirations of numerous inquiry commissions and reform measures could erase its roots in slavery and "apprenticeship."[9]

Meanwhile, Cuba, the Caribbean's premier sugar-producing colony in the nineteenth century, magnified the contradictions presented by British West Indian coolieism. Sugar planters there demanded laborers in numbers and conditions that the illicit trans-Atlantic slave trade—prohibited in Anglo-Spanish treaties in 1817 and 1835 and in Spanish law in 1845—could no longer supply by the 1840s, at least not without deep political and economic costs. Following the British example, a Spanish merchant engaged in the slave trade suggested the procurement of Chinese laborers in 1846, four decades before slavery would be abolished in Cuba. Within a year, his firm had made arrangements for two shiploads of "coolies" bound to eight-year contracts with wages fixed at four pesos per month. This experiment initiated and defined a migrant labor system that Cuban planters found indispensable over the next two decades, especially as their recruiting forays in Africa, Mexico, the Canary Islands, and elsewhere failed to yield the results they had hoped for. Ultimately, almost 125,000 Chinese laborers landed in Cuba between 1847 and 1874 to work under conditions approximating slavery, unbeknownst to them and despite legal distinctions and safeguards. Enslaved and indentured labor flourished side by side in Cuba, casting chattel slavery's dark shadow over the "free" aspects of coolieism.[10] British authorities, in response, laid claim to moral superiority through state intervention, in Africa and India as well as in China, whence 17,904 laborers arrived in the British West Indies under conditions similar to the larger system involving close to half a million South Asian migrants.[11]

These developments on the other side of the Gulf of Mexico immediately captured the notice of Americans engaged in their own struggles over slavery.

As in British denunciations of the Gladstone experiment, abolitionists wasted no time in vilifying "coolie" labor as a new variant of slavery. New England periodicals related to readers in the 1840s that "coolies" in the British West Indies were "in a state of nudity and hardly any of them decently clothed" and "suffering from severe sickness," with many complaining vociferously and running away. The plight of the early "coolies" was so miserable that "their belief is, that they are slaves" and "the negroes appear sincerely to pity them." Trinidad's officials received and distributed "coolies" like slaves "in pure Baltimore or Cuban style," *Littell's Living Age* reported, while "coolies, half naked, scabby, famishing, helpless from ignorance, and overrun with vermin, infest the highways" of British Guiana. "Coolies" faced a cycle of coercion in that colony, where "the authorities have hounded on them . . . drive[n] them into the lock-up house, (surely an illegal act,) and the planters cry out for permission to conclude contracts of indenture, that is, with beguiled strangers, who cannot comprehend the signification thereof." William Lloyd Garrison's *The Liberator* hoped that "the abolitionists of Great Britain will succeed in their efforts to break up entirely a system that produces so much cruelty and misery."[12]

Within a few years though, Caribbean planters' and European officials' propaganda campaigns had their desired effect on American reports, many of which began touting "coolie" labor as a means to expedite and effect emancipation. Chinese emigration heralded a new era across the world, exclaimed an advocate of Chinese labor, that would benefit "both the Chinaman and the Negro, if you can at once relieve the hunger of the former and preserve the freedom of the latter." Four years of Chinese migrants residing in Cuba had proved them to be "laborious, robust—almost as much so as the best Africans—more intelligent, and sufficiently docile, under good management." Similar results prevailed in British Guiana and Hawai'i, but would "prejudice or a mistaken philanthropy" prevent a migration beneficial to all parties? Chinese dispersion across the globe and American expansion across the Pacific and Asia would proceed apace, he concluded. "Instead of the labor-market of the new empires of Oceanica being supplied, like that of Eastern America, by means of violence, and with the captive savages of Negroland, it will be voluntarily occupied by the free and industrious outpourings of China." By 1852, the *New York Times* was imploring U.S. slaveholders to emulate their competitors in the British West Indies, Cuba, and Hawai'i, presenting "coolies" as a conduit toward abolition. "Some happy medium must be struck," an editorial insisted, "and the only medium between forced and voluntary labor, is that offered by the introduction of Orientals."[13] Neither free nor enslaved labor, "coolies" signified an ambiguous contradiction that seemed to hold the potential to advance either.

"Coolies" and Slavery

Humphrey Marshall, the U.S. commissioner to China, likewise felt that "coolies" would spell the end of American slavery. "Should that power [Britain] seriously undertake to populate her West India possessions and her colonies on the coast of South America with Chinese laborers, who have no idea, however, of the right of popular participation in the direction of government," he informed the secretary of state in 1853, "the effect . . . upon the industrial interests of the planting States of the United States, and upon the institutions of the republics of South America, must necessarily be most disastrous to them." Marshall, a Kentucky planter and a future member of the Confederate military and congress, estimated that each Chinese contract laborer cost $80 per year to employ, "far below the cost of slave labor, independent of the risk which the planter runs in his original investment." The Chinese were "patient of labor, tractable, obedient as a slave, and frugal . . . [and] will compel from the earth the maximum production of which it is capable, and, under whatever circumstances, will create a competition against which it must be difficult to struggle." On behalf of American slaveholders, Marshall hoped the president would establish a policy to prevent American ships from advancing the profits of British interests, against whom the United States was competing in the production of tropical goods and Asian commerce. "Coolies," he was convinced, threatened both American imperial ambitions and American slavery.[14]

Marshall articulated a short-lived ideological convergence between U.S. diplomats and slaveholders that would decisively bind "coolies" with slavery in American culture. In the years following his appeal, U.S. officials stationed abroad cast "coolie" labor not only as cheaper than slavery but as a brutal form of slavery that demanded federal intervention. Proslavery ideologues heartily agreed, even as they bristled at the notion of federal meddling in the domestic institution of slavery. The advent of a new system of slavery after emancipation in the Caribbean, they argued, warranted international scorn and laid bare the duplicity of abolition. American slavery, in their view, deserved protection more than ever. On the eve of the Civil War, New England abolitionists and Southern fire-eaters could find common ground in the "coolie" problem, issuing equally strident condemnations that clarified and blurred the limits of slavery and freedom in the process. American calls for the prohibition of "coolie" labor abroad, in turn, also justified and fueled U.S. expansionism in Asia and the Caribbean. Joining the international movement to suppress the "coolie" trade legitimized the U.S. diplomatic mission in China; the abuse of "coolies" in Cuba seemed to affirm the need for American annexation of the

Spanish colony, for many, as a slave state. In and through "coolies," American diplomats and slaveholders found ways to promote the U.S. empire, as a beacon of freedom and slavery in the age of emancipation.

Marshall's admonition against the "coolie" trade conveyed America's longstanding commercial aspirations in China, an economic motive that was in full display in response to the tragedy aboard the U.S. ship *Robert Bowne.*[15] In 1852, Captain Lesley Bryson transported a cargo of contract laborers to Hawai'i and then returned to Amoy the following month to carry another 410 "coolies," ostensibly to San Francisco. On the tenth day out at sea, the Chinese passengers rebelled against the officers and crew, killing Bryson and six others and ordering the surviving crew members to guide the ship to Formosa. Instead, the ship ran aground near a small island on the Ryuku archipelago, to which American and British ships were dispatched to round up as many of the "pirates" as possible. Most of the Chinese passengers were never accounted for—only about a hundred were captured—and hundreds probably died from gunshot wounds, suicide, starvation, and disease, in addition to the eight who had been killed during the original insurrection. Peter Parker, the chargé d'affaires of the U.S. delegation in China, conceded that Bryson had administered "injudicious treatment of the coolies"—such as his order to cut off their queues—but insisted that recent mutinies by "this class of Chinese" aboard French and English ships indicated that the uprising might have been "premeditated before the vessel left port."[16]

The mounting evidence against the American captain and the "coolie" trade in general had no effect on Parker's blind defense of his deceased compatriot and U.S. national honor. Bryson's ship was involved in an intensifying trade in Chinese workers around Amoy operated by European and American shippers and their local suppliers, Chinese brokers (or "crimps"). The insatiable global demand for "coolies" manifested locally in an upsurge of kidnappings and fraudulent schemes in the early 1850s, coercive tactics that drove Chinese residents to equate the trade to "pig-dealing."[17] The growing infamy of the "coolie" trade in Amoy could not deter Parker's quest for justice on Bryson's behalf. Although he claimed U.S. jurisdiction over the entire affair, Parker agreed to hand over seventeen individuals, those deemed the "principal actors" by a court of inquiry aboard a U.S. frigate, to Chinese authorities for a speedy trial and punishment. A month later, however, Parker regretted the "most flagrant breach of good faith" committed by the Chinese commissioners who, from the testimony of the accused, had censured Bryson for engaging in "the style of thing called *buying pigs*" and treating his passengers in a "tyrannical" manner. Only one man was found guilty. The U.S. official angrily defended Bryson as "a kind and humane man" and dismissed the suggestion that the passengers had been coerced into signing contracts. "Hereafter the United States will execute their own laws in cases of piracy occurring upon the high seas," Parker declared.[18]

But the violence aboard *Robert Bowne* turned out to be no exception. U.S. officials in Asia dispatched frightening accounts of the trade that Americans back home read about, including the infamous case of the Boston-based *Waverly.* In September 1855, the *Waverly* left Amoy with 353 "coolies" and added 97 others in Swatow before embarking on its chartered voyage to Peru. Within a short span, four passengers had "sprung overboard" and drowned, while a "good many" fell ill, among them the captain, who died soon afterward. Under the circumstances, the first mate, now the acting captain, decided to switch course to the Philippines. Two more "coolies" died before the ship reached Manila, where Spanish authorities placed it under quarantine. Difficult to control from the outset, the new captain wrote in his log, "all of the coolies came aft, with the intention to kill" him two days later. The crew killed "about four or five" in the ensuing struggle and "drove them all down below, between decks"; the captain later killed another "very impudent" passenger. When the other "coolies" attempted to break through the forward hatch, the crew "shoved them down again and shut the hatches on again." When the captain finally decided to allow the passengers on deck eight hours later, he discovered a grisly scene below. Only 150 "coolies" remained alive. The captain's account of "coolies" attacking him and then killing one another, however, could not be corroborated by witnesses, who testified that he had killed and injured the passengers without provocation. The U.S. consul in Manila reported that "the unfortunate beings had perished by suffocation."[19]

Amid such calamities, U.S. officials moved to prevent American citizens from transporting "coolies," a trade that appeared to threaten America's commercial access to China and its international standing. Four years after his defense of the *Robert Bowne,* Peter Parker heard about the *Waverly* disaster en route to take up his appointment as the new U.S. commissioner to China. Armed with verbal instructions from the secretary of state to "discountenance" the "coolie" trade, he wasted no time in issuing a strong "public notification" in January 1856. Parker denounced the trade as "replete with illegalities, immoralities, and revolting and inhuman atrocities, strongly resembling those of the African slave trade in former years, some of them exceeding the horrors of the 'middle passage,' . . . and the foreign name has been rendered odious by this traffic, hundreds and thousands of lives having been inhumanly sacrificed." Parker instructed U.S. citizens "to desist from this irregular and immoral traffic" that imperiled "amicable relations" and "honorable and lawful commerce" between the United States and China, whose government prohibited it. Parker's proclamation generated immediate public outcries back home that further coupled "coolies" with the banned African slave trade. The abolitionist *Liberator* featured articles on the "new slave trade" and chastised Northerners engaged in it as "doughfaces." And departing from its earlier depiction of "coolies" as a vehicle to free labor, the *New York Times* now hoped the federal government would sustain Parker's declaration "with corresponding vigor" and suppress "this abominable trade."[20]

William B. Reed would reinforce Parker's views shortly after being appointed the new U.S. minister to China in 1857. Reed, too, found that shippers blatantly disregarded his public intimidations and general allusions to Chinese and U.S. laws and treaty obligations. In January 1858, he decided to fortify his warnings with a federal statute already on the books, an 1818 law that prohibited U.S. citizens and residents from transporting from Africa or anywhere else "any negro, mulatto, or person of colour, not being an inhabitant, nor held to service by the laws of either of the states or territories of the United States, in any ship, vessel, boat, or other water craft, for the purpose of holding, selling, or otherwise disposing of, such person as a slave, or to be held to service or labour, or be aiding or abetting therein." Despite "some uncertainty" of its applicability and its original intent for "a different evil," Reed argued for the law's relevance. A "Chinese cooly," he rationalized, was surely "a man of color, to be disposed of to be held to service in Cuba."[21]

In contrast to Parker, who had distinguished between the illegality of the "coolie trade" and the legality of "voluntary emigration of Chinese adventurers," Reed felt that "coolies" raised questions far more significant than coercion. It was, to him, a matter of U.S. racial, national, and imperial interests. Beyond "the practical enslavement of a distant and most peculiar race," the prospect of mass migrations of "free" Chinese male laborers also troubled Reed. Such a demographic shift, he believed, would strengthen "the decaying institutions of colonial Spanish America" that ran contrary to U.S. interests. The Chinese would "either amalgamate with the negro race, and thus increase the actual slave population, or maintain a separate existence, their numbers only to be recruited by new arrivals." Reed thought the latter more likely and envisaged a "bloody massacre" borne from the oppression of "a vast aggregation of troublesome populace" in a foreign colony. Driven to prevent such a scenario, he stressed to shippers that "whether the coolies go voluntarily or not to Havana" did not make "the least difference" under the law, if they were transported "under a contract 'to be held to service.'"[22] In his search for a law to suppress the coercive and corrupt trade in "coolies," Reed turned to a slave trade prohibition that, in turn, defined a "coolie." A "coolie," in his mind, was "a man of color" shipped to labor abroad, a gendered, racialized, and classed figure whose migration, voluntary or not, signified the bounds of slavery.

Reed left his post in November 1858, months before federal officials in Washington rescinded his application of the 1818 statute to the "coolie" trade. Secretary of State Lewis Cass, who criticized British and French efforts to obtain "coolie" and African labor for their colonies, had referred Reed's concerns to Attorney General J. S. Black in April 1858. Black finally ruled almost a year later that he considered the "coolie" trade outside the purview of slave trade prohibitions and other "existing laws." "The evil is one which Congress alone can remedy," he concluded. Washington's delayed and deflective reply provided little comfort or direction to the U.S. legation in China that continued to witness the horrors of the trade firsthand. The "cooly trade to the West Indies," Reed had pleaded repeatedly, was "irredeemable slavery under the form of freedom," with results worse than the African slave trade. The "Asiatic" faced a doomed fate in the Caribbean, he prophesied, marked by racial isolation and "a certain and fatal struggle, in which the Asiatic, as the weakest, fails."[23] To U.S. diplomats in China, it was a matter of life and death, a matter of slavery and freedom.

By 1859, the "coolie" trade from China, in which U.S. clippers had become increasingly involved, generated diplomatic crises that both undermined and bolstered Western imperial designs in China. Popular outrage in southern China against kidnapping and deception, sometimes boiling over into mass antiforeigner riots, drove the Chinese imperial court to request assistance from Western diplomats to suppress a trade that flagrantly violated its prohibition against all emigration. The British—motivated by West Indian planters' demand for labor and London's desire to protect its international image—requested a legalized and regulated system of migration instead. The military occupation of Canton (Guangzhou) by British and French troops beginning in 1858 allowed them to exact such a system. Long aware that the imperial decree on emigration carried no weight among Western shippers, Chinese officials in Canton felt empowered and compelled to collaborate with the British to implement a more pragmatic policy. In November 1859, British and local Chinese motives coalesced into a system of voluntary contract migration to the British West Indies from licensed depots in Canton, with regulations intended to avert the violence heretofore employed in the recruitment of "coolies." Lao Ch'ung-kuang, the provincial governor general of Guangdong, then called on other foreign consuls to instruct their citizens to conduct all

PRESERVING THE PEACE.

Figure 2.
Many U.S. news accounts condemned the inhumanity of the "coolie" trade. From Edgar Holden, "A Chapter on the Coolie Trade," *Harper's New Monthly Magazine* 29 (June 1864): 5. Courtesy of University of Washington Libraries, Special Collections, UW23640z.

Figure 3.
They also dehumanized "coolies." From Edgar Holden, "A Chapter on the Coolie Trade," *Harper's New Monthly Magazine* 29 (June 1864): 10. Courtesy of University of Washington Libraries, Special Collections, UW23641z.

ON THE LOWER DECK.

emigration through Canton under the same guidelines. British and French troops subsequently headed north to Peking (Beijing) and pressured the imperial court to recognize the right of Chinese subjects to emigrate to foreign lands in October 1860.[24]

The regulatory promise of freedom, however, proved illusory, driving U.S. diplomats to lobby more than ever for a new federal law to suppress what they considered a new slave trade. At Lao's insistence, John E. Ward, a Georgia Democrat who replaced Reed, lent his support to inspecting U.S. vessels docked near but beyond Canton's city limits. The testimony of hundreds of Chinese aboard one particular ship, the secretary of the U.S. legation reported, "exhibited a dismal uniformity of the acts of deception, violence, intimidation, and crafty devices practiced by native crimps, to beguile or force them to go on board boats where they were compelled to assent to the demands of their captors, and go with them on board ship or to the barracoons at Macao." Although these particular passengers won their release, Ward and his consuls could do nothing as the American captain proceeded to Macao, a Portuguese colony, and picked up another shipload of "coolies" for Cuba, a Spanish colony. Ward wished for a law to place such cases under his authority, since neither the Canton system nor consular inspection seemed adequate to the task. "When the consul visits the ships to examine into their condition," he noted, "they are questioned under the painful recollection of what they had already suffered, and what they must still endure if a ready assent to emigrate is not given."[25] The United States had an obligation to outlaw "coolies" to American ships, Ward and his predecessors urged, for the sake of free labor and free trade.

Excepting U.S. diplomats in China, no group of Americans studied and criticized the transport of "coolies" to the Caribbean more assiduously than Southern proslavery ideologues. They, however, drew conclusions that had little to do with ending coercive practices in Asia and the Caribbean; rather, their obsession with the Caribbean and "coolies" developed into a defense of slavery and a rebuttal to abolitionism. The racial and economic failings of emancipation and coolieism, proslavery forces argued, confirmed the natural order of slavery, an order that fanatical abolitionists and politicians had destroyed in the Caribbean. While U.S. officials in China appealed for a federal legislation to suppress the "coolie" trade, slavery's supporters emphasized the futility of state intervention in matters concerning race and labor. American slavery, they asserted, protected the nation from the utter decay experienced in the Caribbean and thereby justified its renewal through new importations from Africa and its expansion southward to Cuba and beyond. Their arguments led to neither but contributed to the emerging consensus in antebellum America that "coolie" labor was an evil to be expunged from America's ships and shores.

Not long after the legal end of slavery in the British Empire, American slavery's defenders charged again and again that abolition heralded a new era of duplicity and hypocrisy, characterized by semantic games rather than genuine humanitarianism. British imperial authorities had imposed the slave trade and slavery upon their colonies in North America, the *United States Magazine* claimed, and now ruled over millions of "absolute slaves" in India and elsewhere. Worse yet, they continued deceptively to sell "negroes" into slavery as "immigrants" and inaugurated "the blackest and worst species of slavery" by transporting "Indian Coolies" to the West Indies. "Humane and pious contrivance!" James Henry Hammond accused the British in his widely circulated letters in defense of slavery. "To alleviate the fancied sufferings of the accursed posterity of Ham, you sacrifice, by a cruel death, two-thirds of the children of the blessed Shem, and demand the applause of Christians, the blessing of Heaven!" Under the ruse of "immigration," Hammond added emphatically, "THE AFRICAN SLAVE TRADE HAS BEEN ACTUALLY REVIVED UNDER THE AUSPICES AND PROTECTION OF THE BRITISH GOVERNMENT." West Indian emancipation was a "magnificent farce" that his "humanity" and American slavery's "full and growing vigor" could not allow on U.S. soil. Reverend Josiah Priest likewise castigated the British for "inveigling . . . a yellow, swarthy race" to labor on the other side of the world, a system at odds with "their seemingly noble generosity in manumitting their slaves" but consistent with their recent indenturing of "the negro"—"ignorant" of legal contracts as a "monkey"—in Africa.[26]

New Orleans–based journalist J. D. B. De Bow was perhaps the most influential figure to incorporate British hypocrisy, conspiracy, and degeneracy into the proslavery argument. Great Britain had been the greatest slave dealer in history, he argued, whose conscience turned to "philanthropy" only out of economic self-interest. His conspiracy theory of emancipation was straightforward: "*Liberate your West India slaves; force them [other nations], as you can then, to liberate theirs, and you have the monopoly of the world!*" And exposés of the "wide-spread evils" of Caribbean coolieisms became integral to De Bow's derision of British emancipation and defense of American slavery. Emancipation reverted former slaves to "a state of Pagan cannibalism" in the West Indies and drove up the prices of tropical products in Europe, conditions that "made fillibusters [*sic*] and buccaneers of more than half of christendom." British and Northern abolitionists, De Bow reported, were now shipping "Coolies and

Africans" in a "new system" that was "attended with ten times as much of crime and sacrifice of human life" as the slave trade and slavery. Government and newspaper reports on the *Robert Bowne*, *Waverly*, and other disasters, which he quoted extensively, illustrated the "enormities" being committed everyday in Asia and the Caribbean.[27]

To De Bow, the Caribbean demonstrated the moral superiority of the U.S. South and the dire consequences of interfering in the racial order. The "humane conduct" of American slaveholders, he argued, "preserved" human life and the four million American slaves deserved to be spared "the risk of being exposed to evils" characteristic of other plantation societies. After surveying the various migrant contract labor systems of British, French, and Spanish tropical colonies, particularly the "truly frightful" mortality rates on ships and plantations, De Bow asked how they could be accorded "the specious title of *free labor*": "What is the plain English of the whole system? Is it not just this?—that the civilized and powerful races of the earth have discovered that the degraded, barbarous, and weak races, may be induced *voluntarily* to reduce themselves to a slavery more cruel than any that has yet disgraced the earth, and that humanity may compound with its conscience, by pleading that the act is one of *free will*?" Platitudes on "humane principles" and "righteous decrees" might be "all very plausible and very soothing to the conscience" but the truth, he believed, exposed the unconscionable hypocrisy of abolitionism. De Bow demanded that "decisive means" be taken "to arrest this evil in its infancy," lest the entire world be cursed with the "ineradicable evils" of the "coolie" trade, including the specter of race wars between "half savages and half-civilized idolators" in the tropics. Although slavery protected the South for the moment, he concluded, "a successful insurrection of the negroes" incited by abolitionists would prove "an enormous impulse" toward the introduction of "coolies" to the United States.[28]

If freedom could be worse than slavery, as De Bow insisted, other proslavery propagandists such as Daniel Lee wondered how "immigration," as understood and practiced in the Caribbean, might revitalize the institution of slavery in the United States. "Without making the disastrous sacrifice that ruined the planting colonies," Lee proposed, "we may, if it be wise to do so, import Coolies or Africans, under reasonable contracts to serve for a term of years as apprentices, or hirelings, and then be conveyed back to the land of their nativity." The system would not only fill the South's demand for "a muscular force worthy of its destiny," he argued, but also civilize Asia and Africa as these "pupils" returned home, enlightened. His ultimate objective, however, was to reopen the trans-Atlantic slave trade, a movement that witnessed a resurgence in the late 1850s. By 1858, Lee abandoned the idea of recruiting new races of laborers and advocated the sole importation of "African immigrants" under fourteen-year indentures or longer, as Louisiana legislators were then considering. He claimed that the system, once begun, would convert Northerners to the wisdom of Southern ways, allowing the extension of "the term of the African apprenticeship from fourteen years to the duration of his natural life." Lee's reasoning was, in effect, the mirror image of William Reed's attempt to apply the slave trade laws to the "coolie" trade: since the "coolie" trade and African "immigration" to the Caribbean were like the banned African slave trade, the slave trade itself ought to be legalized. Prominent proslavery thinkers such as George Fitzhugh agreed wholeheartedly.[29]

The drive to enslave peoples, at the same time, did not stop proslavery forces from imagining themselves and their nation as liberators—would-be liberators of "coolies" across the oceans as much as U.S. diplomats. U.S. expansionism in the Caribbean, they suggested, would result in the deliverance of slaves and "coolies" from backward despots. Representative Thomas L. Clingman of North Carolina, for example, attempted to shed light on "how this system of transporting and selling into slavery these Coolies is managed by Great Britain and Spain," to drum up congressional support for a more aggressive policy toward "our American Mediterranean" in peril. The mass importation of Chinese "coolies," Mayan Indians, and Africans intermixing with "the present black and mongrel population," he argued, threatened to make Cuba and other islands "desolate," the permanent "abode of savages." Instead, some "*Norman* or *South-man* fillibuster [*sic*]" ought to go down and force "Cuffee" to produce tropical goods, "which Providence seems to have intended these islands to yield for the benefit of mankind." Senator John Slidell of Louisiana likewise called for the U.S. acquisition of Cuba. In January 1859, he presented a bill to that effect on behalf of the Committee on Foreign Relations, whose accompanying report forecast the humanitarian and financial benefits to come. The United States would put an end to the slave and "coolie" trades—the latter of which resulted in mortality rates and suffering "far worse" than slavery—and thereby improve the value and treatment of Cuban slaves and allow American slaveholders to dominate the world sugar market.[30]

The proslavery argument's critique of Caribbean coolieisms, in the least, frustrated abolitionist attempts to draw sharp contrasts between slavery and freedom and revealed the complex global ties that slavery and coolieism had forged. Developments in Europe, the British West Indies, Cuba, India, China, and Africa produced new anxieties and hopes that informed and challenged universalizing notions. Were the British West Indies really free after emancipation? Weren't Asian and African immigrations merely legalized slave importations? The transport and employment of "coolies" in the Caribbean rendered such questions—whether in diplomatic correspondence from Asia or proslavery pronouncements from the Old South—beyond a black-and-white issue. Initially cast as the "free" advancement from coerced labor, "coolies" came to epitomize slavery in the United States at a time when the national crisis over slavery was about to erupt in open warfare. On the eve of the Civil War, the "coolie" and slave trades had become so intertwined in American culture that an encyclopedic entry for "Slaves and Slave-Trade" devoted a section exclusively to the "Coolie Trade."[31] The project of outlawing "coolies" could not be extricated from the national war over slavery.

Importation and Immigration

The convergent and contrasting denunciations of "coolies" by American diplomats and slaveholders generated simultaneous but distinct initiatives to outlaw "coolies" on U.S. vessels and on U.S. soil. Representative Thomas D. Eliot, a Republican from Massachusetts, led the legislative campaign in the U.S. Congress to ban American participation in the "coolie" trade, beginning with the publication of his report on behalf of the Committee on Commerce in 1860. Encapsulating the frustrations and aspirations of U.S. diplomats in China far more than those of proslavery critics, Eliot and his associates took great pains to distinguish between the status of "coolies" in the British colonies and Cuba. The transport and employment of "East Indian coolies" in British Guiana, Trinidad, and Mauritius, the report argued, were characterized by voluntary contracts and government supervision that obviated outside interference. Chinese migration to California was also "voluntary and profitable mutually to the contracting parties" and, in any case, already subject to federal statutes on passenger ships. The "Chinese coolie trade" to Cuba, on the other hand, was categorically unique and warranted immediate congressional action. That particular trade was "unchristian and inhuman, disgraceful to the merchant and the master, oppressive to the ignorant and betrayed laborers, a reproach upon our national honor, and a crime before God as deeply dyed as that piracy which forfeits life when the coasts of Africa supply its victims." Though targeting "American shipmasters and northern owners" engaged in a trade "as barbarous as the African slave trade"—not Southern slaveholders—the timing and language of the report obviously underscored Eliot's broader antislavery message.[32]

Consistent with a longstanding American rebuke of Cuba as morally backward, the report's geopolitical boundaries also reflected the Republican Party's growing faith in nation-state authority and enduring hope for a peaceful end to slavery. The British Empire stood for state protection, progress, and freedom; the Spanish Empire exemplified state failure, stagnation, and slavery. Antislavery forces therefore vigorously contrasted what the *New York Times* called the "Chinese Coolie-trade" to Cuba and Peru and the "Hindoo Coolie-trade" to the British West Indies, which was "not the ally, but the enemy of Slavery." The "East-India Coolies, taken to the British Islands," John S. C. Abbott wrote in his antislavery tract, seemed to "have their rights carefully protected by the British government," whereas "in Cuba the Coolie trade is merely a Chinese slave-trade under the most fraudulent and cruel circumstances." Juxtaposing the "human misery" in Cuba against the "joy and gratitude" in postemancipation British West Indies, Abbott prayed that "the execrable institution" of slavery would "speedily go down" in the United States, "but not in a sea of flame and blood."[33] State regulation and supervision, it seemed, would guarantee and, in essence, define freedom for all.

Slavery's defenders had no patience to draw distinctions among Caribbean coolieisms and demanded the exclusion of "coolies" from America's shores so as to preserve domestic slavery. Between Lincoln's election and inauguration—and during the secession of one state after another—proslavery unionists desperately turned to the Caribbean and "coolies" to sustain their lost cause, with President James Buchanan going so far as to propose the acquisition of Cuba. At a convention called to draft a constitutional amendment to avert a war in February 1861, a delegate from New York recommended the preservation of slavery as a state institution and ridiculed its abolition in England and France. "True, they have abolished slavery by name," he argued, "but they have imported apprentices from Africa, and Coolies from Asia, and have placed them under the worst form of slavery ever known." In considering a provision to prohibit the importation of slaves from abroad, the convention added the phrase "or coolies, or persons held to service or labor" upon the suggestion of a Kentucky delegate, who contended that "the importation of coolies and other persons from China and the East" was "the slave-trade in one of its worst forms."[34]

In a fracturing nation, those who were fighting hardest to uphold slavery attempted to criminalize "coolie" importations first. In March 1861, congressional leaders of the compromise movement proposed multiple drafts of a constitutional amendment that included the retention of slavery below the 36°30' parallel line and the prohibition of the "foreign slave trade" involving "the importation of slaves, coolies, or persons held to service or labor, into the United States and the Territories from places beyond the limits thereof." At the same moment in Mobile, Alabama, the constitutional convention of the

Confederate States of America considered an identical clause against "the importation of slaves, coolies, or persons held to service or labor into the Confederate States and their Territories, from any places beyond the limits thereof." Politicians on opposing sides of the secession crisis figured that the preemptive exclusion of "coolies" would shore up slavery in the South.[35]

Antislavery Republicans also moved to put a stop to "coolie" importations during the first year of the Civil War. After settling for congressional resolutions requesting more documents from Buchanan and then Lincoln, Eliot and his allies renewed their attempt to disengage Americans from the "coolie" trade in the now Republican-dominated Congress. Upon the receipt of the Lincoln administration's report on the "Asiatic coolie trade" in December 1861, which attested to the violence of the trade and the failure of government inspection, Eliot proposed an amended bill (H.R. 109) for the House's consideration and pleaded for its passage. Aside from procedural objections to his earlier bill, Eliot argued, he had heard only "a solitary objection" to it from his colleagues. "I refer to Mr. [Henry C.] Burnett [of Kentucky], who is now doing what he can to pull down the Government which he was then under oath to sustain and support," he explained, "and that objection, as I recollect it, was based simply upon the assertion that . . . it might by possibility affect some of his constituents who, as he declared, had some cooly laborers upon their plantations." The House passed the bill.[36]

The Senate then made a significant modification to Eliot's bill. Senator John C. Ten Eyck of New Jersey recommended on behalf of his chamber's Committee on Commerce that the phrase "against their will and without their consent" be stricken from H.R. 109. "The committee are of opinion that the cooly trade should be prohibited altogether," Ten Eyck argued. "They are of opinion that persons of this description should not be transported from their homes and sold, under any circumstances; being, as is well known, an inferior race, the committee are of the opinion that these words will afford very little protection to this unfortunate class of people." His racial and moral argument carried the day. The Senate passed the bill with Ten Eyck's amendment; the House concurred two weeks later. And in the throes of military and political battles over slavery, Lincoln signed "An Act to Prohibit the 'Coolie Trade' by American Citizens in American Vessels" in February 1862.[37]

The final version of the bill reproduced the racial logic of the age of emancipation that made the practical enforcement of prohibiting the "coolie" trade a confusing and impossible endeavor. What exactly constituted a "coolie"? And could one ever be emancipated from the status of a "coolie"? The new law answered neither question. Its first section prohibited U.S. citizens and residents from acting as "master, factor, owner, or otherwise, [to] build, equip, load, or otherwise prepare, any ship or vessel . . . for the purpose of procuring from China . . . or from any other port or place the inhabitants or subjects of China, known as 'coolies,' to be transported to any foreign country, port, or place whatever, to be disposed of, or sold, or transferred, for any term of years or for any time whatever, as servants or apprentices, or to be held to service or labor." It was from this section that Ten Eyck removed the words "against their will and without their consent," a clause that might have classified "coolies" more conclusively. Instead, the legislation simply outlawed any shipment of Chinese subjects "known as 'coolies'" abroad "to be held to service or labor." Virtually all Chinese subjects leaving China were known as "coolies." But another section of the law left the door open to Chinese migrations, proclaiming that "any free and voluntary emigration of any Chinese subject" should proceed unabated so long as a U.S. consul attested to the voluntary status of the migrant through a written certificate.[38] The two sections presumably went hand in hand. The United States deplored the importation of human beings; it embraced immigration.

Anti-"Coolie" Legacies

Reflective of the 1862 anti-"coolie" law's origins in wider debates over slavery, postbellum legal battles over its application took place in the U.S. South and its leading antebellum slave market and port city, New Orleans. With the abolition of slavery and the prospect of black enfranchisement, former slaveholders and their allies now looked to the Caribbean and "coolies" for political and economic salvation. A refrain uttered across the region after the war, a journalist reported, was: "We can drive the niggers out and import coolies that will work better, at less expense, and relieve us from this cursed nigger impudence." Alarmed by such brash talk, federal officials responded without delay when the U.S. consulate in Havana reported in 1867 that "certain parties in the State of Louisiana . . . [were] engaged in the business of importing into that state from this Island Chinese or coolies under contracts to serve on stipulated wages for a specified time." The U.S. attorney in New Orleans was dispatched immediately to intercept an American brig en route that was reportedly carrying passengers "purchased" from their Cuban "masters" and signed to contracts establishing "the relation of slavery or servitude." Although the vessel was unquestionably transporting twenty-three Chinese subjects "known as 'coolies' . . . to be held to service or labor" in Louisiana, the U.S. attorney eventually decided to dismiss the case. The failure to obtain consular certificates notwithstanding, he decided, the brig's captain had believed the "coolies" to be "free agents."[39]

The law's creators never contemplated a conflict between the two provisions on "coolies" and "immigrants," rendering its legal enforcement ineffective but its cultural effects enduring. When a labor recruiter from the South requested consular certificates to ship nearly two hundred Chinese workers from Hong Kong to New Orleans in 1869, the local U.S. consul was baffled. "*What constitutes a free and voluntary emigrant?*" he asked the secretary of state. ". . . What is a 'Coolie' as here defined, and what is a free emigrant?" Discovering that his superiors knew no better and that the passengers appeared to be voluntary, he issued the certificates.[40] If the law did little to stem Chinese migrations to the United States, including to a region vocally demanding "coolies," the racial and cultural logic behind it—that "coolies," in contrast to "immigrants," embodied slavery after emancipation—suffused almost every political debate on Chinese migration. When Senator Charles Sumner tried to remove the word *white* from U.S. naturalization laws in 1870, for instance, his opponents dwelled on the racial image of "coolies" overwhelming the United States back to slavery. "These people are brought here under these infamous coolie contracts," a Nevada Republican exclaimed, "the same contracts that have disgraced humanity in the taking of these poor people to the West India islands and various portions of South America as slaves." As Sumner's resolution went down in defeat, unanimous condemnations of "coolies" echoed universal applause for "immigrants," defined explicitly and implicitly as hailing solely from Europe. The act of outlawing "coolies" racialized "immigrants" as decidedly white and European in American culture, negating the legal space afforded to "free and voluntary" Chinese migrants.[41]

For decades preceding and following the passage of the 1862 law, "coolies" occupied the legal and cultural borderland between slavery and freedom, signifying and enabling critical transitions in U.S. history. The 1862 law, unambiguously framed as an antislavery measure by Eliot and others, established a precedent that few politicians would or could resist. What was, in effect, the last slave trade law would lead to a litany of immigration laws ostensibly targeting "coolies" (and prostitutes) in the name of "immigrants" and freedom, including the Page Law of 1875 and the Chinese Exclusion Act of 1882. And the perceived existence of coolieism and other forms of bondage—and the moral imperative to prohibit slavery—infected and rationalized U.S. expansionism abroad, from China and Cuba in the 1850s to the Philippines in the 1890s.[42] Locating, defining, and outlawing "coolies" ultimately evolved into an endless and indispensable exercise that facilitated and justified a series of historical transitions—from slave trade laws to racially coded immigration laws, from a slaveholding nation to a "nation of immigrants," and from a continental empire of "manifest destiny" to a liberating empire across the seas. The violent and mythical legacies of those transitions would go a long way toward defining race, nation, and empire in the twentieth century and beyond.

Notes

I thank Tefi Lamson, Moon-Kie Jung, Lisa Lowe, Jodi Melamed, Chandan Reddy, Leti Volpp, Alys Weinbaum, and fellows at the Simpson Center for the Humanities for reading and commenting on earlier drafts.

1. Congressional Record, 47th Cong., 1st sess., 1482, 1581, 1932, 1936.
2. Ibid., 1934, 1517.
3. On the figure of the prostitute, see Amy Dru Stanley, *From Bondage to Contract: Wage Labor, Marriage, and the Market in the Age of Slave Emancipation* (Cambridge: Cambridge University Press, 1998), esp. 218–63.
4. Scholars of Asian American history all too often stress that Asians in the United States were "immigrants" and not "coolies," presumed to be those coerced to move to the Caribbean (see, for example, Ronald Takaki, *Strangers from a Different Shore: A History of Asian Americans* [Boston: Little, Brown and Company, 1989], 35–36). The habitual assertion of this false binary—"coolies" versus "immigrants"—not only reifies "coolies" and American exceptionalism but ironically reproduces the logic and rhetoric of nineteenth-century debates on whether or not Asians in the United States were, in fact, "coolies." No one, in the United States or the Caribbean, was really a "coolie."
5. *The Oxford English Dictionary*, 2nd ed. (Oxford: Clarendon Press, 1989), 891–92; Hugh Tinker, *A New System of Slavery: The Export of Indian Labour Overseas, 1830–1920* (London: Oxford University Press, 1974), 41–43; Robert L. Irick, *Ch'ing Policy toward the Coolie Trade, 1847–1878* (Taipei: Chinese Materials Center, 1982), 2–6; Vijay Prashad, *Everybody Was Kung Fu Fighting: Afro-Asian Connections and the Myth of Cultural Purity* (Boston: Beacon Press, 2001), 71–72.
6. The term *cooly*, defined as an "East Indian porter or carrier," had first appeared in 1842. Noah Webster, *An American Dictionary of the English Language* (New York: White and Sheffield, 1842), 953; Noah Webster and Chauncey A. Goodrich, *An American Dictionary of the English Language* (Springfield: George and Charles Merriam, 1848), 264.
7. Alan H. Adamson, *Sugar without Slaves: The Political Economy of British Guiana, 1838–1904* (New Haven, Conn.: Yale University Press, 1972), 41–42 (Gladstone quote on 41); Tinker, *A New System of Slavery*, 61–63 (quote on 63).
8. Tinker, *A New System of Slavery*, v (quote), 69–70; Adamson, *Sugar without Slaves*, 42–43; Walton Look Lai, *Indentured Labor, Caribbean Sugar: Chinese and Indian Migrants to the British West Indies, 1838–1918* (Baltimore: Johns Hopkins University Press, 1993), 109, 156–57; Dwarka Nath, *A History of Indians in British Guiana* (London: Thomas Nelson and Sons, 1950), 8–21.
9. See, for example: Adamson, *Sugar without Slaves*, 44–56, 104–53; Look Lai, *Indentured Labor, Caribbean Sugar*, 16, 50–86, 107–35; Tinker, *A New System of Slavery*, 61–287; Walter Rodney, *A History of the Guyanese Working People, 1881–1905* (Baltimore: Johns Hopkins University Press, 1981), 33–42.
10. See, for example: Denise Helly, "Introduction" to *The Cuba Commission Report: A Hidden History of the Chinese in Cuba: The Original English-Language Text of 1876* (Baltimore: Johns Hopkins University Press, 1993), 5–27; Evelyn Hu-DeHart, "Chinese Coolie Labour in Cuba in the Nineteenth Century: Free Labour or Neo-slavery?" *Slavery and Abolition* 14.1 (April 1993): 67–83; Rebecca J. Scott, *Slave Emancipation in Cuba: The Transition to Free Labor, 1860–1899* (Princeton, N.J.: Princeton University Press, 1985), 29–35, 89–110.

11. Look Lai, *Indentured Labor, Caribbean Sugar*, 19, 37–49, 58–61, 70–75, 87–106; Wally Look Lai, "Chinese Indentured Labor: Migrations to the British West Indies in the Nineteenth Century," *Amerasia Journal* 15.2 (1989): 117–35.
12. "Slavery in Jamaica, W.I.," *Littell's Living Age*, May 30, 1846, 429; "Miscellany: West-India Immigration," *Littell's Living Age*, September 19, 1846, 582; *The Liberator*, April 23, 1847.
13. "The Celestials at Home and Abroad," *Littell's Living Age*, August 14, 1852, 289–91, 297–98; *New York Times*, April 15, May 3, 15, June 14, December 10, 1852.
14. Jules Davids, ed., *American Diplomatic and Public Papers: The United States and China*, ser. 1, vol. 17, *The Treaty System and the Taiping Rebellion, 1842–1860: The Coolie Trade and Chinese Emigration* (Wilmington, Del.: Scholarly Resources, Inc., 1973), B13–B15; M. Foster Farley, "The Chinese Coolie Trade, 1845–1875," *Journal of Asian and African Studies* 3.3–4 (July and October 1968): 262; Humphrey Marshall to Secretary of State, March 8, 1853, 33rd Cong., 1st sess., House Executive Document (HED) 123, 78–82.
15. John Kuo Wei Tchen, *New York before Chinatown: Orientalism and the Shaping of American Culture, 1776–1882* (Baltimore: Johns Hopkins University Press, 1999), 3–59.
16. Robert J. Schwendinger, *Ocean of Bitter Dreams: Maritime Relations between China and the United States, 1850–1915* (Tucson, Ariz.: Westernlore Press, 1988), 30–37; Irick, *Ch'ing Policy toward the Coolie Trade*, 32–34; Peter Parker to Secretary of State Daniel Webster, May 21, June 19, 1852, 34th Cong., 1st sess., HED 105, 94–96, 108–10.
17. Schwendinger, *Ocean of Bitter Dreams*, 29–30; Ching-Hwang Yen, *Coolies and Mandarins: China's Protection of Overseas Chinese during the Late Ch'ing Period (1851–1911)* (Singapore: Singapore University Press, 1985), 41–52.
18. Peter Parker to Commodore [J. H.] Aulick, June 5, 1852; J. H. Aulick to [Peter] Parker, June 19, 1852; Peter Parker to Chinese Commissioners, June 22, 1852; Peter Parker to [Secretary of State Daniel] Webster, July 20, 1852; [Chinese Commissioners' Reports], July 9, August 1, 1852; Peter Parker to Seu and Pih, Commissioners, &c., July 12, August 10, 1852; 34th Cong., 1st sess., HED 105, 121–22, 127–28, 130–36, 144, 148–49.
19. T. Hart Hyatt to William L. Marcy, June 1, 1856 (including log excerpts), in Davids, *American Diplomatic and Public Papers*, ser. 1, vol. 17, 356–60; H. N. Palmer to Thomas R. Rootes, February 15, 1856 (including log excerpts), 34th Cong., 1st sess., Senate Executive Document (SED) 99, 8–10; H. N. Palmer to Secretary of State W. L. Marcy, November 9, December 6, 1855, 34th Cong., 1st sess., HED 105, 71–73.
20. Peter Parker to Messrs. Sampson & Tappan, September 8, 1856; Public Notification, January 10, 1856; 35th Cong., 2nd sess., SED 22, 1129–30, 625–26; Irick, *Ch'ing Policy toward the Coolie Trade*, 53; *The Liberator*, April 18, 25, May 9, 16, 1856; *New York Times*, April 21, 1856.
21. William B. Reed to Secretary of State Lewis Cass, January 13, 1858, 36th Cong., 1st sess., SED 30, 59–65. The 1818 law is quoted in Lucy M. Cohen, *Chinese in the Post–Civil War South: A People without a History* (Baton Rouge: Louisiana State University Press, 1984), 37–38.
22. Public Notification, January 10, 1856, 35th Cong., 2nd sess., SED 22, 625–26; William B. Reed to Secretary of State Lewis Cass, January 13, 1858; William B. Reed to E. Doty, February 15, 1858; 36th Cong., 1st sess., SED 30, 59-65, 203–4.
23. *Harper's Weekly*, April 24, 1858; Lewis Cass to J. S. Black, April 28, 1858; Domestic Letters of the Department of State (National Archives Microfilm M40, roll 46); J. S. Black to Lewis Cass, March 11, 1859; Miscellaneous Letters of the Department of State (National Archives Microfilm M179, roll 168); General Records of the Department of State, Record Group (RG) 59; National Archives (NA), Washington, D.C.; William B. Reed to Lewis Cass, September 1, 1858, 36th Cong., 1st sess., SED 30, 422–25.
24. Schwendinger, *Ocean of Bitter Dreams*, 47–55, 60–61, 195; Irick, *Ch'ing Policy toward the Coolie Trade*, 57-60, 67-104, 148-49; Yen, *Coolies and Mandarins*, 84–100.
25. Governor General Laú to John E. Ward, January 30, February 5, 18, 1860; minutes of an interview between Governor General Laú and U.S. officials, February 1, 1860; John E. Ward to Governor General Laú, February 3, 24, 1860; S. Wells Williams, secretary of the U.S. legation, to John E. Ward, February 7, 20, 1860; John E. Ward to Secretary of State Lewis Cass, February 24, 1860; 36th Cong., 1st sess., HED 88, 29–37, 40–46, 48.
26. "Slaves and Slavery," *The United States Magazine and Democratic Review* 19 (October 1846): 243–55; "Gov. Hammond's Letters on Slavery—No. 3," *De Bow's Review* 8 (February 1850): 128–31; Josiah

Priest, *Bible Defence of Slavery; and Origin, Fortunes, and History of the Negro Race,* 5th ed. (Glasgow, Ky.: Rev. W. S. Brown, 1852), 359–60.

27. "The West India Islands," *De Bow's Review* 5 (May and June 1848): 455–500 (quote from 488, emphasis in original); "The Coolie Trade," *De Bow's Review* 23 (July 1857): 30–35.
28. "Asiatic Free Colonists in Cuba," *De Bow's Review* 24 (May 1858): 470–71; "The Coolie Trade; or, The Encomienda System of the Nineteenth Century," *De Bow's Review* 27 (September 1859): 296–321.
29. D[aniel] Lee: "Agricultural Apprentices and Laborers," *Southern Cultivator* 12.6 (June 1854): 169–70; "The Future of Cotton Culture in the Southern States, No. II," *Southern Cultivator* 16.3 (March 1858): 90–92; "The Future of Cotton Culture in the Southern States," *Southern Cultivator* 16.5 (May 1858): 137–39; and "Laborers for the South," *Southern Cultivator* 16.8 (August 1858): 233–36; [G.] Fitzhugh, "The Conservative Principle; or, Social Evils and Their Remedies: Part II—Slave Trade," *De Bow's Review* 22 (May 1857): 449–50, 457.
30. Thomas L. Clingman, "Coolies—Cuba and Emancipation," *De Bow's Review* 22 (April 1857): 414–19; "Monthly Record of Current Events," *Harper's New Monthly Magazine* 18 (March 1859): 543–44; "Continental Policy of the United States—The Acquisition of Cuba," *The United States' Democratic Review* 43 (April 1859): 29–30. On the antebellum movement for the annexation of Cuba, see Philip S. Foner, *A History of Cuba and Its Relations with the United States,* vol. 2, *1845–1895: From the Era of Annexationism to the Outbreak of the Second War for Independence* (New York: International Publishers, 1963), 9–124.
31. J. Smith Homans and J. Smith Homans Jr., *A Cyclopedia of Commerce and Commercial Navigation,* 2nd ed. (New York: Harper & Brothers, 1859), 1726–29.
32. 36th Cong., 1st sess., House Report 443, 1–5, 24.
33. *New York Times,* April 21, 1860; John S. C. Abbott, *South and North, or, Impressions Received during a Trip to Cuba and the South* (1860; New York: Negro Universities Press, 1969), 47–52, 184, 352. A Creole newspaper in British Guiana, on the other hand, described indentured migration as "the enemy, instead of the auxiliary, of freedom" (Look Lai, *Indentured Labor, Caribbean Sugar,* 180).
34. Foner, *A History of Cuba,* vol. 2, 121–22; L. E. Chittenden, *A Report of the Debates and Proceedings in the Secret Sessions of the Conference Convention, for Proposing Amendments to the Constitution of the United States, Held at Washington, D.C., in February, A.D. 1861* (New York: D. Appleton & Company, 1864), 268, 379.
35. 36th Cong., 2nd sess., Journal of the Senate, 373–87 (esp. 382, 386); "Monthly Record of Current Events," *Harper's New Monthly Magazine* 22 (April 1861): 689–90; *Journal of the Congress of the Confederate States of America, 1861–1865,* vol. 1 (Washington, D.C.: Government Printing Office, 1904), 868.
36. 36th Cong., 1st sess., HED 88, 1; 37th Cong., 2nd sess., HED 16, esp. 1, 3–16, 21–36; *Congressional Globe,* 37th Cong., 2nd sess., 350–52. Burnett might have been referring to the Chinese laborers who worked in Kentucky in the 1850s, mostly at iron-refining factories (Cohen, *Chinese in the Post–Civil War South,* 16–19).
37. *Congressional Globe,* 37th Cong., 2nd sess., 555–56, 581–82, 593, 838, 849, 855, 911; *Harper's Weekly,* February 15, March 1, 1862.
38. The full text of the 1862 law can be found in Cohen, *Chinese in the Post–Civil War South,* 177–79.
39. Whitelaw Reid, *After the War: A Tour of the Southern States, 1865–1866,* ed. C. Vann Woodward (1866; New York: Harper & Row, 1965), 417; Thos. Savage to William H. Seward, July 12, 1867, Despatches from U.S. Consuls in Havana, Cuba (NA Microfilm M899, roll 49), RG 59, NA; Cohen, *Chinese in the Post–Civil War South,* 58–61.
40. C. N. Goulding to Hamilton Fish, November 19, 1869, February 9, 1870, Despatches from U.S. Consuls in Hong Kong (NA Microfilm M108, rolls 6 and 7), RG 59, NA.
41. *Congressional Globe,* 41st Cong., 2nd sess., 5121–25, 5148–77 (quote from 5151). These postbellum developments are discussed in greater detail in my *Coolies and Cane: Race, Labor, and Sugar in the Age of Emancipation* (Baltimore: Johns Hopkins University Press, 2006).
42. For the full text and a discussion of the law named after Representative Horace F. Page of California, see George Anthony Peffer, *If They Don't Bring Their Women Here: Chinese Female Immigration before Exclusion* (Urbana: University of Illinois Press, 1999), 32–37, 115–17. On how the antislavery ideology shaped the debates surrounding the U.S. conquest of the Philippines, see Michael Salman, *The Embarrassment of Slavery: Controversies over Bondage and Nationalism in the American Colonial Philippines* (Berkeley: University of California Press, 2001).

Between "Oriental Depravity" and "Natural Degenerates": Spatial Borderlands and the Making of Ordinary Americans

Nayan Shah

In October 1926, Police Chief A. W. Reynolds raided a ranch four miles northeast of Porterville, California, in the foothills of the Sierra Mountains, and arrested forty-eight-year-old ranch hand Arjan Singh for attempting the "crime against nature" on a seventeen-year-old white "local boy," Alexander Quinn. The local newspaper reported Singh's arrest as a "statutory crime," but Alexander Quinn was hardly shielded from police suspicions. The Porterville police arrested Quinn and held him in jail on the charge of vagrancy pending a hearing in juvenile court. Although Singh declared that he would fight the sodomy charge, at the trial he pled guilty and was sentenced to five years in prison.[1]

Arjan Singh and Alexander Quinn were among thousands of seasonal field workers—foreign migrants, tramps, and casual local laborers—engaged in the yearlong cycle of planting, pruning, and harvesting up and down the Pacific Coast in the early twentieth century.[2] This narrative culled from Tulare County Superior Court records could be considered predictable. Arjan Singh's arrest for sodomy fit a pattern of intergenerational, working-class, same-sex relations that early-twentieth-century sociologists, sexologists, and labor economists have conventionally described as situational "homosexuality" common in "mining districts, lumber camps, wheat fields, and fruit ranches." Sodomy was considered a prevailing immoral practice "wherever a large number of men [were] grouped together apart from women."[3] The prosecutor, Assistant District Attorney W. C. Haight, blamed the crimes on socializing between "low down whites and Hindus of the same type." Haight's ability to explain the crimes did not diminish his outrage at Singh's "disgusting Oriental depravity" or temper his ambivalence toward Quinn's behavior. Despite the newspaper's invocation of statutory crime, the prosecutor appeared reluctant to treat Quinn as an innocent victim.[4] What made the Porterville case simultaneously predictable and outrageous?

Like many other prosecutors and police, Haight anticipated immorality and criminality in the social interactions between white adolescent males and Asian migrants. Suspicions had turned the spatial locations of contact—the streets, alleys, boardinghouses, labor camps, and ranches where migrant workers congregated—into borderland spaces characterized by disorder, conflict, and murky social and sexual ties between males. In these borderland spaces of migrant life, the police suspicion of illicit and immoral activity remade transient domestic and leisure spaces into sites of public scrutiny. Two years prior to the sodomy arrest, Singh had been convicted of liquor possession and at the time was reputed for "making his house attractive to depraved boys by having liquor on hand."[5] At the trial, Haight pointedly established the illicit reputation of Singh's house and demonstrated the legal ramifications of de-privatizing a residence. Charging Quinn with vagrancy was a means to punish his association with an allegedly immoral foreign man and his presence in a transient's house that was defined as a disreputable and illicit resort. Policing by the liberal state strictly defined the boundaries of public and private in society. However, in borderland migrant spaces the feverish redefining of the borders of the public, the semipublic, and the private kept the boundaries unclear and unsettled.

The surveillance of spatial borderlands brought another set of ambiguous identities into play: the containment of normative American masculinity from the threats of other interloper masculinities, cast as foreign and degenerate. To this end, prosecutors and judges in the early twentieth century created racialized and sexualized typologies of masculinity to police the relationships of roaming male youth and foreign migrants. Their immediate purpose was to identify the dangers posed to male youth, but the effect was to ensure a future for American normative masculinity.[6] Yet the sexual ambiguity of male youth confounded the jurists, forcing them to consider whether sodomy was an act of violation or invitation, to judge whether a youth was innocent, criminal, or delinquent. The protection of a specific male victim, however, was secondary to the protection of society and civilization and the affirmation of American normative masculinity. As David Bell has argued, the emphasis on public victimization "often deployed in state and legal discourses" on sodomy normalizes the common good and recodes all suspect intimacies as spectacles of public discipline.[7] In the Porterville case, Haight hailed Singh's imprisonment as the removal of a "menace to society" and a "blessing to the community."[8] In political and cultural discourse, Asian men were generally perceived as the importers of "unnatural" sexual practices and pernicious morality.[9] The putative threat posed by the social practices of "amoral" alien migrants, domestic transients, and male adolescents thus simultaneously unsettled and shored up the constitution of normal American masculinity.

Very little of the texture of these tensions bubbles to the surface in the discreet and pithy newspaper accounts of the Porterville case and similar California cases. The court records, however, pulsate with the interests, suspicions, and imperatives of policing, and the corresponding production and regulation of borderland spaces and identities and the threats to normative American masculinity. This article examines how a series of California court cases in the 1910s and 1920s recast the boundaries of American masculinity through tackling the ambiguities of adolescent delinquency and deploying the categories of normality, degeneracy, and natural sex. Understanding how those spaces and identities were constituted and policed necessitates an exploration of how and why the legal statutes—sodomy, statutory rape, and vagrancy laws—were reinterpreted and combined in this era to both explain and punish the dangers of male migrant social and sexual relations. The combination of sodomy, statutory rape, and vagrancy in these cases has particular analytical significance since most historical studies of law and society in the late-nineteenth- and early-twentieth-century United States often isolate the legal prosecution of vagrancy, sodomy, and statutory rape protections as separate problems and as the regulation of distinctive social bodies.[10]

Correlating American national identity with sexual normalcy was a new development of the twentieth century. The categories of deviance and normality and the new definitions of sexual identity shaped the policing of male adolescents' relationships with both external and internal nomadic subjects—the foreigners and transients who were the subject of vagrancy and sodomy prosecution. Policing and judicial reasoning converted these social dangers into the categories of delinquents, vagrants, and degenerates and developed heightened surveillance of the spatial borderlands of interaction. The judicial process revealed how unsettled the ideas of masculinity, adolescence, and normative sexual behavior were. Case by case, the legal archive underlined racialized sexualities that endangered the state as well as national masculinity. Even as the prosecutors, judges, and legal commentators strove in each individual case to put borders around normal masculinity, the process and dilemmas of adjudicating the cases repeatedly subverted any hope of fixed borders.

Sodomy, Statutory Protections, and the Problem of Consent

Until 1976, California law defined the felony charge of sodomy as a "crime against nature" and explicitly prohibited all genital-anal penetration. In sodomy prosecutions in California the penetrator was charged with the "crime against nature" but the status of the "penetrated" was ambiguous. Sex acts between females and males were occasionally punished under sodomy statutes, but historians have noted that since the 1880s in the United States, the prosecution of sodomy mostly involved two males, usually an adult male and a male youth or child.[11] At the turn of the nineteenth century, the greater police and prosecutorial interest in punishing adult male sexual conduct that involved youth paralleled the rise of legislation that created statutory protections for females with regard to rape.

In the last decades of the nineteenth century and the first decades of the twentieth century, U.S. society was undergoing a cataclysmic shift in social consciousness and legal protections for girls and their sexual relations with adult men. Against the backdrop of prolific popular cultural and political representations of child prostitution, female abduction, child marriage, and white slavery, Progressive-era voluntary organizations and municipal government developed a web of social regulatory programs from juvenile courts to homes for unwed mothers to protect and discipline female youth.[12] Jurisdictions in California were at the vanguard of policing and protecting adolescents, and the courts became a key arena for disciplining and rehabilitating youth.[13] State legislatures created statutory rape protections for girls and rapidly revised age-of-consent standards. In the late nineteenth century, in tandem with trends nationwide, the California legislature had increased the age of consent for sexual intercourse for females from the age of ten in 1872 to fourteen in 1883 and sixteen in 1897. The legislature was deadlocked in lifting the age to eighteen until 1913, the year after women exercised suffrage in the state.[14] Despite this highly publicized movement to regulate the sexual activity of young females and their male partners, the California legislators were remarkably silent on similar age standards in sodomy cases. Judges and district attorneys stepped into the breach and formulated legal rules about how to try charges of, and who to protect in cases of, the "crime against nature," often borrowing from more-developed case law on female rape.[15]

Statutory rape protections were supposed to shield girls from interrogation about sexual history, conduct, and comportment. These protections were unevenly enforced, often resulting in greater scrutiny and interrogation of girls and young women. In practice, underage girls were often expected to explain their conduct, behavior, dress, and social history in order to prove their innocence. Defense attorneys, social workers, and even judges often pressed underage females to explain whether the particular sex act and sexual partner was invited, consensual, or forced. Yet raising the age of consent thresholds and creating statutory rape protections for girls carried an implicit understanding that both female and male adolescents possessed sexual maturity and the physical capacity for sexual activity that outstripped their social maturity and moral capacity to make decisions about sexual partners and sexual acts. Underwriting the new protections that defined the age boundary for consensual sex between males and females was a conventional understanding of male aggression and female vulnerability. It was understood that female youth could be forced, persuaded, or duped into sexual relations with male adults and believed that the law must intervene to protect the girl before she would be capable of consent.[16]

In an era when cultural and legal borders of age and legitimate sexual participation for females were being fixed in statute, however, there existed striking ambiguity and uncertainty about how to judge the vulnerability of male youth. In the early-twentieth-century California state courts, the issue of how to adjudicate the innocence or culpability of male adolescents in sodomy cases emerged repeatedly. A 1912 California State Supreme Court decision in the appeal of *People v. Dong Pok Yip* became the ruling precedent for applying statutory protections for male youth and was frequently and authoritatively cited in subsequent sodomy cases.[17] The case involved a Chinese man, Dong Pok Yip, who befriended nine-year-old Albert Hondeville at the Antioch wharf and taught him to fish. Later in the afternoon, Rodrigues, a Portuguese American bookkeeper with offices overlooking the wharf, observed the two "walking hand-in-hand." Suspicious, Rodrigues followed them behind the oil tanks to a brush of willows, where he described them as "stooping . . . with the boy in front and the Chinaman" behind him with his "hands on the sides of the boy's waist." Although he could not testify to penetration of Albert, Rodrigues claimed to see the back of the boy's overalls hung down and that the "Chinaman's" trousers were unbuttoned in front.[18]

At the trial, the eyewitness Rodrigues explained that Dong Pok Yip was "trying to use the boy as a female."[19] This claim gendered the incident into a "crime against nature" by transforming the boy into a passive object that could be sexually acted upon and penetrated. By rendering the boy as a feminized victim, attorneys and judges could analogize the sexual victim status of underage females to the legal experience of male youth. In the appeal to the California State Supreme Court, State Attorney General U. S. Webb elaborated on the analogy of statutory assault. Webb argued that the boy was "overpowered," and that the circumstances were similar to those where a "schoolteacher takes indecent liberties with a female pupil" or a man lays "hold of" a woman and kisses "her against her will."[20] The supreme court agreed and ruled that "consent" must be distinguished from "submission," despite the perception that the "boy was ignorantly indifferent and passive in the hands of the defendant." They argued that a "child of tender years or retarded mental development . . . in the hands of a strong man might be easily overawed into submitting without actually consenting."[21]

The statutory age standards applied from the law on female rape, however, had to contend with the legal category of a criminal accomplice. California statute in 1911 specified that in order to be charged as a criminal accomplice one must be fourteen or above. Female age of consent at the time was sixteen and was raised two years later to eighteen. In sodomy prosecutions, the criminal accomplice became the category for the males who engaged in consensual sex. In 1923, the California Supreme Court affirmed in *People v. Carter Singh* that the age standard of an accomplice created a different baseline of statutory protections for male youth—"a child under the age of fourteen years is presumed incapable of committing a crime and cannot therefore be deemed an accomplice."[22]

Protecting a "child of tender years" was a far clearer proposition, however, than confronting the dynamic of a majority of sodomy cases that involved male adults with male youth between the ages of fourteen and twenty-one. These youth were among a new category—"adolescence"—that emerged from social reform projects and social science knowledge and marked a paradigm shift from conceptualizing youth as "incomplete adults" to a distinctive and recognized intermediate phase of human development.[23] The emergence of scientific and social reformer interest in adolescence became linked to concerns about this period's social and cultural transformations. Changing social mores, the rise of commercialized entertainment in both large cities and towns, shifting patterns of work outside the household for youth and young adults, both male and female, and the tremendous internal migration and immigration of the late nineteenth and early twentieth century all fostered perceptions of the collapse of traditional family and social structures. Social reformers and commentators expressed fears that the widespread social and economic dislocations and social mobility created the conditions for sexual corruption and immorality. Youth were vulnerable to perils of premature sexual activity that could have devastating health and social consequences for individuals as well as spell ruin for society. The perceived vulnerability and needs of adolescents fueled the development of municipal juvenile courts, truancy officers, social workers, psychologists, and counseling programs in the early twentieth century.[24] These programs were charged with protecting the vulnerability of boys and girls from the sexual and moral dangers posed by urban vice and the immigrant male.

Above this age threshold of fourteen, defense and prosecution attorneys struggled over how an individual could be designated an accomplice. The exchange of money or gifts for a sexual act constituted the most decisive material evidence of consent. The problem of consensual sodomy emerged in cases of male youth between the ages of fourteen and twenty-one implicated in activities that raised concerns of prostitution and hustling. In the early twentieth century, male street hustling was identified as a social problem for urban adolescent delinquents. Physicians, psychologists, sociologists, social workers, and sexologists studied the nature of individual pathology and social deviance that led male youth to prostitute their bodies to men. Encounters and transactions between men and male youth were thus seen as part of an ensemble of criminal and sexual activity, on a sliding scale from petty theft, truancy, loitering, intoxication, drug addiction, and socializing with female prostitutes.[25]

The street-level transactions of migrant males allowed the law to define adolescent males as criminal accomplices to adult men. In one incident, on Friday night, February 10, 1918, two police officers were patrolling downtown Sacramento. The officers observed Stanley Kurnick, a "nineteen year old boy of Austrian descent," in the company of a forty-year-old "Hindu," Jamil Singh; both were ranch hands who found temporary work in the surrounding Sacramento and San Joaquin valleys. Their conversation on a street corner led Jamil to offer Stanley seventy-five cents for a meal and to share his room at the Colusa Rooming House. Later that night the police followed a lead from a street informer to their room. Officer Parker "looked through the keyhole and saw a boy lying face downward on the bed with his clothes partly off" and the "Hindu," also with his clothes partly off, lying on top of the boy, "going through the motions" of a man "having sexual intercourse." The officers broke open the door and arrested both men.[26]

Officer Parker's improbable strategy of looking through the "keyhole" was emblematic of sodomy arrests in which the police officer's account produced the third-party corroboration of the accomplice's testimony that was critical to conviction. This characteristic voyeurism, with its framing of anal intercourse, made sodomy a staged, witnessed, and profoundly public act. Sodomy was of such implicit public interest that at the trial neither the prosecution nor the defense attorneys compelled the police officers to explain their interest, justify their search without a warrant, or disclose their source of information. The protection of public morality justified police intervention into the "private" rooms of boardinghouses. In 1918 Sacramento, police surveillance of boardinghouses, brothels, pubs, and gambling houses had increased sharply under federal and public pressure to "clean up" the town in preparation for the construction of a military base. The ostensible concerns about the impact of female prostitution, venereal disease infection, and immoral gambling on male servicemen also drew more police officers into the downtown district and intensified their scrutiny of the interaction of foreign migrants and male youth. In such an atmosphere of intensified moral policing, boardinghouses became recalibrated as "semipublic" spaces along with an array of public leisure sites.

This scrutiny, however, produced different public exposure and punishment for the males involved. When Judge Glenn sentenced Jamil Singh to seven years in San Quentin, he wrestled with how to interpret Stanley Kurnick's behavior and his legal culpability. Glenn offered his opinion that Singh was "probably not any worse than the young man," and pronounced both "equally guilty." Yet he offered defenses for Kurnick's conduct—"he is a young man" and "probably of low mentality."[27] The prosecutors had charged Kurnick as "an accessory to the carnal act of the Hindu" and sent his case to juvenile court. From the prosecution's perspective, the accomplice charge signaled a perception of the delinquent youth as having unformed ethics, yet also the potential for reform that would be enhanced by the confidentiality of juvenile legal proceedings. Judge Glenn's assessment of Kurnick's culpability had much to do with his very suspect association with a foreign man and the heightened suspicion of illicit activity.

The credibility of the "accomplice" hinged on the circumstances and the social status of the adult defendant of the alleged crime. In September 1913, a San Francisco case involving circumstances that transpired in a middle-class home had a very different result upon appeal. In the San Francisco Superior Court, Samuel Robbins, a fifty-six-year-old white bookkeeper, was convicted by the reluctant testimony of sixteen-year-old Sidney, who claimed that Robbins attempted to penetrate him while in a locked bathroom in his house but was interrupted by the housekeeper, Mrs. Nute, trying to open the door. In the appeal to the California Supreme Court, however, the majority of justices argued that Mrs. Nute's testimony, though casting suspicious light on the defendant, did not sufficiently corroborate Sidney's accusation.[28] In overturning Robbins's conviction, the judges gave no credence to Sidney's explanation of trauma and his narration of the assault. The decision implicitly characterized Sidney as an unreliable accomplice and the producer of a false accusation. The judges decided not to heed Mrs. Nute's testimony, because she was a "prying" servant woman who had not expressly witnessed the actual crime.

Instead, the supreme court justices worried about Samuel Robbins's reputation, fearing that "friendship of a middle aged man for the lad" could be misinterpreted as criminal intent or activity. They argued that "in these days of the 'big brother movement' thousands of men throughout the country are systematically cultivating the friendship of boys, to the end that the influence of mature thought and association with men may aid in the development of the best qualities of the children."[29] The judicial intervention focused upon a key middle-class reform strategy for taming delinquent youth. Middle-class reformers advocated the sublimation of sexual energies into physical fitness, organized sports, and scouting, which were expected to impart proper socialization through adult mentorship and gender training into responsible and healthy adults.[30] Ironically, the same activities produced a homosocial environment and possibilities for intimate relations between males. The judges' decision, however, revealed the anxiety that men of middle-class privilege would be considered suspect in their association with boys and young men. The judges maintained that middle-class white men could impart moral development and should, therefore, not "be convicted of degrading crimes upon mere suspicion plus the story of an accomplice."[31] The judges accepted the defense's interpretation that it was "natural" that after a game of tennis the man and boy washed hands together in the bathroom and locked the door after themselves as a "simple precaution . . . to prevent" any interruption from cleansing their bodies.[32] Such homosocial activities between white men and white boys could be perceived as natural, moral, and pedagogically appropriate.

The difference between "natural" intergenerational male friendship and "unnatural" sexual predation thus depended upon the reputation of the adult. The defense attorney's use of "natural" homosociality and modesty from female view reinforced Robbins's credibility. The judges refused the inference that Robbins may have taken advantage of that familiarity and instead let Sidney bear the trauma of sexual predation bereft of state protection. Branding Sidney an unreliable accomplice was all the more startling because Sidney had no history of juvenile delinquency or deceit. Robbins's defense succeeded because his white racial identity and respectable middle-class status overrode suspicions and accusation of sexual assault.

In contrast, the social associations of Asian migrant men with "American" or provisionally "American" youth were perceived as inherently dangerous and catalyzed suspicions of sexual immorality. The same week of Jamil Singh's arrest in downtown Sacramento, police surveillance led to the arrest of another South Asian man for sodomy. On February 13, 1918, eighteen-year-old

Hector McInnes, a Native American who was originally from Truckee in the Sierra Mountains, befriended Tara Singh on the streets of downtown Sacramento. Tara gave Hector fifty cents for a meal and to rent a room at a lodging house on L Street run by a Japanese innkeeper, Koro Shigo. Tara followed Hector and was assigned to the adjoining room. In the early morning hours of Friday, February 15, police officers Malone and Weisler went to Shigo's boarding house pursuing anonymous leads "on the streets" that there "was a boy up there, with a Hindu." The officers found Hector naked in bed alone, and the doors between the adjoining rooms locked.[33] Under pressure from the police, Hector later testified in court that Tara came into his room at nine o'clock that night; Hector had taken off his pants, left his shirt on, and was ready to sleep. Hector claimed that Tara climbed into bed, began to "feel around" his body and then lay on top of Hector, attempting to penetrate him. Despite Tara Singh's denial that he had "never saw [Hector] that night" he was convicted of attempted sodomy.[34] In this case, the circumstantial evidence of the interracial association between an Asian migrant man and a male youth in public and their retreat to adjoining rented rooms overwhelmed any concerns that Hector McInnes's testimony was uncorroborated. In the arraignment hearing, Judge Henderson acknowledged that "the difficulty of these cases lies in the character of the boys who allow themselves to be used," making "their testimony not worthy of belief."[35] These doubts of credibility did little to dissuade the overwhelming suspicions of the dangers of migrant vagrancy that shaped police intervention and state prosecution.

Vagrancy, Nomadic Subjects, and Spatial Borderlands

In the late nineteenth and early twentieth centuries, vagrancy laws became a general umbrella under which migrants and delinquents could be policed, disciplined, and criminalized. The demands of capitalist development created mobile populations, but politicians and moral reformers condemned the social dynamics of unsteady work and temporary housing that were generated in the wake of human mobility. A vagrant was a transient, lacking reliable work, home, or family. Idleness was alone considered a badge of immorality, but vagrancy encompassed a range of disreputable behavior that could be criminalized. In nineteenth-century legal statutes, the crime of vagrancy explicitly identified the unproductive, disreputable, and sexualized character of its policing targets. In 1891 the California legislature amended the 1872 vagrancy statute that criminalized being an "idle or dissolute person, who wanders about the streets at late or unusual hours of the night," with characterization of a "lewd or dissolute person who lives about houses of ill-fame."[36] Vagrancy was thus not just temporary misfortune, unemployment, and poverty but was defined as an aversion to productiveness, an unwillingness to rehabilitate, and a failure of self-discipline. Vagrants were characterized as "lewd or dissolute persons" who were prone to habits of immorality—intoxication, prostitution, gambling, sodomy, or cross-dressing. In California, the shift from an explicit condemnation of prostitution to a broad policing of sex occurred when the vagrancy law was simplified in 1903 to criminalizing an "idle, lewd, or dissolute person."[37]

U.S. legal and historical studies have analyzed the use of vagrancy laws in three ways. The first sees it as a device of labor regulation that has been used since English common law and revived in the nineteenth and early twentieth centuries to force black freed people in the South into wage work and to stifle European, Asian, and Mexican immigrants as well as white native-born workers from labor organization, protest, and bargaining in the North, Midwest, and West.[38] The second arena of scholarly interest recognizes that vagrancy law criminalizes "having a certain personal condition or being a person of specified character" rather than criminalizing a specific act. Police surveillance and arrests could be made on reputation and general suspicion of future criminal activity.[39] The third specifically ties "vagrancy" with sexual and moral charges. The vagrancy complaint could combine with or substitute for specific charges of pimping, sodomy, sex perversion, lewdness, intoxication, indecent assault, or solicitation. Nationwide in the twentieth century, police and justice courts combined these policing targets into a generalized "vag lewd" charge. It was a notoriously vague and broadly applied misdemeanor charge that police employed in sweeps of parks, bars, clubs, toilets, and streets and "became the most deployed criminal sanction against same-sex intimacy" according to legal scholar William Eskridge.[40]

The police surveillance for potential vagrancy also produced scrutiny about the activities and movements of migrants and created the atmosphere to pursue suspicions of interracial social contact and, potentially, the felony charge of sodomy. Male migrant sociability thrived in the nodal hubs of transportation and the urban spaces where transients congregated between jobs. Vagrancy policing spatially mapped spaces of presumed safety and danger and recast social contact in terms of morality and immorality. Encounters between males occurred in the border spaces of streets, alleys, parks, and squares. Police walked the streets on their neighborhood beats, observing public activity and the social relations of the street. The police regulation layered public social spaces of everyday social encounter with nefarious and illicit implications. It also remade the interior spaces of public accommodations—saloons, clubs, halls, hotels, and boardinghouses—into semipublic arenas in which police could intervene upon suspicion. The policing of potential criminal activity included the regulation of improper social and sexual activity, resulting in arrests of soliciting prostitution, public drunkenness, property crime, public disturbance, lewdness, and sodomy. The geography of the rapidly urbanizing town and city provided the settings and spaces for casual, fortuitous, and dangerous encounters between men and boys of different ethnicities, classes, and ages.

In California, vagrancy sweeps were a routine practice of police surveillance in the central valley towns. For instance, in Marysville in February 1928, two police officers on routine patrol after midnight noticed a car parked in a secluded spot about a block away from residences. Officer McAuliffe's suspicions were aroused when he saw a dark man asleep leaning against the passenger window who "looked like a Mexican." When the officers pulled the man out, they discovered a "young man [who] was lying in the seat with his head under the wheel, his pants . . . down to his knees, his union suit underwear split . . . open, his coat . . . turned up and his rectum . . . exposed."[41] What had begun as police curiosity on a routine patrol was thus amplified by racial suspicion. Apparently, the presence of a dark man in a parked car at night was enough cause for suspicion. Although Officer McAuliffe had initially mistaken Rola Singh for a "Mexican," the officer treated his initial confusion over racial identity as irrelevant. The police suspected either "Mexican" or "Hindu" men were typically migrant laborers, unlikely to own automobiles, and suspected vagrants. Racial suspicion quickly turned into a more serious police investigation when they discovered a white male partially undressed and unconscious in Singh's company. The police officers arrested both men and hauled them to the police station for observation. Later that day after two medical inspections, Rola Singh was charged with the "crime against nature."

During the trial and appeal, the perception of youth protected Harvey Carstenbrook, who had accosted Rola Singh on the sidewalk near the stage depot and offered him a ride in his car. Carstenbrook explained that he had parked the car because he was too drunk to drive and that they both passed out until they were roused by the police officers.[42] Throughout the trial, the attorneys referred to him as the "Carstenbrook boy," and the judge presumed statutory protections precisely because of Carstenbrook's unconsciousness and lack of memory of how his pants came undone when the police found him. Carstenbrook's social status as a member of a longtime local small business family may have enabled the statutory protections even though his age was documented as twenty-eight in other legal proceedings before the same court.[43]

In the end, Carstenbrook's "boy" status shielded him from any further scrutiny and interrogation as a potential accomplice and he was released from jail without charges, while Rola Singh was convicted and sentenced to seven years imprisonment in San Quentin.

In all of these legal cases, in the recording of testimony from arrest, arraignment hearing, trial, sentencing hearing, and appeals, the police, prosecutors, and judges transmit their prejudices in revealing interpretations. The judges' decisions at the various levels of court proceedings were a conduit of circulating knowledge of the particular dangers of vagrant migrants and predictions of nefarious interracial sexual encounters between migrant males and youth. During a week of sodomy arrests, an uncommonly blunt police court judge in Sacramento, Judge Henderson, remarked that "Sodom and Gomorrah, Long Beach, California, and other places famous in history as being the scene where was practiced the fornicating of man by man must have spewed some of their descendants upon the city of Sacramento, in the form of several Hindus who have found their sexual gratification in the anus of boys."[44] Judge Henderson's opinion was strongly influenced by the *Sacramento Bee*'s exposé of sex between men in Long Beach restrooms, parks, and homes that led to more than fifty arrests in November 1914.[45] Judge Henderson characterized Jamil Singh and Tara Singh, as two of "the many Hindus that frequent the lower part of town, most of whom are Sodomites." Henderson was disturbed that the Native American male Hector had made himself a sort of "punk," or male prostitute, "for denizens of the lower end of town, of the Hindu race."[46] Hector's Native American origins perhaps defined him more readily as a male street hustler. Unlike European immigrant Stanley, Hector did not receive prosecutorial defenses of his age or culpability.

Judge Henderson's vision of "Hindu Sodomites," delinquent European immigrant youth, and Native American "punks" translated the practices and identities of migrant men into an economy of male prostitution. His concerns focused on the spatial borderlands populated with nomadic subjects whose practices and transient association recast public business locations into vice-suspect semipublic spaces. Henderson's language reterritorialized Sacramento's "lower end of town" as a public site of sexual perversity that required police surveillance, incarceration of its "immoral inhabitants," and protection for the middle-class and respectable families who might unwittingly travel into this vice district. Lower town Sacramento provided cultures of leisure, entertainment, and rest for transitory migrants. Its restaurants, saloons, bars, brothels, boardinghouses, hotels, streets, and alleys provided services for migrant men looking for work between harvest and planting cycles in the adjacent hinterlands.

In the court record and the testimony, gestures of financial assistance and offers of sharing accommodations between migrant males were recoded in law as illicit transactions that were flagged by police and prosecution as vagrancy, sodomy, and male prostitution. Yet, we can also reread in the cracks of this testimony a different story. Reinterpreting fragments from Jamil Singh's testimony at the sentencing hearing reveals an alternate rendering of intimacy and nomadic ethics in migrant social worlds. In the interstices of his responses, which were supposed to confirm his predisposition to criminality, Jamil Singh narrated a moral economy of duty that included financial support for his wife and family; avoidance, for the most part, of intoxicants and vices; and a willingness to work and to keep to his own people—"the Hindus."[47] He expressed incredulity that he was being convicted of a crime. Perhaps he believed that his reputation among his peers and performance of his duty shielded him from scrutiny. Perhaps he believed that his generosity in feeding and housing another worker was a reasonable exchange for physical intimacy. Jamil may have believed that Stanley invited and agreed to physical intimacy and that the police and courts were unreasonable in interfering. Maybe Jamil could not fathom that his interactions with Stanley were criminal. Did those actions that the authorities definitively labeled "unnatural sex" compute as "sexual" or "an assault" in the way that an attempt at physical intimacy with a female would certainly have? Jamil Singh's incredulity may have been a desperate attempt to defend himself and to entreat the judge's mercy, but it also contains within its narration shards of alternative ways of expressing his own reputation for responsibility and generosity to his family, his people, and to the working strangers he encountered.

Where Singh may have seen a moral social universe, Henderson saw a "mass of deviants" that had descended into Sacramento and created a district of immorality where they could satisfy "immoral" and "degenerate" urges. For Henderson, police, and prosecutors, the spatial concentration of male prostitution produced a sexual public for its surveillance and created boundaries of what social status and which actions the umbrella of privacy could protect. Irrespective of the efforts of migrant males to remove their intimate activities from public view, the very transience of migrant life cast all their activities outside the boundaries of domestic privacy. The norms of public morality offered valued public status and the shield of domestic privacy to married couples, but thwarted a similar pursuit of privacy for migrant males.[48]

Normal Man and Natural Degenerate

Early-twentieth-century jurisprudence and legislative politics intensively criminalized a range of sexual acts, practices, and persons. By elaborating upon the illegitimacy of the "unnatural" practices of sodomy and the specific dangers of migrants and vagrants, the contours of "natural" and "normal" male sexuality were constructed. The defense of normal masculinity and sexuality emerged under the threat of alleged degeneracy. James Kerr, a prominent legal scholar who edited the compendium of the *Codes of California* in 1921, illustrated the intensity of the threat when he railed against contemporary judicial decisions that left open the possibility of consensual sodomy as a "travesty of justice." He feared that "a degenerate person or a person of depraved and low character and mind, by consent to the beastly act, could nullify the will of the legislature."[49] In Kerr's reasoning, society must be defended from the "degenerate" and perverse individual, whose consent to anal penetration not only inverted masculinity but also undermined the political and social order. The ferocity of Kerr's response indexed the severity of the perceived threat. Consensual sodomy produced an "alternative mode of being," and its very viability "denaturalized" heterosexuality as the only "true identity."[50] Kerr's demand for the blanket illegitimacy of all male-to-male sexual relations was imperative to fortify the vision of normal male sexuality. Statutory protections for male youth were not enough. Kerr argued for the criminality of all acts of sodomy and the necessity of statutory protections for female youth that buttressed an ideology of natural sex, guiding male sexual activity into regulated sex, marital union, and procreation with adult females.

Although Kerr may have denied and deferred the question of consensual sex between males by nullifying its legitimacy, judges and prosecutors could not ignore its widespread existence. Like sociologists, psychologists, and social workers of the era, they instead created social categories to identify normalcy, degeneracy, and delinquency.[51] A striking example of how these categories converged and were reassembled is the 1928 Stockton case of "sex perversion," a newly created felony category that the California legislature established in 1921 to criminalize oral sex. In the 1910s the legislature had repeatedly attempted to criminalize oral-genital contact in response to its frequent prosecution in county courts, the California State Supreme Court ruling that only anal penetration constituted the "crime against nature," and the dissatisfaction of the frequent police recourse to the misdemeanor "vagrancy" charge to punish it.[52] In 1928, Stockton police arrested thirty-one-year-old Jack Lynch and seventy-year-old Keshn Singh for engaging in "sex perversion," specifically for being caught with Singh's penis in Lynch's mouth. The prosecution designated Keshn Singh as the accomplice who had paid Lynch fifty cents and "upon whom Lynch practiced his vulgar employment."[53]

In the court record, Assistant District Attorney H. C. Stanley deployed the categories of degeneracy, normalcy, and amorality within the framework of the "ordinary American" in order to identify the internal and external threats to American identity. At the sentencing hearing, Stanley, doubting that intoxication impaired Singh's judgment, instead believed his actions evidenced intrinsic amorality that was incompatible with American ethical behavior, despite Singh's having lived in the United States for twenty-three years. Stanley argued that Singh showed no remorse about the "wrong" of his action and he "does not seem to be a person that regards such a practice as the ordinary American would." Stanley advocated Singh's incarceration as a preventive measure to stop him from "prostituting other men by furnishing himself as a subject to be acted upon, whether for or without compensation."[54] Judge George Buck agreed and sentenced Singh to four years at San Quentin. As an amoral foreigner, Singh was cast as incapable of ever becoming an "ordinary American."

On the other hand, Jack Lynch appeared to have the lineage of an "ordinary American," a white man who was born in Wisconsin. But he also possessed all the characteristics of a vagrant—he was unmarried at age thirty-one, migrated from the upper Midwest to California in 1924, had temporarily worked in lumber camps and restaurants throughout the state, and had a long criminal record in California, which included vagrancy arrests and petty theft conviction, as well as the admission to arresting officers that he had practiced oral sex on men in Modesto and Stockton previous to this arrest. Stanley concluded that Lynch was a "natural degenerate," and that his record of vagrancy and habitual sex perversion made him unlikely to "be cured" of his "vulgar" practices that was "the incidental characteristic of the vagrant, who can never be regarded as a fit subject for society."[55] The case, a rare prosecution of two adult males, paired the amoral alien man who incited practices of sexual perversion with the condensation of the vagrant, degenerate, and sex pervert in the body of the white, native-born man. Neither man was considered a victim of the crime; rather, the work of policing their behavior served to ultimately isolate degenerate and amoral subjects from American society and incarcerate unfit subjects of society.

Racial difference had incited police suspicion, but it was the new sexual identities that framed the legal prosecution. The categories of degenerate and pervert fortified an understanding of the normal. While some white middle-class men such as Samuel Robbins could sidestep the indictment of sodomy through their ability to preserve their reputations as moral subjects and normal men, many more men were suspect because of how they were cast as either innately degenerate, through an enumerated criminal history, or amoral foreigners, by their "proven" reputation. In the Lynch and Singh oral sex perversion case, the policing of sex between white males and migrant/vagrant men, white identity was not as it may have first appeared—the sign of the always-innocent victim. Police and prosecutors thus deployed whiteness strategically in scrutinizing social contacts between so-called Americans and foreigner nomadic males, but the fundamental goal became to isolate "natural degeneracy" and amoral foreigners from contaminating American society.

The internal threat of the vagrant degenerate and the external threat of the amoral foreigner most perniciously converged in the potential corruption of male youth. During the 1910s and 1920s, California courts were interpreting the degree of male vulnerability and victimhood on perceptions of age, consciousness, and the ability to narrate sexual transgression. The characterization of the vulnerable and innocent male victim became that of someone who was acted upon without will or knowledge. A child under the age of fourteen occupied this category, as did an unconscious male of an indeterminate youthfulness. Harvey Carstenbrook's silence and protestations that he had no consciousness of sexual assault demonstrated how the age boundaries could be flexed to accommodate unconscious males. Above the age of an accomplice and below the age of legal adulthood, male youth were in a more precarious position in the courtroom. Sidney, Stanley, Alexander, and Hector, ironically because of their reluctant and coerced testimony of sexual assault by adult men, aroused suspicion of their potential consent and complicity. In practice in the lower courts, judges, attorneys, and juries interpreted the conscious choice of teenage males to socialize and participate with adult men on the double-edge of statutory protections. In fact, the parallel prosecution of some of these male youth for vagrancy and other misdemeanor charges in juvenile courts demonstrated how the legal proceedings served to rechannel the conduct of adolescent males and rehabilitate them into respectable sociality and sexuality.

In these early-twentieth-century California court cases, the variability of the ethnic and racial identity of the male youth (European immigrant youth, Native American, and native-born white youth) demonstrated the broadening of subjects for the project of social rehabilitation into moral and normal American men. While the racial boundaries for the social rehabilitation of male youth were malleable, the court cases underscored and justified the insurmountable racial boundary that perpetually defined Asian men as foreigners to the American nation. The amoral Asian could never be an "ordinary American" and was already defined as an unfit subject for American society and at the outer limits of the continuum between the "natural man" and the "natural degenerate." The "foreigner" and the "degenerate" were not legal categories, but were culturally and politically potent contextual categories that served both to identify and to explain moral peril. Racial ascription of external threats such as "Oriental depravity" and "Hindu sodomites" had the taxonomic function of harnessing suspicion and identifying and amplifying targets for both the official police and the informal policing of community residents. But it did not produce a categorical certainty. Not all foreigners were immoral and degenerate; however, an alleged tendency to immorality reinforced racialized suspicions. In sentencing hearings and judicial decisions, the interpretation of criminal behavior shifted focus from the criminal act to criminal identities. And the very process of fixing individual behavior into broad social categories was undergoing transformation. Categories of ethnicity and race had been employed descriptively and analytically, but they were being harnessed to new categories such as degeneracy and normality. These categories were accruing salience in court decisions and were enabling a reconsideration of new liberal life forms. By the mid-twentieth century the broad categories of "normal" and "degenerate" would become interchangeable with the binary opposition of heterosexual and homosexual.[56]

The policing of degeneracy and anxious fixing of categories of unnatural sex and social conduct in spatial borderlands, both urban and rural, illuminated how liberal governance produced authoritative rule and social subjects to regulate the reproduction of a society of normal and ordinary Americans. The conjunction of external danger (amoral foreign migrant), internal danger (degenerate vagrant), and the identification of subjects for flexible rehabilitation (delinquent youth) became the ensemble of social figures that required policing and prosecution. On these grounds, liberal legal adjudication of sodomy and vagrancy in the early twentieth century gave way to a greater coherence of social figures that could be governed. Legal scholar Judith Grbich has encouraged scholarly investigation into "the ways in which legal reasoning transforms the embodied imaginings" of particular lives into that "which passes for the 'normative.'"[57] The process of transforming "embodied imaginings" into normative subjects also produced a wide array of liberal life forms, both valorized and denigrated, that were shaped by legal, political, and cultural logics into a regulative field. In early-twentieth-century U.S. political and legal liberalism, the most valued and valorized life forms were the normal man and ordinary woman, who were seen to constitute normal American sexuality and "fit subjects for society." The healthy, fit, reproductive capacities of normal men and women were affirmed as simultaneously "natural" and "civilized" by the legal regulations that both shaped consensual and contractual monogamous marriage and the curtailment of putatively unnatural habits and vice.

Liberal governance and the policing of liminal social spaces also produced life forms that defined the boundaries of, and threats to, American normalcy—the vagrant, the degenerate, and the delinquent—all of whom inhabited the expansive repertoire of the "abnormal" in law and social life. As Christopher Tomlinson has recognized, these new social subjects of liberal rule generate a paradoxical process of fortifying "the authority of normality and the deviancy of the abnormal."[58]

Theorizing from the geographical specificity of the Mexican American borderlands, Gloria Anzaldúa offered an analytical approach that incisively interprets the density of human associations that straddle spatial and social boundaries. Anzaldúa recognized the strategies of social survival in the borderlands by the "the squint-eyed, the perverse, the queer, the troublesome, the mongrel, the mulatto, the half breed, the half dead; in short those who cross over, pass over or go through the confines of the 'normal.'"[59] This process of traversing the boundaries and confines of the normal embraces the heterogeneity of borderland bodies and practices, which flourish upon and within national borders.

Borderlands historian Emma Perez encourages us to challenge the exclusions of racialized sexualities and the dominant historical narratives that have "chosen to ignore or negate the populations who are on the margins, outside of normative behavior."[60] Perez's self-conscious approach meshes queering with borderlands analysis by encouraging the mining and reinterpreting of the borderlands legal archive for lost and silenced heterogeneities. By casting a queer and critical borderlands perspective on the state's records, Perez advocates reassembling alternative histories embedded in the legal archive of normalization.

This essay critically examines how legal codes, court cases, and jurisprudence contributed to both the sociological and aesthetic knowledge for identifying and regulating aliens, vagrants, and degenerates in spatial borderlands.[61] The policing of internal and external nomadic subjects revealed the ambiguity and insecurity of cross-racial and cross-class intimacy and intensified the fixing of social boundaries and social status. The state's imperative forged a seemingly unassailable defense of American normality and masculinity and an immense legal archive that records its success at maintaining security. Through the process of abstracting legal subjects and rules of law, the legal archive can be harnessed to create authoritative and normalized legal subjects. But the very same repository can also be reinterpreted to expose rifts and crevices where competing narratives have slipped. These residual traces in the case records contradict and confound the normalizing of legal subjects. Just as the judges and prosecutors recognized that they could not guarantee that the borders of normative masculinity or American identity would hold no matter how vigilantly they attempted to curtail specific sexual acts, partners, or practices, so too our own examination should not mistake the indictment and incarceration of nomadic subjects as acquiescence to normativity. Instead, we can continue to reassess the moments throughout when the borders blur and nomadic subjects deflect the normalizing project of making ordinary Americans.

Notes

I am grateful to the Rockefeller Foundation Humanities Fellowship at the Sex, Race, and Globalization Project at the University of Arizona, which supported research for this article. Duke University Press kindly granted permission to use a portion of my article, "Policing Privacy, Migrants, and the Limits of Freedom," in *Social Text* 84-85 (October 2005). Versions of this essay were presented at the Legal Borderlands Conference at Pomona College; the University of California, Irvine; Macalester College; the SSRC Sexual Worlds and Political Cultures Conference (2003); and the American Studies Association Meeting in Hartford, Conn. (2003). My analysis has been strengthened by the engaging questions of audience members at each event. I especially would like to thank the following for their suggestions and trenchant critiques: Sharon Bloch, Yen Le Espiritu, Eileen Findlay, Ken Foster, Rod Ferguson, Tak Fujitani, Gayatri Gopinath, Neil Gotanda, David Guttierez, John Howard, Sara Johnson, Miranda Joseph, Elizabeth Kennedy, Lisa Lowe, Eithne Luibhéid, Martin Manalansan, Scott Morgensen, Chandan Reddy, Vicki Ruiz, George Sánchez, Shelley Streeby, Stephanie Smallwood, Daniel Widener, and Lisa Yoneyama. I am grateful for the passionate engagement of Mary Dudziak, Leti Volpp, and Marita Sturken, who have stewarded this essay through many drafts and provided invaluable conceptual and editorial counsel.

1. *People v. Arjan Singh*, Case No. 2464, 1926, Tulare County Superior Court; "Two Statutory Cases Are Up for Hearings; Probe of One Hindu's Case Results in Another Being Arrested," *Porterville Evening Recorder*, October 9, 1926.
2. Bruce La Brack, *Sikhs of Northern California, 1904–1975* (New York: AMS Press, 1988), 123–24; David Vaught, *Cultivating California: Growers, Specialty Crops, and Labor, 1875–1920* (Baltimore: Johns Hopkins University Press, 1999).
3. Ranjani Kanta Das, labor economist and special agent of the U.S. Department of Labor, charged to study South Asian migrants on the Pacific Coast. Rajani Kanta Das, *Hindustani Workers on the Pacific Coast* (Berlin: Walter De Gruyter and Co., 1923), 83. Other noteworthy scholarship included Carleton H. Parker, *The Casual Laborer and Other Essays* (New York: Harcourt, Brace, and Howe, 1920); Nels Anderson, "Juvenile and Tramp," *Journal of American Institute of Criminal Law and Criminology* 14 (August 1923): 30; Josiah Flynt, "Homosexuality among Tramps, Appendix A," in Havelock Ellis, *Studies of the Psychology of Sex*, vol. 4, *Sex Inversion* (Philadelphia 1904). Recent historical scholarship that has situated this history of male homosociality and homosexuality includes Peter Boag, *Same Sex Affairs: Constructing and Controlling Homosexuality in the Pacific Northwest* (Berkeley: University of California Press, 2003); Dee Garceau, "Bunkies, Cross-Dressers, and Family Men: Cowboy Identity

and the Gendering of Ranch Work," in *Across the Great Divide: Cultures of Manhood in the American West,* ed. Matthew Basso et al. (Minneapolis: University of Minnesota Press, 2000).

4. *People v. Arjan Singh*; "Two Statutory Cases Are Up for Hearings."
5. *People v. Arjan Singh.*
6. David Campbell, *Writing Security: United States Foreign Policy and the Politics of Identity,* rev. ed. (1992; Minneapolis: University of Minnesota Press, 1998), 1–13.
7. David Bell, "Sexual Citizenship," in *Mapping Desire: Geographies of Sexualities,* ed. David Bell and Gill Valentine (New York: Routledge, 1995), 311–13.
8. *People v. Arjan Singh.*
9. The interpretation of "foreign" incitement to vice was typical in all areas, from legislative hearings to published medical studies. For instance, see U.S. Congress, *Senate Reports of the Immigration Commission,* 61st Cong., 3rd sess., 1911, Doc 753, 86; Immigration Commission Reports, Importation and Harboring of Women for Immoral Purposes, S. Doc. No. 61–753, 86 (3rd sess., 1911); Alfred J. Zobel, "Primary Gonorrhea of the Rectum in the Male," *American Journal of Urology* 45.1 (November 1909). For the contextualization of these threats in immigration, labor, and urban vice literature, see Chris Friday, *Organizing Asian American Labor* (Philadelphia: Temple University Press, 1994); Boag, *Same-Sex Affairs*; Nayan Shah, *Contagious Divides: Epidemics and Race in San Francisco's Chinatown* (Berkeley: University of California Press, 2001).
10. The history of sodomy prosecutions has identified and regulated the male homosexual body and mapped the formation of urban sexual subcultures. Vagrancy law was frequently deployed to police transients, migrants, and vagabonds and to regulate public space in small towns and cities. Historically associated with the control of labor, vagrancy arrests policed the leisure activities and intervened in working-class and migrant social spaces under the pretext of preserving public order. The history of statutory age protections for sexual relations focused on protecting female youth from male adults. No statutory legislation at this time protected male youth the way that highly publicized legislative protections for female youth at the turn of the century did.
11. George Chauncey, *Gay New York: Gender, Urban Culture, and the Making of the Gay Male World, 1890–1940* (New York: Basic Books, 1994); and Nan Alamilla Boyd, *Wide Open Town: A History of Queer San Francisco to 1965* (Berkeley: University of California Press, 2003).
12. Kathy Peiss, *Cheap Amusements: Working Women and Leisure in Turn-of-the-Century New York* (Philadelphia: Temple University Press, 1986); David J. Langum, *Crossing Over the Line: Legislating Morality and the Mann Act* (Chicago: University of Chicago Press, 1994); Mara L. Keire, "The Vice Trust: A Reinterpretation of the White Slavery Scare in the United States, 1907–1917," *Journal of Social History* 35.1 (2001): 5–41; Ruth Rosen, *The Lost Sisterhood: Prostitution in America, 1900–1918* (Baltimore: Johns Hopkins University Press, 1982); Pamela Haag, *Consent: Sexual Rights and the Transformation of American Liberalism* (Ithaca: Cornell University Press, 1999).
13. Municipal and county jurisdictions across the United States, including those in California, Oregon, Illinois, New York, and Massachusetts, were at the vanguard of creating partnerships between public agencies and private voluntary associations that both policed juvenile delinquents and protected adolescents.
14. William M. McKinney, ed., "Rape," *California Jurisprudence: A Complete Statement of the Law and Practice of the State of California,* vol. 22 (San Francisco: Bancroft–Whitney Company, 1925), esp. 361–65.
15. Jane E. Larson, "Even a Worm Will Turn at Last": Rape Reform in Late-Nineteenth-Century America," *Yale Journal of Law and the Humanities* 9.1 (1997); Mary E. Odem, *Delinquent Daughters: Protecting and Policing Adolescent Female Sexuality in the United States, 1885–1920* (Chapel Hill: University of North Carolina Press, 1996).
16. Larson, "Even a Worm," 19–20; Odem, *Delinquent Daughters.*
17. The case is cited in the following appellate cases: *People v. Samuel P. Robbins* 171 Cal., 466 (1915); *People v. Kangiesser* 186 P. 388 (Cal. Dist. Ct. App. 1919); *People v. Carter Singh* 62 Cal. App. 450 (Dist. Ct. App. 1923). For summaries of the case law, see Curtis Hillyer, *Consolidated Supplement to the Codes of the State of California, 1927–1931,* pt. 2 (San Francisco: Bender-Moss, 1932), 6922–23, 6929–30; James M. Kerr, *The Codes of California,* vol. 4, *Penal Code 1920* (San Francisco: Bender-Moss, 1921), 277–78, 384–85, 390.
18. Transcript at 1, 4–7, *People v. Dong Pok Yip,* 164 Cal. 143, 145–46, 1912, California State Archives.
19. *People v. Dong Pok Yip,* 22.

20. Ibid., 13, 14.
21. Ibid., 147.
22. *People v. Carter Singh.*
23. Jeffrey P. Moran, *Teaching Sex: The Shaping of Adolescence in the Twentieth Century* (Cambridge, Mass.: Harvard University Press, 2000); Harvey J. Graff, *Conflicting Paths: Growing Up in America* (Cambridge, Mass.: Harvard University Press, 1995); Joseph F. Kett, *Rites of Passage: Adolescence in America, 1790–Present* (New York: Basic Books, 1977).
24. Odem, *Delinquent Daughters*; Michael Willrich, *City of Courts: Socializing Justice in Progressive Era Chicago* (Cambridge: Cambridge University Press, 2003); Anne Meis Knupfer, *Reform and Resistance: Gender, Delinquency, and America's First Juvenile Court* (New York: Routledge, 2001); David S. Tanenhaus, *Juvenile Justice in the Making* (New York: Oxford University Press, 2004).
25. Lilburn Merrill, "A Summary of Findings in a Study of Sexualisms among a Group of One Hundred Delinquent Boys," *American Journal of Urology and Sexology* 15 (1919): 259–69; A. J. Jones and Lee Janis, "Primary Syphilis of the Rectum and the Gonorrhea of the Anus in a Male Homosexual Playing the Role of the Female Prostitute," *American Journal of Syphilis, Gonorrhea, and Venereal Disease* 28 (July 1944): 453–57; F. A. Freyhan, "Homosexual Prostitution: A Case Report," *Delaware State Medical Journal* (May 1947): 92–94.
26. *People v. Jamil Singh*, Case No. 6029, 2–3, 7–9 (1918); Records of the Superior Court, Criminal Division, County of Sacramento, Sacramento Archives and Museum Collection Center (hereinafter "SAMCC").
27. Ibid., 15.
28. See *People v. Kangiesser.*
29. *People v. Robbins*, 145–46.
30. Dominick Cavallo, *Muscles and Morals: Organized Playgrounds and Urban Reform, 1880–1920* (Philadelphia: University of Pennsylvania Press, 1981), 15–48; Martha H. Verbrugge, *Able-Bodied Womanhood: Personal Health and Social Change in Nineteenth-Century Boston* (New York: Oxford University Press, 1988).
31. *People v. Robbins*, 145–46.
32. Ibid., 145.
33. *People v. Tara Singh*, Case No. 6039, 7 (1918), Records of the Superior Court, Criminal Division, County of Sacramento, SAMCC.
34. *People v. Tara Singh*, 9–10.
35. Ibid., 3.
36. 1891 Cal. Stat. 117 sec. 5, 7; William N. Eskridge Jr., *Gaylaw: Challenging the Apartheid of the Closet* (Cambridge, Mass.: Harvard University Press, 1999), 30.
37. See Arthur Sherry, "Vagrants, Rogues, and Vagabonds—Old Concepts in Need of Revision," *California Law Review* 48 (1960): 557–60; "Use of Vagrancy Type Laws for Arrest and Detention of Suspicious Persons," *Yale Law Journal* 59 (1950): 1351.
38. See Ahmed A. White, "A Different Kind of Labor Law: Vagrancy Law and the Regulation of Harvest Labor, 1913–1924," *University of Colorado Law Review* 75 (2004): 668–743; Amy Dru Stanley, *From Bondage to Contract: Wage Labor, Marriage, and the Market in the Age of Slave Emancipation* (New York: Cambridge University Press, 1998); Linda K. Kerber, *No Constitutional Right to Be Ladies: Women and the Obligations of Citizenship* (New York: Hill and Wang, 1998), 47–80.
39. Forrest W. Lacey, "Vagrancy and Other Crimes of Personal Condition," *Harvard Law Review* 66 (1953): 1203–26; William O. Douglas, "Vagrancy and Arrest on Suspicion," *Yale Law Journal* 70 (1960): 1–14.
40. Eskridge, *Gaylaw*, 31; Boyd, *Wide Open Town.*
41. *People v. Rola Singh*, 268 P. 958 (Cal. Dist. Ct. App. 1928); see Transcript of Testimony in District Court of Yuba County, 5–7, 10, 12, 13, California State Archives, No. 359 (June 1928) (hereinafter "Rola Transcript").
42. Rola Transcript, 43–50.
43. Harry J. Carstenbrook, Probate Case No. 3226 (May 18, 1927), Superior Court of Yuba City; Great Register of Yuba County, General Election, 1928, Marysville Public Library.
44. *People v. Jamil Singh*, 2.
45. Sharon Ullman, *Sex Seen: The Emergence of Modern Sexuality in America* (Berkeley: University of California Press, 1997); Christopher Brunnette, B.A. thesis, Critical Gender Studies, University of California, San Diego (in author's possession).

46. *People v. Jamil Singh*, 2–3.
47. Ibid., 4.
48. Lauren Berlant, "Intimacy: A Special Issue," *Critical Inquiry* 24 (1998): 281–86. For an examination of the implications of the 2003 *Lawrence and Garner v. Texas* ruling in the U.S. Supreme Court and the legal and historical problem of coupled intimacy and public recognition, see Katherine Franke, "Commentary: The Domesticated Liberty of *Lawrence v. Texas*," *Columbia Law Review* 104 (2004): 1399–26; and Nayan Shah, "Policing Privacy, Migrants, and the Limits of Freedom," *Social Text* 84–85 (October 2005).
49. Kerr, *Codes of California*, 277–78.
50. Campbell, *Writing Security*, 3.
51. Jennifer Terry, *An American Obsession: Science, Medicine, and Homosexuality in Modern Society* (Chicago: University of Chicago Press, 2000).
52. Concern for the absence of statutes for oral sex led the state legislature in 1915 to pass a statute criminalizing fellatio and cunnilingus specifically; the State Supreme Court overturned the statute because it violated an "anti-Spanish" state constitutional amendment that required laws to be written in English. See Sharon Ullman, *Sex Seen*; Christopher Brunnette, B.A. thesis.
53. *People v. Jack Lynch and Keshn Singh*, Case No. 4680 (1928), San Joaquin County Superior Court.
54. Ibid.
55. Ibid.
56. Terry, *An American Obsession.*
57. Judith E. Grbich, "The Body in Legal Theory," *At the Boundaries of the Law: Feminism and Legal Theory*, ed. Martha A Fineman and Nancy Thomadsen (New York: Routledge, 1991), 69.
58. Christopher Tomlinson, "Subordination, Authority, and Law: Subjects in Labor History," *International Labor and Working Class History* 47 (spring 1995): 56–90.
59. Gloria E. Anzaldúa in *Borderlands/La Frontera: The New Mestiza* (San Francisco: Aunt Lute Press, 1987).
60. Emma Perez, "Queering the Borderlands: The Challenges of Excavating the Invisible and Unheard," *Frontiers* 24.2–3 (2003): 129.
61. Roderick Ferguson, *Aberrations in Black: Toward a Queer of Color Critique* (Minneapolis: University of Minnesota Press, 2003).

Toward a History of Statelessness in America

Linda K. Kerber

Browsing through an electronic card catalog not long ago, I found a new edition of Edward Everett Hale's *A Man Without a Country.*[1] First published during the Civil War, the novella is a frightening cautionary tale. The fiction begins in 1805, when a young naval officer is seduced (Hale's word, not mine) by Aaron Burr, and drawn into the former vice president's conspiracy to detach the Southwest and reconfigure the United States. The voice of the narrator moves between fact and fiction; many readers are still convinced that they are reading history. In the story, the young officer, Philip Nolan, is tried for treason in a regional imitation of Aaron Burr's trial in Richmond, Virginia. When the chief judge asks him whether he has anything to say that will prove his loyalty to the United States, Nolan blurts out, "Damn the United States! I wish I may never hear of the United States again!"

The shocked court, composed of Revolutionary War veterans, grants his wish. Nolan is condemned to perpetual exile, sailing around the globe on American ships for the rest of his life, doomed never to return and never to hear talk of home. He does not question his punishment. Late in life, he cautions another young officer, the narrator, to avoid his fate: "And for your country, boy . . . and for that flag . . . never dream a dream but of serving her as she bids you." The punch line is absolute and uncritical.

The tale is a densely layered fable. Philip Nolan himself may not step on the earth over which his nation's flag waves or claim his nation's protection, but he lives out his life on a floating nation, a ship that flies the American flag and freely moves across the globe, conveying American claims to authority and influence, and in that way constructing the new nation as a player in an international contest for space and power. Aaron Burr figures in the narrative in only one dimension of his many-dimensioned career: only in the guise of the Devil, whispering temptation, the Aaron Burr who killed the hero Alexander Hamilton in a duel. There is no hint of the Aaron Burr who admired Mary Wollstonecraft, the Aaron Burr who raised his daughter, Theodosia, to be an intellectual (as Thomas Jefferson most assuredly did not raise his daughter,

Martha). There is certainly no hint of the Aaron Burr who eloquently opposed the Alien and Sedition Acts and who called on America to be "an asylum to the oppressed of every nation."[2]

Edward Everett Hale intended simply to make an intervention into the politics of his own time, hoping to undermine Confederate sympathizer Clement Vallandigham's race for governor in Ohio.[3] But Hale's novella has had an extraordinarily long life. Reaching back to the founding era for its setting, published as a patriotic narrative in the midst of the Civil War and as a support to Abraham Lincoln's suspension of civil liberties, it was reprinted steadily throughout the nineteenth and twentieth centuries, with flurries of new editions during World War I and again during World War II. During World War I several dramatic versions were staged; shortly after World War II a radio adaptation was broadcast, with voice-over narration by Bing Crosby, and in 1973 a sympathetic made-for-TV version appeared, echoing the anxieties of the Vietnam War, starring Cliff Robertson. And then no more reprints until after 9/11.

A roughly similar drift in the pace of attention paid to the issue of statelessness can be traced in the lineage of nonfiction books and articles, tracking with chilling accuracy the rise and fall of the threat of statelessness throughout the world. Thus a number of legal and political monographs were published in the aftermath of World War I, then their numbers receded. They reemerged in the 1930s; among them the rare monograph on the subject, published a little more than seventy years ago: Catheryn Seckler-Hudson's 1934 *Statelessness: With Special Reference to the United States (A Study in Nationality and Conflict of Laws).*[4] In the aftermath of World War II, the Atlantic world swarming with displaced people, Hannah Arendt wrote what remains the most powerful set of reflections on statelessness—the stunning ninth chapter of *The Origins of Totalitarianism,* written between 1945 and its publication date of 1951, not long before the passage of the notorious McCarran-Walter Immigration and Nationality Act of 1952.[5] Attention to statelessness receded again in the 1960s, reemerged modestly when attention was claimed by refugees from Vietnam and by the contested condition of Palestinians, and then exploded in our own moment.

Today, once again, statelessness matters. With the end of the cold war and fall of the Berlin Wall; with the people made refugees by war in the Balkans, Rwanda, and the Sudan; with the fragility of citizenship in entities like Palestine, increasing numbers of people lack secure citizenship.[6] Although international conventions have long provided protections against *refoulement*—the recirculation of refugees on to other receiving countries or even back to the nations in which they feel themselves in danger—its practice is increasing as asylum seekers are increasingly returned to third countries, many of which will not provide them safety.[7] The United Nations High Commissioner for Refugees recently estimated that some 9.7 million people are now refugees—an increase of close to 50 percent since 1980—and that another 7 million are what UNHCR calls "persons of concern" (stateless citizens of the former Soviet Union who have not obtained nationality in any of the new countries that succeeded the USSR) and "internally displaced persons" (uprooted persons who fall through the cracks of current human rights law).[8] These "persons of concern" introduce a new dimension into our understanding: stateless persons have been commonly understood to be a population made vulnerable by movement; Philip Nolan is forced out of the state he calls home. But citizenship ties can be fractured in stasis as well as in movement; liminal people who have not moved physically sometimes find that state boundaries have shifted, and the protections that citizenship were thought to provide suddenly evaporate.[9]

Imprisonment heightens vulnerability. Citizenship in one country has long been a fragile claim to protection for those in the prisons of another country, but that fragility has been heightened in American military prisons of the post–cold war era, which Amnesty International has recently decried as twenty-first century "gulags" in which even U.S. citizenship has not assured prisoners the civil rights of citizens, such as the right to counsel. U.S. citizens captured in post-9/11 conflicts have been declared to be "enemy combatants" and denied, for varying periods of time, the right to consult their own lawyers. The United States held Yaser Esam Hamdi incommunicado for three years, "without any semblance of normal legal process or rights despite his citizenship." After the U.S. Supreme Court intervened, Hamdi, who was born in Baton Rouge, was finally allowed to leave the country, but only at the price of relinquishing his citizenship.[10]

Extreme economic vulnerability also can propel people into something that looks like statelessness; they dare not ask for asylum, and often have no one from whom to ask for it. In this situation most notably are the millions of laborers, many of whom are women, who can escape the desperate circumstances of their home countries only by accepting airfare from traffickers who transport them to labor situations close to slavery, in which they have no recourse against the exploitation and anger of their employers.[11]

Gender has, in fact, been a key factor in the history of statelessness. Only recently have gender-specific asylum claims such as rape, dowry-related violence, or coerced female circumcision been recognized, and that recognition has been sporadic. Among refugees, in settings in which gender and age demographics are provided by the United Nations High Commissioner for Refugees, adults divide evenly between men and women, but women are much more likely to be accompanied by children. Most significant, as Jacqueline Bhabha has recently emphasized, crude numbers do not describe the situation as women experience it: there is a significant disparity in exposure to statelessness between men and women refugees and asylum seekers in different parts of the world, which emerges only when microclimates are examined. "In every single developing country of asylum neighboring the refugees' country of origin, women and children refugees [representing nearly 80 percent of the refugees] substantially outnumber adult males . . . [I]n every developed state, male asylum seekers far outnumber females." Women historically have had less access than men have to "the formal and informal structures that facilitate migration (state agencies, travel agents, smugglers, family funding), together with dependent family status, resource inadequacy, personal history and social positioning, which militate against a self-perception as an autonomous asylum seeker, [and] are likely to be powerful impediments to individual flight," Bhabha observes.[12]

Statelessness is a subject that most historians of the United States have treated as though it belongs to others—Jews, Gypsies, Palestinians. That U.S. history is taken to be innocent of engagement with the subject is yet another example of the habits of American exceptionalism. Since the *meanings* of statelessness have changed over time, the subject is one that should command the attention of historians as well as humanitarians. In recent years, when some boundaries between states have become more plastic, "statelessness" has been given a positive valence in the form of cosmopolitanism, flexible citizenships, multiple citizenships; statelessness can be made to sustain a dream of unboundedness.[13] The dreamers include many citizens of the member states of the European Union, whose passports carry them over the borders of twenty-five countries, and hundreds of thousands of people who hold more than one passport, often wealthy people with property on two continents. For these people, a destabilized citizenship is an enriched citizenship, and ties to a particular state seem less important than they once were. Such people speak cheerfully of multiplied citizenships, a comfortable cosmopolitanism, being a citizen of the world—an empowered status, an enlargement of the traditional relationship of subject to king, citizen to nation. If citizenship is about what might be called state*full*ness, then some people are rich in it.

When we speak informally of citizenship, the "other" is often constructed as the citizen of another state—the citizen of Mexico, of Japan, rather than of the United States—and is directed to a different line in customs. Or the "other" might be someone with doubled citizenship and dual passports, the enriched citizenship of the multiply stated. But even the enriched state is defined by borders; inside those borders are citizens and subjects, their identity secured by passports. In fact, the ultimate "other" to citizenship lies in its absence, in lack, in state*less*ness. It is possible that the state *needs* its negation in order to know itself. "The boundaries of a state's identity are secured by the representation of [what counts as] danger," David Campbell has observed; a full decade before 9/11 Campbell sensed "a general disquiet about the pervasive nature of ambiguity and uncertainty." Our post-9/11 moment intensifies Campbell's challenge to historians: "What functions have difference, danger, and otherness played in constituting the identity of the United States?"[14] To historicize statelessness is to write a history of the practices of race, gender, labor, and ideology, a history of extreme otherness and extreme danger.

The nightmare of statelessness—of the man or woman without a country—exists everywhere in our own time. But the contours of statelessness are now somewhat different from those Hannah Arendt limned a half century ago. Statelessness is in part the description of a status, fixed in its contemporary moment. But statelessness is also a condition that changes over time, dynamically created and re-created by sovereignties in their own interests, defining the vulnerable in ways that affirm the invulnerable, and in the process revealing changing domestic values and changing power relations across international boundaries. As the meanings of work, racial identity, and gender identity have shifted over time under the stress of war, political struggles, global economic relations, and developing ideologies, vulnerability to statelessness has been reconfigured. To examine the phenomenon as it now presents itself—in the context of new turn-of-the-century wars, in the context of American fears of terrorism, and when, as likely as not, it's the woman who lacks the country—and to attempt to place the matter in the long course of U.S. history, is a long overdue exercise.

***

The work of Hannah Arendt is a crucial starting point for any examination of statelessness. She calls our attention to ironies of the era of the democratic revolutions of the eighteenth century when civil and human rights were reconceptualized. Americans speak of inalienable rights, the French of the "rights of man"—abstractions that gain power from not being rooted in time or place. Yet both democratic revolutions, Arendt points out, situated the practice of those rights in the context of the new national sovereignty. Revolutionaries were convinced that true freedom and true popular sovereignty could be attained only with full national emancipation, that is, within a nation. Inadvertently, as Arendt saw it, they left in limbo people who lacked their own national government. Thus one of our major inheritances from the era of democratic revolutions, an era that generally we honor for its expansive vision, is a narrow understanding of individual human rights. Arendt finds herself thinking Burke was right:

> The Rights of Man, after all, had been defined as "inalienable" because they were supposed to be independent of all governments; but it turned out that the moment human beings lacked their own government and had to fall back on their minimum rights, no authority was left to protect them and no institution was willing to guarantee them. . . . [Instead,] civil rights—that is the varying rights of citizens in different countries—were supposed to embody and spell out in the form of tangible laws the eternal Rights of Man, which by themselves were supposed to be independent of citizenship and nationality. All human beings were citizens of some kind of political community; if the laws of their country did not live up to the demands of the Rights of Man, they were expected to change them, by legislation in democratic countries or through revolutionary action in despotisms.[15]

What was "supposedly inalienable, proved to be unenforceable," Arendt observed. It is a sad irony.

The transformations that we call the era of the democratic revolution—asserting as they did an increase of freedom and civil liberties—simultaneously drew new boundaries and thickened already existing ones until nations constructed themselves out of provinces, principalities, counties, and townships. As Robert Wiebe brilliantly discerned, the democratic transformations of the late eighteenth century paradoxically gathered an increasingly mobile population, one no longer tied to the soil, into populations fictively tied to a nation. Systematized citizenship had its advantages for the state; it simplified taxation, it provided an identifiable pool of male citizens vulnerable to military conscription. And in these redefinitions, it might be added, the space between those who belonged to a state and those who lacked one expanded.[16]

The new American republic made no promises of the rights of man to enslaved people, although they were physically located inside the national state. Slaves were inhabitants who were locked out of the protective aspects of citizenship. While Americans were systematically inventing a political structure in which the fundamental rights of mankind could be practiced, they were simultaneously devising structures that fundamentally deprived a large segment of their population of human rights. Like Arendt's stateless people, slaves were deprived "of a place in the world which makes opinions significant and actions effective . . . belonging to the community into which one is born is no longer a matter of course and not belonging no longer a matter of choice. . . . They are deprived, not of the right to freedom, but of the right to action; not of the right to think whatever they please, but of the right to opinion."[17] In 1773, as Massachusetts patriots were challenging the Tea Act, enslaved inhabitants petitioned the legislature: "We have no Property. We have no Wives. No Children. We have no City. No Country." Three years before Thomas Jefferson articulated a fundamental right to the "pursuit of happiness" they described themselves repeatedly as "unhappy," described their "greatest unhappiness" and signed themselves, wistfully, "FELIX."[18] On the eve of the Civil War, voting with the majority in *Dred Scott v. Sanford*—a decision that arguably helped to bring the war into being—Associate Justice Peter V. Daniel of Virginia stated what he took to be truth: that among Africans "there never has been known or recognized by the inhabitants of other countries anything partaking of the character of nationality, or civil or political polity; that this race has been by all the nations of Europe regarded as subjects of capture or purchase; as subjects of commerce or traffic."[19] His is a chilling definition of permanent statelessness.

No characteristic of slaves' statelessness had been more obvious than their lack of freedom to travel. How to demonstrate that one is no longer stateless? After the Civil War, the presence of freedpeople in public places, dressed in clothes that no longer marked them as slaves, signaled their claim to enter the national state and angered whites who thought that whatever changes in status slaves experienced should be invisible. "Young women particularly flock back & forth by scores to Hilton Head, to Beaufort, to the country simply to while away their time, or constantly to seek some new excitement," complained A. S. Hitchcock, Acting General Superintendent of Contrabands, when the Union Army took over the Georgia Sea Islands.[20] As federal courts removed restrictions on internal travel, establishing that the right to travel within the United States was a right of national citizenship, Congress began to restrict physical entry from outside the nation. Immigration restriction had in it an element of the restoration of some notion of equilibrium, as though the balance among exotic others admitted into the American population had to be reset.[21]

The Chinese themselves—whether or not admitted—were not stateless. But hostility to them led to passage of the Page Law of 1875, which targeted Chinese women as likely to be imported for the purposes of prostitution, and its successors, the Chinese Exclusion Laws of 1882, 1892, and 1902, which forbade the entry of Chinese laborers and severely restricted the entry of others. In struggles over the enforcement of the laws, the Bureau of Immigration often resorted to deportation; in the process, as Lucy Salyer has eloquently described, government agencies "undermined the very principles they accused the Chinese of subverting"—rights to counsel, judicial review, habeas corpus, due process of law.[22] This system of exclusion defined a new category of those who did not deserve to enter, and, because even those Chinese who did enter could not be naturalized, provided the context in which Congress expanded the range of its claims to plenary power over immigration.[23] In the first decades of the twentieth century, Japanese and Indians from South Asia were also made ineligible for U.S. citizenship.[24] Whether by statute or by court decision, by the early twentieth century a vast class of people found themselves vulnerable to being turned back at the border, or faced with deportation should they get in, and a number of individuals with complicated histories of their own, including women born in one country who married a citizen of another, were dragged perilously close to statelessness. There was, for example, the American-born woman citizen married to a Chinese man who went with him to visit China and then tried to return to the United States in 1925. Because she was married to a man who was not eligible for citizenship, and had gone out of the borders of the United States, she had lost her citizenship. Suddenly her passport was no good; she had been involuntarily expatriated.[25]

At the turn of the twentieth century, in the aftermath of the Spanish-American War of 1898 (which stretched, in the Philippines, at least to 1902), the United States invented the ambiguous and unstable category of "noncitizen national" to describe a new status of people who lived under the U.S. flag without the full range of constitutional protections that flag normally carries. When the United States acquired the Philippines, Guam, Cuba, and Puerto Rico, Congress and the Supreme Court devised a series of related statutes, decisions, and conceptualizations that defined the status of these places in ways that simultaneously, as Christina Duffy Burnett eloquently puts it, took "control over territory while avoiding many of the responsibilities that sovereignty implies." Like other imperial powers—the British in India and elsewhere, the Germans in Africa, the French in North Africa and Asia—the United States, through the Supreme Court, simultaneously asserted sovereignty while holding "that these territories were *neither* foreign *nor* part of the United States."[26] Despite the extension of numerous federal statutes to these territories, they could not look forward to developing into states. The U.S. Supreme Court drew a distinction between "incorporated territories," such as those that had been covered by the Northwest Ordinance of 1787, and "unincorporated territories" such as Guam and the Philippines.[27] When Congress provided a Bill of Rights for the Republic of the Philippines after squashing the insurgency in 1902, it omitted the rights to bear arms and to jury trial.[28] The Constitution did not follow the flag.[29] In the aftermath of 1898, as the United States developed an empire, some geographical configurations defined by the United States—states—were fully peopled by citizens; other geographical configurations were colonies, inhabited by subjects who were not, and could not be, citizens. The nation experimented with the creation of ambiguous spaces between the domestic and the foreign, between the national and the international, between sovereignty and subjugation.[30] And in those spaces lay great potential for statelessness.

The legal baggage carried from the colonial era into the republic also included the concept of *coverture*, a set of rules and practices that linked married women to the state through their husbands, defining them as "covered" by their husbands' legal identity. The culture of coverture had no room for the concept that there might be limits to a husband's sexual access to his wife's body. It embedded the husband's control of the wife's property and earnings in the heart of the marriage contract. Married women were thus extremely vulnerable under the law: as one judge in the Supreme Judicial Court of Massachusetts observed in 1805, "a married woman has no more political rights than an alien."[31] In this culture—and Americans were not peculiar; these practices persist in other nations into our own time—the common sense of the matter was that when a male citizen married a foreign woman, his citizenship stretched to embrace her. She did not even have to go through the process of naturalization. But when a woman citizen married a foreign man, she lost her citizenship, and, depending on the laws of the other country, statelessness loomed. Even Ulysses Grant's daughter was denationalized when she married an Englishman in 1874, and it took a special act of Congress to reinstate her citizenship when she was widowed. "Are we aliens because we are women?," demanded abolitionist Angelina Grimke.[32]

No one had definitively answered Grimke's question until 1907, when Congress passed a statute, and 1915 when the U.S. Supreme Court upheld it, that provided that the marriage of a woman citizen to a foreigner produced her denaturalization, even if she had been born here. The Expatriation Act confirmed that hundreds of American-born women were no longer citizens. When World War I began, many hundreds of American-born women who had married men from countries with which the United States was at war were required to register as alien enemies.[33] Yet not all of their husbands' homelands embraced them as citizens. In the United States in the interwar years, gender was a category of instability and potential statelessness; most individual cases of statelessness involved women and arose from marriage.[34]

Indeed, once American women seized the vote, among the first things for which they used it was to press for the integrity of married woman's citizenship. The Cable Act, passed in 1922 in the midst of a movement for immigration restriction, secured married women's nationality—*unless* they had married a man who was ineligible for citizenship and went overseas with him to live. If they resided overseas for two years in their husband's country or five years in another country, they were considered to have renounced their citizenship and could not reclaim it if the marriage ended by death or divorce. Thus, even the legal device intended to protect women from vulnerability increased the vulnerability of some. Moreover, women from nations that expatriated them when they married an alien—from countries including Britain and Canada—now became stateless when they married American men. "Women Without a Country Are in Straits from the New American Nationality Law," was the headline of an article in the *New York Times* in 1922. And, writes Candice Bredbenner, "most resident immigrant women who married Americans after the passage of the Cable Act became stateless on their wedding days and remained so until they earned a naturalization certificate."[35]

By the mid-1920s, women who were naturalized citizens also found themselves with limited citizenship rights. Naturalized women, many of them Jewish, desperately tried to bring husbands and fiancés into the United States during the 1930s. They organized themselves as the Citizen Wives Organization, established in an office by the Hebrew Immigrant Aid and Sheltering Society in New York.[36] In the context of fascist expansion, the inability of American women, whether citizens by birth or by naturalization, to transmit their citizenship to their stateless children or husbands spelled danger.

***

In our time, the opening years of the twenty-first century, the "undocumented alien" describes a condition of danger in relation to statelessness. Documentation or its lack is a defining aspect of the production of statelessness today. By contrast, in the opening years of the twentieth century, before visas were required for entry to the United States, and when the United States understood itself to be in great need of new labor, most of the people who entered at Ellis Island lacked documents of any sort. It was the disruption of national boundaries devised by the Treaty of Versailles in the aftermath of World War I that gave federal claims of absolute power at the borders considerably more frequent occasions on which to be deployed. The fascists' rise to power intensified the pressures. In this context the Nansen Passport, a measure of desperation devised in 1922 by Fridtjof Nansen, the League of Nations' High Commissioner for Refugees, which granted departure without the right of return and was widely used as an identification and travel document by the USSR and Eastern European countries, was a devil's bargain.[37] In its wake, Britain, France, and the United States hastened to stabilize and seal their borders against the millions of refugees and stateless whom the post-Versailles remapping of the European landscape had created.[38] But what contemporaries called "nationality problems" entered anyway. In 1930, political scientist Richard W. Flourney dourly blamed the "increase in facilities of travel, especially through the development of the airplane," for exacerbating population movements and heightening the visibility of the vulnerable.[39]

The United States Immigration Act of 1924 reduced entry to the United States by some 85 percent of what it had been on the eve of World War I. Once the statute was backed by enforcement mechanisms, Mae Ngai writes, deportation "amounted to permanent banishment under threat of felony prosecution."[40] In addition, the clash between the new statute and the explosive aftermath of the war meant that the difference between the immigrant and the refugee began to blur; even more blurred became the difference between the refugee and the stateless. By the 1930s, the United States was no longer excused from the nightmare. Fleeing Nazis, thousands of stateless Jews begged for sanctuary and were turned back at the U.S. borders.[41]

As we have seen, marriage could expose women to statelessness. In the twentieth century, until well after World War II, it was common practice for married women to travel on their husbands' passports. The implications—that husband and wife would always be together, that she would not leave the country without him—are harmless only in times of peace and quiet. In time of disruption, the lack of a passport of one's own could be life threatening. The stabilization of the "national identity of married women" was a key item on the League of Nations' human rights agenda in the 1930s. When Western democracies emerged from World War II, feminists—led by Dorothy Kenyon, the American member of the UN's Commission on the Status of Women—began again to sketch out an agenda that had the independent citizenship of the married woman high on the list of their goals.[42]

Although red-baiting derailed Kenyon's UN career, she and her allies doggedly kept the issue alive. In 1957 the UN created a "Convention on the Nationality of Married Women," forbidding compulsory expatriation. The issue was not solved. The Convention on the Elimination of all Forms of Discrimination Against Women (CEDAW), established in 1979, provides that neither marriage to an alien nor a husband's change of nationality shall render a woman stateless, but there is virtually no enforcement mechanism for any provision of CEDAW.

Children—often subsumed in the category "women and children"—have had and continue to have their own specific vulnerabilities to statelessness. In the United States, where "all persons born . . . are citizens," children are citizens at birth. But the meanings of citizenship are different for children and adults, not least because children are spared or excused from the key rights and obligations of citizenship: to vote, to serve on a jury, to perform military service. Is anything meaningful left to them? "It is only from a perspective that takes the adult male as norm that women and children merge as a group, 'the other,' united by an assumption of common dependency, and socio-political inferiority," Jacqueline Bhabha warns.[43] A crudely drafted American statute of 1802 excluded foreign-born legitimate children of American fathers from citizenship. Had they the misfortune to be born in a nation in which citizenship followed blood rather than birth—a category that grew as the *Code Napoleon* spread—these children could find themselves without any citizenship at all. In 1855, it was American fathers (not mothers) who transmitted citizenship to their children, and that continued to be the case well into the 1930s.

When adults are deported, their citizen children go with them. The most notorious example of this is the U.S. internment camps of World War II, where the birthright citizen children of Japanese-American parents (some of whom were themselves birthright citizens) were confined without recourse.[44] The *bracero* program—the agreement with Mexico that the United States would import some two hundred thousand contract laborers a year—was initiated in 1948. Mexican farm workers had, of course, been entering the United States for decades, forming families, and becoming parents to American citizen children. By the time the *bracero* program was ended in 1964, several million Mexican men had been part of it. Most were individual men who had not brought their families with them, but over the years many built families in America. When the program ended and the *braceros* were forced back to Mexico, their citizen children could not force a pause for reconsideration; they left with their parents.[45] In the aftermath of 9/11, an uncounted number of citizen children have risked or actually faced the deportation of noncitizen parents.[46]

As a 2001 Supreme Court decision, *Tuan Anh Nguyen v. INS*, makes clear, the claim to U.S. citizenship of children born overseas remains unbalanced, and relationships of empire continue to haunt American law. Children born on U.S. soil, whether or not their parents are citizens, whether or not their parents are married to each other, are citizens at birth. Children born abroad whose parents are married to each other, and at least one of whom is a citizen, are citizens at birth, so long as one parent has lived in the United States for five years, at least two of which were after age fourteen—a rule intended to ensure that we do not develop a class of citizens who from one generation to the next have never lived in the United States. But should the parents not be married to each other, and only one is a U.S. citizen, then the sex of the citizen parent has major consequences. In a practice that reaches back to medieval England, when the older rule that the bastard was the child of no one was revised to make the bastard the child of the mother (continuing to free the father from any obligation to the child), extended when the American colonies reified the practice in the form of statutes that provided that children fathered by slave masters "followed the condition of the mother," birthright citizenship for children born overseas to unmarried couples is transmitted only through the mother.

Thus although Tuan Anh Nguyen's father, a civilian employee of a U.S. construction company, kept Nguyen after his Vietnamese mother had abandoned them both, and he raised the child, first in Vietnam and then in Houston, Nguyen was not a citizen. Although Joseph Boulais provided financial support, he did not officially register the birth or demonstrate a blood relationship between them. So long as life moved along quietly, so long as Boulais supported his son, what did formal paperwork matter? But in the early 1990s, Nguyen was found guilty of sexual assault of a minor. While he was serving his prison sentence, Congress, responding to a rising tide of anti-immigrant sentiment, tightened the rules controlling legal resident aliens such as Nguyen. By the time he was ready to emerge from prison, the Illegal Immigrant Reform and Immigrant Responsibility Act of 1996 had been passed. Conviction for what immigration law now termed an aggravated felony now meant deportation. And a five-to-four U.S. Supreme Court majority denied Nguyen's father's claim that he should have been able to transmit birthright citizenship to his child on the same terms that an American citizen woman can.[47]

In reaching this decision, the majority on the Court made two major arguments. One was an argument about gender equity, in which the court expressed doubt that the appropriate comparison was between the ability of birth mothers and birth fathers to transmit birthright citizenship, and emphasized rather that the nonmarital father of a child born overseas was not being burdened more severely than were many nonmarital fathers of children born within the United States who are required to exhibit their relationship to the child.[48] The other, an extended argument that did not receive much press coverage, invoked the danger of statelessness. The Court sustained the Department of Justice's assertion that the reason for different legislative criteria had long been the danger "that the foreign-born children of unwed citizen mothers might become stateless if they were not eligible for United States citizenship, because the children would not be eligible for citizenship in their country of birth or in the country of the unwed father."[49] In the United States, citizenship accompanies birth on American soil, whatever the citizenship or marital status of the parents. But in many nations (though fewer than in 1940, the time of the passage of the original statute), citizenship is traced through bloodline. In dozens of foreign countries, illegitimate children follow the mother's nationality, and it seemed imperative that U.S. law confirm this practice. The 1940 statute and its successors—notably section 1409 of the Immigration and Nationality Act of 1952—was intended to ensure that the child of an unwed citizen mother had U.S. nationality at birth.[50] "Congress minimized the burdens on unwed mothers who seek citizenship for their children," the Department of Justice concluded, ". . . in order to advance its important interest in avoiding statelessness."[51]

A few years before *Nguyen*, in a case that tested similar questions and arrived at similar conclusions, the Department of Justice had revealed the subtext: fear of fraud by the children of American military men stationed abroad:

> The Department of State . . . has consulted . . . with consular officers in six nations in which the United States has or has had a significant military presence and which, not coincidentally, account for a large proportion of citizenship claims by illegitimate children born abroad. The Department reports that the problem of foreign law . . . remains a clear concern today in at least Germany, Great Britain, South Korea and Vietnam. Recent legal changes in the Philippines and Thailand have allowed an illegitimate child born there of a non-national mother to acquire Philippine or Thai nationality, respectively, if the father is a Philippine or Thai national and complies with the requirements of local law. The possibility of statelessness remains, however, in all other cases, unless the mother can transmit her citizenship in accordance with the law of her own country.[52]

In a dissenting opinion in one of the cases that formed a backdrop to *Nguyen*, Judge Andrew Kleinfeld of the Ninth Circuit Court of Appeals had emphasized that Congress had understood full well what they were doing:

> This statute was passed during the Korean War. Members of Congress knew that American soldiers who went abroad to fight wars, and caused children to be conceived while they were abroad, were overwhelmingly male, because only males were drafted, so that the number of children born illegitimately of male citizens might be large enough to affect immigration policy, while the number of illegitimate children of female citizens would be negligible. They may also have sought to minimize the administrative burden on the Department of Defense for paternity and citizenship claims respectively by the women the soldiers left

> behind and their children. This may not be pretty, but it is a rational basis for the sex distinction . . . Some noncustodial fathers of children born out of wedlock do not care to pay child support if it can be avoided.[53]

In other words, even those men representing the United States abroad have the Court's permission to father children out of wedlock and abandon them. "I expect very few of these are the children of female service personnel," Ruth Bader Ginsburg observed to the amusement of the audience during the oral argument in *Nguyen.* "There are these men out there who are being Johnny Appleseed."[54]

After the Illegal Immigration Reform and Immigrant Responsibility Act of 1996 required deportation for what immigration law referred to as aggravated felony convictions and defined as such felonies an expansive range of crimes, minor as well as serious, thousands of permanent legal residents were subject to deportation. Nguyen was unusual among them because he had the hope of making the argument that he was a U.S. citizen. But most who faced deportation came from nations with which the United States has no treaty of reciprocity (Cambodia, Vietnam, Laos) and others whose birth nation refused to take them back, effectively rendering them stateless. In Seattle, Assistant Federal Public Defender Jay Stansell found an entire floor of the Federal Detention Center devoted to the nearly two hundred prisoners who had prospect neither of freedom nor deportation.[55] A hundred such cases were brought together for appeal for habeas corpus proceedings and a limit to the indefinite detention to which they were subject. In the early spring of 2001, defending indefinite detention in response to a series of questions from Justice Ginsburg, Deputy Solicitor General Edwin Kneedler found himself saying, in an eerie reprise of Edward Everett Hale, that "one way to remove the alien [who has no country to go to] would be to put him on a boat."[56] And when Stansell emphasized the vulnerability of one of the youthful prisoners, his inability to speak the language, his lack of contacts if he were to be sent back to Cambodia, Justice Scalia was skeptical: "It is up to you to find a country to get sent back to. The burden is not on us."[57]

But the Supreme Court ruled (although Scalia dissented) that although the attorney general "may" continue to detain aliens who present risks to the community, he does not have unlimited discretion. Drawing on Justice Robert H. Jackson's legendary dissent in *Shaughnessy v. United States ex rel. Mezei* at the height of the cold war, the Supreme Court now ruled that "once an alien enters the country . . . the Due Process Clause applies to all 'persons' within the United States, including aliens, whether their presence here is lawful, unlawful, temporary or permanent."[58] Stansell's clients were spared indefinite detention—a limbo not unlike statelessness—only until the administration found a place to which to deport them. As repatriation agreements were negotiated—with Cambodia, with Vietnam—they were deported to nations where they knew no one, whose languages they did not speak.[59]

Indefinite detention has long been the norm at the U.S. Naval Station at Guantánamo Bay, Cuba, which identifies itself as the United States' "oldest . . . military installation overseas and "host to the Detainee Mission of the War on Terrorism."[60] Guantánamo is now the prison for men captured in Afghanistan and elsewhere who are thought to be fighting for Al Qaeda. In three separate decisions in 2004, justices of the U.S. Supreme Court expressed their suspicion of unlimited detention and simultaneously limited severely the ability of the detainees to test it.[61] Justice Stevens invoked the barons at Runnymede and Justice Jackson's dissent in *Mezei.* In an *amicus brief,* former attorney general Janet Reno invoked the Civil War–era case that had so angered Edward Everett Hale, *Ex parte Milligan*: "The power which the Executive seeks in this case is far broader and far more terrifying."[62] Likening "incommunicado detention for months on end" to torture, Justice Stevens, joined by Justices Ginsburg, Souter, and Breyer, complained that "if this Nation is to remain true to the ideals symbolized by its flag, it must not wield the tools of tyrants even to resist an assault by the forces of tyranny." More than a year after the Guantánamo decisions were handed down, many questions remain unresolved. The International Committee of the Red Cross, its patience at an end, broke its usual commitment to confidentiality in November 2004, charging that psychological and physical coercion, "an intentional system of cruel, unusual and degrading treatment," sometimes "tantamount to torture," was repeatedly used on prisoners on Guantánamo.[63] Yaser Hamdi, a U.S. citizen who had been captured in Afghanistan, was forced to relinquish his American citizenship in order to return to Saudi Arabia, where his family lived and where he had grown up.[64] Almost a year after the Supreme Court remanded the case of José Padilla, an American citizen who had been accused of participation in a bomb plot, to a lower court for reargument, a federal district court judge in South Carolina ordered the administration either to release him or, within forty-five days, charge him formally with a specific crime.[65] The protective dimensions of American citizenship seem gradually to be eroding in the aftermath of 9/11.

The history of the right to citizenship in U.S. law is an ambivalent one. We are inheritors of *Yick Wo v. Hopkins,* the great California case of 1896 that honored the claims of the alien ineligible for citizenship; of *Trop v. Dulles,* in which the Supreme Court held in 1958 that the "use of denationalization as a punishment is barred by the Eighth Amendment"; and of *Afroyim v. Rusk* in which the Court held in 1967 that "every citizen in the U.S. has a constitutional right to remain a citizen . . . unless he voluntarily relinquishes that citizenship."[66] But we are also inheritors of a strongly skeptical countertradition that emphasizes the *alien* ingredient in the "legal resident alien." This suspicion, with its inherent xenophobia, was greatly strengthened after 9/11.[67] The Patriot Act gave the attorney general expanded power to detain noncitizens who are suspected of terrorist activity; he is not required to notify them of the reason for detention or to share the evidence on which detention is based with the detainee.[68] The draft of *Patriot II* contemplated stripping even native-born Americans of their citizenship if they provide support for organizations marked as terrorist.[69] The decisions in *Hamdi*, *Padilla*, and *Rasul* offer citizens accused of being enemy combatants limited protections, aliens even fewer protections. Indefinite detention may be our contemporary opposite of expulsion. Guantánamo, the island prison where the American flag flies, inhabited by men whose own nations cannot assure them decent prisoner-of-war treatment, is today's floating prison of men without a country.

***

The dream of a cosmopolitan citizenship—and the nightmare of its absence in statelessness—in American history is a complicated one, whose presence we are only just beginning to acknowledge. In trying to understand the expansive meanings embedded in the status of statelessness, we come to consider not only questions of who can be a citizen and on what terms, but also to consider some of the instabilities of public/private distinctions, of the way the personal and the political merge, of the way in which the state regularly relies on the microclimates of the workplace, the bedroom, and the birthing room to sustain national citizenship. Behind the public story is a backstory of distrust: today, a distrust of the future complexities of sorting out the claims of thousands of people who might well conclude that they could now claim citizenship retroactively, and in the past, a distrust of women as tricksters, accompanied by a belief that men should be able to pick and choose for which of their children they will be responsible. These issues have such resilience not only because they are stereotypes based on actual trends (U.S. military men, stationed overseas, are indeed culpable of fathering more nonmarital children than are U.S. women who are in other countries), but also because they are rooted in concepts that reach back to the founding era, when the property regime of *coverture* ensured that married women's relation to the state was filtered through their husbands.

The categories that define who is vulnerable to statelessness have been refigured since the 1930s, when Seckler-Hudson sought to provide it with a syntax. Statelessness is not a simple conceptual matter; it now breaks along the fault lines of perceptions of state security, race and ethnicity, ideal workers, and gender. Indeed the fault lines are not themselves always clear. Hannah Arendt has reminded us of the difficulty of distinguishing between stateless refugees and "normal" resident aliens. "Who," she asked, "will guarantee human rights to those who have lost their nationally guaranteed rights?"[70] Statelessness is now made in the daily decisions of immigration officers, deciding who is a guest worker and who is not, and in the daily decisions of captors in prisons like Abu Ghraib and Guantánamo, deciding who is entitled to the protections of international law and who is not.

Today's transnational market in domestic labor is filled with people who are not technically refugees, but are homeless in having left their home country, who are citizens of one country but undocumented aliens where they work. By far most of these people are women, many of whom, like Miss Saigon, slide all too easily into the international traffic in women. If citizenship is linked to work—as it is in Judith Shklar's understanding of citizenship as the "right to earn," T. H. Marshall's understanding of social citizenship as the right to basic material well-being, and Alice Kessler-Harris's understanding of economic citizenship—then what citizenship can be claimed by those trapped jobless in the underworld of the globalized marketplace?[71] Hundreds of thousands of trafficked women are brought to the United States each year.[72] Indeed, anthropologist Aihwa Ong argues that in the last generation "the norms of good citizenship in advanced liberal democracies have shifted from an emphasis on duties and obligations to the nation to a stress on becoming autonomous, responsible choice-making subjects who can serve the nation best by becoming "entrepreneurs of the self."[73] Those who lack resources are almost bound to fail that entrepreneurial challenge. Ambiguous borders cloud the margins between Ong's "mobile homo economicus" and the trafficked, between the trafficked and the refugee, between the refugee (subject to multiple *refoulements* despite its illegality in international law) and the stateless.

If we listen to patriotic public speeches these days in the context of the preemptive war in Iraq, we hear citizenship described as unambivalent, stable, and unidimensional. Even if the Patriot Act is not expanded, it has articulated fresh possibilities of expatriation in an atmosphere already soaked with suspicion, possibilities that are now being explored at Guantánamo. The outcry of dismay that greeted the leaked draft of the expanded Patriot Act in 2003 gave reason to hope that it would be challenged by another, more expansive understanding of citizenship, and that the strongest elements of the new proposals, in particular those threatening expatriation, would quietly be erased. But the initiation of war in Iraq has transformed public attention, making it unlikely that we will find a renewed commitment to the heightened ideals of equal citizenship that emerged out of the principles of fairness that were freshly articulated only a generation ago, in the civil rights, women's, and gay liberation movements.[74]

In this volatile political context, statelessness is no longer so easily measured only by the presence or absence of a passport; it is a state of being produced by new and increasingly extreme forms of restriction and of the creation of new categories of stateless human beings.

It is widely understood—thanks not least to Nansen and to Arendt—that statelessness haunted twentieth-century Europe. Statelessness has also haunted the United States throughout its history, from its oxymoronic founding as a republic of slavery to our own time. "Once they had left their homeland they remained homeless; once they had left their state they became stateless; once they had been deprived of their human rights they were rightless."[75] Arendt's heartbreaking words conspicuously begin not with a crime but with a passive and neutral behavior: "once they had left." It is the leaving that makes the individual or community vulnerable. But if, for Arendt, twentieth-century statelessness was triggered by a single act, statelessness today, in particular in relation to the borders and borderlands of the United States, is most usefully understood not only as a status but as a practice, made and remade in daily decisions of presidents and judges, border guards and prison guards, managers and pimps. The stateless are the citizen's other. The stateless serve the state by embodying its absence, by providing frightening models of the vulnerability of those who lack sufficient awe of the state. The stateless serve the state by signaling who will not be entitled to its protection, and throwing fear into the rest of us.

Notes

1. Edward Everett Hale, *A Man Without a Country* (Annapolis, Md.: Naval Institute Press, 2002).
2. Aaron Burr in the House of Assembly, Legislature of New York, January 8, 1799, "Debate on Proposed Amendments to the U.S. Constitution," *Political Correspondence and Public Papers of Aaron Burr*, vol. 1, ed. Mary-Jo Kline (Princeton, N.J.: Princeton University Press, 1983), 366, 371.

3. Vallandigham's habeas corpus challenge to the claims of military courts to try civilians reached the U.S. Supreme Court in *Ex parte Vallandigham* 68 U.S. (1 Wall.) 243 (1863). For Hale's own reflections on the origins of the story, see E. E. Hale, "The Man Without a Country," *Outlook* 59 (May 5, 1898): 116.
4. Catheryn Seckler-Hudson, *Statelessness: With Special Reference to the United States (A Study in Nationality and Conflict of Laws)* (Washington, D.C.: Digest Press, 1934), published under the auspices of the Department of International Law and Relations of the American University Graduate School, with preface by Ellery C. Stowell, who described statelessness as "an inexcusable anomaly," and an "intolerable condition."
5. Hannah Arendt, *The Origins of Totalitarianism* (New York: Harcourt Brace Jovanovich, 1951); McCarran-Walter Immigration and Nationality Act, Pub. L. No. 82–414 (1952).
6. There is ongoing argument about whether Palestinian refugees are stateless persons. See "The Status of Palestinian Refugees and Stateless Persons in Europe," Briefing Paper prepared by BADIL Resource Center for Palestinian Residency and Refugee Rights, for the Council of Europe, Committee on Migration, Refugees and Demography, December 2002, http://www.badil.org/Publications/Monographs/CoE.2002.pdf (accessed August 10, 2005). The United Nations conventions on statelessness can be found at http://www.ohchr.org/english/law/statelessness.htm (Convention relating to the Status of Stateless Persons, Adopted on September 28, 1954, by a Conference of Plenipotentiaries convened by Economic and Social Council Resolution 526 A [XVII] of April 26, 1954) and (Convention on the Reduction of Statelessness, 1961) (all accessed July 19, 2005).
7. Stephen H. Legomsky, "Secondary Refugee Movements and the Return of Asylum Seekers to Third Countries: The Meaning of Effective Protection," *International Journal of Refugee Law* 15 (2003): 567–677.
8. "2003 Global Refugee Trends: Overview of Refugee Populations, New Arrivals, Durable Solutions, Asylum-Seekers and Other Persons of Concern to UNHCR," June 15, 2004, http://www.reliefweb.int/rw/lib.nsf/db900SID/LHON-634JPE?OpenDocument (accessed July19, 2005).
9. I am indebted to Mary Dudziak for this insight.
10. Speech by Irene Khan, president of Amnesty International, at Foreign Press Association, *Washington Post*, September 24, 2004, A24.
11. For a recent example see Amy Waldman, "Sri Lankan Maids Pay Dearly for Perilous Jobs Overseas," *New York Times*, May 8, 2005, A1, detailing "exploitation so extreme that it sometimes approaches 'slaverylike' conditions, according to a recent Human Rights Watch report on foreign workers in Saudi Arabia."
12. Jacqueline Bhabha, "Demography and Rights: Women, Children, and Access to Asylum," *International Journal of Refugee Law* 16 (2004): 232, 235; see also Jacqueline Bhabha, "'More Than Their Share of Sorrow': International Migration Law and the Rights of Children," *Saint Louis University Public Law Review* 22 (2003): 253, n. 1.
13. Arjun Appadurai, "Patriotism and Its Futures," *Public Culture* 5.3 (1993), 423–24; Aihwa Ong, *Flexible Citizenship: The Cultural Logics of Transnationality* (Durham, N.C.: Duke University Press, 1999).
14. David Campbell, *Writing Security: United States Foreign Policy and the Politics of Identity* (Manchester: Manchester University Press, 1992), 3, 7.
15. Arendt, *The Origins of Totalitarianism*, 291–93.
16. Robert Wiebe, "Framing U.S. History: Democracy, Nationalism, and Socialism," in *Rethinking American History in a Global Age*, ed. Thomas Bender (Berkeley: University of California Press, 2002), 239. For the process in France, see Gerhard Noiriel, "The Identification of the Citizen: The Birth of Republican Civil Status in France," in *Documenting Individual Identity: The Development of State Practices in the Modern World*, ed. Jane Caplan and John Torpey (Princeton, N.J.: Princeton University Press, 2002), 29–47.
17. Arendt, *The Origins of Totalitarianism*, 296.
18. "Petition of the Africans, Living in Boston, 1773," in James Oliver Horton and Lois E. Horton's *Slavery and the Making of America* (New York: Oxford University Press, 2005), 51. In a 1792 debate in the French Assembly, a deputy would say, "Slaves have no civil status. Only the free man has a city, a fatherland."
19. *Dred Scott v. Sanford*, 60 U.S. 393 (1856).
20. A. S. Hitchcock to Provost Marshal General of the Department of the South, August 25, 1864, in *Freedom: A Documentary History of Emancipation 1861–1867*, ser. 1, vol. 3, ed. Ira Berlin et al. (New York: Cambridge University Press, 1982), 316–17.

21. John Torpey, *The Invention of the Passport: Surveillance, Citizenship, and the State* (Cambridge: Cambridge University Press, 1999), 95–96.
22. Lucy E. Salyer, *Laws Harsh as Tigers: Chinese Immigrants and the Shaping of Modern Immigration Law* (Chapel Hill: University of North Carolina Press, 1995), 247–48; and see John R. Wunder's review in the *American Historical Review* 102 (1997): 889–90.
23. See *Fong Yue Ting v. United States*, 149 U.S. 698 (1893).
24. Mae Ngai, *Impossible Subjects: Illegal Aliens and the Making of Modern America* (Princeton, N.J.: Princeton University Press, 2004), 37–50. The key cases were *Takao Ozawa v. United States* 260 U.S. 178 (1922) and *United States v. Bhagat Singh Thind* 261 U.S. 204 (1923).
25. *Ex parte (Ng) Fung Sing* 6 F.2d 670 (D.C. Wash. 1925). See Candice Lewis Bredbenner, *A Nationality of Her Own: Women, Marriage, and the Law of Citizenship* (Berkeley: University of California Press, 1998), 136.
26. Christina Duffy Burnett, "The Edges of Empire and the Limits of Sovereignty: American Guano Islands," in this issue, 798, 799.
27. *Downes v. Bidwell* 182 U.S. 244 (1901); note Justice John Marshall Harlan's eloquent dissent.
28. Sarah H. Cleveland, "Powers Inherent in Sovereignty: Indians, Aliens, Territories, and the Nineteenth-Century Origins of Plenary Power over Foreign Affairs," *Texas Law Review* 81.1 (2002): 211.
29. A good place to start is Sanford Levinson, "Why the Canon Should Be Expanded to Include the Insular Cases," *Constitutional Commentary* 17 (2000): 241ff; and see Burnett, "The Edges of Empire."
30. I am indebted to Amy Kaplan for conversations on this point.
31. *Martin v. Commonwealth*, 1 Mass. 347 (1805).
32. H. R. Joint Resolution No. 238, 55th Cong., 2nd sess., 30 Stat. 1496 (May 18, 1898). John L. Cable, *Decisive Decisions of United States Citizenship* (Charlottesville, Va.: Michie Co., 1967), 41–42. I have discussed this point in chapter 1 of *No Constitutional Right to Be Ladies: Women and the Obligations of Citizenship* (New York: Hill and Wang, 1998).
33. See *Mackenzie v. Hare* 239 U.S. 299 (1915), upholding the denationalization of American women who married aliens. I discuss this case at some length in *No Constitutional Right to Be Ladies.*
34. Seckler-Hudson, *Statelessness*, 23–99.
35. Bredbenner, *A Nationality of Her Own*, 157.
36. See the splendid treatment of these matters in Bredbenner, *A Nationality of Her Own*, 98–102, 157, 170–94.
37. For the Nansen Passport, see Arendt, *The Origins of Totalitarianism*, 281, n. 30, and *passim*; and Torpey, *The Invention of the Passport*, 127–29. When the Germans occupied France, they used the Nansen passport for their own purposes, detaining all the Russians with a Nansen passport. White Russians were released; Jews with Nansen passports were deported to their deaths.
38. Despite the severity of U.S. immigration restriction policies in the 1920s and thereafter, Catheryn Seckler-Hudson estimated that some eighteen and a half million immigrants entered the United States in the first third of the twentieth century. Seckler-Hudson, *Statelessness*, 1.
39. Richard W. Flournoy Jr., "Nationality Convention Protocols and Recommendations Adopted by the First Conference on the Codification of International Law," *American Journal of International Law* 24 (1930): 467, quoted in Seckler-Hudson, *Statelessness*, 2.
40. I am indebted to Mae Ngai's remarkable essay, "The Strange Career of the Illegal Alien: Immigration Restriction and Deportation Policy in the United States, 1921–1965," *Law and History Review* 21 (2003): 69–107, especially notes 11 and 14. In her analysis, immigration restriction makes the illegal alien; she gives relatively little attention to statelessness, although it is implicit in the situation.
41. See the moving testimony by a man himself stateless, Marc Vishniac, *The Legal Status of Stateless Persons* (New York: American Jewish Committee, 1945), 34; and David S. Wyman, *Paper Walls: America and the Refugee Crisis 1938–1941* (Amherst: University of Massachusetts Press, 1968).
42. The original agenda of the UN Commission on the Status of Women expressed a grave concern for the risks of statelessness, and a fear for the fragility of married women's nationality. See Linda K. Kerber, "'I Was Appalled': The Invisible Antecedents of Second Wave Feminism," *Journal of Women's History* 14.2 (summer 2002): 86–97.
43. Bhabha, "'More Than Their Share of Sorrows,'" 253.
44. Hannah Arendt pointed out the irony that the test of statelessness is when you have more rights as a criminal: "A West Coast Japanese-American, who was in jail when the army ordered internment . . . would not have been forced to liquidate his property at too low a price; he would have remained right where he was, armed with a lawyer to look after his interests." *The Origins of Totalitarianism*, 287, n. 42.

45. On Mexican migrant farm workers and *braceros* in particular, see Ngai, *Impossible Subjects*, chap. 4, and Kitty Calavita, *Inside the State: The Bracero Program, Immigration, and the INS* (New York: Routledge, 1999).
46. Jacqueline Bhabha, "The 'Mere Fortuity' of Birth? Are Children Citizens?" *Differences* 15.2 (summer 2004): 91–117; for the vulnerability of children to statelessness in the 1930s, see Seckler-Hudson, *Statelessness*, 196–243.
47. *Tuan Ahn Nguyen v. INS*, 121 S. Ct. 2053 (2001). I have written about this case in "Top Court Took a Step Backward on Gender Bias," *Boston Globe*, June 23, 2001. See also Kristin Collins, "When Fathers' Rights Are Mothers' Duties: The Failure of Equal Protection in *Miller v. Albright*," *Yale Law Journal* 109 (2000): 101–42.
48. Brief for the Respondent, 10, December 13, 2000, *Tuan Ahn Nguyen v. INS* (No. 99-2071). This is a development feminists supported, in an effort to strengthen the rights of unmarried birth mothers within the United States. See *Lehr v. Robertson*, 463 U.S. 248 (1983).
49. Brief for the Respondent, 8, *Nguyen* (No. 99-201).
50. Ibid., 19.
51. Ibid., 34.
52. Respondent's Brief, 33–34 and n. 18, *Miller v. Albright*, 523 U.S. 420 (1998) (No. 96–1060).
53. *United States v. Ahumada-Aguilar*,189 F.3d.1121 (9th Cir. 1999).
54. Oral Argument in *Nguyen v. INS*.
55. Interview by author with Jay Stansell, January 12, 2001; Jonathan Simon, "Refugees in a Carceral Age: The Rebirth of Immigration Prisons in the United States," *Public Culture* 10.3 (1998): 577–607.
56. Oral Argument, *Zadvydas v. Davis*, 533 U.S. 678 (2001) (Nos. 99-7791, 00–38) (argued February 21, 2001).
57. Oral Argument, *Zadvydas v. Davis*, p. 7.
58. *Shaughnessy v. United States ex rel. Mezei*, 345 U.S. 206 (1953). Mezei was a permanent resident, a man, Justice Jackson observed, "who seems to have led a life of unrelieved insignificance," who left the United States to visit his dying mother in Romania for a year and a half. When he attempted to return in 1950, he was excluded by an immigration inspector; the attorney general made that ruling permanent "for security reasons." Unable to find a country that would accept him, Mezei was held in indefinite detention on Ellis Island. In his dissent, Jackson observed: "Executive imprisonment has been considered oppressive and lawless since John, at Runnymede, pledged that no free man should be imprisoned, dispossessed, outlawed, or exiled save by the judgment of his peers or by the law of the land. . . . Realistically, this man is incarcerated by a combination of forces which keeps him as effectually as a prison."
59. Deborah Sontag, "In a Homeland Far from Home," *New York Times Magazine*, November 16, 2003, 48ff.
60. See http://www.ccis.edu/nationwide/newsroom/index.asp?PAFB&story=383 (accessed July 19, 2005).
61. *Rumsfeld v. Padilla*, 124 S. Ct. 2711 (2004); *Hamdi v. Rumsfeld*, 124 S. Ct. 2633 (2004); *Rasul v. Bush* 124 S. Ct. 2686 (2004).
62. *Ex parte Milligan*, 71 U.S. (4 Wall.) 2 (1866), quoted in Brief of Janet Reno, *Rumsfeld v. Padilla* (No. 03-1027).
63. Neil A. Lewis, "Red Cross Finds Detainee Abuse in Guantanamo," *New York Times*, November 30, 2004; for Abu Ghraib, see Mark Danner, *Torture and Truth: America, Abu Ghraib, and the War on Terror* (New York: New York Review Books, 2004) .
64. Joel Brinkley, "From Afghanistan to Saudi Arabia, via Guantanamo," *New York Times*, October 16, 2004.
65. Neil A. Lewis, "Judge Says U.S. Terror Suspect Can't Be Held as an Enemy Combatant," *New York Times*, March 1, 2005, 14.
66. David A. Martin, "Behind the Scenes on a Different Set: What Congress Needs to Do in the Aftermath of St. Cyr and Nguyen," *Georgetown Immigration Law Journal* 16 (2002): 333–38.
67. Rogers Smith, *Civic Ideals: Conflicting Visions of Citizenship in U.S. History* (New Haven, Conn.: Yale University Press, 1997).
68. Center for Constitutional Rights, "The State of Civil Liberties, One Year Later: Erosion of Civil Liberties in the Post 9/11 Era," http://www.ccr-ny.org (accessed July 19, 2005).

69. For a detailed report on the leaked document, see http://www.aclu.org/SafeandFree/SafeandFree.cfm?ID=12234&c=206, "ACLU Fact Sheet on Patriot Act II," March 28, 2003 (accessed July 19, 2005).
70. Arendt, *The Origins of Totalitarianism*, 269.
71. Judith N. Shklar, *American Citizenship: The Quest for Inclusion* (Cambridge, Mass.: Harvard University Press, 1991); T. H. Marshall, *Citizenship and Social Class* (Cambridge: Cambridge University Press, 1950); Alice Kessler-Harris, *In Pursuit of Equity: Women, Men, and the Quest for Economic Citizenship in Twentieth-Century America* (New York: Oxford University Press, 2001).
72. The Trafficking Victims Protection Act of 2000 recognizes something of the scope of the problem in the United States. See also U.S. Department of State, "Trafficking in Persons Report," June 5, 2002, http://www.state.gov/g/tip (accessed July 19, 2005).
73. Aihwa Ong, *Buddha Is Hiding: Refugees, Citizenship, the New America* (Berkeley: University of California Press, 2003), 9.
74. Notably Title VII of the Civil Rights Act of 1964, the Voting Rights Act of 1965, and *Reed v. Reed* (1971).
75. Arendt, *The Origins of Totalitarianism*, 267.

In the Shadow of NAFTA: *Y tu mamá también* Revisits the National Allegory of Mexican Sovereignty

María Josefina Saldaña-Portillo

The year 2004 marked a peculiar convergence in Mexican politics, the tenth anniversary of both the North American Free Trade Agreement (NAFTA) and the Zapatista insurrection. After a decade of permanent structural reforms, NAFTA was declared a resounding success across the continent, even exceeding its economic goals in Mexico by ushering in an electoral democracy. Meanwhile, the Zapatistas appear to have suffered an ultimate defeat, a result of a politics of exhaustion deployed with equal alacrity by the Partido Revolucionario Institucional (PRI) and its democratically elected successor, the Partido Acción Nacional (PAN). Together, these two events—ten years of NAFTA and the Zapatista revolution—present us with two distinct Mexicos, united by one historical process, neoliberalism. The implementation of NAFTA, on the one hand, tells the story of a technocratic elite's vision of Mexico's entry into "democratic capitalism;" an entry pockmarked by displacement and pain, but which, purportedly, redeems the nation in the end through increases in economic indicators. The Zapatistas, on the other hand, tell the story of the displaced, of those subalterns whose present is sacrificed to the nation's future. These two interpretations of Mexico's embrace of neoliberalism provide the context for my psychoanalytic reading of Alfonso Cuarón's *Y tu mamá también*, a seemingly insignificant little film about two teenage boys, Tenoch and Julio, whose homoerotic love for each other is mediated by a beautiful Spanish woman and mother-figure, Luisa.[1] More accurately stated, the homoerotically charged Oedipal complex that provides the plot device, propelling this "on the road" film through narrative time and the Mexican countryside, functions as an allegory, presenting the viewer with a cinematic interpretation of the changing nature of Mexican sovereignty, subaltern positionality, and colonial fantasy in the context of a neoliberalism historically represented by NAFTA.

With its panoramic shots of a bucolic Mexican landscape, and its comedic and beguilingly innocent triangulated "love story," this film would be easy to dismiss as either multicultural "cinema lite" or as adolescent in its themes, particularly when compared to the gritty and violent rendition of Mexican life presented to us in its cross-over predecessor *Amores Perros* (2000). It is possible to read this film as yet another clichéd, misogynistic representation of the homoerotic sexuality of young boys, as a stereotypical Oedipal complex resolved positively in the end, against a backdrop of an exotic and primitive Mexico. However, the narrative trajectory of the triangulated love story is intercut with interstitial scenes that interrupt the filmic text. Each of these interstitial scenes begins with a few seconds of complete silence followed by a voice-over that conveys to the viewer some tangential information about one of the three characters. Equally as often, the voice-over conveys information about something happening *outside* the car on the road, to random people or to the actual landscape.

These scenes, which might otherwise be read as pastoral asides, are a key to understanding the film as anything but innocent or apolitical. They brush up against the "main action" of the film, steadfastly decentering the plot while nevertheless insisting on interdependence between the peripheral and the consequential story lines. Thus, a psychoanalytic reading of the Oedipal complex as it unfolds among the three protagonists allows for an allegorical understanding of their triangulated desire. Their Oedipal desire enacts the final crisis in revolutionary nationalism brought about by the onslaught of NAFTA and neoliberalism. In fact, one can read these interstitial scenes as an irruption of the subaltern onto the scene of masculine nationalism, as an expression of another knowledge of neoliberalism, one existing on the porous borders of the bourgeois elite's experience of Mexican sovereignty during the era of what I call NAFTA's "fiction of development."

Thus, the film itself provides an allegory for the history of how U.S. border-making has shaped Mexican sovereignty. The very experience of Mexican sovereignty is arguably bookended by the defining, delimiting consequences of two treaties promulgated with the United States concerning its borders. The first is, of course, the notorious 1848 Treaty of Guadalupe-Hidalgo; NAFTA is the second. Mexico acquired its independence from Spain in 1821 and had written its first constitution by 1824. This constitution, while based on the U.S. Constitution, extended considerably beyond its liberal vision by recognizing whites, *afromestizos*, mestizos, and all pacified Indians as equal citizens of Mexico, with equal rights to land, voting, public office, and education. In 1829, President Vicente Guerrero abolished slavery throughout the republic.[2] This recognition of all blacks as full citizens was a principal factor in the 1836 Texas War of Independence, since by 1829 slave-owning Anglos made up the majority of the state's population and resented the central Mexican government's interference in their affairs of "property."[3] In 1846, less than three decades after Mexico's formal independence, the United States launched an early version of "preemptive war," invading Mexico on the pretext of protecting its slave-holding constituents in the newly annexed state of Texas. The Treaty of Guadalupe-Hidalgo, then, was the legal resolution to an imperialist war waged against Mexico by the United States in the interest of slave-holding states and of expanding national territory.[4] It permanently reconfigured the geographical boundaries of Mexico, dispossessing it of fully half of its territory, half its natural resources, and a considerable portion of its indigenous and mestizo population.[5] This first treaty between the United States and Mexico not only affected territorial boundaries, but also made evident the tenuous and conditional nature of Mexican sovereignty in the shadow of the United States.

NAFTA was promulgated in 1994, almost 150 years after the Treaty of Guadalupe-Hidalgo, by the United States, Mexico, and Canada. In contrast, this treaty was the result of long-term, peaceful negotiations among the three nations, and it did not change the existing territorial borders between the signatories. Nevertheless, NAFTA radically altered the legal structure of the border between Mexico and the United States, the social geography of the borderland, and, as I argue in this essay, the character of Mexican sovereignty. NAFTA is a trinational legal regime of trade and capital investment, one that "opened up" the borders among the three nations by changing the formal legal controls on the entry and exit of goods and capital, although notably not of people. It did so primarily by requiring the dismantling of the prior import and export tariff structures for each country, as well as the structures of domestic subsidies. Thus, under the new legal regime introduced by NAFTA, any and all tariffs and subsidies explicitly used to protect domestic products and markets from the foreign competition of the other two signatories were removed or scheduled for removal.

While NAFTA facilitated the unencumbered movement of goods and capital across the North American continent, it pointedly did not address the third leg of this capitalist triumvirate: labor. NAFTA is strangely mute on the subject of the movement of laborers across national borders. And significantly, ten years after NAFTA, the United States and Mexico have yet to broker a single agreement on temporary workers, although the U.S. economy, from California to New York, is visibly addicted to the importation of cheap, undocumented labor from the south. This is not an oversight on the part of the negotiators of NAFTA, but is the result of the paradoxical relationship that exists among capitalism, liberalism, and the nation-state form (a relationship I will return to in my concluding remarks). Throughout the last decade, even as NAFTA's legal border regime has ushered in the unprecedented movement of goods and capital across the U.S.–Mexico border, the United States has militarized its border as never before to insure that immigrants—drawn to it by this very treaty—are denied easy entry into its territory.

Fictions of Development

The goals of NAFTA were very specific, limited to (1) the increase in trade among the signatories, and (2) the increase in direct financial investment across the three economies. Proponents of NAFTA argued that these two limited goals would have multiplying effects on the economies of Canada, the United States, and Mexico, predicting that increases in trade and foreign direct investment (FDI) would lead to considerable increases in the gross domestic product (GDP) of all three countries, as well as an increase in job creation. At least according to the major economic indicators, NAFTA has been a success on all counts, especially where Mexico is concerned. For example, the *Free Trade Bulletin*, published by conservative think tank The Cato Institute, reported in 2002: "Since 1993, the value of two-way U.S. trade with Mexico has nearly tripled, from $81,000,000,000 to $232,000,000,000, growing twice as fast as U.S. trade with the rest of the world. Canada and Mexico are now America's number-one and -two trading partners, respectively, with Japan a distant third."[6]

Perhaps more significant than this expected increase in trade, FDI in Mexican manufacture increased dramatically. The Interhemispheric Resource Center (IRC), critical of the overall effect of NAFTA on sustainable development, nevertheless reports: "On the surface, the strategy [of NAFTA] was, at least, a dazzling success. Between 1994 and 2002, FDI inflows into Mexico ballooned to a yearly average of $13 billion, nearly three times more than the yearly average of $4.5 billion between 1988 and 1993. Indeed, Mexico ranks among the top three developing country recipients of global FCI [foreign capital investment]."[7] An average of only $2.2 billion per year of this investment came from the United States, while most of the remainder came from Europe and Japan. During the same period (1994–2004), U.S. manufacturing companies invested a yearly average of $200 billion in domestic manufacture, fully one hundred times the United States' investment in Mexico.[8] Thus, arguably, NAFTA and the deregulation it ushered in have increased investment in Mexico with a negligible effect on domestic investment in the United States.

This increase in FDI has indeed led to increased production of jobs in manufacturing in Mexico. When export-oriented *maquiladora* industries and export-oriented non-*maquiladora* industrial production are combined, it turns out that overall manufacturing has risen, some would say substantially. By 2004, the *maquiladora* industries could be labeled a success story in generating jobs, registering a net gain of 550,000 jobs.[9] When one looks at the non-*maquiladora* industrial sector, the picture gets a bit more complicated for job growth, but nevertheless one can locate positive indicators with relation to NAFTA. There were roughly 1.4 million jobs in this sector of the economy when NAFTA was signed and there were approximately 1.3 million jobs in 2004. However, during the interim, the number of these jobs dedicated to export actually increased by 500,000 (450,000 of these tied directly to exports to the United States), while production for the domestic market decreased proportionally.[10] Arguably, then, even with non-*maquiladora* production losing jobs over the last ten years, manufacturing for export has actually succeeded in creating new jobs. Thus, the aggregate figures look good, at least when considered in light of NAFTA's specific goals. There was an overall increase of 1 million jobs devoted to export-oriented manufacturing. Meanwhile, there have been roughly 450,000 jobs created in export-oriented agriculture and agro-industry spurred by NAFTA. When added together, the net gain of jobs in export-oriented industries is approximately 1 million. Arguably, all of these jobs can be attributed to the effect of NAFTA's opening up of Mexico's economy to trade.

Of course, Mexico's trade deficit with the rest of the world has also increased—indeed exploded—as agricultural and other imports flood Mexico's markets (from the United States, Canada, *and* beyond). Indeed Mexico's trade deficit is at a historical high. Thus, the increase that takes place during NAFTA in Mexican export-manufacture occurs *simultaneously* with an increase in Mexico's dependence on foreign imports (including foodstuffs), and does little to decrease the net outflow of capital. Importantly, this trade deficit is *not* in the *maquiladora* industry, which actually has a positive balance of trade with the United States:

> Although exports grew fast, imports grew faster, generating a persistent and growing current account deficit. The problem was that, rather than buy inputs locally, TNCs [transnational corporations] relied heavily on foreign suppliers. In 2002, locally sourced inputs in export-oriented maquila manufacturing plants accounted for less than 4% of total value added.[11]

As I suggested earlier, NAFTA may not be blamed directly for the loss of jobs in non-*maquiladora* industry geared toward domestic production. However,

FDI in this export-oriented area has failed to produce the backward linkages that could have spurred growth in this sector, and is instead responsible for a significant portion of the trade deficit in imports.

Thus, there is always a flip side to NAFTA-style development. In addition to the blossoming trade deficit, over the course of the last ten years, 1.3 million jobs have been lost in agriculture. While not all of this job loss is singularly attributable to NAFTA (and indeed, NAFTA-stimulated exports in agriculture have created jobs), economists nevertheless attribute a portion of this loss to NAFTA. Mexican peasants who traditionally farmed basic grains simply cannot compete against the cheaper imports in foodstuffs that have flooded the national market.[12] The phasing out of price supports on basic grains, such as beans, corn, and rice, was legally required by NAFTA. In addition, the United States insisted on the removal of constitutional protections against the selling and renting of communal land-holdings.[13] These changes have combined to displace a significant number of the agricultural population.[14] In the end then, there has been a net loss of 300,000 jobs when all the calculus around NAFTA is done.

These figures for job loss (which many would argue are a relatively insignificant price to pay for job increases in the industrial sector), however, do not factor in the exploding growth in Mexico's job-age population. An estimated 1 million new workers are entering the job force each year, and will continue to enter at this rate until the year 2020. Most are entering the informal sector as NAFTA-style development failed to absorb this demographic boom in work-age Mexicans. NAFTA was originally marketed to the skeptical (and xenophobic) United States precisely as a way of protecting a territorial border repeatedly figured as "under siege" by undocumented Mexican workers. Pushing NAFTA as a way of assuaging U.S. citizen's anxiety over this border "problem," Salinas de Gotarí famously declared that Mexico should export products, not people. There were, of course, those scholarly voices that cautioned that the economic restructuring induced by NAFTA-style development would cause an "immigration hump," as economic restructuring inevitably does produce job displacements and short-term increases in migration.[15] Proponents of NAFTA nevertheless won the day in 1994. In 2004, it appeared the naysayers were correct:

> By most measures, illegal immigration to the United States continued to increase after NAFTA came into effect. Apprehensions along the U.S. southwestern border also continued to increase, from about 700,000 in 1994 to more than 1,300,000 at their peak in 2001. The population of unauthorized Mexican immigrants grew as well: The Immigration and Natu-

> ralization service . . . estimated the number of Mexicans present in the United States without authorization rose from 2 million in 1990 to 4.8 million in 2000, increasing from 59.3 percent to 68.7 percent of the estimated total unauthorized population in the United States.[16]

It is also noteworthy that while the percentage of rural immigrants within this general immigrant population has declined significantly (to less than 25 percent of total immigrants), a much greater percentage of those emigrating from rural areas is proceeding to the United States instead of to other rural or urban areas within Mexico: "Thirty percent of migrants from rural Mexico were in the United States in 2002, versus 19 percent in 1994. From 1980 to 1994, migration from the surveyed rural communities to the United States increased by 95 percent. By 2002, migration to the United States was 452 percent higher than in 1980."[17] While it would certainly be incorrect to attribute this increase in migration singularly, or even principally, to NAFTA, it would appear that a good number of those displaced in agriculture, or for whom agriculture is no longer viable, have begun the long trek northward.

I begin with this raw data because it tells what I have referred to earlier as a "fiction of development." Or rather, as I hope my own narrative suggests, it tells at least two fictions of development. Reading the data from the hegemonic perspective of neoliberalism allows us to diagnose NAFTA as a success in terms of its limited goals, for all sorts of economic indicators are up in Mexico: FDI, GDP, job production in industry, volume of trade. Thus, free trade enthusiasts across the Americas point to such statistics as evidence of NAFTA's resounding success, which they interpret as not only bestowing economic well-being, but also ushering in Mexico's transition to an electoral democracy. However, these figures also expose a fiction at the heart of NAFTA's legal regime with regard to territorial boundaries. They expose the liberal paradox suggested above. NAFTA was promulgated under the operative fiction that territorial borders could be porous to goods and capital but closed to those laborers whose impoverishment is often the result of NAFTA-style development. From the counterhegemonic perspective of migration studies, these economic indicators tell a different story, one of displacement and diaspora. According to INS figures, almost three million new immigrants from Mexico have traveled to the United States, many of these from the rural and indigenous areas.[18] They have faced deserts and militarized border patrols, *coyotes* and Mexican police, not to find jobs in the Southwest among established generations of Mexican immigrants, as in previous decades, but rather to settle new urban areas—as delivery boys and maids in English-speaking New York City—or to enter debt peonage—as isolated agricultural laborers in Durham, North Carolina, in Stamford, Connecticut, and on Long Island.

Indeed, the population of Mexican immigrants in the five boroughs of New York City quadrupled in the 1990s, according to the U.S. census. Mexicans are now the fifth largest immigrant group in New York, with 122,550 people living in the city. (Demographers expect the figure is closer to 200,000.) In 1990, Mexicans ranked seventeenth, with a population of only 32,689.[19] These undocumented immigrants live in a metaphoric borderland in New York City. They exist on the very borders of legality, as human rights and labor law controverts immigration law. Thus, undocumented immigrants have the right to obtain drivers' licenses in New York City, but dare not answer juror qualification questionnaires, which are generated from the county DMV rolls and require proof of legal visa status for disqualification. At the same time, undocumented workers have the right to file grievances for exploitative labor conditions (as they frequently do), but do not actually possess the basic right to work legally in the United States. Undocumented college students, many of whom have been in New York City since early childhood, are allowed to attend City and State University of New York systems (CUNY and SUNY) without proof of citizenship, but must constantly battle opportunistic state legislatures wanting to fund higher education by charging these students out-of-state tuition.

From the perspective of these immigrants who live their everyday lives on the border between legality and invisibility, between ascertaining the agencies designated to help undocumented immigrants and avoiding the immigration officers who seek to deport them, the economic indicators of NAFTA's successful stimulus of the economy tell a very different fiction. For how must the conditions of their *rancherías*, *ejidos*, *tierras comunales*, and *colonias* have changed over the course of ten years for them to have decided to leave their homes, their languages, their indigenous cultures, their families, their nation—to leave every form of social relation that marks one's identity—to begin again in this legal limbo? And how does the Mexican imaginary—the citizenry's sense of their own national identity—change in the midst of this migration and the structural changes ushered in by NAFTA's particular legal regime? Where can we locate the shifting positionality of the rural subaltern in the changing landscape of Mexican nationalism? How, in other words, has neoliberalism, whose legal fulcrum is the NAFTA treaty, changed the historical substance of Mexican sovereignty for its citizenry?

Because economic indicators are so malleable, I would suggest that the fictions these statistics can tell, however significant, cannot answer these questions. They can set the stage, provide the context, for such a tale of transformation, but they cannot give us the texture of the change. These economic indicators and statistics on migration cannot capture the transformation in the lives of millions of Mexican subalterns. Nor can such statistics register the ephemeral changes in the national political imaginary, in the quotidian experience of international social relations. For NAFTA, I suggest, as the fulcrum of neoliberalism, has wrought the biggest change to the conception of Mexican national sovereignty since the Mexican revolution of 1910. Indeed, in some ways it is the tangible result of seventy long years of legal counterinsurgency waged by U.S. and Mexican elites against the socialist principles enshrined in the Mexican constitution of 1917. To detect these changes in the everyday lives of subalterns and in the political imaginary of a nation, one must turn to either the ethnographic, literary, or filmic text, which, while it cannot deliver "the truth of the matter," can nevertheless register these richer cultural and political transformations. *Y tu mamá también*, as one such narrative, offers another interpretation of what has transpired in the era of neoliberal Mexico. Economic indicators capture what "is," whereas *Y tu mamá también* captures what is lost, and, in Thomas Pynchon's words, "what remained yet had somehow, before this, stayed away."[20]

National Allegories as Oedipal Desire in the Era of Neoliberalism

Y tu mamá también tells the story of two Mexican teenage boys, Tenoch and Julio, who take Luisa, a beautiful Spanish woman in her late twenties, on a road trip along the Pacific coast of Mexico in the hopes of seducing her.[21] Tenoch is the son of a wealthy, high-level PRI functionary, while Julio is the son of a single mother, who is a secretary for a generic "transnational corporation." Contrasting scenes of each boy's house strikingly convey their distinct class positions to the audience, especially one familiar with Mexican architecture. Tenoch's house is a gated, multilevel, hacienda-style mansion, replete with *retablos*, massive wooden furnishings, maids, gardeners, and guard dogs, all of which the camera slowly pans in wide-angle shots for a good minute of film. Julio's home, on the other hand, is a modest, cluttered apartment in one of the many identical block-style affordable housing complexes built in the 1960s and '70s by the PRI in response to organized popular agitation. The shots of his apartment, a rapid montage of tight-angle shots, convey a claustrophobia proportional to the wealthy spaciousness of Tenoch's home. Through these parallel scenes, Tenoch is established as a member of the most elite political class in Mexico, while Julio's class position is located in the upper echelons of the working class or the lower rungs of a managerial class. The unlikely pair are best friends initially brought together by their girlfriends. Luisa is married to Tenoch's cousin, Jano, a published writer recently returned from an honorary teaching post at a Madrid university, where he met his wife. When Luisa mentions she would like to visit Mexico's beaches, Tenoch and Julio immediately invite her on a quickly improvised trip. Luisa eventually accepts their invitation, and the remainder of the film follows them on their journey, the camera sometimes in the car with the three characters, sometimes shooting them from outside, but always trained on their travels through the Mexican landscape. As each boy enacts his fantasy of having sex with Luisa, a rivalry over the mother figure's affection ensues, which culminates in the boys finally expressing their painfully obvious attraction for each other by having sex together, facilitated by Luisa.

The so-called positive Oedipus complex is resolved through an intensification of the male child's identification with the father, according to Freud. This intensified identification with the father is at once ambivalent, due to the residue of the rivalry it contains, and "consolidate[s] the masculinity in the boy's character."[22] The mother is given up as an object-cathexis precisely because through identification with the father, the child incorporates the father's authority into the ego, and with it a prohibition against incest. The resolution of the Oedipal complex through identification installs an "ego-ideal" or "super-ego" within the subject, which "retains the character of the father," or so Freud initially argues.[23] For Freud, however, this "simple positive" resolution of the Oedipal complex may be regarded as normative, but it is by no means the most common resolution. He also posits a "negative" resolution in which he suggests the child's initial object-cathexis with the mother's breast is extremely mobile, attaching itself equally and indiscriminately to both mother and father, and hence establishing the "originally present" bisexual nature of the child.[24] This negative Oedipal complex elucidates, indeed troubles, Freud's own prior claim that the resolution of the complex occurs through "an *intensification* of his identification with his father," as if to suggest no prior identification with the mother exists.[25] Instead, it would appear that the child (male or female) is already identifying with the mother in the "*more complete*" Oedipal complex before its resolution. This identification follows the pathways of the mother's desire for the father, with the male child even mimicking the "affectionate feminine attitude" of the mother toward the father.[26] Thus, it is perhaps most correct to suggest that the resolution of the Oedipal complex necessarily involves the intensification of a prior identification with both the father *and* the mother. The mother, just as the father, will always remain as an ideal of gender, confronting "the other contents of ego."[27] The recognition of these two caveats to the Oedipal complex—the bisexual desire attached to mother-identification and the intensification of this bisexual identification into an ego-ideal—allows for a series of allegorical readings of the layers of Oedipal desire in the film.

The negative Oedipal desire expressed by Tenoch and Julio for each other through their identification with Luisa is symptomatic, I suggest, of a desire for "*PRI papa*," a system of corporativist patronage represented in the film by Tenoch's father, the party functionary. It is an ambivalent desire, to be sure, especially for Tenoch, who anemically defies his father with his interest in literature rather than economics. Nevertheless, read allegorically, the desire these boys express for each other as substitute father figures reveals the eroticized fulcrum upon which a seventy-year "ego-ideal" of revolutionary masculinity (*PRI papa*) turns: the union of *PRI/pueblo*. Meanwhile, the positive Oedipal desire expressed by the boys *for* Luisa, I suggest, expresses a desire for *mama España* as ego-ideal. Thus, in the scene in which Tenoch and Julio recall images of older women for masturbatory fantasy on the diving board of a private country club, Julio slips metonymically from recalling first the mother of Tenoch's girlfriend and then their teacher, both maternal figures, to recalling the image of Luisa, which immediately prompts both boys' simultaneous ejaculation. Significantly, he does not refer to her by her by name, but as "tu prima, la Españoooola." However, this desire for incorporation of an ideal of imperial whiteness, when read through the dynamics of *mestizaje*, circuitously stands in for a desired *independence* from the foreign investment facilitated by NAFTA.

Luisa is established as the maternal figure at various moments in the film: with the aforementioned elision between mother/teacher/Española, with her instructions to the boys on how to make love correctly, with her subsequent motherly reassurances when the boys ejaculate too quickly during intercourse, and with her explicit acknowledgment of their maternal desire when she berates herself for becoming involved with them: "Mierda, quien me manda coño, jugar con críos y limpiar los pañales." However, when she is first established as a maternal figure for the viewer, she is explicitly associated with a composed, unflappable whiteness. We first see Luisa at the *charriada* wedding of Tenoch's sister, at the same moment that Tenoch and Julio, together, first see her. She is dramatically dressed, from head to toe, in an ivory-white dress that distinguishes her from the rest of the guests. Luisa is standing alone on a landing, overlooking the bull ring when the boys approach her. They try to impress her with clumsy, macho posturing, but it is they who are immediately impressed when she says she is "de Madrid . . . España." Jano, her husband and Tenoch's cousin, interrupts the trio, putting an end to their childish flirtation. By claiming his proper place as father figure, he displaces the boys physically as the objects of her attention. Luisa's attitude toward Jano, though, immediately turns matronly, when she notices he has spilled a drink on his suit. She snatches the handkerchief and water out of his hands to begin scrubbing his jacket herself, her face assuming the distinct expression of motherly scolding.

The film stages Luisa's Spanish colonial heritage as a factor in the boys' attraction to her. She is, after all, iconically named Luisa Cortes.[28] But to understand fully its racial appeal as an ego-ideal for the boys, themselves two emergent political subjects of new, neoliberal Mexico, we must turn to the social text of *mestizaje*. In early-twentieth-century Mexico, the discourse of *mestizaje* was deployed as a strategy of national identification and unification in the aftermath of a divisive revolutionary war against the oligarchic class of the *porfiriato*. This revolutionary *mestizaje*, however, also registered a desire for an anticolonial sovereignty, as the oligarchic class of the *porfiriato* was notorious for its business dealings with U.S. capitalists. Indeed, the revolutionary rhetoric of the war was highly anti-imperialist, emphasizing the need to remove the oligarchic elites who were purloining national interests to the United States. The nineteenth-century discourse of *mestizaje* was perfectly adaptable to such twentieth-century revolutionary aspirations because it not only metaphorized national unity for Mexico through biological coordinates, but also interpellated subjects into a principle of citizenship based on a leaving behind of residual indigenous *and* imperial racial categories and cultures.[29] Indeed, in the essays of such revolutionary intellectuals as Manuel Gamio and Jose Vasconcelos, *mestizaje* is privileged in the evolutionary logic of leaving behind those twin eternal obstacles to modern Mexican sovereignty: indigenous being *and* foreign domination. Thus, I am not suggesting that Tenoch and Julio are cathected onto Luisa as ego-ideal because of a straightforward desire for whiteness. Such privileging of whiteness may correspond to a U.S. racial ideology, but it would contravene the desire for independence and sovereignty expressed in historical *mestizaje*. Instead, I am suggesting that the mestizo's rise to prominence in the twentieth century is traditionally associated with a "golden age" of revolutionary nationalism. *Mestizaje* represents a period when the lofty ideals of Mexican economic and political independence from foreign, and specifically *Yankee*, intervention dominated not only the political imaginary of its citizens, but also the policies of the early PRI state.[30] Tenoch and Julio's desire for Luisa as *mamá España*, and eventual sexual possession of her, allegorically suggests a desire to re-act *mestizaje* precisely as the incorporation of her racial otherness, as emblematic of an incorporation that symbolizes independence from, indeed triumph over, foreign domination. Indeed, the very structure of Oedipal desire harkens back to an early, constitutive moment of subject constitution; in this case, enacted as it is against a prosaic Mexican landscape, it harkens back to an earlier, "simpler time" (to a simpler paradigm of neocolonialism?) in which the nation's foes were discrete (individual U.S. capitalists) rather than immanent (foreign direct investment), and could be easily absorbed within the national category (i.e., nationalized). Luisa functions, then, both as a pathway for Tenoch and Julio's identificatory desire for *PRI papa* as expressive of a political *mestizaje* between the PRI and *el pueblo*, and as the crucible that allows the boys to enact their desire for a *mestizaje* that represents genuine political sovereignty and independence against the eroding of national sovereignty represented in NAFTA.

Luisa as *mama España*, then, enables the performance of a biological *mestizaje* when she has sex with the boys separately and together. In sex, she embodies the principle of the incorporation of the foreign element as the grounds for independence from it. However, Luisa is also called upon as witness to the enactment of their political *mestizaje* as well. Julio and Tenoch desire each other, I suggest, as allegorical stand-ins for the PRI's historical desire for an identificatory relationship with *el pueblo*, and vice versa. In other words, Tenoch and Julio's desire for each other, necessarily expressed through Luisa as identificatory conduit, articulates the cross-class aspirations of the two historical constituencies present in the political machinery of a revolutionary party turned corporativist: the elite party leadership and leadership of the popular classes.

Tenoch's desire for identification with *lo popular* is staged for the viewer at two moments in the film. The first conveys to the viewer the structure of the desire for this identification at the very heart of the political imaginary of the PRI leadership. As the camera offers the viewer a montage of four different exterior and interior shots of Tenoch's opulent house (each containing a servant tending to its upkeep), the voice-over, as always monotone, informs the viewer that Tenoch, second of three children, is born to a marriage "formed" by a Harvard-trained economist, who is the "sub-secretary of state," and a housewife concerned with new age spirituality. The viewer is told that Tenoch's parents initially intended to name him "Hernan," suggesting the parents' identification with the dominant term in the conquest. However, we are told, Tenoch is born just as his father is entering public service, when he is "*contagiado por un nacionalismo inucitado.*" Consequently, his parents decide to give their first-born male an indigenous name, in homage to *lo popular*, to the subaltern but resistant roots of Mexican *mestizaje.* As a "Harvard-trained economist," the father is placed among the generation of technocrats who, like Carlos Salinas de Gotarí and Ernesto Zedillo, received their training at elite U.S. schools and engineered the neoliberal turn in Mexico. This turn toward neoliberalism not only liberalized trade policies and allowed for the wholesale privatization of state-run industries, but also broke the corporativist social contract with *el pueblo,* forever fracturing the political *mestizaje* of *papa PRI* and *el pueblo.* And yet, even as Tenoch's father emblemizes the "new PRI" and the severing of a historical relationship of patronage between *papa PRI* and the popular classes, he nevertheless is compelled to pay tribute to this identification with *el pueblo* as party functionary. Indeed, "*contagiado*" suggests his identification with *el pueblo* is endemic, an infection at the heart of revolutionary nationalism so widespread that it overwhelms the father. Meanwhile, "*inucitado*" suggests an unexpected event, an infectious desire for identification with *lo popular* that surprises even himself with its exaggerated proportion. As if to underscore this desired identification with indigenous, subaltern Mexico structured into the naming of Tenoch, during the voice-over we see Tenoch in the background of the shot, framed through a wide hallway lined with indigenous artifacts.

The second moment of Tenoch's identification with *el pueblo* suggests a desire on Tenoch's part to fulfill the promise of his naming: to renew the bond of political *mestizaje* between the PRI elite and *lo popular* that has been broken by the new generation of technocrats. In the scene in which Tenoch receives Luisa's phone call informing him that she would like to join them on their beach trip after all, Tenoch is wearing a Subcomandante Marcos T-shirt. Tenoch is literally wearing his identification "on his sleeve." Elsewhere I have argued that the Zapatista insurrection occurs in large part because Salinas de Gotarí and his technocratic cohort broke the social contract with the peasant classes, which was put in place by the 1917 constitution and solidified by Lázaro Cardenas's agricultural policies. Salinas de Gotarí's administration dismantled the price supports, basic grain subsidies, and government distribution networks that had kept peasant agriculture viable since the revolution. Most significantly, in compliance with U.S. stipulations for its signing of NAFTA, de Gotarí's administration altered the constitution to allow for the private sale to foreign interests of communal lands.[31] Together, these policies ushered in NAFTA. The T-shirt bearing Marcos's signature image, then, signals Tenoch's naive desire for identification with the Zapatista struggle, with *lo popular, against* this elite, technocratic, capitalist vision. After all, the Zapatistas theatrically burst onto the national stage on the very day NAFTA goes into effect: January 1, 1994. The Zapatistas explicitly represent a *neo*revolutionary movement, an insurrection against the latest modernizing, *de*nationalizing, free trade vision of Mexico represented by Tenoch's father. In his identification with the Zapatistas, Tenoch expresses nostalgia for a previous model of revolutionary nationalism, one in which sovereignty and independence took precedence over comprador capitalism and alignment with the U.S. interests. This desire for the Zapatistas as *el pueblo mexicano* then is echoed in Tenoch's Oedipal desire for Julio, whose last name is, tellingly, Zapata.

This desire for identification with the Zapatistas as emblematic of *el pueblo* is at once idealized and decadent, however, just as the father naming his son Tenoch is at once heartfelt and opportunistic, for we have just witnessed Tenoch's unadorned relationship with *el pueblo*. Leading up to the scene of the telephone call, we see Tenoch's nurse-maid, Leo, as she carries a grilled cheese sandwich from a pristine kitchen with many cooks through a sitting room, across an indoor courtyard complete with fountain, up a stone staircase, across the hallway adorned with indigenous statuettes, and, finally, into the room where we find Tenoch listening to rock music and watching television. This preamble to the main action of the film is rendered interminably long because all the while we hear a phone ringing incessantly. Finally, after ten rings, once Leo has delivered the sandwich to her charge, informed Tenoch that she made it just as he likes it, and patted him lovingly on the head, she answers a phone that is just three steps from Tenoch. In a telling gesture, Leo wipes the phone clean with her sweater before passing it to Tenoch, either because she has been trained to do so or because she identifies with her own abjection before Tenoch, or both. The entire scene conveys Tenoch's unquestioned acceptance of his own pampered privilege vis-à-vis the servile subaltern subjects. By wearing the T-shirt, then, Tenoch is not so much identifying against his own class interests as he is expressing a desire for a return to an era of political *mestizaje*, of political accommodation between PRI leadership and the leadership of the popular classes made possible under a previous model of *papa PRI*. As a social climber from the working class, Julio functions as the appropriate substitute for this desired identification.

Julio's desire for Tenoch is straightforwardly expressed throughout the film as aspiration. Julio desires Tenoch because he baldly desires the power and prestige of the PRI elite. Thus, Julio's Oedipal desire is expressed alternately as a desire to please Tenoch's father or to replace him. For example, Julio has little sympathy for Tenoch's desire to major in literature rather than economics, as Tenoch's father would prefer. When Tenoch informs Julio that his father has threatened to take away his car if he insists on majoring in literature, Julio urges him to please his father in order to keep the car. Indeed, Julio himself plans to major in economics, and dismisses Tenoch's tender request that he switch to literature in order that they may be together. Similarly, when Tenoch's father reprimands his son for drinking too much at the *charriada,* Julio vainly solicits the father's approval by reiterating his criticism of Tenoch. Thus, Julio's desire for identification with the PRI elite is expressed twice as emulation. Subsequently, it culminates in a fantasy of replacing the father. In the scene preceding Julio and Tenoch's love-making, during which the boys are making full confessions of their sexual transgressions with each other's girlfriends, Julio slips in that he has also slept with Tenoch's mother, with the words that give the film its title, "y tu mamá también." Whether or not Julio actually has slept with Tenoch's mother, this statement is the denouement of the film; it lays bear his desire to fulfill the Oedipal complex by replacing the father as a member of the PRI elite. This desire for identification with the PRI leadership is even given historical justification in the film. Moments before Julio confesses to sleeping with Tenoch's mother, he accuses Tenoch of being a *fresa,* a spoiled rich kid. Tenoch turns the tables, accusing Julio of being a striver, who loves visiting all of Tenoch's houses. Julio retorts, "Of course I do, so that I can get back a little of what your father has stolen from the people." Thus, Julio's cross-class aspiration, his desire for Tenoch and the class privilege he will inevitably inherit, makes Julio the perfect accommodationist in the political *mestizaje* that is PRI nationalism, old school.

Y tu mamá también stages an allegorical reading of a national allegory—concerning the identification of PRI and popular interests—at the very moment of this allegory's historical demise. The liberalization and deregulation of the Mexican economy represented in NAFTA—its territorial *de*nationalization—requires a formal democracy that puts an end not only to the PRI dynasty, but to political *mestizaje* as a model of national sovereignty, with its Oedipalized structure of desire, with its anti-imperialist, anti–U.S. legacy, and with its modicum of redistribution of social wealth. Hence, although the boys realize their allegorical desire for cross-class identification at the end of their beach trip, their relationship has no future in the new Mexico, as there is no way to reconstitute the sovereign borders rendered open by NAFTA. In the film's final scene, which takes place one year later in Mexico City, the voice-over tells us first that the boys stop seeing each other shortly after their beach trip, and then immediately proceeds to inform us that Mexico's ruling party lost the national elections for the first time in seventy-one years, as if the two events were causally related. Tenoch then informs Julio that Luisa, the vehicle for expressing their masculinized allegory of revolutionary nationalism, has died of a cancer that had spread all over her body, further implying that the relationship of accommodation between the PRI elite and the upper echelons of the popular classes is also riddled with an infection that leads to its demise.

The film offers two possible readings of the nature of the cancer infecting political *mestizaje*, the first interior to the Oedipalized desire the boys feel for each other, the other exterior to it. Luisa most explicitly functions as the pathway for the fulfillment of their desire for each other in the car, as she listens to the boys recount their adventures and their eleven-point manifesto as fellow "*charrolastras*," or astral cowboys. As the voice-over informs us, Tenoch and Julio's desire for each other is filled with a hidden revulsion and shame:

> Julio and Tenoch told Luisa many more anecdotes. Each story confirmed the strong tie that united them, the link that made them a into a solid and inseparable nucleus. The stories they told, though adorned with their own personal mythologies, were true. Though as always happens, it was an incomplete truth. Among the many things they forgot to mention was how Julio would light matches after he used the bathroom at Tenoch's house to hide the smell. Or how Tenoch would lift the seat of the toilet with his foot when he used the bathroom in Julio's house. These were details the one didn't need to know about the other.

The homophobic aversion the boys express toward each other after they have sex, then, is symptomatic of the revulsion that is at the heart of the PRI elite's appraisal of the popular classes, and the internalized shame felt by the leadership of those very classes. Hence, while the voice-over is telling us this more "complete" truth concerning the ambivalence at the "nucleus" of the boys' mutual desire, the camera shoots from behind the windshield of the car, capturing in the headlights the unadorned *pueblo*: poor mestizos and indigenous shopkeepers and peasants engaged in the bustling exchange of everyday life, amid oxcarts and beat-up cars, under thatched-roofed houses and against graffiti-ridden stucco walls. All this is located safely outside the protection offered by the car, beyond the reach of the mythologies of political *mestizaje*.

This then is the other problem at the heart of political *mestizaje* and the unfulfilled promise of revolutionary nationalism—its exclusion, or more precisely occlusion, of *el pueblo*. Subaltern Mexico has historically sustained political *mestizaje*, enabled it, served it, and enveloped it, while nevertheless remaining marginal to this allegory of revolutionary nationalism. Similarly, in the film, the scenes of rural Mexico and its subaltern residents—frequently shot from inside the car looking out—envelop the station wagon in which Julio, Tenoch, and Luisa travel, sustaining it, serving the central "action" of the plot, enabling their love story to move endlessly forward through the landscape, while nevertheless remaining marginalized by it. Thus, we see *el pueblo* intersect with the trio at various junctures: feeding them at rest stops and in restaurants, pulling the broken-down car with a tractor, fixing the radiator by the side of the road, giving them hats and cigarettes, clarifying the meaning of death and life, performing folkloric backdrop to their unfolding Oedipal affair with flower-adorned wedding trucks and barnyard beauty queens, and finally delivering them by boat to their mythical destination—a beach called *la boca del cielo.* All the while, the camera lingers lovingly on these scenes within scenes, revealing to the viewer what repeatedly remains invisible to the Oedipal trio: women dancing or laboring in kitchens; men forced to bear witness to the trio's sexual exploits; and, most significantly, peasants violently searched by police on the side of the road, or at the numerous army roadblocks where the military has pulled aside the less privileged. These glimpses are tucked into the Oedipal plot, lingering onscreen without comment for the viewer to decode. The camera renders these bits of scenes almost neutrally; however, the political relationship that exists between *el pueblo* and the groups represented in political *mestizaje* is anything but neutral. Instead, these lingering shots, particularly those of the police and military, suggest the high degree of coercion and state violence necessary to maintain the subaltern in service to the dominant national, regional, and local groups. Indeed, it is a violence that is not merely incidental to the Oedipal allegory, but required by it.

Ranajit Guha's discussion of "the politics of people" in India during British colonialism sheds some light on the place of Mexico's political *mestizaje* and of *el pueblo* in the post-NAFTA era. Guha differentiates among four hierarchical groups under the British Raj: dominant foreign groups, dominant indigenous groups at the national level, dominant indigenous groups at the regional and local levels, and finally, the "'subaltern classes,'" representing "*the demographic difference between the total Indian population and all those whom we have described as the 'elite.'*"[32] There is no one-to-one correspondence between Guha's grid of Indian social classes under colonialism and social classes in Mexican politics during the transition to neoliberalism, but there are insightful analogies. While there is no single "dominant foreign group" within Mexican politics, there is now a transnational capitalist class, based in Mexico's export industries, with unprecedented access to political power through the national elites. Meanwhile, the social classes present in politics of political *mestizaje* correspond roughly to Guha's dominant elites: at the national level, party leadership is represented by Tenoch, and at the "regional," or more appropriately, the sectoral, level, popular leadership is represented by Julio. *El pueblo*, or the subaltern class, is all that remain; they are the "demographic difference" between these elite groups and the total Mexican population.

Just as Guha suggests with subaltern politics, the politics of *el pueblo* is "an autonomous domain, for it neither originated from elite politics nor did its existence depend on the latter."[33] The politics of *el pueblo* exist beyond the political *mestizaje* among the leadership that excluded them, as the Zapatista movement makes evidently clear. However, I do not want to suggest that subaltern Mexico prevails, against all odds, in some prosaic, bucolic state. Instead, the film again points us to a more precise articulation of the historical relationship between the political *mestizaje* of the dominant groups and the politics of *lo popular.* Under the political *mestizaje* of a previous era of revolutionary nationalism, *el pueblo* occupied a paradoxical position of mathematical remains: they are the residual elements, which sustain and surround the calculations of political *mestizaje.* On occasion subaltern classes benefited from this political accommodation between elites, able to maintain a degree of political autonomy on their constitutionally protected communal lands through their state-subsidized production and distribution. However, the film documents the demise of political *mestizaje* in the face of neoliberalism. With it, the volatile "peace" brokered over seventy years between the dominant elites and the subaltern classes—a peace that allowed subalterns to remain in Mexico and yet somehow remain autonomous from political *mestizaje*—is also no longer possible. The subaltern can no longer "stay away," in Pynchon's terms.

The film's interstitial scenes thus chronicle the subaltern's movement to the center: from fishing village to tourist resort, from Michoacan to Mexico City, from Mexico City to the United States. These scenes register the effects of NAFTA in the everyday life and death of those alienated from their own labor by the privatization of the economy and the geography of Mexico: fishermen, masons, *campesinos.* They register the brutal migration of the displaced rural subalterns in the face of a pervasive change in social and economic relations. Furthermore, they mark the loss of a national allegory, and with it the ego-ideal of *papa PRI,* of a nationalist state that will provide work and protect workers. The first interstitial scene alerting the viewer to the fact that there is more to the story than the sexual adventures of two teenage boys occurs in the opening minutes of the film. The boys are stuck in traffic. Julio complains that the traffic jam is probably due to another demonstration by malcontents like his sister. Tenoch objects that they are within their rights to protest, and then immediately notes that "lefty" girls are "hot ass." This jaundiced civic lesson is interrupted by a silence, as the camera cuts to the highway as seen from a rooftop. A man lies dead in the road, surrounded by an ambulance and police, as cars make their way around his body. The voice-over begins, telling us there *were* three protests in the city that day; however, this particular bottleneck was caused by the death of Marcelino Escutia, "a bricklayer, immigrated from Michoacan. Marcelino was hit by a speeding bus. He never used the closest pedestrian overpass because its bad location meant that he would have to walk two extra kilometers to get to the construction site at which he worked . . . It took four days for [his corpse] to be identified and claimed." The scene implies not only that Mexico City is in open revolt against economic and political conditions, but also that it is a city overwhelmed by immigration from its own countryside. Mexico City, the largest city in the world, has an infrastructure that cannot keep pace with its growth, a transportation system whose harried drivers endanger the citizens it is meant to serve. More poignantly, Marcelino Escutia's loneliness, isolation, and anonymity in the industrialized metropolis are underscored by the fact that it takes four days for anyone to claim his body.

The next interstitial scene is one in which the death of immigrants is linked to Luisa's own impending death. When the trio stops to get the radiator repaired, Luisa sees a makeshift altar on which sits a stuffed mouse with her name embroidered on it. Next to the altar sits an old woman. A few scenes later, when the trio is back in the car, the mouse hangs from the rearview mirror. As the car passes a funeral procession, the voice-over informs the reader that the old woman has given Luisa the mouse. Doña Martina has told Luisa that the mouse belonged to her great-grandchild, Luisa Obregon, who, along with her parents, died of heatstroke crossing the Arizona desert, "where they went in search of a better future." Once again, this seemingly tangential scene offers the viewer a very different perspective on those 1.3 million peasants who have lost "jobs in agriculture" during the decade of NAFTA. It registers an effect of NAFTA not captured in the calculus of net job gains or job losses, but in the fatalities of those compelled to migrate, forced to leave their homes and families. And it registers the effects of these deaths on those who remain. Thus, the voice-over continues, "Luisa thought that even in their absence, persons continued to be present, and she wondered how long she would remain alive in the memory of others when she no longer existed." The family is remembered by the ninety-eight-year-old grandmother who obscenely survives even her great-grandchild because of the exigencies of neoliberal reform.

The final interstitial scene I will discuss occurs almost at the end of the film. The trio has finally arrived at a beach when a fisherman's family approaches them by boat. The voice-over tells us that Jesus Campos and his wife, Mabel, "were the fourth generation of a family devoted to fishing. They lived close to the beach, at the *rancheria* San Bernabe. Chuy offered to take them to visit the surrounding beaches the following day. He would charge them 350 pesos for the trip, including food." The scene on the beach is idyllic: Mabel is making *empanadas* on an open fire, one child asleep on her shoulder while the older one plays with Luisa. Julio and Tenoch drink and eat, while Chuy naps under a slap-dash tent. All this takes place against a calm bay, surrounded by green hills. The next day, they take the boat to the mythical bay called *la boca del cielo,* where they play soccer, swim, and eat together, all enjoying the fruits of Chuy's family's unalienated labor. For one moment in the film, all exist together and for each other: subalterns, foreigners, national and regional elites. As the day ends, Luisa asks Tenoch and Julio if they wouldn't like to live like this forever, to which they answer in unison, yes.

This idyllic scene, which is perhaps meant to represent the radical potentiality of a national allegory of identification that never came to pass, is immediately undercut by the voice-over that follows:

> By the end of the year, Chuy and his family would have to abandon their home to make way for an exclusive hotel built on the *ejido* lands of San Bernabe. They will move to the outskirts of Santa Maria Colotepec. Chuy will attempt to give boat tours for tourists, but he will be blocked by a licensed collective of boatmen recently arrived from Acapulco and favored by the local tourism board. Two years later he will end up as a janitor at the hotel. He will never fish again.

Meanwhile, the camera remains focused on Chuy's family in the boat returning from *boca del cielo,* speeding through the bay, against the backdrop of the sea and mountains. Tenoch, Julio, and Luisa, though in the boat, are pointedly not onscreen, because this is not their story. They are protected from it. Mabel plays with her two children, as Chuy steers the boat and plays with the wind. This is all that transpires, and yet it communicates the autonomous domain that afforded Chuy's family some degree of dignity and freedom, and that existed for so long alongside political *mestizaje.* Chuy and Mabel will "survive" the neoliberal economics, which allows the *ejido* to sell their beachfront property to a transnational hotel company. However, in the process, Chuy will lose the means of his production and the freedom and dignity associated with this in the film. Again, this loss is outside the calculus of growth indicators in GDP and FDI, but it is all within the calculus of the shifting positionality of the subaltern in the era of neoliberalism.

The voice-over in classic Hollywood cinema, usually spoken by a film's protagonist, is an "ideological operation" that sutures over the "trauma of castration" present in every film experience. As psychoanalytic film critic Kaja Silverman argues, the viewer is always on the verge of discovering this castration—his or her own lack of mastery over the filmic event—as cuts and edits reveal the artifice of the filmic experience.[34] As an ideological operation, the voice-over disavows this lack, "since it restores the viewer to his or her preordained subject-position and re-secures existing power relations." The voice-over restores mastery by informing the viewer of what is presumably going on inside a protagonist's mind, or, alternately, by filling in important bits of storyline that are implied or cut out during the editing process.

In contrast, the voice-over in *Y tu mamá también* adamantly refuses to resecure power relations. Its repeated and seemingly inconsequential interruptions into the "plot" insists the main action of the film is a minor story when told against the drama of subaltern Mexico in transition. The monotone voice-over, bracketed by silences, jars the viewer into realization: the Oedipal love story is not the real story of the film—or even a "real" story. Meanwhile, the neutralized, documentary style of the interstitial scenes hints at a truth that exists in excess of filmic representation. Nevertheless, the viewer who is denied mastery over the central plot is implicated in the peripheral, interstitial one: for is it not the international bourgeoisie who will visit the hotel where alienated and displaced laborers come to work as janitors, maids, and waiters? The viewer's lack of mastery over the film mirrors the subaltern's lack of mastery over a Mexico unmoored from its national allegory, bereft of revolutionary nationalism, overrun by neoliberalism represented by NAFTA. The interstitial scenes are as fleeting as the viewer's ability to comprehend the enormity of the upheaval in the lives of the subaltern classes. In the end, the film is terribly nostalgic, nostalgic for a Mexico that still exists, as the film itself attests, but is somehow condemned to disappear by neoliberalism. It is even nostalgic for the national allegory it allegorically puts to death. But the film's voice-over, its interstitial scenes, rather elusively reveals what the homoerotic, Oedipal allegory of political *mestizaje* historically tried so desperately to conceal for decades: *el pueblo*, that which remained yet had somehow, before this, stayed away.

Conclusion

The recent increase in the flow of immigrants from the periphery to the center, from rural Mexico to urban United States, underscores a paradox at the heart of liberalism. From its inception, capitalism has had global aspirations, ideally predicated on the perfect mobility of capital, commodities, and labor. Similarly, liberalism, as a system of rights, is ideally predicated on the principal right of freedom of movement granted equally, if historically unevenly, to capital, commodities, *and* individuals. And yet paradoxically, both capitalism and liberalism have sought to realize these universal aspirations through the medium of the particularly bounded nation-states. As Etienne Balibar theorizes in "The Nation Form: History and Ideology," "it is quite impossible to 'deduce' the nation from capitalist relations of production . . . [for] in the history of capitalism, state forms other than the national have emerged and have for a time competed with it before finally being repressed or instrumentalized . . . The nascent capitalist bourgeoisie seems to have 'hesitated' between several forms of hegemony."[35] From a historical perspective, according to Balibar, the local bourgeoisie in the mid-sixteenth century could have sought, and frequently did seek, a form of the state that did not rely on nationalist affect. Nevertheless, capitalism ultimately *did* take the nation as its hegemonic form. And so the question before us is why. Why did capital, under capitalism, take the form of nation as its state when in fact its tendency, even under other forms of production, has always been to migrate, to seek profit in a world economic system?

While it is beyond the scope of this essay to explore this question, it is clear that capitalism produces a nationalist affect that it cannot always control, and that it indeed often seeks to evade.[36] This contrary yet constitutive relationship is made all the more evident in NAFTA's legal regime. In the name of unencumbered capitalist production across the continent, NAFTA established the free flow of capital and goods across territorial boundaries. And yet, although NAFTA might well have considered the topic of migrant labor pools as an inevitable component of free trade, negotiators did not even broach the topic for fear of turning racialized national affect within the United States and Canada permanently against the accord. Indeed, it was the U.S. labor movement that most vehemently opposed the signing of NAFTA on strictly nationalist grounds. While global capitalism and national affect may often find themselves at odds, this does not imply an irresolvable contradiction. Rather, anti-immigration and English-only laws may be seen as the new *global* disciplining techniques of governmentality, imposed by the nation-states but for the purposes of furthering exploitation at a supranational level.[37]

This brings us to a paradox of liberalism as a political system, a paradox as productive as it is limiting. Liberalism, as a political system, reflects the politics of hegemonic states, particularly the United States. It is a system based on rights, principally on property rights, especially on the rights of capital. However, it also provides for the extension of rights to individuals (particularly freedom of movement and the freedom to labor under just conditions), as well as to nations (the freedom to insure the national security of its territorial borders). And while clearly not all entities enjoy the same degree of rights under liberalism, the system is theoretically based on the principle of competing rights balancing each other. Thus, for example, the rights of the nation and its citizen-workers are often pitted against the rights of the immigrant laborers and are mediated by the presumed right of capital to have fair and easy access to both forms of labor. Alternately, the rights of capital are often pitted against the rights of immigrant workers, and mediated by a discourse of human and civil rights negotiated, in large part, by national labor movements. Similarly, a nation's right to secure the borders of its territory are pitted against the rights of immigrants to cross those borders safely and thus mediated by an international discourse of human rights. This is the very heart of the "liberal paradox," a term coined and described by James Hollifield.[38] Liberalism is ensconced in the nationally bounded entities, to which it presumably grants the right of territorial integrity. And yet, it also grants individuals the right to migrate; indeed, it enshrines the principle of movement and provides the legal grounds for protecting it, just as it provides capital this right. Indeed, the migrant worker crossing the Arizona desert "in search of a better future" is arguably the enterprising capitalist subject writ small. We see this paradoxical formation of competing rights enacted everyday in the borderland between the United States and Mexico. The border patrol's increased, militarized presence along the Southwest border drives immigrants into the most lethal terrain under the pretext of national security. There, they will meet with vigilante citizen groups, legally armed and ready to perform "citizens arrests" of these undocumented immigrants. If these immigrants are lucky, they will be turned over to the border patrol unharmed for deportation. If they are even luckier, they will meet members of other citizen groups, armed with only a liberal discourse of human rights, who will provide food, shelter, water, and medical care, so that these immigrants may proceed to enter the legal borderland of undocumented status, where they remain and yet somehow stay away.

Notes

1. *Y tu mamá también*, directed by Alfonso Cuarón, written by Alfonso Cuarón and Carlos Cuarón, was produced in Mexico in 2001; DVD by MGM Home Entertainment, 2002.
2. Though it became illegal to introduce new slaves to Mexico in 1824, the remaining ten thousand enslaved people were not immediately freed. Instead, a legal infrastructure was established for emancipating them over a period of ten to fourteen years. This delaying of emancipation was a response to political pressure from the southeastern states, whose representatives pleaded for time for slave owners in their states to switch labor sources. This infrastructure was rendered mute when in 1829, President Vicente Guerrero, himself of African decent, issued an emancipation proclamation with absolutely no exceptions for the territories.

3. For a discussion of the role of slavery in the Texas War of Independence, please see Martha Menchaca, *Recovering History, Constructing Race: The Indian, Black, and White Roots of Mexican Americans* (Austin: University of Texas Press, 2001), 187–215.
4. For an analysis of President James Polk's provocation of the U.S.–Mexican war in the interest of slaveholding states, please see Howard Zinn, *A People's History of the United States, 1492–Present* (1980; New York: HarperCollins, 1995), 146–66.
5. For an analysis of the Treaty of Guadalupe-Hidalgo and its long-term consequences on racial formations in the southwestern United States, see my article "'Wavering on the Horizon of Social Being': The Treaty of Guadalupe-Hidalgo and Its Racial Character in Américo Paredes's *George Washington Gómez*," *Radical History Review* 89 (spring 2004): 135–61.
6. Daniel T. Griswald, "NAFTA at 10: An Economic and Foreign Policy Success," *Free Trade Bulletin* 1, December 17, 2002, published by the Cato Institute, Center for Trade Policy Studies, Washington, D.C.; http://www.freetrade.org/pubs/FTBs/FTB-001.html (accessed July 19, 2005).
7. Lyuba Zarsky and Kevin P. Gallagher, "NAFTA, Foreign Direct Investment, and Sustainable Industrial Development in Mexico," America's Program Policy Brief, America's Program, Interhemispheric Resource Center, January 28, 2004.
8. Griswald, "NAFTA at 10."
9. Sandra Polaski, "Jobs, Wages, and Household Income," in *NAFTA's Promise and Reality: Lessons from Mexico for the Hemisphere*, ed. John Audley et al. (Washington, D.C.: Carnegie Endowment for International Peace, 2004): 11–38, 16.
10. Polaski, "Jobs, Wages, and Household Income," 15–16.
11. Zarsky and Gallagher, "NAFTA."
12. Polaski, "Jobs, Wages, and Household Income," 17–20.
13. See Neil Harvey, *Rebellion in Chiapas: Rural Reforms, Campesino Radicalism, and the Limits to Salinismo*, Transformation of Rural Mexico Series, No. 5, Ejido Reform Research Project (San Diego: Center for U.S.–Mexican Studies, University of California, San Diego, 1994); also see chap. 6 in my *The Revolutionary Imagination in the Age of Development* (Durham, N.C.: Duke University Press, 2003).
14. Demetrios G. Papademetrious, "The Shifting Expectations of Free Trade and Migration," in *NAFTA's Promise and Reality*, ed. Audley et al., 39–61, 52.
15. Please see Phillip Martin, *Trade and Migration: NAFTA and Agriculture* (Washington, DC: Institute for International Economics, 1993).
16. Papademetrious, "The Shifting Expectations," 48–49.
17. Ibid., 51.
18. Office of Policy and Planning, *Estimates of the Unauthorized Immigrant Population Residing in the U.S.: 1990 to 2000* (Washington, D. C.: Bureau of Citizenship and Immigration Services, 2003), cited in Papademetrious, "The Shifting Expectations," 58, n. 20.
19. Nina Bernstein, "Record Immigration Changing New York Neighborhoods," *New York Times*, late edition, January 25, 2005, B1.
20. Thomas Pynchon, *The Crying of Lot 49* (New York: Harper and Row, 1966), 20.
21. In their article "Transnational Cinema and the Mexican State in Alfonso Cuarón's *Y tu mamá también*," Hester Baer and Ryan Long produce a remarkably similar analysis of the film as principally concerned with the allegory of the Mexican national-developmentalist state, but they come to very different conclusions. Baer and Long read the film as nostalgic for the national-developmentalist state, arguing that the male voice-over and social-realist interstitial scenes impose an authoritarian closure on the liberatory potential of the homoerotic and feminine sexuality that is the concern of the central plot: "Through its employment of national allegory, the film suggests, in a teleological, national-developmentalist mode, that allegedly more important work, like social equality and national cohesion (though utterly patriarchal), must be completed before any attention is given to 'minority' concerns like gender equality . . . the film undoes anything liberatory it hints at . . . [it] contains potentially emancipatory meanings through its deployment of narrative closure and the omniscient, authoritative male voice-over" (163). As my argument will make evident, I read the film as invoking Mexican national allegory in order to critique it profoundly and to expose the homoerotics at the heart of revolutionary masculinity. Furthermore, rather than seeing the male voice-over as necessarily misogynist, and interstitial scenes as undemocratically "trumping" the more libidinal (and therefore more emancipatory?) central romantic plot line (an approach that privileges the identity politics of the United States), I argue the film insists on the interdependence of emancipatory narratives in a thoroughly postrevolutionary way. *South Central Review* 21.3 (fall 2004): 150–68.

22. Sigmund Freud, "The Ego and the Id," in *On Metapsychology: The Theory of Psychoanalysis*, ed. Angela Richards, vol. 11 in *The Penguin Freud Library* (1923; New York: Penguin, 1961), 350–408, 371.
23. Ibid., 374.
24. Ibid., 372.
25. Ibid., 371.
26. Ibid., 372.
27. Ibid., 373.
28. Baer and Long also read Luisa as an allegorical stand-in for imperial Spain, casting her as a "vampiric Spanish colonizer, sucking dry the youth of Mexico." From this perspective, she "inflames" Tenoch and Julio's jealousy and "orchestrates" the demise of their friendship ("Transnational Cinema and the Mexican State," 163, 162). I would suggest that Baer and Long not only exaggerate Luisa's role in the demise of the boys' friendship, but also that they, like Julio and Tenoch, misinterpret her positionality in the film. Although Luisa functions as an object of Oedipal desire and as an identificatory ego-ideal, this ideal is a projection of the boys' own desire for *mama España*. The voice-over interruptions about Luisa repeatedly inform the viewer of what Tenoch and Julio ignore: that as a child Luisa was rendered impoverished by her parent's death, utterly dependent upon a tyrannical *franquista* aunt. She marries Jano in part to escape this fate, but his intellectual friends frequently humiliate her for her lack of schooling. Thus, it becomes evident to the viewer that the privilege the boys associate with Luisa's Spanish heritage does not pertain to Luisa specifically. Instead, she has turned to a member of Tenoch's elite Mexican family for a conditional respite from her own poverty and misery. That the boys' misconstrue Luisa's positionality underscores the naiveté of their Oedipal nostalgia, of a desire for return to a (post)colonial fantasy of mestizo liberation in the era of an immanent neoliberalism. Rather than cast Luisa as a mistress-manipulator, as Baer and Long do, the voice-overs reveal another side of Spain, a more subaltern side. Luisa's function as *mama España* occludes her subaltern positionality for Julio and Tenoch; however, it should not occlude it for the critic. Chicana literary scholar Luz Calvo, in comments on an earlier draft of this essay, has instead suggested that we read Luisa as representing a sexual *mestizaje* in her own right, as she repeatedly inhabits the position of polymorphous desire. Not only does she enjoy anal penetration, but she enjoys penetrating her husband. Thus, as Calvo brilliantly suggests, Luisa offers the boys a more emancipatory sexuality, their rejection of which leads to their own dejection. It is Luisa, after all, who remains behind in "heaven's mouth" while the boys return to their repressive heteronormativity.
29. See chap. 6 of my *The Revolutionary Imagination* for the detrimental consequences of *mestizaje* for indigenous peoples.
30. Here I am specifically referring to the PRI's nationalization of U.S.–owned oil interests in the 1930s and 1940s, as well as the nationalization of foreign-held plantations.
31. Please see chap. 6 of my *The Revolutionary Imagination.*
32. Ranajit Guha, "On Some Aspects of the Historiography of Colonial India," in *Selected Subaltern Studies*, ed. Ranajit Guha and Gayatri Spivak (New York: Oxford University Press, 1988), 37–44, 44; emphasis his.
33. Ibid., 40.
34. "The trauma of castration occurs whenever the viewer recognizes his or her discursive impotence, understands that he or she is 'only authorized to see what happens to be in the axis of the glance of another spectator [the camera], who is ghostly or absent.'" Kaja Silverman, *The Acoustic Mirror: The Female Voice in Psychoanalysis and Cinema* (Bloomington: Indiana University Press, 1988), 12.
35. Etienne Balibar and Immanuel Wallerstein, eds., *Race, Nation, Class: Ambiguous Identities* (London: Verso, 1991): 86–106.
36. Please see David Kazanjian, *The Colonizing Trick: National Culture and Imperial Citizenship in Early America* (Minneapolis: University of Minnesota Press, 2003). In it Kazanjian theorizes that the capitalist mode of production brings into being a modern logic of differentiation and abstraction, a logic that then supplements the formation of racialized citizens even as it also supplements a logic of equality.
37. Please see Leo Chavez, "Immigration Reform and Nativism: The Nationalist Response to the Transnationalist Challenge," in *Immigrants Out!: The New Nativism and the Anti-Immigrant Impulse in the United States*, ed. Juan F. Perea (New York: New York University Press, 1997), 61–77; and Saskia Sassen, *Losing Control? Sovereignty in the Age of Globalization* (New York: Columbia University Press, 1996).

38. James F. Hollifield, *Immigrants, Markets, and States* (Cambridge, Mass.: Harvard University Press, 1992). I am indeed elaborating on his conception of the "liberal paradox" as discussed by him in relation to the rights of immigrants under democratic systems. See particularly "Immigration and the Principles of Liberal Democracy," 214–34.

The Edges of Empire and the Limits of Sovereignty: American Guano Islands

Christina Duffy Burnett

One thousand miles south of Honolulu lies Palmyra, an atoll consisting of about fifty islets "generally . . . uninhabited except for a caretaker."[1] Covering an area of six square miles (including water), the fertile Palmyra is "blessed with a propitious climate . . ., covered with coconut palm, puhala, and koa trees," and "surrounded by a deep, reef-encircled lagoon that offered mariners safe anchorage."[2] Blessed in another, more unusual way, Palmyra also enjoys the curious distinction of being the only American jurisdiction outside the fifty states and the District of Columbia to which the U.S. Constitution applies "in its entirety."[3] This is because Palmyra possesses a unique legal status within the framework of U.S. law: it is the only "incorporated" territory of the United States.[4] By dint of this exalted status, little Palmyra enjoys more comprehensive constitutional protections than any other nonstate area claimed by the United States, including its five populated, "unincorporated" territories, home to four million American citizens.[5] How did a lonely little atoll in the middle of the Pacific Ocean come to occupy such a curious constitutional position? How did such a geographically marginal place come to reside in the constitutional heartland? Unfolding the answers to these questions will open to view forgotten dimensions of American expansion in the nineteenth century, and reveal how legal borderlands served as the proving ground for the principles of U.S. imperialism.

New York businessman Alfred Grenville Benson staked a claim to Palmyra in 1859 on behalf of the United States Guano Company, under the Guano Islands Act of 1856.[6] A federal statute that remains on the books, the act empowers American citizens to take possession of uninhabited, unclaimed islets containing deposits of guano (dried bird and bat droppings), and confers upon the executive discretion to treat the islets in question as "appertaining to the United States." In the words of the first section of the act,

> Whenever any citizen of the United States discovers a deposit of guano on any island, rock, or key, not within the lawful jurisdiction of any other government, and not occupied by the citizens of any other government, and takes peaceable possession thereof, and occupies the same, such island, rock, or key may, at the discretion of the President, be considered as appertaining to the United States.[7]

The aim of the Guano Islands Act was simple. As Secretary of State Lewis Cass explained, the act would, it was hoped, supply Americans with affordable guano, nothing more.[8] In fact, the act even made clear that the United States need not keep a guano island once the guano was gone: in the words of the act's final section, "nothing in this chapter contained shall be construed as obliging the United States to retain possession of the islands, rocks, or keys after the guano shall have been removed from the same."[9]

It turned out later that Palmyra contained no guano after all, and that neither Benson's company, nor a second company that claimed the island later that year, had ever even occupied the place, whether to remove its alleged guano "or in fact for any other purpose."[10] Hawaiians did occupy the atoll in 1860; the Kingdom of Hawai'i claimed it in 1862; and the United States officially annexed it in 1898, a year more often associated with American overseas territorial expansion than the 1850s.[11]

Guano or no guano, one hardly expects the Constitution to follow the flag to an uninhabited atoll. Yet Palmyra has ended up as a special sort of place, "incorporated" into the United States, and thus into the core of U.S. constitutional jurisprudence. The Supreme Court long ago held that incorporated territories are "part of" the United States, whereas unincorporated territories merely "belong to" the United States.[12] Is uninhabited Palmyra, then, part of the United States, while U.S. territories inhabited by American citizens merely belong to it? Students of the U.S. territories generally agree that an important distinction between incorporated and unincorporated territories is that the former will eventually become states of the Union, while the latter may or may not. Is Palmyra on its way to becoming the fifty-first state? Statehood is probably not in the cards for Palmyra, but the answer to the first question—whether Palmyra is part of the United States—turns out to be more elusive, and, finally, more significant.

Historians, Guano Islands, and Imperialism

This essay offers a legal history of the relationship between American-claimed guano islands and the United States. Examining American efforts to take control over guano islands in the nineteenth century, and to make sense of their legal status, I use the little-known story of the guano islands to shed light on other episodes of American territorial expansion and on the relationship between territorial expansion and imperialism in the United States. Specifically, I argue that the guano islands help us to understand that American imperialism is ultimately about the management of national boundaries as much as it is about their expansion.

We tend to associate imperialism with the acquisition of territory, the projection of power, and the imposition of sovereignty. The emphasis tends to be on expansion—more territory, plenary power, extended sovereignty. Yet American imperialism has also consisted of efforts to impose limits on expansion: to draw lines around what counts as properly "national" territory (as opposed to, say, territory "belonging" to the nation but not fully part of it), and even to circumscribe national power, for purposes of reducing the number of contexts in which the government must take up the responsibilities that come with such power. In the case of guano islands, as I show here, the United States acquired territory and projected American power, to be sure, but all the while U.S. officials insisted on disclaiming sovereignty, and on denying that such places had become part of the "territorial domain" of the United States. Here, I try to understand this phenomenon, and its troubling legacy.

Historians of the guano mania that began in the 1840s have attempted to characterize the episode as an important and underappreciated early chapter in the story of American imperialism.[13] They have pointed out, for instance, that it was the renowned expansionist William Henry Seward who introduced the bill that became the Guano Islands Act, while he was still in the Senate.[14] Later, "as Johnson's Secretary of State," writes one scholar, "expansionistic Seward would be the chief architect of the purchase of Alaska from Russia in 1867, an action often derided by contemporary critics as 'Seward's Icebox.'" By these lights, it has been playfully suggested, the guano islands might be thought of as "Seward's Outhouse."[15] By the time of the war with Spain in 1898, the United States and its citizens had already claimed scores of guano islands, located in the Caribbean, Pacific, Atlantic, and even Indian oceans.[16]

Citing this activity, scholars have invoked the guano islands to refute a familiar narrative about American imperialism, according to which the United States was only briefly (between about 1898 and 1912) a truly "imperialist" power. But even as this and other work has challenged the "aberration thesis" and its variants, the era on the watershed of the nineteenth and twentieth centuries continues to be characterized as the age of imperialism in U.S. history, and these years still figure prominently as the period in which the United States made its first foray into overseas territorial expansion. Even Donald

Meinig, in his magisterial geographical history of the United States, takes note of only a single earlier instance of such expansion: Midway, claimed by the United States in 1867 (though not as a guano island).[17] "In spite of Seward's tireless and skillful efforts," writes Meinig of Midway and Alaska, "this tiny speck in the vast ocean and that huge but remote and marginal expanse in the boreal extremities of the continent were the only additions to U.S. territory at this time."[18] Yet Seward's own efforts yielded the Guano Islands Act and, with it, the acquisition of not just one but numerous (more than seventy) tiny specks.

Yet whether one may properly refer to guano islands (or to Midway, for that matter) as "additions to U.S. territory" has never been entirely clear (indeed, by omitting mention of them, Meinig may well have been taking sides on the matter). For this reason, what is needed is not another effort to insist that American imperialism had its origins before 1898, but rather a better understanding of the relationship between American claims to these seemingly insignificant places and other episodes of American territorial expansion. Looked at in this way, significant similarities can certainly be discerned between pre-1898 American claims to places beyond the physical borders of the continent and turn-of-the-century U.S. activities in the Caribbean and Pacific, but equally significant differences also emerge. It is with this combination of similarities and differences, continuities and discontinuities, that I will be concerned in the pages that follow. By examining the ambiguous legal status of the guano islands in the second half of the nineteenth century, I will both show their peculiar place within the American legal system and shed light on later episodes of U.S. global projecting. In the process, it will become clear that the guano islands provide an important example of the wide range of fine formal and legal distinctions—the practices of boundary management—that have attended American territorial expansion.

Guano Mania and the Lure of the Islands

American farmers learned of the powerful fertilizing properties of guano in the mid-nineteenth century. As word of guano's agricultural uses spread across rural North America in the 1840s (several years after it had in England, and several centuries after present-day Peru), "the *American Agriculturalist* feared there would be 'a perfect mania' for guano. Within three years this prediction became a reality."[19] The first shipment of guano arrived in the United States in 1844 and consisted of 700 tons of the stuff; a decade later, guano imports into the United States peaked at 175,849 tons.[20] The price had peaked a few years earlier, in 1850, at about $76 per pound, later stabilizing at about $50.[21]

The farmers who had anticipated the arrival of guano soon found cause for complaint—not because guano did not work its magic, but because of the high price and short supply. They blamed Peru, which had a monopoly over the principal source of guano at the time: the Chinca Islands off the Peruvian coast.[22] And they translated their frustrations into an aggressive lobbying campaign, "besieging their representatives in Washington to do something, anything, to assist them in acquiring guano" at a better price.[23]

In the meantime, the United States found itself embroiled in several diplomatic disputes involving guano islands that had been claimed by enterprising American "discoverers" unwilling to wait for government action. The incident that finally triggered legislation centered on the Caribbean island of Aves, an "isolated, uninhabited dot" lying about 350 miles off the coast of Venezuela.[24] In 1854, Americans landed on Aves and "attempted to claim Aves Island as United States territory. To buttress that assertion, they occupied the island, erected a 'liberty pole' (their ballast) on the island, and even transported some 'American females' there."[25] They left temporarily, and when they returned with guano mining equipment, they found the employees of a rival British firm already engaged in the enterprise. At first, the two groups divided up the island between them and went about their business. But Venezuela, which considered the island part of its territory, was unimpressed both by the rituals of possession that had been performed on Aves and by the actual occupation of the place. A Venezuelan warship arrived several months later and expelled everyone. This led to a dispute that would last for decades, even after Aves Island's guano turned out to be "comparatively worthless as a manure."[26]

Concluding that the lack of backing from the U.S. government had contributed to their failure successfully to assert control over Aves, the American firm, led by Boston merchant Philo S. Shelton, submitted a memorial to Congress in the spring of 1856 concerning the disputed claims to Aves.[27] Theirs was not the first petition to Congress relating to guano, but this one also included a proposed bill, which "would have automatically extended United States sovereignty over any unclaimed guano island which was discovered and occupied by American citizens unless either the president or the Congress expressly declined to do so, and authorized the president to use the naval forces of the United States to protect such claims."[28] The basic aim of the proposed bill—to secure a cheap supply of guano for American farmers—would be preserved in the Guano Islands Act passed later that year, but the wording, along with the implications respecting U.S. sovereignty over guano islands, would change.

Figure 1.
"Loading Cars with Guano at the Great Heap, Chinca Islands," photograph by Alexander Gardner circa 1865. Reproduced courtesy of The Rare Book and Special Collections Division, The Library of Congress.

The Guano Islands Act

Shelton's proposal was one of several bills introduced in the wake of the Aves affair. Early drafts contained references to the United States' "sovereignty," "territory," and "territorial domain," but these words would disappear from the final version. The word "appertaining," however, survived. It initially appeared in Senator Seward's first attempt at legislative language, Senate Resolution 15, dated April 16, 1856.[29] Seward's resolution provided that the discoverer of a guano island would acquire property rights in the guano, and that these property rights would include "the privilege of entering upon and occupying the grounds and waters *appertaining* to such islands, for the purpose of preserving, disposing of, and taking away the said deposits and productions."[30] Significantly, the word "appertaining" would be used in the final version in an entirely different manner—not with reference to "the grounds and waters appertaining to such islands," but rather with reference to the islands themselves, which were described as "appertaining" to the United States.

The debate on the final version (Senate Bill 339) took place on July 23–24, 1856.[31] Most of the discussion concerned guano prices, a focus that reflected the fundamental concern that had given rise to calls for legislation in the first place. Some of the discussion, however, addressed the broader implications of the bill in the context of territorial expansion. Early on, Senator Clayton defended Seward's bill in part by noting that nothing in it would require the government "to assume other duties than those which are devolved on it by the general principles of international law. I take it for granted that the Government is bound to take proper care of these discoveries." Senator Hale made the same observation, but in order to question the bill, not to defend it. Hale wondered why there should be a "special rule laid down in relation to guano islands" when under the law of nations the government had a duty to protect its citizens' discoveries.[32] This elicited a clarification from Clayton, who denied "that the Government is bound to protect its citizens in the discovery of an island of any description, or territory anywhere. . . . A different doctrine," he added, "would involve us in a great deal of trouble."[33] In other words, in his view the purpose of the act was not to authorize American control of guano islands, but rather to limit the circumstances in which the United States would exert such control.

Senator Toombs, however, shared Hale's concern, and remained unconvinced of the need for the legislation. The bill seemed to him to imply that title to an island might vest in an individual discoverer rather than in the United States; but this could not be so, under the law of nations, so why the need for this legislation? "By the universal law of nations," he insisted, a discovery "belongs to the nation under whose flag it was discovered. That has been the rule of public law always."[34]

Seward then intervened to explain his bill. He began by reminding his colleagues of the importance of guano as a fertilizer, and of the recent events that had brought about the need for legislation to facilitate the purchase of guano by American farmers. He explained that the bill was simply "necessary for the protection of our own citizens" against the Peruvian monopoly. He then addressed the broader implications of the legislation:

> If there was any such thing as a prospect of dominion to be secured to the United States resulting from the discovery and occupation of these islands, it would be a subject for some jealousy, but the bill is framed so as to embrace only these more ragged rocks, which are covered with this deposit in the ocean, which are fit for no dominion, or for anything else, except for the guano which is found upon them. There is no temptation whatever for the abuse of authority by the establishment of colonies or any other form of permanent occupation there.[35]

Driving home the point, he referred to the final section of the bill, the abandonment clause, which had not been present in earlier drafts. According to that clause, "nothing in this act contained shall be construed [as] obligatory on the United States to retain possession of the islands, rocks, or keys, as aforesaid, after the guano shall have been removed from the same."[36] Thus, Seward reassured his colleagues, "the bill itself . . . provides whenever the Guano should be exhausted, or cease to be found on the islands, they should revert and relapse out of the jurisdiction of the United States."[37]

Although Toombs insisted that he still could not understand why the arrival of a "public armed vessel of the United States" could not render title "as perfect . . . as if you passed a hundred acts of Congress," the discussion turned from there to other concerns, such as the quality of guano and, again, its price.[38] Before the day's discussion of guano concluded, Senator Mason introduced an amendment replacing the phrase "or territory" with "or rocks or keys," which passed without debate.[39] The next day's topics ranged from the incentives created by the bill, to the difficulty of procuring labor to mine guano on the islands in question, to (once again) price. But the debate did not last much longer, and, aside from a passing comment by Senator Mason referring to the possibility that these islands might "become a part of the United States," the discussion that day did not address the formal legal relationship between guano islands and the United States. The Senate proceeded to pass the bill and forward it to the House. There, it passed without any discussion at all, and, on August 18, 1856, President Franklin Pierce signed "an act to authorize protection to be given to citizens of the United States who may discover deposits of guano" into law.[40]

"What the Guano Act Really Did Mean"

An exhaustive analysis of the legal status of American guano islands prepared by the State Department in 1931–1932 summed up an eighty-year history of efforts to make sense of the Guano Islands Act with the remark that "the only conclusion which can fairly be drawn from [these efforts] is that no one knew what the Guano Act really did mean."[41] In particular, no one understood precisely what it meant to say that a guano island could "be considered as appertaining" to the United States. As the same analysis put it, the act's "use of the word 'appertain' is deft, since it carries no exact meaning and lends itself readily to circumstances and the wishes of those using it."[42] And, indeed, interpretations abounded. These efforts ranged from the understandings reflected in the actions of discoverers (who performed, or claimed to have performed, ceremonies of discovery, possession, and occupation in the hope of securing protection under the act) to official analyses of the legislation (such as the Supreme Court's effort to put the issue to rest in *Jones v. United States*).

The earliest official interpretation of the act came from Attorney General Jeremiah S. Black, in an 1857 opinion setting forth the criteria that must be established before the president would have the discretion to consider a guano island as "appertaining" to the United States.[43] Black explained that "in order to consider an island as appertaining to the United States, and protect it accordingly," seven "facts must be established." They included: (1) a deposit of guano had been discovered on it by an American citizen; (2) the island was not within the lawful jurisdiction of any other government; (3) the island was not occupied by the citizens of any other government; (4) the discoverer had taken and kept peaceable possession thereof in the name of the United States; (5) the discoverer had given notice of these facts as soon as practicable to the State Department, on his oath; (6) the notice had been accompanied by a description of the island, its latitude and longitude; and (7) satisfactory evidence had been furnished to the State Department showing that the island had not been taken out of the possession of any other government or people.[44] The opinion pointedly omitted any mention of U.S. "sovereignty" over the islands.

Despite the specificity of these requirements, what followed was not exactly an orderly process of guano island acquisition involving discovery, occupation, the transmission of information and a bond, and a resulting formal declaration of "appurtenance." Instead, something more akin to bureaucratic chaos ensued. While more than seventy islands were declared "appertaining" to the United States within the next thirty years (and even more were claimed by individual discoverers), the proliferation of claims ranged widely in their credibility, and elicited a similarly wide range of responses from the government, from the sought-after declaration (issued by the State Department on behalf of the president), to contradictory replies, to complete silence.[45] Some claimants who seemed to have fulfilled all of the requirements set forth in the act failed to secure declarations; others received declarations almost immediately on the basis of similar evidence; still others succeeded in obtaining declarations on the basis of shoddier evidence; in some cases, even nonexistent islands made the list of "appurtenances."[46] Moreover, at one point the State Department stopped issuing declarations altogether and began simply filing the documentation submitted by claimants. For some reason, however, it did not make this new policy public, consequently failing to stem the tide of applications.

Guano entrepreneurs responded to the act by engaging in rituals designed to convey that a taking of "peaceable possession . . . in the name of the United

States" had occurred, reminiscent of the acts performed on Aves Island in the year prior to the Guano Islands Act (minus the "American females"). Generally these involved raising an American flag, putting up a sign bearing some sort of inscription relating to the discovery, and building a makeshift structure that would communicate to all comers that someone had occupied the island, or would soon return to do so. These rituals, however, did not always succeed in establishing peaceable possession, and disputes arose respecting certain claims. In response to one of these, Black further elaborated on the requirements of the act.[47] An act of possession required actual occupation, not merely symbolic gestures. The mere sighting of an atoll would not do. Moreover, "empty ceremonies . . . could vest no jurisdiction." Only a claim based on "actual, continuous, exclusive possession" could prevail under the act.[48] Yet despite Black's efforts to clarify the legislation, its meaning and implications would remain unclear and contested.

Navassa (U.S.A.)

The events that brought the question of the legal status of guano islands to the Supreme Court took place on the Caribbean island of Navassa. Navassa was declared "appertaining" to the United States by the State Department—over the strenuous objections of Haiti, which considered neighboring Navassa part of Haitian territory—on December 8, 1859.[49] Thirty years later, a group of black workers who had been brought to the island to mine guano by the Navassa Phosphate Company would stage what became known as the Navassa island riot, rebelling against the "horrendous cruelty and mistreatment" imposed upon them by twelve white supervisors (so-called officers) and killing five of them.

Working conditions on Navassa, as on other guano islands, were grotesque. Accounts of the slavelike labor arrangements imposed in the Peruvian Chinca Islands on Chinese workers (who were brought there by force and by fraud) describe workers committing suicide rather than go on with the hellish work of mining guano.[50] As for Navassa, an American sailor on the U.S.S. *Galena*, which landed on Navassa several days after the riot, said that he could "hardly understand how human beings . . . [could] live in such a place and not go mad."[51] Mining dried guano, with its overpowering ammoniac stench, under a hot tropical sun was hard enough. The Navassa Phosphate Company and its "officers" made it even harder by committing innumerable abuses against the nearly 140 workers in their employ: forcing them to work for long hours under needlessly dangerous conditions, docking their pay on days they were injured (as well as charging them twice their daily wage for board on such days), gouging them with wildly inflated prices at the "company store," and punishing insubordination by placing men in "the stocks," a "barbarous instrument" in which a man was cuffed by his hands and feet, his body stretched taut. Anyone who dared to complain would forfeit all accrued pay.[52]

Such were the working conditions on Navassa when a group of workers decided they had had enough. On September 14, 1889, a worker by the name of John Ross emerged from a phosphate hole in which he had been digging to explain to his supervisor, Charles W. Roby, that the phosphate was too hard to remove manually and would have to be blasted out of the hole. Roby responded by kicking Ross back into the phosphate hole, prompting another worker, Edmund Francis, to swing a metal bar at Roby's head, knocking him unconscious.

Thus began the Navassa Island riot. Roby did not die, but as a group of workers brought his bloodied and inert body down the hill toward the company settlement, word of the incident spread, and a number of workers joined in, while the rest simply stopped working and waited. The rioting workers squared off against the company's officers, surrounding the supervisor's house where their bosses had barricaded themselves, and demanded an end to their inhumane treatment. A series of skirmishes left four white supervisors dead; a fifth would soon die of his injuries.

But by the end of the day "the violence was spent."[53] A doctor on the island arranged to send word to a British brig lying off Navassa's Lulu Bay that an American vessel should be sent to retrieve the men and take everyone back to the mainland. In the end, the H.M.S. *Forward* took some of the men to Kingston, Jamaica, whence they were sent back to Baltimore, Maryland. On October 4, the *Galena* arrived. The *Galena*'s Rear Admiral Bancroft Gherardi assigned a five-person board to investigate the incident and, after taking names and stories, settled on six ringleaders, whom he arrested and took on board, along with others he detained as witnesses. By then the company's brigs *Romance* and *Alice* had arrived as well; the remaining men were taken on board, and all headed to Baltimore.

As the *Galena* approached the mainland, Baltimore U.S. attorney Thomas G. Hayes intercepted the vessel off the coast of Virginia, and he too "practically held court on the ship."[54] He identified eighteen men as the instigators, and on November 6 a federal grand jury agreed, issuing five indictments. These charged workers George S. Key, Caesar Fisher, Henry Jones, Edward Smith, Charles H. Davis, Stephen Peters, and Charles H. Smith with the murders of the five supervisors on Navassa, and the rest as accessories. In five separate trials over the next three months, juries convicted George Key, Edward Smith, and Henry Jones of murder, fourteen others of manslaughter, and twenty-three others of rioting.[55] Key, Smith, and Jones were sentenced to death, and appealed their convictions to the Supreme Court.

Jones v. United States

The fourteen-page brief on behalf of the defendants in *Jones v. United States* did not contest the facts, focusing rather on legal arguments.[56] One of these, resting on both international and constitutional law, consisted of the claim that the "peculiar species of discovery" contemplated by the Guano Islands Act could find no sanction in international law—nor consequently, under the Constitution (and that, as a result, Congress did not have the power to create federal court jurisdiction for crimes committed on guano islands, as it had done in the act).[57] Title, went the argument, is acquired by "occupancy, discovery, conquest, or cession."[58] Citing Wheaton's *International Law,* the defendants noted that title to Navassa had not been obtained either by occupancy or by conquest or by cession.[59] Not all of these claims were equally strong: without question, Haiti had not ceded Navassa to the United States, and arguably, the United States had not conquered Navassa; but the agents and employees of the Navassa Phosphate Company had certainly been present on the island, mining its guano, and yet the brief did not elaborate on why title by occupancy should not apply in this case.

In any event, ruling out these three options left only discovery. The brief went on to assert that the United States had sought to acquire title to Navassa "by a peculiar species of discovery described in the statute" but not contemplated by international law. A claim to title by the right of discovery, went the argument, "means a title that is *permanent, fixed,* and *indefeasible.*"[60] Yet the type of discovery set forth in the act did not vest permanent title, because all of the act's provisions "relating to the rights of things and the rights of persons" would terminate once the guano had been removed, under the abandonment provision (section 1419).[61] As a result, the question was whether the Constitution authorized "Congress, which represents the Federation of States[,] to exercise the jurisdiction which is sought to be maintained in this cause by reason of the discovery of [Navassa] . . . [and to legislate] upon the theory of the discovery to which the Act refers, whatever may be said with reference to the power of Congress to deal with any new territory acquired by discovery, conquest, occupancy, or cession."[62] In other words, the brief conceded the power of Congress to legislate over territory acquired in all of the ways recognized under international law (discovery, conquest, occupancy, or cession), but called into question the power of Congress to legislate over territory acquired in a different manner—namely, by a so-called discovery conferring merely *temporary* possession and, therefore, not conveying title at all, under international or constitutional law. Territory taken temporarily, the defendants insisted, cannot form "part of the territorial domain of the United States."[63]

Referring to the Territory Clause of the U.S. Constitution, the brief acknowledged that "the Constitution empowers Congress to make rules respecting territory belonging to the United States." But because the United States had not in fact attempted to acquire title to Navassa (since it did not intend to claim Navassa permanently), the island "[did] not belong to the United States."[64] Distinguishing other nonstate territories addressed in the Constitution from the guano islands subject to the Guano Islands Act, the brief further noted that "dock-yards, navy-yards, arsenal grounds, territories and districts over which the United States exercises its jurisdiction, are claimed under indisputable, indefeasible title."[65] The brief thus drew a boundary around the United States by including only those places permanently within it.

The defending attorneys concluded this argument by taking aim at the word "appertain" and denying that it meant anything at all. "The Act provides that after this peculiar discovery and certain other formalities, the island . . . shall be deemed to 'appertain to' the United States," the brief observed, then asked: "It is respectfully inquired what is the significance or meaning of this desultory phrase, 'appertain to'?" The term's lack of significance was, of course, its great advantage. This would become all the more evident when the Court deployed the term a little more than a decade later to explain the status of the Philippines, Puerto Rico, and Guam in the aftermath of the Spanish-American War. As I show in the next section, in that context, the Court would confirm that territories "appertaining" to the United States are indeed territories "belonging to," but not a "part of," the United States, making them part of the "territorial domain" of the United States but not of the "United States" proper. And it would turn out that the distinction between territories merely belonging to the United States and territories forming a part of the United States mirrored a distinction between territories temporarily (albeit indefinitely) subject to U.S. sovereignty and those bound in permanent union to the United States.[66]

For the time being, however, the novel idea that territory could "appertain to" the nation was only beginning to take shape, and, in their briefs in *Jones*, the government's lawyers focused on more traditional terminology associated with the acquisition of territory under international law. The government's response to the defending attorneys' argument that the United States could establish title to territory only by claiming it permanently began with the dismissive observation that the argument was "not easy to understand."[67] International law, the brief continued, clearly establishes "national title to territory, whether island or continental, by discovery and occupation, or by occupation alone."[68] The assertion did not meet the defendants' argument directly, for their brief had not denied the validity under international law of the acquisition of title by discovery and occupation, but rather had argued that the guano legislation ignored the essential criterion under international law for establishing title pursuant to discovery: namely, permanence.

As for whether the abandonment provision of the legislation (section 1419) was inconsistent with permanent title (and therefore with the criteria for territorial acquisition under international law), the government brief argued that title resides in the government, not in the individual.[69] This distinction between title in the United States and the rights of individuals under the act implicitly responded to the defendants' arguments by suggesting that the temporary nature of individual title did not mean that U.S. title was temporary as well. But the government was not altogether clear about what all of this meant with regard to Navassa's relationship to the United States.

The brief explained suggestively that Navassa, "being thus in the possession of this Government, it must be for the time being regarded as part of the national domain."[70] Here the brief referred not to the "territorial domain of the United States" but to a somewhat more nebulous "national domain"—although it then equated Navassa with territory subject to the Territory Clause, noting that if it was proper for the United States "by discovery and possession to acquire supremacy over this island," then it was proper "for Congress to legislate with reference to the jurisdiction of the courts over the island as with reference to the jurisdiction of the courts over Alaska or any other purchased territory."[71] The assertion of federal "supremacy" over Navassa gestured toward the supremacy clause, which establishes the supremacy of federal law as "the law of the land," but if anything the government was trying here to tease apart the "land" in that clause and the broader scope of American "national" power.

The next assertion took this effort one step further. Without question, "Congress has the power to legislate co-extensive with the national domain," the brief asserted—and "not only co-extensive with the national domain, but co-extensive with the national authority, according to maritime and international law."[72] According to the reasoning in the government's brief, then, Navassa belonged in all three categories: within the national domain, within the maritime domain, and within the realm beyond the national domain (where national authority was projected).

The Court's unanimous decision in *Jones* took sides with the government, holding that the Guano Islands Act was "constitutional and valid" and "that the Island of Navassa must be considered as appertaining to the United States."[73] The Court responded to the defendants' attempt to distinguish between (full) permanent title and (inchoate) impermanent title in two ways: first, it observed that the law of nations encompassed the sort of discovery contemplated by the Guano Islands Act; and, second, it pointed out that the determination of sovereignty over a territory in any case belongs to the political, not judicial, branches.

"By the law of nations," the Court explained, "dominion of new territory may be acquired by discovery and occupation, as well as by cession or conquest," and the nation to which such territory belongs "may exercise such jurisdiction and for such period as it sees fit over territory so acquired."[74] Citing several international law treatises, the Court added that "this principle affords ample warrant for the legislation of Congress concerning guano islands."[75] Then, the Court reasoned that "who is the sovereign, de jure or de facto, of a territory is not a judicial, but a political question, the determination of which by the legislative and executive departments of any government conclusively binds the judges, as well as all other officers, citizens, and subjects of that government."[76] In the pages that followed, the Court discussed the evidence of discovery, possession, and occupation on Navassa in detail—not in order to draw a conclusion regarding sovereignty, but to determine whether the political branches had drawn their own conclusion. Finding convincing evidence that they had done so, the Court accepted it.

The *Jones* opinion used variants of the term "appertain" repeatedly to refer to the relationship between Navassa and the United States, though without shedding any additional light on what it meant: the Court reasoned that the law of nations supported the Guano Islands Act, which used the word "appertaining"; that the government had taken the steps required by the act to establish "appurtenance"; and that Navassa therefore "appertained' to the United States. The opinion also referred to Navassa as a "possession" of the United States, explained that the island was subject to the "exclusive jurisdiction" of the United States (and described "the territorial extent of the jurisdiction exercised by the government" as encompassing the island), discussed certain preconditions to the "annexation" of a guano island (and concluded that annexation had occurred here), and suggested that the United States had extended "sovereignty" over Navassa (when it deferred to the political branches' determination of "who is the sovereign, de jure or de facto, of a territory").[77]

In the end, however, the Court did not settle either of the two principal questions before it: the precise legal status of guano islands and the fate of the defendants. The Court affirmed the defendants' death sentence, but they were spared execution when the news emerged, not long thereafter, that the Navassa Phosphate Company had refused return passage to a worker who had completed the term of his contract, leaving him stranded on the island.[78] Aware that the riot, the abuses that caused it, and the trial that followed had already elicited nationwide press attention, an appalled President Harrison commuted the sentences of the *Jones* defendants to life in prison. Renewed reports criticizing working conditions on Navassa also prompted Harrison, along with the press and even the U.S. Navy, to call for federal intervention to keep order on guano islands.[79] As for the legal status of guano islands, it was now clear that federal courts had jurisdiction over crimes committed on guano islands—but whether such crimes had been committed in the United States, still no one knew.

American Appurtenances

The "sole and exclusive purpose" of the Guano Islands Act may have been the procurement of cheap guano, but Seward's legislation would turn out to have other uses as well.[80] In perhaps the most concrete sign of its lasting influence, the act's unusual terminology for describing the relationship between guano islands and the United States would return for an encore in the better known episode of American overseas territorial expansion at the end of the nineteenth century.

After the acquisition of Puerto Rico, the Philippines, and Guam in the Spanish-American War, the relationship of these new territories to the United States became the subject of intense debate, and eventually came before the Supreme Court in a series of decisions known as the Insular Cases. In one of these, *Downes v. Bidwell*, the term "appertaining," along with the Guano Islands Act and *Jones v. United States*, were invoked in support of the mincing conclusion that the new territories "belonged to" but were not "a part of" the United States. In *Downes*, both Justice Brown (in his opinion for the Court) and Justice White (in an influential concurrence) described the new territories as "appurtenant" to the United States.[81] Brown used the term once, in a concluding passage summing up the Court's holding that "the Island of Porto Rico is a territory appurtenant and belonging to the United States, but not a part of the United States."[82] White, in turn, used the term in the context of a discussion explaining why the Guano Islands Act and the decision in *Jones* offered relevant precedent in support of the holding in *Downes.* White also used the term in a passage that would come to be one of the best known and most frequently quoted descriptions of the relationship of the new territories to the United States.

Under the law of nations, wrote White, "acquired territory, in the absence of agreement to the contrary, will bear such relation to the acquiring government as may be by it determined."[83] Any other principle, he added, would render the United States "helpless in the family of nations."[84] Quoting the first section of the Guano Islands Act, White noted that under its authority "the government now holds and protects American citizens in the occupation of some seventy islands."[85] He explained that *Jones* had held both that the act was constitutional "and that islands thus acquired were 'appurtenant' to the United States."[86] Then came the memorable passage: "whilst in an international sense Porto Rico was not a foreign country, since it was subject to the sovereignty of and was owned by the United States, it was foreign to the United States in a domestic sense, because the island had not been incorporated into the United States, but was merely appurtenant thereto as a possession."[87] That is to say, "appurtenant" had now come to mean neither foreign nor part of the United States (though, in this context at least, emphatically subject to U.S. sovereignty).

In a dissenting opinion, Chief Justice Fuller rejected the relevance of guano islands to the territories at issue in *Downes.* "I am unable to see," he wrote, "why the discharge by the United States of its undoubted duty to protect its citizens on *terra nullius,* whether temporarily engaged in catching and curing fish, or working mines, or taking away manure, furnishes support to the proposition that the power of Congress over the territories of the United States is unrestricted."[88] Fuller had a point—small, uninhabited guano islands differed from large, populated territories in certain obvious ways—but the government's practice with respect to guano islands bore a slightly different, and more relevant, relationship to the territories in question than the one Fuller described.

Recall Senator Clayton's observation in the Senate debate over Seward's bill in 1856 that a doctrine asserting "that the Government is bound to protect its citizens in the discovery of an island of any description, or territory anywhere . . . would involve us in a great deal of trouble."[89] The Guano Islands Act addressed this concern precisely because it did *not* in fact stand for the government's "undoubted duty to protect [American] citizens on *terra nullius,*" as Fuller put it. On the contrary, the act sought to establish clear limits on that duty of protection, by setting forth the criteria that would trigger it. To be sure, the act did not deny the underlying federal power; but it sought by statute to limit the circumstances authorizing its exercise, and it facilitated the assertion of American influence precisely by imposing these limits. The act fulfilled this aim by creating a category of territory that, through American intervention, had ceased to be *terra nullius*, yet had not quite made it within the boundaries of the United States. The term "appertaining" served this purpose well because, as noted above, it "carries no exact meaning and lends itself readily to circumstances and the wishes of those using it."[90] The word "appertaining" then "[gave] rise to such words as 'appurtenant' and 'appurtenances.'"[91] And in *Downes*, such words described territory no longer foreign and yet not a part of the United States. In this way, the precedent of the guano islands provided an essential foundation for the imperialist policies of the McKinley Administration and the constitutional decisions of the Court that sanctioned those policies.

In the process, the uses and meanings of "appurtenance" had evolved: at one point describing waters and grounds (appertaining to uninhabited islands, in Senate Resolution 15); later, referring to the uninhabited islands themselves (appertaining to the United States, in the Guano Islands Act); and, later still, encompassing populated territories (now "appurtenant" to the United States, in *Downes*). No one seemed to doubt that these newest territories were subject to American sovereignty. Yet in the context of guano islands, the term "appertaining" seemed to have been intended to obscure the question of sovereignty—and, whether or not intended that way, had repeatedly been interpreted as leaving the issue unresolved. In the Guano Islands Act, the term "appurtenant" had replaced other, more traditional ways of describing the legal status of American-claimed land. As noted above, early drafts of the legislation had referred to them as "a part of the territory of the United States of America" and as subject to U.S. "sovereignty." But these phrases had been dropped from the final version in favor of the more ambiguous formulation—one that served the Court well when the time came to explain how the United States could extend sovereignty over populated territories without making them a part of the United States.

Empire and Sovereignty

Despite the Supreme Court's deference to the political branches and their purported assertion of sovereignty over Navassa in *Jones*, federal officials repeatedly denied that the United States had sovereignty over these islands, both before and after *Jones*. In a typical disclaimer, an opinion of the attorney general issued in 1918 insisted that the United States had "never acquired sovereignty of any kind or extent over" guano islands under the act; that, instead, the United States "had acquired certain rights over the islands because of their continuous occupation by American citizens;" and, moreover, that "no other country has proper claim to these islands, and the United States Government may at any time assert its sovereignty over them by appropriate action."[92] Discussing a long history of similarly vague declarations, the 1931–1932 State Department analysis observed that it was "difficult," to say the least, "to determine the exact legal significance of acts performed under the Guano Act."[93] The analysis went on to speculate that "the absence of a clearly defined position is attributable, perhaps, to the idea, and in some cases, fact, that guano islands are barren outcroppings of rock in the ocean, possessing no value save their deposits."[94]

But by that time any assumption that guano islands were good for nothing but guano had surely proven mistaken. Some of these islands had come to have great strategic value through their location with respect to trade routes, such as those through the Panama Canal; or as the sites of lighthouses, meteorological stations, and radio stations; or later (most importantly in the Pacific and especially during World War II), as landing strips.[95] In fact, one is tempted to suggest that the absence of a "clearly defined position" may well have been attributable, not to the insignificance of these places, but rather to their real (and changing) importance; not to their being simple, barren rocks, but rather to their being complicated places where people, principles, and politics might run aground.

Seward, it should be recalled, had deemed it necessary during the Senate debate to reassure his colleagues that "there is no temptation whatever for the abuse of authority by the establishment of colonies or any other form of permanent occupation there."[96] As he explained, the prospect of such colonies would have aroused the jealousy of other powers and embroiled the United States in unwanted international controversies. In the case of Aves, as noted earlier, the controversy even continued despite the worthlessness of the manure at issue.

Moreover, guano islands could turn out to be complicated in the way Navassa had, with actual communities taking shape and, however small and transient, requiring some form of governance. Not long after Seward's Senate debate, the Navassa Phosphate Company set up its guano mining operation on Navassa, with its draconian labor contract and slavelike working conditions. The events of 1889 inspired the headlines, such as "Slaves Under Our Flag," that prompted the embarrassed President Harrison to take action.[97] During the earlier debate over the Guano Islands Act, the unspeakable working conditions to which

Chinese workers had been subjected on the Chinca Islands had already received widespread attention; Senator Mason had noted, with respect to the difficulty of procuring guano mining labor, that the "whole world now seems to be resorting, Abolitionists and all, to the great hordes of China, for the unfortunate Coolies."[98] In short, it may well be that the unusual terminology of the act reflected a sense that guano islands could turn out to be more than "barren outcroppings," and that this obscure terminology would help the U.S. government avoid unpredictable complications, by making it possible to assert control while disclaiming sovereignty.

If this interpretation is correct, it suggests that the guano islands episode belongs not only within the history of American imperialism, but also within a broader history of European imperialism in the nineteenth century (and not only because European powers were also trying to assert control over guano islands). That is, the absence of a clearly defined position on sovereignty over guano islands calls to mind other contemporaneous efforts to find ways to take control over territory while avoiding many of the responsibilities that sovereignty implies.

Martti Koskenniemi tells this story compellingly and in some detail in his recent history of international law, in a chapter on the relationship between international law and imperialism in the mid- to late-nineteenth century.[99] There, he describes the unsuccessful efforts of nineteenth-century international lawyers to persuade European political leaders to assert sovereignty over the colonies they claimed. These lawyers reasoned that, because sovereignty implied responsibilities as well as rights, the humanitarian "problems that accompanied colonialism" could be minimized by "includ[ing] sovereignty among the benefits civilization would bring."[100] The political leaders to whom these lawyers addressed their recommendations must have reached the same conclusion, for they adamantly resisted acknowledging sovereignty over their colonies; according to Koskenniemi, they did so precisely to avoid sovereignty's burdens.

Koskenniemi describes numerous examples of this phenomenon. The establishment of "protectorates" in Africa, he explains, "allowed the British, for instance, to uphold their unlimited commercial empire while at the same time avoiding the financial and administrative burdens . . . that would have resulted from formal occupation."[101] Other examples included the Austro-Hungarian Empire's annexation of Bosnia-Herzegovina and the British annexation of Cyprus, each one "veiled as a lease."[102] By avoiding clarity on sovereignty, he explains, colonial powers would gain the flexibility to settle their disputes in an "ad hoc" manner, while depriving people of their land (and more) by all manner of deception and subterfuge.[103] In short, as one critical observer argued, "greed and the wish for exploitation without administrative and policy costs had led European countries to employ hypocritical techniques of annexation without sovereignty."[104]

Such practices, of course, had far worse consequences in Africa and elsewhere than they did on most guano islands, which, even on the rare occasions when they amounted to more than mere "barren outcroppings," were still tiny places, and sparsely inhabited (when inhabited at all). The comparison simply suggests that the disclaimers of sovereignty in the context of American guano islands did not occur in a vacuum, and did not arise merely out of confusion over the meaning of one word in the Guano Islands Act. Rather, just as the ambiguities of the formal legal status of places claimed by imperialist powers facilitated the colonial enterprise in the European context, so too did such ambiguities facilitate this early American foray into overseas territorial expansion, as well as later and more elaborate efforts. In the Insular Cases, for instance, as I have shown, the Court went on to assert that U.S. sovereignty did apply to the new territories, but then perpetuated the uncertainty concerning their formal legal status by borrowing the basic idea behind "appurtenance" (as well as the word) to hold that these territories were *neither* foreign *nor* part of the United States.

In the end, efforts to understand the legal status of American guano islands produced confounding and contradictory conclusions: the islands "appertained" to the United States but did not form part of its "territorial domain"; the islands had been "annexed," but "sovereignty" had not passed to the protecting power. The variations were endless; but always, they combined the assertion of power with qualifications, modified the expansionist thrust with limitations, and worked to make certain boundaries rigid even while making others flexible.

Conclusion

Which brings us back to Palmyra. That an island half the size of Manhattan (including water), with a considerably smaller population (one caretaker), came to be considered an "incorporated" territory of the United States illustrates the role that the management of boundaries has played in the practice of American imperialism. Palmyra ended up in its current constitutional condition as a result of the development of an elaborate system of legal categories designed to mediate the United States' relationships with territories at the margins of the nation.[105] These have included, as we have seen, territories occupied, acquired, annexed, and admitted; unorganized and organized; incorporated and unincorporated; some or all of these, in a variety of combinations. Palmyra's peculiar history—claimed as a guano island, abandoned, claimed by Hawai'i, annexed by the United States along with Hawai'i, included in a statute "incorporating" Hawai'i into the United States, excluded when Hawai'i became a state—explains how Palmyra ended up with its curious and unique designation as an incorporated territory. But the island's peculiar situation matters as a symptom, since Palmyra ended up as it did, constitutionally speaking, as the result of a wobble in the elaborate process of combined inclusion and exclusion, expansion and retraction, projection and limitation, intended for territories at the margins of the nation.[106] In that wobble, as in the broader case of the guano islands, we catch a glimpse of that elaborate process in the making.

As I noted at the outset, historians of American imperialism have tended to focus on one aspect of this process: the acquisition of territory, the projection of power, the extension of sovereignty.[107] Historians of the legal framework of empire too have been drawn to this aspect of the process, emphasizing, for instance, the plenary nature of federal power over American possessions and abroad. Scholars who have studied the American guano islands have reflected this tendency as well, supporting their arguments that the guano islands episode belongs within the history of American imperialism by supplying evidence that U.S. officials pursuing these acquisitions adopted an aggressive posture and clearly harbored a desire to take territory and project power.

None of these views is exactly wrong. And yet, as I hope this essay has shown, a close investigation of the guano islands episode suggests that there is more to the history of American imperialism than a story of voracious expansion and legal overreaching. The practice of imperialism in the United States, and elsewhere, has been tentative and ambiguous as well as aggressive and assertive; it has relied on the creation of legal categories that do their work by withholding, retracting, and assiduously delimiting national power, as well as by increasing and extending it. The Guano Islands Act was no less "imperialist" because it actually *limited* federal power, by enacting criteria that would *reduce* the number of places where the federal government was expected to project its power in order to protect American citizens. Such limits, and the disclaimers of sovereignty that followed, demand the same kind of close attention from historians of American empire that has been bestowed on Teddy Roosevelt charging up San Juan Hill.

Notes

Many thanks to D. Graham Burnett, Mary Dudziak, Hendrik Hartog, Daniel Rodgers, Leti Volpp, and the anonymous readers for their feedback on this essay.

1. General Accounting Office, *U.S. Insular Areas: Application of the U.S. Constitution,* Report to the Chairman, Committee on Resources, House of Representatives (November 1997), 41 (cited hereinafter as "GAO Report").
2. Jimmy M. Skaggs, *The Great Guano Rush: Entrepreneurs and American Overseas Expansion* (London: Macmillan, 1994), 85 (quoting *U.S. v. Fullard-Leo,* 133 F.2d 743, 747 [9th Cir. 1943], Judge Healy dissenting).
3. "GAO Report," 45.
4. Ibid., n. 22. Concededly, not everyone agrees with this classification. See Skaggs, *Great Guano Rush,* 221, n. 2 (describing Palmyra as an "unincorporated territory").
5. These include Puerto Rico, the U.S. Virgin Islands, Guam, the Commonwealth of the Northern Mariana Islands, and American Samoa. See generally GAO Report, 14–22; Arnold H. Leibowitz, *Defining Status: A Comprehensive Analysis of United States Territorial Relations* (Netherlands: Martinus Nijhoff, 1989).
6. Skaggs, *Great Guano Rush,* 85. The act is at 48 U.S.C. sec. 1411–19.
7. Ibid., sec. 1411.
8. See U.S. State Department, "The Sovereignty of Islands Claimed under the Guano Act and of the Northwest Hawaiian islands, Midway and Wake," unpublished typescript ms., 3 vols., 1932–1933 (continuously paginated), 222 (hereinafter quoted as "Sovereignty") (quoting the Cass letter). The "Sovereignty" manuscript is a 969-page typescript document exhaustively analyzing the legal status of guano islands claimed by the U.S. government and by American citizens. Apparently one copy of this document exists, and it is kept in the department's Office of the Legal Adviser.
9. 48 U.S.C. sec. 1419.
10. Skaggs, *Great Guano Rush,* 85 (quoting "Sovereignty").
11. Ibid.
12. *Downes v. Bidwell,* 182 U.S. 244, 287 (1901).
13. Skaggs, *Great Guano Rush,* chap. 4; Dan O'Donnell, "The Lobos Islands: American Imperialism in Peruvian Waters," *The Australian Journal of Politics and History* 39 (1993): 37–55; Dan O'Donnell, "The Pacific Guano Islands: The Stirring of American Empire in the Pacific Ocean," *Pacific Studies* 16 (1993): 43–66; Roy F. Nichols, *Advance Agents of American Destiny* (Philadelphia: University of Pennsylvania Press, 1956), 189–90.
14. Skaggs, *Great Guano Rush,* 56.
15. Ibid. The topic of guano islands seems, perhaps not surprisingly, to inspire no end of scatological humor.
16. See ibid., 230–36 (appendix), for a list of islands claimed by the United States. "Sovereignty" discusses islands claimed by American citizens but not declared "appertaining" to the United States.
17. I do not address the difference between the American claim to Midway (and Wake) and the claims to guano islands in this essay. On this, see "Sovereignty," 920–40.
18. D. W. Meinig, *The Shaping of America: A Geographical Perspective on 500 Years of History,* vol. 2: *Continental America* (New Haven, Conn.: Yale University Press, 1993), 556.
19. Richard A. Wines, *Fertilizer in America: From Waste Recycling to Resource Exploitation* (Philadelphia, Pa.: Temple University Press, 1985), 39.
20. Ibid.
21. Skaggs, *Great Guano Rush,* 10.
22. Ibid., 7–10.
23. Ibid., 11.
24. On the Aves affair, see ibid., 41–49; Wines, *Fertilizer in America,* 59–61; Roy F. Nichols, "Latin American Guano Diplomacy," in *Modern Hispanic America,* ed. A. Curtis Wilgus (Washington, D.C.: George Washington University Press, 1933), 536–40; "Sovereignty," 292–94.
25. Wines, *Fertilizer in America,* 60.
26. Ibid.
27. U.S. Congress, Sen. Exec. Doc. 25, Serial 879 (1857), 93–95.
28. Wines, *Fertilizer in America,* 61.

29. See *Journal of the Senate of the United States of America,* 34th Cong., 1st & 2nd sess. (Dec. 3, 1855–Aug. 21, 1856) (Washington, D.C.: A. O. P. Nicholson, Senate Printer, 1856) (hereinafter cited as *Senate Journal,* 34:1–2), 257; see also *Cong. Globe,* 34th Cong., 1st sess. (May 26, 1856), 1297; Skaggs, *Great Guano Rush,* 49.
30. *Senate Journal,* 34:1–2, 257 (emphasis added).
31. *Cong. Globe,* 34th Cong., 1st sess. (July 23, 1856) (hereinafter "Senate Debate"). The part of the debate that I discuss here appears at 1697–1700.
32. Ibid., 1697.
33. Ibid.
34. Ibid.
35. Ibid., 1698.
36. Codified at 48 U.S.C. sec. 1419. The missing "as" did not appear in the Statutes at Large version (11 Stat., 120) but was inserted in the Revised Statutes version (R.S., tit. 72, sec. 5578).
37. "Senate Debate," 1698.
38. Ibid., 1699.
39. Ibid., 1700.
40. Ibid., 1741.
41. "Sovereignty," 5.
42. Ibid., 316.
43. 9 Ops. 30 (June 2, 1857).
44. Ibid., 30–31.
45. Roy F. Nichols, "Navassa: A Forgotten Acquisition," *American Historical Review* 38.3 (1933): 505–10, at 506; Skaggs, *Great Guano Rush,* 99; "Sovereignty," *passim.*
46. Skaggs's appendix of places "claimed and/or acquired after the Guano Islands Act" lists twenty-four "nonexistent" islands, rocks, or keys. See Skaggs, *Great Guano Rush,* 230–36. The list also includes a number of islands with cross-references to other islands; these exist, but were apparently duplicated on some records, under different names. One appears twice on the list: the island existed at one location, and not at the other.
47. 9 Ops. 364, 369 (July 12, 1859).
48. Ibid., 368.
49. John Cashman, "Slaves Under Our Flag," *The Maryland Historian* 24.2 (1993): 1–22, at 1. The following account of the Navassa island riot is based on Cashman and on Skaggs, *Great Guano Rush,* chap. 10.
50. Even a friendly little pamphlet on the birds of the Chinca Islands put out by the Pan American Union in 1945 notes this grisly fact. Mae Galarza, *The Guano Islands* (Washington, D.C.: Pan American Union, 1945), 14.
51. Quoted in Cashman, *Slaves Under Our Flag,* 1, n. 1.
52. Ibid., 5–6.
53. Skaggs, *Great Guano Rush,* 183.
54. Ibid., 185.
55. Ibid., 185–90.
56. Brief for Plaintiffs-in-Error, *Jones v. United States,* Nos. 1142–44 (1890) (hereinafter cited as "Defendants' Brief"). The defendants had now become the "plaintiffs in error," but I refer to them (as did the Court in its opinion in *Jones*) as the "defendants," and to the opposing party as the "government."
57. Ibid., 3–5.
58. Ibid., 3.
59. Ibid.
60. Ibid.
61. Ibid.
62. Ibid., 4.
63. Ibid.
64. Ibid.
65. Ibid., 5.
66. I develop this argument in "*Untied* States: American Expansion and Territorial Deannexation," *University of Chicago Law Review* 72.3 (2005): 797.

67. "Government's Brief," 5.
68. Ibid.
69. Ibid., 7.
70. Ibid.
71. Ibid. (emphasis deleted).
72. Ibid.
73. *Jones v. United States*, 137 U.S. 202, 211 (1890).
74. Ibid., 212.
75. Ibid.
76. Ibid.
77. Ibid., *passim.*
78. Cashman, *Slaves Under Our Flag*, 17–18.
79. Ibid., 19–20.
80. See "Sovereignty," 222.
81. See *Downes*, 287.
82. Ibid.
83. Ibid., 306.
84. Ibid.
85. Ibid., 306–7; see also ibid., 304–5 (citing guano islands as evidence of the power to acquire territory).
86. Ibid., 307. The scare quotes around "appurtenant," suggesting the novelty of the term, were White's own.
87. Ibid., 341–42.
88. Ibid., 372–73.
89. "Senate Debate," 1697.
90. "Sovereignty," 316.
91. Ibid.
92. Ibid., 35–36.
93. Ibid., 240.
94. Ibid., 244.
95. Ibid., 173; see also Skaggs, *Great Guano Rush*, chap. 11.
96. "Senate Debate," 1698.
97. See Cashman, *Slaves Under Our Flag*, 1, 19.
98. "Senate Debate," 1740.
99. Martti Koskenniemi, *The Gentle Civilizer of Nations: The Rise and Fall of International Law 1870–1960* (Cambridge: Cambridge University Press, 2001), chap. 2 ("Sovereignty: The Gift of Civilization").
100. Ibid., 109–10.
101. Ibid., 125.
102. Ibid., 151.
103. Ibid., 125, 124.
104. Ibid., 151 (paraphrasing one "particularly critical attack" in 1909).
105. That is, if on further examination we could all agree that it really is an incorporated territory. See note 4 above.
106. Compare Koskenniemi, *Gentle Civilizer*, chap. 2 (discussing the dynamic of inclusion and exclusion in the context of late-nineteenth-century European colonialism).
107. Even Koskenniemi, who demonstrates in such rich detail the ways in which European imperialism relied on the withholding of sovereignty, falls into this familiar trap, defining "imperialism" early in the same chapter as "an insistence on the extension of formal European sovereignty in the colonies." Ibid., 100, n. 6.

Romantic Sovereignty: Popular Romances and the American Imperial State in the Philippines

Andrew Hebard

In a 1900 review titled "The New Historical Romances," William Dean Howells deliberately extends his consideration of literary aesthetics into the realm of imperial politics. Asking his readers to shun the romance and return to the more ethically and aesthetically viable works of realism, Howells ends his review with the claim that "we have still a republic and not yet an empire of letters."[1] Not only does Howells's remark register how the heated national debate on imperialism profoundly influenced the dissension in literary journals between romancers and realists, but also it reinforces one of the assumptions of literary politics at the turn of the century: the assumption that the romance was inextricably linked to a national culture of imperial expansion and violence. However, while Howells certainly directs his critique at an imperial culture, the way that he maps literary form onto governmental form raises questions about the aesthetics of imperial governance and administration as well. Much has been written on the connection between the romance and imperial culture, but what rarely gets noted is the extent to which this correlation of romantic aesthetics and empire spoke not just to a "culture" of expansion and violence, but also to the legal and administrative forms that allowed for such violence.

Recently, scholars of American studies have picked up on some of the connections between the romance and American imperialism. Nancy Glazener, for example, notes that

> the new romance also embodied an alternative national mission for legitimate literature: Whereas realism promoted good citizenship through self-discipline and self-denial, the romance was imagined to offer an outlet for antisocial impulses and instincts comparable to the outlet provided by imperialist exploitation and warfare.[2]

Glazener states what Howells insinuates, that the extraordinary actions of the romance translate into the extraordinary actions of an imperial nation, whereas realism's emphasis on the ordinary promoted everyday discipline and good government. Similarly, in her essay "Romancing the Empire," Amy Kaplan traces how the popular romance was complicit in the national project of imperialism because it created a "spectacle of American manhood and nostalgia" that worked to "deny political agency and visibility to the subjects of the American empire."[3] As Kaplan demonstrates, the romance not only personifies imperial agency within the figure of the romantic hero, but also helps to "refigure the relation between masculinity and nationality in a changing international context."[4] The psycho-sexual structuring of the popular romance is remarkably similar to the way that Americans began to reimagine their nation as a part of an empire. Indeed, both of these scholars link the imaginary of an imperial nation to the imaginary of the romance.

These correlations work remarkably well when the object of analysis is a national imaginary or culture, and by connecting the romance to American expansion, Glazener and Kaplan have opened up an important reconsideration of our national culture during the Progressive era. However, if we shift from the discourses surrounding national imaginaries and imperial cultures to the more mundane legal and administrative discourses surrounding the state, the rhetorical conventions change. Just as prevalent as the nationalistic bluster that fired up political speeches and editorial pages were heated debates about how to accomplish the mundane work of running an empire. These debates included technical questions about how to define U.S. sovereignty legally, how to define the scope of administrative activity, and how to define the relation between civil and military governance in the nation's new colonial acquisitions.

One might assume that such exacting questions would require exact answers, but while the imperial nation was given a clear image (at least on its surface) in the figure of the romantic hero, the imperial state, with its administrative and legal demands for precision, was ironically figured through the tropes of ambivalence. For example, Howard Taft, the head of the second Philippine Commission and later governor of the islands, would describe this imperial state as a "quasi-civil government."[5] Similarly, the 1900 Supreme Court cases known as the Insular Cases would ambivalently define American sovereignty by describing the colonial territories as "foreign in a domestic sense."[6] Commenting on this ambivalence in his dissenting opinion, Justice Fuller would famously point out the haziness of these legal definitions when he complained that these territories were like "a disembodied shade, in an intermediate state of ambiguous existence for an indefinite period."[7] The masculine romance of Roosevelt's "strenuous life" provided an apt image for the work of national expansion, but when it came to the legal and bureaucratic work of administrating overseas territories and defining the limits of state sovereignty, the resolve of the hero gave way to the vague agency of a "disembodied shade."

But this is not to say that the romance played no part in creating this "disembodied shade." In what follows, I trace the role of the popular romance in this less romantic side of American imperialism, in the more mundane discourses surrounding the legal and administrative state. The conventions of the popular romance can be found in documents ranging from civil service reports and legal cases to congressional debates on imperial government. However, while the heroics of a "strenuous life" certainly make their appearance in these documents, the turn-of-the-century romance was most complicit in the project of imperial administration in the way that it presented the *contradiction* between romantic and realist literary modes. Far from being purely romantic, the popular romances of this period produced their narratives by displaying the contradiction between the romantic and realist modes, the ordinary and the extraordinary. As I will demonstrate, this contradiction took on the form of an ambivalence, and an ambivalence that corresponded to the way that the "disembodied shade" of an imperial state rose out of the contradiction between the seemingly ordinary norms of colonial administration and the more extraordinary and undemocratic acts of executive oversight and military violence.

One might assume that administrators would avoid the ambivalence that Justice Fuller hurled as an accusation in his dissenting opinion, but, in fact, they embraced it. Far from being an inhibition to the power of the imperial state, the ambivalence I describe served to expand the possibilities of state action. Indeterminacy haunted the legal borders between the colonial state and the national body politic, creating contradictory notions of legitimate state action and even calling into question the ontology of the colonial state (what is, after all, a "quasi-civil government"?). But this form of government was remarkably successful in its ability to combine violence and undemocratic oversight with the regular functions of bureaucratic governance while simultaneously producing a narrative of progress and development. This movement from contradiction to narrative can be understood through the conventions that produced its intelligibility, conventions that are found and sustained in the literature of this period. In other words, the romantic fiction of the period shared in a cultural imaginary that not only conventionalized this contradiction between the ordinary and the extraordinary, but also transformed it into a principle of narrative. Understanding this convention helps one to understand not only how the imperial state was figured as simultaneously permanent and temporary, but also how state violence was figured as extraordinary despite its presence in the everyday workings of imperial governance.

Like Amy Kaplan's recent work in *The Anarchy of Empire*, I see imperialism "as a network of power relations that changes over space and time and is riddled with instability, ambiguity, and disorder, rather than as a monolithic system of domination that the very word 'empire' implies."[8] But whereas Kaplan's analysis of empire looks to the production of a "U.S. culture" that creates an imaginary "where Americans can go out into the world without bearing the foreign into the home," my analysis is centered more specifically on the ambivalent contradiction between governmentality and sovereignty.[9] On the one hand, the United States diligently constructed a bureaucracy that not only claimed to have the welfare of the population as its object, but that also worked gradually to incorporate the population into the running of the bureaucracy.[10] On the other hand, the United States repeatedly expressed its "rightful supremacy over the Philippine Islands," and expressed it through military violence and autocratic oversight.[11]

The importance of examining legal borderlands, which I take to be sites where the state is emerging and where the territorial and legal limits of the United States are being negotiated, is that they force us to bring state sovereignty into our consideration of the relation between representation and power. The state may indeed be what Foucault calls "mythicized abstraction." However, in these administrative sites at the legal boundaries of the nation, state sovereignty was a persistent and pervasive issue wherein the conventions through which this myth was narrated affected the ways that administrative authority and military violence were experienced and made intelligible.[12] These legal borderlands were also sites that produced an almost endless stream of reports and documents, allowing, if not forcing, us to consider the representational conventions of state ambivalence. *Ambivalence* has become a useful term for exploring the relation between representation and power, but too often the term has become a constitutive element of a theory of representation rather than a term with a representational history. Georgio Agamben, for example, has usefully brought sovereignty back into a consideration of governmentality and has done so by examining the ambivalence, the "zone of indistinction," that combines them. But Agamben figures this "zone of indistinction" through the aporetic disjunction between *langue* and *parole* and in doing so turns it into a constitutive element of a theory of representation and the state. The importance of such work should not be discounted, and its ethical impulse is at the heart of what follows. However, faced with the immense archive of legal and administrative writings that both produce and discuss forms of ambivalence, I am left with the sense that while ambivalence was constitutive of state power in the Philippines, these acts of constitution were also mundanely conventional. My goal then is to bring literary history into this ambivalent "zone of indistinction," to understand the ways that ambivalence was conventionalized during the Progressive era and to explore the political implications of these conventions. Subsequently, what follows is not a theory of the state, but rather an exploration of the conventions circulating in yet another borderland, the intersection of literary, legal, and administrative discourses.

"No Middle Ground": Sovereignty between Racial Difference and Racial Uplift

When Justice Edgar Douglas White described the status of the United States' new colonial possessions as unincorporated territories, he reinforced a legal construction of American sovereignty that paradoxically designated territories like the Philippines as both *a part of* and *apart from* the United States. White described sovereignty from two points of view: "while in an international sense Porto Rico was not a foreign country, since it was subject to the sovereignty of and was owned by the United States, it was foreign to the United States in a domestic sense because the island had not been incorporated into the United States."[13] He also insisted that both of these points of view coexist simultaneously, that the territories remain both foreign and domestic. This odd construction of sovereignty lies at the heart of the ambivalences that I described earlier, and it derives its reasoning from the contradictory race ideologies that circulated through the debates about imperial governance. Race is a motivating factor in White's argument as he imagines the consequences of discovering an "island, peopled with an uncivilized race, yet rich in soil, and valuable to the United States for commercial and strategic reasons."[14] Unwilling to relinquish the benefits of acquiring such a territory, White still questions the wisdom of "the immediate bestowal of citizenship on those absolutely unfit to receive it."[15] Justice Brown, in his concurring opinion, similarly argues that "Porto Rico is a territory appurtenant and belonging to the United States, but not a part of the United States."[16] His reasoning also relies on a notion of racial difference, for he notes that when acquiring lands "inhabited by alien races . . . the administration of government and justice, according to Anglo-Saxon principles, may for a time be impossible."[17]

The difference between the Philippines and the American body politic was a point of consensus in debates on imperialism in the United States. In spite of their fundamental disagreements, both anti- and pro-imperial platforms confirmed the idea that both the Filipino territory and the people occupying it were inassimilable to the U.S. body politic. The territory was seen as all but unlivable with respect to an American citizenry because of climate, while the Filipinos were seen as inassimilable to an American citizenry on the basis of race and culture. Anti-imperialists easily incorporated the putative inassimilability of the Philippines into their political platforms. William Jennings Bryan, for example, used this belief to denounce imperialism when he asked, "Are we to bring into the body politic eight or ten million Asiatics, so different from us in race and history that amalgamation is impossible?"[18] Bryan's views were by no means limited to Democratic and anti-imperialist platforms, and he rightly notes in the same speech, "No Republican of prominence has been bold enough to advocate such a proposition" [that amalgamation would be possible].[19]

In contrast to this assumption of absolute racial difference, the Filipinos were simultaneously inscribed within discourses of racial uplift and progress. The project of state building in the Philippines was a pedagogical project whereby the Filipinos were to be trained to be "like" Americans. This project posited a fundamental similarity between Americans and Filipinos. Although clearly paternal, the underlying assumption of this project was that Filipinos (though not modern) existed within the same sliding scale of historical progress. Again, both pro- and anti-imperialists deployed this racial ideology: pro-imperialists to justify colonial occupation as a philanthropic and progressive act, anti-imperialists to argue for the Filipino right to self-determination. In addition to running throughout the debates on imperialism, this idea of racial continuity was also built into actual state practices. Vicente Rafael, for example, demonstrates how the census of 1903 was able to reframe racial difference within the islands as a "great homogeneity" that made the whole population an object of American administrative control. The census accomplished this not because it erased racial difference, but because it was "able to imagine civilized and wild peoples existing side by side on the same map of the Philippines." Rafael is also sure to note, however, the way that a more absolute sense of racial difference qualified this continuity, for "the census not only mapped the structure of racial difference; it also established the privilege of a particular race to determine the borders of those differences."[20]

Out of this contradiction between stark incongruity and progressive continuity emerged a mimetic state-building project. If the extension of U.S. institutions raised anxieties about assimilation while the progressive project of building good government demanded forms of similarity, then one way to mediate such a quandary was to copy U.S. forms of governance into the Philippines rather than extend them. Subsequently, when the Organic Act of 1902 established civil government in the Philippines, it did so in a way that closely mimicked forms of governance in the United States. It created three branches of government: executive, legislative, and judicial. Similarly, the Philippine Commission established a civil code and civil service procedures that were "almost identical to the laws which obtain in this country for the government of our towns, cities, and counties."[21] Such formal similarities existed, however, alongside insurmountable legal and administrative distances between this mimetic state and the U.S. federal government. As Julian Go notes:

> Organic Law called for a legal and economic system that would be discontinuous with the U.S. federal system; U.S. legal statutes would not apply. The Philippines was designated a foreign port, giving Congress the right to establish tariff duties and customs, and it had a local monetary system based on the Philippine peso rather than the dollar. [Additionally], because of the "unincorporated" status of the Philippines declared by the Supreme Court [in the Insular Cases], the inhabitants of the islands would not enjoy full citizenship or all constitutional rights.[22]

The fact that a colonizing government would copy its own system of rule upon its acquired territories is perhaps not all that surprising. More surprising, however, is the way that this mimetic project often produced an ontological ambivalence in both state institutions and the populations they regulated. The government in the Philippines was awkwardly figured as actively copying American institutions, but also as having an existence that was incompletely articulated—a partial object. Howard Taft's description of the government as a "quasi-civil government" is certainly indicative of this ambivalence.[23] Similarly, congressional debates, executive speeches, and civil service reports stressed the *impermanence* of the U.S. civil government. Early commission reports and congressional debates repeat the sentiment that it would have been "premature for the [Philippine] Commission [of 1900] to have announced, on its arrival and in its proclamation, a fixed and definite form of government."[24] Congress actually wrote the impermanence of the government into the 1902 Organic Act, which legislated a more formal civil government. The law passed on the books was "*temporarily* to provide for the administration of the affairs of civil government."[25] This civil government was emergent and would become permanent only at an undetermined point in the future and through unspecified means, remaining in this state of emergence "until otherwise specified by law."[26]

The status of the Filipino citizenry was similarly indeterminate. On the one hand, because of their putative incapacity for self-rule, the Filipinos were subjected to the tutelage of an American sovereignty. On the other hand, they were still to participate in a national and everyday form of modern government—both as citizens and as civil servants. Situated as both subjects and citizens, the Filipinos occupied an ambivalent legal territory. Legal and bureaucratic discourses defined the Filipinos as citizens of the Philippines, but as Senator Teller pointed out in a heated congressional debate, "there must be a sovereignty before there can be a citizen," and the Philippines had no such sovereignty. In relation to the sovereignty of the United States, the status of the Filipino was no clearer.[27] During the same debate, Senator Bacon states,

> As to the ultimate paramount sovereignty [a man] must be either a citizen or a subject. *There is no middle ground for him to occupy.* There is no other place in the world . . . where a man fails to occupy the position of either citizen or subject to the government which is in ultimate and paramount control over him.[28]

Senator Bacon was criticizing a government that he believed turned the Filipinos into imperial subjects. Official policy, however, was not so clear on this matter. It was precisely this impossible "middle ground" that the Filipino occupied according to the legal and administrative framework. One sees this in the Organic Act of 1902, which explicitly states that the constitution does not extend to the islands and that the Filipinos are to be "citizens of the Philippine Islands."[29] Yet the Organic Act also states that Filipinos must "owe allegiance" to the United States as a prerequisite for voting (or enacting their Filipino citizenship) in local and regional elections.[30] In other words, they were to act out a Filipino citizenship without being full citizens of any sovereign entity. Caught between the imperatives of a forced colonial possession and the imperatives of regulatory rule, the Filipinos were subjects to a juridical order from which they were excluded and yet simultaneously citizens of that same order.

Romance, Realism, and the Modes of the Imperial State

While the contradiction between narratives of incommensurate racial difference and narratives of racial uplift helped produce these ambivalent definitions of the colonial state and colonial citizens, they also mapped onto a contradiction between different "ways" that the state went about its business. It is here that we begin to see how the conventions of romance and realism entered into governmental discourses, for the literary modes of the ordinary and the extraordinary were particularly prevalent in figuring the contradiction between the norms of ordinary bureaucratic administration and more extraordinary acts of military violence and executive oversight.

As Howells suggests in his review of historical romances, to speak of the relation between literature and politics at the turn of the century was to speak of the conflict between romance and realism. This conflict had been playing out on the pages of literary magazines since the early 1880s, and at the turn of the century acquired a new sense of urgency with what has been referred to as a "romantic revival."[31] There was a resurgence of the romance during this period, and these novels were not only bestsellers, but also achieved critical legitimacy as they appeared on the pages of respected literary journals such as the *Atlantic Monthly*.

The relation between these novels and broad ideologies of U.S. imperialism is easily traced through their thematic similarities.[32] Their relation to the legal and administrative ambivalence that I examined earlier is also evident, for the ambivalence of an emergent sovereignty is often the very terrain upon which turn-of-the-century romances unfold their plots. Many of these romances are set in places where the institutions of governance are in a nascent state. Take, for example, Mary Johnston's *To Have and to Hold*, set in colonial Jamestown, and Richard Harding Davis's "The Reporter Who Made Himself King," set on a tropical island that lacks government institutions.[33] Similarly, many of these romances are set in places where one form of governance is replacing another. Some examples of this are S. Wier Mitchell's *Hugh Wynne: Free Quaker*, set in Philadelphia during the American Revolution; Richard Harding Davis's *Soldiers of Fortune* and *The White Mice*, both set in South American nations that are experiencing revolutions; McCutcheon's *Graustark, the Story of a Love Behind a Throne*, set in a fictional monarchy where the government must rapidly alter its traditions in order to survive; and Gertrude Atherton's *Rulers of Kings*, set in the Austro-Hungarian Empire at a time when it had to adjust to growing demands for democratization.[34] All of these novels are set in spaces wherein the forms of governance are undecided and new forms are emergent. In each case, the emergent form is one that copies or mimics the turn-of-the-century ideals and forms of American governance.

The relation between these novels and imperial administration can also be traced in the way that administrative discourses adopted their modal conventions. Mode, as I use it here, is that which designates a "world" or representational milieu of intelligibility. In a novel, it consists of the conventions of plot, character, setting, and worldview that make the events of the novel intelligible.[35] Fredric Jameson notes that this world is "something like the frame or the *Gestalt*, the overall organizational category within which the various empirical innerworldly phenomena are perceived and the various innerworldly experiences take place…that supreme category which permits all experience or perception in the first place."[36] Although I will later question the fullness of Jameson's framing, his description of mode as a horizon of intelligibility is useful in the context of these novels, for it allows us to examine the "worlds" that make different state actions intelligible or even possible.

The modes that primarily concern us here are those of romance and realism. The term "romance" designates a horizon of possible actions and outcomes in a world marked by extraordinary circumstances, characters, and settings. "Realism," on the other hand, demarcates the actions and outcomes possible in a seemingly ordinary or everyday world. Romance and realism have a complicated critical genealogy, but this association of realism with everyday life and romance with the extraordinary can be seen in the work of critics ranging from Richard Chase to more recent work by Glazener, Eric Sundquist, and Robert Shulman.[37] It was also the way that literary critics of the period such as William Dean Howells, Agnes Repplier, and Henry James understood this modal difference. More importantly, the ordinary and the extraordinary were the terms by which realism and romance entered into governmental discourses.

Within governmental discourses, the literary modes of the ordinary and the extraordinary were particularly prevalent in figuring the contradiction between the regulative norms of ordinary bureaucratic administration and the more extraordinary acts of military violence and executive oversight. The language of everyday duty, work, and social interaction marked descriptions of the bureaucratic project of the colonial state, while, in contrast to this, the language of heroism, adventure, honor, and the extraordinary marked the descriptions of the military and executive oversight that were seen as an exception to bureaucratic norms.

In terms of the realist mode, the work of producing U.S. forms of governance went hand in hand with teaching the Filipinos the "everyday" art of self-governance. The importance of producing an imperial everyday in the Philippines has been examined in both Rafael's study of women's writing in the Philippines and in Laura Wexler's study of female photography.[38] This concern for the quotidian is easily extended into the administrative and legal discourses surrounding the government-building project in the Philippines. Theodore Roosevelt, for example, stated that good self-government exhibited itself "not merely in great crises, but in the everyday affairs of life [and in] the qualities of practical intelligence."[39] This commitment to the everyday was more specifically a commitment to the *practice* of governance and was a commitment that was central to the discourses of American imperialism. Similarly, William Taft repeatedly argued that "government is a practical, not a theoretical, problem," and that "the best political education is practice in the exercise of political power."[40]

The Filipinos were to get this "political education" by taking part in a kind of dress rehearsal of the everyday workings of a bureaucratic state. They were to take part in the civil service, hold elections, conduct a census, participate in public works projects, and even pass legislation, but all as a way of "practicing" everyday self-governance. Governance was "a matter not of intellectual apprehension, but of character and of acquired habits of thought and feeling," and imperial policies were to help the Filipinos acquire this everyday "habit" of governance.[41] Acquiring such "habits" was to be a gradual process, and one that began at the local level. Subsequently, the civil government gave limited autonomy first to municipal governments, then to provincial governments, and finally in 1907 created a national assembly. The administration also increased the number of Filipinos involved in the day-to-day workings of the civil service by giving preference to qualified Filipinos in low- and mid-level appointments. Although the 1902 Organic Act outlined the broader structure of this government and laid out the rights of its participants, the act primarily details the minutia of how the government would interact with the everyday commerce of the islands. Much of the act is taken up with the details of coinage, processing mineral rights, and establishing public works projects. Unlike a constitution, this founding document was much more concerned with everyday details than with principles and procedures.

Realist themes also enter governmental discourses through the ways that these discourses pay close attention to the social texture of the colonial setting. The first Philippine Commission stated at the outset of their annual report that one aspect of their mission was to

> visit the Philippine peoples in their respective provinces, both for the purpose of cultivating a more intimate mutual acquaintance and with the view to ascertain from enlightened native opinion what form or forms of government seem best adapted to the Philippine peoples, most apt to conduce to their highest welfare, and most comfortable in their customs, traditions, sentiments, and cherished ideals.[42]

While one can see the presence of an ethnographic discourse in this passage, the references to intimacy, customs, and sentiment also place this passage within the concerns of the realist novel. Intimacy in this passage, like the intimacy in the realist novel, is imbedded in social relations and customs. The "enlightened native opinion" also refers to a caste of Filipinos who were increasingly represented as civilized, educated, and within the social horizon of the American civil servants and rulers. This inclusion was not without its anxieties, but nevertheless both imperial and anti-imperial discourses stressed the civility and sociability of Filipino elites, either to posit the future ability of Filipinos to rule themselves, or to make the case for their current ability to do so.[43]

The administrative concern for social custom was so central to the government building project in the Philippines that McKinley's initial instructions to the first Philippine Commission stated that "the measures adopted [when establishing a government] should be made to conform to their customs, their habits, and even their prejudices."[44] This adaptation had its limits and was by no means unidirectional. The United States immediately established an extensive and mandatory school system that not only taught an American curriculum, but also changed the official language of the Philippines from Spanish to English. These schools had effects that extended beyond the classroom and that altered the texture of a Filipino everyday. As Samuel Tan notes,

> New sports from America like baseball, softball, volleyball, tennis, badminton, and basketball were added to *sipa*, *kaldang*, and *pagtanduk* in Muslim Mindanao, and to *horse racing*, *cockfighting*, *patintero*, and fluvial parades and sports in the Christian areas. Games like billiards, bridge, poker, and magic were readily received by people with a penchant for gambling, magic, and mysticism. . . . Even buildings, especially public edifices, acquired the utilitarian influences of American architecture.[45]

The Supreme Court also used social custom to determine which constitutional rights should extend into the colonial possessions. Citing *Downes v. Bidwell* as a precedent, Justice Day would argue in *Dorr v. United States* that the right to a jury trial in the Philippines was not a fundamental constitutional right because, if it were, "the preference of the people must be disregarded, their established customs ignored, and they themselves coerced to accept, in advance of incorporation into the United States, a system of trial unknown to them and unsuited to their needs."[46]

Whether the administration adapted to the habits of Filipinos or Filipinos adapted to the habits of the American administration, the everyday was a central site of struggle for the project of government building. Thus, far from being an anti-imperial mode, realism, as a mode of the everyday, was very much a mode of imperial governance. The ethical investments of realism closely mirrored the legislative narratives of U.S. colonial rule. Glazener's claim that realism "promoted good citizenship through self-discipline" is, I believe, a plausible one, and one that was intimately connected to the pedagogical goals of the American administration.[47] The "education" that Filipinos were to receive through schooling and restricted participation in the government was aimed at producing such self-discipline by engaging with the Filipino population at the level of the everyday and familiarizing them with the mundane workings of an administrative bureaucracy.

This realist mode is, however, only a part of the story or rather only a part of the way the story gets told. The actions and motivations of a more extraordinary worldview appear alongside the everyday. The project of producing an everyday mode of governance was often disrupted by the seemingly incongruous and extraordinary demands of colonial rule, demands that required military violence and undemocratic executive oversight. The everyday administrative responsibilities of American sovereignty were predicated on the often violent acts of establishing that sovereignty. Consequently, a discussion of military violence takes up hundreds of pages of the *Congressional Record.* This violence was often mapped onto the romantic tropes of "heroism" and figured as an extraordinary measure. One can see this in the way that Theodore Roosevelt argued that the United States needed heroic and extraordinary leaders who knew when to depart "from the red-tape regulations of peace."[48] One can also see it in the romantic troping of military actions. For example, after capturing the leader of the insurgency, General Funston went on tour as a war hero, and his exploits were explicitly compared to the plots of adventure novels: "Here was an opportunity that suggested an adventure equal to anything in penny-awful fiction. It was just the kind of a dare-devil exploit that appealed to the romantic Funston."[49] Such accounts of Funston's action appear not just in the popular press, but also in official hearings and congressional investigations. Within congressional debates, politicians even criticized Funston for overplaying this role, a role that had an "official" sanction.

> Funston is a hero *officially acknowledged and proclaimed,* and with all the rights, privileges, and immunities that go with the title. There have been heroes, sir, who were modest and unassuming. There have been heroes who were something more than *licensed* swaggerers and braggarts. But Funston is not one of these . . . The performances of this doughty warrior illustrate the danger of a small man becoming a hero too suddenly. There is always the danger of his overacting the part.[50]

Executive oversight was similarly figured as an extraordinary measure, and one that drew its legitimacy from the more personified and charismatic authority of the executive branch. The civil government may have been seen as an elaborate dress rehearsal for instructing the Filipinos in the art of everyday governance, but it was still a dress rehearsal with a director. Subsequently, all of the legislation providing for civil governance reserved the power of oversight for the appointed American governor.

The romantic tropes of honor and prestige also work their way throughout legal and administrative discourses. Justice White ends his opinion in *Downes v. Bidwell* with the argument that immediate incorporation of the islands should be avoided not because it is unconstitutional, but rather because it is "incompatible with the dignity and honor of the government."[51] Executive oversight was similarly figured not just as a matter of good government but also as a way of preserving national "honor." Honor became a major term in the Senate debates about the Organic Act, for rather than argue about the details of the civil government that the bill would establish, Senators spent days defending and attacking the "honor" and "character" of military and administrative officials who had testified in hearings on the military's use of excessive violence and torture.[52] These themes also converge in a 1902 speech by Secretary of War Elihu Root. Not only does Root state that it "concerned the credit and honor of our country that we should succeed in the Philippines," but he also firmly places this honor within the executive branch: "The sagacity and skill of [McKinley's] sympathetic leadership over men, made his nobility of character an active force for justice and peace and righteousness . . . his policies were the outcome of a strong desire for the peace and happiness and honor of his country."[53]

Figure 1.
"Two Views of the President." This image, which appeared in the September 1904 issue (30.3) of *The American Monthly Review of Reviews*, demonstrates the perceived contradiction between Roosevelt, the staid bureaucrat, and Roosevelt, the violent adventurer. Courtesy of the McCain Library at Agnes Scott College.

One can see a similar romantic troping of imperial leadership in the writings of Theodore Roosevelt. Roosevelt's essay "The Strenuous Life" calls for men of action to embrace the "life of strife" that imperial rule necessitates.[54] This essay came to represent a form of American heroism that constituted American sovereignty through violence, for the initial work of this new American hero was not the mundane work of administration: "The first and all-important work to be done is to establish the supremacy of our flag. We must put down armed resistance before we can accomplish anything else."[55] In another speech, Roosevelt extends this romantic narrative of American empire from military violence into civil leadership. Asking for the public support of American administrative leaders in the Philippines, Cuba, and Puerto Rico, Roosevelt writes:

> We are no less bound to see that where the sword wins the land, the land shall be kept by the rule of righteous law. We have taken it upon ourselves, as in honor bound, a great task,

THE "MILITARY" ROOSEVELT.

Two views of the President.—From the *Eagle* (Brooklyn).

> befitting a great nation, and we have a right to ask of every citizen, of every true American, that he shall with heart and hand uphold the leaders of the nation as from a brief and glorious war they strive to a lasting peace that shall redound not only to the interest of the conquered people, not only to the honor of the American public, but to the permanent advancement of civilization and of all mankind.[56]

While much of the rhetoric here can be attributed to the flourish of a political speech, the discourses of imperialism regularly applied the romantic rhetoric of honor, action, and glory to imperial leaders and administrative oversight, both when they were praised as heroes and when they were criticized as "adventurers."[57]

Although these literary modes mapped onto different modes of imperial governance, the alignment of literary form onto governmental form did not in itself determine the aesthetic politics of empire during this period. Both ordinary and extraordinary modes of governance were at work in overseas territories, and an investigation into the intersection between literature and administration needs to shift away from examining how literary forms reflected governmental ideologies and toward examining the work that these modes did through their relation to one another. It was by projecting a particular relationship between realist and romantic modes that the turn-of-the-century romance engaged with the project of imperial governance.

Modal Incongruity in the Popular Romance and the Imperial State

The literary criticism of the Progressive era reconfirmed this alignment of governance and literary mode. In "The New Historical Romances," Howells makes his distinction between an "empire" and "republic" of letters on the basis of an opposition between heroic violence, the "ignoble ideals of force," and "everyday duty and peace."[58] However, neither the romance, nor imperial governance, is as straightforward as Howells implies. Like the discourses surrounding governance, the turn-of-the-century romance operated through more than one mode. As much as critics such as Howells figured these romances as thoroughly romantic, the novels themselves were by no means homogenous in their construction. Far from being completely filled with violent heroics and extraordinary circumstances, the turn-of-the-century romance was often interrupted by scenes that sit securely within the realist mode of the ordinary. In fact, a tension between realist and romantic modes repeats *within* these romances.

A good example of this tension can be found in Richard Harding Davis's *Soldiers of Fortune*, an adventure romance set in a fictional South American country. Early on in *Soldiers of Fortune*, there is an odd moment of domestic homemaking. Clay, the male protagonist who manages an iron mine, begins to build a bungalow to house his employer's daughters, Alice and Hope. Although the event seems inconsequential from the standpoint of the adventure narrative, it takes up three pages of the novel. Layered with detail, these pages not only convey the layout of the home, but also its color scheme of "blue and green and white tiles" and the "tropical plants and colored mats and awnings" that fill the house. The male characters pay as much attention to the details as the passage does:

> They would be walking together in Valencia when one would say, "we ought to have that for the house," and without question would march into the shop together and order whatever they fancied to be sent out to the house . . . They stocked it with wine and linens, and hired a volante and six horses.[59]

These seemingly contingent details of domestic space recall what Roland Barthes terms the "reality effect" of realism, and could seem out of place within a romance, a genre that privileges the extraordinary over the ordinary.[60] But such scenes are by no means anomalous for the romances of this period. *Soldiers of Fortune*, for example, begins with the "minute perfections" of a parlor room drama that turn-of-the-century critics associated with realism.[61] In fact, many turn-of-the-century romances contain such dramas, and throughout these novels, the motivations and actions of a romantic world share the same spaces with the more realist context of everyday life.[62]

These novels also reinforced the critical commonplace that these modes were incongruous. The popular essayist Agnes Repplier, for example, would write that romance and realism had little to say to one another. "It does not appear to the peace-loving reader that either the realist or the romanticist has any very convincing arguments to offer in defense of his own exclusive orthodoxy . . . Neither of the combatants is likely to be much affected by anything the other has to say."[63] Realism and romance designated not just different worlds, but worlds that had nothing in common.

The same is true of modes of governance. As Senator Bacon claimed, between subject and citizen "there is no middle ground." Ruling over a subjected population through extraordinary acts of military and executive oversight was seen as incompatible with being a citizen of a government and participating in its everyday administration. The incongruity of these modes of governance was by no means only an anti-imperial observation, for it was often legislated into existence. Violence, for example, was seen paradoxically as both incongruous to civil governance *and* necessary for its instantiation in the Philippines. Manifesting such logic, the Organic Act gave the president unfettered powers of military rule while at the same time stating that any need for military violence would delay the establishment of a civil government.[64] Similarly, Elihu Root urged the president to establish a civil government because "the powers of civil government" were "not vested in this [War] Department."[65] Root also pointed out that military rule could not supply the banking and currency laws that regulate everyday economic activity.[66]

Military orders and reports also reinforced the incompatibility of military and civil governance. In a report that received much attention in both Congress and the press, Major Cornelius Gardener noted that "the attitude of the Army, thereby meaning most of its officers and soldiers, is decidedly hostile to the provincial and municipal government in these provinces and to civil government in these islands in general."[67] Just as famous, or perhaps infamous, was the military order stating that the proper procedure characteristic of a bureaucracy could be disregarded within the context of military action: "As long as the war actively exists, it is not necessary to seek or wait for authority from these headquarters to do anything or take any action which will contribute to its termination. It is desired that all battalion commanders give their subordinate officers a degree of confidence and latitude in operation."[68]

The incongruity between military and civil rule is in many ways predictable, and many of the histories written about this period in the Philippines chronicle the tensions between the military and civilian administrations.[69] What still demands an explanation, however, is the way that such divergent modes of governance were repeatedly articulated together in spite of these incongruities and contradictions. Not only were ordinary bureaucratic governance and extraordinary intervention (violence and oversight) both thought to be necessary aspects of American rule, but also the civil government was ironically placed within the War Department. What also demands an explanation is the success of this form of government. How is it that a government that was repeatedly figured as not even fully present was able to assert such strong claims of control and sovereignty? How is it that the seemingly insurmountable contradictions of colonial government (contradictions readily admitted by its supporters) were so easily co-opted into a narrative of progress? This contradiction was not dialectical—there was no sublation of its terms. Instead, this contradiction functioned more like an "ambivalence" in the psychoanalytic sense of the word, an ambivalence in which opposing components are "simultaneously in evidence and inseparable" as a "non-dialectical opposition" that cannot be transcended.[70] And yet, in spite of this ambivalence, the narrative of empire was a progressive one, fundamentally invested in ideas of historical progress. To answer these questions and to understand how this ambivalence was incorporated into narratives of progress, we must look to the ways that these contradictions were conventionalized within the American cultural imaginary, and it is here that a turn to literature is most instructive.

Conventionalizing Contradiction: Romance, Realism, and Narrative Progression in the Popular Romance

Moving from the legal records to the romance, we find that the romance genre repeatedly staged this incongruity between the everyday and the extraordinary, but staged it according to a particular convention. In this convention realist and romantic modes interrupt one another and repeat their incongruity without ever resolving it. One sees this in Richard Harding Davis's *Soldiers of Fortune*, wherein, like many turn-of-the-century romances, a tension between romance and realism arises in the very first chapter. The novel begins with a social gathering in which the novel's hero, Clay, is introduced into high society. This drawing room scene smacks of the concerns of realist drama. The romance, however, retains its presence, and the chapter moves along through a constant reframing of one mode by the other.

Take, for example, the scene that ensues when Reginald King, Alice's suitor, begins to romanticize the life of an engineer. When the dinner conversation turns to the Mexican railroad, King exclaims, "There are no men today . . . who lead as picturesque lives as do civil engineers." King then goes on to compare them to "pioneers and martyrs," and after listing the adventurous aspects of the lives they lead, he claims "they are the bravest soldiers of the present day . . . the chief civilizer[s] of our century." Unaware that Clay is himself an engineer and in fact the very same engineer who built the Mexican railroad, Alice asks Clay sarcastically if he agrees, or whether he prefers soldiers "in red coats and gold lace." Deflating both King's romance as well as Alice's sarcastic alternative, Clay simply states that it is his "trade" and a "livelihood." Clay's comment disrupts the frame of the romance and brings into it an element of work and daily toil that repeats throughout the novel. Davis often portrays Clay in the context of everyday toil, and despite Clay's adventures, "the part he had to play was not that of leading man, but rather one of general utility," a part wherein he does "the work of five men and five different kinds of work."

Just as Clay disrupts King's romance about being a civil engineer, Alice disrupts one of Clay's own romances soon after dinner. Clay tells Alice that though they had never met, he has been carrying a picture of her that he found in a newspaper four years earlier. Alice is made uncomfortable by the story. While Clay's ordinary world is one of daily work, hers is one of social conventions, and she remains "in doubt as to how to treat this act of unconventionality." Finally, she asks him where he keeps the picture, and he tells her that it is in his trunk. Her response is quite revealing, for she exposes the romantic conventions of his tale by stating, "Not in your watch? That would have been more in keeping with the rest of the story." This comment is all the more revealing when "the young man smiled grimly, and pulling out his watch pried back the lid and turned it to her so that she could see the photograph inside." Clay resents the constriction of Alice's surroundings, but his attempt to bring her out of her conventions only reveals the conventionality of his own romance. Just as the romance of being an engineer is reframed as a livelihood of daily work, the romance of an extraordinary love at first sight is reframed as an ordinary convention.

This brings us to an important observation: this constant reframing of modes provides the very rhythm of this novel. These moments mark episodic breaks in the narrative, and every time the romance seems to build up steam, seemingly realist concerns disrupt it. These disruptions help construct the episodic progression of the narrative. At one point in the narrative a desire for "supper" even disrupts the romantic escape and flight of the characters during a political coup. This interruption begins a new chapter and marks an episodic change, for this rest stop breaks up the adventure of their retreat as well as a love scene between Clay and Alice's sister, Hope.

The incongruity of mode constitutes the temporality of the narrative, a temporality that, like a repetition compulsion, repeats a contradiction without ever resolving or changing it. The plot might move along in terms of narrative action, but its modes of storytelling never get anywhere. The novel even ends where it begins, shuttling between realms of ordinary and extraordinary life. The closing scene is on a boat heading into New York, where Clay and Hope are to get married. Clay points out the "electric lights along the ocean drive" and the "glare of the New York street lamps thrown up against the sky," but Hope is also interested in what lies to the east. Her gesture in that direction situates them between a realist urban landscape and an alternative realm of romance.

> "Over there is the coast of Africa. Don't you see the lighthouse on Cape Bon? If it wasn't for Gibraltar being in the way, I could show you the harbor lights of Bizerta, and the terraces of Algiers shining like the *café chantant* in the night."
>
> "Algiers," sighed Hope, "where you were a soldier of Africa, and rode across the deserts."[71]

Such popular romances were not simply a series of extraordinary and improbable actions. They instead alternated ambivalently between worlds of the ordinary and the extraordinary.[72] These modal contradictions rarely find a "middle ground," and there is no totalizing worldview or, in Jameson's words, a *Gestalt.* On the contrary, these novels chart a zone of indeterminacy, and like the final scene on the boat, the modes of realism and romance are uncertain destinations or horizons rather than places that are ever fully inhabited. The result is a process of endless worlding that never achieves the coherence of a world. As a form of contradiction, there are many ways that this modal difference could play out. There could be a dialectical sublation; they could coexist in a kind of equilibrium; the conflict could be displaced. But rather than sublation, equilibrium, or even a movement toward continuity, the modes of the ordinary and the extraordinary in these novels reframe and disrupt one another while maintaining their incongruity. As they disrupt one another, these modes mark the episodic progress of the narrative, but the modes themselves remain both partial and incongruous.

Ordinary Violence and Extraordinary Rule

The modes of realism and romance are the texture of the narrative rather than its text. They are the *way* it is told rather than what is told. While the plot itself has a relatively continuous flow, the *way* this story unfolds, its worlds of intelligibility, repeat ambivalently as the emergent terms of an unresolved contradiction. These modes of storytelling repeat a contradiction without resolving it, but this becomes the very form through which the story moves. The indeterminacy of mode, the repetition of an unresolved contradiction between the mundane world of the everyday and the exceptional world of the romance, beats the very rhythm of the narrative as it separates out events and stages scenes. Here one begins to see the ideological work that this convention does when it enters the discourses of sovereignty, for such a convention begins to render intelligible the transition from the indeterminacy of imperial sovereignty to the narrative of imperial progress.

The ideological work of this convention cannot be situated *within* the genre of the romance. It is not as if by denouncing these novels (the way that Howells does) one would be critiquing an imperial ideology of governance. Ideology, as I am using the term, is not a set of political ideas or practices that embody a political position. It is not for or against empire. It is, instead, something like the social imaginary that Althusser points to in his essay "Ideology and Ideological State Apparatuses," a social imaginary that becomes material through rituals and repeated habits of thought.[73] It is a horizon of intelligibility, an intelligibility that works across different discourses rather than being embodied in a single discourse. To denounce these novels as imperialist would miss the point that they participate in a social milieu that can have a social existence only by repeating across a variety of discourses. No discourse, form, or set of ideas holds a monopoly on the politics of representation, and rather than denounce or praise the politics in these novels, a more useful approach is to inquire into the work they do as participants in a social milieu they help to constitute but that also constitutes them.

So what is the work that this convention does? First, by making indeterminacy a convention of narrative flow, these novels participate in a milieu of intelligibility whereby the imperial state can continually emerge without becoming permanent. The administrative argument for sustaining an American presence was predicated on the idea that the Filipinos could be independent only when there was no longer a need for extraordinary interventions. The indeterminacies of American sovereignty functioned as a reliable or stable instability that served to legitimate a continued American presence abroad by endlessly deferring the full arrival of an ordinary mode of government. But this modal convention also allows the paradoxes and contradictions of imperial sovereignty to become the structuring elements of a narrative. From the perspective of its modes of the ordinary and the extraordinary, the narrative of the Filipino state, like the romance, ends where it began: between partial worldviews, emerging but never arriving. The indeterminacy of these worlds constituted the temporality of a narrative in which the state could remain forever without ever becoming permanent. The episodes of empire would move on; the progressive story of the state would continue to be told; but the worlds that made this story intelligible would repeat compulsively and get nowhere.

Second, such an approach provides wide latitude for different and often contradictory modes of state action to occur together. I would like to suggest that this modal convention distinguishing between realism and romance, between the ordinary and the extraordinary, does much to explain a peculiarity in the representation of colonial violence and executive oversight, a peculiarity whereby these modes of governance were figured as extraordinary despite their existence as a part of everyday colonial administration. To figure violence as a disruptive and extraordinary event might seem like common sense, but what happens if we begin to examine this "common sense" as a convention rather than as truism?

In many ways violence was very much a part of the everyday in the Philippines, where guerilla warfare lasted intermittently from 1898 through the first decade of the twentieth century. Although the colonial administration often peripheralized these conflicts, the fact remains that some of the islands lost a third of their population as an indirect and direct result of these conflicts.[74] Agricultural production, as well as the economy, ground to a halt as a consequence of the war that the United States waged against a resistant population. For example, the number of water buffalo dropped by an overwhelming 90 percent during the war, effectively wiping out Filipinos' ability to produce rice in some regions.[75] Military campaigns against insurgents often used methods of "reconcentration" that depopulated rural areas and placed the former inhabitants in concentration camps near towns and cities.[76] Many of the camps were formed in the years after President Roosevelt officially declared an end to hostilities on July 4, 1902. It is also important to note the scale of this war as well as its continued presence after Roosevelt's declaration of peace. Renato Constantino comments:

> Although 70,000 American soldiers were already fighting on Philippine soil in 1900, their number continued to increase until December 1901, or six months after the establishment of civil government, there were a total of 126,000 troops distributed in 639 military posts. On July 4, 1902, when President Theodore Roosevelt proclaimed the "insurrection" officially ended, 120,000 American soldiers were still trying to suppress Filipino resistance.[77]

Additionally, military and civil authorities continued to divide up the islands into "pacified" and "unpacified" regions well after 1902.

Executive oversight also became a part of everyday administration when it became the ultimate arbiter of land distribution and large-scale public works projects. With its tight control over the budget and the civil service, the executive disrupted and controlled the workings of the bureaucratic state on a regular basis. The Philippine Commission even created an office of the insular auditor that "was given broad powers over the accounts of the insular government and exclusive jurisdiction in determining the legality of all transactions involving these accounts."[78] Though such oversight was often figured as a necessary but extraordinary measure (there was no counterpart to this agency in the U.S. federal government), it was also very much a part of the everyday running of the administration.

To consider how the convention of these romances repeated incongruity is to begin to understand how violence and oversight became intelligible as extraordinary despite their everyday presence in acts of colonial administration. Such a consideration of this convention also allows us to begin to understand how the colonial state could deploy such divergent modes of governance and yet remain a seemingly coherent element in the romantic narrative of American empire. Figured as the most "extraordinary" of these modes of governance, violence was repressed from the representations of everyday bureaucratic governance by being portrayed as incongruous to them. However, this repression was not a matter of making violence unrepresentable. The convention of incongruity that I have been tracing suggests that repression in this case is more usefully understood in terms of its uncanny return. In other words, repression is not about how the incongruous is made to disappear. It is instead about how incongruity comes to be repeated, its convention as a symptom that wracks, not the body in this case, but the body politic.

Notes

1. William Dean Howells, "The New Historical Romances," *The North American Review* 171 (1900): 948.
2. Nancy Glazener, *Reading for Realism: The History of a U.S. Literary Institution, 1850–1910* (Durham, N.C.: Duke University Press, 1997), 148.
3. Amy Kaplan, "Romancing the Empire: The Embodiment of American Masculinity in the Popular Historical Novel of the 1890s," *American Literary History* 2 (1990): 667.
4. Ibid., 661.
5. William H. Taft, "Inauguration Speech to the Philippine Assembly, 1907," in *Present Day Problems: A Collection of Addresses Delivered on Various Occasions* (New York: Dodd, Mead, 1908), 12.
6. *Downes v. Bidwell*, 182 U.S. 244 (1901).
7. Ibid., 372.
8. Amy Kaplan, *The Anarchy of Empire in the Making of U.S. Culture* (Cambridge, Mass.: Harvard University Press, 2002), 14.
9. Ibid., 11.
10. See Organic Act, 57th Cong., 1st sess., ch. 1369 (July 1), "Report of the Philippine Commission," (Washington, D.C.: War Department, 1900), and "Report of the Philippine Commission," (Washington, D.C.: War Department, 1901). The administration gradually increased the number of Filipinos in the civil service throughout the first two decades of U.S. rule and also gradually expanded Filipino participation in the legislative process. This "Filipinization" of the state is analyzed in most of the historical accounts of this period. For recent analysis on the ways that the U.S. administration and Filipinos negotiated this often difficult process, see Julian Go, "The Chains of Empire: State Building and 'Political Education' in Puerto Rico and the Philippines," and Patricio N. Arbinales, "Progressive-Machine Conflict in Early-Twentieth-Century U.S. Politics and Colonial State-Building in the Philippines," in *The American Colonial State in the Philippines: Global Perspectives*, ed. Julian Go and Anne L. Foster (Durham, N.C.: Duke University Press, 2003).
11. "Report of the Philippine Commission," 1900, 4.
12. Michel Foucault, "Governmentality," in *Power*, ed. James D. Faubion, *The Essential Works of Foucault, 1954–1984* (New York: New Press, 2000), 220. While Foucault reexamines the role of state sovereignty in his later work, his dismissal of it in "Governmentality" seems to have a critical legacy within American studies. See, for example, Philip Fisher's argument in his introduction to *The New American Studies* in which he argues for the use of poststructuralism to analyze the relation between rhetoric and power, but then dismisses the importance of the state. Philip Fisher, "Introduction: The New American Studies," in *The New American Studies*, ed. Philip Fisher (Berkeley: University of California Press, 1991).
13. *Downes v. Bidwell*, 341–42.
14. Ibid., 306.

15. Ibid.
16. Ibid., 287.
17. Ibid.
18. Gerald E. Markowitz, ed., *American Anti-Imperialism* (New York: Garland, 1976), 45.
19. Ibid.
20. Vicente L. Rafael, *White Love and Other Events in Filipino History* (Durham, N.C.: Duke University Press, 2000), 35.
21. 57th Cong., 1st sess. (April 28, 1902), *Cong. Rec.*, 4754.
22. Julian Go, "Introduction: Global Perspectives on the U.S. Colonial State in the Philippines," in *The American Colonial State in the Philippines*, 7–8.
23. Taft, "Inauguration Speech to the Philippine Assembly, 1907," 12.
24. "Report of the Philippine Commission," 8.
25. Organic Act, 691 (my emphasis).
26. Ibid.
27. 57th Cong., 1st sess. (April 21, 1902), *Cong. Rec.*, 4477.
28. Ibid., 4478.
29. Organic Act, 692.
30. See ibid., particularly sections 1, 4, and 7.
31. See Glazener, *Reading for Realism*, for a good account of this revival.
32. See ibid.; Martin Burgess Green, *Dreams of Adventure, Deeds of Empire* (New York: Basic Books, 1979); and Kaplan, "Romancing the Empire."
33. Mary Johnston, *To Have and to Hold* (Boston: Houghton Mifflin, 1959); Richard Harding Davis, "The Reporter Who Made Himself King," in *The King's Jackal* (New York: Charles Scribner's Sons, 1909).
34. S. Wier Mitchell, *Hugh Wynne: Free Quaker* (East Ridgewood, N.J.: Gregg Press, 1967); Richard Harding Davis, *Soldiers of Fortune* (New York: Grosset & Dunlap, 1897); Richard Harding Davis, *The White Mice* (New York: Charles Scribner's Sons, 1916); McCutcheon, *Graustark, the Story of a Love Behind a Throne* (Chicago: Herbert S. Stone, 1901); Gertrude Atherton, *Rulers of Kings* (New York: Harper & Brothers, 1904).
35. René Wellek and Austin Warren, *Theory of Literature* (New York: Penguin Books, 1985), 214.
36. Fredric Jameson, "Magical Narratives: Romance as Genre," *New Literary History* 7 (1975): 141.
37. See Richard Chase, *The American Novel and Its Tradition* (Baltimore: Johns Hopkins University Press, 1980); Robert Shulman, "Realism," in *The Columbia History of the American Novel*, ed. Cathy N. Davidson et al. (New York: Columbia University Press, 1991); Glazener, *Reading for Realism*; and Eric J. Sundquist, "Introduction: The Country of the Blue," in *American Realism: New Essays*, ed. Eric J. Sundquist (Baltimore: Johns Hopkins University Press, 1982).
38. See Rafael, *White Love and Other Events in Filipino History*, and Laura Wexler, *Tender Violence: Domestic Visions in an Age of U.S. Imperialism* (Chapel Hill: University of North Carolina Press, 2000).
39. Theodore Roosevelt, "Inaugural Address, March 4, 1905," in *Presidential Messages and State Papers*, ed. Julius W. Muller (New York: Review of Reviews Company, 1917), 3089f.
40. William Taft, *Present Day Problems*, 3, 20.
41. Elihu Root, "Principles of Colonial Policy, Extract from the Report of the Secretary of War for 1899," in *The Military and Colonial Policies of the United States: Addresses and Reports by Elihu Root*, ed. Robert Bacon and James Brown Scott (New York: AMS Press, 1970), 165.
42. "Report of the Philippine Commission," 1900.
43. For a good account of the often personal relations between the administration and Filipino elites, see Ruby R. Paredes, ed., *Philippine Colonial Democracy* (New Haven, Conn.: Yale University Southeast Asia Studies, 1988). The essays in the volume trace client-patron relations in the development of the state.
44. As quoted in Dean C. Worcester, *The Philippines Past and Present* (New York: Macmillan, 1930), 271.
45. Samuel K. Tan, *The Filipino-American War, 1899–1913* (Quezon City: University of the Philippines Press, 2002), 220.
46. *Dorr v. United States*, 195 U.S. 138, 148 (1904).
47. Glazener, *Reading for Realism*, 148.
48. Theodore Roosevelt, *The Strenuous Life, Essays and Addresses* (New York: Charles Scribner's Sons, 1906), 185.

49. 57th Cong., 1st sess. (April 26, 1902), *Cong. Rec.*, 4673.
50. Ibid. (my emphasis).
51. *Downes v. Bidwell*, 344.
52. See the debates on the Organic Act in the *Congressional Record*, particularly between April 25 and May 9, 1902.
53. Elihu Root, "American Policies in the Philippines in 1902, Address of the Secretary of War at Peoria, Illinois, September 24, 1902," in *The Military and Colonial Policies of the United States*, 80, 65–66.
54. Theodore Roosevelt, "The Strenuous Life," in *Theodore Roosevelt: An American Mind*, ed. Mario R. DiNunzio (New York: Penguin Books, 1995), 189.
55. Ibid., 188–89.
56. Theodore Roosevelt, "America's Part of the World's Work," in *Theodore Roosevelt*, 183.
57. See, for example, *Cong. Rec.* (April 26, 1902), 4719, 4720.
58. Howells, "The New Historical Romances," 943, 945.
59. Davis, *Soldiers of Fortune*, 40, 41. All subsequent quotations are cited parenthetically.
60. Roland Barthes, "The Reality Effect," in *The Realist Novel*, ed. Dennis Walder (London: Routledge, 1995).
61. Agnes Repplier, "The Decay of Sentiment," in *Books and Men* (Boston: Houghton Mifflin, 1888), 119.
62. See, for example, Harold MacGrath, *The Carpet from Bagdad* (Indianapolis: Bobbs-Merrill, 1911), and Mitchell, *Hugh Wynne*.
63. Agnes Repplier, *Varia* (Boston: Houghton Mifflin, 1897), 225–26.
64. Organic Act; see particularly sections 2, 3, and 6.
65. "Report of the Philippine Commission," 5.
66. Ibid., 7.
67. 57th Cong., 1st sess. (April 24, 1902), *Cong. Rec.*, 4619.
68. Ibid., 4617. For a good historical account of the scandals surrounding these military reports and the excesses of the military campaign, see Stuart Creighton Miller, *"Benevolent Assimilation": The American Conquest of the Philippines, 1899–1903* (New Haven, Conn.: Yale University Press, 1982).
69. One of the best accounts of some of these tensions appears in the memoir of Dean Worcester, who was on the Philippine Commission between 1900 and 1913. Worcester, *The Philippines Past and Present*.
70. See J. Laplanche and J. B. Pontalis, *The Language of Psycho-Analysis*, trans. Donald Nicholson-Smith (New York: W. W. Norton, 1973), 28.
71. Davis, 12–14, 18, 36, 299, 345. There are many other examples of this. In Charles Major, *When Knighthood Was in Flower* (Indianapolis: Bowen Merrill, 1898), the narrator sets up an opposition between those who would "stoop to trade" (the work of everyday commerce) and "intrigues" with nobility. In MacGrath, *The Carpet from Bagdad*, the protagonist is described as having two sides to his personality, a romantic side and a side that makes him a "marriageable man" because of his sense of everyday duty and work. In Johnston's *To Have and to Hold*, the opening scene oscillates between the protagonist sitting on his porch with a pipe after a long day of work, and the impending threat of Indian attacks. In McCutcheon, *Graustark, the Story of a Love Behind a Throne*, the first chapter is titled "Mr. Grenfall Seeks Adventure," and the chapter establishes a tension between his desire for adventure and familial pressures for him to settle down to work. The chapter begins with a seemingly ordinary set of circumstances and ends with precisely the kind of romantic adventure he is seeking.
72. One can trace this logic through any of the other novels that I have mentioned in this article. In many of them the distinction between these modes is made with direct reference to literary conventions. See, for example, MacGrath, *The Carpet from Bagdad*, in which novels and reading habits help to delineate the split between romance and realism in the protagonist's personality.
73. Louis Althusser, *Essays on Ideology* (New York: Verso, 1993).
74. 57th Cong., 1st sess. (April 24, 1902) *Cong. Rec.*, 4620.
75. Stanley Karnow, *In Our Image: America's Empire in the Philippines* (New York: Ballantine Books, 1989), 194.
76. See O. D. Corpuz, *The Roots of the Filipino Nation*, vol. 2 (Quezon City: Aklahi Foundation, 1989), and Miller, *"Benevolent Assimilation."*
77. Renato Constantino, *A History of the Philippines: From the Spanish Colonization to the Second World War* (New York: Monthly Review Press, 1975), 241.
78. Frank Hindman Golay, *Face of Empire*, as quoted in Arbinales, "Progressive-Machine Conflict," 159–60.

Where Is Guantánamo?

Amy Kaplan

> I think Guantánamo, everyone agrees, is an animal, there is no other like it.[1]
>
> —Ruth Bader Ginsburg

> Strictly speaking, the written accent on the second syllable (Guantánamo) is required to indicate the proper Spanish pronunciation. To Americans this is unnecessary. In the half century of United States occupancy, the accent has disappeared. Guantanamo Bay is in effect a bit of American territory, and so it will probably remain as long as we have a Navy, for we have a lease in perpetuity to this Naval Reservation and it is inconceivable that we would abandon it.[2]
>
> — *The History of Guantanamo Bay*, 1953

In January 2002, the first shackled and hooded men from Afghanistan were incarcerated behind barbed wire at the U.S. Naval Station, Guantánamo Bay, Cuba. In April 2004, when the case challenging the legality of their detention was argued before the U.S. Supreme Court, Guantánamo still appeared to many as a strange aberration, as an "animal," with "no other like it," as Justice Ginsburg stated. Descriptions of Guantánamo as a lawless zone enhanced this image of its exceptional status: a legal black hole, a legal limbo, a prison beyond the law, a "permanent United States penal colony floating in another world."[3] Yet since the revelations of prisoner abuse at Abu Ghraib in Iraq and the leak of the Washington "torture memos," it has become increasingly clear that, more than an anomaly, Guantánamo represents the start of the "road to Abu Ghraib," one island in a global penal archipelago, where the United States indefinitely detains, secretly transports, and tortures uncounted prisoners from all over the world.[4] As a rallying cry against human rights abuses in the U.S. "war on terror," Guantánamo has come to embody what Amnesty International calls a "gulag for our times."[5]

The global dimensions of Guantánamo cannot be understood separately from its seemingly bizarre location in Cuba. Prisoners captured in Afghanistan and around the world were transported here, to a country quite close geographically, yet far politically, from the United States, a country with which the United States has no diplomatic relations. Guantánamo occupies a transitional political space, where a prison housed in a communist nation against whom the U.S. is still fighting the cold war has become an epicenter for the new "war on terror." It also occupies a liminal national space, in, yet not within, Cuba, but at the same time a "bit of American territory," as the 1953 history of the naval base proclaimed. Guantánamo is not clearly under the sovereignty of either nation, nor seemingly subject to national or international law. Where in the world is Guantánamo?

Guantánamo lies at the heart of the American Empire, a dominion at once rooted in specific locales and dispersed unevenly all over the world. The United States first acquired the land around Guantánamo Bay in 1898, when it occupied Cuba in the aftermath of the Spanish-American War. At a critical historical juncture, the United States reached the limits of its expansion westward and southward into lands violently dispossessed from Indians and Mexicans. During the height of the global "Age of Empire," the year 1898 launched the United States onto the world stage as an imperial force in the Caribbean and the Pacific.[6] Ever since, Guantánamo has played a strategic role in the changing exercise of U.S. power in the region, as a coaling station, a naval base, a cold war outpost, and a detention center for unwanted refugees.[7] The use of Guantánamo as a prison camp today demands to be understood in the context of its historical location. Its legal—or lawless—status has a logic grounded in imperialism, whereby coercive state power has been routinely mobilized beyond the sovereignty of national territory and outside the rule of law. Understanding this history can help us decipher how Guantánamo has become critical to the working of empire today. Thus to ask about the location of Guantánamo is to ask: where in the world is the United States?

Given this history, it is not surprising that Guantánamo has become a subject for international debate at the same time that the idea of the American Empire has gained credence across the U.S. political spectrum.[8] Until recently, the notion of American imperialism was considered a contradiction in terms, an accusation hurled only by left-wing critics. Indeed the denial of imperialism still fuels a vision of America as an exceptional nation, one interested in spreading universal values, not in conquest and domination. Yet, since September 11, 2001, neoconservative and liberal interventionists have openly embraced the vision of an ascendant American Empire policing and transforming the world around it through military and political might and economic and cultural power.[9] Other commentators of different political perspectives have viewed the United States as an overstretched empire in chaotic decline.[10] Many have tried to understand the difference between earlier imperial formations based on a nation's territorial conquest and annexation and today's more dispersed forms of globalized power unanchored in particular territorial domains. Some advocates for empire today have in fact turned to the history of U.S. imperialism at the turn of the last century as a model for the present.[11]

The question of empire has rarely entered the important legal debates about the prison camp at Guantánamo, debates about the balance between national security and civil liberties, the rights of the prisoners, the extent of U.S. legal jurisdiction, the domain of international law, and the thorny question of national sovereignty.[12] While Guantánamo's history occasionally provides background for these deliberations, it has remained largely absent from the discussion of Guantánamo as a legal dilemma. This *American Quarterly* volume on "Legal Borderlands" provides the opportunity to bring together the concerns of legal scholars with civil liberties and human rights and those of American studies scholars with the history and culture of imperialism, precisely because it is a phenomenon that does not simply inform foreign policy abroad but, rather, intimately shapes the contours of U.S. national identity.[13] Guantánamo lies at the intersection of these two inquiries.

In this essay, I argue that the legal space of Guantánamo today has been shaped and remains haunted by its imperial history. This complex history helps to explain how Guantánamo has become an ambiguous space both inside and outside different legal systems. Guantánamo's geographic and historical location provides the legal and political groundwork for the current violent penal regime. The first three sections of the essay show that the political, social, and constitutional legacies of U.S. imperialism inform key contemporary debates about Guantánamo: the question of national sovereignty, the codification of the prisoners as "enemy combatants," and the ambiguity about whether the U.S. Constitution holds sway there.

The essay then turns to the 2004 Supreme Court decision in *Rasul v. Bush*, which seems to answer one question about where Guantánamo is as a juridical space. The Court ruled that the federal courts do have jurisdiction over the U.S. naval base, and that the prisoners therefore should have access to the courts to challenge the legality of their detention. The justices were not only interested in restraining executive power to bring Guantánamo within the rule of domestic law; they also showed concern with the scope of U.S. power in the world and the extent to which the judiciary should accompany or limit U.S. military rule abroad. In a close reading of the Supreme Court's decision and dissent, I argue that the logic and rhetoric of *Rasul v. Bush* rely on and perpetuate the imperial history the Court also elides. In concert with its other recent decisions about civil liberties and national security, the Court, in this decision about Guantánamo, is contributing to the global expansion of U.S.

power by reworking the earlier history of imperialism. Its legal decisions respond to the changing demands of empire by creating new categories of persons before the law that extend far beyond Guantánamo Bay, Cuba.

The Imperial Legacy of Limited Sovereignty

The most outrageous claim of the Bush administration about Guantánamo continues to be that the Republic of Cuba has "ultimate sovereignty" over this territory, that therefore neither the Constitution nor U.S. obligations to international treaties apply, and, as a result, that the prisoners at Guantánamo have no rights.[14] Nor, according to this argument, do Cuban laws hold sway there. In other words, because the U.S. *lacks* formal sovereignty, it can do whatever it wants there, and the military can act with impunity to brutally control every aspect of the prisoners' lives. While this legal groundwork was carefully prepared by the Justice Department's legal counsel at the end of 2001, the disavowal of sovereignty over a territory nonetheless controlled by the United States has a long history and was key to U.S. imperial strategy of more than a century ago.

Guantánamo Bay had been a strategic colonial site since the arrival of the Spanish in the fifteenth century. On the southeastern tip of Cuba, it served as a portal for the trade of enslaved Africans, and in the nineteenth century, Caimanera, one of its port cities, became the end point for the railroad that transported sugar and molasses from the plantations of the region to be exported abroad. In 1895, when the Cubans launched their third war for independence against centuries of Spanish rule, the uprising began in the Oriente province, where revolutionary leaders José Martí and General Máximo Gómez landed at a beach near Guantánamo Bay.

In 1898, backed by popular enthusiasm at home, the United States intervened against Spain to aid the anticolonial struggle of *Cuba Libre.* At the outset of the war, U.S. Marines landed at Guantánamo Bay, where they fought a key battle and remained ensconced after the end of the three-month war. Touted as a war of liberation to rescue the Cubans from a brutal Old World empire, the Spanish-American War secured U.S. control over the remnants of Spanish colonialism in the Caribbean and the Pacific. The swift victory against Spain ended in U.S. reluctance to accept the national independence of Cuba, or that of any of the other territories ceded by Spain. While the United States fought to annex the Philippines in a vicious three-year war against Filipino nationalists and turned Puerto Rico and Guam into territorial possessions, the United States occupied Cuba with the professed goal of ceding to Cuban self-

Figure 1.
U.S. Marines raising the American flag. "Hoisting the flag at Guantánamo, June 12, 1898," photograph by Edward H. Hart. Detroit Publishing Company. Courtesy of Library of Congress.

government. Yet after three years of military occupation, Washington agreed to withdraw its troops only after forcing a sweeping amendment it wrote onto the new republic's constitution.

The Platt Amendment reserved to the United States the right to intervene in Cuba militarily and to control its economy and its relations with other countries.[15] It also guaranteed the lease or purchase of coaling and naval stations, a provision that would lead to leasing Guantánamo Bay in 1903. The Platt Amendment legislated U.S. domination of the new republic, as its language perpetuated the paternalistic narrative of rescue. The amendment decreed that "the United States may exercise the right to intervene for the preservation of Cuban independence."[16] This formulation renders the U.S. military intervention, rather than Cuban self-government, as a "right." In this logic of equating intervention with protection, Cuba's independence becomes dependent on the U.S. right to violate its autonomy. Article VII of the amendment guaranteed that the Cuban government would lease or sell lands necessary for coaling or naval stations in order "to enable the United States to maintain the independence of Cuba."[17] In other words, for the United States to protect

Cuban independence, the new government of Cuba had no choice but to accept measures that drastically curtailed that liberty. As military governor Leonard Wood wrote to President Theodore Roosevelt, "There is, of course, little or no independence left Cuba under the Platt Amendment."[18]

After the United States intervened militarily several times in the early twentieth century, with Cuba drawn solidly into the economic and political orbit of the United States, the two parties abrogated the Platt Amendment in 1934. At the same time, they extended the lease for Guantánamo in perpetuity, that is, until both parties agreed to cancel it, or "so long as the United States of America shall not abandon the said naval station."[19] The United States could stay as long as it wanted, regardless of the desires of the Cubans. The language of the treaty places the United States in the active position of agent with the prerogative to stay or leave, and Cuba in the passive role of accepting either occupation or abandonment. Indeed, after the revolution of 1959, Fidel Castro tried unsuccessfully to revoke the lease, but he succeeded only in cutting off the water supply and surrounding the base with cactus fields. The U.S. treasury still sends a check each year of $4,085 for "leasing" the land that the Cuban government doesn't cash, because it demands that the United States cease the occupation of its territory. According to the Cuban government, Guantánamo Bay continues to be an illegitimately occupied territory.

Most of today's legal arguments about Guantánamo have hinged on the interpretation of the 1903 lease, which reads: "While on the one hand the United States recognizes the continuance of the ultimate sovereignty of the Republic of Cuba over the above described areas of land and water, on the other hand the Republic of Cuba consents that during the period of the occupation by the United States of said areas under the terms of this agreement the United States shall exercise complete jurisdiction and control over and within said areas."[20] The language of the lease expresses a hierarchy between recognition and consent, rendering Cuban sovereignty over Guantánamo Bay contingent on the acknowledgment of the United States, in exchange for which Cuba agrees to cede sovereignty over part of the territory it never controlled. The Republic of Cuba had no option but to agree to terms that had already been dictated prior to its independence, terms which founded and undermined its sovereignty as a nation.[21] Although the lease refers to the control of territory, the phrase "the continuance of ultimate sovereignty," key to the government's argument today, implies a strange temporality. "Continuance" is at odds with the fact that Cuba had not yet achieved sovereignty as a nation because it emerged directly from its status as a Spanish colony into the military occupation of the United States. "Ultimate sovereignty" refers to a condition that never quite existed in the past, yet is assured continuity into some unspecified future. Thus as a territory held by the United States in perpetuity, over which sovereignty is indefinitely deferred, the temporal dimensions of Guantánamo's location make it a chillingly appropriate place for the indefinite detention of unnamed enemies in what the administration calls a perpetual war against terror.

The lease and the attribution of limited sovereignty, which the Platt Amendment exemplifies, formed—and continue to form—an effective technology of imperial rule. The United States was following an established practice of other empires at the turn of the twentieth century, as annexation with high administrative costs became less attractive to colonial regimes around the world.[22] In practice, a lease, as opposed to outright annexation, allowed for greater maneuverability of imperial powers, in part because it enhanced their immunity from political and legal accountability to all forms of governance, both in the colony and the metropolis.

The lease of Guantánamo Bay in 1903 also reflected the reigning U.S. imperial strategy and ideology of the "New Empire" as voiced by prominent figures such as Alfred Thayer Mahan and Theodore Roosevelt.[23] Both advocated building a strong navy to support U.S. economic and political expansion around the world, unfettered by the burden of annexing territories with populations to govern. In 1902, Mahan recognized that "it would be difficult to exaggerate the value of Guantanamo, only fifty miles from Santiago de Cuba, to the American fleet off the latter port, which otherwise had to coal in the open, or depend upon a base many hundred miles away."[24] According to Mahan, such stations facilitated the mobility of an empire that would foster economic expansion, through military and political domination. Indeed the key strategic value of Guantánamo Bay for most of the century was not only the control of Cuba, but also its access to the rest of the Caribbean, Central and South America, and the Panama Canal Zone, whose "treaty" was negotiated at gunpoint in the same period.[25] Guantánamo was viewed as a steppingstone to Latin America and across the Pacific, and it was deployed as a launching pad for military interventions in Cuba, the Dominican Republic, Nicaragua, and Guatemala throughout the twentieth century.

Thus the "legal black hole" of Guantánamo did not appear suddenly after September 11, 2001, but is filled with a long imperial history.[26] The government's argument that the United States lacks sovereignty over the territory of Guantánamo has long facilitated rather than limited the actual implementation of sovereign power in the region. In *Rasul v. Bush*, the Court dismissed what Justice Souter called the vague "metaphysics of ultimate sovereignty" in favor of the prisoners' claims that the United States has in practice exercised total control and jurisdiction over the base for a century.[27] Yet the Court's decision still leaves open the question of national sovereignty, and while it supports the prisoners' claim that divorces jurisdiction from sovereignty over territory, this same open-endedness seems to abet a different kind of sovereignty, the executive power to dictate the violent terms of governance over the lives of the prisoners there.

The Racialized Legacy of the Colonial Outpost

In establishing Guantánamo as a space removed from the reach of U.S. domestic law, the administration has concomitantly created the category of "enemy combatants" to deny the prisoners the protections and rights of international law and the Geneva conventions, which they would have as prisoners of war. Secretary of Defense Rumsfeld declared the prisoners to be the "most dangerous, best-trained, vicious killers on the face of the earth."[28] While such statements conjure threatening racist stereotypes of Muslim terrorists as "bad guys" and "evil-doers," the prisoners' presence at the U.S. naval base at Guantánamo has also accrued a history of racialized images from the legacy of U.S. intervention in the Caribbean.

Although Guantánamo was never formally a U.S. colony, the social space of the base has long resembled a colonial outpost. Until the Cuban revolution, the base served as a contact zone of sorts, a site of uneven colonial exchanges between Cubans and Americans, as Cubans entered the base as laborers through a highly regulated passport system, and U.S. sailors used the neighboring towns as an exotic playground for prostitution, drinking, and gambling.[29] In the 1930s through the 1950s, journalists and travelers described the naval station through colonialist discourse as a transplanted Little America and often contrasted its hygienic, well-ordered housing with the reportedly "primitive" and squalid, impoverished conditions of the neighboring Cuban villages. After the revolution, the base became a self-enclosed enclave, where most of the Cuban laborers were replaced with Jamaican and Filipino laborers contracted to work there. The image of the base as small town America, however, continues to circulate today, replete with bowling alleys, video rental shops, golf courses, and McDonald's restaurants. The naval commander has been quoted as referring to the base as "Mayberry RFD with bad neighbors."[30] It is unclear which bad neighbors he was referring to—the Cubans kept out by barbed wire fences and military guards or the prisoners encaged by barbed wire inside the base. With unintended irony, a defense department publication elaborated on the meaning of "Mayberry," the town in television's *Andy Griffith Show* of the 1960s. "Like Mayberry, Guantánamo Bay has virtually no crime."[31]

The current prisoners were not the first to be held in cages in the middle of "Mayberry." In the last decade of the twentieth century, the role of the naval base at Guantánamo changed dramatically: from a way station for the global reach of military might outward, it became a site of detention camps for blocking Haitian and Cuban refugees from entering the United States. Thus, another trajectory that leads to the camps of Guantánamo today is the long history of U.S. imperial relations with Haiti, a nation it occupied from 1915 to 1934. After a military coup ousted Jean-Bertrand Aristide in 1991, tens of thousands of Haitians sought political asylum in the United States, a status the United States had long refused. The coast guard took the unprecedented step of intercepting Haitians on the high seas, and when, under international pressure, the United States stopped repatriating them to the repressive regime at home, they were taken to the base at Guantánamo for "processing," where they were denied any rights to appeal for asylum. Many were held up to three years in makeshift barbed wire camps, exposed to heat and rain in spaces infested with rats and scorpions, with inadequate water supplies and sanitary facilities.[32] Furthermore, a separate camp was built for those who, through forced testing, were found to carry HIV, where they received inadequate medical care and where medicine was often used coercively; their health rapidly deteriorated.[33] The rationale for detaining the Haitians relied on racist hysteria that imagined Haiti as the source of the AIDS virus and Haitians as the bearers of contaminated blood. Newspaper articles and speeches in Congress envisioned hordes of Haitians invading Florida, as though they themselves were the viruses they were purported to carry. This assumption that Haitian bodies carried disease has a long history as well. From the Haitian Revolution that began in 1791, black Haitian bodies were viewed from the north as bearing the contagion of black rebellion that could "infect" slaves in other countries and colonies.

In 1994, Washington constructed another tent city surrounded by barbed wire to detain almost thirty thousand Cubans who were attempting to reach the United States by sea. "Miserable conditions led some Cuban detainees to attempt suicide. Their numerous uprisings were met by U.S. troops in riot gear with fixed bayonets."[34] The Cubans were trapped in a cold war nightmare. Whereas Cubans fleeing from the communist regime long held privileged status as political refugees, the United States viewed these Cubans, whom Castro had released during an economic crisis, as criminals to repatriate. When the detention camps were shut down in 1995, most of those detained were allowed into the United States, though many were repatriated or sent to third countries. A legacy of Guantánamo's unclear sovereignty, Haitians in the United States who were born in detention there remain "effectively stateless, since the camp authorities would not give them U.S. birth certificates and Haiti has not extended citizenship rights to them either."[35]

It is striking that the current prisoners at Guantánamo, purportedly the most dangerous terrorists in the world, have been brought to the geographic threshold of the United States as though they were aspiring immigrants or would-be refugees who have to be kept out forcibly. If the naval base can still be viewed as a colonial outpost, it is a colony devoid of local inhabitants, and the colonized "others" now comprise a transnational population from forty nations, captured in many places besides Afghanistan, including Pakistan, Bosnia, Turkey, Germany, and Gambia and untold other places around the world. Although the government has lumped them together as terrorists, al Qaeda members, and Islamic extremists, their identities are enormously varied. They speak as many as seventeen different languages; many are immigrants or the children of immigrants to different nations around the world.[36]

The current prisoners not only first literally inhabited the camps built for the Haitian and Cuban refugees, but they also continue to inhabit the racialized images that accrued over the century in the imperial outpost of Guantánamo: images of shackled slaves, infected bodies, revolutionary subjects, and undesirable immigrants. The prisoners fill the vacated space of colonized subjects, in which terrorism is imagined as an infectious disease of racialized bodies in need of quarantine. The category of "enemy combatants" effaces all differences among the detainees and also draws on these older imperial codes. The image of the "enemy combatant" also draws on the conflation increasingly made of immigrants and terrorists, at a time when the Immigration and Naturalization Service (INS) has become part of the Department of Homeland Security, immigrants are detained without legal recourse, and there is an "increased intermingling of immigration law enforcement and criminal law policing."[37] Thus "enemy combatant" is a racialized category, not only because of rampant racism toward Arabs and Muslims, but also because of this history. Stereotypes of the colonized, immigrants, refugees, aliens, criminals, and revolutionaries are intertwined with those of terrorists and identified with racially marked bodies in an imperial system that not only colonizes spaces outside U.S. territories but also regulates the entry of people migrating across the borders of the United States.

The Haitians and Cubans in Guantánamo protested their detention through hunger strikes, riots, and legal suits. While they succeeded in shutting down the camps, the government ultimately refused to concede them any constitutional rights, and the courts never definitely ruled on this issue. In response to litigation brought by Haitian refugees, two circuit courts divided over whether the Bill of Rights applied to noncitizens there.[38] Legally, the justification for detaining Haitians and Cubans without constitutional or international rights at Guantánamo was the same one used by the government today, involving the absence of U.S. sovereignty. In 2001, the government's choice of Guantánamo relied in part on the 1995 decision by the Eleventh Circuit Court of Appeals that "Cuban and Haitian migrants have no First Amendment or Fifth Amendment rights which they can assert."[39] The same decision ruled that international human rights treaties "bind the government only when refugees are at or within the borders of the United States."[40] Where then is Guantánamo, if not at the border of the United States?

The Ambiguous Legacy of the Insular Cases

The question of whether the U.S. Constitution holds sway in Guantánamo remains unresolved by the Supreme Court in *Rasul v. Bush*. Save for a mention in a footnote, the Court carefully avoided the question of whether noncitizens in Guantánamo Bay have access to constitutional protections and rights. This indeterminacy about the extraterritorial reach of the Constitution has long accompanied the expansion of U.S. rule beyond its national borders.

At the turn of the last century, the legal debate about imperialism revolved around the question of whether the "Constitution follows the flag" into the new territories taken from Spain and the recently annexed territory of Hawai'i.[41] At stake in this question, which resonates today, was whether the nation could remain a republic if it ruled over lands and peoples governed by laws not subject to its Constitution. In a series of decisions that came to be known as the Insular Cases (1902–1922), the Court answered that question ambiguously: it decided that parts of the Constitution followed the flag, sometimes, and in certain contexts.[42] In the best-known case, *Downes v. Bidwell*, which concerned whether the uniform clause of the Constitution applied to Puerto Rico, the Court created the new category of "the unincorporated territory," a territory not annexed for the ultimate purpose of statehood. The decision deemed Puerto Rico "foreign to the United States in a domestic sense," a space "belonging to" but "not a part of the United States," whose inhabitants were neither aliens nor citizens.[43] In these liminal spaces, the Insular Cases allowed for a two-tiered, uneven application of the Constitution, claiming that some unspecified fundamental or substantive rights were binding in the unincorporated territories. Yet there were no consistent guarantees of due process or the right to criminal and civil juries or full protection under the Fourteenth Amendment; in other words, there were no clear rights to be protected against unfair procedures.

This differential application of the Constitution created the legal edifice for imperial rule. The designation of territory as neither quite foreign nor domestic was inseparable from a view of its inhabitants as neither capable of self-government nor civilized enough for U.S. citizenship. The Insular Cases legitimated a colonial space, inherently based on racism, to protect U.S. citizens from an acquired population that might belong to a race, "absolutely unfit to receive" the full responsibilities and protections of the Constitution.[44] In *Downes v. Bidwell*, both the territory of Puerto Rico and its inhabitants were not therefore treated as part of an autonomous foreign nation, but they were left in "limbo," according to Chief Justice Melville Weston Fuller's dissent. The "occult meaning" of the "unincorporated territory," he argued, gave Congress the unrestricted power to keep any newly acquired territory "like a disembodied shade in an intermediate state of ambiguous existence for an indefinite period."[45] This language uncannily describes Guantánamo today, and the sense of the occult was echoed in Justice Souter's skepticism about the "metaphysics of ultimate sovereignty." The Insular Cases have never been overruled, even though the international scope of the Constitution has changed greatly in the twentieth century, for the most part expanding the constitutional rights of American citizens abroad rather than those of noncitizens. The imperial origins of these cases, which often remain unacknowledged, continue to haunt their subsequent use as precedence in later cases throughout the twentieth century.

Although Guantánamo Bay, Cuba, was never an "unincorporated territory," the two-tiered legacy of the Insular Cases helped construct the naval base there as an ambiguous legal space where the extent of constitutional rights remains indeterminate. While *Rasul* does not rely directly on the Insular Cases as precedent, it indirectly evokes them in the sole footnote in the decision that addresses the constitutionality of the detentions. *Rasul* ruled that the prisoners at Guantánamo have the right to challenge their detention in the federal courts according to a federal statute (28 U.S. Code Sec. 2241), not according to the Constitution. Yet, in note 15, the Court holds that the detainees might have constitutional rights they could assert in the United States, indicating that the detainees' allegations do provide a basis for a constitutional claim. The Court writes that these allegations, namely, "that, although they have engaged neither in combat nor in acts of terrorism against the United States, they have been held in Executive detention for more than two years in territory subject to the long-term, exclusive jurisdiction and control of the United States, without access to counsel and without being charged with any wrongdoing" do "unquestionably describe 'custody in violation of the Constitution or laws or treaties of the United States.'" By relegating this opinion to a footnote, however, rather than incorporating it into the opinion, the Court leaves open the question of constitutional rights, an openness that has led to diametrically opposing positions on the part of the administration and advocates for the prisoners, and between judges in the federal courts.

To trace the lineage of the Insular Cases in *Rasul*, we have to look further at this footnote. Justice Stevens follows this statement by referring to a comparison with a 1990 case that took the opposite direction of denying constitutional protections abroad. In *United States v. Verdugo-Urquidez*, the Court held that the Fourth Amendment was not available to a suspected drug dealer, whose home was searched without warrant in Mexico, when he was captured by U.S. agents and brought to the United States for criminal indictment.[46] The Court in *Verdugo-Urquidez* drew on the precedent of the Insular Cases to hold that not all constitutional provisions pertain to U.S. governmental activity in foreign territories. As in those cases, Chief Justice William Rehnquist's argument relied not only on the territorial scope of the Constitution but also the extent of its reach to noncitizens. Because the Fourth Amendment used the word "people," instead of "persons," he claimed, it refers to a narrower scope of "a class of persons who are part of a national community or who have otherwise developed sufficient connection with this country to be considered part of that community."[47] He thus read a nationalist hierarchy of rights as already written into the language of the Bill of Rights, only some of which are applicable to the general category of "persons" who are not U.S. citizens.

In *Verdugo-Urquidez*, Justice Anthony Kennedy wrote a concurring opinion, and it is to this opinion that Stevens specifically refers in the *Rasul* note. Kennedy rejected Rehnquist's distinction between "the people" and "persons," but he maintained a boundary between foreign and domestic territory: "The Constitution does not create, nor do general principles of law create, any juridical relation between our country and some undefined, limitless class of noncitizens who are beyond our territory."[48] Even though Kennedy insists on this division, he proceeds to cite precedents that blur these boundaries to argue that the Constitution may still apply abroad in particular circumstances. He quotes Justice Harlan in *Reid v. Covert* (1953), a landmark case that involved the right of U.S. citizens abroad to a trial by jury:

> The Insular Cases do stand for an important proposition, one which seems to me a wise and necessary gloss on our Constitution. The proposition is, of course, not that the Constitution "does not apply" overseas, but that there are provisions in the Constitution which do not necessarily apply in all circumstances in every foreign place. . . . There is no rigid and abstract rule.[49]

In 1990, Kennedy concludes from this reasoning that "just as the Constitution in the Insular Cases did not require Congress to implement all constitutional guarantees in its territories because of their 'wholly dissimilar traditions and institutions,' the Constitution does not require U.S. agents to obtain a warrant when searching the foreign home of a nonresident alien." In pursuing this racially inflected differential logic, he argues that "the absence of local judges or magistrates available to issue warrants, the differing and perhaps unascertainable conceptions of reasonableness and privacy that prevail abroad, and the need to cooperate with foreign officials all indicate that the Fourth Amendment's warrant requirement should not apply in Mexico as it does in this country."[50] With this reasoning, Kennedy concurred with the majority in denying that the Fourth Amendment should cross the border to Mexico to accompany the actions of U.S. agents.

The import of this reference in *Rasul* is far from clear. Is the Court suggesting that the prisoners in Guantánamo may indeed have constitutional rights in contrast to the prisoner in *Verdugo-Urquidez*? Or is the Court evoking Kennedy's reasoning in sustaining both limits and flexibility to the extension of constitutional provisions? In *Rasul*, Kennedy concurred with the majority in favor of extending U.S. jurisdiction to the prisoners, but he wrote a separate opinion in order to uphold a dividing line between foreign and domestic territory as he did in *Verdugo-Urquidez*. His reasoning construed Guantánamo in the imperial language of the Insular Cases as "a place that belongs to the United States."[51] By claiming that "Guantánamo Bay is in every practical respect a United States territory," as the basis for extending some rights to the prisoners, he implicitly insists that these rights do not necessarily apply to other locations under U.S. control.

Neither Stevens nor Kennedy answers the question, where is Guantánamo?—whether it is located in foreign or a domestic space as far as the Constitution is concerned. For the legacy of the Insular Cases does not lie primarily in delimiting the extraterritorial scope of the Constitution. It lies more powerfully in legislating an ambiguity that gives the U.S. government great leeway in deciding whether, when, and which provisions of the Constitution may apply overseas, and indeed in determining what territories may be considered "foreign to the United States in a domestic sense."

Because of this historical ambiguity, the Insular Cases have been marshaled both for and against the prisoners. The Justice Department, in its motion to dismiss the prisoners' habeas corpus cases drew on the interpretation of the Insular Cases in *Verdugo-Urquidez* to argue that there is "nothing in the Supreme Court's opinion in *Rasul*" to undermine the conclusion "that aliens, such as petitioners, who are outside the sovereign territory of the United States and lack a sufficient connection to the United States may not assert rights under the Constitution."[52] In January 2005, Federal District Judge Richard J. Leon accepted this argument that no "viable legal theory" accords rights to the prisoners, and he granted the government's motion to dismiss seven of the prisoners' habeas corpus cases.[53]

Two weeks later, however, his counterpart, Federal District Judge Joyce Hens Green, came to the opposite conclusion and relied on the same footnote in *Rasul* to reveal an "implicit, if not express, mandate to uphold the existence of fundamental rights through the application of precedent from the Insular cases."[54] Her decision went farther to declare illegal the Combatant Status Review Tribunals at Guantánamo conducted by the Department of Defense, and she held that the detainees should be treated as prisoners of war. With both decisions still under appeal at the time of this writing, the petitioners remain imprisoned with no change in their status, and the unanswered question may yet return to the Supreme Court to resolve its own ambiguity as to whether the Constitution follows the flag, not only to Guantánamo, but also to other extraterritorial sites under the control of the U.S. military.

The Supreme Court's refusal to squarely rule on the constitutional status of Guantánamo is in part a product of the Insular Cases, which remain doctrinal precedent today. Gerald Neuman, in a brief for the petitioners, wrote that "the *Insular Cases* forged a compromise between the forces of constitutionalism and the forces of empire by guaranteeing that the most fundamental constitutional rights would be honored wherever the U.S. rules as sovereign."[55] Judge Green's decision powerfully endorses this view. Yet history has shown that the Insular Cases resolved that conflict by forging a compromise in favor of empire. In not clearly deciding on whether the prisoners at Guantánamo have constitutional rights, the Supreme Court may have implicitly supported the executive's unrestricted power given to Congress by the Insular Cases, to keep any domain, "like a disembodied shade, in an intermediate state of ambiguous existence for an indefinite period." This ambiguity increases the range and mobility of the exercise of U.S. power abroad, and this uncertainty legitimates a crushing certainty of dominion over the lives of those imprisoned in Guantánamo and other locations around the world.

Imperial Spaces in *Rasul v. Bush*

In *Rasul v. Bush*, the Court ruled that the federal courts do have jurisdiction over the U.S. naval base at Guantánamo "to determine the legality of the Executive's potentially indefinite detention of individuals who claim to be wholly innocent of wrongdoing." Therefore the Court deemed that the prisoners should have access to the federal courts and the right to bring a petition for habeas corpus to challenge whether they are being unlawfully denied their freedom. This judicial check of excessive executive power is often narrated in spatial terms: the administration placed the prisoners outside the reach of the law in an extraterritorial domain where the courts were unavailable to them, and the Supreme Court decision brought Guantánamo—and executive authority—inside the rule of law and opened the doors of the federal court to the prisoners there. The trajectory of *Rasul*, however, can be seen to move in the opposite direction as well, not only to include the prisoners inside the realm of domestic law, but also to expand the realm of U.S. juridical dominion beyond its national borders.

The Supreme Court ruling in *Rasul* perpetuates the imperial logic of the Insular Cases by contributing to the development of a two-tiered flexible legal system to serve the global reach of a U.S. military penal regime. Important as this decision may be as a curb on unbounded executive power, it is not a decision against empire. Indeed, the majority decision written by Justice Stevens and the dissent by Justice Scalia can be read as supporting two different juridical modes of imperial rule. The Supreme Court ruling in *Rasul* does not directly address the history of Guantánamo, except in its brief reference to the lease. Nonetheless, the language of both the decision and the dissent is suffused with imperial metaphors and references that evoke this absent history and implicitly place the Court rulings in an imperial genealogy.

In carefully crafting the question before the Court, Stevens maps Guantánamo in the ambiguous space of the Insular Cases, as a location that is neither foreign nor domestic:

> These two cases present the narrow but important question whether United States courts lack jurisdiction to consider challenges to the legality of the detention of foreign nationals captured abroad in connection with hostilities and incarcerated at the Guantánamo Bay Naval Base, Cuba.[56]

This formulation delineates four interrelated spaces. It opens with the domestic legal space of the U.S. courts and poses the question of their territorial jurisdiction as an absence, a "lack." It then moves to unnamed places "abroad," where "foreign nationals" were captured, using phrases that can include any place in the world outside the United States. In contrast to this global arena of unspecified "hostilities," there is the confined space of incarceration at the Guantánamo Bay Naval Base, for which Cuba serves as mere backdrop. In dropping "the United States" from the name of the base, Stevens implicitly conflates "bay" and "base," as many do in common parlance, as though no distinction exists between a U.S. military installation and Cuban geography. Cuba then recedes into the background, divorced from the arena of foreign nations "abroad" while it also stands outside the United States. The majority opinion then proceeds to answer its own question with a double negative, that is, the U.S. courts do not lack jurisdiction. The question and answer, however, do not thereby remap Guantánamo as a space inside the law, but as an indefinite legal borderland between the domestic and the foreign.[57] Even though the Court deems this as a space where the right to habeas corpus is equally available to noncitizens and citizens, the unresolved question of Guantánamo's legal status maintains the prisoners in a limbo between military rule and civil rights.

Justice Stevens expresses his support of the principle of habeas corpus as a narrative of historical and territorial expansion. Stevens's rhetorical power stems from the sweeping scope of habeas corpus, as though it were the main agent in this drama, marching across time and space. He notes its "explicit recognition" in the Constitution and the Judiciary Act of 1789, and traces the expansion of courts' power to review applications for habeas relief throughout U.S. history in war and peace from the Civil War to World War II, on U.S. soil and in "its insular possessions."[58] In stressing its increasing inviolability over time, he does not note Lincoln's suspension of habeas corpus during the Civil War. However, he does refer to this possibility by quoting the Constitution, "which forbids suspension of '[t]he Privilege of the Writ of Habeas Corpus . . . unless when in Cases of Rebellion or Invasion the public Safety may require it."[59] These possible exceptions still shadow the space of Guantánamo, where the prisoners are figured both as rebels within and invaders from without, and where their imprisonment is represented by the administration as the protection of public safety.[60]

As if to shore up the principle of habeas corpus against its potential suspension, Stevens quotes earlier cases to stress its "ancestry," which long precedes the founding of the nation, "a writ antecedent to statute, . . . throwing its root deep into the genius of our common law."[61] Arising with the Magna Carta centuries ago, the Great Writ's venerable "ancestry" receives more historical emphasis when Stevens quotes Justice Jackson in a dissenting opinion: "Executive imprisonment has been considered oppressive and lawless since John, at Runnymede, pledged that no free man should be imprisoned, dispossessed, outlawed, or exiled save by the judgment of his peers or by the law of the land."[62] An unintended irony informs Stevens's narrative. The phrase *habeas corpus*, from the Latin "you shall have the body," refers to the act of actually bringing a person physically before a court or a judge to determine whether that person is being unlawfully denied his or her freedom. Yet the writ of habeas corpus itself becomes the protagonist in Steven's narrative, standing in for the bodies of the prisoners while the violence of their captivity and incarceration remains invisible throughout the case.

To the venerable lineage of habeas corpus, Stevens joins its "extraordinary territorial ambit."[63] To demonstrate this expansiveness, he includes Ellis Island, Guam, and the Philippines, but he refers primarily to examples from the British Empire. His examples range widely from Scotland and the Channel Islands to Jamaica, India, Kenya, and China, from 1759 through 1960. He stresses that the sovereign crown of England extended habeas corpus across its dominions: "At common law, courts exercised habeas jurisdiction" over "all other dominions under the sovereign's control."[64] In addition, when he concludes that "application of the habeas statute to persons detained at the base is consistent with the historical reach of the writ of habeas corpus," this consistency relies primarily on the history of the British Empire.[65] Although he avoids mention of the American Empire, its presence is implied by analogy: just as the United States inherits the "genius of our common law," it also inherits the imperial scope of the British Empire's legal system. While Stevens rejects the administration's claim that Cuba's nominal sovereignty constitutes Guantánamo as a space outside the purview of habeas corpus, he does not thereby claim that the United States has sovereignty over Guantánamo. By historical analogy, however, he renders Guantánamo as "a dominion under the sovereign's control." In Stevens's argument, the British Empire serves implicitly as a model for the expansion of U.S. law, while permitting an elision of the history of U.S. imperial rule as an aspect of law that bears on the present. Stephens thus maintains a view of American exceptionalism by defining the United States as a nation that embodies the values of liberty inherited from England but abjures its path of colonial conquest.

In a scathing dissent, Justice Scalia explicitly rejects the analogies with the British Empire, while he offers his own version of the imperial role of the judicial branch. U.S. rule over Guantánamo, he argues, does not resemble the dominance of the British Empire: "All of the dominions in the cases the Court cites—and all of the territories Blackstone lists as dominions . . . are the sovereign territory of the Crown: colonies, acquisitions and conquests, and so on. It is an enormous extension of the term to apply it to installations merely leased for a particular use from another nation that still retains ultimate sovereignty."[66] Divorcing U.S. actions in Guantánamo from the history of colonial conquest, Scalia accuses the Court of judicial imperialism and condemns "the unheralded expansion of federal-court jurisdiction."[67] He declaims: "In abandoning the venerable statutory line drawn in *Eisentrager*, the Court boldly extends the scope of the habeas statute to the four corners of the earth."[68] Thus, what Stevens maps as the narrow scope of the ruling, Scalia finds to have global proportions. He expresses outrage that the Court has blurred inviolable lines between aliens and citizens, between foreign and domestic territory, and between the executive power to wage war and the judicial power of review. These are lines he claims the Supreme Court held as doctrinal precedence in *Johnson v. Eisentrager*, a 1950 decision about German "alien enemies" in World War II, "the position that United States citizens throughout the world may be entitled to habeas corpus rights . . . even while holding that aliens abroad *did not have* habeas corpus rights."[69] Scalia envisions a different "territorial ambit" of habeas corpus—a concept he derides in the majority, one that protects the mobility of U.S. citizens around the world, while simultaneously excluding aliens from its reach.

Scalia excoriates Stevens for placing aliens and citizens on a continuum when Stevens concludes that if the habeas corpus statute applies to U.S. citizens at the base, then it should apply to aliens held in U.S. custody there.[70] Scalia criticizes the Court for not explaining how "'complete jurisdiction and control' without sovereignty causes an enclave to be part of the United States for purposes of its domestic laws."[71] He emphasizes the word *domestic* several times to point out the danger of eroding the boundaries between home and abroad: "The habeas statute is (according to the Court) being applied *domestically*, to 'petitioners' custodians,' and the doctrine that statutes are presumed to have no extraterritorial effect simply has no application."[72] For Scalia this erosion of boundaries leads to several nightmare scenarios. According to the logic of the majority, he argues, because "jurisdiction and control" obtained through a lease is no different in effect from "jurisdiction and control acquired by lawful force of arms, parts of Afghanistan and Iraq should logically be regarded as subject to our domestic laws."[73] Thus, with the images of Abu Ghraib before the world's eyes, he imagines that any person subject to U.S. military rule would also have unfettered access to a hearing in the U.S. court, that the federal courts will entertain petitions from "around the world." While Scalia is primarily concerned that the courts will thereby tie the hands of the executive's ability to wage war, he expresses the concomitant fear that the decision in *Rasul v. Bush* will spread domestic law to foreign spaces and give aliens the rights of citizens.

Scalia is by no means an isolationist, but he does present a different model of empire from that of Stevens, one in which the executive power rules abroad unhindered by judicial checks, and a strict boundary similarly exists between domestic and foreign territories, and between citizens (who are governed by the Constitution) and aliens (who are ruled by the force of executive authority and its military arm). For him there is no compromise between the forces of constitutionalism and empire, for no conflict exists in the first place.

If Scalia accuses the majority of extending domestic law to foreign places that should remain under military rule alone, his rhetorical overkill expresses anxiety about the opposite direction as well. He concludes with an image of lowering floodgates, as Guantánamo detainees, like unwanted Haitian refugees or illegal aliens, storm the courts of the ninety-four federal judicial districts. Worse than the image of the teeming hordes, these aliens would not break down the doors of the court; rather, they would work the system to "forum shop" for the most favorable conditions.[74] Thus to Scalia, "judicial adventurism of the worst sort" threatens to expand domestic law outward beyond its proper limits and risks incorporating undesirable aliens inward in a "monstrous scheme in a time of war." While he means that the Court's decision will unnecessarily tie the hands of the military leaders and the executive, the word "monstrous" also conjures the image of a grotesque body composed of threatening intermixtures: bodies of aliens and citizens, foreign and domestic spaces, and civil, martial, and international laws.[75]

Scalia is reiterating a long-standing fear that imperial expansion will be accompanied by the invasion or incorporation of those unwanted aliens inhabiting conquered territories. In *Downes v. Bidwell*, for example, Justice Edward Douglass White raised the specter that "millions of inhabitants of alien territory . . . if acquired by treaty, can . . . be immediately and irrevocably incorporated in the United States and the whole structure of the government overthrown."[76] Scalia's critique combines fantasy with reality in the sense that an expanded legal terrain may indeed be a consequence of the government's tactic in not labeling the detainees on Guantánamo as prisoners of war, which would have shored up the legal and spatial boundaries between international treaties and domestic law. If the Department of Defense had done so, the Justice Department would not be now in the situation of facing potential federal lawsuits from Afghanistan to Iraq.[77]

Guantánamo Is Everywhere

Although Scalia's dissent may sound characteristically extreme, it does shed light on the majority opinion: the constraints imposed on executive power by the Court also may abet the juridical expansion of empire. Though it is too soon to tell, the Court's decision in *Rasul*, in conjunction with their decisions on the same day about citizen enemy combatants in the *Hamdi v. Rumsfeld* and *Rumsfeld v. Padilla* cases, may together facilitate the global reach of U.S. power by creating a shadowy hybrid legal system coextensive with the changing needs of empire.

The Court never fully answers the question of where Guantánamo is. It extends and legitimates the ambiguous legacy of the Insular Cases by ruling that Guantánamo is domestic for some purposes and foreign for others. *Hamdi* blurs the distinctions between aliens and citizen, not by giving them shared rights, but by giving judicial legitimacy to the figure of the "enemy combatant," a designation by executive fiat.[78] Many critics today are outraged that the administration has been ignoring these legal decisions and "treating a historic loss in the Supreme Court as though it were a suggestion slip."[79] But perhaps the administration has not been defeated by these rulings. *Rasul*, read alongside *Hamdi* and *Padilla*, suggests that the Court is not extending the protections of domestic law to the "four corners of the earth," but rather that it is legitimating a second-tier legal structure that can extend the government's penal regime, all the while keeping itself immune from accountability and keeping prisoners from the safeguards of any of these systems. This penal regime cuts a wide swathe across national borders, from Guantánamo to detention centers in Iraq and Afghanistan, to undisclosed military prisons around the world, and to immigrant detention centers and prisons within the United States.[80]

To follow this reasoning, it is necessary to turn briefly to the *Hamdi* decision, the one most heralded by the press as the victory of judicial restraint against unbounded executive power. Yet, in this case, Justice O'Connor, writing for the plurality, accepted Bush's position that the nation is at war and that this open-ended "war on terror" gives the president and the executive branch sweeping powers to jail anyone they accuse of being an "enemy combatant"—citizens and noncitizens alike—without the approval of Congress. The ruling accepted the administration's position that such "enemy combatants" are not entitled to the protections either of the Geneva Conventions on prisoners of war or to full due process rights accorded to criminal defendants in the U.S. courts. This decision thus legitimated an evolving category of persons before the law, who are not defined primarily by citizenship or their relation to national or international law but by their designation by the executive. While the Court upheld Hamdi's right to counsel and to petition for habeas corpus, it also endorsed a legal process skirting both constitutional restrictions and international law, with a weakened adherence to due process, with an assumption of guilt until proven innocent, and with the admission of hearsay as evidence. The Court's decision allows for an unspecified military tribunal in lieu of a civilian trial or a military court-martial, itself a kind of parody of the Geneva Convention provisions for prisoners captured on the battlefield.[81]

In *Rasul*, the Court made clear that it would not specify any procedures or venues for addressing the petitioners' claims. In its response to the Supreme Court's decision, the Justice Department capitalized on this by quickly adopting part of the Court's logic in the *Hamdi* case to argue that aliens in foreign territory (Guantánamo detainees) would certainly not be afforded more constitutional protections than those deemed appropriate for citizens within the United States, such as José Padilla and Yaser Hamdi. To argue for denying due process to the Guantánamo prisoners, the government, in its response, quotes from the Hamdi decision, "that the full protection that accompanies challenges to detentions in other settings may prove unworkable and inappropriate in the enemy combatant setting."[82] Thus, the government relies on *Hamdi* specifically to claim that the Guantánamo detainees have no protections under the Fifth Amendment, and they use the district court's ruling in *Padilla* to claim that the detainees have no constitutional rights to counsel unmonitored by military security.[83]

Although these issues remain unresolved, the Justice Department has been consistent in arguing that the detainees in Guantánamo have no constitutional protections. And it has been aided here by the gaps in the Court's decision. It left mainly unanswered the century-old question of whether the Constitution follows the flag, and the government has called on both the Insular Cases and *Verdugo-Urquidez* to argue that the inmates at Guantánamo have no constitutional protections whatsoever. Although the arguments may sound staggeringly cynical, nothing in the Supreme Court decision really works against them. The Justice Department argues against the Sixth Amendment right for the accused in a criminal proceeding to have "assistance of counsel for his defense" because "petitioners are being detained solely because of their status as enemy combatants, not for any other criminal or punitive purpose."[84] The counsel claims that *Verdugo-Urquidez* established that "aliens receive constitutional protections when they have come within the territory of the U.S. and *developed substantial connections with this country*."[85] Beyond its ongoing insistence that Guantánamo is not "within the territory of the U.S.," the government argues that the detainees do not have "voluntary connections" to the United States, because they were captured involuntarily by the military, and therefore—like slaves—they do not have sufficient connection with the United States to warrant constitutional protection. In other words, the act of imposing arbitrary power—the forced transport to Guantánamo, the lack of criminal charges—tautologically justifies the imposition of arbitrary power immune from constitutional restrictions and international treaties.

Outrage has rightfully been expressed at the government's dismissive response to the Supreme Court's decision, and military and civilian lawyers have persistently challenged these practices and even succeeded in halting them before lower court reviews.[86] Since *Rasul* in June 2004, however, the administration continues its effort to block the access of the prisoners to the lower courts. Despite its many legal defeats, it continues to ignore the courts and to treat the prisoners according to its own rules: by staging farcical administrative hearings to determine the enemy combatant status of prisoners who have already been labeled enemy combatants, by planning military tribunals to judge war crimes run by officers with little training who have the power to condemn the accused to death, by releasing some prisoners at its whim, and by building two maximum security prisons for the indefinite detention of others.[87]

By understanding the long imperial history that fills the black hole of Guantánamo, we can see how the Court decision in *Rasul v. Bush* does not simply rein in executive power or bring Guantánamo inside the rule of law. In perpetuating the differential logic of the Insular Cases, the Court remaps an arena only partially and indiscriminately subject to constitutional restraints, wherein the executive can still exert power with impunity. In creating this ambiguous territory, the Court contributes to reclassifying persons as "enemy combatants," a category that erodes the distinctions among citizens and aliens, immigrants and criminals, prisoners and detainees, terrorists and refugees. Yet this erosion is not moving toward granting more rights to noncitizens. On the contrary, it moves both citizens and noncitizens further toward the lowest possible rung of diminished liberties. Ultimately, these persons are codified as less than human and less deserving of human, international, or constitutional rights. This dehumanization is shaped by racial, national, and religious typologies and shored up by revamped historical imperial taxonomies, which rebound across national borders. The blurring of legal boundaries between domestic and foreign, and aliens and citizens, does not weaken executive and military authority, as Scalia fears. Instead it creates ever-widening spheres to the "four corners of the earth," where the U.S. administration, abetted by the courts, might manipulate habeas corpus to conceal rather than to "show the bodies" that have been indefinitely detained, sexually humiliated, and medically and psychologically abused and tortured. Haunted by the ghosts of empire, Guantánamo Bay, Cuba, remains an imperial location today. From here the borders of the law are redrawn to create a world in which Guantánamo is everywhere.

Notes

I am grateful to the following colleagues for their helpful responses to different versions of this essay: Muneer Ahmad, Mary Dudziak, Katherine Franke, Carla Kaplan, Mary Renda, Teemu Ruskola, Rogers Smith, Marita Sturken, Paul Statt, Priscilla Wald, and Leti Volpp.

1. Justice Ruth Bader Ginsburg, Oral Arguments, *Rasul v. Bush*, 542 U.S. 466 (2004) (Nos. 03-334, 03-343), 51. Oral arguments (April 20, 2004) are available at http://www.supremecourtus.gov/oral_arguments/argument_transcripts/03-334.pdf (accessed July 11, 2005).
2. Rear Admiral M. E. Murphy, *The History of Guantanamo Bay, 1494–1964*, chap. 1, "Under the Spanish Flag" (U.S. Naval Base, 1953), available at http://www.nsgtmo.navy.mil/gazette/History_98-64/hischp1.htm (accessed July 11, 2005).
3. Many of these phrases have become commonplace. "Legal black hole" was first used in the British Supreme Court in *Abbasi v. Secretary of State for Foreign & Commonwealth Affairs* (2002); see also Joseph Margulies, "A Prison Beyond the Law," *Virginia Quarterly Review* 80.4 (fall 2004): 37–55; for "legal limbo," see Neil A. Lewis, "Red Cross Criticizes Indefinite Detention in Guantánamo Bay," *New York Times*, October 10, 2003, 1; for "penal colony" see Michael Ratner, "The War on Terrorism: The Guantánamo Prisoners, Military Commissions, and Torture," January 14, 2003, http://www.humanrightsnow.org/guantanamoprisoners.htm. (accessed July 11, 2005).
4. "The Military Archipelago," editorial, *New York Times*, May 7, 2004, A24. Karen J. Greenberg and Joshua L. Dratel, eds., *The Torture Papers: The Road to Abu Ghraib* (New York: Cambridge University Press, 2005).
5. "Amnesty International Report 2005," speech by Irene Khanat, Foreign Press Association, May 25, 2005, at http://web.amnesty.org/library/index/ENGPOL10014200 (accessed July 11, 2005).
6. Eric Hobsbawm, *The Age of Empire, 1875–1914* (New York: Random House, 1987).
7. See Murphy, *The History of Guantanamo Bay*.
8. For a brief review of these changing attitudes toward American imperialism, see Amy Kaplan, "Violent Belongings and the Question of Empire Today—Presidential Address to the American Studies Association, October 17, 2003," *American Quarterly* 56.1 (March 2004): 1–7. For recent books on the subject of diverse political perspectives, see Andrew Bacevich, *American Empire: The Realities and Consequences of U.S. Diplomacy* (Cambridge, Mass.: Harvard University Press, 2002); Bacevich, *The Imperial Tense: Prospects and Problems of American Empire* (Chicago: Ivan R. Dee, 2003); Patrick J. Buchanan, *A Republic, Not an Empire: Reclaiming America's Destiny* (Washington, D.C.: Regency, 1999/2002); David Harvey, *The New Imperialism* (New York: Oxford University Press, 2003); Chalmers Johnson, *The Sorrows of Empire: Militarism, Secrecy, and the End of the Republic* (New York: Metropolitan Books, 2004); John Newhouse, *Imperial America: The Bush Assault on the World Order* (New York: Knopf, 2003); Joseph S. Nye, *The Paradox of American Power: Why the World's Only Superpower Can't Go It Alone* (New York: Oxford University Press, 2002). One of the major intellectual proponents of American Empire is Niall Fergusson. See, for example, his *Colossus: The Price of America's Empire* (New York: Penguin, 2004).
9. This vision was propounded before 9/11 by the neoconservative Project for the New American Century in their 2000 report "Rebuilding America's Defenses: Strategy, Forces, and Resources for a New

Century," available at http://www.newamericancentury.org/RebuildingAmericasDefenses.pdf (accessed July 12, 2005). For a recent essay bringing together U.S. imperialism and universalism, see Michael Ignatieff, "Who Are Americans to Think That Freedom Is Theirs to Spread?" *New York Times Magazine*, June 26, 2005.

10. See Charles A. Kupchan, *The End of the American Era: U.S. Foreign Policy and the Geopolitics of the Twenty-First Century* (New York: Knopf, 2002); Michael Mann, *Incoherent Empire* (London: Verso, 2003); Emmanuel Todd, *After the Empire: The Breakdown of the American Order* (New York: Columbia University Press, 2003); Immanuel Wallerstein, *The Decline of American Power* (New York: New Press, 2003).
11. Max Boot, *The Savage Wars of Peace: Small Wars and the Rise of American Power* (New York: Basic Books, 2002), 341–42. See Robert Kaplan, "Rule No. 7: Remember the Philippines," in "Supremacy by Stealth: Ten Rules for Managing the World," *Atlantic Monthly*, July–August 2003, 80; and Michael Ignatieff, "Why Are We in Iraq? (And Liberia? And Afghanistan?)," *New York Times Magazine*, September 7, 2003. Imperial sites conquered in 1898, such as the Phillipines and Guam, are being retooled by the military to support the current wars. See James Brooke, "Threats and Responses: U.S. Bases: Guam Hurt by Slump, Hopes for Economic Help From Military," *New York Times Magazine*, March 10, 2003, A14.
12. See, for example, Diane Marie Amann, "Guantánamo," *Columbia Journal of Transnational Law* 42.1 (2004): 263–349; Ronald Dworkin, "What the Court Really Said," *New York Review of Books*, 51.13, August 12, 2004; Neal K. Katyal, "Executive and Judicial Overreaction in the Guantanamo Cases," in *Cato Supreme Court Review*, 2003–2004, at http://www.cato.org/pubs/scr/docs/2004/executiveandjudicial.pdf (accessed July 11, 2005); Gerald L. Neuman, "Closing the Guantánamo Loophole," *Loyola Law Review* 50.1 (spring 2004): 1–66; Kal Raustiala, "The Geography of Justice," *Fordham Law Review*, 73.6 (May 2005): 2501–2560; Michael Ratner and Ellen Ray, *Guantánamo: What the World Should Know* (White River Junction, Vt.: Chelsea Green, 2004); Kermit Roosevelt III, "Guantánamo and the Conflict of Laws: *Rasul* and Beyond," *University of Pennsylvania Law Review*, 153 (June 2005): 2017–71. Neuman has long written of Guantánamo in the context of its imperial history, and for my understanding of its legal status, I am indebted to him. Raustiala identifies Guantánamo's imperial history as evidence of an outdated anachronistic attachment to legal spatiality.
13. See, for example, Matthew Jacobson, *Barbarian Virtues: The United States Encounters Foreign Peoples at Home and Abroad, 1876–1917* (New York: Hill and Wang, 2000); Amy Kaplan, *The Anarchy of Empire in the Making of U.S. Culture* (Cambridge, Mass.: Harvard University Press, 2002); Melanie McAlister, *Epic Encounters: Culture, Media, and U.S. Interests in the Middle East, 1945–2000* (Berkeley: University of California Press, 2001); Mary Renda, *Taking Haiti: Military Occupation and the Culture of U.S. Imperialism, 1915–1940* (Chapel Hill: University of North Carolina Press, 2001); Neil Smith, *American Empire: Roosevelt's Geographer and the Prelude to Globalization* (Berkeley: University of California Press, 2003); Penny Von Eschen, *Race Against Empire: Black Americans and Anticolonialism, 1937–1957* (Ithaca, N.Y.: Cornell University Press, 1997).
14. This argument was prepared in "Possible Habeas Jurisdiction over Aliens Held in Guantanamo Bay, Cuba," U.S. Justice Department memo to the Department of Defense concerning the applicability of International Humanitarian Law to the prisoners in the war on terrorism, written by Deputy Assistant Attorney Generals Patrick F. Philbin and John C. Yoo, December 28, 2001, from "The Philbin/Yoo Memo," *Newsweek*, accessible at http://www.yirmeyahureview.com/archive/documents/prisoner_abuse/011228_philbinmemo.pdf (accessed July 11, 2005). See also Brief for the Respondents, *Rasul v. Bush*.
15. The Platt Amendment, 1901, Modern History Sourcebook available at http://www.fordham.edu/halsall/mod/1901platt.html (accessed July 11, 2005).
16. Ibid.
17. Ibid.
18. Philip Sheldon Foner, *The Spanish-Cuban-American War and the Birth of American Imperialism, 1895–1902, vol. 2* (New York: Monthly Review Press, 1972), 632.
19. Treaty Defining Relations with Cuba, May 29, 1934, U.S.–Cuba, Art. III, 48 Stat. 1683, T. S. No. 866 at http://www.nsgtmo.navy.mil/gazette/History_98-64/hisapxd.htm (accessed July 11, 2005).
20. Lease of Lands for Coaling and Naval Stations, February 23, 1903, U.S.–Cuba, Art. III, T. S. No. 418 at http://www.nsgtmo.navy.mil/gazette/History_98-64/hisapxd.htm (accessed July 11, 2005).
21. The Platt Amendment was approved by the U.S. Congress in 1901, two years before its adoption in the Cuban constitution.

22. Thank you to Teemu Ruskola for pointing this out to me in the case, for example, of the Hong Kong lease of 1862. See Martti Koskenniemi, chap. 2, "Sovereignty: A Gift of Civilization: International Lawyers and Imperialism, 1870–1914," in *The Gentle Civilizer of Nations: The Rise and Fall of International Law, 1870–1960* (Cambridge: Cambridge University Press, 2001).
23. Walter LaFeber, *The New Empire: An Interpretation of American Expansion, 1860–1898* (Ithaca, N.Y.: Cornell University Press, 1963).
24. Alfred Thayer Mahan, "Conditions Determining the Naval Expansion of the United States," in *Retrospect and Prospect: Studies in International Relations Naval and Political* (Boston: Little, Brown, 1902), 48.
25. The opening epigraph by Justice Ginsburg is followed by: "The closest would be the Canal Zone, I suppose." Although the government counsel rejected this analogy, the reference implicitly evokes another space colonized by the New Empire at the turn of the last century.
26. While the phrase "black hole" evokes its most immediate connotations from astronomy, it also has a prior imperial history. The "black hole of Calcutta" refers to the barracks in Fort William, Calcutta, where in 1756, the Nawab of Bengal allegedly imprisoned more than a hundred Europeans who died overnight, an incident that became a cause celebre in the idealization of British imperialism in India.
27. Oral Arguments, *Rasul v. Bush*, 52.
28. *Newsweek*, July 8, 2002.
29. Louis A. Perez, *On Becoming Cuban: Identity, Nationality, and Culture* (New York: HarperCollins, 1999), 238–42; Jana Lipman, "Guantanamo: Cubans, Marines, and Migrants, 1955–1965," paper presented at Global Studies Association, Brandeis University, April 2004.
30. "Cuban Base Has American Flavor," *Morning Call Online*, January 2, 2004.
31. Kathleen T. Rhem, "From Mayberry to Metropolis: Guantanamo Bay Changes," *American Forces Press Service*, March 3, 2005, at http://www.dod.mil/news/Mar2005/20050303_77.html (accessed July 11, 2005).
32. Paul Farmer, "Pestilence and Restraint: Guantánamo, AIDS, and the Logic of Quarantine," in *Pathologies of Power: Health, Human Rights, and the New War on the Poor* (Berkeley: University of California Press, 2003), 51–59; Lizzy Ratner, "The Legacy of Guantánamo," *The Nation*, July 16, 2003, at http://www.thenation.com/doc.mhtml?i=20030721&s=ratner (accessed July 11, 2005); Jane Franklin, "How Did Guantánamo Become a Prison?" *History News Network*, April 11, 2005, at http://hnn.us/articles/11000.html (accessed July 11, 2005).
33. Medicine is again being used coercively in Guantánamo. The Red Cross has asserted that currently "some doctors and other medical workers at Guantánamo were participating in planning for interrogations," in what the report called "a flagrant violation of medical ethics." Neil A. Lewis, "Red Cross Finds Detainee Abuse in Guantánamo," *New York Times*, November 30, 2004, 1; Neil A. Lewis, "Interrogators Cite Doctors' Aid at Guantánamo Prison Camp," *New York Times*, June 24, 2005.
34. Franklin, "How Did Guantánamo Become a Prison?"
35. Ratner, "The Legacy of Guantánamo."
36. The administration has not released the names or exact numbers of prisoners at Guantánamo. For the most comprehensive record, see the Web site Cageprisoners.com at http://www.cageprisoners.com/index.php (accessed July 11, 2005).
37. Rogers Smith, "Citizenship Rights, Alien Rights, and the New American Empire," forthcoming in *Radical History Review*. See also Mark Dow, *American Gulag: Inside U.S. Immigration Prisons* (Berkeley: University of California Press, 2004).
38. Neuman, "Closing the Guantánamo Loophole," 42.
39. Ibid.; *Cuban Am. Car Ass'n v. Christopher*, 43 F.3d 1412 (11th Cir.1995).
40. Ibid.
41. See Brook Thomas, "A Constitution Led by the Flag: The *Insular Cases* and the Metaphor of Incorporation," in *Foreign in a Domestic Sense: Puerto Rico, American Expansion, and the Constitution*, ed. Christina Duffy Burnett and Burke Marshall (Durham, N.C.: Duke University Press, 2001), 82–103.
42. For the most comprehensive examination of the Insular Cases from different perspectives, see Burnett and Marshall, eds., *Foreign in a Domestic Sense*.
43. *Downes v. Bidwell*, 182 U.S. 244, 341 (1901); Efrén Rivera Ramos, "The Legal Construction of American Colonialism: The Insular Cases,1902–1922," *Revista Jurídica de la Universidad de Puerto Rico* 65 (1996): 227–328.
44. *Downes*, 306.

45. Ibid., 373.
46. *Rasul,* 564, n. 15.
47. *United States v. Verdugo-Urquidez,* 494 U.S. 259, 265 (1990).
48. Ibid., 275.
49. Ibid., 278.
50. Ibid.
51. *Rasul,* 565 (Kennedy concurring).
52. Response to Complaint in Accordance with the Court's Order of July 25, 2004, *Odah v. United States,* 355 F. Supp. 2d. 482 (D.D.C. 2005) (No. 02-CV-0828).
53. *Khalid v. Bush,* 355 F. Supp. 2d. 311 (D.D.C. 2005).
54. Memorandum Opinion Denying in Part and Granting in Part Respondent's Motion to Dismiss or For Judgment as a Matter of Law, *In re Guantanamo Detainee Cases,* 355 F. Supp. 2d. 443 (D.D.C. 2005) (No. 02-CV0299).
55. Neuman, "Closing the Guantánamo Loophole," 19. The argument of this article is based on his contribution to Brief Amici Curiae of Former Government U.S. Government Officials in Support of Petitioners, *Rasul v. Bush.*
56. *Rasul,* 554.
57. In posing the question this narrowly in the passive voice, the Court does not narrate how the prisoners were transported to Guantánamo from horrendous conditions in the prison of Khandahar, Afghanistan, where many were beaten and tortured, and others died of suffocation, cold, and the lack of medical care and food. They also do not mention how, in scenes evocative of the middle passage of slavery, they were tied together and blindfolded in the belly of a transport jet, seated below an American flag.
58. *Rasul,* 557.
59. Ibid., 556.
60. On the relation of habeas corpus to the possibility of its suspension in British colonial rule, see Nasser Hussain, chap. 3, "'The Writ of Liberty' in a Regime of Conquest," in Hussain's *The Jurisprudence of Emergency: Colonialism and the Rule of Law* (Ann Arbor: University of Michigan, 2003). On Guantánamo as an exception and its relation to the U.S. Civil War, see Scott Michaelsen and Scott Cutler Shershow, "The Guantánamo 'Black Hole': The Law of War and the Sovereign Exception," *Middle East Report Online,* January 11, 2004, at http://www.merip.org/mero/mero011104.html (accessed July 11, 2005).
61. *Rasul,* 556.
62. Jackson in *Shaughnessy v. United States ex. Rel. Mezei,* 345 U.S. 206, 218–19, quoted in *Rasul v. Bush,* 557.
63. *Rasul,* Stevens, 562, n. 12.
64. Ibid., 561–62.
65. Ibid., 561.
66. Ibid., 575 (Scalia dissenting).
67. Ibid., 572.
68. Ibid., 571–72.
69. Ibid., 574.
70. Ibid., 561.
71. Ibid., 574 (Scalia dissenting).
72. Ibid., 573 (Scalia's emphasis).
73. Ibid., 574.
74. Ibid., 577.
75. This dissent is consistent with what may seem like a surprisingly "progressive" position on *Hamdi* (see n. 79, following). There he also upheld the absolute dividing line between citizen and alien by arguing that as a citizen, Hamdi should either be criminally charged with treason or released, unless the government exercised its constitutional right to suspend habeas corpus. For Scalia, in the case of the aliens in foreign territory, no domestic laws apply, but for the citizen, the laws of the land are clear.
76. *Downes,* 313.
77. Thank you to Muneer Ahmad for pointing this out; see Katyal, "Executive and Judicial Overreaction."
78. On the Department of Defense's definition of "enemy combatant," see William J. Haynes II, General Counsel of the Department of Defense, "Enemy Combatants," presentation to Council on Foreign Relations, at http://www.cfr.org/publication.php?id=5312 (accessed July 11, 2005). For an analysis of this designation by executive fiat (see Amann, "Guantánamo").

79. Quoted in Adam Liptak, "In First Rulings, Military Tribunals Uphold Detentions of 4," *New York Times*, August 14, 2004, 11.
80. On the relation of the torture of prisoners at Guantánamo and Abu Ghraib to the treatment of prisoners in the U.S. prisons, see Joan Dayan, "Cruel and Unusual: The End of the Eighth Amendment," *Boston Review*, October/November 2004, at http://bostonreview.net/BR29.5/dayan.html (accessed July 11, 2005).
81. *Hamdi v. Rumsfeld*, 542 U.S. 507 (2004) (No. 03-6696).
82. Response to Complaint, July 2004, 19.
83. Ibid., 23.
84. Ibid., 17.
85. Ibid., 13.
86. Prior to Judge Joyce Green's ruling declaring the Combatant Status Review Tribunals unconstitutional and that the prisoners should be treated as prisoners of war, in October 2004 U.S. District Judge Colleen Kollar-Kotelly ordered the Pentagon to stop intelligence eavesdropping on lawyer-client conversations at Guantánamo; Carol D. Leonnig, "U.S. Loses Ruling on Monitoring of Detainees," *Washington Post*, October 21, 2004, 4. In November, U.S. District Judge James Robertson ordered the Pentagon to halt the war crimes trial of a Yemeni who allegedly worked as Osama bin Laden's driver, saying the Military Commissions are flawed, and likewise called the Pentagon's Combatant Status Review Tribunals (CRSTs) an inadequate, nonjudicial alternative to habeas proceedings in federal courts; Warren Richey, "Court Puts off Guantánamo War-Crimes Case," *The Christian Science Monitor*, January 19, 2005, 2. On July 15, 2005, a three-judge panel of the United States Court of Appeals for the District of Columbia Circuit ruled unanimously to reverse Judge Robertson's decision and to resume military tribunals. Neil A. Lewis, "Ruling Lets U.S. Restart Trials at Guantanamo," *New York Times*, July 16, 2005, 1.
87. In the case of *Hamdi*, rather than abide by the Court's decision, the Department of Justice released Yaser Hamdi to return to Saudi Arabia on the condition that he relinquish his U.S. citizenship.

Canton Is Not Boston: The Invention of American Imperial Sovereignty

Teemu Ruskola

> We have a separate and different Law of Nations for the regulation of our intercourse with the Indian tribes of our own Continent; another Law of Nations between us and the woolly headed natives of Africa; another with the Barbary Powers and the Sultan of the Ottoman Empire; a Law of Nations with the inhabitants of the Isles of the Sea . . . and lastly with the Flowery Land, the Celestial Empire, the Mantchoo-Tartar Dynasty of Despotism.[1]
>
> John Quincy Adams (1841)

China, according to received wisdom, was never colonized, except for the minor British and Portuguese outposts of Hong Kong and Macao, respectively, and the United States never established even its own little Hong Kong in the Chinese empire. To be sure, in 1856–57 the American commissioner in China tried to sell the idea of a U.S. occupation of Taiwan, arguing that under international law it "ought not to be allowed to exist in the hands of such a people" who could not even control the island's "cannibals."[2] The commissioner went so far as to bring to the State Department's attention Americans who would be willing to assist in Taiwan's "colonization,"[3] but the State Department nevertheless rejected the plan, and President McKinley was equally unsuccessful half a century later in trying to talk his secretary of state into acquiring a "slice" of China—as if the Middle Kingdom were a pizza.[4] (Nevertheless, the government did ask the Supreme Court to consider, in adjudicating the constitutional status of the territorial spoils of the Spanish-American War in 1901, that "the question might arise as to the powers of this government in the acquisition of Egypt and the Soudan, or a section of Central Africa, or a spot in the Antarctic Circle, or a section of the Chinese empire.")[5]

In the end, the formal sovereignty of the Chinese emperor was never seriously challenged throughout the nineteenth century. However, recent critical scholarship in Asian studies has come to question just what "sovereignty" meant in conditions in which foreign powers came to dictate, increasingly, not only how China should conduct its external relations, but how it should reform even its domestic constitutional structure.[6] At the same time, scholars in American studies are increasingly analyzing America's territorial expansion in North America, the Caribbean, and the Pacific as an imperial project. It is noteworthy that most students of colonialism in China have focused on the actions of the British, rather than those of the United States. At the same time, most legal scholars of American imperialism have focused on America's legal maneuvers in its various territorial possessions, rather than on nonterritorial forms of American legal imperialism.[7]

Yet there is a largely forgotten story to be told of U.S. legal imperialism in China as well, despite China's location far outside of America's territorial borders.[8] The story's protagonist is a rather arcane sounding legal doctrine, extraterritorial jurisdiction. Exclusive territorial jurisdiction is one of the defining features of the sovereignty of the modern nation-state. With limited exceptions, it is *where* a person is that determines *what law* applies to him or her. However, when a state asserts extraterritorial jurisdiction, it claims the right to apply its laws beyond the borders of its territory.

To anticipate the story, the extraordinary treaty that laid the foundation for American extraterritoriality was negotiated by Caleb Cushing, the first American minister to China as well as a Massachusetts congressman, a lawyer, and a future attorney general of the United States. Cushing was charged by President John Tyler with the pretextual mission of going to Peking to inquire after the emperor's health and to carry out the president's wishes for his longevity. Backed by his own little armada as well as the presence of the U.S. naval forces in the Pacific, Cushing persuaded the Qing Empire to enter into a Treaty of Peace, Amity, and Commerce with the United States. The treaty was signed on July 3, 1844, in the village of Wanghia in Macao. Under its terms, China was obligated to allow Americans to trade freely in Canton as well as in four other previously closed ports. Moreover, Americans obtained the right of extraterritorial jurisdiction in China.[9] From 1844 until 1943, U.S. citizens in China were formally subject only to the laws of the United States. Stated differently, when Americans entered China, American law traveled with them, effectively attaching to their very bodies.

How did the relatively recently emancipated world's leading anticolonial power reconcile its extraterritorial jurisdiction in China with Chief Justice Marshall's ringing statement in 1812, "The jurisdiction of a nation within its territory is necessarily exclusive and absolute . . . being alike the attribute of every sovereign and incapable of conferring extraterritorial power"?[10] It turns out that the forgotten century of American extraterritorial jurisdiction in China is a story not only about China and the United States but also of international law. This essay is thus also a story about law's operation transnationally, and a case study of how law dynamically both constitutes and deconstitutes sovereigns at both national and international levels. In the end, Western extraterritorial jurisdiction in China served to constitute it as a state in the international legal system, while at the same denying it full admission into the international society into which it was apparently being inducted.

In outlining a brief history of the origins of American extraterritorial jurisdiction in China, I consider its operation together with the free trade rationale that it was deemed to serve. In their classic article on "free trade imperialism," John Gallagher and Ronald Robinson caution against a rigid qualitative distinction between formal and informal empire in the analysis of British expansion in the nineteenth century. As they put it, studying imperialism in terms of formal empire alone is "rather like judging the size and character of icebergs solely from the parts above the water-line."[11] Specifically, they observe that in the mid-Victorian era "perhaps the most common political technique of British expansion was the treaty of free trade and friendship made with or imposed on a weaker state."[12] This essay argues that in the Treaty of Wanghia the United States laid the foundation for this imperial practice in Asia, where it utilized and refined the practice even beyond the British precedent—up to the point where it was the updated, American version that in turn became a model for the British themselves and other European states with imperial aspirations in Asia.

The notion of an informal American empire is of course not new. However, the vocabulary for analyzing U.S. power overseas is largely military and economic, as evidenced by terms such as "gunboat diplomacy" and "dollar diplomacy." This essay analyzes law as an important currency in its own right in American overseas imperialism. The exercise of American power has been rarely based merely on the assertion of sheer economic and military might. From the beginning, it has been mediated through the language of law, as a matter of *right.* Although the United States' independence was premised on the view that not only all men but also all states were born to be equal, in the mid-nineteenth century the liberal notion of sovereign equality gave way to an imperial American sovereignty in the Pacific. In China, Caleb Cushing essentially renarrated the nation's early diplomatic history and substituted in its place an invented tradition of U.S. extraterritoriality in "Oriental" states. This extraterritoriality in turn protected American commercial interests in Asia, while real or alleged violations of extraterritorial privileges justified the occasional use of military power to protect America's "rights" under the law of nations.

To explain the ideological transformation in American diplomacy from an assumption of equality among states to an expectation of extraterritorial privileges for American citizens among "uncivilized" peoples, I first consider

America's historic place in the global expansion of (Western) international law and then analyze how the United States reconfigured its legal relationship to Europe and the rest of the world in the post–Revolutionary War era. After a short account of America's early trade relations with China, I analyze the conventional narrative about Britain's aggressive role in opening China for free trade in the Opium War, and I then contrast it with the received wisdom about America's "special relationship" with China. Questioning the latter view, I suggest that the Treaty of Wanghia was a constitutive moment in U.S. political relations with Asia. It laid the foundation for an imperial American sovereignty in the Pacific in the second half of the nineteenth century and, moreover, it became the model for various European states that entered into their own extraterritoriality treaties in the following years. Finally, I turn to the Chinese Exclusion Laws in the United States, to analyze how the differential construction of sovereignties operated on this side of the Pacific.

Two caveats are in order. First, the core of this essay focuses on changing conceptions of sovereignty in the nineteenth century. To examine those conceptions in context, I provide thumbnail sketches of long stretches of American, Chinese, and British political and economic history. Necessarily simplified and selective, these interpretive summaries are intended only to illuminate relevant parts of the core thesis. Second, this essay is part of a larger study of the legal encounter of China and the West. The part of the story that appears here is narrated primarily from the perspective of the United States. Consequently, in this essay China comes across as an all but inert object of Euro-American actions. That of course is a limitation of the perspective chosen, not a fact about China.

America and the Law of Nations

Standard accounts of the origin of modern international law trace its birth to the Treaty of Westphalia in 1648 and the end of the post-Reformation religious civil wars in Europe. Thereafter, each sovereign was to determine the religion of his state, and without regard to domestic differences, all states were to enjoy formal equality under the law of nations.[13] Collectively, these accounts provide a history of the emergence of the liberal norm of sovereign equality among nation-states. The picture changes significantly when it is reframed geographically, beyond Europe, and temporally, to an earlier date. Consider Carl Schmitt's invitation to view the Discovery of the New World in 1492 as the origin of modern international law.[14] From this perspective, the narrative is no longer one of increasing inclusion and equality *within* Europe.

Rather, it becomes a story of the violent exclusion of others *outside* of Europe, first on the basis of religious, then cultural, difference.

Viewing the history of international law from this earlier date, then, how did the New World fit into what was still by and large the public law of the "Christian republic" of Europe? It is important to recall that Columbus ended up in America while looking for a route to India. America hence began its European career as Asia: Columbus believed until his dying day that the New World he had found was in fact Asia. Thus, America originated as the "West Indies" in European historical consciousness, in contrast to the East Indies in the "real" Asia.

Originally both the East and West Indies were regarded as lying beyond the pale of civilization, or as Locke put it epigrammatically, "in the beginning, all the world was America."[15] Yet with the Declaration of American Independence, the United States rose to assume, "among the powers of the Earth, the separate and equal station to which the Laws of Nature and Nature's God" entitled it. Although the new nation emerged from what had once been the West Indies, the United States now claimed to exceed, and supersede, that categorization. It confidently asserted its political parity with Europe, and ultimately even its superiority. With the Revolution, Americans came to believe that theirs was the *real* West: the New World embodied the true values of Europe *better* than Europe did, so that the Old World really became just that—old and anachronistic.

Whatever may have remained of the Indies in the New World was expelled geographically outside of North America proper, where it still languishes, mostly in the islands of the Caribbean. And insofar as some "Indians" still remained physically within the borders of the United States, they were certainly not citizens of the new polity but mere "domestic dependent nations," in the memorable words of Chief Justice Marshall.[16]

As far as Europe was concerned, in 1776 the law of nations was limited in its application to the "Family of Nations," or European international society consisting of "civilized" states. Nevertheless, despite some early hesitation, the admission of the United States into this European political family was fairly uncontroversial: given the colonists' indisputable genealogical connection to the Old World, the young nation was soon recognized as civilized and hence fully sovereign.

But although the American Revolution reconstituted America's legal relationship to Europe on the novel basis of sovereign equality, it remained an open question how the young nation would organize its political relations with the rest of the world. Even after the American Revolution, Europeans deemed themselves fully authorized by the law of nations to continue their project of colonizing the extra-European world. With a high degree of self-consciousness, the young United States rejected that European understanding of sovereignty and the "will to empire" that it implied.[17] It was self-evident to patriotic early Americans that they ought not to establish territorial colonies on the European model (but rather on their own, American one, which was not seen as imperialism at all, only the young nation's manifest, preordained destiny).[18]

Nineteenth-century international law, however, did not divide the world simply into civilized states that were fully sovereign and savages whose lands were either mere *terra nullius* that was simply there waiting to be "discovered" or else could be won through colonial conquest. In certain circumstances, less-than-civilized peoples might have some degree of sovereignty, yet they could not impose their laws on civilized men even when they entered their territory. This exemption from local law became established as the right of extraterritorial jurisdiction.[19]

The secular international law of the nineteenth century justified the practice of extraterritoriality on explicitly civilizational grounds, but its origins date to the much earlier system of the so-called Capitulations, which once mediated Europe's relations with the Ottoman Empire. In the pre-Westphalian era when religion provided the predominant framework for European interstate relations, the privileges of the law of the European *Respublica Christiana* could not be extended to infidels and, concomitantly, Christians sojourning in the Ottoman Empire could not be subjected to Muslim law but adjudicated their disputes under their own law. The arrangement, known as the Capitulations, began as a favor granted by Turks to Europeans. Yet as the Ottoman Empire became increasingly weak relative to Europe, the system ultimately solidified into a resented imperial imposition. By the nineteenth century, it was a well-established, nonterritorial form of imperialism.

As the newborn United States began looking outside its borders and turned its gaze across the South Seas—that is, the Pacific Ocean—how was it to constitute its relationship to Asia? Having (ostensibly) rejected outright territorial colonialism, would it decline to follow the European practice of extraterritorial jurisdiction in Asia as well? The matter was far less urgent than the relations with Europe, for example (the clarification of which required a revolution), or the relations with Africa (which were troubled because of slavery). Unsurprisingly, it was also decided much less self-consciously. China figured only minimally in the early American diplomatic consciousness, and from the beginning, U.S.–China relations were inextricably intertwined with questions of trade. Moreover, "Asia" was hardly the relevant contemporary category anyway: America's China trade was viewed as part of the larger "East Indies trade"—a legacy of Columbus's mistaking America for a West Indies.

China and the American East Indies Trade

Before 1776, Americans were not legally permitted to trade with China directly. During the colonial period, the East India Company enjoyed a Crown monopoly on Britain's China trade and Americans were permitted to function only as middlemen. In the case of Chinese tea, for example, the company first shipped the tea to England, and Americans then transported it to the colonies, subject to much resented import duties. This basic framework was altered by the notorious Tea Act of 1773. It gave the company the right to sell tea directly to the colonies, thus displacing the American middlemen from the trade. Outraged American patriots responded by raiding the company's boats in Boston and dumping the tea into the harbor. (To compound the irony, as they attacked the property of the East India Company, the Americans were dressed as Indians, the original inhabitants of Columbus's "West Indies.")

It was thus one of the consequences of American independence from Britain that the Chinese market now opened legally to the United States for the first time. In 1784, China trade was inaugurated with the celebrated voyage of the *Empress of China* from New York to Canton. (Notably, in his journal the captain described the ship's destination as "Canton in India.")[20] The following year, excited by the prospect of entering China's mythically vast markets, the Continental Congress appointed one of the supercargoes of the *Empress of China* as consul in Canton.[21] Yet the gesture was purely unilateral and the Chinese government in no way recognized the consular post.[22]

Although American trade grew considerably in volume over time and many fortunes were made from it, overall it did not live up to the unrealistically wild expectations that had inspired it. Even the consular post remained unstaffed for most of the time during the first several decades of its existence. The main Western presence in Canton continued to be the British East India Company, and British sailors in particular appear to have gotten into violent, drunken brawls with the local Cantonese with some frequency. In an oft-repeated pattern, if and when British subjects were tried under Chinese law, the British government voiced its protest.[23]

In the one major controversy involving the United States, in 1821 sailor Francis Terranova, who served onboard an American ship, was accused of killing a Chinese woman who had come to the ship to sell food. The Chinese government demanded the surrender of Terranova and ultimately ended up convicting him to death by strangling. In response, some American merchants—most notably the fur merchant John Jacob Astor—voted with their feet and withdrew from China trade altogether.[24] Others wrote in protest to the Chinese authorities ("We consider the case prejudiced"), but even they recognized the legal weakness of their complaint: "We are bound to submit to your laws while we are in your waters, be they ever so unjust. We will not resist."[25] The State Department evidently also believed that Americans in China violated the empire's laws at their own risk, for it made no protest in the matter. The British, meanwhile, took notice of American "weakness" in submitting to Chinese jurisdiction.[26]

Indeed, in an 1815 communication to the British representative in Canton, the American consul expressly acknowledged China's jurisdiction over Americans in the city, stating "that the citizens of the United States have for many years visited the city of Canton in the pursuit of honest commerce, [and] that their conduct during the whole period of intercourse has been regulated by a strict regard and respect for the laws and usages of this Empire, as well as the general law of nations."[27] Even the Americans who most resented Chinese jurisdiction observed reluctantly that, "as a question of the law of nations and casuistry, it would bear an argument whether the United States could rightfully go to war against the Chinese for administering their own laws on persons voluntarily coming within their jurisdiction."[28]

These perceptions of Americans about their status in China reflected what had been made explicit by treaty in the only existing political relationship into which the United States entered with an Asian state prior to its extraterritoriality treaty with China. In addition to providing commercial access, the 1833 Treaty of Amity and Commerce with Siam stated expressly that Americans in Siam would be subject to Siamese law.[29] And as early as 1808, Thomas Jefferson had agreed to make an exception to the Embargo Act for a Chinese mandarin, which he justified as a matter of "national comity"; he evidently believed that China qualified fully for the respect and courtesies that sovereign nations owe one another.[30] Until the outbreak of the Sino-British Opium War in 1839, it thus appeared that the United States would in fact respect the sovereign equality of "Oriental" states such as China—unlike European imperialists such as the British, who had a tradition of extraterritoriality in dealing with barbaric and semicivilized peoples.

China and Britain: Through Opium into Modernity

Yet in 1844 the United States insisted on formalizing its right to extraterritorial jurisdiction in the nation's first trade treaty with a major Asian state. Before analyzing this change in U.S. policy, it is useful to consider briefly the conventional account of the Opium War and the role of the British in opening China for Western trade.

In the field of Asian studies, the Opium War is universally regarded as the beginning of "modern" Chinese history. From this perspective, the war is seen as an unfortunate but unavoidable stimulus for the modernization of China. It is viewed as having played a necessary role in displacing the native Sinocentric worldview and inducting China into the global economic and legal order. The official Chinese worldview—as described by historians of modernization—regarded China as a universal empire that defined itself against uncivilized "barbarians" at its borders. Nevertheless, the borders did not constitute a point of absolute exteriority: barbarians who paid economic and symbolic tribute could become Sinified and included in the purportedly universal Chinese civilization.[31]

The standard illustration of China's smug isolationism is the fate of the Macartney embassy in 1793. Since 1744, all Western trade in China was restricted to Canton, where foreigners were permitted to trade only as a matter of imperial grace. Lord Macartney was the first British ambassador to China, sent by George III to negotiate an agreement that would open up the Celestial Empire for British trade. The Qianlong emperor treated Lord Macartney much as he treated his other tributaries coming from Vietnam, Korea, and elsewhere. In keeping with imperial protocol, the emperor expected the British ambassador to perform the requisite kowtow—a series of prostrations and "knockings" of the forehead on the ground. From the perspective of the British ambassador, to perform the kowtow would have constituted nothing less than a scandal of sovereign equality. He declared that he could not show greater deference to an Oriental monarch than he did to his own sovereign, before whom he would only kneel, not prostrate himself in slavish abjection.

A series of complicated diplomatic negotiations ensued. To gain access to the emperor without surrendering his insistence on equality, Lord Macartney at one point even offered to kowtow to the emperor on the condition that an imperial official of equivalent rank perform the same series of prostrations before a portrait of George III that Macartney had brought with him. This offer was declined and followed by further negotiations. The end result was a tense imperial audience (it is unclear to this day whether the ambassador in fact kowtowed or not), no trade agreement, and the beginning of a British obsession with Chinese "arrogance."[32]

Taking this iconic diplomatic fiasco as its point of reference, much of postwar area studies scholarship views the Sino-Western encounter in the nineteenth century as a tragic cultural misunderstanding: the Chinese simply did not understand modernity and the West in general. As a corollary, they were also unable to appreciate the political concept of sovereign equality, as well as the economic idea of free trade among independent states. The main piece of evidence was the notoriously condescending message which the Qianlong emperor asked Lord Macartney to deliver to George III. After thanking the British monarch for sending an ambassador to pay tribute to the Middle Kingdom, the emperor declared, "We have never valued ingenious articles, nor do we have the slightest need of your Country's manufactures."[33]

Indeed, the Chinese economy was self-sufficient, and stubbornly remained so—despite heroic British hopes of convincing the Chinese of the superiority of knives and forks over chopsticks, for example.[34] At the same time, the British appetite for Chinese tea and silk was only growing: "for nearly three centuries, China was the tomb of European silver—from which none ever returned."[35] The East India Company ultimately devised a brilliant solution to its ever-increasing trade deficit. It started shipping opium grown in India to pay for Chinese tea and other goods, which it then shipped to England. Finally, here was a commodity that created its own demand, once introduced to the Chinese market.

The only problem with this solution was that it constituted an open violation of Chinese law, which prohibited the importation of opium. Despite repeated official Chinese protests and even an appeal to Queen Victoria's moral conscience and the rules of the law of nations, the British refused to stop the trade.[36] When the Chinese in 1839 finally confiscated some of the smuggled opium and destroyed it, Britain condemned this as a violation of its subjects' private property. Determined to "open" China for free trade once and for all, the British declared war—freedom of trade evidently not including the right *not* to buy opium.

At the end of the Opium War in 1842, China signed the Treaty of Nanking as well as the supplemental Treaty of the Bogue the following year. Together, these treaties required China to open four additional ports for British trade and to cede the island of Hong Kong to Britain in perpetuity. Additional Regulations of Trade that accompanied the treaties also provided for the privilege of extraterritorial jurisdiction.

United States and China: A "Special Relationship"

In short, the conventional history of the Opium War is a story of Chinese modernization and of China's introduction into free trade organized under the rules of international law—notions the Chinese originally "misunderstood" but subsequently learned to appreciate, even if the lesson regrettably had to be learned at gunpoint. There is also a prominent narrative of these events that is told from the perspective of American studies, primarily by American diplomatic historians. Theirs is a story about America's "special relationship" with China.[37] Unlike the British in Hong Kong and Portuguese in Macao, Americans never set up colonies in China on the European imperial model. Equally important, they also declined the British invitation to join the Opium War and subsequent European military campaigns in China (with the important but again largely forgotten exception of American participation in the punitive multinational expedition sent to North China in the wake of the Boxer Rebellion). Indeed, American diplomatic historians tend to emphasize that throughout a century of increasing European encroachments in China, Americans typically actively *opposed* such encroachments.

Admittedly, after Britain did "open" China in the Opium War, Americans were perfectly happy and indeed very eager to participate in the "free trade" that the war had made possible. No sooner had the British won in Canton than President Tyler turned to Congress for an authorization to send the first American minister to China. The New England lawyer and congressman, Caleb Cushing, was charged with the task of matching the British treaties, although he was sent on the official pretext of inquiring after the emperor's health.

Aware of the Qianlong emperor's demand half a century earlier that Lord Macartney kowtow before him, Tyler and his secretary of state, Daniel Webster, were both at least somewhat concerned about China's putative arrogance. On the matter of the kowtow, Webster's instructions to Cushing emphasized that, should he receive an imperial audience, Cushing should "do nothing which may seem, even to the Chinese themselves, to imply any inferiority on the part of your government, or anything less than perfect independence of all nations." However, it was left ultimately to Cushing's discretion to determine just what a kowtow would signify and whether its performance would compromise U.S. sovereignty. He was also specifically instructed to "avoid[ ], as far as possible, the giving of offence either to the[ ] pride or the[ ] prejudices" of the Chinese.[38]

This concern about Chinese pretensions was reflected also in President Tyler's letters to the Son of Heaven, which Cushing was charged with delivering. So as not to feed the Celestial Emperor's inflated ego, the letters opened with the shockingly familiar salutation, "Great and Good Friend."[39] Cushing himself also wished to impress the emperor, and he had a special uniform made for his mission—"a Major-General's blue frock-coat with gilt buttons and some slight additions in the way of embroideries, gold striped trousers, spurs, and a hat with a white plume."[40] (The uniform was lost, alas, when one of Cushing's four ships was destroyed in Gibraltar.[41] However, according to an eyewitness account by an American in Canton, upon his arrival Cushing nevertheless cut a dashing figure, with "spurs on his heels, and mustachios and imperial, very flourishing!")[42]

In the end, Cushing never made it to the Chinese capital and thus never had to confront the audience question, with or without his uniform. However, he did succeed in negotiating a commercial treaty. In accordance with his instructions, Cushing obtained free commercial access to the same five ports as the British had. In addition, the treaty provided for extraterritorial privileges for Americans in China. Finally, it also contained a most favored nation clause, which was to guarantee that the United States would not find itself in a position inferior to anyone else in China: it would share equally in all the privileges that any European imperial power might obtain from China in the future.

Over the ensuing decades, as more gunboats appeared at its doorstep and further wars were fought against the British and the French, China in fact surrendered further privileges. The process culminated in the Scramble for Concessions at the turn of the century, which for the first time presented the real possibility that China might indeed be divided up among various European powers as well as Japan (which had just succeeded in overthrowing its regime of Western extraterritoriality). This race provided the immediate impetus for President McKinley's behind-the-scenes plea for a "slice" of China, but Secretary of State John Hay talked McKinley out of his China fever and into condemning the actions of the Europeans and Japan in China. In an articulation of what had been implicit in the terms of the Treaty of Wanghia, in 1899 and 1900 Hay issued the so-called Open Door notes: all foreign powers were to have commercial access to China on equal terms, while at the same time they were to respect China's territorial integrity.[43]

Admittedly, the policy was not designed with the primary goal of advancing China's interests. As a very recent owner of the Philippines and other newly obtained "insular possessions," the United States was a late-comer to territorial imperialism in the Pacific and would likely have been left behind in a race for the acquisition of territory. However, it was evident to both critics and supporters of the Open Door policy that in an economic competition with the European powers the United States would come out ahead. As *The Nation* put it succinctly in 1901, "We do not need to seek an unfair advantage. An open door and no favor infallibly means for the United States . . . the greater share and gain in the commercial exploitation of China."[44]

At the same time, however, until the Chinese reformed their "despotic" legal system, Westerners would remain exempt from Chinese jurisdiction. It was quite evident that the United States did not intend to surrender its extraterritorial privileges anytime soon. Like its European counterparts, the United States continued to exercise its extraterritorial jurisdiction in so-called consular courts, in which U.S. consuls adjudicated disputes involving Americans in China. These consuls exercised a dubious mix of executive, legislative, and judicial functions, and many were notorious for their incompetence and corruption. Nevertheless, the continuation of American extraterritoriality in China was justified in part by the pedagogical function it served, as an example of the rule of law. Although American extraterritoriality in China ostensibly violated the principle of exclusive national territorial jurisdiction, its very point—the Chinese were told—was to prepare for its own demise and help China take full legal control of its territory.

Why Canton Is Not Boston: American Imperial Sovereignty

For all the differences between the British and American attitudes to China, at least retrospectively it seems natural and self-evident that Americans sided in principle with the British on the question of free trade. Although Americans refused to join in a war to gain commercial access with force, any disagreement between the two countries was over the means, not the end—namely, how best to emancipate China into modernity and absorb it into the emerging capitalist world system. Ultimately, Britain and the United States represented modernity and freedom, while China stood on the side of constraint of tradition.

It is noteworthy, however, that many American contemporaries in fact sided with the *Chinese* in the events leading up to the Opium War. When John Quincy Adams argued in a lecture in 1841 that "the cause of the war is the Ko-tow!" and "the arrogant and insupportable pretensions of China,"[45] this position was considered so extreme and controversial that the *North American Review*, which had previously agreed to publish the piece, ultimately declined to do so.[46] Even most merchants recognized that China had "a perfect right to regulate her imports"[47] and many considered the Opium War "one of the most unjust wars that one nation had ever waged against another."[48] The fact that the immediate *casus belli* was opium hardly made the war any more respectable.

Indeed, with confiscated British opium being flushed into the Canton harbor, it was difficult *not* to view the event as a kind of Canton Opium Party, analogous to the Boston Tea Party: these were two heroic acts of struggle against British imperial regulation of trade, in China and America, respectively. Admittedly, John Quincy Adams, for one, rejected this analogy strenuously: "It is a general, and altogether mistaken opinion that the quarrel is merely for certain chests of opium imported by British Merchants into China, and seized by the Chinese Government for having been imported contrary to Law. This is a mere incident to the dispute; but no more the cause of the War, than the throwing overboard of the Tea in Boston Harbor was the cause of the North American Revolution."[49] The point, however, is that this *was* the analogy to be rejected and that many Americans did in fact find the analogy persuasive.

However, while it was still plausible on the eve of the Opium War for many Americans to see China's struggle against British imperialism in the light of their own recent past, by the end of the century America itself had become an imperial power in Asia and its fate aligned with that of Britain *against* China. Admittedly, the United States rejected British territorial imperialism (at least in China, except for its erratic interest in Taiwan), but it adopted, with a vengeance, the key form of British *nonterritorial* imperialism: the cultivation and elaboration of the privilege of extraterritoriality in connection with various Treaties of Peace, Amity, and Trade (or some combination of the trinity). Indeed, the Treaty of Wanghia of 1844 can be viewed as a turning point in American political relations with Asia more generally. Not only did it "plac[e] our relations with China on a new footing, eminently favorable to the commerce and other interests of the United States," as President Tyler happily informed the Congress, but once ratified it became the model for subsequent American extraterritoriality treaties elsewhere as well.[50]

In short, prior to America's adoption of the European practice of extraterritoriality in Asia, it was still possible to view China as a sovereign state that enjoyed a political status equal to that of the United States, and to condemn England as a nation that cloaked itself in an illegitimate imperial sovereignty that purportedly made it politically superior to both China and the United States. However, by taking on the practice of extraterritoriality, America adopted a form of imperial sovereignty that rendered it *Britain's* equal in nonterritorial imperialism in China.

Below, I sketch an outline of the genesis of American imperial sovereignty in China and analyze its rhetorical justifications by Caleb Cushing.

Caleb Cushing and America's Honor in China

If the privilege of extraterritoriality itself is extraordinary, it is equally extraordinary how the United States came to obtain that privilege in China and how the main author of the Treaty of Wanghia renarrated the history of the law of nations to justify the extraterritoriality clause—and even played an important role later on, as attorney general, in interpreting extraterritoriality's meaning.[51]

Caleb Cushing's primary charge in 1844 was to match the British trade concessions. However, in the Treaty of Wanghia he in fact far exceeded his mandate. The instructions he received were admittedly ambivalent in tone, but they certainly did not call for him to acquire the right of extraterritoriality for American citizens. Indeed, President Tyler's letter to the emperor (which Cushing was charged with delivering) expressly pledged the president's respect for the emperor's jurisdiction over Americans: it assured the emperor solemnly that "we shall not uphold them that break your laws." To be sure, the letter ended on an ominous note, asking the emperor to agree to a "just" commercial treaty in order that "nothing may happen to disturb the peace between China and America," but the letter provided no suggestion whatsoever that "just" trade relations might require American extraterritoriality in China.[52]

Cushing's eventual decision to obtain extraterritoriality is all the more surprising given that, in keeping with the early American tendency to recognize Oriental states as relative equals, only a few years before his mission, in 1840, Cushing himself had proudly declared in the House of Representatives that "the Americans in Canton, and they almost quite alone, have manifested a proper respect for the laws and public rights of the Chinese Empire, in honorable contrast with the outrageous conduct of the English there."[53] Cushing's statement constituted both an unequivocal admission that the Chinese empire apparently *had* "public rights" under the law of nations, as well as an inspired condemnation of the British imperial policy in China.

However, during his stay in China Cushing evidently became convinced that China's disinterest in trade and diplomatic relations was not motivated by a mere harmless desire to be left alone. Rather, he came to see it as evidence of a civilizational superiority complex—what the British for a long time had called Chinese "arrogance." When subsequently confronted by his earlier inconsistent remarks, he did not deny the contradiction but simply unhesitatingly disavowed his earlier views, declaring, "I do not admit as my equals either the red man of America, or the yellow man of Asia, or the black man of Africa."[54] From such a perspective of racial superiority, it was only a short step to conclude China's isolationist foreign policy was nothing less than an *insult* to the honor and dignity of the United States as a sovereign nation.

Indeed, Cushing's correspondence from China is filled with accounts of various "indignities" he suffered. When he was told, for example, that it would not be appropriate for him to proceed to Peking for an imperial audience, as there was no precedent for American ambassadors being received in the capital, he promptly informed the Chinese that a refusal to receive an envoy constituted among Western nations "an act of national insult and a just cause of war."[55] Disingenuously, he huffed that the "sole object" of his diplomatic efforts was "to signify my high personal respects and that of my Government for the August Sovereign, by seizing the earliest moment, after my arrival in China, to make inquiry for his health."[56]

And when one of Cushing's ships was requested not to fire twenty-one guns in salute—because, he was told, "China has no such salute as firing twenty-one guns"[57] and gunfire from a foreign vessel would therefore likely have caused terror among the population[58]—Cushing declared in response that not only was it his "duty at the outset not to omit any of the tokens of respect customary among Western nations," but that "China will find it very difficult to remain in peace with any of the Great States of the West" if it was unwilling "either to give or to receive manifestations of that peace, in the exchange of the ordinary courtesies of national intercourse."[59]

Inventing an American Tradition of Extraterritoriality

As to the extraterritoriality clause of the Treaty of Wanghia itself, Cushing was well aware that obtaining it had not been part of his instructions and that it was in fact quite extraordinary. His ship had barely departed the South China Seas when he started composing a long and remarkable memorandum to the State Department. He reviewed the origins of extraterritoriality in the religious exemption of Christians from the jurisdiction of the Ottoman Empire, seeking to prove that general principles of international law "only apply to the intercourse of no states but those of Christendom."[60] Moreover, he observed that the United States had, in fact, already entered into a series of extraterritoriality treaties with "the Barbary states, the Porte, and the Imam of Muscat."[61] With the issue of "Mohammedan states" thus settled, Cushing concluded that the right of Western extraterritoriality certainly applied with equal force in the "pagan" states of Asia.

Yet if the law of nations, as well as American diplomatic practice, were so clear on the matter, why had the United States not apprehended their relevance in its political relations with China until after the Opium War? The problem was, in Cushing's view, the secularized nature of nineteenth-century international law: its main justification for imperialism was the *mission civilisatrice*, rather than the older Christian mission of religious conversion (accompanied, when necessary, with the conduct of a "just war" against infidels). To the extent that the law of nations provided for the exemption of subjects of "civilized states" from the laws of barbaric peoples, China provoked a catachresis in this classification. The civilizational discourse worked perfectly well in dealing with the "savages" of the New World or Africa, but not with the states of East Asia, which had all the conventional markers of a "high" civilization. Cushing's solution was thus to recall the original *religious* justification of the doctrine of extraterritoriality and to reinstitute Christianity as the standard of admission into international society.

Despite its rhetorical appeal, Cushing's account of the history of extraterritoriality does not bear scrutiny. For example, most of the U.S. treaties with the Barbary States provided for a *reciprocal* right of (primarily civil) extraterritorial jurisdiction, whereas the Treaty of Wanghia had not even a hint of such reciprocity.[62] Cushing also completely ignored the 1833 Treaty of Amity and Commerce with Siam, although it was presumably the only directly applicable precedent, as the sole prior treaty with a "pagan" state in Asia. That treaty, of course, provided expressly for American *submission* to Siamese jurisdiction. Other relevant precedent of relations with "non-Mohammedan states" in the Pacific would have included U.S. treaties with the Sandwich Islands (i.e., Hawai'i, 1826), Tahiti (1826), Samoa (1839), and Sulu (1842), none of which provided for American extraterritoriality.[63]

Yet all of this was conveniently left out of Cushing's narrative explaining why extraterritoriality in China was "essential" to the "honor" of the United States, as he put it.[64] Remarkably, the United States made its signal contribution to a seemingly modern form of nonterritorial imperialism in Asia by justifying its precedent-setting extraterritoriality claims by invoking a medieval religious discourse of a *Respublica Christiana.* Whatever hesitation it might have had, the United States now took on unambiguously the European discourse of imperial, aristocratic sovereignty, which made sovereignty available only to the states with the right genealogy: *viz.*, members of the Euro-American Family of Nations. Only these states were born to be equal and possessed their sovereignty as a matter of birthright. All others would have to earn their sovereignty and prove that they deserved it.

From Invention to Institution

Indeed, Cushing seems to have been largely successful in convincing the State Department that the extraterritoriality provisions of the Treaty of Wanghia, far from providing a novel basis for American political relations with Asia, was simply a continuation of what had been implicit, and even explicit, prior policies. Over the next several decades, extraterritoriality turned into a settled expectation in U.S. relations with states in Asia and the Pacific. The 1850 Treaty of Peace, Friendship, Commerce and Navigation with Borneo provided for full extraterritoriality, civil and criminal.[65] In 1854, Commodore Perry arrived in Japan with the task of opening it for the West, as Britain had done in China. Using the Treaty of Wanghia as his model, Perry acknowledged encountering "great difficulties" in winning immunities for Americans at first, but in 1857 the United States obtained an express right of extraterritoriality in Japan.[66] Despite the minor delay in getting Japan to fit into the emerging structure of American extraterritoriality in the Pacific, in 1856 the United States revised its treaty with Siam and insisted on extraterritoriality in Siam as well.[67] In the last quarter of the nineteenth century, the United States obtained similar privileges in Samoa (1878), Korea (1882), and Tonga (1886) as well.[68]

Not only did the United States adopt British practices of empire in its political intercourse with Asia, but it perfected them so effectively that it came to serve as an imperial model in its own right. Although the British had been the first to obtain extraterritoriality in China, the American statement of extraterritorial rights in the treaty language itself was regarded as "superior" in terms of precision and coverage, and it came to be hailed as "one of the distinct contributions of the treaty to the diplomacy of the Far East."[69] In the envious admission of a high-ranking contemporary Briton, "the United States in their treaty with China, and in vigilant protection of their subjects at Canton, have evinced far better diplomacy and more attention to substantive interests than we have done."[70] In the end, it was the American, rather than the British, extraterritoriality provision that became the model for the other European nations that entered into their own treaties with China in the following years. Hence, the United States played a crucial role in designing the legal architecture of the semicolonial century of Unequal Treaties that structured China's entry into modernity.

Similarly, the 1858 revision of Perry's original treaty with Japan provided the first clear statement of extraterritoriality in Japan, and it too came to serve as the model for subsequent European treaties.[71] And in a repetition of the same pattern, the American treaty with Korea in 1882 was also that country's first treaty with a Western state, and again it set the precedent for later treaties by other powers.[72]

Within decades, Cushing's invented tradition had become an institutionalized norm in U.S. diplomatic practice, which in turn was eagerly emulated by others.

Open Door vs. Chinese Exclusion

Although Americans in China were exempt from the operation of Chinese law starting in 1844, Chinese in America were absolutely subject to American law. Moreover, American law absolutely discriminated against them—sometimes with considerable effort and ingenuity. For example, the California Supreme Court held in 1854 that the prohibition of "Indians" witnessing against white persons applied to the Chinese witnesses as well—on the dubious ground that Columbus *thought* he was in Asia when he called the natives of North America "Indians."[73]

And although the United States was pleased to refer to its China policy as "Open Door," it hardly escaped the Chinese that the door swung one way only. Starting in 1882, a series of Chinese Exclusion Laws enacted by the Congress barred the Chinese from entering the United States and from naturalization.[74] In 1888, for example, the Congress retroactively terminated the right of some twenty thousand Chinese residents to reenter the United States after visiting China, without permitting the excluded to recover or sell any of their personal property left in the United States.[75] These racially motivated laws were not only harsh in consequence, but also in direct violation of the nation's obligations to China under the 1868 Burlingame Treaty and its subsequent amendments. This treaty was one of several revisions and extensions of Cushing's Treaty of Wanghia, and in it the United States solemnly pledged to permit Chinese immigration.

The Chinese exclusion laws had been justified in part on the premise that the Chinese, as born slaves of Oriental despots, were incapable of understanding the notion of individual rights and could therefore never assimilate into America's republican values. Ironically, the Chinese responded to their exclusion by immediately taking the matter to federal court and challenging it under the Constitution. The Supreme Court held unequivocally that the United States had an absolute right to exclude aliens from its territory. This right was an inherent power of sovereignty, a core attribute of what it means to be an independent nation. It did not derive from the Constitution, but from the law of nations and the very notion of sovereignty itself, and hence it simply could not be constrained by the Constitution. Quoting the authoritative words of Chief Justice Marshall from 1812, the Court declared, "'All exceptions, therefore, to the full and complete power of a nation within its own territories, must be traced upon the consent of the nation itself. They can flow from no other legitimate source.'"[76]

Yet even if only the United States government itself could limit its sovereign right to exclude the Chinese from within its borders, had it not done precisely so in the Burlingame Treaty, which presumably *was* a binding obligation under international law? After all, if it was not, then all American privileges in China, including the right of extraterritoriality, would also be in doubt. With breathless indifference to this implication, the Court "conceded" that the 1888 legislation was "in contravention of express stipulations of the treaty of 1868, and of the supplemental treaty of 1880," but that it was not, because of any such technicality, "invalid, or to be restricted in its enforcement."[77] The Court held that since the power to exclude "foreigners" was "an incident of sovereignty," a core attribute of nationhood itself, it "cannot be granted away or restrained on behalf of any one." That is, despite its apparent willingness to restrict its sovereign right to exclude immigrants from China, the United States had in fact not succeeded in doing so: it *could not* impair its sovereignty in such a radical way as to surrender its right to exclude Chinese immigration. Hence, any promises it had made to China on the subject amounted merely to a moral, rather than legal, obligation. Sovereign states, like individuals, were simply not free to give away their inalienable rights. In the end, the right to exclude Chinese could not be "the subject of barter or contract."[78]

To add insult to injury, the Court noted that if the Chinese government was displeased with the result, it was free to pursue diplomacy or "resort to any other measure which, in its judgment, its interests or dignity may demand."[79] Of course, it was evident to all informed observers that the exclusion of the Chinese from the United States could not possibly injure China's "dignity" in the same way that American dignity was offended at not being allowed to exercise its "right" to trade freely with China.

Yet in discussing the American policy of Chinese exclusion, the Court made no mention of how the United States had responded to the *Chinese* policy of seeking to exclude Americans and Europeans. While the American right to exclude the Chinese was an inalienable right of sovereignty that inhered in the United States' nationhood, the efforts of the Chinese government to exclude Americans from China outside of Canton were seen as antisocial behavior that could not be tolerated in international society. And while the United States *could* not—even if it wanted to—give away its ontological freedom to keep foreigners outside, the extraterritoriality treaties by which China had signed away far bigger chunks of its sovereignty were regarded as perfectly valid exercises of whatever "sovereignty" China had.

As Sarah Cleveland characterizes the Supreme Court's nineteenth-century jurisprudence on the government's foreign affairs power, "the Court repeatedly utilized international law as a source of authority for United States governmental action, but did not recognize it as a source of constraint."[80] Remarkably, the law of nations was thus seen to give Americans *both* the right to exclude Chinese from the United States *and* the right to "open" China for the entry of Americans.

American Empire and the Rise of Racial Anglo-Saxonism

By the end of the nineteenth century, the global expansion of Western international law was well on its way to turning the entire planet into a juridical formation consisting of nation-states. At the same time, it was eminently clear that even in a world structured on the notional basis of formal sovereign equality, some sovereigns were more equal than others. It was not only a geographical, but also a social, historical, and political fact that Canton was not Boston and that access from the "Mantchoo-Tartar Dynasty of Despotism" (in John Quincy Adams's lyrical phrase) to the shores of New England was far more limited than the other way around. Treaties of "free trade" with imperial conditions became one of the pillars of the informal empire on which the emerging global structure rested.

Although the United States still prefers to view itself historically as China's "special friend," the story of the Treaty of Wanghia casts it in the role of a precedent-setting imperial power in its own right, in China as well as elsewhere in the Pacific region. It is noteworthy that in their analysis of British free trade imperialism, Robinson and Gallagher cite as one of their main examples Britain's 1858 treaty with Japan—when that treaty was in fact modeled on the prior American precedent, as I have noted. A conventional distinction between a British policy of "imperialism" in Asia and an American one of "free trade" thus masks a fundamental continuity in the two nations' practices.

Nevertheless, American exceptionalism retains much persuasive force in the telling of the history of America in China. Although few would state the point quite as starkly today, Tyler Dennett's statement is exemplary:

> England was approaching China through the old world, through India and other Oriental countries, where every precedent was in favor of the policy she was laying down; the United

> States was approaching China as one independent nation another, and the negotiations were in the hands of Yankees who recognized no color line and prided themselves as they yielded to no race prejudice.[81]

Caleb Cushing was certainly a Yankee, but I hope to have shown that he wore his racial prejudice on his sleeve, with great Anglo-Saxon pride.

Indeed, it is noteworthy, and hardly coincidental, that the rise of American extraterritoriality in Asia maps the development of what Reginald Horsman calls American racial Anglo-Saxonism.[82] He observes that while the beginning of the nineteenth century is dominated in the United States by a pervasive sense of the country's Manifest Destiny, the notion did not yet connote the "rampant racialism" that was evident by midcentury.[83] At that time, the country's "sense of idealistic mission" was replaced with the view "that the people of large parts of the world were incapable of creating efficient, democratic and prosperous governments; and that American and world economic growth, the triumph of Western civilization, and a stable world order could be achieved by American commercial penetration of supposedly backward areas."[84]

The United States' territorial conquest ended on this side of the Pacific Coast, culminating in a congressman's exuberant declaration that with title to Oregon, "we shall be neighbours of the Chinese!" Yet even if America ended at the water's edge, its mission did not. From Oregon, "civilization was to be carried into Asia along the paths of commerce."[85] Indeed, as this essay suggests, commerce did not replace an earlier discourse of civilization, nor even a prior one of religion. All three discourses survived, each available for invocation when the other two failed in their imperial purpose.

In sum, during the first decades of the nineteenth century, while relatively positive views of Asia still prevailed (or, at a minimum, the picture remained radically ambivalent), the United States paid little or no diplomatic attention to Asia. When the nation finally focused on Asia around midcentury (only to be distracted again by the Civil War, and to remain so until the Spanish-American War), the policies that developed reflected the increasingly negative views of Orientals in general and the Chinese in particular. With growing contact, what had once been "fabulous had become mundane,"[86] and the notion of "race" took the place an earlier concept of merely strange, alien peoples.[87] Chinese discovered that they were "yellow," along with all the other attributes that this implied—and by definition, they did not include what Cushing called "the marvellous qualities of Anglo-Saxon blood."[88] Accordingly, the United States took upon itself the imperial sovereignty to which its heritage entitled it, and the civilizing mission that it implied.

While many important recent studies of American imperialism have focused on law's role in America's territorial possessions, it is crucial not to ignore law's role in nonterritorial forms of American imperialism as well. For one thing, the story of American extraterritorial jurisdiction in the Asia-Pacific region puts in question our epistemological commitment to such discrete, sovereign categories as "China" and the "United States." We may well recognize that nations are "imagined communities" as far as their social and cultural constitution is concerned, yet legally at least we incline to think of nations as defined by their territorial borders.[89] However, in China, among other places, American law did not attach to American territory but to the *bodies* of American citizens—each one of them representing a floating island of American sovereignty. In effect, the story of American law in China helps us see "law" as an almost ontological character of American *being*—the glory of the law-loving Anglo-Saxon race, a kind of White Lawyer's Burden.[90]

Notes

I have presented versions of this essay at the Hart Institute for American History at Pomona College as well as at American University, City University of Hong Kong Law School, Columbia Law School, Michigan Law School, Temple University Beasley School of Law, and the University of Helsinki. I thank the audiences for their critical feedback. I owe special thanks to Mary Dudziak, Leti Volpp, David Eng, Randle Edwards, Muneer Ahmad, and Susie Lee for their careful reading of the essay, and to Michael McLellan and Brian Fiorino for research assistance. Adeen Postar, deputy director of the Pence Law Library at American University, was extraordinarily helpful in obtaining the materials. Dean Claudio Grossman of the Washington College of Law at American University and the Charles A. Ryskamp Research Fellowship from the American Council of Learned Societies provided financial support for this project.

1. "John Quincy Adams on the Opium War," *Proceedings of the Massachusetts Historical Society* 43 (February 1910): 324.
2. Tyler Dennett, *Americans in Eastern Asia: A Critical Study of the Policy of the United States with Reference to China, Japan, and Korea in the Nineteenth Century* (New York: Macmillan, 1922), 288. For details, see Message from the President Communicating the Correspondence of Commissioners to China, S. Doc. No. 35–22, 1083, 1148 (1858).
3. Ibid., 1204.
4. See Thomas J. McCormick, *China Market: America's Quest for Informal Empire, 1893–1901* (Chicago: Quadrangle Books, 1967), 168–75.
5. *Downes v. Bidwell*, 182 U.S. 144, 374 (1901).
6. See James L. Hevia, *English Lessons: The Pedagogy of Imperialism in Nineteenth Century China* (Durham, N.C.: Duke University Press, 2003); Tani Barlow, "~~Colonialism~~'s Career in Postwar China Studies," 1 *positions* 1.1 (1993): 224.
7. There is a considerable literature on the subject. A limited sample includes Christina Duffy Burnett and Burke Marshall, eds., *Foreign in a Domestic Sense* (Durham, N.C.: Duke University Press, 2001); Gerald L. Neuman, *Strangers to the Constitution: Immigrants, Borders, and Fundamental Law* (Princeton, N.J.: Princeton University Press, 1996); and T. Alexander Aleinikoff, *Semblances of Sovereignty* (Cambridge, Mass.: Harvard University Press, 2002); as well as Sarah H. Cleveland, "Powers Inherent in Sovereignty: Indians, Aliens, Territories, and the Nineteenth Century Origins of the Plenary Power over Foreign Affairs," *Texas Law Review* 81 (2002): 1.

8. Important exceptions to the general neglect of the topic include Elaine Scully, *Bargaining with the State from Afar* (New York: Columbia University Press, 2001), and David J. Bederman, "Extraterritorial Domicile and the Constitution," *Virginia Journal of International Law* 28 (1988): 451. In addition, Tahirih Lee has explored American extraterritorial jurisdiction in China in unpublished papers, e.g., "U.S. Extraterritorial Courts in the Twentieth Century as a Means of Exercising Jurisdiction in the Pacific," paper presented at the annual meeting of the Association of American Law Schools, San Francisco, January 2001.
9. Both the English and Chinese texts of the treaty, with background notes, can be found in Hunter Miller, ed., *Treaties and Other International Acts of the United States of America*, vol. 4 (Washington, D.C.: U.S. Government Printing Office, 1934), 559.
10. *Schooner Exchange v. McFaddon*, 11 U.S. 116, 136 (1812).
11. John Gallagher and Ronald Robinson, "The Imperialism of Free Trade," *Economic History Review* (2nd series) 6.1 (1953): 1.
12. Ibid., 11.
13. See Lassa Oppenheim, *International Law*, vol. 1 (London: Longmans, Green, 1905): 60–61.
14. See Carl Schmitt, *The Nomos of the Earth in the International Law of the Jus Publicum Europaeum, trans. G. L. Ulmen* (*New York*: Telos Press, 2003). See also Antony Anghie, "Finding the Peripheries: Sovereignty and Colonialism in Nineteenth-Century International Law," *Harvard International Law Journal* 40.1 (1999): 1.
15. John Locke, *Two Treatises of Government* (Cambridge: Cambridge University Press 1988), 301.
16. *Cherokee Nation v. Georgia*, 30 U.S. 1, 16 (1830).
17. I borrow the term from Robert A. Williams, *The American Indian in Western Legal Thought: The Discourses of Conquest* (New York: Oxford University Press, 1990), 326.
18. See Amy Kaplan, *The Anarchy of Empire in the Making of US Culture* (Cambridge, Mass.: Harvard University Press, 2002).
19. See Travers Twiss, *The Law of Nations Considered as Independent Political Communities* (Oxford: Clarendon Press, 1884), 267.
20. Philip Chadwick Foster Smith, *The* Empress of China (Philadelphia: Philadelphia Maritime Museum, 1984), 8.
21. James Morton Callahan, *American Relations in the Pacific and the Far East, 1784–1900* (Baltimore: Johns Hopkins University Press, 1901), 14, 84.
22. John W. Foster, *American Diplomacy in the Orient* (Boston: Houghton Mifflin, 1903), 43.
23. See R. Randle Edwards, "Ch'ing Legal Jurisdiction over Foreigners," in *Essays on China's Legal Tradition* (Princeton, N.J.: Princeton University Press, 1980), 222.
24. Jonathan Goldstein, *Philadelphia and the China Trade, 1682–1846: Commercial, Cultural, and Attitudinal Effects* (University Park: Pennsylvania State University Press, 1978), 61.
25. Dennett, *Americans in Eastern Asia*, 89.
26. Edwards, "Ch'ing Legal Jurisdiction over Foreigners," 249.
27. Dennett, *Americans in Eastern Asia*, 84.
28. Ibid., 88.
29. Treaty of Amity and Commerce, Art. 9, in Miller, *Treaties*, vol. 3, 757.
30. John Kuo Wei Tchen, *New York Before Chinatown* (Baltimore: Johns Hopkins University Press, 1999), 41–42. See also Dennett, *Americans in East Asia*, 77.
31. The established reference for a description of the "tributary system" in East Asia is John King Fairbank, ed., *The Chinese World Order: Traditional China's Foreign Relations* (Cambridge, Mass.: Harvard University Press, 1968).
32. The literature on the Macartney embassy is far too large to cite in a single footnote. See generally James Hevia, *Cherishing Men from Afar: Qing Guest Ritual and the Macartney Embassy of 1793* (Durham, N.C.: Duke University Press, 1995), and the sources cited therein.
33. Ibid., 238.
34. J. L. Cranmer-Byng, ed., *An Embassy to China: Being the Journal Kept by Lord Macartney During His Embassy to the Emperor Ch'ien-lung, 1793–1794* (London: Longman's, 1962,) 225–26.
35. Marshall Sahlins, "Cosmologies of Capitalism: The Transpacific Sector of 'The World-System,'" *Proceedings of the British Academy* (1988), 13.
36. See Ssu-yu Teng and John K. Fairbank, eds., *China's Response to the West: A Documentary Survey, 1839–1923* (Cambridge, Mass.: Harvard University Press, 1954), 24–28.

37. See Michael Hunt, *The Making of a Special Relationship: The United States and China to 1914* (New York: Columbia University Press, 1983).
38. "Webster's Directions to Cushing," in *The Works of Daniel Webster*, 5th ed., vol. 6 (Boston: Little, Brown, 1853), 468.
39. For the full language of the letters, see Message from the President Communicating Instructions Given to the Late Commissioner to China, S. Doc. No. 28–138, 8–9 (1845).
40. Jack Beeching, *The Chinese Opium Wars* (New York: Harcourt Brace Janovich, 1975), 174.
41. Claude M. Fuess, *The Life of Caleb Cushing*, vol. 1 (New York: Harcourt, Brace, 1923), 423.
42. Dennett, *Americans in Eastern Asia*, 143.
43. See Jerry Israel, *Progressivism and the Open Door: America and China, 1905–1921* (Pittsburgh: University of Pittsburgh Press, 1971), 4–6.
44. *The Nation*, May 9, 1901, 368.
45. "John Quincy Adams on the Opium War," 324.
46. John Quincy Adams, *Memoirs*, vol. 11 (Philadelphia: J. B. Lippincott & Co., 1876), 31.
47. Dennett, *Americans in Eastern Asia*, 105 (quoting *Hunt's Merchant Magazine*, March 1843, 205).
48. William C. Hunter, *The "Fan Kwae" at Canton Before Treaty Days: 1825–1844* (London: Kegan Paul, Trench & Co., 1882), 154.
49. "John Quincy Adams on the Opium War," 314.
50. Message from the President Transmitting an Abstract of Treaty, H. R. Doc. No. 28–69, 1 (1845).
51. See 7 Op. Att'y Gen. 503 (1855).
52. Message from the President Communicating Instruction, 8.
53. Dennett, *Americans in Eastern Asia*, 104.
54. Fuess, *The Life of Caleb Cushing*, vol. 2, 230–31.
55. S. Doc. No. 28–67, 12 (1845).
56. Ibid.
57. Ibid., 16.
58. Fuess, *The Life of Caleb Cushing*, vol. 1, 430.
59. S. Doc. No. 28–67, 18.
60. Message from the President Transmitting an Abstract of Treaty, 10.
61. Ibid.
62. See the treaties with Tripoli (1796–97 and 1805), Tunis (1797–99), and Algiers (1815, 1816), reproduced, respectively, in Miller, *Treaties*, vol. 2, 348, 529, 386, 585, and 617.
63. See, respectively, Miller, *Treaties*, vol. 3, 269, 249; vol. 4, 241, 349.
64. Message from the President Transmitting an Abstract of the Treaty, 14.
65. See Miller, *Treaties*, vol. 5, 819.
66. Ibid. On Perry's negotiations and his use of the Treaty of Wanghia as a model, see Perry, *Narrative of the Expedition of an American Squadron to the China Seas and Japan* (Washington, D.C.: Beverly Tucker, 1856), 376 ff.
67. Miller, *Treaties*, vol. 7, 329.
68. For these treaties, see, respectively, William M. Malloy, *Treaties, Conventions, International Acts, Protocols and Agreements Between the United States of America and Other Powers, 1776–1909* (Washington, D.C.: Government Printing Office, 1910), vol. 2, 1574; vol. 1, 334; and vol. 2, 1781.
69. The assessment is by Kenneth S. Latourette, *The History of Early Relations Between the United States and China, 1784–1844* (New Haven, Conn.: Yale University Press, 1917), 140–41.
70. Foster, *American Diplomacy in the Orient*, 89–90.
71. Louis G. Perez, *Japan Comes of Age: Mutsu Munemitsu and the Revision of the Unequal Treaties* (Cranbury, N.J.: Associated University Presses, 1999), 51–52.
72. Ibid., 37, 39.
73. *People v. Hall*, 4 Cal. 399, 401–02 (1854).
74. Act of May 6, 1882, ch. 126, 22 Stat. 58.
75. Act of Oct. 1, 1888, ch. 1064, 25 Stat. 504.
76. *Chae Chan Ping v. United States*, 130 U.S. 581, 604 (1889), quoting *Schooner Exchange v. McFaddon*, 11 U.S. 116, 136 (1812).
77. *Chae Chan Ping*, 130 U.S. at 600.
78. Ibid., 609.
79. Ibid.

80. Cleveland, "Powers Inherent in Sovereignty," 280.
81. Dennett, *Americans in East Asia,* 169.
82. See Reginald Horsman, *Race and Manifest Destiny: The Origins of American Racial Anglo-Saxonism* (Cambridge, Mass.: Harvard University Press, 1981). As Sarah Cleveland observes, from the domestic perspective this racial Anglo-Saxonism coincided with the consolidation of the so-called plenary power doctrine, grounded in the "inherent sovereignty" of the United States, which not only permitted racial immigration bars, but also gave the federal government essentially unconstrained power in its treatment of the Indian nations and U.S. territories. See Cleveland, "Powers Inherent in Sovereignty."
83. Horsman, *Race and Manifest Destiny,* 1, 297.
84. Ibid., 298.
85. Ibid., 288.
86. The phrase is from P. J. Marshall, "Britain and China in Late Eighteenth Century," in *Ritual and Diplomacy: the Macartney Mission to China, 1792–1794,* ed. Robert Bickers (London: Wellsweep/British Association for Chinese Studies, 1992), 11.
87. Hannah Arendt, *The Origins of Totalitarianism* (San Diego: Harcourt, 1968), 206.
88. Fuess, *The Life of Caleb Cushing,* vol. 2, 233.
89. See Benedict Anderson, *Imagined Communities: Reflections on the Origins and Spread of Nationalism,* rev. ed. (London: Verso, 1991).
90. I have analyzed the contrasting, conceptually linked idea of the Chinese as an ontologically "unlegal" people in "Legal Orientalism," *Michigan Law Review* 101 (2002): 179; and "Law Without Law, or, Is 'Chinese Law' an Oxymoron?", *William and Mary Bill of Rights Journal* 11 (2003): 655.

Liberation under Siege: U.S. Military Occupation and Japanese Women's Enfranchisement

Lisa Yoneyama

One year after the United States attacked Afghanistan, a *New York Times* article, headlined "U.S. Has a Plan to Occupy Iraq, Officials Report," informed its readers that the Bush administration was developing a plan for postwar Iraq "modeled on the postwar occupation of Japan."[1] To be sure, the occupation of Japan (1945–1952) was not the only instance of a past U.S. military involvement that was invoked during this national emergency. Throughout different phases of the crisis that followed the 9/11 incidents, U.S. cultural apparatuses mobilized divergent memories of past wars fought against different enemies at different times and places. Indeed by September 2003, White House reporters were noting that the Bush administration was viewing the Iraqi situation—in which militant opposition against the occupying U.S. forces appeared much more formidable than the administration had led the public to expect—as closer to that of postwar Germany than Japan. Furthermore, during his October 2003 visit to the Philippines, President George W. Bush spoke to the Philippine Congress and suggested that the 1898 Spanish-American War ought to be recalled as a model for the postwar rebuilding of Iraq. In challenging such selective amnesia and the distortion of history, Amy Kaplan poignantly cited Mark Twain to point out: "What Bush called liberation, Twain decried as a bloody campaign against the Philippine struggle for independence, a campaign that would usher in five decades of occupation by the United States."[2] Before and during the 2004 presidential election, the seemingly endless attacks against U.S. troops, roadside bombings, hostage abductions, and the obscurity of intelligence ineluctably evoked memories of the Vietnam War quagmire and the perils of guerilla warfare.

What is remarkable, therefore, is not so much whether Washington policymakers were seriously modeling the postwar occupation of Iraq on the occupation of Japan. The analogy Washington officials drew between the U.S. occupation of Japan and the postwar plans for occupying Iraq were publicized precisely at the moment when the United States was threatening to attack, when millions of people throughout the world were vigilantly protesting the illegality of the war. It remains crucial that remembering the occupation of Japan as a "success" *prior to* the beginning of war proved effective in preparing the public, both here and abroad, for the preemptive military strike the U.S. government was about to launch against Iraq.

This anachronism, which enabled the American public to foresee the "success" of the postwar U.S. occupation of Iraq antecedent to the war itself, is arguably one instantiation of the discursive power the dominant memory of the U.S.–Japan War and its aftermath can exert over the production of "just war" narratives. This dominant memory not only remembers the U.S. war against Japan as a "good war" that liberated the people of Asia, including the Japanese themselves, from Japan's military fanaticism, cultic imperial worship, and feudalism—all of which helped define U.S. modernity and democracy as their antitheses. It also remembers that those liberated by the United States were reformed into free and advanced citizens of the postwar democratic world. Insisting that the war's mission was rescue and rehabilitation, this memory shapes and feeds the American myth that allows people to at once anticipate and explain that the enemy can be freed and reformed through U.S. military interventions and territorial takeovers. The ability to anticipate Iraq's successful postwar recovery while planning its destruction stemmed precisely from the compelling power of this myth—a myth that allows for the simultaneous enunciation of violence and recovery.

Underlying this myth and the "just war" it endorses is the "women question." In the midst of mounting difficulties and increasing violence in post–cease-fire Iraq, the Bush administration continued to draw parallels between its "war on terror" and the World War II missions that led to the demise of totalitarian regimes and "women's freedom."[3] Earlier, in countering the European and other nations' challenges to U.S. "unilateralism," George F. Will defended the Bush administration's abrogation of the Kyoto environmental protocol and the United Nation's Convention on the Elimination of All Forms of Discrimination Against Women, among other policies, by claiming that American democracy is so "uniquely well developed" that it surpasses the standards of international supervision. For proof of such uniqueness, Will reminded us that "the most important emancipator of Japanese women was Gen. Douglas MacArthur, who made women's suffrage occupation policy. The liberators of Afghan women wore U.S. battle dress."[4] The knowledge that Japanese women gained constitutional rights at this U.S. imperial border of occupied space is thus integral to American exceptionalism.[5] If, as Kaplan astutely put it, the Bush administration confuses occupation with liberation in its justification of the U.S. military presence in Iraq, American popular memories of Japanese women's liberation under U.S. occupation are key to enabling such a confusion to persist.

As I have argued elsewhere, Japanese women embodied and enacted both the changes the U.S.–led military occupation brought about, and the renewal of the national polity at large. The transformation of the Japanese national polity from a wartime belligerent nation to a postwar demilitarized and peaceful one was a highly gendered process.[6] This radical shift was especially punctuated by the postwar constitution's granting of full civil rights to Japanese women. Furthermore, as political scientist Susan Pharr once noted, Americans viewed Japanese women's increasing presence in the formal political arena as an eloquent demonstration of the extent to which occupation reforms were "improving women's status" overall.[7] The occupation forces, particularly the United States, regarded Japanese women's suffrage and women's visibility in the national election as a barometer with which to measure the overall improvement of life under occupation. Japanese women's political liberation thus showcased the success of occupation policy to the international community.

Yet, if publicizing Japanese women's liberation and their improved status was central to U.S. postwar/cold war propaganda at that time, and if indeed the issue of women's liberation and other democratizing projects helped justify the continuing U.S. occupation of Japan, how did this discourse become so powerful that it even foreshadowed the manipulation of American public opinion nearly sixty years later? How have the various representations of the liberation of Japanese women come to proffer such an overwhelming faith in the possibility of the enemy's rehabilitation, so much so that they preempt any effective counterargument to the deployment of military force? How have the memories of Japanese women's enfranchisement come to provide material credibility for the myth of rescue and rehabilitation?

In a modest attempt to address these questions, this essay analyzes U.S. media coverage of occupied Japan. It traces the emergence of the problematic association between the U.S. democratization of Japan and U.S. exceptionalism at the initial moment of the production of knowledge—that is, by investigating the ways in which the American public came to be informed about Japanese women's enfranchisement and improvements in their legal and other social statuses. To put it differently, this essay undertakes what Michel Foucault once called a "history of the present." It proposes to illuminate the critical juncture at which memories of America's mid-twentieth-century imperial project of democratization and reform came to be shaped, and then became effective in abetting the expansion of U.S. military, politico-legal, and moral borders in the postwar years and its invasive reterritorialization of the world in the twenty-first century. While a number of excellent studies of the U.S. occupation of Japan have scrupulously documented the detailed processes whereby the reforms of Washington and the Supreme Commander for the Allied Powers (SCAP) became instituted through active Japanese collaboration, there has been virtually no analysis of the ways in which the occupation was presented and conveyed to the American public.[8] The American media's portrayals of Japanese women were no less unstable or inconsistent than the complex realities of occupied Japan. Yet this paper is not primarily concerned to reestablish the historical realities of occupied Japan. Rather, its chief objective is to examine the discursive processes of enduring ideological implications—a process whereby knowledge about Japanese women's liberation was produced through its travels from the fringe of the American empire to the mainland.

Scholars in recent years have observed how sovereignty is constituted through confined spaces of exception, such as camps. Following Giorgio Agamben, who noted that the temporary suspension of law under the Nazi regime's concentration camps became normalized as juridical rule itself, feminist political scientist Jenny Edkins has observed that during the Kosovo conflict, NATO forces effectively demonstrated their sovereign power through the creation of refugee camps.[9] Both Nazi and NATO sovereignty were made possible through the establishment of spaces in which human beings were reduced to bare life, a state of nondistinction between human and nonhuman, where a human as a political being bestowed with rights, dignity, morality, and numerous other relational identities became suspended. Agamben observed the state of sovereignty under Nazi rule as where "an unprecedented absolutization of the biopower to *make live* intersects with an equally absolute generalization of the sovereign power to *make die*, such that biopolitics coincides immediately with thanatopolitics."[10] The Nazi concentration camps were spaces wherein the Nazis claimed sovereignty through the production of those who could be excluded and expended as their constitutive others. The NATO camps offered humanitarian aid but also policed the refugees fleeing from violence—even though, according to Edkins, NATO might have been responsible for such violence in the first place. It is through generating such a threshold space of biological life and social death that the sovereign decides on the exceptions.

The space of military occupation is not unlike these camps, though the circumstances are obviously distinctive. Military occupations are ruled by the state of exception. Here the law, social and political rights, and forms of belonging as imagined through citizenship, territory, or nationality are temporarily confiscated. Thus Japan under U.S. occupation was a site at which the United States could claim itself as sovereign by categorically suspending the existing rights and identities of those who had belonged to the Japanese empire, including Taiwanese, Koreans, Okinawans, and so on, while unilaterally granting newly defined rights, agency, and subjectivities to the chosen (that is, Japanese women, conservative nationalists, pro-American anticommunists, etc.). Japan under U.S. occupation was a legal borderland as such, a threshold space through which the new subjects of U.S. occupation policy, and the postwar/cold war governmentality of which it was a part, were generated out of a people under siege. The insistence on the United States' granting of constitutional rights to Japanese women obscures the occupation as a space of unfreedom, a place of nonrights, and thus masks the paradox of its simultaneous violence and benevolence. As such, the memories of Japanese women's enfranchisement remain critically vital to American understandings of the national self-image, the nation's military and political aspirations, and the political and moral supremacy it confers upon itself.

Finally, in articulating how certain stories of Japanese women's liberation acquired remarkable consistency and dominance, this article also seeks to problematize the subjugation of other stories that contradicted and yet were constitutive of that very same trajectory of knowledge. Primarily, I discuss how U.S. media representations of Japanese women under occupation helped naturalize the American audience as the subject of rescue and liberal democracy, while simultaneously containing desires for radical social transformation. This is another dimension of occupied Japan as a U.S. legal borderland. Japan under U.S. occupation—a state of exception wherein Japanese women were unfree yet granted constitutional rights by the United States—has existed as an outside that is simultaneously an inside, a liminal border that helps define the mainland United States as the principal space for freedom and rights-bearing subjects, including American women. Yet third world, anti-imperialist, postcolonial, poststructuralist, and other feminists of color—those whose positions I shorthand as critical feminisms—have taught us that the cultural logic that posits the United States and the rest of the West as the normative site of democratic rights and emancipation has been inseparably linked to feminist universalism. Such a feminism has measured women's status singularly through gender relations while ignoring other equally constitutive networks of power.[11] In critiquing feminist emancipation ideals that do not take into account the intersectionality of power, critical feminisms have interrogated the identitarian concept of "women" and debunked the binary notion of gender that posits women as universally victimized by male dominance.

Through an examination of U.S. representations of Japanese women under occupation and the memories (and repression) it has spawned, I hope to build upon critical feminist perspectives to show how the U.S. discourse on the rights and democratization of Japanese women established a normative cold war subject at this legal borderland, even as it proceeded to marginalize and subordinate a number of other diverse feminist modalities and aspirations.

From "Woman Warrior" to the "Unhappiest Women in the World"

In July 1944, when many began to vaguely foresee the war's end, the *Saturday Evening Post* featured an article titled "The Unhappiest Women in the World."[12] The white European woman author, who had apparently gained authoritative knowledge of Japanese women when she accompanied her Polish minister husband on a visit to Japan, explained how, after having lived in Japan for three years, she had come to discover that "the graceful, smiling Japanese women were the unhappiest [she] had ever known." Japanese women were "intended as either the servant or pretty toy of men" who demand "unquestioning obedience." They are "not regarded as a person" according to Japanese law and "marriage is her only career unless she becomes a geisha." In Japan, even the empress was a "frightened, timid, little" being who was "unable to break through the wall of her own shyness and sense of inferiority." The author then concluded that "the Japanese wife has very few pleasures" regardless of wealth or class, while "the only pleasure to which a Japanese wife can look forward is the satisfaction of becoming a mother-in-law," whose abuse of their daughters-in-law was "another case of the legalized traditional sadism of the Japanese."[13]

While deploring Japanese women's subordination to their men, the author of this article forgot that she too was no less an appendage to her husband's travel to Japan. Such asymmetry and occlusion in representation reveals more about the writer's ideological position than the objects under observation. Yet my concern here is neither the accuracy of the article's representation of Japanese gender relations nor the white female author's subjectivity. Rather, I wish to underscore the abrupt timing of the article's appearance—abrupt, because media coverage since the beginning of the war had for the most part represented Japanese women not as the timid little "unhappiest women," but as "women warriors."

A quick survey of *New York Times* articles that dealt with Japanese women from around the time of the U.S.–Japan War's outbreak to the occupation reveals that the media was concerned less with Japanese women's inferiority and traditional submissiveness than with their modern progressiveness and eccentricity. An article published on the eve of the Pearl Harbor attack introduced the modern transformation of Japanese women since the emergence in the 1920s of the "modern girl" and their active presence as industrial and white-collar workers as well as consumers. The article went on to note that since the 1930s national emergency, women were gaining increasing importance as they had come to fill in for men sent overseas for military service.[14]

After Japan's all-out military attack on China and continuing into the period of the U.S.–Japan War, news reports repeatedly emphasized the mobilization of Japanese women into unconventional gender roles under wartime state policy. Less than three months into the war with Japan, a news report noted that the government urged Japanese women to wear gender-neutral traditional trousers for war-related activities.[15] "Women of Japan Called Fanatical," an article that solicited wartime U.S. women volunteers, described the speech given by former ambassador to Japan Joseph C. Grew at a Red Cross Nurses' Aide Rally. Grew had told the mass audience of mainly American women just how Japanese women were "supporting their men with that same fanatical loyalty and valor" and that "in Japan, women, too are made of strong stuff."[16] Alongside reports on Japanese women's mobilization into the nation's war effort there were occasional yet consistent references to Japanese women warriors who were willing to "take up arms." Between 1942 and 1944, media images of Japanese women were underlined by fear of women "in uniform," of even dangerously armed women and those "killed in action."[17] Considering that Japanese women were not officially mobilized as combatants until 1945, it is reasonable to conclude that rather than reflecting any actual policy for mobilizing women, such a portrayal of Japanese "women warriors" aimed, as the report on Grew's speech did, to inspire and mobilize American women for the U.S. war effort.[18] At the same time, the gender transgressive "women warrior" image effectively suggested that Americans were at war with an "unconventional" enemy that confounded the boundary between the battlefield and home, one that needed to be met with unconventional military strategies.[19]

Breaking away from such earlier portrayals of female Japanese combatants, the *Saturday Evening Post* article "Unhappiest Women in the World" emerged with the onset of a discourse that attempted to make differentiations within the ranks of an enemy that had until then been portrayed as racially uniform and ideologically monolithic. A similar argument distinguishing the virtuous yet self-deprecating Japanese women from evil, tyrannical Japanese men can also be found in "Slave Women of Japan," published in a 1943 issue of the popular magazine *Women's Home Companion.* It detailed that despite the fact that "millions of women have entered industry, managed farms single-handedly and made the major sacrifices in the spectacular decline of Japan's standard of living," they "have gained little or no public recognition." The article predicted that "Japan's women may begin to assert themselves" as a result of the indispensable work they do for the war-torn society and went on to conclude: "Japan would be a far better nation if this should happen. The Japanese men and the Japanese women appear to come from different races—the men being brutal and fanatical, while the women appear kind and reasonable."[20]

In observing how racism shaped the U.S. war against Japan, John Dower astutely pointed out that while the evils of European enemies were confined to particular individuals and groups such as Hitler, Mussolini, or the Nazis, prewar and wartime anti-Japanese racism collectively vilified the Japanese as a whole and represented them as "swarms" of faceless insects or "hordes" of subhumans.[21] Yet, while effective in stirring bellicose sentiments, such totalizing representations of the enemy would prove impractical, if not useless, in building relations beyond hostility. To ensure stability in the relationship between the victor and the defeated, the occupier and the occupied, the elements of evil had to be separated out discursively.

The representation of Japanese women as victims of the male-dominant military state emerged as Washington policymakers anticipated Japan's near defeat. The prewar to postwar transformation of Japanese nationhood was gendered in part because of the need to deploy women as differentiated from Japanese men, who were singularly made to bear the burden of evil. The gender binary in depictions of the Japanese continued to frame postwar reports on the democratization of Japan. As a *Life* magazine article published half a year after the start of occupation put it: "The U.S. can properly take credit for giving a higher degree of freedom to the Japanese schools, press, radio, theater. . . . [T]he Japs are doing some things for themselves. Women are voting for the first time. If they can shake off their status as dolls and chattels, Japanese women may become an effective brake on militarism."[22] The occupation authorities encouraged and sometimes actively propagated the view of Japanese women as exclusively victims of Japanese men and traditional gender norms. In this process, "Japanese women" were discursively constituted as passive victims of male-dominant militarism and the devastations of war who were liberated as a result of the nation's defeat and the postwar occupation. As we shall see, this gender binary—positing women as a uniform entity universally victimized by patriarchy and male dominance regardless of race, class, age, and other relations—facilitated the representation of Japanese women as objects of liberation under the U.S. occupation and recipients of American liberal feminist tutelage.

Representations of Japanese Women's Liberation under U.S. Occupation

General Douglas MacArthur, who as Supreme Commander for the Allied Powers led the six and a half years of the occupation of Japan, listed the enfranchisement of women at the top of his so-called Five Great Reforms. Although MacArthur is known to have not been particularly keen on women's equal rights or feminisms, the U.S. media presented Japanese women's liberation and enfranchisement primarily as his accomplishments. As early as October 12, 1945, the *New York Times* outlined the Five Great Reforms and SCAP's plans to liberalize the Japanese constitution. Under the rather ironic headline "Democratic Rule Ordered in Japan," the article highlighted the fact that MacArthur had directed the Japanese premier Kijuro Shidehara to "Give Women [the] Vote and Encourage Labor Unions."[23] Two days later, another article followed, announcing that in response to SCAP directives the Japanese cabinet had voted to amend the Japanese election law to grant women suffrage. It once again underscored women's enfranchisement in its headline, "Japanese Cabinet for Women's Vote."[24] As we have seen, these stories that had been widely circulated at the beginning of the U.S. occupation were conjured up before and during "Operation Iraqi Freedom," remembering MacArthur as "the most important emancipator of Japanese women."

The idea that the Japanese heartily welcomed U.S. troops was often visually disseminated to the American audience through the image of the bodily intimacy of Japanese women and white male soldiers. News about Japanese women's acquisition of civil rights was also accompanied by such representations. For instance, "Japanese Cabinet for Women's Vote" included two photos, each pairing a smiling white male solider with an Asian woman with an even merrier smile. One was captioned: "Bob Johnson, Reading, Mass., is assisted by geisha girl, Miss Gama, in the selection of a new record for their next dance"; the other, "Corp. Orvel Stone, Randolph, Wiss., waltzing with geisha girl, Teru Shiduse, in the Japanese capital." These two images also appeared in the military services section of the October 22 issue of *Newsweek*, along with several other similar photos that were captioned "Servicemen in Tokyo are teaching geisha girls a few things about American jive and dancing."[25]

What is intriguing about these particular sets of visual images coupling Japanese women and white male soldiers is that height differences are not accentuated. Though this observation might appear trivial, such physical images are in fact striking when contrasted to the familiar, well-circulated, two-shot photo image of MacArthur and Hirohito. In the latter, the stunning gap

SIGNAL CORPS
U.S. ARMY
211627-S

in the two men's height and physicality was astounding, its shattering visual effects allegedly impressing many Japanese of their newly subordinate status to the United States. In contrast, the above images not only underplayed the height differences; they also differed from the MacArthur-Hirohito image in that the Japanese women and white American men do not face the camera, but rather each other. The article and photos together inscribe the Japanese women who are about to receive full citizenship from MacArthur as "geisha girls." Needless to say, "geisha girls" have little to do with actual "geishas." Rather, they are figures born out of the nineteenth-century Western fantasy about the submissive yet licentious "Oriental woman" that has continued to persist into the twentieth and twenty-first centuries. Yet in evoking "geisha," these texts insinuate that the newly enfranchised Japanese women were insignificant and trivial as those "geisha girls" of the Western male fantasy. At the same time, this rhetoric also implies that, unlike their male counterparts, Japanese women liberated under the U.S. occupation might not only embrace white men, as well as the United States and the postwar international community that these men signify, but also could be capable of literally "facing up" to them, or standing "shoulder to shoulder."

Figure 1.
General MacArthur with Emperor Hirohito at the U.S. Embassy in Tokyo, September 27, 1945. © 2005 Corbis.

Propaganda concerning the U.S.–led emancipation of Japanese women was constantly plagued with anxiety toward the sexuality of "Oriental women." The image of the newborn, rehabilitated Japan as visually illustrated through the interracial bodily intimacy between Japanese women and white American men simultaneously elicited fear of miscegenation. News reports on the historic first vote ever cast by Japanese women were supplemented by commentaries that warned against the "promiscuous relationships" between U.S. occupation troops stationed in Japan and local women.[26]

U.S. newspaper and magazine articles reflected Washington's and SCAP's overall propaganda policy to accentuate women's liberation as one of the primary indices of the occupation's "success." They reported extensively on Japanese women's enfranchisement and the overall improvement in their legal status, as well as the surprisingly high female voter turnout in the first postwar general election of 1946, which resulted in the election of a number of female candidates. A few examples may suffice to give us a sense of how these events were reported to the American audience. A *Newsweek* foreign affairs column introduced the liberation of Japanese women under the title "Free Butterfly": "The humble, plodding little female for untold centuries has trotted quietly along in the footsteps of the lordly Japanese male. But last week Japanese women made history on their own account. Of the 2,500-odd Diet candidates who applied for certification in the April 10 general elections, 75 were women."[27] Following the report on the April election, the *New York Times* also ran several articles on the changing status of women under the occupation. They emphasized that women voter turnout far exceeded expectations, while in some areas women voters surpassed male voters in number.[28] Still another article, titled "New Laws to Free Japanese Women," reported on the occupation's initiatives to reform the Japanese civil code to end the "ancient custom" of primogeniture and to make women "the equal economic partners of their husbands."[29]

The enthusiastic reporting of the legal reform that enabled Japanese women to join the ranks of police officers is not only further evidence of the high visibility of Japanese women in media reports coming out of the occupation; it also reflects a sudden amnesia about the fear of wartime Japanese women warriors.[30] A *Senior Scholastic* article titled "The Rising Sun of Japan" argued that Japan's future "depends largely on the present—how successful we are today in reeducating the Japanese people toward a democratic and peaceful way of life" and noted as the first sign of success that "women were permitted to vote for the first time and they turned out in large numbers."[31] The article included a photo of a Japanese female police officer choking a fellow male officer by the neck. The caption read, "Under Allied occupation, Japanese police have opened their ranks to women. Police women learn art of judo."

Likewise deploying the image of a woman police officer to convey Japanese women's new legal status, the *Christian Science Monitor* featured an article titled "New World for Japanese Women." "The little woman who has for generations been walking a respectful two steps behind honorable husband is stepping out in front today." Opening with such a familiar narrative of oppression, the article introduced the activities of Lieutenant Ethel B. Weed, the low-ranking yet central figure in promoting gender reforms through the SCAP Civil Information and Education (CI&E) Office. It emphasized the compatibility of U.S. occupation policymakers' policies with Japanese women's progress: "After centuries of suppression and subservient obedience, [Japanese women] suddenly find themselves not only enjoying equal rights with men, but given great political and social privilege. Those who planned the strategy of our occupation gave great consideration to the women of Japan and counted confidently on their co-operation. Granting equal rights and suffrage to Japanese women was one of the first steps of the occupation."[32] The "unhappiest women in the world" thereby became discursively reconstituted as the liberated subjects of the occupation. As a highly visible sign of freed and rehabilitated Japan for the American audience, they were at once made to vindicate and welcome the trans-Pacific, cold war U.S. regime.

To be sure, not all U.S. media reports represented Japanese women's liberation as a simple top-down achievement. A series of articles by Lindesay Parrott, Tokyo Bureau chief for the *New York Times,* observed how the colonized space of occupation had instituted revolutionary changes in the status of Japanese women. Parrott's article "Out of Feudalism: Japan's Women" begins with a familiar lead about oppressed Japanese women: "The dawn has slowly begun to break in the Land of the Rising Sun for Japan's most depressed class—the patient, plodding Japanese women. For uncounted generations the Japanese woman has tramped along the muddy roads three paces behind her lord and master. For centuries there has been dinned into her little ears 'obedience and modesty are essential virtues of the Japanese woman.'" At the same time, through an interview with the "veteran feminist" Fusae Ichikawa, Parrott introduced the long history of the prewar Japanese women's suffrage movement and the presence of Japanese feminists who sought equal rights.[33] In her interview with Parrott, Ichikawa apparently suggested that Japanese women would have sooner or later gained suffrage without the occupation, primarily as a result of their active participation in the war effort. A year later, in a *New York Times Magazine* article reporting on the 1946 election, Parrott pointed to a female police officer, female labor activists, and a woman politician as representatives of three career professions that occupation reforms had introduced to Japanese women; but he also warned against a simple generalization and stereotyping of them: "The Japanese woman never was either such a fool or such a chattel as some have represented her to be. . . . I know quite intimately a small village down in the Chiba Prefecture. I have heard these women talk. There is no question that they are 'illiterate,' if one takes the standard of literacy to be a knowledge of Chinese characters. . . . Nevertheless, I always found them 'smart'—precisely as a New England farm woman might be called 'smart.'"[34]

Representations drawing such parallels between women in Japan and the United States were not necessarily common. Moreover, Parrott's narrative does not reject the liberal feminism promoted by SCAP. Rather, it reauthenticates occupation policy by labeling prewar and wartime Japan "feudal" as well as by presenting women's suffrage and other constitutional rights as gains that Japanese women themselves had aspired to, yet could not achieve without MacArthur's intervention. At the same time, the article betrays that the representation of Japanese women's liberation could not help but to serve as a mirror, bringing women's issues back home, even as it undoubtedly constructed

American women as the feminist forerunners who would teach Japanese women proper understandings of gender, equality, and liberal democracy.

Cold War Feminism

As many scholars have noted, the Allied occupation of Japan was powerfully structured by U.S. cold war policy.[35] After the post-1947 "Reverse Course"—in which occupation authorities instituted a series of reactionary measures to contain the spread of radical democracy, including the "red purge," remilitarization, the armed suppression of Korean ethnic schools, the release of A-class war criminals, and a ban on the general strike—it is difficult to overlook a remarkable contraction in the U.S. media's coverage of Japanese women's political participation. It reported on debates over the civil code reforms, albeit sparsely, but virtually ignored women's prominence in the 1947 upper house election.

Though not specifically pertaining to women's issues, a May 1947 *Newsweek* column poignantly indicates how the production of knowledge about Japan's democratization during the occupation years was intimately linked to the ideological regimentation of American readers: "Democracy was more than skin deep in Japan. . . . [O]ne Japanese asked an American: 'When were you last on strike?' The American replied that he had never been on strike in his life. The bewildered Japanese remarked: 'But then how can you be democratic?' This Japanese misconception [of democracy] is, to a considerable extent, based on the actions of American officials, in allowing the return to Japan or release from prison of Japanese Communists at the end of the war. The Americans failed entirely to foresee the Japanese misinterpretation of this action."[36] An article in *The Commonweal* defended the occupation's overall plan to democratize Japan, but ended up suggesting the superiority of antilabor, anticommunist American-style democracy and explained radical democratic movements in Japan as the effects of political immaturity: "Japanese have been guilty of excesses in the name of democracy. Laborers have seized factories under the guise of being democrats. Mass demonstrations, openly led by communists, were becoming more and more unruly. . . . These excesses, however, are the exception to and not the rule. They are excesses of a newly liberated people, taking the first wobbly, uncertain steps toward establishment of freedom and equality."[37]

Mirroring the general cold war retraction of democratic radicalism both within and at the outposts of the United States, the "Reverse Course" in media representations of Japanese women depoliticized and desocialized the understandings of gender, liberation, and democratization.[38] An *Independent Woman* article by Gertrude Penrose reveals this shift most eloquently. The piece gave an account of the activities of Dorris Cochrane, a liaison officer for the State Department who had visited Japan to help promote women's issues for SCAP's CI&E section: "From the beginning of the occupation, Miss Cochrane stated, General MacArthur encouraged the women's emancipation movement, and the Civil Information and Education section set up a program to show the women of Japan how women in other countries organize and further their causes by democratic processes." The article attempted to show how Cochrane's visits to various villages and towns successfully mobilized and inspired many women and that Japanese women were the most "earnest and energetic follower-uppers" of American women's guidance. At the same time, by emphasizing that Japanese women themselves felt that the major obstacle to their participation in public affairs was "the traditional attitude of Japanese men toward women," the report intimated that women's liberation meant for them the improvement of personal relationships between women and men, as well as their spontaneous participation in self-governing, women-only community organizations.[39] Similarly, the *New York Times* article that contained Weed's perfunctory comment on the three-year anniversary of women's suffrage in Japan was reticent about securing the newly instituted women's political rights and legal status, instead dwelling primarily on the occupation's efforts in "building confidence" to increase women's leadership and participation in various cultural and other organizations.[40] Such representations stand in particular contrast to Parrott's aforementioned article, in which he had introduced a Japanese labor activist—a woman who had devoted herself to organizing coal mine workers, about one third of whom were former Korean colonial subjects—as an instance of women's liberation and democratization.

Here we can identify what might best be termed a "cold war feminism."[41] Cold war feminism can be understood as a variant of liberal and radical feminism in that it values equality between the two sexes, autonomy, individual choice, and spontaneity. Insisting on a pure notion of gender by disavowing race, class, and other social relations, it prescribes equal opportunity for men and women as well as the dissolution of gender inequities and barriers within the given liberal public sphere. In occupied Japan, its notions of liberation and democratization confiscated the language with which to address economic and political subordinations rooted in the Japanese history of colonialism and racism, as well as the freedom of speech that might otherwise be used to advocate alternative political formations such as communism or to criticize the presence of the occupying forces. Cold war feminism thereby subordinates and de-legitimizes other forms of feminist ideals equally aspiring for antiracist, anticolonial, or anticapitalist agendas. In short, the U.S. media's cold war feminism, by framing stories of Japanese women's liberation within the binary logic of gender relations between Japanese men and Japanese women, worked as the *Independent Woman* article and Weed's commentary did, to contain desires for transformations on multiple fronts of sociality. By the time the occupation drew to a close, cold war feminism had appropriated the meanings of liberation and democratization for Japanese women and recast them as simply having the aim of achieving equality and freedom in conjugal relations within an imagined bourgeois domesticity.

Most crucially, cold war feminism's representation of Japanese women's liberation was intimately tied to disciplining of the American audience. Certainly, many scholars have observed analogous processes at work at various other U.S. imperial locations, whereby the discourse on racialized, colonial women helped constitute white, middle-class American women as the bearers of modernity and progress.[42] However, each one of those instances needs to be scrutinized in its relations to differing global and national configurations specific to particular geohistorical moments. Popular knowledge about Japanese women and their liberation under U.S. occupation was constitutively linked to the U.S. drive for cold war global hegemony and the ideologies of modernity, equality, rights, and democracy. These were specific to the mid-twentieth-century context in which postcolonial independence and the disavowal of racial segregation had become imperative.

Historians and critics have noted that during the postwar and cold war years U.S. women, no less than their Japanese counterparts, came to be contained within the bourgeois, heteronormative family. The postwar U.S. government's official policies explicitly and implicitly encouraged women to withdraw from jobs they had acquired as a result of the wartime male labor shortage.[43] Elaine Tyler May, among others, has elucidated the unambiguous linkages between the cold war ideology of communist containment and discursive practices that aimed at the regulation and disciplinization of gender and sexuality within the parameters of bourgeois domesticity.[44] Yet the cold war rivalry required that the containment process be pursued without disturbing the image of the United States as the prime patron of liberation, democratic rights, and equality. Mary Dudziak, Penny Von Eschen, and Christina Klein, among others, have shown how the championing by the United States of the ideas of racial equality and tolerance in cold war propaganda generated contradictions between "security and liberty" at home, and as a result both advanced and compromised civil rights pursuits.[45] Moreover, in her analysis of the ways in which the meanings and representations of the "Middle East" have shaped the United States in the latter half of the twentieth century, Melani McAlister has argued that in the early 1950s, desires for social transformation—unintendedly set loose by the United States through its counter-Soviet propaganda of independence and liberation—were contained discursively through the strategic deployment of heterosexualized, bourgeois gender relations. McAlister finds one instantiation of such containment in Hollywood films of the 1950s, where it is "the spunky, independent woman who nonetheless chooses to take up the subservient position in marriage."[46]

The rhetoric of liberation, rights, and democratization was indeed crucial for U.S. world domination during the cold war. At the same time, the hopes and desires unleashed by such a rhetoric of emancipation and social transformation had to be kept in check in the interests of managing global, as well as domestic, security. Similarly, the stories of Japanese women's liberation under the occupation were told in such a way that gender relations, normalized through a particular class and sexuality, contained and managed unruly concepts of women's liberation and autonomy. Yet they also reveal that this process of containment required the presence of "Japanese women" who could securely center "American women" within cold war global politics. In other words, the discursive containment of gender equality and sexual independence was racially mediated.

A *New York Times* article on General Douglas MacArthur's wife illustrates just how integral the Japanese presence was to this process of cold war gender containment. Headlined "M'Arthur's Wife Refused to Reign: By Choosing to Stay in Role of Head of Household She Won Applause of Japanese," the piece reported to its American readers that "Mrs. MacArthur has become a celebrity in this country by trying to avoid attention. As wife of the Supreme Commander, she could have reigned as a queen. She chose to remain a housewife. The Japanese applauded her decision. . . . General MacArthur loves a fight. But at the end of the day, when he goes home, from a war or from the office, the first thing he does is to embrace his wife. 'Hello, boss,' she always says."[47] Through its depiction of the passionate love and praise that "Japanese office girls and executives" lavished on MacArthur's wife, the article suggested that the respectable path for an American woman who might lead the Japanese, as well as other people of the world, toward democracy and liberation, was to choose to stay home to serve as a good wife and wise mother.

Shortly before and after the end of the occupation, a dire prognosis began to fill the media that despite the best efforts of the occupation authorities, Japanese women's liberation might be doomed to failure. Indeed, coverage emphasizing the vicious tenacity of sexist Japanese culture and tradition increased after the occupation's formal closure.[48] These stories foretold that with the departure of the occupation forces, the centuries-old Japanese tradition would compromise Japanese women's newly acquired freedom and legal rights. Two years after Japan recuperated its sovereignty, a *New York Times* article featured an interview with the daughter of Shigeru Yoshida, the prime minister of Japan between 1948 and 1954, who led Japan out of the occupation by staying the pro–U.S. course.[49] Speaking with the authority of a native informant, the newspaper quoted Yoshida's daughter as saying that Japanese women's new status "was as enthusiastically received as it was undigested . . . because you cannot change concepts so deeply imbedded in Japanese tradition. . . . Japan is essentially a country for men and most men would prefer to keep the women at home." She predicted that it would take another generation to "create a new trend" as "Japan does not have a society in the Western sense."

What is remarkable here is that, in contrast to MacArthur's American wife who "chose to remain a housewife," this narrative assumed that "old habits" and "Japanese tradition" were depriving Japanese women of their will and independence. Even when similarly subordinated to husbands or fathers, the American woman's case was considered the outcome of spontaneous choice, whereas the Japanese woman's situation was regarded as stemming from the stranglehold imposed by a centuries-old sexist feudal tradition. As Leti Volpp has astutely noted in her critique of representations of domestic violence against women of color in the United States, such an "asymmetrical ascription of culture" is not only allowed by the persistent assumption that non-Western cultures are inherently more sexist than those considered mainstream in the United States. By obscuring the equally profound cultural limitations imposed on mainstream, white American women, it establishes them as subjects of free will, agency, and choice, while casting nonwhite, non-American women as objects of their rescue.[50] Cold war feminism's relationship to racial and cultural differences is thus one of disavowal: it insists on the pure and universal category of gender unfettered by other relations of power, while establishing its normative subject by marking others with the disavowed racial and other critical differences. In this sense, Japanese women came to exist as "the other woman" for women in cold war containment discourse.[51] By contrasting Japanese women to white American women and by depicting the latter as subjects of free will who are not bound by tradition but who spontaneously choose heteronormative, bourgeois domesticity, U.S. media representations of Japanese women's liberation—or more precisely, its failure despite the U.S. occupation's institution of de jure gender equality—helped constitute white American bourgeois women as the authentic practitioners of cold war American feminism.

Conclusion

The legacies of cold war feminism are clearly evident in the gendered dynamics of U.S. imperialism, and have served in many ways to not only legitimate the current U.S. war on terror. This feminism also extends the boundaries of U.S. power by mobilizing the formerly converted as new recruits. In April 2003, shortly after "Operation Iraqi Freedom" led to the U.S. military's seizure of Baghdad, the *Rocky Mountain News* featured an article covering a lecture by Beate Sirota Gordon in Boulder, Colorado. The article reads: "Japanese women who lived through the reconstruction of their country after World War II could help the United States rebuild Iraq and Afghanistan, says the woman who helped Gen. Douglas MacArthur write the Japanese Constitution." At the age of twenty-two, Gordon joined the committee that drafted the Japanese Constitution and worked specifically on the women's rights clause during the U.S. occupation of Japan. According to the newspaper's account, Gordon maintained that the Japanese women who "had no rights" before the new constitution are successful in "politics and business" today and that, as "a colored people," they could "bolster U.S. credibility with Iraqis and Afghans" by demonstrating that the U.S. military occupation "did not run their islands into a colony."[52] The memories of Japanese women's liberation under U.S. occupation thus continue to haunt America's "just war" narratives.

It is important to note that the postwar discursive construction of "Japanese women" as mere victims of male-dominated militarism, who became liberated and gained power only as a result of the postwar occupation, has contributed to a popular amnesia about Japanese women's active participation in colonialism and wars of aggression.[53] Since the 1970s feminist historians have scrutinized the absence of critical reflection on Japanese women's complicity in imperialism. Yet the contemporary redeployment of these Japanese women in relation to the war in Iraq suggests that this narrative has entailed another problematic memory effect. Remembering Japanese women exclusively as gender victims saved by MacArthur and his advisors—that is, remembering them according to the cold war feminism that once mobilized Japanese women as its constitutive others—may well risk rallying them as agents in the current U.S. imperial imaginary of rescue and rehabilitation.

Though far from uniform, critical feminisms have interrogated precisely the unitary concept of feminist liberation that obliterates the overlapping power relations that make up the category of "women," as well as the histories of racialization, global capitalism, colonialism, and foreign military domination through which they must seek transformation. Critical feminists have questioned the posture of pursuing a feminist politics based on the unified, the authentic, and the originary subject, while still others have noted that the white American radical feminist view of women as a universal victim of male violence fails to grasp the "simultaneity of oppressions" and their own complicity in it.[54] Furthermore, those who have observed the discursive dimensions of colonialism and the uneven history of global capitalism have pointed out that the universalist and progressive ideology of Western(ized) feminist discourse on the racialized, non-Western woman, has enabled a paternalistic, missionary position.[55] Chandra Talpade Mohanty, in particular, was among the first to show that the homogeneous category of "women," abstracted out of the web of social relations and represented as the universal victim of patriarchy and male dominance, projects a uniform, progressive course of women's liberation.[56] Once feminist emancipation is envisioned in such a single, linear trajectory, it creates a hierarchy among the more and less advanced women according to the unitary ladder of feminist progress. These multiple insights of critical feminisms suggest that the universal prescription for women's liberation sought exclusively within the gender relation can easily lead to the capitulation of certain feminist positions to practices that would extend U.S. dominance through the rhetoric of liberation, freedom, and democratic rights.

Japanese women obtained suffrage under the U.S. occupation. The constitution guaranteed equal treatment of all national subjects regardless of their differences, including gender. The new civil code stipulated equal inheritance among male and female heirs and legalized women's rights to initiate divorce. To be sure, occupation reforms intended to secure women's rights and to eliminate gender inequalities in the law and other spheres of social life stopped short of achieving their full ideals. Occupation reformers' Orientalist assumptions about the Japanese "reality," coupled with the tenacious maneuvering of conservative male bureaucrats and legislators, discouraged the total dismantling of such disparities.[57] For instance, the Family Registry Law continues to this day to uphold the heteronormative constitution of families and the nation through the codes of marriage, monogamy, conjugality, and heterosexism. The Nationality Law also retained patrilineality until its renunciation in 1985. Historians have generally charged the "Reverse Course" with primary responsibility for the short-circuited character of Japan's democratization under U.S.

occupation. Some scholars have described how the Bureau of Women and Minors—the office established in 1947 by the Socialist Party government under the U.S. occupation to oversee women's issues—became ultimately "ineffective in resolving the problems of de facto gender inequality in employment and society" because cold war SCAP policy not only deprived the office of legal enforcement power but also alienated it from the majority of women's associations that sought more radical reforms.[58]

As I stressed earlier, the hypervisibility of Japanese women's enfranchisement under the occupation was achieved *in exchange with* the invisibility of the disenfranchisement and elimination of the social and political rights of women and men from Japan's former colonies, including their right to be considered Japanese nationals.[59] The U.S. media was not concerned to report on the categorical political disenfranchisement of adult Korean and Taiwanese men residing in mainland Japan. Under prewar and wartime Japanese law these men had been able to vote and hold public office in mainland Japan as long as they could establish residency in the metropole. However, under the new state of exception these rights were summarily denied, depriving them of any ability to represent the postcolonial minorities' interests in the formal political arena. To grasp the full implications of this suppression, we should note that the United States had been competing with the Japanese empire in its promises of world liberation and racial equality before it began a campaign to counter such claims by the Soviet Union with the onset of the cold war. More urgently, with the extension of its power, especially over Asia and the Pacific, the United States was compelled to repudiate the powerful rhetoric of racial emancipation Japan had championed prior to the end of the war.[60] This is a point usually overlooked by most American studies scholars, who tend to locate the exploitation of U.S. multiracial, multicultural self-portraits at a much later stage in the cold war confrontation.

While the pronouncement of Japanese women's acquisition of new rights enhanced the image of the United States as the benefactor of equality, freedom, and democracy, the knowledge about the disenfranchisement of Japan's former colonial subjects contradicted the celebration of multiethnicity and multiraciality, and thus had to be silenced. The current analogy drawn between the occupations of Iraq and Japan completely occludes the fact that when Japan is recalled as the site of the "successful" American imperial project of reform and rebuilding, such a view is limited to the metropolitan core of the vast prewar Japanese empire. Crucially, the Japan/Iraq analogy forgets that Korea and other parts of Japan's former empire emerged as necrospaces, so to speak, where fierce insurgencies and bloody resistance to the new occupying forces, as well as the outbreak of civil war, stand out in glaring contrast to the media image of peaceful "occupied Japan" as a reformed space of rights-bearing, free subjects. Finally, denying these knowledges also risks occluding the multiple affiliations and agency that Korean, Taiwanese, and other colonized women might have possessed to challenge Japanese imperial rule as well as to contest and negotiate with U.S. dominance in the postcolonial, postindependence era.

While ultimately attributing the failure of reform to Japanese racial and cultural differences rather than cold war containment, representations of occupied Japan conveyed to the American audience that U.S. policies had liberated Japanese women by enfranchising them and by enforcing various legal changes. If securing formal rights and equality was undeniably "liberation" in the limited sense of democratic procedure, it did not necessarily liberate women in other sites of power, particularly across the intersections of class, race/ethnicity, colonial relations, and other biopolitical differences of marital and reproductive status. We must thus ask, for which women, along which fronts of power relations, and in what specific respects did the U.S. occupation bring liberation and progress?

The modalities of critical feminisms have called our attention to the intersectionality of power and challenged universalist and unitary notions of oppression, victimization, and emancipation. As memories of occupied Japan are invoked and mobilized to sanction U.S. wars and military occupations in the twenty-first century, it becomes even more urgent to cast such a critical gaze on the past and to dissect how stories about this mid-twentieth-century imperial location were originally told and gained dominance. Remembering Japanese women's enfranchisement from the perspectives of critical feminisms cautions us against the seductive rhetoric of liberation and helps us challenge the unilateral expansion of American power that is fueled and safeguarded by the unitary notion of feminist emancipation. It urges us to reflect on competing visions of liberation, as well as the violent processes of disciplinization and assimilation under U.S. power and governmentality.

Notes

I am indebted to Yuko Nishikawa's international phone call that initially inspired me to write an earlier version of this article. Stephanie Moore worked as a most competent research assistant. I also would like to thank the following individuals for their invaluable support and critical suggestions at various later stages: Jody Blanco, Yen Le Espiritu, Takashi Fujitani, Rosemary George, Nicole King, Lisa Lowe,

Nayan Shah, and Shelley Streeby. I also received insightful comments from participants in the "U.S. Wars in Asia" workshop at UCSD, May 2004, as well as from Mary Dudziak, Marita Sturken, Leti Volpp, and anonymous reviewers for the *American Quarterly*.

1. David E. Sanger and Eric Schmitt, "U.S. Has a Plan to Occupy Iraq, Officials Report," *New York Times*, October 11, 2002.
2. Amy Kaplan, "Confusing Occupation with Liberation," *Los Angeles Times*, October 24, 2003.
3. "Bush Says War on Terror Led to Women's Freedom," *Los Angeles Times*, March 13, 2004; "Bush Likens War on Terror to WWII," *Los Angeles Times*, June 3, 2004.
4. "Another Pose of Rectitude," *Newsweek*, September 2, 2002, 70.
5. On the concept of American exceptionalism, see Amy Kaplan, *The Anarchy of Empire in the Making of U.S. Culture* (Cambridge, Mass.: Harvard University Press, 2002).
6. See chap. 6, "Postwar Peace and Feminization of Memory," 190–91, in Lisa Yoneyama, *Hiroshima Traces: Time, Space, and the Dialectics of Memory* (Berkeley: University of California Press, 1999).
7. Susan J. Pharr, *Political Women in Japan: The Search for a Place in Political Life* (Berkeley: University of California Press, 1981), 30–31.
8. For instance, Robert E. Ward and Yoshikazu Sakamoto, eds., *Democratizing Japan: The Allied Occupation* (Honolulu: University of Hawai'i Press, 1987); John W. Dower, *Embracing Defeat: Japan in the Wake of World War II* (New York: W. W. Norton, 1999); Eiji Takemae, *The Allied Occupation of Japan* (New York: Continuum, 2002). Seminal studies that focused specifically on the occupation policies' effect on Japanese women's status, as well as Japanese women's active involvement in the SCAP programs are: Yasuko Ichibangase, *Kyōdō tōgi sengo fujin mondaishi* (Tokyo: Domesu Shuppan, 1971); Kiyoko Nishi, *Senryōka no Nihon fujin seisaku: sono rekishi to shōgen* (Tokyo: Domesu Shuppan, 1985); and Susan Pharr, "Politics of Women's Rights," in *Democratizing Japan*.
9. Jenny Edkins, *Trauma and the Memory of Politics* (Cambridge: Cambridge University Press, 2003), 179.
10. Giorgio Agamben, *Remnants of Auschwitz: The Witness and the Archive* (New York: Zone Books, 1999), 83.
11. For collective works of critical feminisms, see among others, Cherríe Moraga and Gloria Anzaldúa, eds., *This Bridge Called My Back: Writings by Radical Women of Color* (New York: Kitchen Table, 1981, 1983); Teresa de Lauretis, ed., *Feminist Studies/Critical Studies* (Bloomington: Indiana University Press, 1986); Judith Butler and Joan W. Scott, eds., *Feminists Theorize the Political* (New York: Routledge, 1992); Inderpal Grewal and Caren Kaplan, eds., *Scattered Hegemonies: Postmodernity and Transnational Feminist Practices* (Minneapolis: University of Minnesota Press, 1994); M. Jacqui Alexander and Chandra Talpade Mohanty, eds., *Feminist Genealogies, Colonial Legacies, Democratic Futures* (New York: Routledge, 1997); and Gabriela F. Arredondo et al., eds., *Chicana Feminisms: A Critical Reader* (Durham, N.C.: Duke University Press, 2003).
12. Helen Moscicki, "The Unhappiest Women in the World," *Saturday Evening Post*, July 8, 1944, 19, 37.
13. The image of subservient and oppressed Japanese women has been dominant not only within the United States but also among Japan's modernist elites. However, the feminine ideal of chastity, subservience, and subordination to men had been shared only among a limited elite segment of society until the late-nineteenth-century modernization and westernization. See, for instance, Robert J. Smith and Ella Lury Wiswell, *Women of Suye Mura* (Chicago: University of Chicago Press, 1989).
14. *New York Times*, December 7, 1941.
15. "Japan's Kimono Eclipsed by 'Uniform' for Women," *New York Times*, February 21, 1942. For similar reports in popular magazines, see, for instance, Bataviaasch Nieuwsblad, "An End to the Flippant Kimono," *The Living Age*, April 1941, 112; "Japanese 'Girls in Uniform,'" *Asia*, May 1941. Later, "Japan Mobilizes Women" reported that Japanese premier Hideki Tojo spoke to the public of the "necessity for mobilization of women." *New York Times*, November 12, 1943.
16. *New York Times*, September 23, 1942.
17. "2 Japanese Women Die in Action," *New York Times*, May 18, 1944, for the quote. For similar emphasis on the fear of the armed Japanese women warriors, see also "Japanese Women Get War Duty in Burma," May 19, 1942; "Japanese Women Snipers Reported at Guadalcanal," December 1, 1942; "Japanese Women Are Told to Fight," June 17, 1945.
18. See Sasaki Yōko on the official stipulation of Japanese women as "combatants" in 1945. *Sōryokusen to josei* (Tokyo: Seikyksha, 2001), 124.

19. I thank Shelley Streeby for calling my attention to this aspect of Japanese women warrior representation.
20. Robert Bellaire, "Slave Women of Japan," *Woman's Home Companion*, February 1943, 29, 62, 64; 64 for the quote.
21. John Dower, *War Without Mercy: Race and Power in the Pacific War* (New York: Pantheon, 1986).
22. "U.S. in Japan," *Life*, February 18, 1946.
23. *New York Times*, October 12, 1945.
24. *New York Times*, October 14, 1945.
25. *Newsweek*, October 22, 1945, 64.
26. See, for instance, "Chaplain's Aid Asked to End Fraternizing," *New York Times*, April 3, 1946.
27. *Newsweek*, March 25, 1946, 51.
28. *New York Times*, April 11, 1946; June 2, 1946; August 23, 1946.
29. *New York Times*, August 23, 1946.
30. Lindesay Parrott, "Now a Japanese Woman Can Be a Cop," *New York Times Magazine*, June 2, 1946, 18, 56.
31. "The Rising Sun of Democracy," *Senior Scholastic* 48 (May 13, 1946): 12–13; 12 for the quote.
32. Marion May Dilts, "New World for Japanese Women: Elevation to Eminence Offers Opportunities and Makes Problems," *Christian Science Monitor*, August 23, 1947, 1–2.
33. Lindesay Parrott, "Out of Feudalism: Japan's Women," *New York Times Magazine*, October 28, 1945, 10, 44, 46; 10 for the quote.
34. Parrott, "Now a Japanese Woman," 18, 56. Ichikawa's name is misspelled as "Ishikawa." A similar remonstration concerning U.S. women's sense of superiority toward Japanese women was communicated personally from Mary R. Beard to Ethel B. Weed in 1946. Chikako Uemura, "Nihon ni okeru *senryō* seisaku to josei *kaihō*: *rōdoshō* fujin *shōnenkyoku* no seiritsu kate wo *chūshin* toshite," *Josegaku kenkyū* 2 (1992): 5–28.
35. See for instance, John Dower, *Empire and Aftermath: Yoshida Shigeru and the Japanese Experience, 1878–1954* (Cambridge, Mass.: Council on East Asian Studies, Harvard University, 1988), and his "Occupied Japan and the American Lake, 1945–1950," in *America's Asia: Dissenting Essays on Asia-American Relations*, ed. Edward Friedman and Mark Selden (New York: Random House, 1969–71).
36. "Japan: Fumbling Toward Democracy," *Newsweek*, May 12, 1947, 38, 40; 40 for the quote.
37. Lafe Franklin Allen, "Democracy in Japan," *The Commonweal*, September 1947, 542–46; 546 for the quote. For the enduring implications of the CIO's suppression of workers' direct actions and wildcat strikes under the cold war, see George Lipsitz, *Rainbow at Midnight: Labor and Culture in the 1940s* (Urbana: University of Illinois Press, 1994). Women CIO members were also active in occupied Japan.
38. In her analysis of official U.S. policy over Japanese women's issues under occupation, Mire Koikari notes that the occupation authority promoted "a white, middle-class progressive motherhood" from the beginning. "Rethinking Gender and Power in the U.S. Occupation of Japan, 1945–1952," *Gender and History* 11.2 (July 1999): 313–35; 319 for the quote. To a great extent, the U.S. media representation loyally reflected this official policy, but not without contradiction or significant shift in emphasis.
39. Gertrude Penrose, "Reporting on Japan's Women," *Independent Woman*, November 1948, 322–24; 322, 324 for the quote.
40. *New York Times*, April 9, 1949.
41. See my piece "Hihanteki feminizumu no keifu kara miru Nihon *senryō*," *Shisō*, November 2003, 60–84.
42. Vicente L. Rafael, "Colonial Domesticity: White Women and United States Rule in the Philippines," *American Literature*, 67.4 (December 1995): 639–66; Amy Kaplan, "Manifest Domesticity," *American Literature* 70.3 (September 1998): 581–606; Shelley Streeby, *American Sensations: Class, Empire, and the Production of Popular Culture* (Berkeley: University of California, 2002); Mari Yoshihara, *Embracing the East: White Women and American Orientalism* (New York: Oxford University Press, 2003); Yu-Fang Cho, "Narrative of Coupling in the Shadow of Manifest Domesticity: Transnational Politics of U.S. Cultures of Benevolence, 1890s–1910s" (Ph.D. diss., University of California, San Diego, 2004).
43. Miriam Frank et al., *The Life and Times of Rosie the Riveter: The Story of Three Million Working Women During World War II* (Emeryville, Calif.: Clarity Educational Publication, 1982).
44. Elaine Tyler May, *Homeward Bound: American Families in the Cold War Era* (New York: Basic Books, 1988). For further analyses of gender, sexual, and others forms of cold war domestic containment, see Caroline Chung Simpson, *An Absent Presence: Japanese Americans in Postwar American Culture, 1945–*

1960 (Durham: Duke University Press, 2001); Joanne Meyerowitz, "Sex, Gender, and the Cold War Language of Reform," and Jane Sherron De Hart, "Containment at Home: Gender, Sexuality, and National Identity in Cold War America," in *Rethinking Cold War Culture*, ed. Peter J. Kuznick and James Gilbert (Washington, D.C.: Smithsonian Institution, 2001); John D'Emilio, "The Homosexual Menace: The Politics of Sexuality in Cold War America," in *Making Trouble: Essays on Gay History, Politics, and the University*, ed. John D'Emilio (New York: Routledge, 1993).

45. Mary L. Dudziak, *Cold War Civil Rights: Race and the Image of American Democracy* (Princeton, N.J.: Princeton University Press, 2000); Penny M. Von Eschen, *Race Against Empire: Black Americans and Anticolonialism, 1937–1957* (Ithaca, N.Y.: Cornell University Press, 1997); Christina Klein, *Cold War Orientalism: Asia in the Middlebrow Imagination, 1945–1961* (Berkeley: University of California Press, 2003); Thomas Borstelmann, *The Cold War and the Color Line: American Race Relations in the Global Arena* (Cambridge, Mass.: Harvard University Press, 2001); Eric Foner, *The Story of American Freedom* (New York: W. W. Norton, 1998).
46. Melani McAlister, *Epic Encounters: Culture, Media, and U.S. Interest in the Middle East, 1945–2000* (Berkeley: University of California Press, 2001), 76.
47. *New York Times*, April 15, 1951.
48. See, for instance, "Japan's 'Second-Class Citizens,'" *New York Times*, August 22, 1954; "Japan: The Women," *Time*, April 26, 1954, 37–38; Beryl Kent, "Is Democracy Making Japanese Women Neurotic?" *The American Mercury*, June 1954, 139–40.
49. *New York Times*, November 7, 1954.
50. Leti Volpp, "Feminism Versus Multiculturalism," *Columbia Law Review* 101.5 (June 2001): 1181–218. Further, in calling for alternative alliances across multiple differences, Volpp also extended her critique of "absolution of responsibility" by mainstream American women in ignoring their complicity in minority women's oppression to the transnational feminists' women's rights regime that tends to practice "a missionary feminist effort assuming West is Best." See 1190, 1215, and 1216 for the quote.
51. Gayatri Chakravorty Spivak, "Three Women's Texts and a Critique of Imperialism," in *"Race," Writing, and Difference*, ed. Henry Louis Gates Jr. and Kwame Anthony Appiah (Chicago: University of Chicago Press, 1985; 1986), 262–280. Of course, racialized American women's participation in this discursive process complicates such a simple dichotomy. See Caroline Chung Simpson's observations on Yuri Kochiyama's involvement in the American attempt to physically rehabilitate a group of severely disfigured women survivors of the atomic bombing. Simpson, *An Absent Presence*.
52. "Japan's Women Could Be Model in Postwar Iraq," *Rocky Mountain News*, April 16, 2003. A few months later, Gordon wrote a letter to the editor of *The New York Times* and reiterated her point. See the *New York Times*, October 1, 2003. Gordon also recounts her work during the occupation in *Only Woman in the Room: A Memoir* (Tokyo: Kodansha, 1997).
53. A fuller exploration of the links between the forgetting of women's complicity in imperialism and this discourse on Japanese women as victims is beyond the scope of this paper. I reflected further on this problem in *Hiroshima Traces*.
54. In exploring how the discourse of feminist theories has rendered the voices of women of color writers illegible, Norma Alarcón has succinctly stated: "The pursuit of a 'politics of unity' solely based on gender forecloses the 'pursuit of solidarity' through different political formations and the exploration of alternative theories of the subject of consciousness." "The Theoretical Subject(s) of *This Bridge Called My Back* and Anglo-American Feminism," in *Making Face, Making Soul/Haciendo Caras: Creative and Critical Perspectives by Feminists of Color*, ed. Gloria Anzaldúa (San Francisco: Aunt Lute Books, 1990); 364 for the quote. Alarcón's insight that identifies a nonunitary, multiple-voiced subjectivity and process of disidentification in women of color feminism resonates with the poststructuralist rearticulation of gender categories offered by Judith Butler and many others. See Butler's *Bodies That Matter: On the Discursive Limits of "Sex"* (New York: Routledge, 1993); Lisa Lowe, *Immigrant Acts: On Asian American Cultural Politics* (Durham, N.C.: Duke University Press, 1996); Angela Y. Davis, *Women, Race, and Class* (New York: Random House, 1981); Cherríe Moraga, "From a Long Line of Vendidas: Chicanas and Feminism," in *Feminist Studies, Critical Studies*, ed. Teresa de Lauretis (Bloomington: Indiana University Press, 1986). For theorization of the simultaneity of oppression, see also Biddy Martin and Chandra Talpade Mohanty, "Feminist Politics: What's Home Got to Do with It?" in the same volume.
55. Gayatri Chakravorty Spivak, "Can the Subaltern Speak?" in *Marxism and the Interpretation of Culture*, ed. Cary Nelson and Lawrence Grossberg (Urbana: University of Illinois Press, 1988); Inderpal Grewal, *Home and Harem: Nation, Gender, Empire, and the Cultures of Travel* (Durham, N.C.: Duke University Press, 1996).

56. Chandra Talpade Mohanty, "Under Western Eyes: Feminist Scholarship and Colonial Discourses," *Boundary 2* 12.3/13.1 (spring/fall 1984): 338–58. Republished in *Feminist Review* 30 (1988): 65–88.
57. Kurt Steiner, "The Occupation and the Reform of the Japanese Civil Code," in *Democratizing Japan*, 188–220.
58. See, for example, Yoshie Kobayashi, "A Path toward Gender Equality: State Feminism in Japan" (Ph.D. dissertation, University of Hawai'i, 2002), 52–82; 81 for the quote.
59. See *Hiroshima Traces*, 191.
60. For more details, see Takashi Fujitani, "The Reischauer Memo: Mr. Moto, Hirohito, and Japanese American Soldiers," *Critical Asian Studies* 33.3 (2001): 379–402.

Between Camps: Eastern Bloc "Escapees" and Cold War Borderlands

Susan L. Carruthers

For two weeks in August 1948, U.S. media dwelt obsessively on a news story brimming with B-movie melodrama. Billed as the most perilous moment yet in a nascent cold war, the story's focus was neither the escalating crisis in Berlin nor Whittaker Chambers's revelations but the desperate actions of a widowed Ukrainian schoolteacher. Leaping from a third-floor window of the Soviet consulate on New York's Upper East Side, she insisted that she would sooner die in America than be forcibly returned to the "worker's fatherland."[1] Oksana Kasenkina's feted "leap for freedom" announced the arrival of a new cold war protagonist: the escapee. Crossing the territorial boundary between East and West while often blurring the line between fantasy and reality, this character soon became familiar to American audiences. Hollywood recast the escapee as an imperiled Bolshoi ballerina, and rescue romances such as *Sofia, The Red Danube*, and *Never Let Me Go* formed a distinct early cold war subgenre.[2] If the vision of Clark Gable rowing across the Baltic to retrieve a prima ballerina from Stalin's sadistic clutches strained credulity, "real life" could be equally improbable—as an unsuspecting French customs official found when Rudolph Nureyev leapt into his arms at a Paris airport in 1961, proclaiming "I want to be free!"[3]

Whether dancers or diplomats, physicists or polemicists, Eastern bloc defectors achieved considerable prominence over the cold war's forty-five-year life span. On the surface, the escapee's contribution to superpower competition and cold war identity construction appears self-evident. That thousands of people risked death in order to move west while so few traveled in the opposite direction affirmed the "free world's" superior attractions, and attested to the tyrannous character of regimes from which departure required *escape*. In traversing the fortified divide between East and West, the escapee anchored rhetorical figurations of a world rent between "slave" and "free," making a metaphorical "curtain" meaningful: "a world without easy cross-border movements is a world of concentration camps, forced labor, and cold war," opined a *Life* editorial on the Kasenkina episode.[4] Bearer of lucrative symbolic freight, the escapee also offered Western states much of material value to cold war policy projections. New arrivals provided intelligence on conditions in countries as hostile to foreigners' entry as to their own citizens' exit and were selectively recruited to undertake propaganda initiatives in the West and clandestine operations in the East.[5] Presuming that defectors burned with nationalist zeal, Republican champions of rollback alighted on "single stateless young men" as the raw material for a "Volunteer Freedom Corps": the shock-troops of Eastern Europe's liberation. In the opinion of Senator Henry Cabot Lodge, escapees represented "the biggest, single, constructive, creative element" in U.S. foreign policy during the cold war's formative phase.[6]

Since Washington's instrumental investment in Eastern bloc defectors was so forthrightly announced, it stands to reason (many commentators insist) that legal statutes and instruments were hastily reconfigured to facilitate these prized individuals' entrance to America. This entailed parallel adjustments to domestic and international law. The terms of admission into the United States had to be eased if Washington were to "win ideological points" by welcoming those in flight from communism. Selectively opening national borders to escapees, the Truman and Eisenhower administrations exhibited "calculated kindness" in amending U.S. immigration legislation, claim Loescher and Scanlan.[7] Students of refugee policy further argue that the Truman administration molded *international* law purposely to encourage flight from communism, providing escapees with superior access to relief and resettlement assistance at the expense of less strategically valuable stateless individuals.[8] Before 1950, refugee status remained imprecisely defined. The onset of the cold war coincided (not uncoincidentally) with the solidification of an international refugee regime, with Washington encouraging malleable UN organizations to draw the contours of this new category around the person of the escapee. The resultant 1951 Geneva Convention Relating to the Status of Refugees duly privileged victims of *political* oppression over others who were pushed from, or elected to leave, their countries of citizenship.[9] With Eastern Europeans and Soviets monopolizing this new status, the refugee functioned as a boundary-maintaining device to keep others out of America's protected domestic space, proposes Rachel Buff. Where the escapee was freed from racialized suspicion by an impeccable political pedigree, other (generally darker skinned) migrants found themselves slurred as economic opportunists, and debarred from entry.[10]

Had superpower rivalry over humanity as a manipulable resource structured immigration and refugee legislation as straightforwardly as these scholars maintain, there might be little more to say about Eastern bloc emigrants' recruitment for this particular west side story. But on closer inspection, assumptions about the ease with which Washington converted the symbolic capital vested in escape into the hard currency of geopolitical profit appear more questionable, as do assertions about the ease with which law was sculpted around the escapee's accommodation. Instead, what emerges is not only how neglected the escapee has been as an object of study but how liminal the individuals who embodied, or aspired to, this status remained during the early cold war. Neither the politics of escape nor persons in flight turned out to be as tractable as Washington's early cold war projections assumed.

Focusing on the United States Escapee Program (launched in 1952), this essay highlights the international and internecine conflicts that surrounded the orchestration of cross-border flight, the fabrication of a unique legal subject, "the escapee," and the production of meaning from this phenomenon. For those seeking to tap symbolic and practical payoffs from east-west population movement, none of this proved straightforward. The exhortation to flight, delineation of a specific escapee identity, and "disposal" of its incumbents were processes simultaneously enabled and constrained by law. Manipulation of escapology pushed against international legal norms and ran headlong into domestic legislative obstruction. More than a package of measures to assist individuals encamped on Western Europe's perimeter, the Escapee Program strove to *encourage* flight: "a bright beacon to induce large scale defections from satellite Europe," as one State Department official put it.[11] Yet few commentators have remarked how unorthodox, in international legal terms, it was for Washington to inspire foreign nationals' exodus. Nor have scholars scrutinized the ingenuity required to delineate the escapee as a distinct "person" who was *not* simply a refugee by any other name. In parallel (and in opposition) to the 1951 Convention, U.S. officials configured a typology of statelessness that plotted individuals along a spectrum of functionality to cold war policy, mandating discriminatory humanitarianism in Europe's refugee camps.[12] Near the apex of this anomaly-ridden hierarchy—neither defector, displaced person, nor refugee—stood the escapee.

Washington did, then, differentiate among the stateless. But for all that the escapee appears a privileged recipient of cold war patronage, reading the cultural narratives spun from escape against the conflicted circumstances of escapees' lives reveals something different. The intimation of inclusion extended by a "nation of escapees" often proved chimerical. Encamped between camps, suspended in both space and time, unable to go back or move forward, those who breached the iron curtain existed in precarious limbo—caught between the administration's desire to promote escape and powerful legislators' disinclination to accommodate those who did so within the United States. Summoned to both defy and define cold war borders, escapees were commonly relegated to the shadowy interstices of sovereign space: the borderland where East and West, foreign and domestic, symbolic and material awkwardly overlapped.

In this reading, escapees find a place alongside other "impossible subjects" assigned the task of advertising the desirability of U.S. citizenship while being largely excluded from its entitlements. Like Mae Ngai's "illegal aliens" and Bonnie Honig's "foreign founders," such figures' marginality simultaneously troubles and affirms national projects and international projections: their insecurity at once a rebuke and a reminder that there's "no place like home."[13]

Inspiring Defection

To appreciate the unorthodoxy of "inspired defection" as a practice of statecraft, it is worth pausing to note the degree to which sovereign statehood typically assumes subjects' fixity within territorially bounded polities. Modern states differ from earlier and alternative forms of community in their jealous possessiveness. Since Westphalia, subjects have been required to submit to one sovereign jurisdiction alone, while states have undertaken ever more invasive measures to manage population and to control both its composition and mobility. Few have matched Russia (and, after 1917, the USSR) in prohibiting their own citizens' exit, but by the start of the twentieth century, regulation of foreigners' entry had become—and still remains—a significant attribute and privilege of sovereignty. Borders rigidified as states legislated restrictive terms under which aliens were eligible for inclusion, and putatively for citizenship.[14]

As states sought legitimacy in nationhood, they increasingly figured immigrants ("voluntary" migrants) and refugees ("involuntarily" stateless) as a troublesome threat to what Liisa Malkki terms "the national order of things." The "principle of sedentariness" underlying the modern states system presumes that people properly stay put. Nationalism has served to make rootedness appear natural, with the "nation-state" presenting itself as not only a political expression of a distinct people but its organic home.[15] Stateless individuals thus appear disintegrative to international order and national coherence alike—their displacement threatening to turn borders between sovereign spaces into congested corridors. For this reason, both scholars and states typically represent refugees as a profound "problem."[16] That a state might systematically attempt to *stimulate* exodus from another sovereign entity—setting others' citizens in motion—seems so unlikely an expedient that it has barely received consideration in the voluminous literature on statecraft and refugees.[17]

In the statist imagination, the problem of "displacement" has an obvious solution. As human lost property, refugees should (wherever conditions permit) be restored to their countries of origin: a move often presented as "returning home." Since the post–World War I genesis of an international refugee regime, repatriation has duly undergirded the practice of multilateral relief organizations. Even when dislocated individuals announce a desire to remake lives in fresh destinations, refugee agencies typically presume a universal yearning for home as the place left behind.[18]

Allied policy after World War II underscores states' commitment to these norms, irrespective of resistance from those forcibly "re-placed." Following Germany's collapse, Europe's mobile population numbered more than thirty million: humanity in flux on a scale almost impossible to imagine. The Allies had, however, anticipated massive human dislocation well before Germany's defeat, founding the United Nations Relief and Rehabilitation Administration (UNRRA) in 1943.[19] By 1947, UNRRA had repatriated seven million refugees, working on the agreed principle for postwar resettlement.[20] But hundreds of thousands of displaced persons had no wish to return, and multiple reasons to fear its consequences.[21] Many of the estimated five and a half million Soviet citizens outside the USSR's borders fell into this category: Red Army soldiers aware that their state treated returning POWs as traitors, those who had in fact collaborated with the Wehrmacht, and Balts whose countries had been swallowed by the USSR.[22]

Under provisions agreed upon at Yalta, British and U.S. authorities delivered more than two million people into Soviet custody, including several thousand Russians who had never been Soviet citizens. Many such individuals feared that the Red Army would swiftly dispatch them to the gulag, and their fears were not unwarranted. Nevertheless, British and American troops assisted the USSR's repatriation operations, at gunpoint when necessary. On occasion, displaced Soviets scheduled for return east chose suicide over repatriation: a scenario reworked in *The Red Danube*, whose Russian ballerina heroine, denied sanctuary in the British occupation zone of Austria, throws herself from an upper window—Kasenkina-style—as the Red Army approaches.[23] The granting of asylum ("a right of States, not of the individual") remained largely absent from early postwar practice, and until 1949 Washington formally undertook to return defectors of "Soviet nationality" who appeared in the U.S. occupation zone of Germany.[24] Similarly, the U.S. government made no substantial protest in 1945 at Soviet moves to relocate ethnic

Beautiful Maria... the four lives that touched hers were never the same again!
WALTER PIDGEON
ETHEL BARRYMORE
PETER LAWFORD
ANGELA LANSBURY
JANET LEIGH
with LOUIS CALHERN • FRANCIS L. SULLIVAN
Screen Play By GINA KAUS AND ARTHUR WIMPERIS
Based on a Novel by BRUCE MARSHALL
Directed by GEORGE SIDNEY • Produced by CAREY WILSON
A METRO-GOLDWYN-MAYER PICTURE
THE RED DANUBE
An exciting MGM Picture!
M-G-M 25¢

Germans and other population groups en masse as a form of "human reparations" from defeated enemies.[25]

But then a complete *volte-face* occurred. Truman's administration began to encourage flight west and to castigate the Soviet Union for its forcible movement east of millions of unwilling repatriates and prisoners. A contest often described by its Western architects as a "battle for men's minds" turned human bodies into a key site of interstate competition—"captive peoples" most particularly. Armistice negotiations in Korea stalled over U.S. insistence that prisoners of war *not* be forcibly repatriated: an unconventional departure from the Geneva Conventions, which mandate a straightforward exchange of prisoners on termination of hostilities. Aspiring to a measure of victory in the stalemated war, Washington hoped that repudiation of "Red China" by thousands of North Korean and Chinese POWs would enunciate a clear message of free world superiority.[26] Espousing "freedom of movement" as something akin to a "fifth freedom," Truman simultaneously made the Escapee Program the centerpiece of efforts to stimulate Soviet and Eastern Europeans' exodus. This initiative was accompanied by a concerted international campaign to indict "slave labor" in the Soviet gulag—and to press for the release of those illicitly moved east at the end of the war, together with German and Japanese POWs Moscow had still not relinquished.[27]

Figure 1.
The escapee as doomed dancer: "beautiful Maria" leaps from an upper window, preferring death to forcible repatriation to Russia by the Red Army. Poster from *The Red Danube* (1949).

Summoning "The Escapee"

It is not hard to fathom the origins of this about-turn. Plans to encourage escape—necessarily conducted in secrecy, given their affront to sovereign norms—drew inspiration from the intensity of U.S. media interest in prominent defectors such as Victor Kravchenko, Igor Gouzenko, and Oksana Kasenkina. In the estimation of George Kennan's Policy Planning Staff (PPS), their stories had done more "to arouse the Western world to the realities of the nature of communist tyranny than anything else since the end of the war," leaving "a wide breach in the Iron Curtain."[28] In parting this curtain, defectors not only provided a peephole for those in the West but a navigational light by which others in the East might steer the same course. Such individuals provided a "gold mine of vital information [to] be systematically exploited to the fullest possible extent." Functional to a whole array of "psychological" cold war schemes, "outstanding personalities from the Soviet world" appeared lucrative chips in a zero-sum game whereby America's gains represented the Kremlin's direct losses. As key personnel left its orbit, Moscow's control over its discontented sphere would weaken.

In elaborating plans, Kennan's staff imagined ideal-typical defectors as "important government and party officials, military officers, the intelligentsia, the managerial class and highly qualified technicians."[29] "Convinced that the Stalinist system is evil," these individuals would voluntarily place themselves in U.S. hands. But only a small proportion were likely to be such impeccable ideologues. Some would depart "for primarily economic, personal or other reasons not essentially of a political nature," together with "ordinary military deserters or other persons escaping from Soviet or satellite jurisdiction to escape the consequence of a crime or misconduct not of a political nature."[30] The PPS staked a possessive claim to the first category alone: the "defector." Noting that there might be as many as 700,000 Soviet bloc refugees in Western Europe, its plans recommended admission into the United States of up to 150 scientists, broadcasters, and scholars—the sole group that Kennan's staff sought to accommodate within the United States in productive cold war–oriented employment. Noting "the inflexibility of our present immigration legislation," the PPS took it for granted that "no significant proportion"—even of the ideologically pure—could "be brought to the U.S."[31]

The "escapee," then, had yet to crystallize as a distinct category, and the PPS exhibited some caution in its projections. Eager to entice well-placed defectors west, Kennan's staff appreciated the dangers posed by aggressive moves to undermine national borders. Clumsily handled, initiatives that flaunted the norms of sovereign statehood risked exceeding their destabilizing aim—instead sparking a general war. Even had Washington desired a mass defection, the PPS doubted that it could be engineered "so long as the police controls of the Soviet World remain as effective as they are now."[32] And of course schemes to generate a massive exodus threatened to consolidate defenses against the very action they aimed to promote: the more flagrantly Washington encouraged escape, the more strenuously Moscow and its satellites would prevent and punish it. Leaving dissatisfied citizens in place had the additional advantage of encouraging indigenous resistance—soil that U.S. intelligence operatives sought to fertilize.[33]

However, Truman came under increasing pressure from Republicans eager to "roll back" communism to adopt a more combative stance toward the USSR. Eyeing several thousand Eastern bloc citizens encamped in Western Europe, Congressman Charles Kersten and Senators Henry Cabot Lodge and Alexander Wiley perceived a deep reservoir of military recruits.[34] Two legislative moves entrenched this dual masculinization and militarization of a figure that now began to take specific shape as the "escapee." The Lodge Bill of 1950 authorized the United States Army to enlist 12,500 "unmarried aliens."[35] With the Korean War straining U.S. military resources, the attractiveness of large-scale escapee enlistment appeared to grow—so much so that "unlimited and indiscriminate encouragement of defection" from the USSR became official policy in April 1951, enshrined in NSC 86/1.[36] However, one year after passage of the Lodge Act, only 113 new recruits had been admitted into the army, and this dilatory pace made an alternative plan to form Eastern European emigrants into national units under NATO command more attractive. The chance to join a Volunteer Freedom Corps—Lodge's pet project—would, he believed, provide an incentive for mass desertion among the ranks of disaffected Soviet forces holding down the satellites. In October 1951, Congress duly authorized the Kersten Amendment, permitting expenditure of $100 million from Mutual Security Act funds,

> for any selected persons who are residing in or escapees from the Soviet Union, Poland, Czechoslovakia, Hungary, Rumania, Bulgaria, Albania, Lithuania, Latvia, and Estonia, or the Communist dominated or Communist occupied areas of Germany and Austria . . . either to form such persons into elements of the military forces supporting the North Atlantic Treaty Organization or for other purposes.[37]

The insurrectionary intent of this amendment was underlined by Kersten's exhortation that the United States "make some trouble for Joe Stalin in his own back yard"—which, to a degree unknown to the congressman, special forces already were doing.[38]

Moscow immediately brought Washington's scheme to cultivate subversive elements "residing in" the Soviet bloc before the UN General Assembly as an "aggressive act" that contravened the cornerstone of international law: sovereign inviolability.[39] Privately, State Department staff considered that the United States had "taken a beating" on this issue, and in 1951 it looked as if escapee initiatives were floundering. Candid internal assessments and newspaper reports alike noted the dismal conditions that greeted those who fled the Eastern bloc. According to a secret report on how best to perforate the iron curtain (code-named Project TROY), a "virtual concentration camp" awaited exiles from the "slave world." Some were literally accommodated in former Nazi camps assigned a new carceral function; all were repeatedly interrogated by overlapping agencies who sought to strip new arrivals of usable intelligence. Confined "under needlessly unpleasant conditions," they were "turn[ed] loose to shift for themselves after they [had] been squeezed dry of information."[40]

To make matters worse, resettlement assistance hitherto provided by the International Refugee Organization (UNRRA's successor) would evaporate in January 1952.

Many aspiring escapees never even got this far, however. With undocumented entrants often treated as illegal trespassers, a significant proportion of Eastern Europeans were arrested or turned back at the borders of their intended destinations—by *Western* authorities. According to a September 1951 *New York Times* report (corroborated by the State Department), escapees stood "a better than two-to-one chance of being jailed promptly like a common criminal" on arrival in the Western zones of Austria and Germany.[41] Moreover, this criminalization occurred with the sometime participation of U.S. officials, despite an explicit statement in May 1951 by the U.S. Commissioner for Germany, John McCloy, that asylum-seekers would no longer be turned back.[42]

"An Investment in Humanity": The Escapee Program

Against this dispiriting backdrop, Truman's Psychological Strategy Board (PSB) unveiled a dual-track "Psychological Operations Plan for Soviet Orbit Escapees" in December 1951. Phase A, the genesis of the Escapee Program, outlined "the best means . . . to employ, resettle, and care for current escapees" (estimated at twelve thousand), hoping that their better treatment would quicken the flow of defectors suitable for Phase B. Code-named "Operation ENGROSS," this clandestine track included plans to train some émigrés for future political leadership roles, assigning others to outfits pursuing "unconventional war" behind the iron curtain.[43] ENGROSS, as far as the PSB was concerned, formed the essential—but necessarily submerged—core of all escapee planning, from which other secondary effects could be spun. Fearing that the State Department had succumbed to the sentimental lure of humanitarianism, jettisoning martial aspirations for escapee enlistment, a skeptical Congressman Kersten was assured that "the primary purpose of escapee provision as a whole is to contribute directly toward the military strength of free Europe rather than to provide for the care of refugees in general."[44] However, State Department planners feared that without improved opportunities in the West, Easterners might cease undertaking the hazardous journey, losing faith in the sincerity of America's declarations of support for "captive peoples." Worse yet, some might even head back in the wrong direction, to the free world's considerable embarrassment.

Such naked instrumentalism, however, could hardly form the avowed purpose of the United States Escapee Program (USEP). As Truman announced this initiative in March 1952, the program's $4.3 million budget was linked not to military projections but to the resettlement of escapees along with other Displaced Persons and refugees for whom no permanent location had been found after World War II.[45] Appealing to "long-established humanitarian traditions," Truman urged Congress to authorize some three hundred thousand visas for both escapees and "surplus" Europeans of various nationalities.[46]

This presidential program necessarily gave more precise definition to the escapee—a "person" self-consciously crafted in distinction to the refugee. Eight months before the USEP's inauguration, the 1951 Geneva Convention defined refugees as those beyond the boundaries of their state owing to a "well-founded fear of being persecuted for reasons of race, religion, nationality, membership of a particular social group or political opinion." Having lost the "protection" of their state, refugees could not return.[47] Nor could they *be* returned. This principle, *non-refoulement*, constituted the sole entitlement of a status that extended its bearers no automatic right of asylum, but only prohibited their repatriation to places of origin in which they had suffered persecution prior to the convention's temporal cut-off date of January 1951. As scholars of refugee policy point out, this codification appears to privilege precisely those whom the U.S. government styled as escapees: elevating sufferers of political oppression above victims of natural disaster, and favoring those displaced across state boundaries over those made homeless within their country of origin.[48] The 1951 convention also assumed a clear distinction between migrants who *chose* to move in search of a better life, and refugees who were figured as involuntarily mobile—pushed from states that, under more benign governance, they would have had neither desire nor reason to leave.

Yet for all that this convention apparently conformed to U.S. preferences for marking some mobile individuals as more deserving than others, Washington refused to subscribe. Preferring to avoid open-ended commitments, the Truman administration delineated a separate status, at once more and less than the refugee. To channel assistance to escapees, the U.S. government provided funds to Western European states that hosted new arrivals from Eastern Europe, and built parallel international agencies (primarily the International Committee on European Migration) wholly under its control. In the process, Washington snubbed the United Nations High Commissioner for Refugees (UNHCR)—whose Dutch high commissioner, Dr. G. J. van Heuven Goedhart, was mistrusted by the State Department—by refusing to supplement its scant fifty-thousand-dollar budget.[49]

More was at work here than the self-protective sovereign state's reflexive mistrust of multilateralism. The orchestration of escapology required a different framework—definitional and institutional—than the Geneva Convention and its associated bodies provided. The 1951 status did not, after all, precisely capture the condition of many Eastern bloc emigrants. Its underpinning assumptions were problematic when applied to the Soviet bloc, not least its figuration of the normal relationship between a state and its citizens as "protective"—with the refugee cast as one who had "lost" this protection. The Soviet Union, in contrast, was understood to oppress its *entire* population, incarcerating millions (more or less arbitrarily) in the gulag, and depriving all citizens of their right to leave. Those who found a way out were not, then, necessarily political persecutees according to a narrow application of the 1951 Geneva Convention. Although some contemporary commentators insisted that the escapee was invariably a refugee, historians Loescher and Scanlan point out that the new category was less specific in its conditionality (while more restricted in its territorial remit) in tacit recognition that not all who traveled west had belonged to a *directly* persecuted constituency.[50] Only in leaving did many become members of an imperiled group, liable to persecution if caught. That they had *elected* to leave, and far from suffering expulsion had risked death in order to escape, begged the question whether many who departed the Eastern bloc were in fact "migrants" rather than "refugees"—if (as contemporary discourse held) the former were defined by their active search for material betterment, and the latter by exclusion from an intolerant political community.

As U.S. officials who debriefed new arrivals in Western European camps soon found, the tangled determinants of flight—the interplay of desire and dread, the "pull" of opportunity versus the "push" of oppression—made it impossible to sustain a rigid demarcation between economic opportunists and political refuseniks. Interrogators' attempts to distinguish "worthy patriots from self-seeking promoters" led some to conclude disparagingly that most Eastern bloc exiles were driven more by pecuniarism than principle: those who got out were simply the luckiest, not the most fervently anticommunist.[51] Frustrated by the dwindling flow of high-grade defectors, U.S. intelligence began springing "honey traps" as bait. Putting targeted individuals "under suspicion with the Soviet secret police," the CIA also deployed smear tactics to secure assets who were forced into flight in fear of "liquidation or severe punishment."[52] But other contemporary analysts were slower to conclude that only avarice—or blackmail—impelled flight and readier to dispute the viability of conceiving the economic and political as discrete domains of either state action or individual motive. In searching for economic advantage were Soviet bloc citizens not rejecting the *political* system that reserved a measure of prosperity for party apparatchiks alone?[53]

The escapee category offered a way to avoid public arbitration of Eastern bloc emigrants' motives by accentuating the fact of escape itself: the risks run in fleeing "from barbarism." Its crystallization sprang from a decision in December 1951 that "some definitive language" be found "for escapees as persons who have actually escaped from the Iron Curtain to differentiate [them] from people who are otherwise called refugees."[54] Privately, government discussion still distinguished between "defectors," "potential guerrillas," and (in an idiosyncratic usage) "refugees": "persons who escape from Iron Curtain countries, including both displaced and merely disaffected personnel from within those countries."[55] As this characterization of the largest but least serviceable group suggests, the predicament of such "refugees" animated scant sympathy in the State Department, whose primary focus remained that small segment of defectors for whom a separate program was maintained throughout the 1950s. But Eastern bloc exiles could not be neglected en masse without potential damage to the multiple objectives vested in escape. Furthering these ends required U.S. public support and public finance. Given congressional and popular reluctance during the 1940s to sanction generous provision for displaced persons, some ennobling language was required to transform the "merely disaffected" flotsam of the Eastern bloc into more deserving recipients of America's "investment in humanity."

In popular parlance, the term *escapee* summoned images of inventive extrications from prison or POW camp, with cinema's current vogue for wartime great escapes furnishing the Escapee Program's imaginative *mise en scène*. (*Stalag 17*, Billy Wilder's classic of the genre, appeared in 1953, preceded by several British films—notably *The Captive Heart* [1946] and *The Wooden Horse* [1951]—that dealt with similar material in more subdued fashion.)[56] Transferred from Colditz to cold war, the term's usage conjured the Soviet sphere as one vast prison, surrounded by barbed wire, watchtowers, and guards zealously poised over automatic weapons.

The escapee mantle appeared to valorize all who "heroically pushed through the Iron Curtain."[57] But in practice its constituency was narrower and certainly did not include all those who fled communism. Intersecting geopolitical calculations and racialized discrimination drew anomalous boundaries around this new status. USEP title was limited to "persons from the territory or control of the USSR, the Baltic States, Poland, Czechoslovakia, Hungary, Bulgaria, Rumania, and Albania, who escape into Western Europe, ranging from Turkey to Sweden."[58] Strikingly, this definition excluded the largest group that departed the Soviet orbit: the ten to fifteen thousand East Germans who headed west each month. After the Berlin Wall's completion in 1961, Easterners' attempts to breach this heavily fortified frontier provided the quintessential escapee drama of a later phase of superpower conflict. East Germans were not "stateless," however. The extension of citizenship to all *Volksdeutsche* formed a key plank of the Federal Republic's sponsorship of German reunification under its own leadership. Supporting this objective, Washington underwrote Bonn's absorption of some eight and a half million refugees, omitting Germans from the escapee category.[59]

A different diplomatic calculus led the State Department to exclude refugees from Yugoslavia. Eager to promote Titoism, Washington balked at the implications of extending assistance to refugees from the Balkans when the Escapee Program appeared—and indeed *was*—so obviously directed against the Kremlin. To treat Yugoslavs as escapees risked "getting into a major fuss with Tito" over the implied equivalence between Belgrade and Moscow at a time when Washington aspired to encourage separatism.[60]

More glaringly, Truman's program avoided any reference to thousands of Chinese in flight from Mao's revolution, despite urgings from prominent opinion-formers to capitalize on this outpouring of anticommunists. Privately, Truman's PSB analysts doubted whether such refugees held sufficient potential to merit a financial outlay that threatened to be "overwhelming." Extending Escapee Program assistance to all refugees from "Soviet orbit areas in the Far East, excluding Korea" would instantly add more than one and a quarter million claimants. Keen to restrict spending to those whose aid would do most to bolster the program's psychological objectives, PSB recommended assisting a "manageable segment" of Chinese intellectuals to resettle in Taiwan: just enough (they hoped) to enable Washington to rebut charges of "alleged neglect" while keeping in abeyance the issue of who would accommodate Asia's refugees.[61]

From Iron Curtain to "Paper Wall"

To what, then, were escapees entitled? The Escapee Program strove first to ameliorate camp life in ways that would facilitate residents' interrogation, then to accelerate their resettlement overseas.[62] Neither objective was easily achieved. Since refugees, displaced persons, and escapees mingled in the same overcrowded camps, often unsure as to how these identities (and their differential entitlements) were assigned, America's discriminatory preferences could not

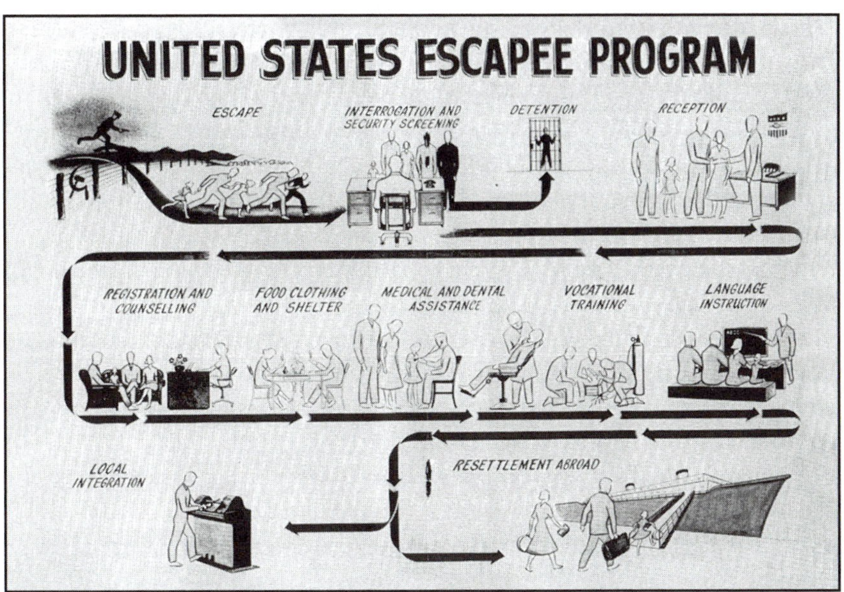

Figure 2.
The escapee life-cycle in idealized form: from border-crossing to an unnamed resettlement destination, with the bogus ("black") escapee screened and detained. From the U.S. government publication *Escape to Freedom*, (Washington: Foreign Operations Administration, 1954). Courtesy of the Lehman Archive, Columbia University.

be exercised without animating considerable tension among encamped communities. Moreover, as U.S. officials ruefully remarked, to improve conditions only for some camp residents and not others proved a practical impossibility: either one sprayed a whole camp against infection, or one did not. Communicable diseases were no respecters of classificatory hierarchy, yet the fact that U.S.–funded agencies attempted to inscribe one sent a clear signal—to stateless individuals, relief workers, and Western European governments—that the Escapee Program was more a strategic instrument than a humanitarian initiative.[63]

From a U.S. perspective, however, the most vexed question was resettlement. Where? Escapees could not remain encamped in ravaged postwar Europe indefinitely, yet the prospect of a significant Russian and East European influx into America animated deep hostility at a moment when nativism and anticommunism found common cause. At the height of the McCarthy era, to be non-American was often to be eyed as suspiciously un-American—a possible bearer of communist contagion. In the same year that containment strategy's foundational statement, NSC-68, hailed the United States' derivation of "strength from its hospitality even to antipathetic ideas . . . secure in its faith that free men will take the best wares," the 1950 Internal Security [McCarran] Act closed this vaunted marketplace for "free trade in ideas" to members and one-time members of the Communist Party.[64] Better remembered for requiring registration of all party and front organization members, and for rendering literary luminaries ineligible for entry into the United States (such as Graham Greene, who had joined the Communist Party briefly as an undergraduate lark), the McCarran Act debarred any alien who had belonged to the party, simultaneously expanding the state's powers of deportation over such individuals already in the country. Since many escapees had been compelled to join the Communist Party, this legislation offered a blow to their hopes of entering the United States via other legal avenues formerly open to them, such as the Displaced Persons Act of 1948.[65]

Truman insisted that this omnibus bill sponsored by his tenacious nemesis, Pat McCarran, would destroy a "great incentive to defection." Decisively ignored, the president could scarcely hope to secure congressional approval for escapees' wholesale resettlement in the United States.[66] His March 1952 escapee proposals thus requested only seven thousand visas—to be spread over three years—for Eastern bloc emigrants. Anticipating Congress's prompt rejection, some State Department architects of the program cautioned against floating even such a modest proposition. Escapee status, they insisted, offered no entry ticket to America; rather, it was a mechanism through which Washington subsidized Western European governments' care for escapees, financing their subsequent passage to Canada, Australia, and South American destinations.

In State Department eyes, Truman's visa proposal jeopardized congressional approval for the USEP by linking it with immigration legislation. Escapees' "reception, care and training" were "essentially matters of important foreign policy"—with escapees best serving American interests by remaining beyond U.S. borders. Immigration, on the other hand, was "essentially a matter of domestic internal policy."[67] Where Truman hoped that the popularity of escapee assistance would leaven Americans' disinclination to admit stateless Europeans, State Department advisers thought the linkage of "unpopular" immigration proposals to the politics of escape would lead Congress to reject the USEP altogether.[68] And indeed immigration liberalization was unpopular in 1952. A presidential veto notwithstanding, Congress endorsed the McCarran-Walter Act as the cornerstone of immigration policy on June 21, 1952: a three-hundred-page statute that, among multiple other provisions, relaxed slightly the ban on ex-Communists but expanded deportation powers and enhanced surveillance over aliens.[69]

Debates surrounding this new Immigration and Nationality Act, and subsequent attempts to transcend its more exclusionary measures, reveal the multiple layers of suspicion that shrouded Eastern bloc escapees. On the surface, arguments against admitting them in any great number spoke a language of security consciousness—fearful of KGB plants among the uprooted. McCarran's supporters speculated that the Kremlin might exploit the Escapee Program as a Trojan horse with which to breach the defensive wall erected by the Internal Security Act of 1950, smuggling spies and saboteurs into the United States under the innocent guise of escapees. Some even asserted that the USSR might push its "unreliable and feeble" elements west to embarrass America by forcing it either to embrace these social undesirables or expose the shallowness of its humanitarianism—foreshadowing similar charges that Castro cast off a "flotilla of criminals and deviants" on the *Mariel*.[70]

To restrictionists, Eastern bloc exiles occupied a murky region of epistemological and legal indeterminacy. How much could be taken on trust about individuals who lacked official identification papers and passports? Ironically, given the illegitimacy they attached to communist regimes (themselves prodigious producers of paperwork), critics of immigration liberalization insisted that such documents—certifying citizens as legal persons—formed the sine qua non of legitimate cross-border circulation. But escapees often arrived paperless. Furthermore, as McCarran repeatedly noted, thousands of Russians and Ukrainians had disguised their nationality in 1945, hoping to avoid repatriation to the USSR. If an individual could simply *assert* something as fundamental to selfhood as citizenship, how else might escapees dissemble as they scripted self-serving new life histories at the border of the free world? What convictions (criminal or political) might such people conveniently erase in their eagerness for admission to the United States?[71]

McCarran-Walter did authorize admission to former Communist Party members who, under stringent screening, could prove they had joined under duress or while still a minor.[72] But this amendment did little to dent the stubborn nativist streak that still regarded certain ethnicities as irredeemably other. Nor did it abolish the national origins quota system to which such sentiments had given rise in the 1920s, severely curtailing entrance except for those of "Anglo-Saxon" or "Nordic" stock. "Slavs" had never figured near the racial imaginary's apex. With Russia conceived as Europe's outer limit, taxonomists of race often cast Slavs as more "Asiatic" than "Caucasian," remarking on alleged propensities toward barbarism, despotism, and cruelty.[73] Such characterizations lingered into the mid-twentieth century. Former U.S. ambassador to the USSR Walter Bedell Smith insisted that Russians were set "apart from other civilizations" by a "Chinese wall": the "Slavonic language and character."[74] Like others of questionable fitness for citizenship, Slavs and East Europeans were thus construed as not only untutored in the habits of liberty but incapable of adaptation.

According to Rachel Buff, the "enduring ideological success of the McCarran-Walter Act . . . lay in its ability to conflate racial distinction and political loyalties": ushering in "political refugees" from the second world while closing the door to "economic migrants" from the third.[75] But its provisions did not, in fact, align race and rectitude quite so readily. Given that the act only gestured toward terminating Chinese exclusion, thousands of Mao's opponents found that their "political loyalties" failed to redeem their lack of "racial distinction." Kuomintang Chinese were passed over by McCarran-Walter just as they were excluded from the escapee category. "Racial distinction" did not spare Soviet bloc immigrants from exclusion either, however. Even white Russians remained of questionable whiteness. This discrimination struck Truman as "fantastic."[76] Yet stringent protectionism is exactly what the 1952 act sought to maintain, with Walter insisting that would-be Eastern bloc entrants were not "the kind of people our ancestors were."[77] His cosponsored act therefore "contained few provisions relevant to the plight of the political refugee." Rather, it proliferated "undesirable" categories by which asylum seekers might be debarred, extending sanctuary only to "the disenchanted diplomat who chose to stay in the United States."[78]

Following America's lead, other states earmarked as possible resettlement destinations started to emulate U.S. restrictionism, leaving escapees stranded.[79] A modified Refugee Relief Act of 1953 only aggravated their predicament. It purported to liberalize admissions policy, promising 120,000 special nonquota visas for each of the two following years. Yet as critics pointed out, it remained rooted in the same racialized discriminations as the McCarran-Walter Act, together with "new ones, so drastic in scope as to destroy the hopes of many who have been dreaming of a safe haven in the United States."[80] As amended and finally passed, the act reduced the upper limit of annual admissions from 120,000 to 58,000. In practice, the number of "escapees and refugees" admitted was considerably lower—the conditions of visa issuance willfully prohibitive. Even those Eastern bloc emigrants who found American sponsors to guarantee them jobs and accommodation were confined to camps for a protracted period. Admission to the United States rested on the ability to produce a documented two-year history that corroborated "character, reputation, mental and physical health, history and eligibility."[81] Since no one emerged from the Soviet bloc with documentation that could possibly satisfy such exacting empiricism, this stipulation effectively required escapees to "wait out their two years' probation in a state of such exemplary grace as to prove to the most skeptical that they just *couldn't* be Communists."[82] Camps in West Germany, Austria, Italy, Greece, and Turkey duly became manufactories of evidence, with inmates subjected to repeated screenings, interrogations, and medical examinations—the strategies of "authentification." Two years after the act's passage, the former solicitor general doubted whether as many as 1,000 "actual escapees, expellees and refugees not eligible under any other category" had entered the United States. A *Harper's* feature—lambasting the "national disgrace" of this "compassion by slide rule"—put the total, in April 1955, at only 563 visas for refugees and escapees.[83]

To some critics, the contradiction between America's promotion of flight and its jealously guarded borders proved the dangers of conceiving immigration legislation as a domestic province rather than "a fundamental instrument in the conduct of our relations with other nations": the site where degrees of foreignness are determined.[84] Yet despite the many policy objectives vested in escape, escapees' liminality was never resolved in the early cold war by a decisive adjudication in favor of their admission into the United States. Summoned to sharpen an ideological boundary, the escapee was repeatedly relegated to the margins of sovereign space: a borderland whose material embodiment was the refugee camp.

In escapee schemes, congressional reluctance to accept these "impossible subjects" was disowned and projected as indelible nationalism on the part of Eastern bloc emigrants—temporary sojourners in the West, merely awaiting the collapse of Soviet power to return home. Interview data revealed a different picture, however. Rather than hanker wistfully for their places of origin, most hoped to settle in the United States or Canada, with Australia a "poor second," and the majority preferring "to stay in the camps in Europe rather than go to Latin America."[85] But since these destinations proved reluctant hosts, cold war strategists concocted increasingly fanciful schemes to locate empty—or emptied—land for reconstitution as "national homelands":

> If grounds of security, politics, and present laws make it impractical to bring the remainder to the continental United States, the possibility of establishing a center on one of the Virgin Islands, from which all other inhabitants were evacuated, or on some other insular possession should be most carefully investigated. Conceivably Nova Scotia would be more suitable for climatic reasons and because of the absence of a "racial" problem if arrangements could be made with the Canadian government.[86]

With indigenous occupants spirited away, Russians and Eastern Europeans would cultivate the art of self-government, nurturing national essence in exile.[87] Shut out by the "paper wall" that immigration restrictionism erected around the United States, escapees were imagined reenacting the founding drama of a territory similarly conceived by its first colonists as "unused" land.[88]

Bloc Busters: The Cultural Politics of Escape

By the mid-1950s, escapee projects were proving slower to yield results than heady projections of a "mass exodus" had anticipated a few years earlier. The flow of people leaving the Soviet orbit dwindled as border controls intensified on the Eastern side and barely relaxed in the West. Meanwhile, Lodge's plan for a Volunteer Freedom Corps, enthusiastically endorsed by Eisenhower, foundered on interagency disagreement over whether U.S. citizenship should be offered as an incentive to service, and on Western European disinclination to host such a provocative presence.[89] Without adding armed units primed for Eastern Europe's liberation, these states already housed large numbers of refugees. According to one report from 1956, more than 250,000 individuals eligible for USEP assistance were "still languishing" in West German and Austrian camps.[90] Tangible achievements thus appear few. But since an explicit aim of escapee projections was to "exploit all aspects of the psychological value inherent in escape from Soviet tyranny," an assessment of how persuasively meaning was marshaled takes us far from the realm of quantifiable results.[91] To ponder the symbolic work of the escapee is necessarily to deal in more impressionistic evidence, leavening any sense that escapee projects simply "failed."

As is clear from the volume of Voice of America and Radio Free Europe airtime devoted to the heroics of escape and escapees' warm reception, such narratives sought to write the West's identity "as a free community with basic concern for the dignity and worth of the individual": a magnetic pole of attraction.[92] To facilitate dissemination of this message, a Psychological Warfare Working Group in Frankfurt supplied broadcasters with "exploitable information," including "special stunts" such as the airlift of sixty-four escapees directly from Munich to Washington, D.C., to commemorate the USEP's second anniversary.[93] Under the terms of the Smith-Mundt Act of 1948, American audiences were ruled off-limits to manipulation of this kind. But this legal proscription was creatively circumvented as Truman's advisers recognized that the distillation of superpower competition into compelling human drama offered an avenue by which Americans "restless to take a personal part

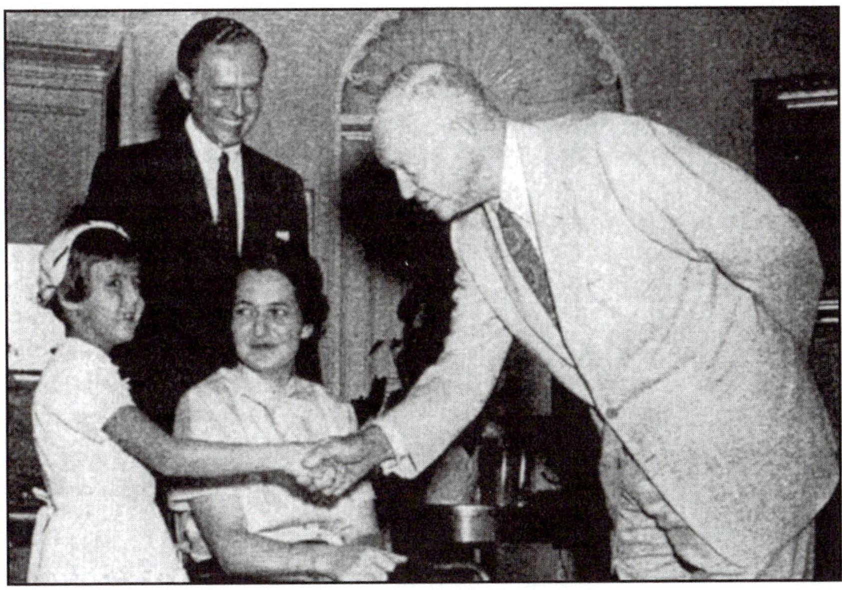

Figure 3.
"I shall be happier with one leg in America than I would have been with two legs in Communist Hungary," Mrs. Kapus was reported to have announced on arrival in the West. From *Escape to Freedom*, 1954. Courtesy of the Lehman Archive, Columbia University.

in the East-West struggle" might participate.[94] Worried that Americans still lacked the kind of "emotional support" for foreign policy goals that would sustain a "larger degree of mobilization for a long time," Kennan's staff turned to "men of the press and radio . . . interested in this problem" for assistance.[95] They found it. Intricate webs of personal and corporate connection wove news and entertainment organizations with the world of intelligence, and specifically with the realm of escapee endeavor.[96]

Popular media bombarded U.S. audiences with particularly ingenious breaches of the curtain. Much drama hinged on the hijacking of trains, planes, trucks, or tanks, and, in the grand tradition of POW movies, on tunneling to freedom. Newsreels showcased the Ollarek family who fled Czechoslovakia in a "freedom duck"—an amphibious jeep stolen and steered across the Morava River into Austria "under dramatic circumstances." Ivan Pluhar, a Czech who tunneled out of a prison camp near uranium mines where he had been sentenced for anticommunist activity, was subsequently admitted into Yale Law School with much fanfare.[97] Some escaped in airplanes, while others defected from Soviet ships; a handful departed diplomatic missions, while rather more deserted their army postings.[98] Almost all personal narratives ended with a ringing declamation that explicated the larger meaning of escape. Having lost a leg when a landmine exploded, impeding—but not preventing—her escape, Mrs. Kapus told her American rescuers: "I shall be happier with one leg in America than I would have been with two legs in Communist Hungary." A Polish pilot who flew his MiG to Denmark was reported by *Life* as jubilantly announcing, "Kommunizm Kaput!" And when a Czech "freedom train" crashed into West Germany in September 1951, carrying an engineer and thirty-two passengers, its driver exclaimed, "We are all here in the West—and the climate is wonderful!"[99]

Stories of dramatic exit afforded entry points for U.S. citizens into what Richard Fried terms cold war "pageantry." The very vehicles of escape were enlisted into efforts to raise "truth dollars" for Radio Free Europe in its mission of relaying word of successful escape back behind the iron curtain. Under the National Committee for a Free Europe's aegis, a "Freedom Tank" toured America in 1954, with onlookers entreated to place donations in this "piggy bank for freedom"—an armoured car in which eight "plucky Czechs" had careened through the cold war frontier.[100] With the Escapee Program announced as an "investment in humanity," such enterprises presented a mobilized citizenry with its chance to contribute.[101] For those of a sedentary disposition, escapee drama could be enjoyed vicariously. A steadily increasing number of memoirs, such as Peter Pirogov's *Why I Escaped*, Vladimir Petrov's *My Retreat from Russia*, and Louis Fischer's collection, *Thirteen Who Fled*, detailed grim conditions behind the iron curtain and the hair-raising adventure of curtain crossing.[102]

Escape lent itself to emplotment in a variety of genres and registers: from all-male action adventure to the heavily gendered romance of rescue. In Hollywood's imagination, women did not escape the Eastern bloc: they were rescued by male romantic leads or died tragically, encircled by Red Army troops. Men, however, plotted inventive ways to evade murderous border patrols. In Elia Kazan's *Man on a Tightrope* (1953), a Czech circus troupe is driven to dissidence by the communist regime's insistence that the clown act depict a "Wall Street capitalist" oppressing an "American Negro worker." In the final reel, they effect a carnivalesque rupture of the iron curtain: lions, fire-eaters, strongmen, and all.[103]

As a form of escapism, escape exerted considerable—but varied—appeal. Enquiring as to why such stories were "even more than usually in demand today," one critic speculated in 1954 that Americans absorbed this material avidly because they existed "in the Dark Ages again": "Boys who grew up down the street have had their brains washed in the brutality of Communist

Figure 4.
Saved from Stalin: Clark Gable rows across the Baltic to claim his Bolshoi ballerina bride from the sexually voracious dictator in *Never Let Me Go* (1953).

imprisonment . . . And the bell can toll for us too with equally loud clangor. It can happen here, and instinctively we want to know about it."[104] But what was "it"? Was the more dreadful prospect that of communist takeover, or (as other critics feared) the passive surrender of self—a latent desire for submission that hinted at a masochistic psychosexual urge? Certainly, as the 1950s wore on, popular accounts of U.S. prisoner of war behavior in Korea increasingly accentuated not communist "brainwashing" but prisoners' passivity and abjection: a condition labeled "give-up-itis" by the *New Yorker*'s Eugene Kinkead, which Betty Friedan saw as a mirror for the "feminine mystique" afflicting suburban housewives.[105] Was it possible that "captive peoples" *desired* their captivity? That "escape *from* freedom" promised lassitudinous release?

This ambivalence was only one tension to strain the smooth surface of congratulatory identity constructions that the phenomenon of escape and condition of captivity seemed to invite. In promotional material for the Escapee Program, emphasis on U.S. humanitarianism masked—or attempted to mask—the instrumentalism that characterized the state's attitude toward its commodified cold war assets. That the program strove primarily to secure military, intelligence, and "psychological" objectives was, of course, excised from the public record in favor of its charitable dimensions.[106] But even here problems arose. Welfare delivered under the USEP banner may have marginally mitigated camp conditions, but many escapees' lives remained so wretched that any forthright account risked exposing the program's rather meager investment in humanity. Motioning the dangers of "overselling" the Escapee Program, an internal USIA report noted that "the hard fact of the matter is that most escapees find it necessary to remain in reception centers for some time before the process of arranging acceptable resettlement is completed. More often than not they experience major difficulty in adjusting to and fitting themselves constructively into the life of resettlement."[107] While this verdict located the burden of failure with escapees (ill-equipped for "the life of resettlement"), press reports were quicker to indict government agencies when they detailed cases of suicide by individuals who despaired of ever leaving camps, and the unceremonious abandonment of those such as the Czech "freedom train" escapees who found the "free world" less than hospitable.[108]

By the mid-1950s, "re-defection" had also become a major concern for the State Department.[109] It was an article of faith, after all, that movement across the curtain occurred in only one direction: Americans did not defect, and escapees, on arrival in the West, stayed put. Neither condition entirely corresponded to reality, however. A thirty-three-year-old Pennsylvania woman caused a brief stir in 1948 when—reversing Hollywood's script—she deserted her embassy post in Moscow, married a Russian opera singer, and wrote a scurrilous exposé, titled *The Truth about American Diplomats.*[110] Five years later, twenty-one American POWs animated even greater consternation at the end of the Korean War when, no longer subject to involuntary postwar repatriation (thanks to Washington's insistence), they elected lives in "Red China" over return home.[111] The most compelling initial explanation for such inexplicable behavior was that these American boys had been "brainwashed." Similarly, some U.S. press commentators attributed instances of escapees' return east to malfeasance on Moscow's part.[112] "Re-defection" seemed to confirm that the Soviets thought nothing of kidnapping their citizens, or variously terrorizing and entrapping them. Some returnees appeared to have been blackmailed into going back by threats against family members still in the USSR; others were framed as Nazi war criminals or "compromised by women" (tactics that bore some resemblance to those employed by the CIA to secure highly placed Soviet defectors).[113] Perhaps certain escapees had been dispatched west by Moscow with the express mission of re-defecting at a later date? But the secret project TROY report concluded that while "some of these cases of 're-defection' may well have involved Soviet 'plants' . . . by no means all of them could fall into this category."[114] Many, in other words, left disillusioned by the gulf separating promises of deliverance from the squalor and suspicion that greeted them in the West. "All had come hoping much from the free world," opined influential columnist Joseph Alsop in 1951. "All had got nothing, except to be utterly cut off from the world they knew."[115]

From the Margins

How do state borders assume a guise as geographical givens rather than limits constructed by law and regulated by force? Interrogating this question, constructivist scholars have recently paid particular attention to the work of refugees in naturalizing the boundedness of life within sovereign jurisdictions. For all that states announce refugee outpourings as problematic, "refugeeness" provides "affirmative resources for statist practices," claims Nevat Soguk.[116] The precarious condition of statelessness encourages a better appreciation of what it means to enjoy state "protection," heightening awareness that only as *citizens* do individuals enjoy rights. Who, then, would shirk their state's embrace? In the early cold war the answer was that only those fleeing tyranny would embark on such a perilous path. Thus Randy Lippert proposes that "*refugeeness* became a moral-political tactic," marking a schism between the barbarous East and civilized West, and fostering "cohesion of the Western Alliance nations."[117]

But while the "sovereignty effect" undoubtedly requires work, Lippert's estimation of "refugeeness" as a cold war resource fails to capture what was specific to—and much more ambiguous about—"escapeeness." Certainly U.S. strategists hoped that escape would demonstrate the desirability of movement in one particular direction. In practice, however, escapees tended to *destabilize* the very boundaries and identities they were meant to consolidate. Paradoxically, the only border that they fixed more securely was the physical one they traversed and, in so doing, helped to solidify. For some U.S. strategists, tightened Soviet border controls were an unfortunate by-product of escapee schemes. Others, seeing intensified repression as likely to hasten communism's implosion, were less troubled that American initiatives to manufacture defection tended to make departure all the more difficult.

As for the identity politics bound up in escape, the pugnacity of U.S. cold war strategy animated increasing concern in Western Europe, tugging at the seams of NATO rather than knitting the alliance together. In the United States,

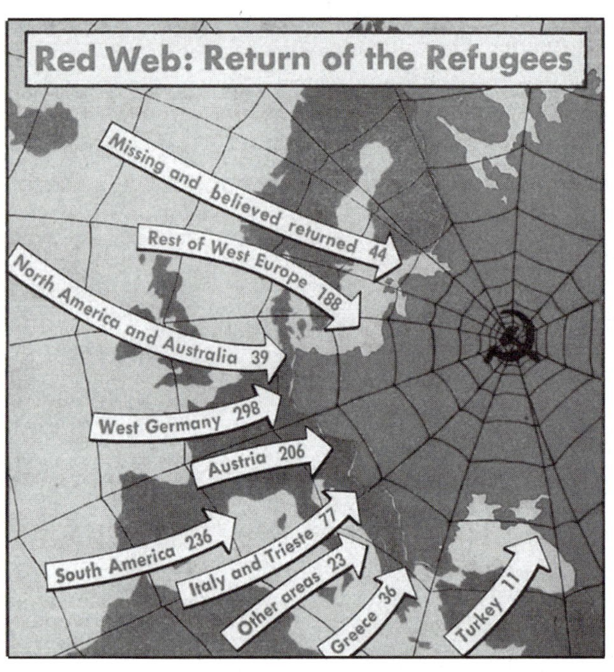
Red Web: Return of the Refugees
Missing and believed returned 44
Rest of West Europe 188
North America and Australia 39
West Germany 298
Austria 206
South America 236
Italy and Trieste 77
Other areas 23
Greece 36
Turkey 11

escapee schemes aspiring to produce a coherent and valorous identity for the free world struggled to keep only the "usable past" in focus. Proclamations of American eagerness to assist escapees invoked a Puritan back-story, with the exodus of "captive peoples" from Europe anchoring a cherished self-image of the United States as "asylum of all asylums." In Lodge's words: "The fact that the U.S. was founded by escapees from oppression is precedence for U.S. solicitude for escapees from behind the Iron Curtain."[118] But the effacements required in imagining the United States as a "nation of escapees"—a place of sanctuary for redeemed captives not of perdition for those brought to America in chains—surely troubled those whose ancestors' enslavement had not been purely figurative. The term "escapee," after all, had another meaning absent from a cold war lexicon intent on suppressing American history as both slave *and* free: that of the escaped or "fugitive" slave, fleeing from bondage but liable (in the era of the Fugitive Slave Act) to be returned to slavery by free Americans.[119]

Figure 5.
The Escapee Ensnared? By mid-decade a significant number of escapees were on the move again, in the wrong direction—East. *Newsweek*-Bensi, March 12, 1956, 49. © Newsweek, Inc. All rights reserved. Reprinted by permission.

Washington's conflicted posture toward "captive peoples"—and toward "freedom of movement" as an (in)alienable right—made "escapeeness" a peculiarly complex resource to manipulate. The contradictions complicated more than the fashioning of a laudatory self-image. Ultimately, they forced a relaxation of immigration restrictions in the wake of Hungary's failed uprising in 1956. Believing that U.S. forces would intervene to assist in effecting "regime change," the Hungarian rebels found Washington prepared to do no more than announce its condemnation of the Red Army as its tanks moved to flatten the revolt. A CIA enquiry into American broadcasting later exonerated VOA and RFE from charges of reckless incitement. Yet the taint of bad faith remained. At the very least, U.S.–financed radio broadcasts—echoing Eisenhower's own apparent endorsement of "rollback"—had raised expectations of assistance.[120]

The crushed Hungarian revolt sharply exposed the limits of Washington's commitment to liberation. In so doing, however, it expanded willingness to admit Eastern bloc emigrants into the United States in significant numbers. The hollowness of commitment to "rollback" had to be recuperated by making Washington's posture toward escapees more than rhetorical. Eisenhower's administration was not, ultimately, prepared to risk a general war over Hungary. But having hemorrhaged so much credibility, it could hardly compound the damage to its self-image by denying a significant number of Hungarians access to America.[121] From a total of almost two hundred thousand who fled

Hungary in November 1956 into neighboring Austria and Yugoslavia, approximately thirty-five thousand were eventually admitted into the United States.[122] According to several commentators, many were not active participants in the revolt but had simply slipped through the Austro-Hungarian border during its temporary rupture. Now, however, no one asked too loudly whether these Hungarians were possible saboteurs, spies, or "self-seekers." On the contrary, *Time* magazine bestowed its "Man of the Year" accolade on a composite "Hungarian freedom fighter." The escapee's moment, it seemed, had finally come—a possible subject and putative citizen after all.

Notes

During this essay's long gestation I have incurred many debts. Audiences at the American Studies Association convention in Detroit (2001) and the American Historical Association convention in Washington, D.C. (January 2004), as well as members of the seminar "Cold War as Global History" at the International Center for Advanced Study at New York University (October 2003) heard and helpfully commented on very different versions of this work-in-progress. In particular, I offer special thanks to Eric Ortiz and Christina Strasburger for their superior scanning skills, Allen Hunter and Marilyn Young for incisive comments on an earlier manuscript, Tom Doherty for zeal in tracking down obscure ballerina movie memorabilia, and the editors of this special issue for their encouragement.

1. "The Mystery of the Kidnaped Russian," *Life*, August 23, 1948, 23–27. Kasenkina's story received a twenty-five-part serialization in the *New York Journal and American*, from September 26, 1948.
2. John Reinhardt, director, *Sofia* (Arpi Productions, 1948); George Sidney, director, *Red Danube* (MGM, 1949); Delmer Daves, director, *Never Let Me Go* (MGM, 1953).
3. David Caute, *The Dancer Defects: The Struggle for Cultural Supremacy during the Cold War* (New York: Oxford University Press, 2003), 486.
4. "Freedom to Move," *Life*, August 30, 1948, 18.
5. Gregory Mitrovich, *Undermining the Kremlin: America's Strategy to Subvert the Soviet Bloc* (Ithaca: Cornell University Press, 2000); Scott Lucas, *Freedom's War: The U.S. Crusade against the Soviet Union* (Manchester: Manchester University Press, 1999); Bennett Kovrig, *Of Walls and Bridges: The United States and Eastern Europe* (New York: New York University Press, 1991); Jim Marchio, "Resistance Potential and Rollback: U.S. Intelligence and the Eisenhower Administration's Policies Toward Eastern Europe, 1953–56," *Intelligence and National Security* 10.2 (April 1995): 219–41.
6. Henry Cabot Lodge, "An Army of the Free," *Life*, October 2, 1950, 38; "An American Foreign Legion?" *Look*, September 14, 1948, 100.
7. Gil Loescher and John Scanlan, *Calculated Kindness: Refugees and America's Half-Open Door, 1945 to the Present* (New York: Free Press, 1986). See also T. Alexander Aleinikoff, "State-Centered Refugee Law: From Resettlement to Containment," in *Mistrusting Refugees*, ed. E. Valentine Daniel and John Knudsen (Berkeley: University of California Press, 1995), 260; Richard Robbins, "The Refugee Status: Challenge and Response," *Law and Contemporary Problems* 21 (spring 1956): 330.
8. Aleinikoff, "State-Centered Refugee Law"; Aristide Zolberg, "Contemporary Transnational Migrations in Historical Perspective: Patterns and Dilemmas," in *U.S. Immigration and Refugee Policy. Global and Domestic Issues*, ed. Mary M. Kritz (Lexington, Mass.: D. C. Heath, 1983), 31; Randy Lippert, "Governing Refugees: The Relevance of Governmentality to Understanding the International Refugee Regime," *Alternatives* 24.3 (1999): 295–328.
9. Paul Weiss, "The International Protection of Refugees," *The American Journal of International Law* 48.2 (April 1954): 193–221; John Stoessinger, *The Refugee and the World Community* (Minneapolis:

University of Minnesota Press, 1956); Kim Salomon, *Refugees in the Cold War: Toward a New International Refugee Regime in the Early Postwar Era* (Lund, Sweden: Lund University Press, 1991).

10. Rachel Buff, *Immigration and the Political Economy of Home* (Berkeley: University of California Press, 2001), 59.
11. Meeting with Congressman Kersten, August 27, 1952, 383.7, Report of Richard Brown on Escapee Program [hereafter EP], File 2, Harry S Truman Presidential Library [hereafter HSTL].
12. Elfan Rees, "The Refugee and the United Nations," *International Conciliation* 492 (June 1953): 295–96; Jacques Vernant, *The Refugee in the Postwar World* (London: Allen & Unwin, 1953), 53.
13. Mae Ngai, *Impossible Subjects: Illegal Aliens and the Making of Modern America* (Princeton, N.J.: Princeton University Press, 2004); Bonnie Honig, *Democracy and the Foreigner* (Princeton, N.J.: Princeton University Press, 2001).
14. Nevzat Soguk, *States and Strangers: Refugees and the Displacements of Statecraft* (Minneapolis: University of Minnesota Press, 1999); Michael R. Marrus, *The Unwanted: European Refugees in the Twentieth Century* (New York: Oxford University Press, 1985).
15. Liisa H. Malkki, "Refugees and Exile: From 'Refugee Studies' to the National Order of Things," *Annual Review of Anthropology* 24 (1995): 508; Christian Joppke, *Immigration and the Nation State: The United States, Germany, and Great Britain* (New York: Oxford University Press, 1999), 1.
16. Peter Nyers, "Emergency or Emerging Identities: Refugees and Transformations in World Order," *Millennium* 28.1 (1999): 1–26.
17. Leon Gordenker, *Refugees in International Politics* (London: Croom Helm, 1987), 66–67, 84–85.
18. Daniel Warner, "Voluntary Repatriation and the Meaning of Return to Home: A Critique of the Liberal Mathematics," *Journal of Refugee Studies* 7.2–3 (1994): 160–74.
19. Marrus, *The Unwanted*, 309, 319.
20. Ibid., 297.
21. Malcolm Proudfoot, *European Refugees, 1939–52: A Study in Forced Population Movement* (London: Faber and Faber, 1957), 214.
22. George Ginsburgs, "The Soviet Union and the Problems of Refugees and Displaced Persons, 1917–1956," *American Journal of International Law* 51.2 (April 1957): 325–61.
23. Jason Kendall Moore, "Between Expediency and Principle: U.S. Repatriation Policy toward Russian Nationals, 1944–1949," *Diplomatic History* 24.3 (summer 2000): 381–404; Proudfoot, *European Refugees*, 207–20.
24. "U.S. Policy toward Resistance within the Soviet Orbit," Records of the Policy Planning Staff [hereafter PPS], 1947–53, RG 59, Box 37a, National Archives, College Park, Md.
25. "Shall German Labor Rebuild Europe?" *The New Republic*, May 7, 1945, 638–39.
26. Barton J. Bernstein, "The Struggle over the Korean Armistice: Prisoners of Repatriation?" in *Child of Conflict: The Korean-American Relationship, 1943–53*, ed. Bruce Cumings (Seattle: University of Washington Press, 1983).
27. On the enlistment of a prominent African American into the campaign to indict Soviet "slavery," see Scott Lucas and Helen Laville, "The American Way: Edith Sampson, the NAACP and African-American Identity in the Cold War," *Diplomatic History* 20.4 (fall 1996): 565–90.
28. PPS 54, "Policy Relating to Defection and Defectors from Soviet Power," June 28, 1949, Records of the PPS, RG 59, Microfiche 1171, 62. Such plans began in 1948 with PPS 22, "Utilization of Refugees from the Soviet Union in U.S. National Interest," February 5, 1948; RG 59, Records of the PPS, Microfiche 1171, 23.
29. PPS 22/1, "Utilization of Refugees from the Soviet Union in U.S. National Interest," March 4, 1948, Records of the PPS, RG 59, Microfiche 1171, 24.
30. PPS 22, February 5, 1948.
31. PPS 22/1, March 4, 1948.
32. Ibid.
33. Joyce to Webb, January 29, 1952, Lot File 62D333, PSB Working File, 1952–53, RG 59, Box 2.
34. Bennett Kovrig, *The Myth of Liberation: East-Central Europe in U.S. Diplomacy and Politics Since 1941* (Baltimore: Johns Hopkins University Press, 1973).
35. Alien Enlistment Act of 1950, P.L. 81-597 (64 Stat. 316), June 30, 1950; PSB D-18/a, "Psychological Operations Plan for Soviet Orbit Escapees," December 20, 1951, Executive Secretariat, PSB Working File, 1951–53, Lot File 62D 333, RG 59, Box 2.
36. NSC 86/1 remains classified, but its central aim is obvious from discussions of escapee policy.

37. Section 101(a)(1) of the Mutual Security Act of 1951, Godel to Cutler, October 19, 1951; ENGROSS, File 1, HSTL.
38. Kovrig, *Myth of Liberation*, 103; Peter Grose, *Operation Rollback: America's Secret War behind the Iron Curtain* (Boston: Houghton Mifflin, 2000).
39. A. M. Rosenthal, "Vishinsky Asks UN to Make U.S. Cease Help to Anti-Reds," *New York Times*, December 20, 1951.
40. Report of Project TROY, Annex 12, February 1951, PPS Working Papers, 1947–63, Lot File 64D 563, RG59, Box 70 [hereafter TROY]. On the redesignation of former Nazi camps, Malkki, "Refugees and Exile," 499; Drew Pearson, "Iron Curtain Refugees Neglected," *Washington Post*, October 11, 1951.
41. Michael Hoffman, "West Bitter Haven for Red Refugees," *New York Times*, September 19, 1951; Godel to Cutler, October 19, 1951; ENGROSS, File 1, HSTL.
42. Bureau of European Affairs; Records relating to Psywar, 1951–53, RG 59, Box 1.
43. PSB D-18/a; PSB D-18a/1, "A National Psychological Program with Respect to Escapees from the Soviet Orbit: Phase B," December 5, 1952, Lot File 62 D 333, PSB Working File, 1951–53, RG 59, Box 2.
44. Meeting with Kersten, August 27, 1952; EP, File 2, HSTL.
45. George L. Warren, "The Escapee Program," *Journal of International Affairs* 7.1 (1953).
46. Message of the President to the Congress, March 24, 1952, *Department of State Bulletin* 36.667: 551–55.
47. 1951 Convention Relating to the Status of Refugees (July 28, 1951), http://www.ufsia.ac.be/~dvanheul/genconv.html (accessed June 27, 2005).
48. See notes 8 and 9, above.
49. The State Department did not regard the UNHCR director, Dr. G. J. Van Heuven Goedhart, as "wholly reliable"; ENGROSS, File 1, HSTL.
50. Loescher and Scanlan, *Calculated Kindness*, 24.
51. Townsend Hoopes, "The Question of Exploiting Anti-Stalinist Exiles and Escapees for Military and Other Purposes," November 27, 1951; EP, File 1, HSTL.
52. TROY, 3.
53. Richard C. Sheldon and John Dutkowski, "Are Soviet Satellite Refugee Interviews Projectable?" *Public Opinion Quarterly* 16.4 (winter 1952–53): 588.
54. The escapee category excluded Soviet citizens in DP camps since 1945, taking its starting date as 1948. Meeting, 12/14, on Defector Problem, December 14, 1951, EP, Section 1, HSTL.
55. Godel to Cutler, October 19, 1951; ENGROSS, File 1, HSTL; Terms of Reference for Coordination of the Implementation of NSC 86/1, October 18, 1954, RG 59, Box 38.
56. Billy Wilder, director, *Stalag 17* (Paramount, 1953); Basil Dearden, director, *The Captive Heart* (Ealing Studios, 1946); Jack Lee, director, *The Wooden Horse* (London Film Productions, 1951).
57. Department of State publication 5804, *Assistance to Escapees—Its Significance for America* (April 1955), 10.
58. PSB D-18/a, n. 1.
59. *Assistance to Escapees*, 3.
60. Phase A meeting, September 25, 1952, 383.7 EP, Section 5, HSTL.
61. PSB D-18a/5, October 23, 1952, FY 1954 Escapee Budget, ENGROSS, File 1, HSTL.
62. PSB D-18, Meeting, September 18, 1952, 383.7 EP, Section 5, HSTL.
63. Progress Report on the Escapee Program, June 30, 1952, EP, File 2, HSTL. On the "bad feeling" that discrimination produced, Rees, "The Refugee," 295–96; Vernant, *Refugee in the Postwar World*, 53.
64. NSC-68, reproduced in Thomas H. Etzold and John Lewis Gaddis, *Containment: Documents on American Policy and Strategy* (New York: Columbia University Press, 1978), 387–88. On the 1950 McCarran Act, John Higham, "American Immigration Policy in Historical Perspective," *Law and Contemporary Problems* 21.2 (spring 1956): 235.
65. Loescher and Scanlan, *Calculated Kindness*, 29.
66. Ibid., 25. On Truman's tortured relationship with McCarran see Michael Ybarra, *Washington Gone Crazy: Senator Pat McCarran and the Great American Communist Hunt* (Hanover, N.H.: Steerforth Press, 2004).
67. Comments of the Department of State on Draft Presidential Message to Congress, March 7, 1952, David D. Lloyd Collection, Box 2, HSTL.

68. Sherman to Taylor and Browne, March 10, 1952, 383.7 EP, Section 3, HSTL.
69. Meeting on Legislative Strategy to Support Administration's Bill on Immigration and Escapees from Communism, May 12, 1952, EP, File 2, HSTL.
70. PSB considered that "dumping" would demonstrate Soviet desperation in a way that would afford the United States "a major propaganda victory"; Working Draft, Phase B, PSB D-18a/1, November 5, 1952, EP, File 2, HSTL. On the *Mariel*, see Joppke, *Immigration*, 51.
71. These sentiments appear as the minority view, dissenting from Eisenhower's proposed Emergency Immigration legislation of 1953. 83rd Cong., 1st sess., HR Rep. 974, Emergency Immigration Program, July 27, 1953, Minority Views, 19–20, Senate Research Files of William B. Welsh, File 17, Lehman Papers, Columbia University.
72. Report to the National Security Council by the Operations Co-ordinating Board concerning the Admission into the United States of Certain Escapees from Communist Domination, January 28, 1955, RG 59, Box 37.
73. Larry Wolff, *Inventing Eastern Europe: The Map of Civilization on the Mind of the Enlightenment* (Stanford, Calif.: Stanford University Press, 1994).
74. Alphonse de Custine, *Journey for Our Time: The Journals of the Marquis de Custine*, (London: Arthur Baker, 1953), introduction by Walter Bedell Smith,12–13.
75. Buff, *Immigration and Political Economy of Home*, 59.
76. Immigration and Nationality Act—Message from the President of the United States (H. Doc. No. 520), reproduced in *Cong. Rec.*, 82nd Cong., 2nd sess., vol. 98, part 6, 8082–85.
77. Walter cited by Cabell Phillips, "That Phony Refugee Law," *Harper's Magazine*, April 1955, 71.
78. Alona E. Evans, "Political Refugees and the United States Immigration Laws: A Case Note," *The American Journal of International Law* 62.4 (October 1968): 921–26, 921; Otto Kirchheimer, "Asylum," *The American Political Science Review* 53.4 (December 1959): 992.
79. Cox to Morgan, December 31, 1952, EP, File 2, HSTL.
80. Statement by Philip B. Perlman to the Subcommittee on Escapees and Refugees of the Senate Committee on the Judiciary, June 16, 1955, Senate Research Files of William B. Welsh, D 362, Folder 13, Lehman Papers.
81. "New York Democratic Delegation Points Out Utter Failure of the Operation of the Refugee Relief Act of 1953," press release, May 16, 1955, Senate Research Files of William B. Welsh, D 362, Folder 13, Lehman Papers.
82. Phillips, "Phony Refugee Law," 69.
83. Ibid., 72.
84. Statement to the President's Commission on Immigration and Naturalization by Edward M. O'Connor, "Escapees from Communism," October 27, 1952, ENGROSS, File 1, HSTL.
85. Cox to Morgan, December 31, 1952, EP, File 2, HSTL.
86. TROY, 11. In December 1955, Washington still expressed interest in "land settlement projects in Latin America"; OCB, "Report on Assistance Programs in Behalf of Refugees and Escapees of Interest under NSC 86/1," December 2, 1955, RG 59, Box 37.
87. Isaac Don Levine, "A Weapon for the West: Here Is a Way to Induce Soviet Occupation Troops to Desert," *Life*, March 23, 1953, 98.
88. The "paper wall" phrase was coined by Claiborne Pell (D-RI) in 1962; cited by Cheryl Shanks, *Immigration and the Politics of American Sovereignty, 1890–1990* (Ann Arbor: University of Michigan Press, 2001), 156.
89. H. W. Brands, "A Cold War Foreign Legion? The Eisenhower Administration and the Volunteer Freedom Corps," *Military Affairs* 52 (January 1988): 7–11; James Jay Carafano, "Mobilizing Europe's Stateless: America's Plans for a Cold War Army," *Journal of Cold War Studies* 1.2 (spring 1999): 61–85.
90. Stoessinger, *The Refugee and the World Community*, 176.
91. PSB D-18/a.
92. PSB D-18a/5, October 23, 1952, FY 1954 Escapee Budget, ENFROSS, File 1, HSTL. On broadcasting behind the iron curtain, Robert T. Holt, *Radio Free Europe*, (Minneapolis: University of Minnesota Press, 1958), 285.
93. Escapee Program Report to the OCB, August 17, 1954, RG 59, Records Relating to State Department Participation in NSC and OCB, Box 38.
94. Draft Program for Soviet Orbit Escapees, December 11, 1951, EP, File 1, HSTL.

95. Marshall D. Shulman, March 15, 1951, Records of the PPS, 1947–53, Subject Files, RG 59, Box 11a; Trends Favoring Communism and Possible Remedial Action, Records of the PPS, 1947–53, RG 59, Box 8; Draft Program for Soviet Orbit Escapees, December 11, 1951, EP, File 1, HSTL.
96. C. D. Jackson, Henry Luce, DeWitt Wallace, General William Donovan, and David Sarnoff played active roles in the National Committee for a Free Europe and its fund-raising wing, the "Crusade for Freedom." Loescher and Scanlan, *Calculated Kindness*, 39.
97. Department of State Recommendations on Agenda Item No. 5(a)—Progress Report on Escapee Phase A Program, August 7, 1952, EP, File 2, HSTL.
98. Izydor Modelski, "I Saw Red Spies at Work in Washington," *Look*, May 10, 1949, 10, 49–57.
99. *Escape to Freedom*, (Washington: Foreign Operations Administration, 1954), 18–20; "A MiG from a Red Renegade," *Life*, March 16, 1953; Franciszek Jarecki, "Flights for Freedom Pierce Iron Curtain," *Life*, April 6, 1953.
100. Richard Fried, *The Russians Are Coming! The Russians Are Coming! Pageantry and Patriotism in Cold-War America* (New York: Oxford University Press, 1998), 48.
101. *Assistance to Escapees*, 10.
102. Peter Pirogov, *Why I Escaped* (New York: Duell, Sloan, and Pearce, 1950); Vladimir Petrov, *My Retreat From Russia* (New Haven, Conn.: Yale University Press); Louis Fischer, *Thirteen Who Fled* (New York: Harper, 1949).
103. Elia Kazan, director, *Man on a Tightrope* (Twentieth Century Fox, 1953).
104. Thomas Caldecott Chubb, "The Ingenuity of Freedom," *Saturday Review*, February 20, 1954, 27.
105. Susan L. Carruthers, "*The Manchurian Candidate* and the Cold War Brainwashing Scare," *Historical Journal of Film, Radio, and Television* 18.1 (March 1998): 75–94.
106. Memo by W. Bradley Connors, August 12, 1952, EP, File 2, HSTL.
107. USIA Progress Report on U.S. Escapee Program, October 13, 1954, Records relating to State Department Participation in OCB and NSC, RG 59, Box 38.
108. Pearson, "Iron Curtain Refugees Neglected."
109. Minutes of the Interdepartmental Escapee Committee, Records relating to State Department Participation in OCB and NSC, RG 59, Boxes 6 and 7.
110. "U.S. Embassy Aide Quits in Moscow," *New York Times*, February 28, 1948.
111. Virginia Pasley, *21 Stayed* (New York: Farrar, Straus, and Cudahy, 1955).
112. Ginsburgs, "Soviet Union and the Problem of Refugees," 359.
113. "Baiting the Trap," *Newsweek*, March 12, 1956; "A Diplomatic Kidnapping on U.S. Soil," *Newsweek*, April 23, 1956.
114. TROY, 4.
115. Joseph Alsop, "Men Without Countries," *International Herald Tribune*, March 21, 1951.
116. Soguk, *States and Strangers*, 16.
117. Lippert, "Governing Refugees," 305.
118. Lodge, Record of Meeting of the Ad Hoc Committee on NSC 143, March 27, 1953, *Foreign Relations of the United States*, 1952–1954, vol. 8, 199.
119. Given the intersection of superpower competition and civil rights activism such issues were hardly invisible; Mary L. Dudziak, *Cold War Civil Rights: Race and the Image of American Democracy* (Princeton, N.J.: Princeton University Press, 2000).
120. George Urban, *Radio Free Europe and the Pursuit of Democracy* (New Haven, Conn.: Yale University Press, 1997).
121. Aaron Levenstein, *Escape to Freedom: the Story of the International Rescue Committee* (Westport, Conn.: Greenwood Press, 1983), 36, 55; Loescher and Scanlan, *Calculated Kindness*, 54.
122. Marrus, *The Unwanted*, 360–61.

The Biopolitics of Security: Oil, Empire, and the Sports Utility Vehicle

David Campbell

In the wake of 9/11 the Bush administration has called upon established foreign policy discourses to cement the idea of a nation at war.[1] Given the amorphous and often virtual nature of the "war on terror," in which the adversary is by definition largely unseen, the association of other resistant elements with terrorism has become a mechanism for materializing the threat. Notorious in this regard was the Bush administration's linking of internal and external threats by aligning individual drug use at home with support for terrorism abroad. In itself, this is not a new argument, with alleged links to terrorism having been featured in previous episodes of the country's "war on drugs."[2] However, the Bush administration went one step further by making a causal connection between individual behavior and international danger. In 2002, the Office for National Drug Control Policy (ONDCP) launched a campaign of hard-hitting advertisements in which the social choices of hedonistic youngsters were said to directly enrich and enable terrorists threatening the United States.[3]

Others at Home and Abroad Post-9/11

This argument, which was controversial, sought to discipline domestic behavior by linking it to external danger. One ironic response to the campaign, first made by columnist Arianna Huffington, was to argue that if funding terrorism was the concern, then "soccer moms" driving sport utility vehicles (SUVs) were more easily linked to the problem through the increased revenues for Middle East oil producers their reliance on an uneconomical family vehicle generated. Huffington reported that two Hollywood producers had written spoof scripts for advertisements that parodied the ONDCP campaign. Linking individual consumer choice with the international threat of the moment, one of these scripts declared the SUVs parked in families' driveways to be "the biggest weapons of mass destruction."[4]

Huffington's column generated considerable debate, and a new lobby group—the Detroit Project—was launched so the anti-SUV advertisements could be produced and broadcast as part of a campaign to link improved fuel efficiency with national security. Although most television stations refused to air the commercials (demonstrating a corporate fear of controversy), they garnered much attention, and came to highlight the cultural clash between SUV manufacturers and users and those concerned about the vehicles' communal effects.[5]

This controversy raged in the months leading up to the U.S.–led invasion of Iraq in 2003 and was part of a larger discourse about the relationship between oil and security. While the ONDCP campaign targeted the casual narcotic user, the Detroit Project advertisements in effect saw the United States as an addict whose oil habit could be satisfied only by an act of international crime. Both arguments sought to individualize responsibility by positing a tight causal connection between personal choice and political effect, thereby following in a long line of issues whose social and political context have been subsumed by the politics of individualization. While the Detroit Project advertisements simplified issues in a manner akin to the ONDCP campaign, in the context of the relationship between oil and security, they did raise difficult issues with respect to the relationship between the domestic and the foreign.

While individual SUV owner-drivers cannot be said to directly endorse terrorism simply as a result of automotive choice, it is the case that the SUV has come to underpin U.S. dependence on imported oil. This dependence in turn underpins the U.S. strategic interest in global oil supply, especially in the Middle East, where the American military presence has generated such animus. As a result, the SUV symbolizes the need for the U.S. to maintain its global military reach. Given the dangers this global military presence provokes, it might be possible to say the SUV is one of America's greatest national security threats. This article explores the validity of those connections as part of a critical examination and retheorization of the relationship between oil and security. Its aim is to conceptualize the relationship between individual choices and geopolitical effects, yet to do so without adopting the moral leveling of crude arguments that demonize certain individual behaviors in the correlation of drugs, oil, and terror.

Central to this rethinking of the relationship between oil and security is an appreciation of the role law has played in making the SUV possible, and the way different laws have combined to produce a series of cultural, social, and political effects that stretch beyond America's borders. U.S. environmental legislation in the early 1970s—especially the Clean Air Act of 1970 and the

Energy Policy Conservation Act of 1975, which established fuel economy standards—permitted the differential treatment of cars and light trucks, which the automakers exploited to the detriment of both efficiency and the environment. The rise of the SUV has also been made possible by building codes, zoning regulations, and legislation such as the Interstate Highways and Defense Act of 1956, all of which have materialized urban America's reliance on private transport. Supported further by tax rebates and trade tariffs, the SUV has come to embody a form of radically individualistic citizenship that is being underwritten by new developments in jurisprudence.[6] However, the impact of domestic law reaches beyond domestic society. Contrary to the new citizenship's ethos of autonomy and disconnection, the SUV has played a role in creating a number of international legal effects, most notably the United States' rejection of the Kyoto Protocol to the United Nations Framework Convention on Climate Change and the illegal invasion of Iraq.

The conceptual starting point for the required rethinking of the relationship between oil and security is that the interconnections between what appear as individual consumer preferences for certain vehicles and their geopolitical effects should be regarded as part of a complex called "automobility." In John Urry's assessment, "automobility can be conceptualized as a self-organizing autopoietic, non-linear system that spreads worldwide, and includes cars, car-drivers, roads, petroleum supplies and many novel objects, technologies and signs."[7] As a complex system, automobility has profoundly affected the social and geographical structure of daily life. In the environment it has spawned, the territorialities of home, leisure, and work have been "unbundled" such that urbanism has been "splintered."[8]

While automobility is recognized as a worldwide system, notwithstanding the occasional references to oil rich states, petroleum supplies, and import dependence, the focus of the literature is principally domestic, with relatively little attention to the global security context.[9] This essay argues that with the unbundling of domestic territorialities in the context of new global networks, we need to appreciate the way (especially though not exclusively in the United States) the "unbounded" consumption of automobility produces an "unbordered" sense of the state in which security interests extend well beyond the national homeland.

At the same time, this deterritorialization of the space of automobility and its security effects does not mean we exist above and beyond territory. To the contrary, the globalization of automobility and its security implications results in the creation of new borderlands with uneven consequences. These borderlands are conventionally understood as distant, wild places of insecurity where foreign intervention will be necessary to ensure domestic interests are secured. They include zones of exploration and the spaces traversed by pipelines, both of which involve the further marginalization of impoverished indigenous communities. The fate of these people and places is subsumed by the privilege accorded a resource (oil) that is central to the American way of life, the security of which is regarded as a fundamental strategic issue.[10]

However, if we understand borderlands as spatially disparate contact zones where practices intersect, actors and issues meld into one another, and conflicts potentially arise, then the translocal borderlands of automobility encompass networks that connect cultures of individual consumption with practices of global security. They do so through multiple sites of materialization and territorialization at "home" and "abroad." As a consequence, this argument intends not only to supplement the automobility literature's focus on the "inside," but also to overcome the way arguments about resource conflicts emphasize the "outside." This essay thus aims to bring the question of security into the heart of the concern with automobility to demonstrate how these consumer practices contribute to the production of national identity.

The first step in this argument is to reconceptualize the relationship between foreign policy, security, and identity so we can appreciate what is at stake in linking internal behaviors with external threats at this juncture in American politics. This allows us to set the grounds for a spatial understanding that goes beyond the "domestic" versus the "foreign." The second step is to consider how the domain of the cultural, social, and political can be conceptualized so that the complexity of the interconnections can be appreciated. Central to this is an understanding of the way "domestic" law, regulation, and policy work to create the geopolitics of identity in the new borderlands of automobility. This is illustrated in this essay's third and fourth sections, which tell the story of U.S. oil consumption, automobility, and regulation. Regulation refers to more than governmental policy; it encompasses the question of the production of desire. An account of the SUV's rise to popularity as family transport in the United States thus demonstrates how questions of geopolitics and identity are linked to a cultural politics of desire that exists beyond the institutionalized sites of the state. The SUV is the icon through which the relationship of security to automobility can be best understood, precisely because the SUV constitutes a cultural site that transgresses the inside and outside of the nation and—through the conceptualizations of security it both embodies and invokes—because the SUV folds the foreign back into the domestic, thereby rendering each problematic.

Figure 1.
Photograph by Amy Alkon, advicegoddess.com.

Together these elements will demonstrate that the predominant representation of oil as simply an external, material cause of insecurity is insufficient for a more comprehensive and nuanced understanding of contemporary geopolitics. However, while this article was prompted by and written in the context of the U.S.–led invasion of Iraq and its aftermath, the argument is not seeking to explain the causes of and reasons for that invasion (fig. 1).[11] Instead, it seeks to articulate an understanding of the conditions of possibility for the specific decisions that led to that invasion as a particular moment of U.S. (and allied) global strategy. The effect of this U.S.–led security strategy is to "reborder" the state in a multitude of cultural and political sites as a way of containing the social forces that have splintered both conventional locales and frames of reference.

Foreign Policy, Security, and Identity: From Geopolitics to Biopolitics

As an imagined community, the state can be seen as the effect of formalized practices and ritualized acts that operate in its name or in the service of its ideals. This understanding, which is enabled by shifting our theoretical commitments from a belief in pregiven subjects to a concern with the problematic of subjectivity, renders foreign policy as a boundary-producing political performance in which the spatial domains of inside/outside, self/other, and domestic/foreign are constituted through the writing of threats as externalized dangers.

The narratives of primary and stable identities that continue to govern much of the social sciences obscure such an understanding. In international relations these concepts of identity limit analysis to a concern with the domestic influences on foreign policy; this perspective allows for a consideration of the influence of the internal forces on state identity, but it assumes that the external is a fixed reality that presents itself to the pregiven state and its agents. In contrast, by assuming that the identity of the state is performatively constituted, we can argue that there are no foundations of state identity that exist prior to the problematic of identity/difference that situates the state within the framework of inside/outside and self/other. Identity is constituted in relation to difference, and difference is constituted in relation to identity, which means that the "state," the "international system," and the "dangers" to each are coeval in their construction.

Over time, of course, ambiguity is disciplined, contingency is fixed, and dominant meanings are established. In the history of U.S. foreign policy—regardless of the radically different contexts in which it has operated—the formalized practices and ritualized acts of security discourse have worked to produce a conception of the United States in which freedom, liberty, law, democracy, individualism, faith, order, prosperity, and civilization are claimed to exist because of the constant struggle with and often violent suppression of opponents said to embody tyranny, oppression, anarchy, totalitarianism, collectivism, atheism, and barbarism.

This record demonstrates that the boundary-producing political performance of foreign policy does more than inscribe a geopolitical marker on a map. This construction of social space also involves an axiological dimension in which the delineation of an inside from an outside gives rise to a moral hierarchy that renders the domestic superior and the foreign inferior. Foreign policy thus incorporates an ethical power of segregation in its performance of identity/difference. While this produces a geography of "foreign" (even "evil") others in conventional terms, it also requires a disciplining of "domestic" elements on the inside that challenge this state identity. This is achieved through exclusionary practices in which resistant elements to a secure identity on the "inside" are linked through a discourse of "danger" with threats identified and located on the "outside." Though global in scope, these effects are national in their legitimation.[12]

The ONDCP drugs and terror campaign was an overt example of this sort of exclusionary practice. However, the boundary-producing political performances of foreign policy operate within a global context wherein relations of sovereignty are changing. Although Michael Hardt and Antonio Negri have overplayed the transition from modern sovereignty to imperial sovereignty in *Empire*, there is little doubt that new relations of power and identity are present. According to Hardt and Negri, in our current condition,

> Empire establishes no territorial center of power and does not rely on fixed boundaries or barriers. It is a decentered and deterritorializing apparatus of rule that progressively incorporates the entire global realm within its open, expanding frontiers. Empire manages hybrid identities, flexible hierarchies, and plural exchanges through modulating networks of command. The distinct national colors of the imperialist map of the world have merged and blended in the imperial global rainbow.[13]

As shall be argued here, the sense of fading national colors is being resisted by the reassertion of national identity boundaries through foreign policy's writing of danger in a range of cultural sites. Nonetheless, this takes place within the context of flow, flexibility, and reterritorialization summarized by Hardt and Negri. Moreover, these transformations are part and parcel of change in the relations of production. As Hardt and Negri declare: "In the postmodernization of the global economy, the creation of wealth tends ever more toward what we will call biopolitical production, the production of social life itself, in which the economic, the political, and the cultural increasingly overlap and invest one another."[14] While the implied periodization of the term *postmodernization* renders it problematic, the notion of biopolitics, with its connecting and penetrative networks across and through all domains of life, opens up new possibilities for conceptualizing the complex relationships that embrace oil, security, U.S. policy, and the SUV. In Todd Gitlin's words, "the SUV is the place where foreign policy meets the road."[15] It is also the place where the road affects foreign policy. Biopolitics is a key concept in understanding how those meetings take place.

Michel Foucault argues that biopolitics arrives with the historical transformation in waging war from the defense of the sovereign to securing the existence of a population. In Foucault's argument, this historical shift means that decisions to fight are made in terms of collective survival, and killing is justified by the necessity of preserving life.[16] It is this centering of the life of the population rather than the safety of the sovereign or the security of territory that is the hallmark of biopolitical power that distinguishes it from sovereign power. Giorgio Agamben has extended the notion through the concept of the administration of life and argues that the defense of life often takes place in a zone of indistinction between violence and the law such that sovereignty can be violated in the name of life.[17] Indeed, the biopolitical privileging of life has provided the rationale for some of the worst cases of mass death, with genocide deemed "understandable" as one group's life is violently secured through the demise of another group.[18]

However, the role of biopolitical power in the administration of life is equally obvious and ubiquitous in domains other than the extreme cases of violence or war. The difference between the sovereign and the biopolitical can be understood in terms of the contrast between Foucault's notion of "disciplinary society" and Gilles Deleuze's conception of "the society of control," a distinction that plays an important role in Hardt and Negri's *Empire.* According to Hardt and Negri, in the disciplinary society, "social command is constructed through a diffuse network of *dispositifs* or apparatuses that produce and regulate customs, habits, and productive practices." In the society of control, "mechanisms of command become ever more democratic, ever more immanent to the social field, distributed throughout the brains and bodies of the citizens." This means that the society of control is "characterized by an intensification and generalization of the normalizing apparatuses of disciplinarity that internally animate our common and daily practices, but in contrast to discipline, this control extends well outside the structured sites of social institutions through flexible and fluctuating networks."[19]

Network is, therefore, the prevailing metaphor for social organization in the era of biopolitical power, and it is a conception that permits us to understand how the effects of our actions, choices, and life are propagated beyond the boundaries of our time-space location.[20] It is also a conception that allows us to appreciate how war has come to have a special prominence in producing the political order of liberal societies. Networks, through their extensive connectivity, function in terms of their strategic interactions. This means that "social relations become suffused with considerations of power, calculation, security and threat."[21] As a result, "global biopolitics operates as a strategic game in which the principle of war is assimilated into the very weft and warp of the socio-economic and cultural networks of biopolitical relations."[22]

This theoretical concern with biopolitical relations of power in the context of networked societies is consistent with an analytical shift to the problematic of subjectivity as central to understanding the relationship between foreign policy and identity. That is because both are concerned with "a shift from a preoccupation with physical and isolated entities, whose relations are described largely in terms of interactive exchange, to beings-in-relation, whose structures [are] decisively influenced by patterns of connectivity."[23] At the same time, while conceptual approaches are moving away from understandings premised on the existence of physical and isolated entities, the social and political structures that are produced by network patterns of connectivity often appear to be physical and isolated. As Lieven de Cauter argues, we don't live in networks; we live in capsules. Capsules are enclaves and envelopes that function as nodes, hubs, and termini in the various networks and contain a multitude of spaces and scales. These enclaves can include states, gated communities, or vehicles—with the latter two manifesting the "SUV model of citizenship" Mitchell has provocatively described.[24] Nonetheless, though capsules like these appear physical and isolated, there is "no network without capsules. The more networking, the more capsules. Ergo: the degree of capsularisation is directly proportional to the growth of networks."[25] The result is that biopolitical relations of power produce new borderlands that transgress conventional understandings of inside/outside and isolated/connected.

Together these shifts pose a major theoretical challenge to much of the social sciences, which have adhered ontologically to a distinction between the ideal and the material, which privileges economistic renderings of complex social assemblages.[26] As we shall see, overcoming this challenge does not mean denying the importance of materialism but, rather, moving beyond a simplistic consideration of objects by reconceptualizing materialism so it is understood as interwoven with cultural, social, and political networks. This means that "paying increased attention to the material actually requires a more expansive engagement with the immaterial."[27]

The Biopolitics of Oil and Security

Most accounts of the role of oil in U.S. foreign policy embody economistic assumptions, rendering oil in materialistic terms as an independent variable that causes states to behave in particular ways. In the prelude to the invasion of Iraq, even the best commentaries represented oil as the real reason motivating the buildup to war.[28] In this vein, a Greenpeace campaign pictured the (oil) "drums of war" and invited people to read about "what's really behind the war on Iraq."[29] In addition to manifesting specific epistemological assumptions, these views regard resource geopolitics as primarily a question of supply. Before we move beyond this frame of reference to explore what goes unexplained by this focus, we need to appreciate the infrastructure of oil resource geopolitics that makes this issue so important.

Securing global oil supply has been a tenet of U.S. foreign policy in the post–World War II era. Because the Middle East holds two-thirds of the known reserves of oil, this objective has made the region an unavoidable concern for successive U.S. administrations. As the largest and most economical supplier of Middle East oil, Saudi Arabia has had a central place in this strategic calculation, with the United States agreeing to defend (internally and externally) the Saudi regime in return for privileged access to Saudi oil. Over the years, this arrangement has cost the United States tens of billions of dollars in military assistance.[30] This strategy was formalized in the Carter Doctrine of 1980, which, in the wake of the Soviet invasion of Afghanistan, declared that any power that threatened to control the Persian Gulf area would be directly challenging fundamental U.S. national security interests and would be seen as engaged in an assault on the United States.

None of this would be required if the United States did not rely on imported oil for its economic well-being. However, in 2002 oil imports fueled 53 percent of domestic consumption, and the U.S. Department of Energy forecasts only increasing dependence. By 2025 oil import dependence is expected to rise to around 70 percent of domestic needs.[31] These percentages mean the United States will consume an additional 8.7 million barrels of oil per day by 2025. Given that total petroleum imports in 2002 were 11.4 million barrels per day, this is a very substantial increase.

In recent years, faced with increased dependence on oil imports, the United States has been seeking to diversify supply, with some paradoxical outcomes. As the country was preparing to go to war with Iraq, the United States was importing half of all Iraqi exports (which satisfied only 8 percent of America's needs), even though this indirectly funded the regime of Saddam Hussein.[32] Some Republicans in Congress used this data to smear then-Democratic Senate leader Tom Daschle as an Iraqi sympathizer, arguing that the Democrat's failure to support drilling in the Arctic National Wildlife Refuge (ANWR)—as the Bush administration desired—forced America into unholy commercial alliances.[33] While this argument conveniently overlooked the fact that ANWR's 3 billion barrels of reserves could supply only six months of the United States' total oil needs, it demonstrated how the internalization of a cleavage between business and environmental interests is sustained through an association with external threat.[34]

The drive for diversification is now a major security objective. In the 2001 review of energy policy chaired by Vice President Dick Cheney, the final chapter of the report focused exclusively on strengthening global alliances with energy producers to achieve that goal.[35] However, the geopolitical pursuit of energy security is likely to produce new and intensive forms of insecurity for those in the new resource zones, which are located in some of the most strategically unstable global locations.[36] As a result, the United States has been providing increased military support to governments in the Caspian Basin area, Latin America, and sub-Saharan Africa—regardless of their ideological complexion or human rights record.[37]

A geopolitical understanding of these developments is necessary but not sufficient. That is because the geopolitical frame focuses solely on the supply of oil without interrogating the demand for this resource that makes it so valuable. Possession of a material resource is meaningless unless social networks value that resource. As such, an analysis of the demand side, and attention to the politics of consumption as much as the problem of production, is a first step toward understanding the biopolitics of security.

The Production and Regulation of Oil Consumption in the United States

The value of oil comes from its centrality to one of the defining characteristics of U.S. society—mobility. It is mobility that drives U.S. oil consumption as the transportation sector accounts for two-thirds of petroleum use. In turn, passenger vehicles are the largest consumers of oil in the transportation sector, using 40 percent of the 20 million barrels of oil consumed each day. Their central role in the consumption of oil is only going to expand, as increases in the number, size, and usage of vehicles propel America's petroleum appetite. Of the additional 8.7 million barrels of oil that will be required each day by 2025, 7.1 million barrels (more than 80 percent) will be needed to fuel the growth in automobility. In global terms, this appetite is staggering, with the U.S. passenger vehicle fleet alone responsible for one-tenth of all petroleum consumption.[38]

There is a regulatory regime designed to address the consumption of oil and the foreign dependence it produces, which, over time, has produced new borders of identity at home and abroad. In response to the oil price hikes of the early 1970s, Congress passed the Energy Policy Conservation Act of 1975, which, in part, established fuel economy guidelines for vehicles.[39] The governance of fuel economy is centered on the Corporate Average Fuel Economy (CAFE) standards, which establish a target figure for the combined output of a particular manufacturer. The objective was to double the 1974 fleet fuel economy average by 1985, with a graded series of improvements up to 27.5 miles per gallon, where it has remained since 1990.[40]

At the heart of the CAFE standards is the distinction between a "car" and a "light truck." Cars are defined simply as "4-wheel vehicle[s] not designed for off-road use" while light trucks are four-wheel vehicles

> designed for off-road operation (has 4-wheel drive or is more than 6,000 lbs. GVWR and has physical features consistent with those of a truck); *or* which is designed to perform at least one of the following functions: (1) transport more than 10 people; (2) provide temporary living quarters; (3) transport property in an open bed; (4) permit greater cargo-carrying capacity than passenger-carrying volume; *or* (5) can be converted to an open bed vehicle by removal of rear seats to form a flat continuous floor with the use of simple tools.[41]

This distinction is significant because when the CAFE regime was established, in contrast to its treatment of cars, Congress did not set a target for the improvement of light truck fuel economy. The first standard came in 1979 (15.8 mpg) and rose to 20.7 mpg in 1996 with a marginal increase to 22.2 mpg required by 2007.[42] These standards fall well short of what is technologically possible in automotive efficiency, with 20.7 mpg being no more than what had been achieved on the road in 1983.[43]

It was a consumer politics of identity that motivated the distinction between cars and light trucks. Automotive manufacturers, industry groups, and their political allies in Congress argued that light trucks were the "workhorses of America," and "commercially vital" for the blue-collar businessmen and farmers who needed cheap transport for their materials. However, by the late 1960s manufacturers had started to stress the family and leisure benefits in advertisements for light trucks, and by the time Congress was creating the distinction between cars and light trucks on the grounds of commercial utility, more than two-thirds of the light trucks on the road were being used as family transport, with nearly three-quarters carrying no freight whatsoever.[44] Moreover, each time the regulations changed, automakers altered their models so they could escape the restrictions set by CAFE standards. When the weight limit for light trucks subject to CAFE standards rose from 6,000 lbs. to 8,500 lbs., automakers kept their products free from the standards by increasing the size of their models to 8,550 lbs. or more. As a result, the regulatory regime turned many light trucks into the heaviest passenger vehicles on the road.[45]

Light trucks did not only benefit from more lenient fuel economy standards. They were granted less restrictive environmental standards and exempted from "gas guzzler" and luxury taxes, and their purchase can be written off against income tax.[46] These benefits were granted because light trucks were a market sector U.S. automakers had almost exclusively to themselves following the imposition in 1964 of a 25 percent tariff on imports. In place for nearly thirty years (and still in place for pickup trucks), these benefits gave U.S. automakers comparative advantage in an underregulated sector of the market, and policymakers have been lobbied incessantly about the need to protect this valuable sector.[47] It is this dynamic that has led the automotive industry to be one of the principal opponents to international climate control agreements. Faced with pressure to improve fuel efficiency in order to reduce emissions, the major manufacturers argued such requirements would harm their economic position, a claim that was pivotal in the Bush administration's decision to withdraw U.S. support for the Kyoto protocol.[48]

Creating Inefficiency and the SUV

The CAFE regulatory regime has helped reduce American oil imports—without these minimal standards the United States would be currently using an additional 2.8 million barrels of oil per day.[49] However, overall this legal framework has failed to curb import dependence. Indeed, the CAFE regulatory regime has had two profoundly negative effects. The first has been to permit an overall *decline* in U.S. automotive efficiency in the last twenty years. While the original goal of the 1975 legislation was achieved in its first decade, fuel economy has been getting worse ever since. Because of the popularity of light trucks, the U.S. vehicle fleet is currently 6 percent less efficient than the peak achieved in 1987–88.[50]

The second consequence of the CAFE regulatory regime is that it has *created* the market position of light trucks that in turn have undermined the original gains in automotive fuel efficiency. The distinction between cars and light trucks created a market niche in which the automakers could profitably produce heavy, inefficient, polluting, and unsafe vehicles. And as the policymakers have made incremental steps toward tightening the regulations, the automakers' drive to escape these controls has meant the production of even larger and less efficient vehicles. According to the Union of Concerned Scientists, this regulatory-induced expansion is "almost like an arms race."[51] This interplay in the network connecting policymakers, auto manufacturers, and consumers is, therefore, a classic example of the strategic interactions that define social relations in a biopolitical context.

Given the favorable regulatory regime, the auto manufacturers have exploited the opportunities afforded light trucks to such a degree they have changed the character of the new vehicle market. With the weak regulatory regime permitting old technology as the basis for light trucks, low production costs mean these vehicles are particularly profitable. As a result, the big three American automakers now make more light trucks than cars, and light trucks (a category including pickups, minivans, and SUVs) outsold cars for the first time in 2001.[52] In particular, the boom in SUV sales (which increased by a factor of 10 to 25 percent in this time) has seen light trucks overtake the car as the favored form of passenger vehicle in the United States.[53] With light trucks constituting 54 percent of the new vehicle market in 2003–04, large pickup trucks became increasingly popular, and automakers ensuring their new "luxury crossover vehicles" are officially classified as light trucks, this sector looks set to dominate family motoring in the United States for some time.[54]

SUVs and the Politics of Desire

While the regulatory regime has constructed the market position of the "light truck," and while the automakers have developed and exploited this market development to profitable ends, it nonetheless took consumers to purchase these products in large numbers for light trucks to surpass the car as the favored passenger vehicle. What, then, is it about light trucks, especially the SUV, which appeals so to American consumer desire?

The genealogy of the SUV can be traced to the Jeep, a small vehicle that came to prominence in World War II. The U.S. Army wanted a light four-wheel-drive truck that could transport troops and a heavy machine gun, and more than half a million were produced. Highly successful in all its tasks, "the Jeep became a sign, the emblem, the alter ego of the American fighting machine."[55] From the outset, then, the SUV has been marked by the military. Once the war had been won, Jeep traded on its military background and attempted to modify and sell its vehicles to the family market. Never very successful, given that the U.S. market then favored stylish and comfortable station wagons for large families, the company stumbled along and was sold to the American Motors Corporation (AMC) in 1969.[56]

When AMC undertook to revitalize the Jeep brand, it noticed that the Wagoneer model was sold mostly to affluent families in urban areas who respected Jeep's military heritage and wanted to be associated with its outdoor image. On the back of this assessment, Jeep sales expanded rapidly in the early 1970s, with *Time* magazine calling the basic model a "macho-chic machine." However, as a basically primitive piece of technology, built on the same World War II truck chassis that made it famous, the Jeep was a vehicle swimming against the tide of environmental consciousness and safety regulation in 1970s America. But Washington policymakers were very reluctant to regulate a weak

Midwest auto producer out of business, so Jeep executives successfully lobbied to have Jeep classified as a truck, thus freeing it from new legislation such as the Clean Air Act of 1970.[57] This established the precedent for differentiating light trucks from cars that the CAFE standards enshrined to such devastating effect.

The military background of the Jeep was part of the heritage that played a role in the development of the model that launched the boom in SUVs—the Ford Explorer. In 1986 when Ford designers began the process of developing a new model line for the 1990s, their methods were more anthropological than automotive:

> They started by trying to take the cultural pulse of the time, paying special attention to the evolving values of the baby boomer generation. They watched some of the most popular movies of the time: *Rambo First Blood, Part II, Rocky IV,* and *Top Gun.* They clipped photographs from magazines and arranged them into a series of large collages, each for a different period of a few years, and were struck by how many people were wearing cowboy hats and other Western attire in their collage of contemporary photos. They took note of the wide media attention give[n] to the two Jeeps that Reagan kept at his ranch near Santa Barbara, California.[58]

The most important SUV was conceived in a time dominated by the paramilitary culture that emerged after, and in response to, America's defeat in Vietnam. Obvious in the Hollywood movies the Ford designers watched, it was manifested as well in "techno-thriller" novels by the likes of Tom Clancy and the emergence of paintball as a popular national game. In this energetic cultural militarism, which saw the remasculinization of American identity, heroes were those individuals who overcome the bureaucratic constraints of daily life, braved abnormal environments to fight America's enemies, and often traveled in exotic vehicles.[59]

Incorporating some of the codes of cultural militarism, the Explorer also embodied elements of the classic rhetoric of American identity, thus demonstrating the way in which vehicles are part of the imaginaries, geographies, and practices of national identity (fig. 2).[60] Baby boomers did not want vehicles akin to the old-fashioned station wagons that had dominated the family vehicle market until the 1990s. Instead, they wanted to use their increasing affluence to express a rugged individualism by purchasing vehicles that allowed them to "to feel a bond with the great outdoors and the American frontier."[61] Central to this was four-wheel-drive technology. Prospective buyers told consumer researchers they almost never used this capacity but wanted it anyway. The fact that 80 percent of SUV owners live in urban areas and no more than 13 percent of their vehicles have been off road does not diminish this

Figure 2. "No Boundaries." Ford Explorer advertisement.

desire (fig. 3).[62] The reasoning behind this paradox was that four-wheel drive

> offered the promise of unfettered freedom to drive anywhere during vacations. These customers might have given up their childhood dreams of becoming firefighters, police officers or superheroes, and had instead become parents with desk jobs and oversized mortgages. But they told Ford researchers that SUVs made them feel like they were still carefree, adventurous spirits who could drop everything and head for the great outdoors at a moment's notice if they really wanted to do so.[63]

Combined with this fantasy of vehicular freedom, SUV owners manifest a concern with social insecurity. French medical anthropologist turned marketing consultant Claude Rapaille argues that SUVs offer the physical embodiment of Americans' concern with "survival and reproduction." According to Rapaille, the United States is a society riven with the fear of crime and other insecurities (even in the period prior to September 11). The same conditions that have led to the private security guard industry and the growth in gated communities are behind the consumer's desire to ensure that the family vehicle offers a high level of personal security. Amidst this neo-medievalization of society, as Americans retreat to our fortified enclaves (or capsules) secure against others, SUVs become "armored cars for the battlefield."[64]

With high front ends, towering driving positions, fenders designed to replicate the haunches of wild animals, and grills intentionally designed to evoke snarling jungle cats, SUVs give their owners an aggressively panoptic disposition to the world.[65] With names like Tracker, Equinox, Freestyle, Escape, Defender, Trail Blazer, Navigator, Pathfinder, and Warrior—or designations that come from American Indians (Cherokee, Navajo) or places in the American West (Tahoe, Yukon)—SUVs populate the crowded urban routes of daily life with representations of the militarized frontier.[66] In the words of one marketing consultant, they say to the outside world: "America, we're risk takers; America, we're rugged."[67] This comes across in interviews with SUV owners in California who, while acknowledging the problems caused by the motoring choice, explain it in terms of security: "The world is becoming a harder and

Figure 3.
"Spread Your Wings." U.K. Land Rover Discovery advertisement.

more violent place to live, so we wrap ourselves with the big vehicles." In the words of another: "It gives you a barrier, makes you feel less threatened" (fig. 4).[68] Crucially, both those voices belong to mothers and indicate how SUVs find particular favor among women. Keen on the high riding position for maximum visibility, women also find that the large ground clearance of their four-wheel drive vehicles intersects with their concerns about security. In one study, respondents surprised researchers by telling them this feature meant "it's easier to see if someone is hiding underneath or lurking behind it."[69] Together these desires coalesce into a sense of the SUV being an "urban assault vehicle" for the homeland city at war—albeit with the expected comforts that also make it a form of "portable civilization"—with the driver as a military figure, confronting, but safe from, an insecure world.[70]

Nowhere do the vectors of security, war, and the SUV intersect more clearly than in the production of the Humvee and Hummer. In 1981 the U.S. military determined that a larger vehicle was required to replace the Jeep. The resulting High Mobility Multipurpose Wheeled Vehicle (or Humvee) came to prominence during the first Gulf War in 1990–91, carrying forward the place of these four-wheel-drive vehicles in the global construction of American identity.[71] The Hummer gained notoriety when Arnold Schwarzenegger purchased

Jeep
THERE'S ONLY ONE
673 DWS
OK, IT'S MASSIVELY OVER-ENGINEERED FOR THE SCHOOL RUN.
AND THE PROBLEM WITH THAT IS WHAT, PRECISELY?
NEW JEEP CHEROKEE 2.8 CRD AUTOMATIC It's not the only vehicle on the road with a torquey, fuel-efficient, common rail diesel engine, a 5 speed automatic gearbox, independent front suspension or a highly sophisticated 4-wheel drive system. But it is the only one that's built like a Jeep Cherokee. For a limited period, prices start at £16,995* for the 2.4 Sport and £20,525* for the 2.8 CRD Sport shown. Reasonable enough, when you think what goes into it. www.jeep.co.uk or call 0800 616 159.
Model featured Jeep Cherokee 2.8 CRD Sport (Auto) with Alloy Wheels and Special Paint £20,525* OTR. *Cherokee prices include £1000 cashback available on all models registered before 30.09.03.
Jeep Cherokee 2.8 Common Rail Diesel mpg(L/100km), 20.6(13.7) urban, 33.6(8.4) ex-urban, 27.4(10.3) combined (CO2 274 g/km).

one for civilian use, provoking the manufacturers to see how they could benefit from the then-emerging SUV boom. As with early Jeeps, the first Humvee was a crude vehicle, so in 2001 the company produced a more refined but still gargantuan Hummer H2. Said to be infused with "military-derived DNA," the H2 was regarded by its owners as embodying "testosterone."[72] In the wake of the September 11 attacks, the already favorable consumer ratings for the Hummer soared as people prioritized personal security at a time of permanent and unconventional war.

Figure 4.
"Massively Over-Engineered for the School Run." U.K. Jeep Cherokee advertisement.

With televised coverage of the invasion of Iraq once again foregrounding the Humvee, the Hummer H2 became the best-selling large luxury SUV in America (with women accounting for one-third of all purchases). Hummer owners have exhibited a profound patriotism, and the vehicles have come to occupy a special cultural place (as the featured vehicle on the popular TV show *CSI: Miami*, for example). As one H2 owner declared, "When I turn on the TV, I see wall-to-wall Humvees, and I'm proud . . . They're not out there in Audi A4's . . . I'm proud of my country, and I'm proud to be driving a product that is making a significant contribution."[73] Advertisements for the Hummer have called up all the reasons people favor SUVs and are leavened with some measure of self-parody. Alongside images of the H2, the tag lines include "When the asteroid hits and civilization crumbles, you'll be ready"; "It only looks like this because it is badass"; and—with special appeal to the prospective female customer—"A new way to threaten men." One Hummer poster, for which the copywriters might not have appreciated the contemporary geopolitical significance of their statement, inadvertently encapsulated the H2's meaning: "Excessive. In a Rome at the height its power sort of way" (fig. 5).[74]

Unsurprisingly, the in-your-face-attitude of the Hummer (part of "the axles of evil") has made it a favorite target of protest groups campaigning against SUVs, ranging from Web sites abusing H2 owners to the satire of Bill Maher and Micah Ian Wright, the evangelical "What Would Jesus Drive?" campaign, and the Earth Liberation Front's (ELF) arson against the vehicles.[75] Responding to what the FBI regards as "domestic terrorism" by the ELF, Hummer owners have wrapped the flag ever more tightly around their vehicle. According to the founder of the International Hummer Owners Group (IHOG [*sic*]), "the H2 is an American icon . . . it's a symbol of what we all hold so dearly above all else, the fact we have the freedom of choice, the freedom of happiness, the freedom of adventure and discovery, and the ultimate freedom of expression. Those who deface a Hummer in words or deeds . . . deface the American flag and what it stands for."[76]

Figure 5.
"Excessive. In a Rome at the Height of Its Power Sort of Way." Hummer print advertisement, 2002.

Excess in the automotive world is not restricted to the Hummer, however. In many ways it has been only the most obvious manifestation of a recent trend. At the 2003 Detroit motor show, on the eve of war with Iraq, many new models with vast engines and enhanced power were displayed. With styling cues taken from the muscle cars of the 1960s (which were produced prior to the onset of the "Vietnam syndrome"), these new designs were read as bold assertions of "American technological virtuosity" and "American self-confidence." At the same time, this bravado—what Claude Rapaille labeled a "return to pride and power"—was seen as a response to the political climate of crisis and fear.[77]

This trend was epitomized when Ford unveiled its new concept vehicle, the SYN^{US} (a name derived from "synthesis" and "urban sanctuary" to emphasize that the outside is about security while the inside is about a high-tech life) at the 2005 Detroit motor show (fig. 6).[78] Although a small SUV, the SYN^{US} demonstrates how the foreign is folded back into the domestic by reference to the border zones of contemporary urban life. As the promotional blurb argues, "as the population shifts back to the big cities, you'll need a rolling urban command center. Enter the SYN^{US} concept vehicle, a mobile techno sanctuary sculpted in urban armor and inspired by the popular B-cars of congested international hotspots." The styling is "intimidating"; it deploys protective shutters when parked and has bullet-resistant windows, all designed to make

Figure 6.
"Vaulting into the Urban Future." Ford SYN[US] ad from http://www.fordvehicles.com/autoshow/concept/synus/ (accessed June 29, 2005).

"any mission possible." At the same time as it takes the notion of an urban assault vehicle to its logical conclusion, it also parades a fine sense of portable civilization, with an interior that can be "a mini-home theater with multi-configuration seating and multi-media work station . . . Plus, you can monitor your surroundings in real time as seen by the rear-mounted cameras."[79] There could be no finer transport for the new SUV citizen.

What these developments indicate is the extent to which the discourses of homeland security are being materialized in automotive form. As De Cauter argues, the fear produced by networks unbundling and splintering our locales means we retreat to capsules, but this increased capsularization only enhances fear, which in turn drives further capsularization. By addressing cultural anxieties with embodiments of material power, the U.S. auto industry is therefore pursuing a path familiar to national security policy. But this response is also paradoxical, because meeting insecurities founded on oil dependence with products that will consume ever more petroleum is simply to promote the conditions of crisis.

Paradoxes of the SUV

Much about the rise of the SUV appears paradoxical. Given the centrality of security to the appeal of the SUV, the foremost paradox of these vehicles concerns safety. SUV owners are convinced the size of their vehicles is synonymous with their safety, while accident records show SUVs are more dangerous than cars. The occupant death rate per million SUVs is some 6 percent higher than the equivalent for cars, meaning that an additional three thousand people die annually because they are in SUVs rather than cars, thereby replicating the death toll of September 11 every year.[80] The principal reason for the SUV's poor safety record is its tendency to roll over in accidents. The vehicle height that owners cherish for its ground clearance and visibility makes SUVs prone to tip easily. Rollovers account for one-third of all road deaths in the United States, and the fatality rate for rollovers in SUVs is three times higher than for rollovers in cars, but neither the industry nor the regulators have addressed this problem.[81]

In collisions that do not result in rollovers, SUVs do offer their occupants greater safety when compared with those in the other vehicle. However, the safety of SUV occupants comes at the cost of substantially higher death rates for those they collide with. When SUVs hit a car from the side, the occupant of the car is twenty-nine times more likely to be killed than those riding in the SUV.[82] What this means is that in collisions that do not result in rollovers, SUVs achieve their relative safety by externalizing danger. Keith Bradsher has concluded that "for each [Ford] Explorer driver whose life is saved in a two-vehicle conclusion by choosing an Explorer instead of a large car, an extra five drivers are killed in vehicles struck by Explorers."[83] This has led the current head of the NHTSA to lament that "the theory that I am going to protect myself and my family even if it costs other peoples lives has been the operative incentive for the design of these vehicles, and that's just wrong."[84] But in the absence of regulation, individuals faced with growing numbers of SUVs on the road are going to opt for these vehicles, even though this will increase the collective danger. The result, in Bradsher's words, is a "highway arms race."[85]

Other paradoxes in the rise of the SUV also involve the relationship between the individual and the collective. The SUV's popularity is drawn from its association with the freedom and rugged individuality of the frontier, but the dominant market position of the light truck sector would not have been possible without the regulatory designs of Washington bureaucrats and politicians. The SUV invokes notions of wilderness and adventure, even though its owners, who rarely if ever venture beyond the urban, are driving a vehicle that is highly damaging to the environment.[86] And SUV owners defend their vehicle choice against criticisms of these kinds by invoking an American's right to be free of government and regulation, even though the entire infrastructure of motoring that makes it possible to choose one model over another—road construction, maintenance, law enforcement, and the like—requires a state subsidy upward of $2.4 trillion annually.[87] The pervasiveness of these paradoxes stems from the way individual choices are part of a biopolitical whole with geopolitical consequences, something signaled by the concept of automobility.

The Auto Social Formation of Automobility

The concept of automobility—or that of the "auto social formation" or "car culture"—calls attention to the hybrid assemblage or machinic complex that the apparently autonomous entities of car and driver compose.[88] In the "automobilized time-space" of contemporary society we can observe a networked, sociotechnical infrastructure that is in process, an infrastructure in which there is "the ceaseless and mobile interplay between many different scales, from the body to the globe."[89] Automobility thus is one dimension of empire, in the sense proposed by Hardt and Negri.

The relationship between the auto and the urban has always been at its strongest in the United States. The beautification of cities through the construction of avenues, malls, and parkways in the early twentieth century coincided with and furthered the rise of the automobile.[90] While the development of technology was obviously important, a transformation in American urban culture—wherein streets came to be viewed as traffic ways rather than recreational social spaces—was fundamental to the creation of the auto social formation.[91] Most obvious in the urban planning of Robert Moses, whose bridges, expressways, and parkways transformed New York City and its environs, these infrastructural developments came to be the leitmotif of modernity.[92] National highway systems became the centerpieces of utopian plans—as in General Motors' "Futurama" in the 1939 World's Fair in New York—and were realized in the cold war years as a consequence of the Interstate Highways and Defense Act of 1956.[93]

Although constructed as a means to achieve the unification of social life, the web of traffic routes that permeate urban space have in practice furthered the fragmentation of the urban and its peri-urban and suburban spaces, creating in the process new borderlands (which in turn require new capsules of security).[94] The distanciation of life elements (home from work, family from friends, haves from have nots) that are part of this urban fissure in turn promotes further reliance on automobility as people seek to overcome, traverse, or bypass these divisions. Importantly, this partitioning of the urban world has been codified in and encouraged by planning legislation. Embodying a functionalist view of the city as an organized machine, American urban planners from the 1920s on relied on a system of zoning controls that separated uses and imposed homogenous criteria on specified areas. Hostile to mixed usage or hybrid formations, these uniform zoning codes (known as Euclidean zoning after a 1926 Supreme Court decision in favor of the village of Euclid) have produced urban sprawl and the elongation of travel routes.[95] In the absence of public transport systems, these urban forms have further increased reliance on the car. For residents of the border zones known as "edge cities," there is little choice but to rely on private transport for mobility. Contemporary urban life is both sustained by oil in the form of the car and requires increasing oil consumption through the use of the car urban life promotes. Citizens are thus coerced into a limited flexibility, creating a situation that is "a wonderful testament to the ability of a sociomaterial structure to serve its own reproduction."[96]

Not that this is exclusive to America. The United States remains the archetypical case of the auto social formation, with more automobiles than registered drivers, and a per capita fuel consumption rate that is ten times the rate of Japan's and twenty times as much as European city dwellers.[97] Nonetheless, the social forces behind automobility are global, and societies other than the United States (China, for example) are witnessing profound growth in private vehicle usage. SUVs are growing in popularity—while equally attracting opprobrium—in Australia, New Zealand, South Africa, the UK, and other EU states.[98] As the icon of automobility, the SUV is imperial.

Concluding Themes

The SUV is a vehicle of singular importance. It is a node in a series of networks that range from the body to the globe, which, when combined, establish the conditions of possibility for U.S. strategic policy and demonstrate that geopolitics needs to be understood in the context of biopolitics. In the story outlined here, it is the central role of mobility in American society that grants oil its social value. This article has outlined the key moments of connectivity in those networks that have given rise to the American auto social formation—the way the transport sector dominates petroleum use; the importance of passenger vehicles as the major consumers of oil in the transport sector; how light trucks have come to be the auto manufacturers' dominant product, overtaking the car as the choice for the majority of families, who find themselves with little choice other than the private vehicle as they move through the domains of their lives. All this—the auto social formation of automobility—has resulted in a situation in which energy efficiency declines and dependence on oil from unstable regions increases as Americans drive further in less economical vehicles. Pivotal in this account is the role played by various laws and regulations—including fuel economy standards, exemptions for light trucks, tax rebates, trade tariffs, international environmental agreements, and zoning codes—in enabling and supporting automobility. Indeed, the story is tragic insofar as the regulatory regime designed to increase energy efficiency and reduce oil dependence (the CAFE standards) has in fact created inefficiency and given rise to a class of vehicles (SUVs) that undermine the overall objective. Those vehicles are the embodiment of a new articulation of citizenship that effaces its social and global connectivity, but SUVs are unquestionably implicated in (if not solely responsible for) the United States' rejection of the Kyoto Protocols and its initiation of an illegal international conflict.

The SUV's importance goes well beyond these instrumentalized concerns, because a renewed emphasis on the material requires an extended engagement with the immaterial. As such, the SUV is the icon of automobility in contemporary America, invested with codes drawn from the militarized frontier culture of post-Vietnam America and manifesting the strategic game animating social and cultural networks in contemporary liberal society. The SUV is the vehicle of empire, when empire is understood as the deterritorialized apparatus of rule that is global in scope but national and local in its effects. The SUV is a materialization of America's global security attitude, functioning as a gargantuan capsule of excess consumption in an uncertain world. With its military genealogy and its claim to provide personal security through the externalization of danger, the SUV is itself a boundary-producing political performance inscribing new geopolitical borderlands at home and abroad through social relations of security, threat, and war. The SUV draws the understanding of security as sizeable enclosure into daily life, folds the foreign into the domestic, and links the inside to the outside, thereby simultaneously transgressing bounded domains while enacting the performative rebordering of American identity.

Because of the SUV's cultural power and pivotal place in the constitution of contemporary America, challenging its encoded performances is a difficult proposition. Instrumentally, rectification could begin with changes in the regulatory regime to increase economy standards (perhaps via efforts to reduce greenhouse gas emissions, as the state of California proposes) and a political recognition that energy conservation is itself "the first and cheapest rapid-deployment energy resource."[99] But bringing about change involves something more incisive than fine-tuning public policy. As this article makes clear, a biopolitical understanding of automobility is necessary, because we are dealing with dispositions and practices that exceed the structured sites of social institutions. Transformation therefore requires so much more than the individualization of responsibility proposed in the advertisements encouraged by the Detroit Project. Can the politics of desire be remodeled to make the SUV an "unpatriotic relic"?[100] Only if America's security attitude can resist the reinscription of the homeland at war and begin to work with the networks of the biopolitical that exceed yet effect the borders of our communities.

Notes

This article has been a long time in the making and incurred many debts along the way. The argument was first tried out in a roundtable on Hardt and Negri's *Empire* at the 2002 American Political Science Association annual meeting in Chicago, where the conversation included William Connolly and Michael Hardt. Since then audiences in Politics and International Relations departments at the Universities of Birmingham, Durham, Leeds, Newcastle, St. Andrews, Sussex, the Open University, Sun Yat Sen University, and the National University of Taiwan have been helpful interlocutors. Thanks for comments, citations, and encouragement is due to Steve Graham, Jef Huysmans, Kate Manzo, Gordon MacLeod, Mat Paterson, Simon Philpott, Robert Warren, and Geoff Vigar. Special mention needs to be made of the participants at the "Legal Borderlands" symposium at Pomona College in September 2004 for their contributions. In particular, the comments of Mary Dudziak, Inderpal Grewal, Leti Volpp, and two anonymous readers for *American Quarterly* were of great benefit. All, however, are absolved of responsibility for the final version.

1. David Campbell, "Time Is Broken: The Return of the Past in the Response to September 11," *Theory and Event* 5.4 (2001), http://muse.jhu.edu/journals/theory_&_event/toc/archive.html#5.4 (accessed June 29, 2005).
2. David Campbell, *Writing Security: United States Foreign Policy and the Politics of Identity*, rev. ed. (Minneapolis: University of Minnesota Press, 1998), chap. 7.
3. "Bush Tars Drug Takers with Aiding Terrorists," *Guardian*, August 8, 2002, 15, at http://www.guardian.co.uk/international/story/0,3604,770783,00.html (accessed June 29, 2005). The ONDCP Web pages, http://www.theantidrug.com/drugs_terror/index.html (accessed June 29, 2005), outline the administration argument and host copies of the advertisements.
4. Arianna Huffington, "An Ad George Bush Would Love," October 22, 2002, *Salon.com*, at http://www.salon.com/news/col/huff/2002/10/22/oil/print.html (accessed June 29, 2005).
5. See http://www.detroitproject.com (accessed June 29, 2005) for the advertisements, and Woody Hochswender, "Did My Car Join Al Qaeda?" *New York Times*, February 16, 2003, at www.nytimes.com/gst/abstract.html?res=F50C14F6395E0C758DDAB0894DB404482&incamp=archive:search (accessed June 29, 2005), for a critical response.
6. Don Mitchell, "The S.U.V. Model of Citizenship: Floating Bubbles, Buffer Zones, and the Rise of the 'Purely Atomic' Individual," *Political Geography* 24 (2005): 77–100.
7. John Urry, "The 'System' of Automobility," *Theory, Culture and Society* 21.4 (2004): 27.
8. Ibid., 28; Stephen Graham and Simon Marvin, *Splintering Urbanism: Networked Infrastructures, Technological Mobilities, and the Urban Condition* (New York: Routledge, 2001).
9. Urry, "The 'System' of Automobility," 26, 27, 33.
10. Michael Klare, *Blood and Oil: How America's Thirst for Petrol Is Killing Us* (London: Hamish Hamilton), 2004; Catholic Relief Services, "Bottom of the Barrel: Africa's Oil Boom and the Poor," June 2003, at http://www.catholicrelief.org/get_involved/advocacy/policy_and_strategic_issues/oil_report_one.cfm (accessed March 23, 2005).
11. For an argument that does see domestic oil consumption as the reason for the war, see Ian Rutledge, *Addicted to Oil: America's Relentless Drive for Energy Security* (London: I. B. Tauris, 2005).
12. Campbell, *Writing Security*.
13. Michael Hardt and Antonio Negri, *Empire* (Cambridge, Mass.: Harvard University Press, 2002), xii–xiii.
14. Ibid., xiii.

15. Quoted in "In California, S.U.V. Owners Have Guilt, but Will Travel," *New York Times*, February 8, 2003, at www.nytimes.com/2003/02/08/automobiles/08SUV.html (accessed June 29, 2005).
16. Michel Foucault, *Society Must Be Defended: Lectures at the College de France 1975–76*, trans. David Macey (London: Allen Lane, 2003), lecture 11.
17. Giorgio Agamben, *Homo Sacer: Sovereign Power and Bare Life*, trans. Daniel Heller-Roazen (Stanford, Calif.: Stanford University Press, 1998).
18. Foucault, *Society Must Be Defended*, lecture 11.
19. Hardt and Negri, *Empire*, 23. It would be incorrect, however, to argue that this conception was radically different from Foucault's articulation of the role practices of governmentality played in constructing a "society of security." See my discussion of this in *Writing Security*, 151–52, 199–200.
20. William J. Mitchell, *Me++: The Cyborg Self and the Networked City* (Cambridge, Mass.: MIT Press, 2003), 5. For an argument that network is an insufficiently fluid understanding, see Mimi Sheller, "Mobile Publics: Beyond the Network Perspective," *Environment and Planning D: Society and Space* 22 (2004): 39–52.
21. Julian Reid, "War, Liberalism, and Modernity: The Biopolitical Provocations of 'Empire'," *Cambridge Review of International Affairs* 17.1 (April 2004): 74.
22. Michael Dillon and Julian Reid, "Global Liberal Governance: Biopolitics, Security, and War," *Millennium: Journal of International Studies* 30.1 (2001): 42.
23. Ibid., 55.
24. Mitchell, "The S.U.V. Model of Citizenship."
25. Lieven De Cauter, *The Capsular Civilization: On the City in the Age of Fear* (Rotterdam: NAi Publishers, 2004), 85.
26. See Marieke de Goede, "Beyond Economism in International Political Economy," *Review of International Studies* 29.1 (2003): 79–97.
27. Alan Latham and Derek P. McCormack, "Moving Cities: Rethinking the Materialities of Urban Geographies," *Progress in Human Geography* 28.6 (2004): 701. This is complementary with but different from the sense that objects such as cars are material expressions of cultural life. See David Miller, ed., *Car Cultures* (London: Berg, 2001).
28. See, for example, Michael T. Klare, "Bush's Real Casus Belli," *AlterNet.org*, January 27, 2003, at www.alternet.org/story.html?StoryID=15036 (accessed June 29, 2005).
29. Advertisement in the *Guardian*, February 26, 2003, 13.
30. Patricia S. Hu, *Estimates of 1996 U.S. Military Expenditures on Defending Oil Supplies from the Middle East: Literature Review* (Oak Ridge, Tenn.: Oak Ridge National Laboratory for the Office of Transportation Technologies, U.S. Department of Energy), revised August 1997.
31. Energy Information Administration, *Annual Energy Outlook 2004* ("Market Trends—Oil and Natural Gas") at http://www.eia.doe.gov/oiaf/archive/aeo04/index.html (accessed March 23, 2005).
32. "U.S. Companies Slash Imports of Iraqi Oil," *Washington Post*, August 20, 2002, A1.
33. "Republicans Aim to Smear Tom Daschle," *CNN.com*, December 23, 2001, at www.cnn.com/2001/ALLPOLITICS/12/23/column.press/ (accessed June 29, 2005).
34. Thomas L. Friedman, "Drilling in the Cathedral," *New York Times*, March 2, 2001, at www.nytimes.com/2001/03/02/opinion/02FRIE.html (accessed June 29, 2005).
35. National Energy Policy Development Group, *National Energy Policy*, May 2001, at http://www.whitehouse.gov/energy/ (accessed June 30, 2005).
36. Michael T. Klare, *Resource Wars: The New Landscape of Global Conflict* (New York: Henry Holt, 2001); Klare, *Blood and Oil*.
37. For a sample of reports touching on these developments, see Ken Silverstein, "U.S. Oil Politics in the 'Kuwait of Africa'," *The Nation*, April 22, 2002, at www.thenation.com/doc.mhtml?i=20020422&s=silverstein (accessed June 29, 2005); and "U.S. Sidles up to Well-Oiled Autocracy," *Guardian*, July 2, 2004, 20.
38. Energy Information Administration, *Annual Energy Outlook 2004* ("Market Trends—Oil and Natural Gas") at http://www.eia.doe.gov/oiaf/archive/aeo04/index.html (accessed March 23, 2005); and Natural Resources Defence Council, *Reducing America's Energy Dependence*, July 2004, at http://www.nrdc.org/air/transportation/gasprices.asp (accessed March 23, 2005).
39. National Highway Transport Safety Administration (NHTSA), Corporate Average Fuel Economy (CAFE), at http://www.nhtsa.dot.gov/cars/rules/cafe/ (accessed June 29, 2005).
40. NHTSA, CAFE Overview and Frequently Asked Questions, at http://www.nhtsa.dot.gov/cars/rules/cafe/overview.htm (accessed June 29, 2005).

41. Ibid. (emphasis added).
42. Energy Information Administration, *Annual Energy Outlook 2004*, at http://www.eia.doe.gov/oiaf/archive/aeo04/index.html (accessed March 23, 2005).
43. Jack Doyle, *Taken for a Ride: Detroit's Big Three and the Politics of Pollution* (New York: Four Walls Eight Windows, 2001), 406.
44. Doyle, *Taken for a Ride*, 399–402.
45. Keith Bradsher, *High and Mighty: SUVs—the World's Most Dangerous Vehicles and How They Got That Way* (New York: PublicAffairs, 2002), 29–30.
46. Doyle, *Taken for a Ride*, 398–99; Union of Concerned Scientists, "Tax Incentives: SUV Loophole Widens, Clean Vehicle Credits Face Uncertain Future," November 2003, at http://www.ucsusa.org/clean_vehicles/cars_and_suvs/page.cfm?pageID=1280 (accessed June 29, 2005).
47. Bradsher, *High and Mighty*, 11–13.
48. Doyle, *Taken for a Ride*, 373–94.
49. NRDC, *Reducing America's Energy Dependence.*
50. *Light-Duty Automotive Technology and Fuel Economy Trends: 1975 through 2004* (EPA420-R-O4-001), i, April 2004, at http://www.epa.gov/otaq/cert/mpg/fetrends/420s04002.pdf (accessed June 29, 2005).
51. Doyle, *Taken for a Ride*, 418.
52. Ibid., 405–6; "The Station Wagon Is Back, but Not as a Car," *New York Times*, March 19, 2002, at http://query.nytimes.com/search/advanced (accessed June 29, 2005).
53. *Light-Duty Automotive Technology*, iv.
54. "Sales of Big S.U.V.'s Rebounded in May," *New York Times*, June 3, 2004, at http://query.nytimes.com/search/advanced (accessed June 29, 2005); "Big and Fancy, More Pickups Displace Cars," *New York Times*, July 31, 2003, at http://query.nytimes.com/search/advanced (accessed June 29, 2005); "Bumper-to-Bumper Details of the Crossover Era," *New York Times*, October 22, 2002, www.nytimes.com/2002/10/22/automobiles/23PATTON.html (accessed June 29, 2005).
55. Manuel A. Conley, "The Legendary Jeep," *American History Illustrated* (June 1981), 27, quoted in Michael VanderPloeg, "The Jeep, a Real American Hero," at www.off-road.com/jeep/jeephist.html (accessed June 29, 2005). The Jeep also inspired the British Land Rover, which first went into production in 1947 and has furthered the SUV phenomenon beyond the U.S. by combining post–WWII military heritage with upper-class cultural values. Bradsher, *High and Mighty*, 385–87.
56. Bradsher, *High and Mighty*, chap. 1.
57. Ibid., 20–25.
58. Ibid., 50.
59. James William Gibson, *Warrior Dreams: Paramilitary Culture in Post-Vietnam America* (New York: Hill and Wang, 1994); Susan Jeffords, *The Remasculinization of America: Gender and the Vietnam War* (Bloomington: Indiana University Press, 1989).
60. Tim Edensor, "Automobility and National Identity: Representation, Geography, and Driving Practice," *Theory, Culture and Society* 21.4/5 (2004): 101–20.
61. Bradsher, *High and Mighty*, 51. Similar valences are evident in other locales; for the way four-wheel drive vehicles have played a part in Australian national identity, see Peter Bishop, "Off Road: Four Wheel Drive and the Sense of Place," *Environment and Planning D: Society and Space* 14 (1996): 257–71.
62. Stacy C. Davis and Lorena F. Truett, *An Analysis of the Impact of the Sport Utility Vehicles in the United States*, Oak Ridge National Laboratory, Oak Ridge Tennessee, ORNL/TM-2000/147, prepared for the Office of Transportation Technologies, U.S. Department of Energy, August 2000.
63. Bradsher, *High and Mighty*, 51.
64. Ibid., 95, 97. For a compelling analysis of gated communities, see Setha Low, *Behind the Gates: Life, Security, and the Pursuit of Happiness in Fortress America* (New York: Routledge, 2003).
65. Bradsher, *High and Mighty*, 98–99.
66. "The Shifting Geography of Car Names: Go West, Young Van," *New York Times*, October 22, 2003, at http://query.nytimes.com/search/advanced (accessed June 29, 2005).
67. "Rollover: The Hidden History of the SUV," *Frontline*, Public Broadcasting Service, February 21, 2002, at http://www.pbs.org/wgbh/pages/frontline/shows/rollover/unsafe/theme.html (accessed June 29, 2005).
68. "In California, S.U.V. Owners Have Guilt."

69. Bradsher, *High and Mighty*, 150. Although the majoritarian popularity of SUVs suggests their cultural codes resonate across class, gender, and racial lines, further study is needed to see which "Americans" are most attracted to these vehicles.
70. Andrew Garnar, "Portable Civilizations and Urban Assault Vehicles," *Techné: Journal of the Society for Philosophy and Technology* 5.2 (winter 2000): 1–7; Stephen Graham, "Constructing 'Homeland' and 'Target': Cities in the 'War on Terror,'" unpublished paper, at http://eprints.dur.ac.uk/archive/00000048/01/Graham_constructing.pdf (accessed March 23, 2005).
71. The U.S. Army is developing a larger and heavier replacement for the Hummer, the "Smart Truck 3." "Just What America Needs—a Car Even Bigger than the Hummer," *The Independent*, November 10, 2004, 30.
72. The description comes from the General Motors Hummer media site at http://media.gm.com/division/hummer/index.html (accessed June 30, 2005); the owners quote from "IN OUR SUVS: Guilt-Tripping," *Pittsburgh Post-Gazette*, Jan. 19, 2003, at http://www.americansforfuelefficientcars.org/readmore/ppg_011903.htm (accessed June 29, 2005).
73. "In Their Hummers, Right Beside Uncle Sam," *New York Times*, April 5, 2003, www.nytimes.com/2003/04/05/business/05AUTO.html (accessed June 29, 2005).
74. Modernista (the Hummer advertising agency), at http://www.modernista.com/ (accessed March 23, 2005); and "Spinning the Axles of Evil," *New York Times*, January 19, 2003, at http://www.nytimes.com/gst/abstract.html?res=F7091FF83D540C7A80894DB404482&incamp=archive:search (accessed June 29, 2005).
75. "Spinning the Axles of Evil." Anti-SUV Web sites include *Stop SUVs.org* (www.stopsuvs.org) and *FUH2.com* (http://www.fuh2.com/); Bill Maher, *When You Ride ALONE You Ride with Bin Laden* (Beverley Hills: New Millennium Press, 2002); and Micah Ian Wright's site (http://www.micahwright.com/index3.htm); "Now, Add God to the List of Enemies of the S.U.V.," *New York Times*, November 24, 2002, at http://www.nytimes.com/2002/11/24/weekinreview/24HAKI.html (accessed June 29, 2005).
76. "In Their Hummers, Right Beside Uncle Sam."
77. "A Proud and Primal Roar," *New York Times*, January 12, 2003, at www.nytimes.com/2003/01/12/fashion/12CULT.html (accessed June 29, 2005).
78. "SYN^{US} Ignites a Gen-Y Debate," *Detroit Free Press*, January 19, 2005, at http://www.freep.com/money/autoshow/2005/synus19e_20050119.htm (accessed March 22, 2005).
79. Ford SYN^{US}, at http://www.fordvehicles.com/autoshow/concept/synus/ (accessed June 29, 2005). While the SYN^{US} is a concept vehicle, those with US $300,000-plus can purchase the "Bad Boy Truck," a nuclear-biological-chemical safe supertruck based on the U.S. Army's Medium Tactical Vehicle, being sold by Homeland Defense Vehicles of Texas. See http://www.badboytrucks.com (accessed March 22, 2005).
80. Bradsher, *High and Mighty*, xvii.
81. "The Nation: By the Numbers; S.U.V.'s Take a Hit, as Traffic Deaths Rise," *New York Times*, April 27, 2003, at http://query.nytimes.com/search/advanced (accessed June 29, 2005); "Regulator Reaffirms Focus on S.U.V.'s," *New York Times*, January 15, 2003, at www.nytimes.com/2003/01/15/business/15AUTO.html (accessed June 29, 2005). The story of this negligence is told in "Rollover: The Hidden History of the SUV." The offices of the attorney general and consumer protection agencies across the United States have a public service campaign offering driving advice to prevent rollovers (see www.esuvee.com, accessed June 29, 2005), which represents the SUV as a mammoth-like creature.
82. "Regulators Seek Ways to Make S.U.V.'s Safer," *New York Times*, January 30, 2003, www.nytimes.com/2003/01/30/automobiles/30AUTO.html (accessed June 29, 2005).
83. Bradsher, *High and Mighty*, 198.
84. "Regulators Seek Ways to Make S.U.V.'s Safer."
85. Bradsher, *High and Mighty*, xix.
86. For an excellent analysis of the way the natural imagery in SUV advertising manages people's relationship with the urban environment, see Shane Gunster, "'You Belong Outside': Advertising, Nature, and the SUV," *Ethics and the Environment*, 9.2 (2004): 4–32.
87. Robert Cervero, *The Transit Metropolis: A Global Inquiry* (Washington, D.C.: Island Press, 1998), 35.
88. George Martin, "Grounding Social Ecology: Landscape, Settlement, and Right of Way," *Capitalism, Nature, Socialism* 13.1 (March 2002): 3–30; Matthew Patterson, "Car Culture and Global Environmental Politics," *Review of International Studies* 26.2 (April 2000): 253–70; Mimi Sheller and John

Urry, "The City and the Car," *International Journal of Urban and Regional Research* 24.4 (December 2000); and Urry, "The 'System' of Automobility."
89. Sheller and Urry, "The City and the Car," 738; Graham and Marvin, *Splintering Urbanism,* 8.
90. Jane Holtz Kay, *Asphalt Nation* (Berkeley: University of California Press, 1998), 144–45.
91. Clay McShane, *Down the Asphalt Path: The Automobile and the American City* (New York: Columbia University Press, 1994).
92. Marshall Berman, *All That Is Solid Melts into Air: The Experience of Modernity* (New York: Penguin, 1988), 290–312.
93. Roland Marchand, "The Designers Go to the Fair II: Norman Bel Geddes, the General Motors 'Futurama,' and the Visit to the Factory Transformed," *Design Issues* 8.2 (Spring 1992): 29; Tom Lewis, *Divided Highways: Building the Interstate Highways, Transforming American Life* (New York: Viking, 1997).
94. Graham and Marvin, *Splintering Urbanism,* 118–21.
95. Jay Wickersham, "Jane Jacob's Critique of Zoning: From *Euclid* to Portland and Beyond," *Boston College Environmental Affairs Law Review* 28.4 (2001): 547–64.
96. Sheller and Urry, "The City and the Car," 744; Martin, "Grounding Social Ecology," 27.
97. Cervero, *The Transit Metropolis,* 33, 46.
98. See "The Cars That Ate Cities," Background Briefing, Radio National, Australian Broadcasting Corporation, June 15, 2003, at http://www.abc.net.au/rn/talks/bbing/stories/s881845.htm (accessed June 29, 2005); and George Monbiot, "Driving into the Abyss," *Guardian,* July 6, 2004, at http://www.guardian.co.uk/comment/story/0,,1254763,00.html (accessed June 29, 2005).
99. R. James Woolsey, Amory B. Lovins, and L. Hunter Lovins, "Energy Security: It Takes More than Drilling," *Christian Science Monitor,* March 29, 2002, at www.csmonitor.com/2002/0329/p11s02-coop.htm (accessed June 29, 2005).
100. Rob Nixon, "A Dangerous Appetite for Oil," *New York Times,* October 29, 2001, available at http://www.peterussell.com/WTC/NYTimes.html (accessed June 29, 2005).

"Setting the Conditions" for Abu Ghraib: The Prison Nation Abroad

Michelle Brown

> I am referring to a state of doubleness of social being in which one moves in bursts between somehow accepting the situation as normal, only to be thrown into a panic or shocked into disorientation by an event, a rumor, a sight, something said, or not said—something that even while it requires the normal in order to make its impact, destroys it. You find this with the terrible poverty in a Third World society and now in the centers of U.S. cities too, such as Manhattan; people like you and me close their eyes to it, in a manner of speaking, but suddenly an unanticipated event occurs, perhaps a dramatic or poignant or ugly one, and the normality of the abnormal is shown for what it is. Then it passes away, terror as usual, in a staggering of position that lends itself to survival as well as despair and macabre humor.
>
> Michael Taussig, *The Nervous System*[1]

Terror as Usual

At Abu Ghraib, the normality of the abnormal was placed on spectacular display when photographs of American GIs proudly humiliating and torturing Iraqi detainees suddenly and surprisingly achieved worldwide media coverage.[2] The shock value of the Abu Ghraib photos lies not in their images of torture during wartime or in prison but in the apparent patriotic delight of the torturers, in America "out of place." In them, we are presented with a seemingly unsustainable contradiction: an image of liberators engaged in torture, of a democracy acting sadistically in a totalitarian setting. We are confronted with America decentered publicly and unavoidably, its "imagined community" disrupted by way of a hyper-aggressive patriotism.

Simultaneously, we are not surprised at all. Mark Danner identifies the soldiers' actions at Abu Ghraib as "a logical extension of treatment they have seen every day under a military occupation that began harshly and has grown, under the stress of the insurgency, more brutal."[3] Slavoj Žižek insists that "in the photos of the humiliated Iraqi prisoners, what we get is, precisely, an insight into 'American values,'" a "flipside" to public morality, premised in the obscene, where soldiers perceive torture and humiliation as acceptable.[4] In other contexts, some neoconservatives express outrage at the outrage itself: war is war after all and prisons house "dangerous" people.[5]

As the story of Abu Ghraib unfolds, the limits of such conflicting discourses are being constructed primarily by and through law. This legal contest centers in many ways upon how various kinds of law will come to view events at the Baghdad prison while under American occupation and which vision of law will be privileged. As is clear from the first wave of legal hearings and courts-martial, the stakes of that contest, much like the conditions of Abu Ghraib, are centered in a vocabulary of punishment, including its correlates: interrogation, accountability, and blame. Culpability is and will be based ultimately upon a legal judgment as to Abu Ghraib's uniqueness or its typicality, its abnormalcy or its normalcy, when, in reality, it is the combined qualities of normal abnormalcy that make Abu Ghraib possible at all. Nowhere is this more apparent than in the penal contexts at home, which mirror the kinds of technologies, techniques, and discourses found at Abu Ghraib.

As a site of unseemly conjunctures between various kinds of competing law, Abu Ghraib is an unusually complex instance of American imprisonment. Its gates mark encounters with United States, Islamic, military, criminal, and international human rights law. Its walls mark not simply the contours of sovereignty and the boundaries of the nation/state but, more significantly, their violation as an immense superpower engages in a preemptive strike, invasion, occupation, and torture. Within this configuration of power, transnational exportations of punishment materialize in a variety of manifestations: (1) in the sociopolitical contexts that define the lives of the primary actors caught up in the prison/military-industrial complex and its increasingly global economies; (2) through the international implementation of U.S. penal technologies with unprecedented exclusionary capabilities, epitomized in President Bush's desire to raze Abu Ghraib and build a "state of the art" supermax prison in its place; and (3) in the unregulated use of force outside of the boundaries of law, a violence juxtaposed and conflated with the memory and backdrop of penal horror under the regime of Saddam Hussein. Abu Ghraib, then, is the kind of place always caught in a double gesture. Regimes and governments attempt to deny and erase the prison's existence. Yet we are simultaneously unable to turn away from its grotesqueness, a site that demands investigation and thus constitutes, as ordered by military judicial ruling, "the scene of the crime."[6]

Prisons have long served as liminal spaces both inside and outside the boundaries of constitutional law, belonging to (in fact, invented by) but not *of* the United States. The birth of the penitentiary, a form of punishment defined entirely upon the denial of freedom, is culturally grounded in democratic values. As historian David Rothman points out, incarceration emerged "at the very moment when Americans began to pride themselves on the openness of their society, when the boundless frontier became the symbol of opportunity and equality . . . as principles of freedom became more celebrated in the outside society."[7] Sociolegal scholar David Garland depicts the penitentiary as a regime constructed upon notably American value systems, including "the targeting of 'liberty' as the object of punishment" and the "intensive focusing upon the individual in prison cells."[8] However, as an institution fundamentally constructed through the inverse of these values, the American penitentiary rests upon a crucial cultural contradiction, the removal of liberty in a nation that would seek to preserve it, the use of violence to counter violence. As Michael Ignatieff writes: "Outside was a scrambling and competitive egalitarianism; inside, an unprecedented carceral totalitarianism."[9] The prison is built upon an interior secret, a union of antithetical ideas and values. Its invocation always risks disclosing the weakness not simply of the sovereign state but of American democracy, founded in distinctly penal terms, including genocide and slavery. Prisons, then, are strategic research sites, from which we may always uncover the contradictions of American power.

For these reasons, special attention must be given to how recent assertions of sovereignty by the United States, coded in penal terms, set the conditions for what Judith Butler refers to as the "new war prison," where "the current configuration of state power, in relation both to the management of populations (the hallmark of governmentality) and the exercise of sovereignty in the acts that suspend and limit the jurisdiction of law itself, are reconfigured," a context rife with possibilities for the violation of human rights.[10] This corruptibility is, in part, an intrinsic property of punishment. To borrow Ignatieff's terminology, prisons are inherently "lesser evil" institutions. Even as democratic defense, such institutions always risk, in any invocation, the violation of foundational commitments to democracy. Even when applied in the context of legislative deliberation, judicial review, and adversarial constraint, they remain necessarily tragic and ultimately evil.[11] However, events at Abu Ghraib and other contemporary domestic and war prisons prove most disconcerting not simply because of the absence of open, adversarial justification, but because of the larger absence of any perceived *need* for justification. As evidence emerges that Abu Ghraib was simply one site of detainee abuse among many in the war against terror,[12] we realize the fear, as expressed by Amy Kaplan in her 2003 presidential address to the American Studies Association, that Guantánamo would become a story of our future, a world where "this floating colony will become the norm rather than an anomaly, that homeland security will increasingly depend on proliferating these mobile, ambiguous spaces between the domestic and foreign."[13] Abu Ghraib is, consequently, the kind of "unanticipated event," dramatic, poignant, and ugly all at once, in which the "normality of the abnormal is shown for what it is"—terror as usual. For these reasons, it also marks a critical site from which to consider how what it means to do American studies is irrevocably bound up with the practice and conjugation of U.S. punishment, not simply at home but abroad, and especially in those "mobile, ambiguous spaces" lost somewhere in between in a time of empire.

What the Law Can Name

The photographs of abuse at Abu Ghraib constitute a compelling case of Amy Kaplan's "anarchy of empire," a distinct site in which we witness how "domestic and foreign spaces are closer than we think" and "how the dynamics of imperial expansion cast them into jarring proximity" (fig. 1).[14] Kaplan observes, "If 'the anarchy of empire' refers to the destruction and exploitation inflicted on the colonized world, it also suggests the internal contradictions, ambiguities, and frayed edges that unravel at imperial borders, where binary divisions collapse and fractured spaces open."[15] In the United States, these "fractured spaces" simultaneously materialize and are eclipsed in the legal debate surrounding Abu Ghraib, which, by definition, permits particular kinds of understandings and discussions to emerge while postponing or closing off others. Two seemingly oppositional accounts of law emerged in the immediate aftermath of the release of the Abu Ghraib photos, both indicative of primary discourses that seek to make meaningful American actions through penal terms. The first frame is grounded in one of individual responsibility—the "few bad apples" theory. This prosecutorial perspective centers upon an assumption launched by the state that Abu Ghraib is an instance of a small group of out-of-control army reservists who decided to photograph detainees in degrading positions. As General Mark Kimmitt, the Deputy Director of Coalition Operations in Iraq, declares at the conclusion of the *60 Minutes II* episode that broke the story: "So what would I tell the people of Iraq? This is wrong. This is reprehensible, but this is not representative of the 150,000 soldiers that are over here. I'd say the same thing to the American people. Don't judge your army based on the actions of a few."[16] This has been the singular rhetoric of the Bush administration, and such a framing permits the

Figure 1.
Spc. Charles Graner and Spc. Sabrina Harmon give a thumbs up over a human pyramid of naked Iraqi detainees, heads covered in sandbags, at Abu Ghraib prison.

depiction of these actors, much like prisons themselves, as "in" but not "of" the nation. From this perspective, the instances of abuse at Abu Ghraib are an "aberration," the result of a particular institutional pathology during a single shift, among a single unit, or between seven individuals.

However, such a narrow explanation is difficult to sustain, as evidenced by the administration's consistent conflation of both individualistic and systemic accounts. The two seemingly oppositional discourses persistently, relentlessly converge. For instance, in an interview with ABC News, Secretary of Defense Donald Rumsfeld equivocates: "There certainly is no excuse for anyone in the armed forces to behave the way these photographs indicate some individuals behaved. We also know that the 1.4 million men and women in uniform on active duty and the terrific Guard and reserve forces are filled with fine, talented, honorable people who don't do that type of thing. No human being, regardless of their training or anything else, would engage in those kinds of acts in a normal, acceptable way. They're, it's unacceptable."[17] Rumsfeld's public statements, much like this one, in the aftermath of Abu Ghraib are marked by a persistent hesitance and incoherence, which speak to the centrality of the tropes of vagueness and uncertainty in the war on terror. Are these actors "some" or "individuals"? Are they human beings or monsters? What constitutes a "normal, acceptable way" to interrogate, detain, punish, torture? His pauses reveal the way in which legal ambiguity successfully blurs categories of "humanness," normalcy, and torture into an official language of denial, culminating in the use of law to evade responsibility and Rumsfeld's now famous declaration concerning acts at Abu Ghraib: "What has been charged so far is abuse, which I believe technically is different from torture. I'm not going to address the 'torture' word."[18] Across rhetoric, reports, "torture memos," and recently released Department of Defense files, the legal architecture of the war on terror is visible only in an elusive language that makes border zones like Abu Ghraib not simply susceptible to human rights violations, but renders dramatic dislocations of cultural responsibility acceptable.

The second legal frame relies upon the rule of law in the form of the military order with its dispersal of responsibility through chain of command and hierarchy to create the "obedience to authority" explanation. In interviews, diaries, and letters home, the soldiers at the center of the Abu Ghraib scandal explain the manner in which "soft" torture tactics were being employed to "set the conditions" for military intelligence to conduct interrogations. As former CIA counterterrorism coordinator Cofer Black insisted in congressional hearings, "All I want to say is that there was 'before 9/11' and 'after 9/11.' After 9/11 the gloves came off."[19] Seymour Hersh argues similarly that the "roots" of Abu Ghraib converge in the predominance of military and penal strategies as appropriate courses of action in response to 9/11, not "in the criminal inclinations of a few Army reservists, but in the reliance of George Bush and Donald Rumsfeld on secret operations and the use of coercion—and an eye-for-an-eye retribution—in fighting terrorism," including the administration's expansion of covert special access programs into prison settings.[20]

These kinds of tactics are what journalist Mark Bowden refers to as "torture lite," methods that, in the aftermath of September 11, are interpreted by some as "not quite" torture, including "sleep deprivation, exposure to heat or cold, the use of drugs to cause confusion, rough treatment (slapping, shoving, or shaking), forcing a prisoner to stand for days at a time or to sit in uncomfortable positions, and playing on his fears for himself and his family," and are perceived by many, including Bowden, to be, in times of emergency, now necessary.[21] At Abu Ghraib, Sgt. Ivan Frederick, the senior enlisted man convicted in the scandal, wrote in a letter home: "Military intelligence has encouraged and told us 'Great job.' They usually don't allow others to watch them interrogate, but since they like the way I run the prison, they've made an exception. We help getting them to talk with the way we handle them. We've had a very high rate with our style of getting them to break. They usually end up breaking within hours."[22] The kind of prisoner exploitation implied in Frederick's statement is an exemplar of the loose manner in which the rule of law has been redefined by the Bush administration in the context of a "new" kind of war with "new" enemies. In the systemic explanation, responsibility and accountability for the abuse at Abu Ghraib must be distributed across a network of agencies and security levels, including private contractors, civilian interrogators, military intelligence, the CIA, and the Department of Defense. This particular frame demonstrates how a particular kind of legal interpretation that privileges the narrowing of human rights protections culminated in lax and abusive patterns in leadership, training, and communication across the military and within the Department of Defense. It is a defense that permits explanation by foregrounding patterns, hierarchy, and networks of institutions rather than viewing Abu Ghraib through the lens of individual actors in a single incident. Each of these legal frames, however, with its strict insistence upon the rules of evidence and emphasis upon direct lines of causality permits only the most formal articulations of law and does not get at the ways in which law and punishment permeate our daily lives and actions in indirect, informal ways.

Consequently, we are left with only two primary discursive frames from which to work through the complexity of Abu Ghraib, two legal frames that, in an even more limiting manner, are presented as irreconcilable—a zero sum game—whereas, Judith Butler writes, "the framework for hearing presumes that the one view nullifies the other."[23] In such a context, explanation itself is suspect, "as if to explain these events would involve us in a sympathetic identification with the oppressor, as if to understand these events would involve building a justificatory framework for them."[24] Both kinds of frames limit discussions of the origins of violence and the cultural conditions necessary for extreme punitiveness, such as torture, in democratic contexts. Both also position the actors and agents involved in the violence at Abu Ghraib outside of the culture from which they emerge, thus promoting a particular kind of cultural denial. This kind of denial and evasion constitutes a third frame that falls outside of or beyond the law and includes what the law cannot name, the cultural conditions and structural contexts that culminate in acts of violence. The dominance of this denial has precluded as well any thorough elaboration of the causes and conditions of terrorism. Benjamin Barber observes that "terrorists swim in a sea of tacit popular support and resentful acquiescence, however, and these waters—roiling with anger and resentment—prove buoyant to ideologies of violence and mayhem."[25] Along these lines, Mark Juergensmeyer writes that "because I want to understand the cultural contexts that produce these acts of violence, my focus is on the ideas and the communities of support that lie behind the acts rather than on the 'terrorists' who commit them. . . . the word 'terrorist' is problematic."[26] Abu Ghraib positions these predicaments in relief and inverts the subjects of these kinds of statements, insisting that no one is caught outside of culture, however far from home they might be.

As the legal dispositions of these cases are slowly decided, it is clear, based upon the first wave of courts-martial, that it is the first frame, centered upon individual culpability, that has achieved dominance. Although the scandal has resulted in at least eight major investigations, one thousand interviews, more than fifteen thousand pages of reports, a series of congressional hearings, the release of Department of Defense files, and a suspended general, all documenting widespread abuse internationally across American military prisons, no one above the rank of staff sergeant has been charged at this point. Those who have been prosecuted and convicted are serving sentences that range anywhere from demotion to prison time. A two-day court-martial for shift supervisor Ivan Frederick ended in a ten-year sentence reduced to eight by way of a pretrial agreement. Charles Graner, the most visible actor in the Abu Ghraib photos, has received the harshest sentence to date, ten years in prison. Graner's mother, in the aftermath of his conviction, insisted "my son was convicted the day that President Bush went on television and said the seven bad apples disgraced the country."[27] It appears that the cases will end in the same context of democratic irony from which they emerged, the invocation of imprisonment to resolve problems exacerbated by the unacknowledged impacts of punitiveness.

In an attempt to move beyond these simplifying frames, I would like to examine the specific penal conditions that gave rise to events at Abu Ghraib and that exist, in many ways, beyond the formal articulations of the law. In this pursuit, I rely carefully upon Judith Butler's nuanced distinction between conditions and causes and her insistence that "conditions do not 'act' in the way that individual agents do, but no agent acts without them."[28] Certainly, the acts that took place at Abu Ghraib deserve attention as distinct, discrete events involving specific perpetrators and victims, but it is also crucial to any understanding of the meanings of those acts that they be contextualized within the paradoxical conditions of imprisonment, democracy, and military occupation. At Abu Ghraib, soldiers in the 372nd Military Company engaged in brutality and torture. According to the Taguba report, the first internal investigation of the 800th Military Brigade (which oversaw Iraqi prisons), the company, amid riots, escapes, and insurgency, engaged in "sadistic, blatant, and wanton criminal abuses" against prisoners.[29] These documented acts include shooting and beating detainees; acts of sodomy and rape; videotaping and photographing naked male and female detainees, many in sexually explicit postures and forced sexual performances; arranging detainees in human piles and jumping and sitting on them; simulating electrocution; using dogs to intimidate and in some instances injure detainees; keeping detainees naked and awake for days at a time; holding detainees in isolation cells without recourse to running water, toilet, ventilation, or windows; exposing detainees to extremes of heat and cold; pouring chemicals and cold water on detainees; and posing with photographs of dead detainees. According to the primary investigative reports and the legal defenses mounted on their behalf, these soldiers were individual actors caught inside an institutional contradiction.[30] Poorly trained, inexperienced, understaffed, and facing limited resources and extensive service in prisons (not unlike correctional officers at home) and war zones, soldiers were being asked to "provide a safe, secure, and humane environment" that simultaneously supported "the expeditious collection of intelligence" by "setting the conditions for successful exploitation of the detainees."[31] It was also a world in which the patterns of punishment in the United States were more broadly applied in the extralegal setting of Guantánamo and then imported into Iraq. In making the terrible decisions to perform acts of torture, the 372nd found themselves in an ill-defined world with ambiguous expectations in a setting inherently designed to be retributive and loosely regulated enough for torture to be seen as permissible and desirable. In negotiating that ambiguity, they committed crimes, acts that depended upon their cultural beliefs and values, their work experience and ideologies, all of which led to particular assumptions about the meaning of the rule of law, the worth of human life, and the routine use of a particular mode of punishment: torture.

What the Law Cannot Name

The register in which Americans are continuing to render meaningful the terrorist attacks of September 11 as well as the expansive war on terrorism in Afghanistan and Iraq is one that has dominated American notions of crime and punishment for more than three decades.[32] It is a distinctly penal discourse centered upon a particular philosophy of punishment, retribution, with its attendant oppositional, binary, and dehumanizing logic. Retributive frames of punishment marked the contours of the war on terror from the beginning, as evidenced when President Bush assured the American public and the world in the hours after the events of September 11: "Make no mistake: The United States will hunt down and punish those responsible for these cowardly acts," those responsible being individuals, to employ the administration's binary rhetoric, who had "burrowed" into the everyday life of Americans, the hidden "cowards," "barbarians," and "evil-doers," lurking in the "shadows" and "caves," afraid to show their faces.[33] It was also an event that occurred in an already entrenched penal context, in which the privileging of retribution, individual responsibility, and cultural denial had become the hallmarks of American justice. This hyper-penal context creates the necessity for a reconceptualization of the way in which punishment is present and at work in the lived spaces and practices of everyday life, well beyond the institutional forms punishment may take. In the story of Abu Ghraib, punishment circulates beyond the prison walls into every facet of social experience. It is apparent in the political rhetoric of war, in the rise of a nationalist solidarity built upon retribution and aggression. It is found in the architecture and configuration of Abu Ghraib's "hard" site, the tiers in which the abuse occurred, in the policies and practices that defined life there, borrowed from the penal system at home. It is apparent in the precedents and policies reformulating and restricting the rights of prisoners, not just in war zones abroad, but in the domestic interior of the United States. And it networks through the biographies of those involved in the scandal, which have become the focus of soap-opera-style media coverage and thus constitute primary signs in the cultural decoding of the case.

Several of the reservists at the center of the prisoner abuse scandal were assigned to Abu Ghraib precisely because they had experience working in prisons. Ivan Frederick was described by Dan Rather as "well suited" for his job at Abu Ghraib as a former Virginia corrections officer (along with his wife), described by his warden as "one of the best."[34] Charles Graner worked as a guard at a high-security prison in Waynesburg, a former Pennsylvania mining town, home to most of the state's death row inmates (including Mumia Abu-Jamal) and subject to numerous complaints of human rights violations and prisoner abuse. Sgt. Joseph Darby, the Abu Ghraib whistle-blower, testified in Article 32 hearings that Graner had said of the abuse at Abu Ghraib: "The Christian in me knows it was wrong, but the corrections officer in me can't help but want to make a grown man piss himself."[35] Specialist Sabrina Harman, a former pizzeria manager, had no explicit ties with prisons but had hoped to follow her father and brother into law enforcement. She is now charged with taking photographs of naked detainees while they were abused and of having attached electrodes to the fingers, toes, and penis of a hooded prisoner who was then threatened with electrocution. The military war machine converges with the prison-industrial complex in the biographies of these Abu Ghraib actors, often overtly, otherwise indirectly.

The other actors involved are remarkably similar in their class status and work experience, all of which are consistent with the kinds of work available to individuals who are more likely to enlist in the Army Reserve and/or go to work in a prison. These include Jeremy Sivits, a former McDonald's employee, who pled no contest and is now serving a one-year prison sentence; Megan Ambuhl, who insisted in her defense that she thought humiliating treatment of detainees was normal and acceptable and no one had taught her otherwise; Javal S. Davis, a New Jersey–born father of two who was the only African American convicted in the scandal (now serving an eighteen-month sentence); and Lynndie England of Forth Ashby, West Virginia, who worked at a chicken factory and bagged groceries before joining the Army Reserve to earn money for college in order to become a meteorologist. England, whose photo once

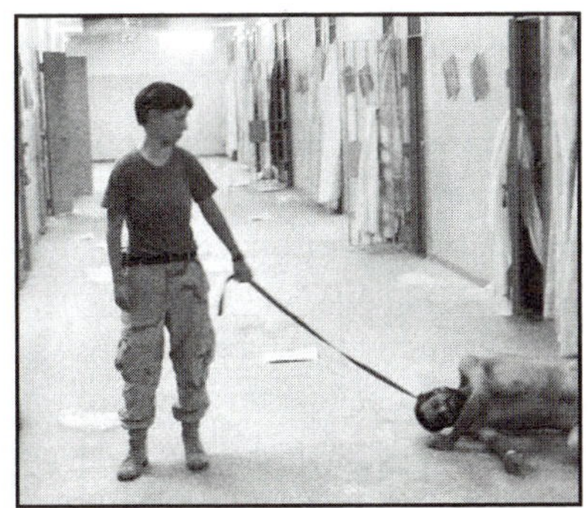

Figure 2.
Pfc. Lynndie England posing with prisoner on leash.

hung on the "wall of honor" at the Cumberland, Maryland Wal-Mart where the reservists were based, is now routinely presented in the media as the "anti–Jessica Lynch" and the "poster child" for Abu Ghraib, notorious for having been photographed while holding a leashed prisoner on a dog chain and pointing and smiling at detainees forced to simulate sexual positions (fig. 2). At Abu Ghraib, she engaged in an affair with Graner, her supervisor, which resulted in her pregnancy, and is, at the time of this writing, undergoing preliminary hearings in preparation for a general court-martial in the United States, following a recent mistrial. Her case is the last to be tried in connection with the scandal.

These biographies reveal little specifically about soldiers and correctional officers in general, and perhaps even less about these specific individuals. However, they do depict the chain of signs and linkages that are being made across media outlets and in legal settings concerning accountability at Abu Ghraib. The primary narrative is one itself based upon voyeuristic sadism, the fascination and relentless public speculation concerning how average Americans come to be private, now public, torturers. However, faintly in the background context of these biographies, a larger cultural narrative is implied, one built upon class, prisons, and labor—work in fast food restaurants and factories, rural prisons built in old mining towns, military and law enforcement families, unrealized dreams of college and careers. The prison-industrial complex and military-industrial complex converge in a sociopolitical economy grounded in rural and lower-class life. The prison itself brings together the elements that have marked their work experience: assembly line efficiency, people and objects as aggregate numbers, an emphasis upon process, routine, and petty rules. The sheer scale and design of American incarceration shapes their lives and stories, supplying work and a particular kind of prison logic to their labor and life experience. Former military bases, now renovated prison-industrial complexes, are rapidly providing economically depressed regions with a new labor base and a new emphasis upon security, the kinds of public works that are unlikely to go away anytime soon. As these sites pull teachers, police, doctors, nurses, cooks, and other professionals out of local economies and into the prison-industrial complex, as they accumulate contracts with some of the world's largest commercial industries, commentators argue that a "new American city" develops—one whose self-sustaining abilities depend upon the production of hard-line attitudes, more prisons, and, equally significant, more prison towns. These kinds of complexes are to be found in nearly all states at this point, communities built around multiple prisons that, in turn, serve as primary sources of livelihood for entire regions, culminating in a reconfiguration of social and economic life in distinctly penal terms.[36]

These kinds of penal contexts have been the direct source for much of the exportation process. Several million dollars were set aside in the war package to hire prison consultants to advise construction abroad. Most of these justice envoys include former directors of corrections, predominantly from border states, such as Texas, Arizona, and New Mexico. Their expertise centers upon illegal immigrant detention and the privatization of prisons, while their professional histories reflect the same questionable patterns of human rights complaints and documented abuses as those found at Abu Ghraib. In the aftermath of the scandal, a steady stream of Internet articles published largely by alternative media have chronicled the shared features of abuse at home with that of Abu Ghraib, including nearly identical acts under the tutelage and directorship of these consultants.[37] The context of imprisonment continues to materialize at Abu Ghraib in other instances emblematic of recent transformations in patterns of American punishment. Civilian interrogators are suspected to have played primary roles in the scandal, routinely brought in to question detainees at Abu Ghraib precisely in order to evade the rule of law (as they are exempt from U.S. military law), implying another story of commercial contractors, the privatization of prisons, and the global expansion of the security sector. A recent estimate suggested that there are at least twenty thousand private military contractors in Iraq alone.[38] Before September 11, numerous private prison companies had begun to remodel themselves as private security agencies focused upon a global market, and they represented some of the first stocks to rise when the markets reopened.[39]

We also witness the inverse as prisons at home become transnational sites for punishment. Within American borders, we find a longstanding history of the detention of foreign nationals outside the rule of law, and not simply in times of crisis. It has been estimated that before September 11, more than twenty thousand undocumented immigrants were held in custody for long periods of time and in harsh conditions, many placed outside of INS facilities in the general populations of U.S. jails and prisons, and many of whom spoke little or no English.[40] This process takes place while asylum seekers await background checks with little or no legal representation, while facing no charges. Since the 1980s, immigration policy has consistently hardened amid increasing documentation of human rights abuse.[41] In the aftermath of September 11, the number of detainees held indefinitely without charges by American forces is estimated to be at or above fifty thousand.[42] In conjunction with these developments, the war on terror brings about new patterns of penality in the offshore, off-limit prisons such as Guantánamo Bay, the myriad undisclosed locations at which detainees are being held, the "rendering" of suspects or exporting of prisoners to other countries for torture, and U.S. "disappearances" that are occurring internationally.[43]

Although these practices have garnered little popular attention, they are identified by some as evidence of a trend toward "criminal justice militarization," in which social relations are redefined through a convergence of militaristic, police, and penal contexts. Much of this transformation, however, is concealed in the rise of incapacitation, a justification for imprisonment that seems to flow from the prison's very structure, lending itself to an easy, seemingly natural morality of convenience that in turn naturalizes the logic of expansion, exclusion, and detention. That logic is exemplified in the social reality of prisons as institutions. Erving Goffman's classic work on total institutions exemplified how prisons, as "social hybrids," attempt to manage individuals through the creation of persistent tensions and strategic leverages defined by power differentials (the "staff/inmate split") and the use of institutional force ("mortification processes")—a world, in Goffman's terms, sociologically defined by abasement, degradation, humiliation, and profanation.[44] In this way, total institutions, including the prison, are ultimately "the forcing houses for changing persons in our society. Each is a natural experiment, typically harsh, on what can be done to the self."[45] These classic "pains of imprisonment" are to be carefully considered as "a set of threats or attacks which are directed against the very foundation of the prisoner's being."[46] Prisons, thus, are best understood in the context of democracies as laboratories of the self, wherein control is directed precisely at the regulation of individuals and individualism. In American rhetoric and penal practice, prisoners are rationalized as being in prison because they "chose" to commit a crime and consequently are in need of "breaking down," as it is the burden of the state to restructure "free" will.[47] This function, as exemplified by Foucault, is distinctly similar to a military model itself, particularly the boot camp, and is apparent in the imagining of the prison as a pedagogical instrument, teaching patterns of obedience and discipline, creating a "good," albeit unthinking, citizenry.

These institutional patterns extend beyond prison walls in the cultural circuits and behavioral maps that make up the social order. As Alexis de Tocqueville first and Foucault later make clear, democracy would necessitate a subtle mechanism for the enforcement of social order, one that would not be perceived as violating individual autonomy and civil liberties, but one that would be pervasive and invisible. Both point out that the model for that form of power would necessarily be the twin of democracy, the birth of the prison following from the birth of the republic. It is Tocqueville who first insists that the conditions of democracy in the United States offered up the possibility of an entirely new form of repression, one so unique that its articulation was not entirely possible, "unlike anything that ever before existed in the world; our contemporaries will find no prototype of it in their memories."[48] Tocqueville imagined this order as "an immense and tutelary power" that "covers the surface of society with a network of small complicated rules, minute and uniform, through which the most original minds and the most energetic characters cannot penetrate, to rise above the crowd."[49] In such a society, he writes, "the will of man is not shattered, but softened, bent, and guided; men are seldom forced by it to act, but they are constantly restrained from acting. Such a power does not destroy, but it prevents existence; it does not tyrannize, but it compresses, enervates, extinguishes, and stupefies a people."[50] These ideas emerged for Tocqueville while visiting the United States and touring its prisons. These markers of democratic despotism are, of course, the very patterns of the penitentiary, whose sociology demonstrates a nearly identical phenomenon, culminating in a disciplinary force that expands beyond institutional walls into the very fabric of social life, where abuse and torture are no longer necessarily recognized as such, and, if they are, are perceived as necessary and acceptable.

This logic has reached its zenith in a particular style of contemporary punishment, the control prison or "supermax" confinement. The institutional similarities between Abu Ghraib and the rise of the supermax prison in the United States mark a particularly dangerous pattern in the exportation of punishment. Most of the human rights violations and detainee abuse at Abu Ghraib took place in a particular wing of the prison, the "hard site," where, it is argued, the "worst" detainees were being held. The "hard site" follows the logic of an emergent form of custody at home that sees all prisoners as violent threats. Commonly described as a new type of prison and/or classification level, supermax prisons are the prisons-within-prison systems, sites where the total lockdown of one unit or facility becomes standard daily operating procedure. The basic premise of supermax units is to apply the absolutely highest level of security to those inmates whose behavior has been defined administratively as manageable only through isolation from other inmates and staff. Most states in the United States have added or are in the process of adding a supermax unit to preexisting institutions or building entire facilities designed solely for supermax purposes.

Designed to house what is increasingly being referred to as "the worst of the worst," the supermax unit is a place to which an inmate can be assigned by engaging in any serious rule violation through disruptive behavior (threatening or injuring other inmates or staff, participating in escapes or escape attempts, or possessing contraband, including deadly weapons or drugs). However, there are a number of more loosely defined ways in which an inmate can end up in isolation, including association with groups that are perceived as security threats (usually based upon gang, political, or religious associations—which, in practice, have often been linked to racial identity—as well as organized crime, terrorist, or drug cartel associations). Others who are likely to be segregated include the mentally ill, those with HIV, and offenders who have been placed in protective custody (informants, for instance). The manner in which supermax classification occurs is similar to the manner in which terrorists are being identified and detained in and out of the United States, with little public notification or legal recourse.

Although "supermax confinement" is often used synonymously with the older "solitary confinement," in practice, and in its proliferation, it represents a new and distinctive phenomenon. Whereas solitary confinement centered upon punishment, supermax classification is a managerial strategy, focused upon the redistribution of individuals on the basis of risk. The guiding principle of supermax design, consequently, centers upon isolation and exclusion, including the restriction of all communication and face-to-face contact with staff and visitors for *security* purposes. The most typically shared features of the supermax prison include the creation of an entirely self-contained unit or facility where inmates spend twenty-three hours a day in confinement, with one hour for recreation, showering, and visitation. Confined in sterile cells, with no movable parts, prisoners live in worlds of concrete and steel "tamper-proof" environments. Cell doors, usually solid steel with a narrow opening for food, materials, and handcuffing procedures, are electronically opened from a control center where staff maintain contact with the inmate via intercom and often conduct regular observations through video surveillance systems. If cells have windows at all, they are narrow, shatterproof glass slats that are usually smoked to prevent visibility to the outside. When removed from cells, prisoners are handcuffed, placed in leg irons, and escorted by two to three guards. Recreation takes place in high-walled, concrete exercise yards ("cages" or "kennels"), where usually the sky is the only visible point of reference. Restrictions in movement and the absence of points of reference are designed to make the institution's layout difficult to ascertain. In many supermax units, all services are automated and provided door-to-door in a manner designed managerially to counter inmates' abilities to throw materials or engage in disruptive behavior. Visitation occurs in "no contact" settings. In short, supermax facilities are so technologically advanced that prisoners can go for days, months, and years with the virtual elimination of human interaction. Institutionally, total isolation is the index of design success.

Prisoners, much like detainees in the war against terror, may be placed in supermax confinement for indeterminate periods of time, with limited review procedures in place to monitor the reasons for and length of time spent in segregation. The average time spent in segregation nationally is not known; however, inmates have been known to spend years, some being released directly from these high-security units to the street with no transition programming. Given that inmates are assigned to these facilities for various reasons, many of which are based upon subjective criteria and the discretion of prison staff, supermax classification has been subject to a good deal of legal scrutiny, centered upon two constitutional claims. The first argues that supermax settings exhibit a degree of harshness in conditions that violates international guidelines for the minimum standards for the treatment of prisoners, including the prohibition of torture, and also challenges Eighth Amendment protections against cruel and unusual punishment. A number of human rights organizations have documented the highly disturbing conditions of supermax settings, including high noise levels; the throwing of food, urine, feces, and belongings; the flooding of toilets; the destruction of clothes; and the widespread practice of self-mutilation (many of the same kinds of conditions documented at Abu Ghraib and visible in photos).[51] These surroundings are argued to be highly punitive, dehumanizing, and potentially volatile living conditions for both inmates and staff, resulting in higher levels of hostility, an enhanced psychological setting of "us versus them," and a generally more confrontational daily institutional setting with an increased likelihood of the use of force. Such sensory and socially deprived environments, in which confrontation is a routine part of daily existence, are argued to have often deeply adverse psychological effects. The sparse amount of research that addresses the psychology of supermax confinement provides evidence for increased problems with concentration, thinking, impulse control, and memory, as well as the development of severe anxiety, paranoia, psychosis, depression, rage, claustrophobia, and hallucinations. When the Red Cross documented identical psychological patterns in its examination of detainees subjected to U.S. interrogation practices, military intelligence officers explained these tactics and effects as "part of the process."[52] Many argue that these conditions increase the likelihood of self-fulfilling prophesies. By placing troublesome prisoners who cannot adapt well to prison life in segregation, supermax settings potentially render them less able to return not only to the general prison population, but to society as well. Such treatment also makes them angrier, more conspiratorial and alienated, fundamentally disconnected from the basic commitments to social life.

The second constitutional critique follows the logic of detention and centers upon the absence of full due process in supermax assignments. Staff decision making and practices, much like the current administration's approach to the war on terror, are argued to be unrestricted and often unreviewable, specifically when addressing the provision of services and supermax admission requirements. Classification and disciplinary hearings are argued to base assignment to supermax settings upon suspicions, hearsay, informers, staff, and anonymous tips as well as simply the potentiality of threatening behavior (gang association, for instance) rather than its exhibition. This operational procedure epitomizes the logic of incapacitation and detention in the war on terror, wherein penal policy is set by potential behavior rather than past actions. Critics of the supermax system argue that the necessity of an extensive, highly intensified level of security for certain populations, with its attendant strict movement restrictions, is unclear and may lead to more complications through an excessive pursuit of security.

The growth in supermax prisons in the United States represents an important penological moment, particularly since supermax confinement is a largely American phenomenon, which other countries with similar governing structures and economic status have openly rejected. It is even more significant in the manner in which it maps contemporary patterns of global action in the post–9/11 new world order. In his discussion of the control prison at California's Pelican Bay, Zygmunt Bauman writes that "as a (thus far) distant ideal, a total isolation beckons, one that would reduce the other to a pure personification of the punishing force of law."[53] That future now seems much less distant as we witness the logic of custody and incapacitation at home converging with the global application of detention by the United States. In retrospect, it is clear that most of the detainees held at the Abu Ghraib "hard site" were common criminals who were of little intelligence value. Here again, we find "domestic and foreign spaces" cast "into jarring proximity" against global correlates of isolation, exclusion, and immobility.[54] In the words of anthropologist Lorna Rhodes, who has published the most systematic cultural analysis of the control prison,

> the contemporary prison has developed a new technology—in the form of the control prison—for the creation of a potentially absolute social exclusion. Historically, and in many prison systems in the United States, this exclusion is correlated with and profoundly linked to race. The current proliferation and expansion of the technology suggests that it is being enlisted to manage other projects of separation and isolation as well. When these projects of exclusion are framed in entirely individualistic and non-rehabilitative terms, they confront us with disturbing questions about what it means to be a human—a social—being. I believe this is the issue most deeply at stake in the contemporary prison.[55]

Rhodes argues that it is this widespread emphasis upon absolute exclusion that makes the will of the individual prisoner the only proper object of the law. In such a setting, what it means to be human and to be social devolve into arbitrary legal categories concerning the amount of natural light a human should have, the level of noise that is unbearable to human ears, the kind of punch or slap that is permissible, the essence of punishment denied.

Abu Ghraib and the Future of Prisons and Borders

> The work of *mestiza* consciousness is to break down the subject-object duality that keeps her a prisoner and to show in the flesh and through the images in her work how duality is transcended. The answer to the problem between the white race and the colored, between males and females, lies in healing the split that originates in the very foundation of our lives, our culture, our languages, our thoughts. A massive uprooting of dualistic thinking in the individual and collective consciousness is the beginning of a long struggle, but one that could, in our best hopes, bring us to the end of rape, of violence, of war.
>
> Gloria Anzaldúa, *Borderlands/La Frontera*[56]

Abu Ghraib, like Guantánamo and other U.S. military prisons, marks the kind of penal expansion that takes place in the context of wars with no end: wars on drugs, crime, and terror. In the U.S., we imprison more than anyone in the world and more than any other society has ever imprisoned for the purposes of crime control, and we do so in a manner that is defined by race.[57] This unprecedented use of imprisonment has largely taken place outside of democratic checks or public interest, in disregard of decades of work by penal scholars and activists who have introduced a vocabulary of warning through terms such as "penological crisis," "incarceration binge," "prison-industrial complex," and the "warehousing" of offenders. Such massive expansion has direct effects upon the private lives of prisoners, prison workers, their families, and their communities. I have tried, at least, to point to the ways in which these effects may extend far beyond their immediate contexts into a potential reconfiguration of public life. Such unprecedented penal expenditures mark the global emergence of a new discourse of punishment, one whose racial divisions and abusive practices are revised into a technical, legal language of acceptability, one in which Americans are conveniently further distanced from the social realities of punishment through strategies of isolation and exclusion, all conducted in a manner and on a scale that exacerbates the fundamental class, race, and gender contradictions and divisions of democracy. In this respect, the "new war prison" is constituted by both material practices and a discursive language whose expansion and intensification need recognize no limits, no borders, no bounds.

I have used punishment and torture interchangeably across this piece, not because I believe they are without distinction or difference, but because I believe, as history and social theory teach us, that they are grounded in the same fundamental practice: the infliction of pain. Because punishment carries pain, rupture, and trauma with it, its implementation will always be fundamentally tragic. Torture, then, is not incidental to punishment. It is at its core. Instead of accepting this reality, the history of the practice and study of punishment is marred by an assumption that intention matters, that explanations and justifications define punishment and its appropriate use, and that the law can control its violence. However, these kinds of assumptions conceal the presence of the law itself. When punishment is invoked, it is always intended to remind the people of the power and presence of the state. However, this is an invocation that is precisely meant to be avoided in democratic contexts, as strong governments have no need to rely upon force. According to both Nietzsche and Durkheim, it is a weak state that will resort to a display of force and violence. Any regime that decides to inflict pain and harm will inevitably find itself caught up in a unique social institution whose essence is violence and whose justifications are inherently problematic. Punishment is, thus, always most usefully understood at its most elemental level: as a bloodlust for revenge, one whose essence is passion, unreason, anger, and emotion, whose invocation is highly individualized, subjective, and personal, an insatiable urge that knows no limits. In such a setting, as sociolegal scholar Austin Sarat argues, a "wildness" is introduced into the "house of law," wherein "private becomes public and public becomes private; passion is introduced into the temple of reason, and yet passion itself is subject to the discipline of reason. Every effort to distinguish revenge and retribution nevertheless reveals that 'vengeance arrives among us in a judicious disguise.'"[58] The vengeance that underlies the implied calm reason of systematic, procedural, proportional retribution cannot be repressed and is evidenced in contemporary patterns of punishment in the United States that often defy a rational logic of any kind. Any solidarity or sociality gained at the price of such punishment, then, speaks not only to the end of democracy but of humanity as well. And so we went from September 11 to a war on terror, from Abu Ghraib to the summer of beheadings in an endless repetition whose limits are defined currently only in the possibility of sheer exhaustion.

For American studies, this means that Abu Ghraib operates at a series of intersections and borders that have rendered the fundamental contradictions of imprisonment in a democratic context acutely visible, if only temporarily. As the impossible case for democracy, the "scandal" at Abu Ghraib reveals how an unmarked proliferation of penal discourses, technologies, and institutions not only "set the conditions" for the grossest violations of democratic values but revealed the normalcy and acceptability of these kinds of practices in spaces beyond and between the law. Consequently, Abu Ghraib falls within a distinct category of legal and territorial borders, those spaces that sociolegal scholar Susan Bibler Coutin observes "defy categories and paradigms, that 'don't fit,' and that therefore reveal the criteria that determine fittedness, spaces whose very existence is simultaneously denied and demanded by the socially powerful." Capturing the sense of doubleness that characterizes Abu Ghraib, she describes these "targets of repression and zones of militarization" as contradictory spaces that "are marginalized yet strategic, inviolate yet continually violated, forgotten yet significant."[59] Many peoples exist at these borders, and all stories may be told there. But, and this is of crucial significance, there is no guarantee that these stories will be told. So much of the writing and thought surrounding the borderlands has been directed at the development of a new social vision, derived from the pain of history and experience, but grounded in the celebratory justice of the inevitable, vindicating arrival of the hybrid. As Gloria Anzaldúa insists, "*En unas pocas centurias*, the future will belong to the mestiza."[60] Yet Abu Ghraib falls squarely into the kind of border zone that cannot be celebrated, a subaltern site where many stories and voices will never be told or heard, no matter how we reconstruct its history and its events.

Judith Butler observes that the subject outside of the law "is neither alive nor dead, neither fully constituted as a subject nor fully deconstituted in death."[61] Under Saddam Hussein's rule, numberless thousands were lost in the prison. Under American occupation, "ghost detainees" were a prevalent problem, unidentified, vanished inside the institution's own lost accountability. As Žižek points out, these individuals constitute the "living dead," those missed by bombs in the battlefield, "their right to life forfeited by their having been the legitimate targets of murderous bombings." This positioning has direct impact upon the legal privilege of their captors: "And just as the Guantánamo prisoners are located, like *homo sacer*, in the space 'between two deaths,' but biologically are still alive, the U.S. authorities that treat them in this way also have an indeterminate legal status. They set themselves up as a legal power, but their acts are no longer covered and constrained by the law: they operate in an empty space which is, nevertheless, within the domain of the law."[62] The spectacle of abuse at Abu Ghraib makes plain the consequences of putting prisoners and custodians in this space "between two deaths," a legal borderland filled with spectral violence, a space packed with people and yet profoundly empty of its humanity. Bibler Coutin writes, "I cannot celebrate the space of nonexistence. Even if this space is in some ways subversive, even if its boundaries are permeable, and even if it is sometimes irrelevant to individuals' everyday lives, nonexistence can be deadly."[63] When writing of Abu Ghraib, I find myself in a similar space, peering in at a border whose history, purpose, and foundations prevent it from being redeemed or reclaimed, its terrorized inhabitants the essence of Anzaldúa's "zero, nothing, no one."[64] Abu Ghraib reminds us then of the pains we had hoped to transcend, of the "intimate terrorism" we had hoped to end, of the bloody sovereignty we had hoped to eclipse in a postnational context.[65] As Anzaldúa observed of "life in the borderlands" nearly two decades ago:

> The world is not a safe place to live in. We shiver in separate cells in enclosed cities, shoulders hunched, barely keeping the panic below the surface of the skin, daily drinking shock along with our morning coffee, fearing the torches being set to our buildings, the attacks in the street. Shutting down . . . The ability to respond is what is meant by responsibility, yet our cultures take away our ability to act—shackle us in the name of protection. Blocked, immobilized, we can't move forward, we can't move backwards. That writhing serpent movement, the very movement of life, swifter than lightning. Frozen.[66]

In the working vocabulary and memory of a penal culture, Abu Ghraib remains a border lost to us, accessible only through the fixed and frozen images that remind us of its irrevocableness. We find ourselves, in a sense, at a new border that is very old, caught at the crossroads, left alone with America, asking, and with considerable trepidation, what will our futures be?[67]

Epilogue

At Camp Delta in Guantánamo, the planning of execution facilities has begun as U.S. military leaders and prison coordinators anticipate the outcome of future military tribunals in which death would be sentenced secretly, without judicial review, and in the absence of international support.[68] A short time ago, accompanied by a small group of students and colleagues, I visited a men's maximum security prison in which nearly six hundred prisoners, more than half the population, were held in control units in a perpetual state of lockdown. The prison also served as the state's execution facility. At the conclusion of the tour they took us to the death house and permitted us to have a lengthy conversation with a member of the execution team while we stood in the witness room, peering through the glass at the lethal injection gurney and the large digital clock on the wall above it. The team had executed two men in the two weeks before and had already, only halfway through the year, executed more than in any of the previous years. Our speaker was a friendly, amiable man who took his job very seriously. When asked why he did his job, he explained that it was totally voluntary. Somebody had to do it. If he didn't, someone else would. The law was the law and it was his job to follow it. But also, as long as he was there, he knew that the individual about to be executed was treated with dignity and respect in the seventy-two hours before he or she was killed. He implied that there were others that might not take the job seriously, who might "botch" the execution, make the state look unprofessional, or even, sadistically, enjoy the process. Preventing that was important to him. In the penal state, the contradictions proliferate at a maddening pace. Terror as usual.

Notes

I would like to extend my sincerest appreciation to Bruce Hoffman, Marita Sturken, Leti Volpp, Mary Dudziak, the editorial staff at *American Quarterly*, and this issue's anonymous reviewers for their insightful comments on earlier drafts of this essay. Also, a special note of thanks to Danielle Fagen for her dedicated research assistance.

1. Michael Taussig, *The Nervous System* (New York: Routledge, 1992), 18.
2. The photographs aired during the *60 Minutes II* episode that broke the Abu Ghraib prison scandal are posted at http://wwwimage.cbsnews.com/images/2004/05/06/image615902x.jpg. (accessed June 15, 2005). There is also an interactive tool titled "Abuse at Abu Ghraib": http://www.cbsnews.com/elements/2004/05/05/iraq/interactivehomemenu615771.shtml.
3. Mark Danner, "Torture and Truth," *New York Review of Books* 51, June 10, 2004, 4.
4. Slavoj Žižek, "Between Two Deaths," *London Review of Books* 26.11, June 3, 2004, online edition http://lrb.veriovps.co.uk/v26/n11/zize01_.html (accessed January 1, 2005).
5. Rush Limbaugh, for instance, garnered critical and supportive attention when he publicly argued that the soldiers were just "blowing off steam" and having "a good time" in a war zone where people were trying to kill them.
6. "Abu Ghraib a Crime Scene Says Military Judge," *ABC News Online*, June 21, 2004, http://www.abc.net.au/news/newsitems/200406/s1137076.htm (accessed June 29, 2005).

7. David Rothman, "Perfecting the Prison," in *The Oxford History of the Prison: The Practice of Punishment in Western Society*, ed. Norval Morris and David J. Rothman (New York: Oxford University Press, 1995), 100.
8. David Garland, *Punishment and Modern Society: A Study in Social Theory* (Chicago: University of Chicago Press, 1990), 40.
9. Michael Ignatieff, *A Just Measure of Pain: The Penitentiary in the Industrial Revolution, 1750–1850* (New York: Pantheon, 1978), 212.
10. Judith Butler, *Precarious Life: The Powers of Mourning and Violence* (London: Verso, 2004), 53.
11. Michael Ignatieff, *The Lesser Evil: Political Ethics in An Age of Terror* (Princeton, N.J.: Princeton University Press, 2004).
12. Both the International Committee of the Red Cross and Human Rights Watch have expressed concern over possible human rights violations at U.S. detention facilities since the beginning of the war on terror, including at twenty detention facilities in Afghanistan (Bagram airbase as well as bases at Kandahar, Jahalabad, and Asadabad). In Iraq, cases are being investigated at Camp Bucca, Abu Ghraib, and other undisclosed facilities. The interrogation practices first implemented at Camp X-Ray (now Camp Delta) at Guantánamo are argued to be the prototypes for emergent patterns of abuse in U.S. detention facilities across the world. See Reed Brody, *The Road to Abu Ghraib* (Human Rights Watch, June, 2004), http://www.hrw.org/reports/2004/usa0604/ (accessed June 28, 2005).
13. Amy Kaplan, "Violent Belongings and the Question of Empire Today—Presidential Address to the American Studies Association, October 17, 2003," *American Quarterly* 56.1 (March 2004): 14.
14. Amy Kaplan, *The Anarchy of Empire in the Making of U.S. Culture* (Cambridge, Mass.: Harvard University Press, 2002), 1.
15. Ibid., 14.
16. "Court-Martial in Iraq; U.S. Army soldiers face court-martials for actions at Baghdad's Abu Ghraib Prison," *60 Minutes II*, April 28, 2004, available at http://web.lexis-nexis.com/universe/document?_m=b7ab631df5dd018146b1dc7f308f81f5&_docnum=1&wchp=dGLbVtz-zSkVb&_md5=69059fbd99c2b3fded07622bd7733b64 (accessed June 28, 2005).
17. "Defense Secretary Donald Rumsfeld Reaction to Abuse in Iraq," ABC News, *Good Morning America*, May 5, 2004, at http://web.lexisnexis.com/universe/document?_m=d76dc228811ec3bf0b237cfb9358758b&_docnum=2&wchp=dGLbVzz-zSkVA&_md5=f3ed76662b03985cac5806edac98bc29 (accessed June 28, 2005).
18. Adam Hochschild, "What's in a Word? Torture," *New York Times*, May 23, 2004, at http://nytimes.com/2004/05/23/opinion/23HOCH.html (accessed June 28, 2005).
19. Mark Bowden, "The Dark Art of Interrogation: A Survey of the Landscape of Persuasion," *The Atlantic Monthly*, October 2003, 56.
20. Seymour Hersh, *Chain of Command: The Road from 9/11 to Abu Ghraib* (New York: HarperCollins, 2004).
21. Bowden, *The Dark Art*, 53.
22. "Court-Martial in Iraq," *60 Minutes II.*
23. Butler, *Precarious Life*, 13.
24. Ibid., 8.
25. Benjamin Barber, *Jihad vs. McWorld* (New York: Ballantine Books, 2001), xiv.
26. Mark Juergensmeyer, *Terror in the Mind of God: The Global Rise of Religious Violence* (Berkeley: University of California Press, 2001), 7.
27. See *The O'Reilly Factor*, "Unresolved Problem: Update on Abu Ghraib Scandal," Bill O'Reilly, 8:21 p.m., Monday, January 17, 2005, Fox News Network, at http://web.lexis-nexis.com/universe/document?_m=b99676829b2678cc4b9c95b970097bad&_docnum=1&wchp=dGLbVzb-zSkVA&_md5=c3c569c472ca6557fdcbfb579408b457 (accessed June 29, 2005).
28. Butler, *Precarious Life*, 11.
29. Article 15-6 Investigation of the 800th Military Police Brigade, conducted by Major General Antonio M. Taguba, issued May 2004, at http://news.findlaw.com/hdocs/docs/iraq/tagubarpt.html (accessed June 28, 2005).
30. See ibid.; *The Final Report of the Independent Panel to Review DoD Detention Operations*, chaired by James R. Schlesinger, issued August 2004, http://news.findlaw.com/hdocs/docs/dod/abughraibrpt.pdf; the army's internal investigation of the Abu Ghraib prison and detention facility, conducted by Lieutenant General Anthony R. Jones and Major General George R. Fay, http://news.findlaw.com/hdocs/docs/dod/fay82504rpt.pdf (access dates for both sites: June 28, 2005).

31. Taguba, Article 15-6, 5.
32. See Katherine Beckett, *Making Crime Pay: Law and Order in Contemporary American Politics* (New York: Oxford University Press, 1997).
33. Presidential remarks given at Barksdale Air Force Base, Louisiana, September 11, 2001. See http://multimedia.belointeractive.com/attack/news/bushtext.html (accessed June 28, 2005).
34. "Court-Martial in Iraq," *60 Minutes II.*
35. "Agent: England Described 'Humiliation' Techniques," cnn.com, August 6, 2004, http://www.cnn.com/2004/LAW/08/06/lynndie.england.hearing/index.html (accessed June 29, 2005).
36. See Joseph T. Hallinan, *Going up the River: Travels in a Prison Nation* (New York: Random House, 2001); Eric Schlosser; "The Prison-Industrial Complex," *The Atlantic Monthly* 282.6 (December 1998): 51–77 ; and Sasha Abramsky, *Hard Time Blues: How Politics Built a Prison Nation* (New York: Thomas Dunne Books, 2002).
37. See Judith Greene, "From Abu Ghraib to America: Examining Our Harsh Prison Culture," *Ideas for an Open Society: Occasional Papers from OSI–U.S. Programs,* 4.1 (October 2004): 6; Sasha Abramsky, "Incarceration, Inc.," at http://www.duckdaotsu.org/070504-incarceration.html; Anne-Marie Cusac, "Abu Ghraib, USA," at http://www.prisonactivist.org/pipermail/prisonact-list/2004-June/009105.html; Earl Ofari Hutchinson, "Iraq 'Supermax' Prison Won't Wipe Away Abu Ghraib Stain," at http://www.alternet.org/story/18819 (access date for all sites: January 31, 2005).
38. Anthony Dworkin, "Security Contractors in Iraq: Armed Guards or Private Soldiers?," http://www.crimesofwar.org/onnews/news-security.html (accessed June 28, 2005).
39. See Paul Tharp, "Private Prison Stocks Hot—New Internment Camps, Cells Coming," at http://www.rense.com/general15/privateprisonstocks.htm (accessed June 29, 2005); Andrew Stein, "Prison Stocks: A Secure Pick?." *Money,* April 30, 2004, online edition, at http://web.lexis-nexis.com/universe/document?_m=8334a5eaf61266e5c847958c13a850da&_docnum=3&wchp=dGLbVlz-zSkVb&_md5=0b2bf5ebd6fa79cb0f3bed7f4cfb183c (accessed June 29, 2005); and Abramsky, "Incarceration, Inc."
40. See Michael Welch, *Detained: Immigration Laws and the Expanding I.N.S. Jail Complex* (Philadelphia: Temple University Press, 2003).
41. Human Rights Watch, *Locked Away: Immigration Detainees in Jails in the U.S.* (New York: Human Rights Watch, 1998); Human Rights Watch, *Slipping Through the Cracks: Unaccompanied Children Detained by the U.S. Immigration and Naturalization Service* (New York: Human Rights Watch, 1997).
42. *The Final Report of the Independent Panel to Review DoD Detention Operations.*
43. Brody, *The Road to Abu Ghraib.*
44. Erving Goffman, *Asylums: Essays on the Social Situation of Mental Patients and Other Inmates* (Garden City, N.Y.: Anchor Books, 1961), 13.
45. Ibid.,12.
46. Gresham Sykes, *The Society of Captives: A Study of a Maximum Security Facility* (New York: Atheneum, 1970), 79.
47. For an excellent recent application, see Lorna A. Rhodes, "The Choice to Be Bad," in *Total Confinement: Madness and Reason in the Maximum Security Prison* (Berkeley: University of California Press, 2004).
48. Alexis de Tocqueville, *Democracy in America* (New York: Vintage Books, 1990), 318.
49. Ibid., 318–19.
50. Ibid., 319.
51. For human rights documentation, see Jamie Fellner and Joanne Mariner, *Cold Storage: Super-Maximum Security Confinement in Indiana* (New York: Human Rights Watch, 1997); Jamie Fellner, *Red Onion State Prison: Super-Maximum Security Confinement in Virginia* (New York: Human Rights Watch, April 1999); Jamie Fellner, *Out of Sight: Super-Maximum Security Confinement in the United States* (New York: Human Rights Watch, February 2000). Other useful sources include Craig Haney, "'Infamous Punishment': The Psychological Consequences of Isolation," *The National Prison Project Journal* (ACLU, spring 1993); and Rhodes, *Total Confinement.*
52. Danner, "Torture and Truth."
53. Zygmunt Bauman, *Globalization: The Human Consequences* (New York: Columbia University Press, 1998), 108.
54. Kaplan, *The Anarchy of Empire,* 1.

55. Rhodes, *Total Confinement,* 7.
56. Gloria Anzaldúa, *Borderlands/La Frontera: The New Mestiza* (San Francisco: Aunt Lute Books, 1987), 80.
57. In 2003, the United States incarcerated 2.1 million people, or 1 in every 140 Americans. Nearly half of the prison population is African American. Another 18 percent are Hispanic or Latino. Currently, African American males have a one-in-three chance of serving time in their lifetime and one in seven is currently or permanently disenfranchised with no right to vote due to felony convictions. These statistics are available at the U.S. Department of Justice, Bureau of Justice Statistics, "Prison and Jail Inmates at Midyear 2003" (May 2004), NCJ 203947. See http://www.ojp.usdoj.gov/bjs/prisons.htm (accessed June 29, 2005). They are also drawn from reports and briefs published by the Sentencing Project, a nonprofit organization well known for its research and advocacy on criminal justice policy. See http://www.sentencingproject.org (accessed June 29, 2005).
58. Austin Sarat, *When the State Kills: Capital Punishment and the American Condition* (Princeton, N.J.: Princeton University Press, 2001), 43.
59. Susan Bibler Coutin, "Illegality, Borderlands, and the Space of Nonexistence," in *Globalization Under Construction: Governmentality, Law, and Identity,* ed. Richard Warren Perry and Bill Maurer (Minneapolis: University of Minneapolis Press, 2003), 171.
60. Anzaldúa, *Borderlands/La Frontera,* 80.
61. Butler, *Precarious Life,* 98.
62. Žižek, "Between Two Deaths."
63. Susan Bibler Coutin, "Illegality, Borderlands, and the Space of Nonexistence," 193.
64. Anzaldúa, *Borderlands/La Frontera,* 85.
65. Ibid.
66. Ibid., 42–43.
67. See Amy Kaplan, "'Left Alone With America': The Absence of Empire in the Study of American Culture," in *Cultures of United States Imperialism,* ed. Amy Kaplan and Donald E. Pease (Durham, N.C.: Duke University Press, 1993), 3–21; and Donald E. Pease and Robyn Wiegman, eds., *The Futures of American Studies* (Durham, N.C.: Duke University Press, 2002).
68. "Camp Delta Death Chamber Plan," *BBC News World Edition,* June 10, 2003, http://news.bbc.co.uk/2/hi/americas/2979076.stm (accessed June 28, 2005).

Contributors

Michelle Brown

Michelle Brown's research explores the intersection of culture, punishment, and law. She is working on a monograph exploring the meanings of U.S. imprisonment in cultural practice while serving as an assistant professor and criminologist in the Department of Sociology and Anthropology at Ohio University. She is coeditor of *Media Representations of September 11* (2003).

Christina Duffy Burnett

Christina Duffy Burnett is coeditor, with Burke Marshall, of *Foreign in a Domestic Sense: Puerto Rico, American Expansion, and the Constitution* (2001) and author of "*Untied* States: American Expansion and Territorial Deannexation," *University of Chicago Law Review* (2005). She has a J.D. from Yale Law School, an M.Phil. in political thought and intellectual history from Cambridge University, and a master's degree in American history from Princeton University, where she is completing a doctorate in nineteenth-century American legal history. She has served as a law clerk to Judge José A. Cabranes on the Second Circuit Court of Appeals and to Justice Stephen G. Breyer on the U.S. Supreme Court.

David Campbell

David Campbell is a professor of cultural and political geography at Durham University in the U.K., where he convenes the Politics-State-Space Research Group and serves as associate director of the Durham Centre for Advanced Photography Studies and associate director of the International Boundaries Research Unit. His research deals with the visual culture of international politics, political theory and global geopolitics, and U.S. security policy.

Devon W. Carbado

Devon W. Carbado is a professor of law at the University of California, Los Angeles. He writes and teaches in the areas of criminal procedure, constitutional law, and critical race theory. He was recently awarded a Fletcher Foundation Award, which, modeled after the Guggenheim Awards, is part of a larger Fletcher Foundation program to mark the fiftieth anniversary of *Brown v. Board of Education*. His most recent coedited book, *Time on Two Crosses: The Collected Writing of Bayard Rustin* (with Don Weise), received the Lambda Literary Award for lgbt studies in 2003. In 2002, his coedited collection,

Black Like Us: A Century of African American Lesbian, Gay and Bisexual Literature (with Dwight McBride and Don Weise) won the Lambda Literary Award for best anthology.

Susan L. Carruthers

Susan L. Carruthers is an associate professor of history at Rutgers University, where her field is the United States and the world. She is the author of *Winning Hearts and Minds: British Governments, the Media and Colonial Counterinsurgency* (1995) and *The Media at War: Communication and Conflict in the Twentieth Century* (2000). She has also written several articles on captivity and conversion in the early postwar period, in settings that range from occupied Germany to Korean War POW camps and colonial Kenya. Her essay on the escapee derives from a larger project titled *Cold War Captives: Prisoners, Traitors, and Escapees in Superpower Struggle.*

Mary L. Dudziak

Mary L. Dudziak is the Judge Edward J. and Ruey L. Guirado Professor of Law, History, and Political Science at the University of Southern California, and a visiting professor of law at Harvard Law School. She is the author of *Cold War Civil Rights: Race and the Image of American Democracy* (2000), editor of *September 11 in History: A Watershed Moment?* (2003), and the author of numerous articles on civil rights history and twentieth-century U.S. constitutional history in law reviews and other journals. Her work centers on international approaches to U.S. legal history. She is currently writing about Thurgood Marshall's work on the Kenya independence constitution, and on law and war in the twentieth-century United States. She is a member of the managing board of *American Quarterly* and is a Distinguished Lecturer for the Organization of American Historians.

Andrew Hebard

Andrew Hebard is an assistant professor of American literature at Agnes Scott College. He is working on a book that examines the relation between late-nineteenth-century literary aesthetics and the forms of ambivalence found in the administrative and legal discourses surrounding the state regulation of race relations.

Moon-Ho Jung

Moon-Ho Jung is an assistant professor of history at the University of Washington, Seattle, and the author of *Coolies and Cane: Race, Labor, and*

Sugar in the Age of Emancipation (2006). He is currently working on a book on antiradicalism, anti-Asian racism, and Asian American political struggles in the 1890s through the 1930s.

Amy Kaplan

Amy Kaplan is a professor of English and the Edmund J. and Louise W. Kahn Endowed Term Professor in the Humanities at the University of Pennsylvania, as well as a former president of the American Studies Association. She is the author of *The Anarchy of Empire in the Making of U.S. Culture* (2003) and *The Social Construction of American Realism* (1988), and coeditor with Donald E. Pease of *Cultures of United States Imperialism* (1994).

Linda K. Kerber

Linda K. Kerber is a professor of history, lecturer in law, and the May Brodbeck Professor in the Liberal Arts & Sciences at the University of Iowa; a fellow of the American Academy of Arts and Sciences; and forthcoming president in 2006 of the American Historical Association. Her most recent book is the prize-winning *No Constitutional Right to Be Ladies: Women and the Obligations of Citizenship* (1998). She is a past president of both the Organization of American Historians and the American Studies Association.

Teemu Ruskola

Teemu Ruskola is a professor of law at American University in Washington, D.C. His publications on comparative law and the cultural study of law have appeared, among other places, in *Michigan Law Review, Stanford Law Review,* and *Yale Law Journal.*

María Josefina Saldaña-Portillo

María Josefina Saldaña-Portillo is an associate professor in the Department of English at Rutgers University, where she is also affiliated with the Departments of Comparative Literature and Women and Gender Studies. She has published several articles in English and Spanish on revolutionary subjectivity, race and representation in the Americas, United States imperialism in Latin America, and subaltern politics. She is the author of *The Revolutionary Imagination in the Americas and the Age of Development* (2003).

Austin Sarat

Austin Sarat is the William Nelson Cromwell Professor of Jurisprudence Political Science at Amherst College and Five College Fortieth Anniversary

Professor. He is former president of the Law and Society Association; former president of the Association for the Study of Law, Culture, and the Humanities; and president of the Consortium of Undergraduate Law and Justice Programs. He is editor of the journal *Law, Culture, and the Humanities* and of *Studies in Law, Politics, and Society*. He is also author or editor of more than fifty books including *When the State Kills: Capital Punishment in Law, Politics, and Culture* (2001); *Law, Violence, and the Possibility of Justice* (2001); and *Pain, Death, and the Law* (2001). His next book, *Mercy on Trial: What It Means to Stop an Execution*, will be published by Princeton University Press.

Nayan Shah

Nayan Shah is an associate professor of history at the University of California at San Diego. His research and teaching interests focus on the political practices and cultural meanings that both define and unsettle categories of race and sexuality in Asian migrations to North America. His book, *Contagious Divides: Epidemics and Race in San Francisco's Chinatown* (2001), received the Association of Asian American Studies History Book Prize. He is at work on a new study of South Asian migrant workers, sexuality, and law in Canada and the United States, 1900 to 1950. He has published articles from this project in *Social Text* and in *Tense and Tender Ties* (2005, ed. Ann Stoler).

Siobhan B. Somerville

Siobhan B. Somerville teaches in the Department of English and the Gender and Women's Studies Program at the University of Illinois, Urbana-Champaign. She is the author of *Queering the Color Line: Race and the Invention of Homosexuality in American Culture* (2000).

Leti Volpp

Leti Volpp is a professor of law at Boalt Hall School of Law at the University of California, Berkeley. She is the author of numerous articles examining questions of citizenship, migration, culture, and identity, including "The Citizen and the Terrorist," *UCLA Law Review* (2002); "Feminism versus Multiculturalism," *Columbia Law Review* (2001); and "(Mis)Identifying Culture: Asian Women and the 'Cultural Defense,'" *Harvard Women's Law Journal* (1994). She is the recipient of two Rockefeller Foundation Humanities Fellowships and a MacArthur Foundation Individual Research and Writing Grant. Before entering academia, she was a public interest lawyer primarily defending the rights of immigrants.

Lisa Yoneyama

Lisa Yoneyama teaches cultural studies, U.S.-Japan studies, and critical gender studies in the Department of Literature at the University of California, San Diego. Her research interests center on the politics of history and memory, gender and militarism, and the cultural dimensions of transnationalism in cold war and post-cold war U.S. relations with Asia. Yoneyama is the author of *Hiroshima Traces: Time, Space, and the Dialectics of Memory* (1999) and *Violence, War, Redress: The Politics of Multiculturalism* (in Japanese, 2003). She also coedited *Perilous Memories: The Asia-Pacific War(s)* (2001). Her current project, *Cold War Ruins*, explores the struggles over memory of cold war violence and the pursuit for historical justice in the three-way nexus of the United States, Asia, and Asia/America.

Index

9/11, 193, 386; after, 6, 16, 136–37, 139, 146, 150–51, 351, 386, 397; before, 262n9, 386
60 Minutes II, 384, 402n2
372nd Military Company, 388
800th Military Brigade, 388

ABC News, 385
Abbott, John S. C., 103
Abu Ghraib, 12, 16, 20, 152, 239, 266n80, 381–405; images of, 257; prisoner abuse at, 239, 390
Abu-Jamal, Mumia, 390
Adams, John Quincy, 267, 279, 280, 287
Afghanistan, 14, 150, 239, 248, 257–59, 311, 360, 389, 403
Agamben, Giorgio, 21–22, 35n25, 46, 216, 296; concept of "bare life," 46–47, 296
Alsop, Joseph, 343
Althusser, Louis, 233
Ambuhl, Megan, 390
America, America, 60
American exceptionalism, 8, 10–11, 107n4, 138, 256, 287, 294
Amnesty International, 154, 239
Amores Perros, 160
Andy Griffith Show, 247
Anzaldúa, Gloria, 2, 47, 129, 398, 400–401
Arctic National Wildlife Reserve (ANWR), 360
Arendt, Hannah, 9, 136, 139–40, 152–53, 155n44; *The Origins of Totalitarianism,* 136, 154–57
Aristide, Jean-Bertrand, 247
Article 32 hearings, 390
Astor, John Jacob, 274
Atherton, Gertrude: *Rulers of Kings,* 221
Aves Island, 191, 196
Bacon, Robert (senator), 220, 229
Balibar, Etienne, 181
Barber, Benjamin, 387
Barthes, Roland, 229
Bauman, Zygmunt, 397
Bell, David, 112
Benson, Alfred Grenville, 187–88
Berlant, Lauren, 67, 69
Berlin Wall, 136, 332
Bhabha, Jacqueline, 138, 146
Biddle v. Perovich, 38n87
Bill of Rights, 30, 143, 249, 251
biopolitics, 357–59, 363, 372, 374–75, 376; of security, 361
Black, Cofer, 386
Black, Jeremiah S., 96, 195–96
Blackstone, William, 5, 23–24, 25, 27, 36nn43, 44, 38n102, 256
borderlands, 129; cold war, 319; geopolitical, 375; legal, 1–17, 20–21, 25, 187, 216, 353–54, 359, 373; spatial, 111–13, 120, 123, 128–29
borders: Austro-Hungarian, 346; crossing, 319, 321, 333, 335; national, 62, 259, 261, 320, 322, 328, 343; patrols, 182, 340; racial, 42, 44; states, 392; territorial, 69, 161, 164, 181, 182, 289; U.S., 62, 248, 249, 254, 268, 271–72, 286, 334, 337, 392; U.S.–Mexico, 66n69, 162, 252; USSR, 323
Boston Tea Party, 280
Bowden, Mark, 386
Boxer Rebellion, 277
braceros program, 3, 146, 156
Bradsher, Keith, 372
Bredbenner, Candice, 144
British Anti-Slavery Society, 88
Brown, Henry B. (Supreme Court justice), 54–55, 202, 217

Bryan, William Jennings, 218
Bryson, Lesley, 93–94
Buchanan, James, 103–4
Buck, George (judge), 126
Buff, Rachel, 320, 336
Bureau of Immigration and Naturalization, 73
Burlingame Treaty, 285–86
Burnett, Christina Duffy, 142
Burnett, Henry C., 104, 109n36
Bush, George W., 293–94; administration, 242, 293–94, 351, 360, 363, 384, 386
Butler, Judith, 82n21, 317n54, 383, 387–88, 400

Cable Act, 144
Caimanera, 242
Campbell, David, 139
camps, escapee, 321
Captive Heart, The, 331
Cardenas, Lázaro, 172
Carstenbrook, Harvey, 122–23, 127
Case Concerning Avena and other Mexican Nationals, Mexico v. United States of America, 39n115
Cass, Lewis, 96, 188
Cass, Ronald, 19–20
Castro, Fidel, 244, 247, 335
Cato Institute, 162
Chambers, Whittaker, 319
Chase, Richard, 222
Cheney, Dick, 360
Chinese exclusion, 61, 85–86, 336
Chinese Exclusion Act, 74, 106, 141, 270, 285–86
Christian Science Monitor, 304
Cisneros, Henry, 20
citizenship, 41, 62, 67–82, 135–57, 170, 217, 219–20, 224, 296, 303, 320, 332, 335–36, 353; and enemy combatants, 259; first- and second-class, 64n22, 250; naturalized, 67–82; new articulation of, 375–76; proof of, 166; rights, 248; sexual, 67; U.S., 45–51, 53, 56–60, 322, 338
Citizen Wives Organization, 144
Civil War, 75, 85–86, 92, 102, 104, 135–36, 141, 150, 255, 288
Clancy, Tom, 365
Clayton, John Middleton (senator), 192–93, 203
Clean Air Act of 1970, 352, 364
Cleveland, Sarah, 287
Clingman, Thomas L., 101
Cochrane, Dorris, 397
Code Napoleon, 146
Codes of California, 125
Cohen, William, 20
Columbus, Christopher, 271, 273, 285
Committee on Foreign Relations, 101
Commonweal, 306
Conquergood, Dwight, 34
Constantino, Renato, 235
"coolies," 85–109
Cooper, Davina, 68
Corporate Average Fuel Economy (CAFE), 361
counterterrorism, CIA, 386
court of equity, 23–24, 27, 30, 36n44
Coutin, Susan Bibler, 400
coverture, 79, 143, 152
Crèvecoeur, J. Hector St. John de: *Letters from an American Farmer,* 77
CSI: Miami, 369
Cuarón, Alfonso, 159. See also *Y tu mamá también*
Cuba, 142; Guantánamo Bay, 150, 239–64
Cuba Libre, 242
Cushing, Caleb, 268–69, 277, 281–85, 288

Daniel, Peter V., 141
Danner, Mark, 381
Darby, Sgt. Joseph, 390
Daschle, Tom, 360
Davis, Charles H., 199
Davis, Javal S., 390
Davis, Richard Harding, 221, 228–29, 231; "The Reporter Who Made Himself King," 221; *Soldiers of Fortune,* 228–29, 231; *The White Mice,* 221
De Bow, J. D. B., 99–100

De Cauter, Lieven, 359, 371
Declaration of Independence, 72
Deleuze, Gilles, 358
Dennett, Tyler, 287
Derrida, Jacques, 22–23
Detroit Project, 351–52, 375
displaced persons, 322–23
Displaced Persons Act, 334
dollar diplomacy, 269
Dorr v. United States, 224
Dower, John, 300
Downes v. Bidwell, 51, 202, 224, 226, 249–50, 258
Dred Scott v. Sanford, 6, 50–54, 56, 62, 141
Dudziak, Mary, 308, 315
Durkheim, É mile, 399

Earth Liberation Front (ELF), 369
East India Company, 273, 276
Edkins, Jenny, 296
Eighth Amendment protections, 396
Eisenhower, Dwight D., 338, 345, 341n71; administration, 320
Eisgruber, Christopher, 51
Eleventh Circuit Court of Appeals, 249
Eliot, Thomas D., 102, 104, 106
Ellis Island, 144, 156n58
el pueblo, 171–73, 175–77, 180
Emancipation Proclamation, 86
Embargo Act, 274
Empire (Hardt and Negri), 357, 358
Empress of China, 273
enemy combatants, 241, 246, 248, 259–61, 265n78; Combatant Status Review Tribunals of, 253, 266n86
Energy Policy Conservation Act of 1975, 352, 361
England, Lynndie, 390–91
Equal Protection Clause, 33
Eskridge, William, 121
European Union, 138
Ex parte Crump, 31–32
Ex parte Garland, 38n82–84
Ex parte Grossman, 29
Ex parte Wells, 27–28
Expatriation Act, 143
extraterritoriality, 267–89

Family of Nations, 271, 283
Family Registry Law, 312
Fanon, Frantz, 43
Farley, Anthony, 52
Federal Detention Center, 149
feminism: cold war, 306–8, 310–11; critical, 297, 312, 314, 315n11
Field, Stephen (Supreme Court justice), 29
Fifth Amendment, 249, 260
Fillmore, Millard, 27
First Amendment, 249
Fischer, Louis, 340
Fitzhugh, George, 101
Five Great Reforms, 301
Flourney, Richard W., 145
Foucault, Michel, 68, 216, 236n12, 295, 377n19, 393–94
Fourteenth Amendment, 7, 54–56, 250; due process clause of, 32
Fourth Amendment, 251–52
Francis, Edmund, 197
Frederick, Sgt. Ivan, 386, 388, 390
Free Trade Bulletin, 162
Fried, Richard, 340
Friedan, Betty, 341
Fugitive Slave Act, 345
Fuller, Melville W. (Supreme Court chief justice), 203, 214–15, 250
Funston, Gen. Frederick, 225

Gable, Clark, 319, 341
Gallagher, John, 269, 287
Gamio, Manuel, 170
Gardener, Cornelius, 230
Garland, David, 383
Garrison, William Lloyd, 91
Geneva Convention, 320, 325, 329–30; on prisoners of war, 246, 259–60
George III, 275–76
Gestalt, 222–33

Gherardi, Bancroft, 197
Ginsburg, Ruth Bader (Supreme Court justice), 149–50, 239
Gitlin, Todd, 357
Gladstone, John, 87–88
Glazener, Nancy, 213–14, 222, 224
Go, Julian, 219
Goffman, Erving, 393
Gómez, Máximo, 242
Gordon, Beate Sirota, 311
Gotanda, Neil, 52, 325
Gouzenko, Igor, 325
Graner, Charles, 385, 388, 390–91
Green, Joyce Hens, 253, 266n86
Grimke, Angelina, 143
Guano Islands Act of 1856, 187–208
Guantánamo, 4, 9, 11–12, 150–52, 239–66, 383, 393, 398, 401, 403n12; extralegal setting of, 389; prisoners in, 401
Guerrero, Vicente, 160, 182n2
Guha, Ranajit, 176–77
gunboat diplomacy, 269

H.M.S. *Forward,* 197
H.R. 109, 104
habeas corpus, 253–57, 260, 262, 265n60
Haight, W. C., 111–12
Hale, Edward Everett, 135–36, 149–50; *A Man Without a Country,* 135
Hale, John Parker (senator), 193
Hamdi, Yaser Esam, 260, 265n75, 266n87. See also *Hamdi v. Rumsfeld*
Hamdi v. Rumsfeld, 259, 265n75, 266n87
Hamilton, Alexander, 23–25; "Federalist 74," 24
Hammond, John Henry, 99
Hardt, Michael, and Antonio Negri, 15, 350, 356–57, 373. See also *Empire*
Harlan, John Marshall (Supreme Court justice), 251
Harman, Sabrina, 390
Harrison, William H., 202, 205
Hay, John, 278
Hayes, Thomas G., 197
Hebrew Immigrant Aid and Sheltering Society, 144
Hersh, Seymour, 386
Heuven Goedhart, G. J. van, 329, 348n49
HIV virus, 247
Hoar, George F., 85–86
Hollifield, James, 182, 185n38
Holmes, Oliver Wendell (Supreme Court justice), 29–31, 33
Hondeville, Albert, 115
Honig, Bonnie, 322
Horsman, Reginald, 288
Howells, William Dean, 221–22, 233; "The New Historical Romances," 213, 228
Huffington, Arianna, 351
Hugh Wynne: Free Quaker (Mitchell), 221
Hummer, 367, 369–70
Hungarian revolt (1956), 345
Hurston, Zora Neale, 53
Hussein, Saddam, regime of, 360, 382, 400

Ichikawa, Fusae, 305
identity: American, 4–8, 10, 16, 41–63, 365, 367, 375; black, 6, 41–63; cold war, 319; consumer politics of, 362; escapee, 321; foreign policy and, 358; law and, 3–4, 143; national, 2, 5, 7, 354, 356–57; politics, 343; relations of power and, 357
Ignatieff, Michael, 383
Illegal Immigrant Reform and Immigrant Responsibility Act of 1996, 147
imagined communities, 289, 355, 381; American, 59
Immigration and Nationality Act. *See* McCarran-Walter Act
Immigration and Naturalization Service (INS), 164–65, 248
Independent Woman, 307–8
In re Sapp, 38n97
Insular Cases, 6, 12, 51, 202, 207, 214, 219, 249–54, 259–61
Interhemispheric Resource Center, 162
Internal Security Act of 1950, 334–35
International Committee of the Red Cross, 150

International Committee on European Migration, 329
International Hummer Owners Group (IHOG), 369
International Law (Wheaton), 198
International Refugee Organization, 328
Interstate Highways and Defense Act of 1956, 356, 373
Iraq, 12, 14, 16, 20, 139, 152, 157–59, 193–95, 311, 313; war in, 15, 20, 154, 311, 352–53, 355, 359–60, 369–70
Iron Curtain, 321, 325, 327–28, 331–32, 340, 345

Jackson, Andrew, 26–27
Jackson, Robert H. (Supreme Court justice), 149–50, 156n58
James, Henry, 222
Jameson, Fredric, 221–22, 233
Jamison v. Flanner, 38n94
Jeep, 364–65, 367, 369
Jefferson, Thomas, 77–80, 83n45; *Notes on the State of Virginia,* 77, 79
Johnson, Robert L., 58
Johnson v. Eisentrager, 257
Johnston, Mary, 221, 238n71; *To Have and to Hold,* 221, 238n71
Jones v. United States, 194, 198–204
Judiciary Act of 1789, 253
Juergensmayer, Mark, 387
jus sanguinis, 71, 75–76, 82n20
jus soli, 71, 76, 82n20

Kaplan, Amy, 293–94, 383–84; *The Anarchy of Empire,* 216; "Romancing the Empire," 214
Kapus, Mrs., 339–40
Kasenkina, Oksana, 319–20, 325, 346n1
Kazan, Elia, 60, 340
Kennan, George, 325–26, 339
Kennedy, Anthony (Supreme Court justice), 251–52
Kenyon, Dorothy, 145
Kerber, Linda, 82n19, 179
Kerr, James, 125
Kersten, Charles (congressman), 326–28
Kersten Amendment, 327
Kessler-Harris, Alice, 152
Kettner, James H., 73
Key, George S., 197–98
Kimmitt, Gen. Mark, 384
Kinkead, Eugene, 341
Klein, Christina, 308
Kleinfeld, Andrew, 148
Kneedler, Edwin, 149
Korean War, 148, 327, 342
Korenmatsu v. United States, 61
Koskenniemi, Martti, 206, 211n107
kowtow, 275–77
Kravchenko, Victor, 325
Kurnick, Stanley, 117–18
Kyoto Protocols, 353, 363, 375

Lao Ch'ung-kuang, 96, 98
Lee, Daniel, 100–101
Lee v. Murphy, 38n93
Leon, Richard J. (federal district judge), 253
Liberator, 91, 95
Life magazine, 300, 320, 340
light trucks, differential treatment of cars and, 352, 361–64, 372, 374
Lincoln, Abraham, 34, 86, 103–4, 136, 255; administration, 104
Lippert, Randy, 343
Lippman, Jonathan (chief administrative judge of New York), 20
Littell's Living Age, 91
Locke, John, 24, 37n46, 271
Lodge, Henry Cabot (senator), 320, 326–27, 338, 345
Lodge Bill of 1951, 327
Loescher, Gil, and John Scanlan, 320, 330
López, Ian Haney, 45; *White by Law,* 45
Luibhéid, Eithne, 68
Lynch, Jack, 125–27
Lynch, Jessica, 391

MacArthur, Gen. Douglas, 294, 301, 303, 305, 307, 309, 311
Macartney, Lord George, 275–77

Magna Carta, 255
Mahan, Alfred Thayer, 245
Malkki, Liisa, 322
Manifest Destiny, 288
Man on a Tightrope, 340. *See also* Kazan, Elia
Mao Zedung, 332, 336
maquiladora, 163
Mariel, 335
Marshall, Humphrey, 92–93
Marshall, John (Supreme Court justice), 26–29, 31–33, 268, 271, 286
Marshall, T. H., 152
Martí, José, 242
Mason, James Murray (senator), 194, 206
Mayberry, 246–47
McAlister, Melani, 309
McCarran, Pat, 334–35, 348n66
McCarran Act. *See* Internal Security Act of 1950
McCarran-Walter Act, 136, 334–36
McCloy, John, 328
McCutcheon, George Barr: *Graustark, the Story of a Love Behind a Throne,* 221, 238n71
McInnes, Hector, 120
McKinley, William, 224, 226, 267, 278; administration, 204
Meinig, Donald, 189–90
mestizaje, 169–73; political, 173–77, 179–80
Middle East, 352, 359; oil producers of, 351
military-industrial complex, 391
Mitchell, Don, 359
Mohanty, Chandra Talpade, 312
Montoya, Margaret, 19
Morrison, Toni, 60–61; "On the Backs of Blacks," 59
Moses, Robert, 373
Mutual Security Act, 327

NAFTA. *See* North American Free Trade Agreement
Nansen, Fridtjof, 145
Nansen Passport, 144, 155n37
Nation, 279
National Committee for a Free Europe, 340, 350n96
Nationality Law, 312
NATO. *See* North Atlantic Treaty Organization
Naturalization Act of 1790, 69, 75, 80
Navassa, 196–202, 204–5; Phosphate Company, 196–98, 202, 206; riot on, 196–97, 210n49
Negri, Antonio, and Michael Hardt, 356–57. See also *Empire*
networks, 353, 357–59, 371, 373–76, 377n20; global, 354
Neuman, Gerald, 253
Never Let Me Go, 319, 341
Ngai, Mae, 3, 17, 145, 322; "impossible subjects," 15, 322, 337
Nietzsche, Friedrich, 399
North American Free Trade Agreement (NAFTA), 9, 159–82
North American Review, 279
North Atlantic Treaty Organization (NATO), 327
Northwest Ordinance of 1787, 142
NSC 86/1, 327, 347n36
Nureyev, Rudolph, 319

Oakeshott, Michael, 19
O'Connor, Sandra Day (Supreme Court justice), 33, 39n109, 259
Office for National Drug Control Policy (ONDCP), 351; drugs and terror campaign of, 351–52, 356
Ohio Adult Parole Authority v. Woodard, 32
Ollarek family, 339
Ong, Aihwa, 152, 154, 157
Operation ENGROSS, 328
Opium War, 279–280, 283
Organic Act of 1902, 219–20, 223, 230; debates about the, 226

Padilla, José, 150–51, 260. See also *Rumsfeld v. Padilla*
Page, Horace F., 85

Page Law (Page Act), 74, 141
Palmyra, 188, 207, 208, 209n4
Parker, Peter, 93–94, 95
Parrot, Lindesay, 305
Partido Acción Nacional (PAN), 159
Partido Revolucionario Institucional (PRI), 159, 167, 169–75, 177, 184n30
Patriot Act, 151–53
Patriot II, draft of, 151
Pelican Bay Prison, 397
Penrose, Gertrude, 307
People v. Carter Singh, 116
People v. Dong Pok Yip, 115
Perez, Emma, 129
Perry, Matthew (commodore), 284, 291n66
Persian Gulf, 360
Peters, Stephen, 197
Petrov, Vladimir: *My Retreat From Russia,* 340
Pharr, Susan, 295
Philippine Commission, 214, 219, 223–24, 235; second, 214
Pierce, Franklin, 194
Pirogov, Peter, 340
Platt Amendment, 243–45
Plessy v. Ferguson, 54
Pluhar, Ivan, 339
Policy Planning Staff (PPS), 325–26, 339
porfiriato, 170
Priest, Josiah, 99
prisoners of war (POWs), 246, 253, 258–59, 266n86, 323, 325, 331; American, 342; movies about, 339
prisons: industrial complex, 390–91, 398; supermax, 394, 397. *See also* Abu Ghraib
Project TROY, 327, 343
Psychological Strategy Board (PSB), 328, 332
Psychological Warfare Working Group, 338
Pynchon, Thomas, 167

Quinn, Alexander, 111–12

Race Trap, The, 58
Radio Free Europe, 338, 340
Rafael, Vicente, 218, 222
Rambo First Blood, Part II, 365
Rapaille, Claude, 366, 370
Rasul v. Bush, 245, 249, 254–58, 261
Rather, Dan, 390
Red Cross, 397
Red Danube, The, 319, 323, 325
Reed, William B., 95–96, 98, 101
refoulement, 136, 152
Refugee Relief Act, 336
Rehnquist, William (Supreme Court chief justice), 32–33, 38n102, 39n109, 251
Reid v. Covert, 251
repatriation, 323, 325, 329, 335, 342
Repplier, Agnes, 222, 229
resettlement, 320, 323, 328–29, 332–34, 336, 342
Respublica Christiana, 272, 283
Revolutionary War, 272
Reynolds, A. W., 111
Rhodes, Lorna, 398
Robbins, Samuel, 118–19
Robert Bowne, 93, 94, 100
Robinson, Ronald, and John Gallagher, 269, 287
Roby, Charles W., 197
Rocky IV, 365
Rocky Mountain News, 311
Roosevelt, Theodore, 208, 244, 245; "The Strenuous Life," 226
Root, Elihu, 226, 230
Ross, John, 197
Rothman, David, 383
rule of law, 19–24, 31, 33–34, 240, 254, 261, 386, 389, 392
Rumsfeld, Donald, 246, 385–86
Rumsfeld v. Padilla, 259. *See also* Padilla, José

Salinas de Gotarí, Carlos, 164, 172
Salyer, Lucy, 142
Sarat, Austin, 399
Saudi Arabia, 360
Scalia, Antonin (Supreme Court justice), 149
Scanlan, John, 346; and Gil Loescher, 320, 330

SCAP Civil Information and Education Office (CI&E), 296, 301, 303–5, 307, 313
Schmitt, Carl, 21, 270
Schuck, Peter, 70
Seckler-Hudson, Catheryn, 136, 152, 155n38; *Statelessness,* 136
security, 353–54, 375
Senate Bill 339, 192
Senate Resolution 15, 192, 204
Senior Scholastic, 304
Seward, William Henry, 189
Shaughnessy v. United States ex rel. Mezei, 149, 156n58
Shelton, Philo S., 191
Shulman, Robert, 222
Silverman, Kaja, 179, 184n34
Simring, Steven, 58
Singh, Arjan, 111–12
Singh, Jamil, 117, 123–24
Singh, Keshn, 125–27
Singh, Nikhil Pal, 61
Singh, Rola, 122
Singh, Tara, 120, 123
Sivits, Jeremy, 390
Sixth Amendment, 260
Shklar, Judith, 152
slavery, 54, 56, 64n29, 65nn43–44; slave identity, 50–53
Slidell, John, 101
Smith, Charles H., 197
Smith, Edward, 197–98
Smith, Rogers, 70
Smith, Walter Bedell, 335
Smith-Mundt Act, 338
Sofia, 319
Soguk, Nevat, 343
sole fiat, 24
Souter, David (Supreme Court justice), 246, 250
Spanish-American War, 142, 240, 242, 293
sport utility vehicles (SUVs), 16, 351, 363–66, 369, 371–75, 378nn55, 68–69, 81, 379
Stalag 17, 331
Stalin, Joseph, 319, 327
Stanley, H. C., 126
stateless persons, 9, 135–57, 321, 343
Stevens, Jacqueline, 68, 81n6
Stevens, John Paul (Supreme Court justice), 33, 150, 251–52, 254–58
Sullivan v. Askew, 38n96
Sumner, Charles, 106
Sundquist, Eric, 222
Supreme Commander for the Allied Powers (SCAP), 296, 301

Taft, Howard, 214, 219
Taft, William, 223
Taguba Report, 388
Tan, Samuel, 224
Taney, Roger (Supreme Court justice), 51–52, 56, 62
Taussig, Michael, 381
Tea Act, 141
Teller, Henry Moore (senator), 220
Ten Eyck, John C., 104–5
Terranova, Francis, 273–74
Territory Clause, 199–200
terrorism, 351–52, 356, 369
Texas War of Independence, 160
Thirteen Who Fled (Fischer), 340
Time, 364
Tocqueville, Alexis de, 19, 394
Tomlinson, Christopher, 129
Toombs, Robert (senator), 193–94
Top Gun, 365
Torpey, John, 63
Treaty of Guadalupe-Hidalgo, 160–61
Treaty of Nanking, 276
Treaty of the Bogue, 276
Treaty of Versailles, 144
Treaty of Wanghia, 269–70, 280–85, 287, 291n66
Treaty of Westphalia, 270
Trop v. Dulles, 150
Truman, Harry S, 347n11; administration, 320, 329
Truth about American Diplomats, The, 342

Tuan Anh Nguyen v. INS, 146
Twain, Mark, 293
Tyler, John, 268
Tyler May, Elaine, 308

Union of Concerned Scientists, 363
United Nations Commission on the Status of Women, 145, 155n42
United Nations Convention on the Elimination of all Forms of Discrimination Against Women (CEDAW), 145, 294
United Nations Convention on the Nationality of Married Women, 145
United Nations High Commissioner for Refugees (UNHCR), 137–38
United Nations Relief and Rehabilitation Administration (UNRRA), 323, 328
United States Department of Defense, 253, 258, 263n14, 265n78, 385–87
United States Department of Energy, 360
United States Department of Homeland Security, 2, 248
United States Department of Justice, 147–48
United States Department of State, 148
United States Escapee Program (USEP), 321, 329, 331, 334, 338, 342
United States Guano Company, 187
United States Information Agency (USIA), 342
United States–Japan War, 294, 298–99
United States Magazine, 99
United States v. Verdugo-Urquidez, 251
United States v. Wilson, 26
United States v. Wong Kim Ark, 56
Urry, John, 353
U.S.S. *Galena,* 196

vagrancy, 103–30; laws about, 113, 121, 131n10
Vasconcelos, Jose, 170
Victoria I, 276
Vietnam War, 293
Voice of America, 338
Volpp, Leti, 310, 317n50
Volunteer Freedom Corps, 320, 327, 338
Von Eschen, Penny, 308

war on drugs, 351
war on terror, 20, 259, 294, 311, 351, 385, 389, 393, 397, 400
Ward, John E., 98
Waverly, 94, 100
Wayne, James (Supreme Court justice), 28
Webb, U. S., 115
Weed, Ethel B., 304, 316n34
Wexler, Laura, 222
White, Edward D. (Supreme Court justice), 202–3, 211n86, 217, 226, 258
whiteness, 45, 60
Why I Escaped (Pirogov), 340
Wiebe, Robert, 140
Wilder, Billy. See *Stalag 17*
Wiley, Alexander, 326
Women's Home Companion, 300
Wood, Leonard, 244
Wooden Horse, The, 331
World War I, 136, 143–45
World War II, 14, 136, 145–46, 255, 257, 294, 311

Yalta, 323
Yick Wo v. Hopkins, 150
Yoshida, Shigeru, 310
Y tu mamá también, 9–10, 159–83

Zapatistas, 159, 172–73
Žižek, Slavoj, 381